CRIME and the LEGAL PROCESS

WILLIAM J. CHAMBLISS
Associate Professor of Sociology
University of California, Santa Barbara

McGRAW–HILL BOOK COMPANY
New York, St. Louis, San Francisco
Toronto, London, Sydney

Crime and the Legal Process

Library of Congress Catalog Card Number 68–30555

1 2 3 4 5 6 7 8 9 0 M A M M 7 5 4 3 2 1 0 6 9 8

This book is dedicated to Chief Justice Earl Warren
who, more than most men, understands the potential as well as the
problems of the American criminal law.

PREFACE

The law touches every man. In varying degrees it is one of the shaping influences in every life; and in that word "varying" lurk a wealth of insistent questions, urgent problems of profound scope and significance to scholars and laymen alike. More often than not, when one speaks or writes of "the law" the subject matter is shrouded in an aura of mystery. In some respects the law appears even more magical in character than comparable social institutions, such as education or medicine. No doubt part of the mystery of the law reflects the fact that for the most part inquiry into the law has engaged in what Mark Twain saw as the distinguishing characteristic of science—the production of "wholesale returns of conjecture out of such a trifling investment of fact." This book is intended to provide the scholar, layman, and student with a compendium of the social sciences' (and I include here legal scholarship) "investment in fact" and to lace this investment with enough theoretical "conjecture" to give it meaning.

The impetus for this book derived from a desire to provide a sourcebook in the sociology of criminal law. It was apparent to me from working In this area that its interdisciplinary nature had the undesirable consequence of keeping persons in different disciplines relatively ignorant of the work being done by others. I was continually impressed by the law-related literature which appeared in journals of political science, philosophy, anthropology, and law, but I was depressed by the realization that so many of the scholars working in these areas were not aware of one another's works or of the soclological studies which were relevant to their problems. Similarly, I was constantly surprised to discover pieces of research pertinent to my own and other sociologists' interests in various journals of other disciplines. My intention, then, was to bring together a selection of the best pieces in the various journals and monographs in the fields of anthropology, law, philosophy, political science, psychology, sociology, and economics bearing on the criminal-law process.

As I began surveying the literature, however, I realized that one book could scarcely do justice to both the ideas *and* the empirical research contained in these journals. Furthermore, it was my impression that scholars, laymen, and students were more likely to have been exposed to the Ideas prevailing about the law than to the facts which have been gathered. I decided, therefore, that the book should be limited to empirical studies of the legal system. But facts without theory are blind and theory without facts is misguided—so I have taken it as my responsibility to provide the empirical studies with a theoretical framework, in the form of the Introductions to each of the sections of the book.

The book is divided into what I take to be the three major questions of concern to the sociology of criminal law: the emergence of legal norms, the administration of criminal law, and the impact of legal sanctions. The administration of criminal law, which comprises the largest and, in many ways, the most important area of inquiry, is subdivided into the processes which characterize arrest, prosecution, and trial and sentencing. In each section the intention is to present to the reader a theoretical framework that makes sense of the empirical studies that follow (as well as of those cited in the references and bibliography but which could not be included) and then to provide a collection of the best research studies available. In the final section of the book, the epilogue, I have attempted to spell out the general implications of research and theory for the social organization of the criminal law.

In making the selection of what to incorporate in this volume, I have left out some areas which are as important as those which have been included. Two areas that have been omitted deserve special mention:

The focus of the book is purposefully, and at the same time unfortunately, on Anglo-American law. This focus is necessitated by the lack of comparable data from studies of the law in other cultures. Although I have included a few studies from other countries, the framework remains Anglo-American out of necessity. It is to be hoped that the few studies of a comparative nature included in the volume will suggest fruitful areas for further research. Another limiting feature of this volume is that the numerous studies of the legal profession *qua* profession (with the accompanying questions of recruitment, training, and professional-association membership) are not represented. This decision was dictated by the desire to keep the volume relatively compact. Another reason for omitting the research on the legal profession is that the focus of this volume is more narrowly limited to the everyday events which take place in the legal process.

The systematic study of the law is still in the embryonic phase; therefore, it would be a mistake to expect our efforts to have yielded definitive answers. Beginning is always hesitant—and tentative. It is hoped that this book will stimulate some inquiring minds to produce other works which will benefit from the mistakes as well as the truths contained in this volume.

William J. Chambliss

ACKNOWLEDGMENT

Robert Seidman, of the University of Wisconsin School of Law, and Gerald MacCallum, of Wisconsin's philosophy department, provided encouragement, insight, and assistance at many critical stages in the development of this book. I am deeply indebted to them for their help, and I know that the book has been greatly improved as a result of their comments. Victor Doyno, of the department of English at New York University, and Marion F. Steele, of the department of sociology at Long Beach State College, read the entire manuscript and made many valuable suggestions. I am grateful to them for their help as well. Many of the ideas expressed in this volume were formed during an informal faculty seminar at the University of Washington, and I wish to thank Pierre Van der Berghe, Si Ottenberg, Bud Winans, and Gerald MacCallum for many intellectual leads provided during that seminar. The book was completed during a year as a Russell Sage resident in law and sociology at the University of Wisconsin, and I am indebted to the Russell Sage Foundation for that year. Finally, I want to express my deep appreciation to Ann Wallace, administrative assistant of the Russell Sage Program in Law and Sociology at the University of Wisconsin, for supervising the typing of the manuscript and for providing editorial assistance.

CONTENTS

PART ONE

THE EMERGENCE of
LEGAL NORMS

PART ONE

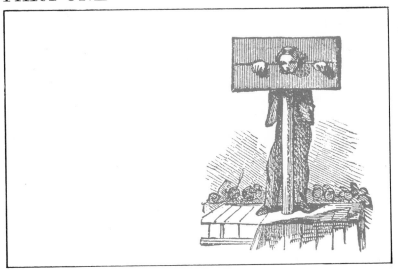

INTRODUCTION

To inquire into the criminal-law process is to embark on an investigation of one of the cornerstones of all modern societies. Nations have increasingly turned to the legal system in an effort to bring order out of chaos or to maintain stability in the face of dramatic changes in the fabric of society. Even efforts to control international conflicts are being seen as problems to be handled by legal processes, and it is "the law," with all its mystery and its presumed integrity, which is viewed as the means through which international conflicts can be controlled. The scope of the problem faced in attempting to establish the boundaries of this vast system of activities provides an intellectual challenge second to none. Although the emphasis in this book is primarily upon contemporary legal processes, it is essential that we have an understanding of the historical events which have been so significant in shaping the current state of the legal system. Let us therefore begin our inquiry with a brief overview of the historical background of Anglo-American law.

Anglo-American Law in Historical Perspective

William the Conquerer was faced with a formidable task when he took the throne of England. The kingdom he had conquered in 1066 was composed of a number of groups of people with quite divergent ways of looking at the world and equally diverse sets of values. The various social groups were not organized in such a way that they paid homage, much less taxes, to one central authority. By contemporary standards, William had conquered an anarchy whose salient characteristic was a pluralistic value system: a land divided into eight subdivisions, each with its own king. The country's only unifying characteristic was the presence of Christianity, a remnant of the Roman occupation six centuries earlier. One of

William's first acts was to declare this heterogeneous conglomeration subject to his leadership and to claim all land for the crown.

He attempted to gain control over the church, which was at that time a major landholder, and as a means of achieving this, William separated the lay and ecclesiastical courts of law. His moves constituted a grave threat to the economic well-being and the political power of the church. Not surprisingly, the conflict between church and state played a major part in the history of England for several centuries, coming to a head during the reign of Henry II. The crown also asserted that it was solely responsible for peace ("the king's peace") throughout the realm. To enforce this peace, the king sent judges into the countryside. By so doing, the crown took away much of the power of the barons, and the lines of conflict between the crown, the barons, and the church were drawn.

From the time of William until the reign of Henry II a quasi-legal structure prevailed which was strongly influenced by the tribal heritage of England prior to the Norman conquest. But during the reign of Henry II, most of the fundamental features of the structure of Anglo-American law emerged.

First and foremost, Anglo-American law has inherited a reliance on force and coercion as the appropriate mechanisms for handling disputes. At an earlier time in England, the emphasis in settling disputes had been on reconciliation rather than on coercion. Thus, if a member of one kinship group had violated the rights of someone from another group, the guiding principle was to effect a reconciliation of the individuals and the groups. But the legal system emerging from the reign of William through that of Henry II emphasized the use of force by the state as the right and proper means of settling disputes.

An equally important inheritance from the earlier years of the Anglo-American legal system is the view that personal wrongs are transgressions against the *state* and that the state and *only* the state has the right to punish such acts. This principle contrasted sharply with the norms of English society prior to the time of William, when wrongs were considered a highly personal matter.

Other characteristics emerging at this time include the state's use of an ostensibly independent and unbiased government official to handle disputes between individuals and the state or between two or more persons. In modern times this is, of course, the judge.

It is also significant that the judicial function was separated from the legislative functions. The legal system was so designed that those who would decide disputes would not be the same as those who made the laws. Finally, there emerged in this early period the use of a group of the accused's peers as the rightful body for determining guilt and innocence.

These innovations more than any others can be said to represent the salient structural features of the Anglo-American legal system. Much of the content and most certainly the focus of the legal norms have undergone dramatic shifts over the centuries; but the reliance on coercion through force, the use of judges, the differentiation of functions between the judiciary and the legislature, and the use of peers (juries) have remained firmly ingrained features of the legal order.

Thus, this heritage from feudal England has been more important in establishing the *structure* of the legal system than in determining the *content* of the laws. The bulk of the offenses which occupy the attention of the legal order today were unheard of in early English law, and even laws which have roots in early England, such as the Law of Theft and the Vagrancy Statutes, differ so in their content today that they are more appropriately to be seen as new laws than as continuations of old ones.

The content of the legal system has also changed through the death of many laws which at one time occupied a central place in the legal order, laws that provided penal sanctions for indebtedness being but one example of this attrition.

There have also been dramatic changes in the types of sanctions meted out for various types of offenses. In early England, punishment for even minor offenses was exceedingly severe: "[I]n medieval England peasants were hanged for stealing a few eggs." [1]

Compliance, Coercion, and Rule Makers

Although the legitimate use of violence has remained the exclusive right of the state, such a device is not sufficient for maintaining social order. Indeed, it is not the most efficient means of ensuring even so relatively simple a goal as the collection of taxes. It is thus not surprising that rulers should attempt to legitimize the morality of the legal system. The use of peers to decide guilt and innocence represents an effort on the part of the government to underpin the legal system with an acceptable moral base. As Lenski has pointed out:

> Though force is the most effective instrument for seizing power in a society, and though it always remains the foundation of any system of inequality, it is not the most effective instrument for retaining and exploiting a position of power and deriving the maximum benefits from it. Therefore, regardless of the objectives of a new regime, once organized opposition has been destroyed it is to its advantage to make increasing use of other techniques and instruments of control, and to allow force to recede into the background to be used only when other techniques fail. [2]

More important than the use of peers as a mechanism for legitimizing the legal order is the fact that throughout the centuries the dominant Christian religion in England and America has lent spiritual support to the legal system. The Christianizing of England thus eventually led to the fusion of the coercive power of the state with religious morality.

Under these conditions, the prevailing view of the law came to be one of respect, though not necessarily compliance. Then, as now, the legal order came to be looked upon with reverence, and the morality of the legal order was seen as containing sets of "eternal truths" and "natural laws."

---

[1] Gerhard Lenski, *Power and Privilege*, New York: McGraw-Hill Book Company, 1966, p. 271; H. S. Bennett, *Life on the English Manor: A Study of Peasant Conditions, 1150–1400*, London: Cambridge University Press, 1960.

[2] Lenski, *op. cit.*, p. 51.

In this atmosphere, "the law" came to stand for what the legal order was in blueprint. No one was so presumptuous as to attempt to see how, in fact, the law operated. It was assumed even by those involved in the process that the legal system in its day-to-day acitvities bore a close resemblance to the way in which, with all its presumed morality, it was supposed to operate.

It is a tribute to the strength of the coalescence between the church and the state that this perspective dominated scholarly as well as lay thinking until very recently. Among legal scholars, members of the intellectual movement, generally referred to as the "legal realists," have done (and are doing) much to challenge this traditional view. The apt phrase, "the living law," captures the essence of this movement. The point made by the realists is that the law cannot be understood merely by looking at the blueprint of the legal system. Rather, the law is a living institution, and it can be described and understood only by systematically studying what is taking place at all phases of the legal process, from the making of laws to the release of law violators.

Once the law is viewed in this way, it becomes apparent that the legal system, like all other social institutions, reflects the character of the times. New laws are passed in an effort to solve perceived problems of prevailing social conditions. Old laws are given new interpretations and applications; the judiciary and the police focus efforts on some laws during one period and on other laws during another.

Recent Trends

The last 200 years have brought profound changes in the Western world, and with these changes we also find equally significant alterations of the legal order. The most important of these changes are not to be found in the types of behaviors which are prohibited or in the types of punishments applied; on the contrary, the most significant changes occur in the institutionalized procedures and the institutionalized conceptions of the basic values of the legal order. For it is these perspectives which ultimately shape the legal system, although their immediate impact may be seen more readily in an alteration of the idea rather than an alteration of the fact of the legal system.

Of the changes to be mentioned here, none is more important than the twentieth-century trend toward an ever-increasing secularization of the legal system. The jury system, as it has developed, illustrates this general process.

Initially, the wisest composition of the jury was seen as consisting in peers chosen because they were familiar with the facts of the case. Being familiar presumably made them better able to establish the truth. Today, of course, the criteria for jury selection are almost the exact opposite: A prospective juror is not allowed to serve if he knows very much about the case prior to the trial. A similar example is the rule governing venue: If a defendant can show that the community at large is too intimately familiar with the case, then it is possible to force the trial to take place elsewhere. The tendency to conceive of deterrence as the most important, if not the only, legitimate justification for the existence of punishment is still another example of this process, for an emphasis on deterrence places increasing emphasis on the role of the law in achieving objectively defensible goals. The more traditional arguments for punishment, which suggested the need for "retribution" or the necessity for obtaining "an eye for an eye and a tooth for a tooth," have become much less persuasive in modern legal thinking than they once were. More and more the law is being structured and judged according to how well it meets certain explicit societal goals; it is no longer sufficient that the law supposedly represents a system of "natural" rights and obligations.

We have seen in very recent years what is perhaps the most important outgrowth of this trend to secularize the legal order, in that courts and legislatures have increasingly turned to empirical evidence of how the legal system works *in fact*—as opposed to simply reifying the beauty of the logical structure of the law. In England, for example, criminal laws against prostitution, drug use, homosexuality, and gambling were abolished in part because there was evidence that requiring agencies to enforce these laws led more often to the corruption of the enforcers than to the reduction in the frequency of such "immoral" acts.[3]

The Supreme Court in the United States has recently shown an equally impressive tendency to look for empirical evidence of the "law in action" as a basis for making legal decisions. The recent "Miranda decision" represents a landmark case in criminal law illustrating this tendency.

The issue in the Miranda case was whether or not the police could interrogate a suspected criminal without the suspect's having first been given the right to refuse to submit to such interrogation. The Supreme Court held in this classic decision that evidence (including confessions) thus gathered was inadmissible in court and could not be used as a basis for finding a defendant guilty. It was certainly not a new principle: the Court had always held that a defendant's civil liberties had to be protected and that the police could not use undue pressure (such as physical brutality) to obtain a confession. As an illustration of the increasing sensitivity of the legal system to empirical data, however, what is significant about the Miranda decision is the fact that the Court did not rest its case simply by reaffirming the rights which are guaranteed by the logical structure (the blueprint) of the legal norms; rather, the Court attempted to assess what was in fact taking place in police stations as officers enforced the laws. To accomplish this, the Court analyzed the contents of police training manuals to determine the tactics and strategies suggested in these manuals for police to use to obtain confessions. It was on the basis of the contradiction between these practices and the spirit of the legal system that the Supreme Court established new rules for ensuring that defendants not receive undue pressure from police.[4]

In addition to this shift to ever-increasing rationalism of the legal sys-

3 Wolfenden Report in Parliament, *Criminal Law Review,* England: 1959.

4 *Miranda v. Arizona in Official Reports of the Supreme Court,* vol. 384, 1966, U.S. part 3, pp. 436–718, 982–995.

tem, two other deep-seated changes deserve at least passing mention. One is the increasing reliance on statutes as the proper source of the law. Although Jerome Hall's analysis of the court's lawmaking function in early England stands as a classic illustration of the fact that the judiciary does, in fact, perform a lawmaking function, it seems to be the case that this is less often true today than it was 100 years ago. Judges do occasionally make decisions which contradict statutes, but more and more the statutes are viewed by the judiciary as the ultimate source of authority, and the judge's role has been more and more circumscribed with respect to its lawmaking ability.

Finally, we have seen in recent years the emergence of administrative boards as institutionalized mechanisms replacing activities previously contained within the legal system. The juvenile-court movement begun at the turn of the century has resulted in the virtual withdrawal of the traditional legal processing of juveniles after arrest. Although the juvenile court retains a judge, this is in most cases simply an anachronism with little real consequence for the functioning of the court. In point of fact, the juvenile court is manned and manipulated, for better or for worse, by professionally trained social workers whose tie to the legal order is only tangential.

A further illustration of the trend toward replacing the legal system with administrative boards is found in Nils Christie's analysis of the use of welfare boards to handle alcoholics.[5] Although we have seen only the beginnings of such programs in the United States, the change has been virtually complete in England and in many other European countries. It seems likely that the trend will take on increasing importance in the future and that we shall see a gradual withdrawal of strictly legal handling of more and more types of heretofore criminal behavior.[6]

The climate of the legal order is thus dramatically different in the twentieth century from what has ever been the case in our history. There is widespread agreement on the value of developing an increasingly rational system for meting out justice. Equally important is the fact that there is a willingness to consider the events which actually take place in the legal process, and not just the structure of the law in its abstract majesty, as evidence to be reckoned with in guiding changes in the legal structure. In recent years we have also seen the trend toward an increasing reliance on statutes combined with a gradual shift away from using the criminal law as the sole entity prescribing the handling of persons who have violated the law.

Theories of Legal Change

How can we account for the changes which have taken place and what are the dynamics through which these changes occur? Two general ex-

---

[5] Nils Christie, "Temperance Boards: A Study of Welfare Law," *Social Problems,* vol. 12, pp. 415–428, Spring, 1965.

[6] For an elaboration of the role of the lawyer in this process, see Willard Hurst, "The Legal Profession," *Wisconsin Law Review,* vol. 1966, pp. 969–978, Fall, 1966.

planations which compete with one another among legal scholars and social scientists as models to explain changes in the legal order deserve special attention: these may be referred to as the "value-expression" and the "interest-group" hypotheses.[7]

The value-expression theory is well summarized by one of its chief exponents among contemporary legal theorists: "Criminal law represents a sustained effort to preserve important social values from serious harm and to do so not arbitrarily but in accordance with rational methods directed toward the discovery of just ends." [8]

The crux of this position is that legal norms are an expression of those societal values which transcend the immediate interests of individuals or groups. Legal norms are seen as emerging through the dynamics of cultural processes as a solution to certain needs and requirements which are essential for maintaining the fabric of society.

Interest-group theorists are not inclined to see the legal system as an expression of values which fulfill the needs of the society as a whole. Rather, the emphasis in this perspective is on the power of interest groups to influence the legal system. Those at the extreme of this position view legal norms as simply a device by which persons in positions of power maintain and enhance their advantaged position by using state power to coerce the mass of people into doing what is consistent with the "power elite's" best interests.[9]

A resolution of this debate is clearly beyond the scope of this book, and, in any case, such an attempt would be premature. Ultimately, the debate will be settled not by polemics but by empirical data such as those provided by the studies in Part I. It is noteworthy, however, that in all the studies incorporated in this volume, the role of interest groups in determining the content of legal norms is paramount. Hall's analysis of the emergence of the laws of theft suggests the operation of interest groups as does Chambliss's analysis of the shifts and alterations in the vagrancy statutes. In both these cases, however, the interest groups were sufficiently influential and sufficiently powerful (representing, as they did, the upper classes of the society) that their ability to influence legislation stemmed from the fact that the legislators and judges never questioned the desirability of passing laws which would benefit these groups. Consequently, no organized intervention by these social classes was really necessary to bring about legislation favorable to them.

The use of a more direct kind of influence by interest groups can be

[7] There is an obvious parallel between these two perspectives and the debate in social science theory between the "conflict" and "functional" theorists. For an excellent analysis of this debate, see Lenski, *op. cit.,* pp. 1–23; Pierre L. Van den Berghe, "Dialectic and Functionalism: Toward a Theoretical Synthesis," *American Sociological Review,* vol. 28, pp. 695–705, October, 1963.

[8] Jerome Hall, *General Principles of Criminal Law,* Indianapolis: The Bobbs-Merrill Company, Inc., 1947, p. 1.

[9] It is generally recognized that interest groups play an exceedingly important role in determining the content of legislation dealing with economic matters. For an excellent case study of an instance of this, see Daniel J. Dykstra, "The History of a Legislative Power Struggle," *Wisconsin Law Review,* pp. 402–429, Spring, 1966.

seen in the behavior of police agencies, both federal and state, in obtaining legislation which expresses their own point of view and which also assists them in developing and expanding their bureaucracies. Policing agencies tend to be unusually successful in campaigns to obtain favorable legislation in part because there is rarely any organized opposition to their efforts. Then, too, the fact that the law-enforcement agencies are expected to publish "authoritative" reports on crime and criminals has the effect of having interest groups defined culturally as authorities on matters which are of direct concern to their own welfare. It is as if the National Association of Manufacturers were looked upon as the ultimate authority on the proper laws governing manufacturing. The history of the Federal Narcotics Bureau is a case study illustrating these points.[10]

Antidrug laws in the United States emerged initially as tax-revenue measures, with the explicit intention that they were to be used to provide a constitutional basis for federal control. The FNB was established in an effort to enforce these laws. But subsequent to their passage, the efforts of the FNB have altered the official reason for the laws, the interpretation of the laws, and the content of subsequent legislation to such an extent that the original tax-revenue purpose has been totally lost. The laws are currently viewed by most law enforcers as a necessary device for eliminating the immoral practice of taking drugs and reducing the crime which is alleged to be associated with addiction. Despite the fact that objective and systematic investigation of the drug problem has clearly indicated that these laws have little or no positive effect on the drug problem but have instead the effect of making criminals out of persons who would otherwise be law-abiding citizens, the influence of the police agencies has been sufficiently great so that the laws have steadily increased in harshness over the years. Equally important, other so-called drugs, such as marijuana, peyote, and LSD, have come in for the same kind of treatment as the opiates (the group of drugs originally covered by the laws), and the use and possession as well as the distribution of these drugs has been made a felony.[11]

It is interesting to compare the emergence of the prohibition laws with that of the drug laws, both in terms of the forces bringing the laws into effect and in terms of the ability of the laws to withstand public sentiment in opposition to them. To a large extent, the prohibition laws represented the effective campaign of a small but highly vocal and well-organized interest group convinced of the moral degeneration of the country, which they believed stemmed from the availability of alcoholic beverages. There is little doubt that the efforts of this group of moral entrepreneurs did not

[10] The Federal Bureau of Investigation, especially in view of its emphasis on communism in recent years, is a similar illustration. In another context, so is the Military Establishment.

[11] The two best studies of the emergence of these laws are Alfred R. Lindesmith, *The Addict and the Law*, Bloomington, Ind.: Indiana University Press, 1965, and Howard S. Becker, *The Outsiders: Studies in the Sociology of Deviance*, New York: The Free Press of Glencoe, 1963. See also Edwin M. Schur, *Drug Addiction in America and England*, Bloomington, Ind.: Indiana University Press, 1964.

in any sense represent the spirit of the times but was effective primarily because opposition to the movement was unorganized and apathetic. This is essentially the same set of circumstances which has characterized the emergence of laws dealing with drugs, except that in the latter case the interest group pushing for the laws has had the added advantage of working from a position of influence and power within the legal system. On the other hand, prohibition laws were rapidly repealed, and enforcement was sporadic and totally ineffective. Drug laws, by contrast, have gained increasing strength and vigor over the years, and although enforcement remains pretty much a matter of arresting drug addicts rather than distributors, the laws have at least been effective in providing policing agencies with a ready supply of persons to be processed for what the community sees as relatively serious offenses.

These analyses of the emergence of criminal laws, then, suggest that many, and perhaps most, of the laws emerge through the efforts of vested-interest groups. The efforts of these groups, however, may be only remotely activist in their nature. More often than not, the views of the groups in power will be expressed in criminal legislation simply because their perspective prevails among those who make the laws. In democratic societies it is assumed, though by no means empirically established, that this view also represents the values of the majority.

It would be a mistake to interpret the foregoing remarks as meaning that all laws represent the interests of persons in power at the expense of persons less influential. In many cases there is no conflict whatsoever between those in power and those not. For most crimes against the person, such as murder, assault, and rape, there is consensus throughout society as to the desirability of imposing legal sanctions for persons who commit these acts. It is also true that laws are passed which reflect the interests of the general population and which are antithetical to the interests of those in power. The Sherman Antitrust Laws which, among other things, make it a crime to enter into agreements to fix prices, are examples of laws which presumably benefit the majority at the expense of the more powerful minority of American corporations.[12] The influence of interest groups, then, is but one aspect of the processes which determine the emergence and focus of the legal norms.

Crime and Middle-class Morality [13]

The single most important characteristic of contemporary Anglo-American society influential in shaping the legal order has been the emerging domination of the middle classes. Indeed, the pervasiveness of this domination has frequently led observers to the conclusion that American society is best characterized as containing one all-encompassing value system agreed upon by everyone. Although such a point of view is under-

---

[12] In subsequent sections we shall take up the question of the enforcement of these laws; as we shall see, their existence as statutes does not guarantee consistent enforcement.

[13] See the insightful analysis in Svend Ranulf, *Moral Indignation and Middle Class Psychology*, New York: Schocken Books, 1964.

standable in view of the trend to middle-class domination of institutions, like all caricatures, it misrepresents the facts. To understand the workings of the legal order in contemporary America and England, one must also comprehend that many of the problems within the legal institution stem from the attempt by the middle class to impose their own standards and their own view of proper behavior on groups whose values differ.

The urban Negro, probably more than any other single group, represents a large segment of contemporary American society that shares a value system and a "view of the world" quite at variance with the prevailing middle-class morality.[14] Since this group alone represents some twenty million Americans, it is certainly a significant social fact that the legal system is expected to force a set of values upon this group which is incompatible with their own version of American culture.

To this group of twenty million Negroes must be added some nine million Mexican-American immigrants (of even more recent immigration than the Negro) and large groups of Japanese, Chinese, Southern "hillbillies," and Puerto Ricans [15] as well.

Although the presence of these groups may not justify describing America as a "pluralistic" society in the same sense that one can so categorize other nations, in Africa, for example, the fact remains that the attempt by the dominant middle class to impose their version of morality on the lower classes generally and on the above-mentioned groups specifically is a source of considerable strain in the legal institution. Thus, with the historical emergence of the middle class as the dominant group, we have inherited a source of legal changes and also a source of inherent conflicts which are played out in the arena of the law.

Summary

No readily available answer is to be found to the question of how legal norms and legal institutions emerge and take their particular shape. The preceding analysis and the studies that follow concentrate on the emergence of legal norms and legal structures in England and their transplantation to the United States. The general conclusion can be reached that the legal institution is a reflection of the social setting in which it exists. As that setting changes, the legal system changes; even the particular source of changes varies with variations in the social setting.

From the legal tradition passed down from early England, contemporary Anglo-American law has inherited a legal structure with these outstanding features: a reliance on state power to enforce rules; the view that a violation of any rule is a violation against the state and not simply a matter of personal injury; the principle that the law enforcers should be separated from the lawmakers; the designation of a judge to settle disputes between the state and individual citizenry; and, finally, the use of peers as the ultimate group for deciding disputes.

[14] For evidence of subcultural differences among the Negroes see Charles Keil, *Urban Blues,* Bloomington, Ind.: Indiana University Press, 1965, and *The Autobiography of Malcolm X,* New York: Grove Press, Inc., 1963.

[15] Oscar Lewis, *La Vida,* New York: Random House, Inc., 1965.

These structural characteristics of the legal system provide, then, a framework within which the legal order has shifted and moved during successive centuries. Substantive law has changed appreciably through the years, and one would scarcely recognize the list of "crimes" which occupied so much legal attention in early England as being of the same general category as those that concern the law today.

More important, however, than changes in substantive law are the alterations of the structure which have occurred. Increasing rationality is certainly of paramount importance among these changes, and this has been accompanied by an increased reliance on statutes as opposed to judge-made laws and an increased reliance on the replacement of certain functions of the legal order by administrative boards. Finally, we have seen an increasing emphasis upon deterrence as the primary, if not the only, justification for the legal system.

Cutting across these structural and substantive changes in the legal order is the rise of the middle class as a dominating force in determining the shape of the law. Although this shift may be responsible for a general lessening of the degree to which the law can be said to represent the interests of particular groups, the fact remains that the middle class imposes on other groups adherence to rules which are in their own best interest. Thus, although we may in a general way have expanded the size of the interest groups which shape the law, it remains the case that groups which lack effective political and economic power are the ones which are most affected by the changes in the legal order.

The law, like everything, has a history, and the studies which follow detail that history. In succeeding sections we shall bring together investigations which attempt to show how, given the inheritance spelled out in this section, the legal system functions in the contemporary world.

1. The Development of Crime in Early English Society

Clarence Ray Jeffery

The purpose of this paper is to trace the development of crime and criminal law in England from 400 A.D. to 1200 A.D. This period of history was selected for two reasons. First, early Saxon laws were recorded, and thus the changes which occurred in the legal structure over a period of years can be traced and analyzed; and second, it was during this period of English history that the tribal law of the Saxons gave way to the common law system which is now basic to Anglo-American law. Whatever social forces produced the common law system had to be present during this period.

SOURCE: "The Development of Crime in Early English Society," *Journal of Criminal Law, Criminology and Police Science*, vol. 47, pp. 647–666, March–April, 1957. By permission of the author and publisher.

It is the intent of the writer to analyze these legal changes in terms of changing social conditions.

The method used was that of institutional legal history.[1] A basic assumption of sociological jurisprudence is that law is related to institutional history and change. The social changes that occurred in England during the period studied produced crime and criminal law as we know them today.

PART I

Anglo-Saxon Social Structure

The Iberians and Celts. The earliest settlers of Britain were the Iberians and the Celts. These people were organized along tribal lines, and there is no evidence of a social structure other than the tribal structure. They were bound together by the "legal and sentimental ties of kinship as the moral basis of society." [2] Trevelyan estimates that the Celts and Iberians were in the iron age. Agricultural practices were very crude. Pigs and cattle were kept as a part of their economic life, along with hunting, fishing, herding, weaving, and metal work.[3]

Between 55 B.C. and 400 A.D. the Romans occupied Britain, but for the exception of roads, walls, and town sites the Romans never did Latinize the Celts. Celtic tribalism still survived beyond the city walls.[4]

The Anglo-Saxons. Caesar and Tacitus describe the Anglo-Saxons as tribal units occupying the territory of North Germany. They had an iron-age culture: they utilized metals for tools and war weapons; they grew corn; they herded cattle.[5] They had a very crude and extensive type of agricultural system. These tribes possessed a very loose type of military organization and were quite warlike.[6] The consanguine family was the important social unit; the blood-tie was the important social relationship. The primitive fusion of institutional functions in the kinship group is undoubtedly the most important characteristic of this social arrangement.

Each tribe was in theory a group of kinsmen. The tribe performed the economic, political, religious, and familistic functions performed by separate and distinct institutional structures in a modern society. The tribe was the land-owning unit, and the land was cultivated by a group of kinsmen who formed plough-teams and who cultivated the land in an open-field system. Political control was in the hands of the armed warriors who met in the folk-moot or tribal council to elect a king or to pass laws. The king was elected from a given hereditary line, and he was the king of a tribe, never of a territorial unit. "The notion of a territorial influence was never for a moment involved in it." [7] The conjugal family unit was less important than the kinship group. "In general the mores of this period were bound up with the assumption that every-

---

[1] Jeffery, C. Ray, *Crime, Law, and Social Structure.* Jour. Crim. Law, Criminol. and Pol. Sci. 47, 4 (1956).

[2] Trevelyan, G. M., *History of England,* New York: Doubleday and Co., vol. I, p. 25.

[3] *Ibid.,* pp. 26–28.

[4] *Ibid.,* p. 43.

[5] Stubbs, William, *The Constitutional History of England,* Oxford: Clarendon Press, 1891, vol. I, p. 15 ff.

[6] *Ibid.,* p. 16 ff.

[7] Kemble, John M., *The Saxons in England,* London: Bernard Quartich, 1879, vol. I, p. 137. See also Trevelyan, *op. cit.,* p. 50.

one belonged to a localized kinship group to which he is answerable." [8] "The tie which united these smaller pastoral communities was simply that of kindred." [9]

The Feudal System

Disintegrating Tribalism. The change that was taking place in English social structure has been characterized as "disintegrating tribalism." [10] "But even before the migrations to Britain, tribalism was yielding to individualism, and kinship was being replaced by the personal relation of warrior to his chief, which is the basis of aristocracy and feudalism." [11]

> The whole economic and political structure of society was undergoing a great change. If by any two words we could indicate the nature of this elaborate process we might say that "tribalism" was giving place to "feudalism." [12]

Even before their invasion of Britain these Teutonic tribes had developed the *comitatus,* a military leader and his followers. They were bound to one another by a code of honor, and the relationship between a military leader and his followers was a personal one. The military leader supplied certain necessities and the warriors shared in the booty whenever a raid was carried out.[13] This military system was replacing the familistic system. The social class system even before the invasions included an *eorl,* a military leader; the *ceorl,* his follower and the *laet,* a slave or conquered man.[14]

The British invasions, between 400 and 600 A.D., accentuated this transition from a tribal state to a feudal state. These invasions were of two different types. First came bands of warriors, the *comitatus,* without women and children; followed by kinship groups, farmers with their families.[15] These "war bands were one of the features of disintegrating tribalism." [16] The warriors settled the land which they were granted as rewards for their military service. Later on the kinship groups settled the land. "They were not so much territories as communities of tribesmen who felt themselves bound together by common customs and blood-ties; sometimes one or two hundred families, sometimes considerably more." [17] Each patriarchal family unit was allotted a share of land, called a *hide,* from which it gained economic subsistence.[18] At the beginning of Saxon history in England we find a distinction between the military man and the agricultural man, a distinction which was to play an important role in the development of feudalism in England.

Feudalism. In his discussion of feudalism Ganshof makes a distinction between two different but related meanings of the term "feudalism." As a *society* feudalism refers

[8] Queen, Stuart A. and Adams, John B., *The Family in Various Cultures,* New York: J. P. Lippincott Co., 1952, p. 175.

[9] Stubbs, *op. cit.,* p. 15.

[10] Gibbs, Marion, *Feudal Order,* New York: Henry Schuman, Inc., 1953, p. 10 ff.

[11] Trevelyan, *op. cit.,* p. 51.

[12] Maitland, F. W. and Montague, F. C., *A Sketch of English Legal History,* New York: Putnam and Sons, 1915, p. 10.

[13] Kemble, *op. cit.,* vol. I, pp. 163–184.

[14] Vinogradoff, Paul, *The Growth of the Manor,* London: George Allen and Unwin, 1904, pp. 123–124.

[15] Trevelyan, *op. cit.,* p. 56.

[16] Gibbs, *op. cit.,* p. 17.

[17] *Ibid.,* p. 19.

[18] *Ibid.,* p. 20.

to a system of personal dependence, with a military class occupying the higher levels in the social scale, and with a subdivision of rights in real property corresponding to this system of personal dependence. As a *legal* system feudalism means a body of institutions creating obligations of service and duty—a military service on the part of the vassal and an obligation of protection on the part of the lord with regard to the vassal.[19]

Land System. The feudal system began in England with the invasions. The conquering warriors were granted land by their chiefs as a reward for military service. The land settlement pattern was mixed, that is, it included both military and family units. The granting of land to a follower by a chief was called a *beneficium* or benefit. The recipient of the land was able to cultivate it for his own use, to use it as a benefit free from obligations of service and taxation.[20] Land held in *alod*, an original grant of land to a military follower, was held free of service and rent. Land held in *fief* or *feud* was held in return for service and rent. Land grants were originally made for services rendered, as in the case of the invasions; however, by the ninth century the process was reversed. Service was now rendered in return for a benefice.[21] By the tenth century all land in England was bookland, land held in *fief*. A grant of land by a lord to a vassal came to be known as a *fief* or *feud*, and these terms replaced the term *beneficium*.[22] Land was now under the control of private landlords, and any man who occupied the lord's land owed the lord services. This concept of land-ownership replaced the system found during the tribal state of Saxon history when the tribe owned the land and each man as a tribesman shared in this ownership.

Vassalage. There was a legal union between vassalage and the benefice since the land relationship created by the grant also created a personal relationship between lord and vassal.[23] *Commendation* was the legal process by which a freeman placed himself under the protection of a lord in return for his services. The act of *commendation* was the way in which the personal tie between men replaced the kinship tie which was disintegrating as a result of the migrations and population growth. An act of *manumission*, usually performed on the altar of a church, freed the serf from his lord. A serf could also be freed by joining the holy orders, being knighted, or by fleeing to a free town and remaining there for a period of a year and a day.[24]

The tenure system, or system of service, developed as an expression of the *fief*. The most common service was knight's service, or military service. In this way military service was connected to the occupation of land. A distinction was made between the man who owed military service and the man who owed other types of services, especially agricultural services.[25] A *thegn* was a man with five hides of land who owed military service to a lord. He was liable for the *trinoda necessitas;* the *fyrd* or military expedition, the repairing of military fortifications, and the repairing of roads and bridges.[26]

[19] Ganshof, F. L., *Feudalism*, New York: Longmans, Green and Co., 1952, p. xv.

[20] *Ibid.,* p. 11.

[21] *Ibid.,* p. 47; p. 237.

[22] *Ibid.,* p. 96.

[23] *Ibid.,* p. 37 ff.

[24] Pollock, Frederick, and Maitland, F. W., *The History of English Law before the Time of Edward I,* Cambridge: University Press, 1932, vol. I, pp. 427–429.

[25] Gibbs, *op. cit.,* p. 55.

[26] Stubbs, *op. cit.,* p. 208–210.

The *ceorl* was a freeman with one hide of land. He paid a fee to his lord, but performed no services. The *geneat* was free from week work. The *gebur* was bound to the land and he did week work, work of an uncertain nature required every day of the week. The man who did week work was in a servile position because his services could be demanded every day by the lord. The more specific the demands on a man, the freer he was in this feudal arrangement.[27] As the kinship system disintegrated the *ceorl* sought protection from economic want and from the Danes during the Danish invasions of the ninth and tenth centuries. In return for security he would perform services for his lord.[28] By the time of Aethelstan (925) a law required that every man have a lord. ". . . the manorial system arises at the end of the Old-English period mainly in consequence of the subjection of a labouring population of free descent to a military and capitalistic class . . ." [29]

> The practice of a man seeking lordship increasingly provided an alternative social discipline. For a good Lord gave his man the material support which a father gave his sons, and the social protection which the kindred gave its members.[30]

Besides military and agricultural services several other types of tenure emerged. Tenure by frankalmoin was held by ecclesiastical groups in return for prayers and saying masses. Tenure by serjeanty was personal service, such as carrying a lord's sword or working in his kitchen. Tenure by socage was a personal tenure involving gifts to the lord on special occasions, such as birthdays and holidays.[31]

Political Unification. The political unification of these militaristic-tribalistic settlements came about as a result of three forces: (1) civil wars among local military leaders, (2) the Danish invasions of the tenth century, and (3) the acceptance of Christianity as the religion of the land.[32] By the tenth century England was united into six or eight large Kingdoms or Earldoms.

The constitutional system of the Saxon tribes was organized around the tribe and the chief. The tribal chief was replaced by a king. The king was a landlord, a military leader. The Saxon invasions plus tribal warfare produced in England a number of such local kings. The concept of kingship changed from a tribal to a territorial concept. The king was elected by the *witan*, usually from a given royal family.[33]

The tribal council was replaced by the *witenagemot*, or the *witan*, a meeting of the large landlords of the community. The *witan* declared law, elected kings, and granted land to lords and churchmen.[34]

Within a kingdom the local subdivisions were known as *shires*, and each *shire* was ruled by an *ealdorman*. The *shire* was a political, military, and fiscal unit of government, and the *shire-moot* was an important feudal court. The *hundred* was a smaller

---

[27] Gibbs, *op. cit.*, p. 55 ff. See also Vinogradoff, *The Growth of the Manor, op. cit.*, pp. 232–233.

[28] Stenton, Frank, *Anglo-Saxon England*, Oxford: Clarendon Press, 1950, pp. 463–464.

[29] Vinogradoff, *The Growth of the Manor, op. cit.*, p. 235.

[30] Gibbs, *op. cit.*, p. 21.

[31] Pollock and Maitland, *op. cit.*, vol. I, pp. 282–295.

[32] Stubbs, *op. cit.*, vol. I, p. 187 ff.

[33] Kemble, *op. cit.*, vol. II, p. 142. See also M. M. Knappen, *Constitutional and Legal History of England*, New York: Harcourt, Brace and Co., 1942, p. 28.

[34] Kemble, *op. cit.*, vol. II, pp. 195–221.

unit than the *shire,* controlling the judicial and agricultural affairs of several agricultural villages.[35]

Village and Manor. With the disintegration of the kinship settlements the local agricultural village came into prominence. These villages were centers for administering agricultural policy, as well as centers of trade and commerce. The manor was the official residence of the lord. It included his house and land. It also represented the agricultural system based on tenure. It included the agricultural classes who worked the land. An open-field system of cultivation was used, along with certain areas designated as pasture land, waste land, and forest land. The manor was also a military and political unit. Each unit furnished so many men for the *fyrd.* The manorial court maintained the judicial control of the manor.[36]

Christianity

Trevelyan has stated that "the change of religion was the first great step forward of the English people." [37] "Anglo-Saxon Christianity transmuted Anglo-Saxon society." [38] When the Saxons invaded Britain Celtic Druidism still existed in the isolated regions of northern England. However Britain was soon converted to Christianity. By 597 Aethelbert, the king of the Kentians, had married a Christian woman and had accepted Christianity himself. The Pope sent Augustine to England to effect a conversion, and by 735 there were two archbishoprics in England. The Germanic warlords allowed the Church to exist and eventually became its converts because it was useful to them.[39]

Christianity and the State. The Church furnished the Teutonic tribes with their only contact with Roman civilization. The Church furnished a model for the state system that was to come. The political unity of England was in a large part due to the spiritual unity of the people under one God and one Pope.[40] The Church also furnished the people with a new moral and social philosophy. A new philosophy of human nature and society emerged. Man was basically weak and immoral. He was born with original sin as a result of his fall from Eden. The purpose of life on earth was salvation, and the body of the church offered to man the means to this salvation. The State was viewed as an agent of God. ". . . the authority of the secular power in administering justice and punishing crime is derived from God." [41] The purpose of the State was to control these sinful individuals during their stay on earth. The major philosophical issue of this period was the question of the nature of the power of the State, the relation between sacred and secular power. The Church claimed prior control over the prince through the Pope because all power was derived from God. Christianity prepared man for the acceptance of a secular ruler, and the rapid growth of the State is in no small measure a reflection of this Christian notion of

---

[35] Stubbs, *op. cit.,* vol. I, pp. 104–108. See also Kemble, *op. cit.,* vol. II, pp. 125–149.

[36] Vinogradoff, *The Growth of the Manor, op. cit.,* p. 296 ff. See also Frederic Seebohm, *The English Village Community,* and F. W. Maitland, *Domesday Book and Beyond.*

[37] Trevelyan, *op. cit.,* p. 74.

[38] *Ibid.,* p. 79.

[39] Gibbs, *op. cit.,* p. 29.

[40] Trevelyan, *op. cit.,* p. 90. See also Stubbs, *op. cit.,* vol. I, p. 266.

[41] Carlyle, R. W., and Carlyle, A. J., *A History of Medieval Political Theory in the West,* London: William Blackstone and Sons, 1915, vol. III, p. 101.

society. Christianity taught people to accept their position on earth as God-given. Man should worry about the hereafter, not the here-and-now.[42]

Christianity and Feudalism. The Church was more than a spiritual force; it was a feudal system with its land grants, laws, courts, and secular officials. The bishops were great landlords. The priests and bishops were members of the witan; they sat on the hundred-moot and the shire-moot. It was the Church who first taught the kings to use written charters and wills to alienate land.[43] The Church supported the feudal system which was emerging in England at this time. "The Church, in elaborating the legal and learned aspects of daily life, was thereby promoting the feudal system based on territorialism, the sharp distinction of classes, and the increasingly unequal distribution of wealth and freedom." [44]

> The fundamental social cleavage in England, as on the continent, was formed by exploitation of peasants by landlords. A section of these landlords were soldiers, another section priests; with sword and cross they protected the people, or so it was said to justify their privileged position in society.[45]
>
> Catholic discipline, as defined and sanctioned by the law of the Church, the canon law, was created in the feudal period. So we need not be surprised that it was well adapted to the needs of a class divided society. Nothing more sharply differentiates feudalism from tribalism and the society of our own time.[46]
>
> What we have written so far may suggest that the effects of conversion to Christianity, including the psychological effects, worked themselves out at two levels; the economic and political. In England, as in many other parts of Europe, the formation of ecclesiastical estates was part of a wider movement—the extension and improvement of agriculture and the subjection of the peasantry to the power of landlords.[47]

At this time there was no separation of Church and State. The Church was an important part of the feudal system. A new system of social order and control emerged "when Christianity and territorial feudalism were beginning to lay new restraints on the individual. . . ." [48]

The Norman Invasion

When William became King of England in 1066, the Saxon era of English history ended and the Norman began. There were few changes in the social structure already described. The land tenure system was accentuated and extended by William. He proclaimed himself to be the "supreme landlord" of all England, and all men who held land held *his* land.[49] The Domesday Survey was a complete survey of the tenure

[42] *Ibid.,* vol. III, p. 170.

[43] Knappen, *op. cit.,* p. 42.

[44] Trevelyan, *op. cit.,* p. 94.

[45] Gibbs, *op. cit.,* p. 7.

[46] *Ibid.,* p. 9.

[47] *Ibid.,* p. 42.

[48] Trevelyan, *op. cit.,* p. 97.

[49] Stubbs, *op. cit.,* vol. I, p. 274 ff.

system. This survey attached all men to the soil and reduced all social relationships to a land tenure system. It redistributed the land to Norman nobles who replaced the Saxons as the new upper class. The principle of *nulle terre sans seigneur*, no land without its lord, was now universal in England.[50] The new class system had the Norman noble at its apex with the Saxon population in various agrciultural positions. The thegn became a Norman knight; the ceorl became a villein. Villeins, bordarii, cotters—agricultural classes—were of Saxon descent.[51] The separation of the military and agricultural classes was now complete. "Between the two epochs (tribalism and the state) stands feudalism as an attempt to connect military organization directly with the agricultural husbandry." [52]

> After the breakdown of the tribal and clan organization, and before the rise of the State, feudalism was the only method by which a help-less population could be protected, war efficiently conducted, coloniza-tion pushed forward, or agriculture carried on with increased profits. For it was a process of differentiating the functions of warrior and hus-bandman.[53]

The split between the Church and State came after the Norman invasion. William attempted to gain control of ecclesiastical affairs whenever he could. The Triple Concordat limited the authority of the Pope. Under William the lay and ecclesiastical courts of law were separated. The controversy and struggle between Church and State continued through the reigns of William Rufus, Henry I, and Stephen. It came to a head during the reign of Henry II with the Becket controversy.[54]

After the death of William the Conqueror the nobles and churchmen gained power at the expense of the crown. It was a period of civil war and peasant uprisings, espe-cially during the reign of Stephen. At this time nobles and bishops reached the height of their power.[55]

PART II

Anglo-Saxon Legal System

Tribal Law. The Anglo-Saxon legal system was originally a system of tribal justice. The old legal codes were recorded from the time of Aethelbert on (570) so that a complete record of the changes which occurred in the legal system is available.[56] Aethelbert followed the Roman practice of recording the laws. These laws are a

[50] Trevelyan, *op. cit.*, p. 172.

[51] Vinogradoff, Paul, *English Society in the Eleventh Century*, Oxford: Clarendon Press, 1908, p. 213.

[52] *Ibid.*, p. 213.

[53] Trevelyan, *op. cit.*, p. 124.

[54] Stenton, *op. cit.*, pp. 650–651.

[55] Poole, A. L., *From Domesday Book to Magna Carta: 1087–1216*, Oxford: Clarendon Press, 1951, pp. 178–192.

[56] The following books contain collections of the early laws of the Saxons: B. Thorpe, ed., *Ancient Laws and Institutes of England*, London: Commission of Public Records, 1840. F. L. Attenborough, *The Laws of the Earliest English Kings*, Cambridge: University Press, 1922. George Rightmire, *The Law of England at the Norman Conquest*, Columbus: Herr Printing Co., 1932. A. J. Robertson, *The Laws of the Kings of England from Edmund to Henry I*, Cambridge, University Press, 1925.

record of Anglo-Saxon tribal custom, based on the principle of kinship. There is no evidence of borrowing from the Roman legal system. Whenever a migration or invasion occurred the laws were recorded so as to make them familiar to all. The family or kinship group, not the State, was regarded as the injured party.[57]

> All crime was crime against the family: It was the family that was regarded as having committed the crimes of its members; it was the family that had to atone, or carry out the blood-feud. In time, money payments were fixed as commutations for injury; but, even as late as the twelfth century, Welsh blood-feuds were fought. . . .[58]

The feud was a kinship matter. If a slaying occurred within a family group no feud took place. The offender was either ignored or exiled. Feuds occurred only between kinship groups.[59]

Feudal Law

Wer, Wite, and Bot. As feudalism and Christianity changed the organization of Saxon society, the blood-feud was replaced by a system of compensations: the *wer, wite,* and *bot.* The *wer* or *wergild* was a money payment made to a family group if a member of that family were killed or in some other way injured. The *bot* was a general payment of compensation for injuries less than death. The *wite* was a public fine payable to a lord or king. The only other punishment referred to is outlawry, or *friedlos.* A man who was an outlaw could be slain by anyone without fear of reprisal or feud. Anyone offending the folk-peace could be placed outside this peace, or be made peaceless. Imprisonment was a punishment unknown to the Saxons.[60]

Like the blood-feud, the *wergild* contained within it the idea of collective responsibility. The clan as a group was responsible for the offenses of its members, and for the collection and payment of the *wer.*[61] Gradually the *wer* replaced the feud. By Alfred's time (871) the feud could be resorted to only after compensation had been requested and refused.[62] A law of Aethelred's made it a breach of the king's peace to resort to the feud before demanding compensation. (Aethelred IV.4.) The collective responsibility of the kin was gradually destroyed and absorbed by other groups.

> If a breach of peace be committed within a "burh" let the inhabitants of the "burh" go get the murderers, or their nearest kin, head for head. If they will not go, let the ealdorman go; if he will not go, let the king go; if he will not go let the ealdordom lie in "peacelessness." (Aethelred 11.6.)
>
> Henceforth, if anyone slay a man, he shall himself bear the vendetta, unless with the help of his friends he pay compensation for it within twelve months to the full amount of the slain man's wergild, according to the inherited rank.

[57] *Select Essays in Anglo-American Legal History,* Boston: Little, Brown and Co., 1907, vol. I, pp. 35–37.

[58] Traill, H. D., *Social England,* New York: Putnam and Sons, 1899, vol. I, p. 5.

[59] Seebohm, Frederic, *Tribal Custom in Anglo-Saxon Law,* London: Longmans, Green and Co., 1902, pp. 20–31.

[60] Pollock and Maitland, *op. cit.,* vol. II, pp. 450–451.

[61] Kemble, *op. cit.,* vol. I, pp. 231–236.

[62] Law of Alfred: 42.

1. If, however, his kindred abandon him and will not pay compensation on his behalf, it is my will that, if afterwards, they give him
neither food nor shelter, all the kindred, except the delinquent, shall
be free from the vendetta. (Edmund 11.1.)

The authorities must put a stop to the vendettas. First, according to
public law, the slayer shall give security to his advocate and the advocate to the kinsmen of the slain man, that he, the slayer, will make
reparation to the kindred.

1. After this it is incumbent upon the kin of the slain man to give security to the slayer's advocate that he, the slayer, may approach
under safe conduct and pledge himself to pay the wergild. (Edmund 11.2.)

And no monk who belongs to a monastery anywhere may lawfully
either demand or pay compensation incurred by vendetta. He leaves
the law of the kindred behind when he accepts the monastic rule.
(Aethelred VIII.25.)

As feudalism developed in England between 700 and 1066, the lords and bishops
replaced the kinship group as the recipients of the *wer* and *wite*. The *wer* was now
determined by the amount of land owned by a man, his feudal rank, rather than by
his rank in the family.

If anyone grants one of his men freedom on the altar, his freedom shall
be publicly recognized, but the emancipator shall have his heritage
and wergild. (Wihtred 8.)

If anyone slays a foreigner, the king shall have two-thirds of his wergild, and his relatives one-third. (Ine 23.)

If an Englishman living in penal slavery absconds, he shall be hanged,
and nothing shall be paid to his lord. (Ine 24.)

He who begets an illegitimate child and disowns it shall not have
the wergild at its death, but its lord and the king shall have it. (Ine
27.)

At this time no distinction is made between intentional and unintentional slayings,
or between private and public wrongs.

If one kills another unintentionally by allowing a tree to fall on him the
tree shall be given to the dead man's kindred, and they shall remove it
within 30 days from the locality. (Alfred 13.)

If a beast injures a man, its owner must hand over the beast to the
injured man or come to terms with him. (Alfred 24.)

If a man has a spear over his shoulder, and anyone is transfixed
thereon, he shall pay the wergild without the fine. (Alfred 36.)

If a bone is laid bare, 3 shillings shall be paid as compensation.
(Aethelbert 34.)

If a bone is damaged, 4 shillings shall be paid as compensation.
(Aethelbert 35.)

If a shoulder is disabled, 30 shillings shall be paid as compensation.
(Aethelbert 38.)

Today we would view such a schedule of payments as belonging to the law of tort, personal injuries for which compensation may be due at law. An insurance policy provides exactly the type of protection provided above by the early Saxon law. Whether or not we call this law criminal law or tort law depends upon the way we use these terms. This is not criminal law as we know it today. Even in the case where the king or lord inherited a wergild it was in the spirit of being an heir, and is not analogous to a criminal action. A man can fall heir to a suit at civil law, but a man cannot fall heir to a criminal law suit, nor can he collect damages and compensation as a result of a crime.

Some crimes were "botless," that is, no compensation was allowed. In such a case the feud had to be resorted to. Secret murder was a "botless" crime.[63]

> We can watch a system of true punishments—corporeal and capital punishments—growing at the expense of the old system of pecuniary mulcts, blood-feud, and outlawry; but on the eve of the Norman Conquest mere homicide can still be atoned for by payment of the dead man's price or "wergild", and if that be not paid, it is rather for the injured family than for the state to slay the slayer.[64]

The Mund and the King's Peace. In the *wite* we see the germ of the idea that a wrong is not simply the affair of the injured party and his kin, but rather it involves a breach of a *mund* of a king, lord, or bishop.[65] Early Germanic justice was based on a folk-peace, a peace of the community. This idea gave way to the *mund*. A *mund* was the right a king or lord had to protect a person or area. At first the *mund* was restricted to special persons and areas; gradually it was extended to include the king's court, army, servants, hundred-court, and finally the four main highways in England. It was now referred to as the "king's peace." [66] The kings, lords, and bishops now received the compensation rather than the kinship group. They had a *mund* which had to be protected.

Other Teutonic tribes had a legal system similar to that of the Saxons. The Welsh tribes had a *galanas*, or murder fine, that was allowed in lieu of the bloodfeud. Among the Irish tribes the *eric*, or a death fine for homicide, was shared by the kin. The Frankish law book, *Lex Salica*, described the same system of feuds and compensation for the Frankish tribes in France.[67]

The Administration of Justice. The Teutonic tribes placed the administration of justice in the hands of local tribal councils, popular assemblies known as folk-moots. As feudalism replaced tribalism these folk-moots were replaced by hundred-moots and shire-moots. The hundred-moot, the court of the hundred, was gradually restricted to lords, stewards, priests, reeves, and four men from each township. It also contained a body of twelve men who heard arguments, which committee later emerged as our petit jury.[68] The shire-moot was attended by ealdormen, bishops, lords, and shire-

---

[63] *Select Essays in Anglo-American Legal History,* op. cit., vol. I, p. 100.

[64] Traill, *op. cit.,* vol. I, p. 172.

[65] Holdsworth, W. S., *A History of English Law,* Boston: Little, Brown and Co., 1923, vol. II, p. 47.

[66] Pollock and Maitland, *op. cit.,* vol. I, p. 44; vol. II, pp. 453–454.

[67] Seebohm, *Tribal Custom in Anglo-Saxon Law,* op. cit., pp. 32–145.

[68] Rightmire, *op. cit.,* pp. 19–26.

reeves. In these courts precedence was given to the pleas of the Church, or kings, and complaints involving individuals, pleas known as "common pleas." [69]

In later Saxon history an important development in the hundred was the tithing. The tithing represented a local grouping of ten men who stood as surety for one another. If one of them broke the law, the other nine would make good the harm. The tithing was based on the notion that every man ought to have a lord. Only lord-less men belonged to a tithing since men with a lord had a surety. "As long as the family remained strong, and the duty of giving up or paying for an offending member and avenging an injured member was acknowledged and carried out, the place of general police was fairly filled; but as population growth, migration, and new ideas loosened family ties, the kings began to substitute local mutual responsibility of free-holders arranged in little groups. . . ." [70] "This was the way, apparently, that a sub-stitute was found in the towns for the absent kindreds." [71]

In these courts the responsibility for initiating a trial was placed with the injured party, who in turn summoned the defendant to court. There was no prosecuting official.[72] Proof was by compurgation or ordeal. If compurgation were used, the parties involved secured the aid of oath-helpers who swore to the truthfulness of the charge. These oath-helpers were originally kinsmen; later on, they were members of the tithing. The number of oath-helpers needed depended upon the rank of the parties and the seriousness of the offense. Trial by ordeal included the hot iron ordeal, the hot and cold water ordeal, and the dry bread or *corsnaed* ordeal.[73] The ordeal was administered with the aid of a priest. Just prior to the Norman invasions a new trial procedure, the jury of presentment, came into existence. It was composed of twelve men who presented facts to the court. It resembled the grand jury of today in many respects.[74]

Sac and Soc. The administration of justice is inseparable from the exercise of jurisdiction. Jurisdiction was now based on a land tenure system, and was related to the feudal system. Those people on the land of a lord or king are in his *mund,* under his protection, and therefore, in his jurisdiction. The right to jurisdiction was given to lords along with a grant of land in grants called *sac* and *soc.* These words, when added to a grant of land, meant that the grantee could hold private court for his subjects and keep the returns therefrom. Such justice was a profitable business for lords and bishops.[75]

By the time of Canute (1016) most of the hundred-moots had passed into the hands of private lords. The manorial court developed as an important aspect of the legal system. Justice was now in the hands of the landlords. "The man who had land judged the man who had not. . . ." [76]

The Church and the Law. There was no separation of lay and ecclesiastical courts until the time of William, which meant that most of the court business was of an

[69] *Ibid.,* pp. 16–20.

[70] Traill, *op. cit.,* vol. I, p. 138.

[71] Seebohm, *Tribal Custom in Anglo-Saxon Law, op. cit.,* p. 413.

[72] *Essays in Anglo-Saxon Law,* Boston: Little, Brown and Co., 1905, pp. 185–205.

[73] Attenborough, *op. cit.,* note on Law of Ine, 37.

[74] Stubbs, *op. cit.,* vol. I, pp. 125–128.

[75] *Ibid.,* pp. 119–121.

[76] *Ibid.,* pp. 207–208.

ecclesiastical nature. The church accepted the system of compensation and compurgation, assigning various values to its own ranks. The bishops and priests sat on the various courts, and they held grants of *sac* and *soc*. Excommunication was used as a punishment for secular as well as sacred offenses.[77] A church law provided benefit of clergy, which meant that people within the sanctity of the church could not be subject to the feud. The Church also demanded compensation for itself for many offenses. "The judicial matters of the Church were apparently transacted in the ordinary *gemots* of the hundred and of the shire." [78] The following laws are selected to illustrate the ecclesiastical nature of these Saxon codes.

Men living in illicit union shall turn to a righteous life repenting their sins, or they shall be excluded from the communion of the Church. (Wihtraed 3.)

If a servant, contrary to his lord's command, does servile work between sunset on Saturday and sunset on Sunday, he shall pay eighty sceattas to his lord. (Wihtraed 9.)

In the first place, we command that the servants of God heed, and duly observe, their proper rule. (Ine 1.)

A child shall be baptized within thirty days. If this is not done, the guardian shall pay forty shillings compensation. (Ine 5.)

If anyone is liable to the death penalty, and he flees to a church, his life shall be spared and he shall pay such compensation as he is directed to pay by legal decision. (Ine 5.)

If anyone withholds Peter's Pence, he shall pay *lahslit* in a Danish district, and a fine in an English district. (Edward and Guthrum, 5.1.)

We enjoin upon every Christian man, in accordance with his Christian profession, to pay tithes, and church dues, and Peter's Pence, and plough-alms. (Edmund 1.)

He who has intercourse with a nun, unless he makes amends, shall not be allowed burial in consecrated ground any more than a homicide. (Edmund 1.)

Priests know full well that they have no right to marry. (Aethelred V.9.)

[Every Christian man shall make amends for] horrible perjuries and devilish deeds, such as murder, homicide, theft, robbery, gluttony, covetousness, greed, and intemperance, fraud, and various breaches of the law, violations of holy orders, and of marriage, and misdeeds of any kind. (Aethelred V.25.)

Norman Law

One of the first acts of William the Conqueror was to claim that he was the guardian of the laws of Edward. The Saxon legal system was accepted in its entirety.[79] A few changes were introduced by the Normans. Willian separated the lay and ecclesi-

---

[77] Thomas Oakley, *English Penitential Discipline and Anglo-Saxon Law in Their Joint Influence*, New York: Columbia University Studies in History, Economics, and Public Law, 1923, p. 86.

[78] *Ibid.*, p. 139.

[79] Maitland and Montague, *op. cit.*, p. 27.

astical courts, so that from this time on two distinct legal systems existed: state law and canon law.[80]

> The differentiation of the functions of lay and spiritual courts was a lone step towards a higher legal civilization. Without it neither Church nor State could have freely developed the law and logic of their position.[81]

William required all freemen to swear fealty to him as King of England.[82] The practice of Englishry and the murder-fine were introduced. Any man found dead under suspicious circumstances was deemed to be a Frenchman unless Englishry were proven, and the district in which the body was found had to pay a murder-fine.[83] The frankpledge replaced the tithing in order to enforce the law of Englishry. Trial by battle replaced the trial by ordeal. The lords grew in power through grants of *sac* and *soc;* they controlled the administration of justice. The kings were too weak to centralize the control of judicial functions in their own hands.[84] The law of Henry I was still the law of *wer, wite,* and *bot.* The central problem of Henry I's time was: "Who in the myriad of possible cases has *sake* and *soke,* the right to hold court for the offender and to pocket the profits of jurisdiction?" [85]

PART III

The Emergence of Crime and Criminal Law in England

It was during the reign of Henry II (1154–1189) that the old tribal-feudal system of law disappeared and a new system of common law emerged in England. A comparison of the laws of Henry I and Henry II reveals that a revolution occurred in the legal field. The former described a system of *wer, bot,* and *wite;* the latter described a system of writs, procedures, and common law.[86]

> In this period we are at a turning point in the history of English law. We still see traces of old tribal divisions and old tribal rules—divisions and rules which an unmitigated feudal system would have modified but perpetuated. But we can see also that a strong centralized court, in touch with the main currents of the intellectual life of Europe, is beginning to make some general rules for all England.[87]

The sources of this new law were the Constitutions of Clarendon, the Constitutions of Northampton, and the records of the Curia Regis. These records, known as Pipe Rolls, were kept by Glanvil and Bracton, court officials. Glanvil's work, *"A Treatise on the Laws and Customs of England Composed in the Time of Henry II,"* was a

---

[80] Episcopal Laws of William I.

[81] Trevelyan, *op. cit.,* p. 176.

[82] Ten Articles of William I.

[83] Holdsworth, *op. cit.,* vol. II, p. 150.

[84] Maitland, F. W., *Domesday Book and Beyond,* Cambridge: University Press, 1897, pp. 80–96.

[85] Pollock and Maitland, *op. cit.,* vol. I, p. 106.

[86] *Ibid.,* vol. II, p. 458.

[87] Holdsworth, *op. cit.,* vol. II, p. 173.

record of the proceedings of the Curia Regis, and it revealed a system of writs, which were necessary in order to be admitted to court. The important legal question now is: "What writ do I need to gain admittance to the King's court?" No mention is made here of tribal justice, or wergilds and bot.[88]

The Court System. During the reign of Henry I the Curia Regis was a court of the nobility. Between 1166 and 1178 great changes occurred in the Curia Regis. It came to be a court of common law for the common man. It gave the peasant the right to a court hearing, a right he had been denied by the manorial court. Thus developed a court of common law as a result of the growth of a strong centralized government. As Henry II gained control of the government from the feudal lords, he also gained control of the administration of the justice. The peasant now looked to the king, not his lord, for justice. Henry opened Westminister Hall, where the Court of the King's Bench met, to all who possessed the proper writ. In 1285 the Statute of Westminister II provided that jury cases could be tried in local communities rather than at Westminister.[89]

In time the King's Court came to be several courts. The Court of Common Pleas heard minor pleas without the presence of the king being required. The Court of the Exchequer heard tax and fiscal cases. The Court of the King's Bench was held in the presence of the king to hear difficult and important cases. After 1268 the king did not have to be present in court personally. An official acted in the name of the Crown. The Court of Chancellory issued royal writs. A system of royal justice emerged. This is a system of common law, law common to all England and available to all men.[90]

The hundred court and the shire court continued in existence for several centuries; however, as the common law developed these courts declined in importance, and finally disappeared. In 1278 Edward made an attempt to gain jurisdiction over all land through the Quo Warranto Inquest, an inquest into the titles held to jurisdiction by various lords.[91] As the Crown grew in strength it reserved to itself the right to hold court and dispense justice. Feudal justice was absorbed and replaced by royal justice.

The shire-reeve, or sheriff, before the time of Henry II, had been an important judicial official in the county. Henry, through an Inquest of Sheriffs, subordinated this office to the Crown, and after his time the sheriff was a minor official who represented the interests of the Crown in local counties. This was an important step in the extension of royal control and justice into the various counties.[92]

Henry II also made use of itinerant justices, called justices in *eyre*. These men travelled about England, holding court sessions in the various hundreds and shires. They declared law in the name of the king. A jury of twelve men would present the facts to the judge whenever he was in their particular hundred.[93]

Trial by oath and ordeal was replaced by trial by battle and trial by jury. The Fourth Lateran Council of 1215 forbade the clergy to participate in trial by ordeal,

[88] *Ibid.*, pp. 188–190.

[89] Maitland, F. W., *The Constitutional History of England,* Cambridge: University Press, 1931, pp. 61–64. See also Maitland and Montague, *op. cit.*, p. 36.

[90] Knappen, *op. cit.*, pp. 166–168.

[91] Trevelyan, *op. cit.*, pp. 256–257.

[92] Stubbs, *op. cit.*, vol. I, pp. 649–652.

[93] Knappen, *op. cit.*, pp. 170–172. See also Stubbs, *op. cit.*, vol. I, pp. 652–654.

which meant that alternatives had to be used. During the time of Henry II a defendant was allowed the alternative of a jury trial or trial by battle. Many men refused to accept a jury trial because if they were convicted their property escheated to the king's treasury rather than going to their families. Many were forced to accept a jury trial by means of the *peine forte et dure,* a system of torture whereby heavy stones were placed on a man's chest until he consented to a jury trial or died. It was not until the Abraham Thornton case in 1818, in which the defendant used the ordeal, that Parliament abolished the ordeal.[94]

A new writ, the writ of trespass, came into existence to replace trial by appeal. It allowed a litigant to collect damages. Indictment was now by jury, and charges were brought by the Crown. Private appeals were no longer allowed. The initiation of criminal trials was in the hands of the Crown.[95] "The new procedure, though accusatory, was a true criminal procedure and the king prosecuted, and every indictment alleged that the accused had offended against the peace of our lord, the king, his crown and dignity." [96]

The King's Peace. By the time of Henry II the King's peace extended to all persons and all places in England. The special *munds* of the lords and bishops were devoured by the king's peace. The king was now a territorial king and his peace extended throughout the land. The king was now the source of law. He had jurisdiction in every case. The State, and not the family or the lord, now was the proper prosecutor in every case.[97]

Crime and Criminal Law. "Sometime in the twelfth century this ancient system of *writ* and *bot* disappeared, leaving in its place the beginnings of a common law of crime." [98]

> On no other part of our law did the twelfth century stamp a more permanent impress of its heavy hand than on that which was to be criminal law of after days. The change that it made will at first sight seem to us immeasurable. At the end of the period we already see the broad outlines which will be visible throughout the coming ages. . . . We go back a few years . . . and we are breathing a different air. We are looking at a scheme of *wer,* blood-feud, *bot* and *wite.*[99]
>
> In that most revolutionary of all centuries, under the influence of the East, of the idealism induced by the Crusades, of the reality of the Christian story brought home by nearer knowledge of the Holy Land, of the re-discovery of Roman law, of a world enlarged by contact with a greater civilization, all forms of thought were in process of revision; great minds were questioning accepted beliefs and customs; the Western world suddenly ceased to regard murder, arson, rape, and theft as regrettable torts which should be compensated by payment to the

---

[94] Maitland and Montague, *op. cit.,* pp. 60–63. See also Traill, *op. cit.,* p. 293.

[95] Holdsworth, *op. cit.,* vol. II, p. 364.

[96] *Ibid.,* vol. II, p. 621.

[97] Pollock and Maitland, *op. cit.,* vol. II, pp. 463–464. See also Maitland, *Constitutional History of England, op. cit.,* p. 107.

[98] Walsh, William, *Outlines of the History of English and American Law,* New York: New York University Press, 1923, p. 371.

[99] Pollock and Maitland, *op. cit.,* vol. II, p. 448.

> family—such and other offenses came to be regarded not only as sins
> for which a penance was required by the Church, but as crime against
> society at large to be prosecuted by the community through its chief;
> the ever-recurring blood-feud was gradually discredited in men's
> minds. The transfer of the receipt of payment from the kinsfolk to the
> king disinclined men to favor violence.[100]
>
> *The State Takes the Place of the Kinsmen*—The very core of the
> revolutions in law and finance that took place in Henry's reign was the
> transfer of the initiative in criminal matters from the kindred of the
> injured man . . . to the king as public prosecutor.[101]
>
> *Pleas of the Crown*—The king's jurisdiction finally ousted the com-
> munal courts and tended to control the courts of the barons, because
> the king . . . could give a hearing which, if not as speedy, was very
> likely to be more impartial than the court presided over by local great
> men.[102]

By 1226 an agreement between the criminal and the relatives of a slain man would
not avail to save the murderer from an indictment and a sentence of death. The state
no longer allowed a private settlement of a criminal case.[103] During Glanvil's time
pleas were for the first time divided into civil and criminal.[104] By adding the words
de pace domini regis infracta to a plea any offense could be made a plea of the
crown.[105]

Blackstone defined a crime as a public offense.

> The distinction of public wrongs from private, of crimes and misde-
> meanors from civil injuries, seems principally to consist of this: that
> private wrongs, or civil injuries, are an infringement or privation of
> the civil rights which belong to individuals, considered merely as in-
> dividuals; public wrongs, or crimes and misdemeanors, are a breach
> and violation of the public rights and duties due to the whole com-
> munity, considered as a community, in its social aggregate capacity
> . . . treason, murder, and robbery are properly ranked among crimes;
> since besides the injury done the individual, they strike at the very
> being of society; which cannot possibly subsist where actions of this
> sort are suffered to escape with impunity.[106]

A new doctrine of criminal responsibility was emerging, the doctrine of *mens rea*
or intent. Murder was now divided into murder with malice aforethought and
murder without malice aforethought. Malice aforethought can be dependent upon
other conditions, such as infancy, lunacy, drunkenness, and so forth. The psychiatric

---

[100] Jeudwine, J. W., *Tort, Crime and the Police in Medieval England*, London: Williams and Norgate, 1917, p. 84.

[101] *Ibid.*, p. 85.

[102] *Ibid.*, pp. 110–111.

[103] Holdsworth, *op. cit.*, vol. II, p. 257.

[104] Pollock and Maitland, *op. cit.*, vol. I, p. 165.

[105] Reeves, John, *History of the English Law*, Philadelphia: M. Murphy Co., 1880, vol. I, p. 384.

[106] Blackstone, William, *Commentaries on the Laws of England*, 8th ed., Oxford: Clarendon Press, 1778, Book IV, p. 5.

view of personality development clashed with this legal view of free will and moral responsibility. A major issue in criminal law today is: "How can a man be guilty of a crime, possess mens rea, if his actions are determined by sociological and psychological conditions?"

The notion of natural crime, a crime against a law of nature rather than against a legal law, was present in the criminal law at its inception. This led to the definition of crimes as *mala in se,* acts bad in themselves, and *mala prohibita,* acts which are crimes because they are prohibited by positive law. This led to the current confusion in criminology between anti-social behavior and anti-legal behavior.[107]

> Criminal law is related to acts which, if there were no criminal law at all, would be judged by the public at large much as they are judged at present. If murder, theft, and rape were not punishable by law, the words would still be in use and would be applied to the same or nearly the same actions.[108]
>
> Which has occasioned some to doubt how far a human legislature ought to inflict capital punishment for *positive* offences; offences against the municipal law only, and not against the law of nature. . . . With regard to offences *mala in se,* capital punishments are in some instances inflicted by the immediate *command* of God Himself to all mankind; as, in the case of murder. . . .[109]

The English common law is based on the assumption that there is a higher moral order which is a part of the law of nature and from which positive laws are derived.

> Throughout the Middle Ages the Law of Nature, identified by Gratian with the law of God, was regarded by the canonists and civilians as the reasonable basis of all law . . . in English law not so much is heard of the law of nature. . . . As a matter of fact, the work done elsewhere by the law of nature was done in England by "reasons.". . . Similarly this appeal to reason and expediency has led in later law to talk about the distinction between *malum prohibitum* and *mala in se.* . . .[110]

Church and State. Although Church and State had been separated under William, the separation was not complete. The practice of "benefit of clergy" had existed for some time. All clerks of the court had a right to be tried in an ecclesiastical court. Henry II attempted to overcome the abuses of this practice when in the Constitutions of Clarendon he provided that criminous clerks were to be sentenced in lay courts. Thomas Becket, the archbishop, opposed the sentencing of clerks in a lay court, and after a bitter struggle Becket was slain. The immediate effect of Becket's death was to postpone the issue until a later date, but gradually the Church lost its right to punish crime through the use of force.[111] The Church could punish offenders of the

[107] Jeffery, *op. cit.*

[108] Stephen, J. F., *A History of the Criminal Law of England,* London: Methuen and Co., 1883, vol. II, p. 75.

[109] Blackstone, *op. cit.,* Book IV, p. 9.

[110] Holdsworth, *op. cit.,* vol. II, pp. 603–604.

[111] Poole, *op. cit.,* pp. 197–212.

canon law through excommunication and a system of penances, but this was a spiritual rather than a secular jurisdiction.

This does not mean, however, that State and Church developed separately and independently of one another. They functioned as an interdependent system. The moral code of the Church was made an important part of the common law. The legal system borrowed a great deal from the Church in those areas concerning marriage, sexual practices, morals, wills, property rights, and so forth.

The notion of crime contains within it the notion of sin, for which punishment is required. The concept of *mens rea* was derived from the Christian view of sins of the mind. Sin can be punished individually, not collectively, so that the individual and not the clan or family is responsible. Only individuals have a soul that can be saved; social groups do not possess souls, and for that reason tribal responsibility gave way to the Christian notion of individual responsibility.

The concept of crime thus developed as it did as a result of this interaction of the Church and State. However, it was the State, not the Church, that became the agent for punishing sin.

> Although the religious might preach that it was a sin to kill, the conception of killing as an offence against the community is co-existent only with the conception of the power and the will of the State to enforce penalties for offences against the community. So long as overlords of the tribes, whether the king of Ireland or the king of France, contented himself with collecting customary dues and took no notice of wrongs as between individuals . . . crime as such did not exist.[112]

Kemble has summarized this social change when he stated: "And thus, by slow degrees, as the State itself became Christianized, the moral duty became a legal one." [113] Before a moral offense is a crime it has to become a legal offense.

The transition from tribalism to feudalism to territorialism was complete. The State was not yet complete in all its aspects, but territorialism as we know it was emerging from feudalism. This is especially true in the case of criminal law. The *wer, wite,* and *bot* had disappeared, and in their place a new system of common law emerged.

> The State replaced the family as the agent of social control.
>
> The main fact in the development of the State, manifesting itself roughly from the end of the twelfth century, is that the citizens are protected by a central power . . . with its national councils and courts. Between the two epochs stands again the doctrine, and to a certain extent, the practice of feudalism.[114]
>
> In the end the king or the parliament, or both, came to be directly related to all individuals who compose the State, and in their authority the local and personal authorities and jurisdictions of feudalism were finally lost. . . . The royal justice at last absorbs all feudal justice . . . but it was not feudalism that triumphed, but territorialism.[115]

---

[112] Jeudwine, *op. cit.,* p. 89.

[113] Kemble, *op. cit.,* vol. II, p. 516.

[114] Vinogradoff, *English Society in the Eleventh Century, op. cit.,* p. 213.

[115] Carlyle and Carlyle, *op. cit.,* vol. III, p. 20.

CONCLUSIONS

Social Structure and Social Change in England

The pattern of social change in England from 400 to 1200 was a change from tribalism to feudalism to nationalism. The *land-tie* replaced the *blood-tie* as the basis for social order.

During the tribal period there was a fusion of institutional functions in the kinship unit. This body was the political, economic, family, religious, and ecological unit. By 1200 separate institutions existed in these several areas. Political authority was now in the hands of landlords. By the time of Henry II the king emerged as the surpreme landlord in this feudal hierarchy. Economic organization shifted from a hunting, fishing, and pastoral economy, where the kinship group was the economic unit, to an agricultural economy, where the feudal manor was the economic unit. Each man occupied land belonging to his lord, rather than to his kin, and he was attached to this land through a personal-legal relationship known as the tenure system. Status was now based on this tenure system. Feudalism was based on a division of men into two classes: military and agricultural. Religion was now controlled by a professional hierarchy of priests and bishops who acted as both church officials and landlords. Christianity was an important aspect of the feudal system. The conjugal family did not perform the many functions performed by the tribal family. This shift from an institutional family to a companionship family is a familiar theme in sociological literature today.[116]

A new social structure emerged in England, and as a result of these changes a new legal system came into existence. During the tribal period the legal system was in the hands of the tribal group, and justice was based on the blood-feud. As tribalism gave way to feudalism, the feud was replaced by a system of compensations. Justice passed into the hands of landlords. There was no separation of lay and ecclesiastical courts until the time of William. State law and crime came into existence during the time of Henry II as a result of this separation of State and Church, and as a result of the emergence of a central authority in England which replaced the authority of the feudal lords. Henry replaced feudal justice with state justice by means of justices in eyre, the king's peace, a system of royal courts, and a system of royal writs. Common law emerged as the law of the Crown available to all men. The myth that the common law of England is the law of the Anglo-Saxons is without historical foundation.[117] The family was no longer involved in law and justice. The State was the offended social unit, and the State was the proper prosecutor in every case of crime. Justice was now the sole prerogative of the State. "Custom passes into law." This shift occurred historically when a political community separate from the kinship group emerged as a part of the social organization. A comparison of tribal law and state law reveals these basic differences.

Tribal Law	*State Law*
Blood-tie	Territorial-tie
Collective responsibility	Individual responsibility
Family as unit of justice and order	State as unit of justice
Feud or compensation	Punishment

[116] Burgess, Ernest W., and Locke, Harvey J., *The Family, from Institution to Companionship*, New York: American Book Co., 1953.

[117] Radin, Max, *The Law and You*, New York: Mentor Book, 1948, p. 103.

The basic thesis presented in sociological and anthropological literature concerning law and society is that the development of law has been from tribal law to State law. This idea is developed in one way or another by Maine, Weber, and Hoebel.[118] The growth and development of English law from Saxon tribal law to State law supports Maine's thesis that there has been a transition from kinship authority to territorial authority. It likewise supports Weber's thesis that a change from traditionalistic to rationalistic authority occurred when the State emerged as the unit of social order.

In this paper I have attempted to make the sociology of law the subject of study rather than the criminal. One of the basic difficulties in criminological research is that very little use is made of such basic sociological concepts as institution, history, social change, social organization, and social theory. This orientation is clearly seen in a statement from Sutherland and Cressey that "criminal behavior is not affected directly or significantly by variations in the form of the general social institutions—economics, government, religion, and education. . . ." [119] Group behavior is affected by the institutional structure within which it occurs. But more to the point, the system of social control used to judge behavior as legal or illegal is functionally interrelated with the social institutions: political, economic, familial, and educational. As sociologists we should be interested in sociological jurisprudence. A theory of crime depends upon an institutional study of law and society.

2. Theft, Law and Society: The Carrier's Case

Jerome Hall

Every legal problem arises within the framework of a particular set of social institutions. The interrelations of these institutions and the interaction between them and the body of legal sanctions existing at any given time create innumerable problems, in the solution of which the materials of legal history are made. In these problem-situations, one sees an interplay of impersonal forces as well as the unceasing efforts of man directed at the considered use of means to gain ends, and applied in the actuality or under the illusion of power to modify his course of life.

The law of theft provides a superb opportunity to study these problems. Related immediately to the development of property interests and characterized by its concern with relatively refined methods of illegal acquisition, this body of law has a long and well-marked history which can be definitely and significantly traced. For each ultimate link in the chain of its history is a specific case or statute.

The report of any law case is a human document. Illuminated with but a bit of imagination, even the technical words written in a musty volume portray a vivid drama. The dead awaken, contestants battle hotly for the things they value; and powerful forces penetrate the courtroom, driving the actors to extend themselves to

SOURCE: *Theft, Law and Society* (revised edition), Indianapolis: The Bobbs-Merrill Company, Inc., 1952. By permission of the author and publisher.

[118] Jeffery, C. Ray, *Crime, Law, and Social Structure.* Jour. Crim. Law, Criminol. and Pol. Sci. 47, 4 (1956).

[119] Sutherland, Edwin H., and Cressey, Donald R., *Principles of Criminology,* 5th ed., New York: J. P. Lippincott, 1955, p. 217.

their uttermost limits. The final opinion, deliberately expressed, may conceal within its austere form a life-struggle. Most cases, to be sure, are merely cumulative in their effect, moving in well beaten paths, with some inevitable deviation but by and large within the lines laid down. Occasionally, however, comes a case of tremendous importance. It affects the gentlemen on the bench greatly; despite their efforts to preserve the appearance of conformity to precedent, it is clear that they struck out in a definitely new direction.

Such a case, decided in 1473, was designated the Carrier's Case.

I. THE FACTS AND THE LAW

The facts are simple enough: the defendant was hired to carry certain bales to Southampton. Instead of fulfilling his obligation, he carried the goods to another place, broke open the bales and took the contents. He was apprehended and charged with felony.

The case was discussed at length, at least on two occasions, before and by the most illustrious judges of the time, among whom were Brian, the Chief Justice, Choke, and Nedham; attorneys Hussey and Molineux represented the Crown.[1]

Brian, one of the soundest of English judges, contended throughout the proceedings that no felony had been committed. The defendant had possession, said Brian, "by a bailing and delivery lawfully"; and "what he himself has he cannot take with *vi et armis* nor against the peace; therefore it cannot be felony nor trespass."

Against this position, it was argued:

> **1.** There was no bailment but, instead, "a bargain to take and carry" which did not vest possession if the carrier's intention was unlawful at the time he received the goods.
> **2.** Granted that there was a bailment, felony was committed by subsequently taking the property *animo furandi*.
> **3.** The bailment was terminated by taking the goods to a place other than Southampton and "breaking bulk," that is, opening the bales.
> **4.** The defendant had possession of the containers or wrappers only but not of the contents of the bales.
> **5.** The case should be decided not according to common law but "according to the law of nature" (this was urged by the Chancellor).

The defendant was finally held guilty of felony by a majority of the judges. In order to understand the meaning of the decision and its effect upon the law of theft, it is necessary to project an inquiry in several directions. The traditional professional approach runs in terms of an analysis of the law existing at the time of the trial. Since the *corpus juris* was well known to the judges and was, avowedly at least, given

[1] The Carrier's Case, Y. B. 13 Edw. IV. f. 9, pl. 5, is interesting from a procedural point of view for several reasons: First, it was heard in the Star Chamber (and later in the Exchequer), although the beginning of the Court of the Star Chamber is generally set at 1487, fourteen years after the Carrier's Case was decided. Second, the trial of a felony in the Star Chamber was extraordinary. Finally, its later hearing in the Exchequer, an inferior tribunal, is also unusual. Possible reasons for the appearance of the case in the Star Chamber are (1) the fact that an alien merchant was involved. There are numerous cases in which foreigners appear as parties in the early history of the court; (2) the question of waif, to which the king might have a right, although it was actually decided otherwise. As to the date of the case with reference to the origin of the Star Chamber, it is indicated that the statute of 1487 (3 Hen. VII, c. 1) did not create a new tribunal but that the court was in process of formation for some years prior to the passage of the act. *Cf.* Dicey, The Privy Council (1887) 95.

particular consideration, this approach suggests itself quite naturally as the necessary initial investigation.

It must, however, be borne in mind that in 1473 *stare decisis* was not the solid structure that it has become, if for no other reason than that the number of past cases was relatively small and the reporting of them was still a rather haphazard affair. No abridgement had yet been published (Statham's was printed in 1490); but, on the other hand, the Year Books had been compiled for two centuries, and the judges were undoubtedly familiar with the important cases. Moreover, despite the fact that the Chancellor's remark regarding the law of nature went unchallenged, it is perfectly clear that the judges regarded themselves as bound by the common law. Such difference, then, as existed regarding the extent of precedent and the attitude of the judges with reference to the binding effect of past cases, was one of degree.

We may start with the fact that it was agreed that:

>   1. Trespass is an essential element of larceny.
>   2. A person in possession of property cannot commit a trespass upon that property.
>   3. A bailee has possession.

Trespass as an essential element of larceny simply meant taking a chattel from one who had possession of it. It is as clear as anything can be that, prior to the Carrier's Case, "taking," as an element of larceny, had no artificial meaning. Anglo-Saxon and early Norman economic conditions limited both the objects and the methods of theft. Movable property consisted of cattle, farm products, and furniture. "To carry it [movable property] away manually was, in practice, the only way by which he was likely to be deprived of it." [2]

Since theft of cattle by armed bands was by far the most important crime against property,[3] it requires no stretch of imagination to see what was meant by "trespass" in the early law.[4] Quite appropriately, the old form of indictment charged "that J. S. on etc. one etc. of the goods and chattels of J. N. feloniously did steal, *take and carry away against the peace*," etc.[5] Theft was either "manifest" or "non-manifest," depending upon whether or not the offender was caught in the act of stealing. In either event, the trespass was identical. The final effect was likely to be the same if the property taken was worth more than a fixed minimum amount; but the manifest thief was disposed of on the spot. This distinction between types of theft persisted into the thirteenth century when new procedural developments introduced by the Normans gradually established a different classification.[6]

When we turn to the professional literature we find no use or interpretation of the word "trespass" as an element of theft, which fitted the facts in the Carrier's Case. Glanvil, the first author of a text of the procedural common law, stated specifically

---

[2] Stephen, General View of the Criminal Law of England (1863) 51.

[3] See *infra*.

[4] "The most striking fact about the use of *cum vi (sua) et armis* and kindred expressions in the early appeals is that they were used only in connection with an invasion of land by an armed force, never of the act of an individual of and by himself." Woodbine, *Origins of the Action of Trespass* (1925) 34 Yale L. J. 361.

[5] "In truth, the limitation [that felony required a taking from the possession of the owner without his consent] seems to have been inherent in the nature of a common law felony. That act alone was punishable by appeal or indictment which was done *contra pacem regis*, or, in other words, *vi et armis*." (Citing Brian J. in Carrier's Case, and in 3 Hen. VII, 12, pl. 9.) Beale, *The Borderland of Larceny* (1892) 6 Harv. L. Rev. 245.

[6] 2 Pollock and Maitland, H. E. L. (2nd. ed. 1911) 496.

that "the party, indeed, shall be absolutely excused from the imputation of Theft, by reason that his possession of the thing detained originated through the owner of the property." [7] Bracton, influenced by his Latin training, emphasized the *animo furandi*,[8] and provided the basis for one of the arguments made in the Carrier's Case. The definition of theft in the *Mirror of Justices,* though embedded in considerable irrelevancy, particularly emphasized the "taking . . . for bailment or livery excludes larceny." [9]

As for actual case materials, there were only two or three very fragmentary decisions in point. In an early anonymous case [10] the defendant was indicted because *"felonice abduxit unum equum rubrum price de tant."* In the King's Bench, to which the case had been removed from the sheriff's tourn, it was held that the indictment could not lie because it did not appear whether the defendant had *taken* the horse feloniously or whether he had led it away *after* he had come lawfully into possession of it.[11]

In the debate on the Carrier's Case there was also some suggestion of another legal principle which was in the process of formation. It referred to larceny by a servant. A special rule applicable to servants only was mentioned as early as 1339, but was disregarded in 1344–1345.[12] The earliest case which presented the doctrine in some detail was reported in the Year Books [13] where it was stated:

> If a taverner serve a man with a piece, and he take it away, it is felony, for he had not possession of this piece; for it was put on the table but to serve him to drink: and so it is of my butler or cook in my house; they are but ministers to serve me, and if they carry it away it is felony, for they had not possession, but the possession was all the while in me; but otherwise peradventure if it were bailed to the servants, so that they are in possession of it.

Although this decision was discussed, apparently with general approval, in Carrier's Case, the doctrine was repudiated several years later by Brian and his associate judges.[14] Not until 1506 was it held that property in or about the house of the master was in his possession, and that his servant had mere custody of this property and was guilty of felony if he converted it.[15]

I have extended the discussion of the emerging distinction between custody and

---

[7] Book X, c. 13 (*circa* 1187).

[8] Vol. 2, Twiss ed. 509.

[9] Sel. Soc. ed. 25.

[10] 2 Edw. III, p. 1, no. 3 (1328).

[11] In commenting on the case, Stephen writes: "This is a judicial recognition of part of the doctrine of the *Mirror* as to the proper definition of theft." 3 History of the Criminal Law of England (1883) 136.

[12] Y. B. 18, 19 Edw. III (R. S.) 508.

[13] 49 Hen. VI, Mich. pl. 9.

[14] "HUSSEY put a question. If a shepherd steals the sheep which are in his charge, or a butler the plate which is in his charge, or servants other things which are in their charge, whether it shall be called felony. And it seemed to him that it would. And he cited a case which was, that a butler had stolen certain stuff which was in his charge, and was hanged for it. HAUGH (J.) cited the case of Adam Goldsmith of London, who had stolen certain stuff which was in his charge, and was hanged for it. BRIAN (C. J.)—It cannot be felony, because he could not take *vi et armis*, because he had charge of it. And the justices were of the same opinion, and so no discussion, etc." Note, Mich. Y. B. 3 Hen. VII, f. 12, pl. 9 (1487).

[15] Hil. Y. B. 21 Hen. VII, f. 14, pl. 21. The point, about which there apparently remained some doubt, was finally settled by 21 Hen. VIII, c. 7 (1529). *Cf.* 1 Hale, P. C. 667; 3 Stephen, H. C. L. 151–2.

possession somewhat beyond 1473 to indicate the full implications of existing legal sanctions as they might have appeared to the judges who decided Carrier's Case. The point was argued in the Exchequer Chamber, and the case of a servant was definitely distinguished from that of a bailee, it being agreed that the latter had possession and not mere custody. It must be concluded that this rule played no part in the decision of the case.

Finally, it may be noted that modern scholars agree that trespass as an element of larceny meant, prior to the Carrier's Case, a direct, simple, overt taking from another's possession.[16]

How, in the face of such a definite legal rule, was it possible to hold a bailee guilty of larceny? The judges were too well versed in the law to concur in Hussey's argument that a subsequent taking *amino furandi* (following Bracton) was sufficient. Nor did Vavisour's point that there was "a bargain to take and carry" rather than a bailment, lie any better (except with Laicon, J.).[17] An additional, quite ingenious theory was suggested which finally carried the day for the Crown. Choke J.,[18] advanced this argument:

> I think that where a man has goods in his possession by reason of a bailment he cannot take them feloniously, being in possession; but still it seems here that it is felony, for here the things which were within the bales were not bailed to him, only the bales as an entire thing were bailed *ut supra* to carry; in which case if he had given the bales or sold them etc., it is not felony, but when he broke them and took out of them what was within he did that without warrant, as if one bailed a tun of wine to carry, if the bailee sell the tun it is not felony nor trespass, but if he took some out it is felony; and here the twenty pounds were not bailed to him, and peradventure he knew not of them at the time of the bailment. So is it if I bail the key to my chamber to one to guard my chamber and he takes my goods within this chamber, it is felony, for they are not bailed to him.

No comment is reported regarding Choke's argument concerning the contents of the bales. The decision, expressing an attempted reconciliation with precedent, was that "breaking bulk" terminated the carrier's possession and that "where a man has possession and that determines, he can then be felon of the things, as if I bail goods

---

[16] "There can we think be little doubt that the 'taking and carrying away,' upon which our later law insists, had been from the first the very core of the English idea of theft. 'He stole, took and carried it away:' this is the charge made against the thief. The crime involves a violation of possession; it is an offence against a possessor and therefore can never be committed by a possessor." 2 Pollock and Maitland, H. E. L. 498.

"This change of possession has from the earliest times been essential to larceny; so that there can be no larceny where there is no trespass." 3 Holdsworth, H. E. L. 361.

"If there was a delivery by the owner, the opinion of Brian, C. J., is the only one that can be supported on principle." Beale, *op. cit.*, 251.

[17] As Professor Beale has suggested, if the carrier took the bales before he was authorized to do so under the agreement, the case might be supported on principle. Beale, *op. cit.*, 251.

[18] Little is known about the judges except the steps in their legal careers. About Choke, who provided the principal theories upon which the decision was based, we are told "that he was a useful judge, and did not unnecessarily interfere with the violent politics of the time, may be presumed from his successive reappointments on the temporary restoration of Henry VI in 1470, on the return of Edward IV in the following year, and on the accessions of Edward V and Richard III in 1483. . . .

"By the inquisition taken after his death it appears that besides Long Ashton he possessed several other manors and lands in the same county, and also the manor of Randolveston in Dorcetshire." 4 Foss, Judges of England 486–7.

to one to carry to my house, and he bring them to my house and then take them thereout it is felony; for his possession is determined when they were in my house."

Holmes called this "an unnecessary as well as inadequate fiction." "The rule," said he, "comes from the Year Books, and the theory of the Year Books was, that, although the chest was delivered to the bailee, the goods inside of it were not, and this theory was applied to civil as well as criminal cases. The bailor has the power and intent to exclude the bailee from the goods, and therefore may be said to be in possession of them as against the bailee." [19] In any event, it was held that "breaking bulk" terminated the bailment. Somewhat simplified, the theory was that the property at once reverted to the constructive "possession" of the bailor, and the removal of it from the bales supplied the "trespass." By this refinement the door was opened to admit into the law of larceny a whole series of acts which had up to that time been purely civil wrongs.[20] The case also provides an illuminating example of legislation by judges who assert that they are applying the principle of *stare decisis* in all its rigor! [21] The judicial technique involved in such decisions has been discussed at length.[22]

The discussion has been confined thus far to legal analysis and the traditional professional technique employed in such analysis. Such an approach can only lead to one conclusion—that the decision in a particular case is or is not in accord with precedent. This type of analysis is not designed to explain the *causes* of any departure from precedent or, for that matter, of adherence to precedent. Its function ends when it appears that a departure *exists*. The demonstration that new law has been made is obviously important; but the very assertion that a decision is *new* law is tantamount to alleging that it was not found among existing legal rules or deduced from them.

Modern legal scholars agree that the Carrier's Case was an important innovation in the law of larceny.[23] The difficulty of formulating an objective standard to deter-

---

[19] The Common Law 224.

Cf. "That [opinion] of Choke J., though it rested upon a rule then well established, seems hardly justified by the facts. It may well be that when a chest is delivered, there is no delivery of the goods within the chest; but this can be true only if the chest is an article of sufficient importance in itself to be the subject of delivery. One cannot say as a matter of fact that bagging in which a bale of goods is wrapped, or paper about a parcel, or twine with which a bundle of clothes is tied, is delivered, while the goods thereby inclosed are not delivered; and these bales appear to have been of that sort. The view of Choke, J., seems, however, now to be the prevailing one, and to have been carried to extreme lengths." (Citing Com. v. James, 1 Pick, 375, Reg. v. Poyser, 2 Den. C. C. 233.) Beale, *op. cit.* 251.

[20] Professor Beale points out (*id.*) that later treatises did not adopt Choke's rationale but placed the decision upon the more persuasive, though unprecedented, ground that, "There are some tortious acts before the regular completion of a contract, on which goods are delivered, which may determine the priority of it, and amount in law to a new taking from the possession of the owner." 2 East, P. C. 695.

[21] The ease with which a fiction, once invoked, may be expanded can be seen from an early American case. In Commonwealth v. Joel Brown, 4 Tyng. 580 (Mass. 1808), the defendant, who was employed to carry several articles, converted one entire package. The defendant was held guilty on two grounds: first, that he was a servant and not a carrier; and, second, that *by removing one package from several*, he· was "breaking bulk."

That the Carrier's Case is very much alive today may be seen in Rupert Cross, *Larceny De Lege Lata* (1950) 66 L. Q. R. 499, and J. Edwards, *Possession and Larceny*, in Current Legal Problems (Keeton and Schwarzenberger eds. 1950) 139.

[22] See Maine, Ancient Law c. 2 and 3; Pound, *Spurious Interpretation* (1907) 7 Col. L. Rev. 379; Pound, Interpretations of Legal History (1923) 131 ff.; L. L. Fuller, *Legal Fictions* (1930–31) 25 Ill. L. Rev. 363, 513, 877.

[23] Stephen writes: "This has always appeared an extraordinary decision. . . . This [decision] required a deviation from the common law, which was accordingly made." 3 H. C. L. 139. Holdsworth writes: "That this was a departure from principle is obvious." 3 H. E. L. 366. Beale, *op. cit.* 251.

mine the existence and extent of departure from precedent which any case represents, arises from the fact that it is impossible to fix the meaning of many decisions with a high degree of precision.[24] Moreover, for various reasons, but chiefly because of a felt need to perpetuate traditional theories of the judicial function, the courts almost invariably assume, if their opinions are to be taken at face value, that their decisions necessarily result from the logical application of prior rules. We have seen the expression of this judicial assumption in the Carrier's Case. Indeed, if this case be read and accepted literally, it represents no change in the law. Trespass was and trespass remained an essential element of the law of larceny. There was a "trespass," *Quod erat demonstrandum!*

As suggested, it may be stated, in general, that a court departs from precedent when it redefines a concept or adopts and introduces into its decision a proposition of law which can neither be found among existing legal rules nor logically derived from them. Clearly, however, the *application* of this standard is difficult because of the infinite variation of facts and the consequent opportunities for expansion or contraction of concepts.[25]

If Carrier's Case represents a purely formal compliance with precedent and a substantial departure from it, our problem becomes more complicated. For we are then confronted by a *change* in law which cannot be explained in terms of precedent and the continuity thereof; by definition, we are seeking to understand a *departure* from, and, in effect, *a renunciation* of precedent.

This type of problem may be approached from many points of view.[26] If we ask the specific question, *why* did Carrier's Case (or any other event) occur when it did, we turn quite naturally for an explanation to the events which *preceded* it.[27] Such explanations have been provided by narratives of events occurring between a chosen point of "origin" and the phenomenon for which an explanation was sought.

Historians have recently broadened the scope of their inquiry to include *thorough* consideration of social, economic,[28] political and religious conditions.[29] This approach

---

[24] Oliphant, *A Return to Stare Decisis* (1928) 14 A. B. A. J. 73.

[25] The opinion may be hazarded, however, that, in fact, as a result of the conditioning of legal specialists over a period of many years, a relatively high degree of uniformity (for the purpose in hand) in the interpretation and application of legal rules has been attained. Thus the unanimity of expert opinion regarding the Carrier's Case is evidence of the existence of sufficiently objective criteria to insure a relatively high degree of uniform judgment in many cases. See Hall, General Principles of Criminal Law (1947) 32–50.

[26] *Cf.* Pound, Interpretations of Legal History (1923).

[27] "Answers to questions Why? can only therefore be found in the antecedents of the developments under consideration; and if we want to know why the Reformation took place in the sixteenth century, why America was discovered in 1492, why learning came to its new birth at the end of the fifteenth century, we must search the records of preceding generations." Pollard, Factors in Modern History (1907) 34.

[28] ". . . from the lawyers the historical method passed to the economists." Ashley, English Economic History and Theory, Preface ix.

[29] This raises interesting questions regarding history and sociology. "When he begins to generalize, the historian is no longer a historian, but becomes, in a large way, a sociologist." J. W. Swain, *What Is History?* (1923) 20 J. of Phil. 282.

    Cf. "The controversy turns, in first instance, on the question of what is the proper province of the historian; whether History should concern itself only with unique and hence unrepeatable phenomena, or whether it may not also be concerned with studying the underlying forces and influences that condition social growth and which, by their very nature, seem to be constantly operative. . . . As a matter of fact, the two points of view are not mutually exclusive. It would seem folly to deny that there are two aspects of the history of man. One consists of the exceptional or extranormal happenings; the other of the common or persistent factors." Schlesinger, *History,* Research in the Social Sciences (Gee, ed. 1929) 227.

    And *cf.* Teggart, Theory of History; and R. L. Schuyler, *Law and Accident in History* (1930) 45 Pol. Sci. Quar. 273.

is based upon (*a*) the alleged fact that the behavior of any people is, by and large, uniform, standardized, and habitual,[30] and that, as a result, social life may be thought of in terms of "institutions" which denote such behavior; and (*b*) that social change (departures from institutional modes of behavior which are generally recognized as permanent and important) is to be explained as a result of conditions determined by and arising from a large network of institutions which are closely interrelated and the impact of these institutions upon each other. An institutional interpretation of history [31] does not ignore human factors but emphasizes common and recurring, rather than infrequent or individual, modes of human behavior.[32]

II. THE POLITICAL CONDITIONS

Carrier's Case was decided in England in 1473. A glance at the political scene immediately preceding Edward IV's accession indicates the nature and extent of the change in government which he introduced. In 1450 Cade's Rebellion occurred. In 1452 the Hundred Years' War terminated with the English driven from France. The War of the Roses started in 1455 and lasted until 1459; then, after a short truce, the war again broke out and continued intermittently until 1471, when Edward defeated the Lancastrians at Tewkesbury and recaptured the throne. These and many similar events provide the basis for the uniform conclusion of historians of Lancastrian

---

[30] *Cf.* Cooley, Social Organization 313 ff.; Allport, Institutional Behavior, and K. N. Llewellyn, *The Constitution as an Institution* (1934) 34 Col. L. Rev. 1.

[31] Three limitations are apparent. (1) The interpretation will obviously be incomplete. All of the facts are not known, and of those which were known at one time, only a few have been recorded. Yet even this very incomplete history which has come down to us is of enormous proportions, despite the disinclination of historians to delve into fifteenth century England. It will, therefore, be necessary to condense the existing, incomplete history very considerably.

(2) History is not only incomplete, but it is also conditioned by accepted ideas about the importance and relevancy of the factors regarded as causal, and by the selection and interpretation of particular data by certain individuals. "But it is the historian in every case who presents the evidence; strive for impartiality as he may, his presentation and arrangement of the evidence will have something to do with the verdict given." J. W. Swain, *op. cit.* 284. *Cf.* "But even under these auspicious circumstances, with the student seeking objective truth as his only goal, the preconceptions of the age, as well as his own human shortcomings, almost certainly refract the historian's vision and affect the result of his researches." A. M. Schlesinger, *op. cit.* 211. This difficulty is increased in the following discussion due to the fact that an explanation is sought for specific legal developments. This renders it impossible merely to reproduce or summarize sections of the commonly accepted history, but requires a further special selection of data which can be significantly related to the criminal law and Carrier's Case.

(3) Most important is the question, how far does an institutional interpretation of changes in law provide a satisfactory "explanation" of these changes? It would be fatuous to expect an explanation of the *precise form* that changes in the law have taken. It may accordingly be argued that this type of analysis does not *explain* change at all, but merely describes the antecedent and concomitant conditions of change. In any event, all that will be attempted is to discover the *various possibilities for certain changes* in the law which were determined by the conditions established by existing, interrelated, interacting institutions.

[32] It is possible to write a history of law in terms of great judges and lawyers. Such phenomena as dissenting opinions, reversals by upper courts, and other changes *within a short period of time* suggest the operation of individual, unique influences, or at least make such a hypothesis defensible. Certainly it seems clear that judges like Brian, Choke, Coke, Mansfield, and Buller have left many distinctive marks upon the law and have greatly influenced its development. These judges and all the others functioned in a milieu which was determined very largely by existing legal, social, political and economic institutions and their interaction. The interpretation of the law of theft that follows emphasizes this latter aspect of the complex pattern set by the operation of many converging forces. *Cf.* Vinogradoff, *Aims and Methods of Jurisprudence* (1924) 24 Col. L. Rev. 1; and L. K. Frank, *An Institutional Analysis of the Law* (1924) 24 Col. L. Rev. 480.

The two views indicated above are represented by Carlyle's Heroes and Hero Worship at one extreme and, at the other, by Tolstoy's War and Peace.

England that the entire period was marked by disorder and discontent.[33] This chaotic condition was due chiefly to the existence of a powerful baronial class which the Lancastrians were impotent to hold in check. That the instability and turbulence of the times affected the administration of the criminal law is also clear. "The livery of a great lord was as effective security to a malefactor as was the benefit of clergy to the criminous clerk." [34] The subserviency of the courts to the militant power of the nobility became a commonplace.[35]

This, then, provides the central basis for contrasting Lancastrian impotence and "administrative anarchy," as Pollard characterized it,[36] with the powerful New Monarchy of Edward. With Edward's victory came the annihilation of Warwick, whom Hume called "the last of the barons," and of the most powerful family in England, except the king's. The Church was reduced to its lowest level of influence; enormous confiscations brought about by wholesale attainders severed the treasury from the will of the Commons. For several years Edward hardly summoned Parliament at all.[37]

So extreme was the concentration of power in the king that several historians have severely condemned his reign as despotism. Green maintains that the liberty from arbitrary government which the English had won over a period of many years was lost at the end of the War of the Roses.[38] Hallam is even bitter. To him "the reign of Edward IV was a reign of terror." [39] "No laws favorable to public liberty, or remedial with respect to the aggressions of power, were enacted, or, so far as appears, even proposed in Parliament during the reign of Edward, the first since John to whom such a remark can be applied." [40]

This leads directly to the next factor to be considered, namely, the relationship of the judges to the Crown. The sharp struggle for independence of the judiciary and the supremacy of law did not arise until a century and a half later in Coke's desperate battle with James over Peacham's Case. There had been, to be sure, an occasional expression of discontent by a courageous judge; and we are told that Sir William Hussey, who had represented the Crown in the Carrier's Case, "in the first year of this reign [Henry VII's] successfully protested against the King's practice of consulting the judge beforehand upon Crown cases which they were subsequently to try." [41] Coke was dismissed in 1614, and the Crown's practice of "consulting" the

---

[33] For a brief account of the lawlessness during this period, see V. B. Redstone, *England during the War of Roses* 16 (n. s.) Trans. of the Royal Hist. Soc. 186–90.

[34] 3 Stubbs, Constitutional History 533.

[35] "Nothing is more curious than the way in which it is assumed that it is idle to indict a criminal who is maintained by a powerful person; (quoting from 1 Paston Letters 190) 'ther kan no man indyte him for Sir T. Todenham mayteynyth him.' " Plummer, Introduction to Fortescue, The Governance of England 29. See Plummer's Introduction, 20–25, for a description of lawlessness in the fifteenth century.

[36] *Op. cit.* 71.

[37] 1 Innes, A History of England and the British Empire (1913) 461–2.

[38] "Parliamentary life was almost superseded, or was turned into a mere form by the overpowering influence of the Crown. The legislative powers of the two Houses were usurped by the royal Council.

"The old English kingship, limited by the forces of feudalism or of the religious sanctions wielded by the priesthood, or by the progress of constitutional freedom, faded suddenly away, and in its place we see, all-absorbing and unrestrained, the despotism of the new Monarchy." J. R. Green, A Short History of the English People (1899) 290.

[39] 3 Constitutional History 198.

[40] 1 *Id.* 10.

[41] Y. B. 1 Hen. VII. p. 26, quoted in Foss, Lives of the Judges.

judges beforehand continued for a long time after that.[42] Indeed, contemporary sources reveal Edward's domination of public officials generally. Thus, Charles Plummer, relying on the Paston Letters,[43] declares that occasionally royal letters were sent to justices or to sheriffs ordering them to show favor to a particular person.[44]

Green, whose dislike of the new despotism militates against his impartiality, declaims against the degradation of justice brought about by "servility of the judges, [and] by the coercion of the juries." [45] He charges that "it was to Edward that his Tudor successors owed the introduction of an elaborate spy system, the use of the rack, and the practice of interfering with the purity of justice." [46]

The Carrier's Case was heard first in the Star Chamber [47] and later in the Exchequer; conceivably, the judges in these august tribunals might have been free from royal interference. On the contrary, we are informed on every hand that Edward reduced the formerly powerful Council to complete subservience to his wishes. The inclusive and undifferentiated function of this tribunal,[48] the special interests of the Crown together with the relations that existed between the judges of the Star Chamber, the king, and his chief representative, the Chancellor, made the likelihood of royal control extremely probable. We may accept the opinion of the leading authority on the subject, that, "Instead of a ruling or guiding council there was at every step an emphasis of the royal authority." [49]

The above changes, ushered in with the Yorkist reign, present nothing short of a profound transformation in both the state and the judiciary. This in itself might provide, for some purposes, a sufficient explanation of the decision of the judges in the Carrier's Case. Indeed, so great a master of the criminal law as Stephen, in commenting upon Carrier's Case asserts, "I think it obvious from the report that the de-

---

[42] Independent judges were dismissed. This was the fate of Crew in 1626, of Walter in 1629, and of Heath in 1634.

[43] Vol. 3, 428.

[44] *Op. cit.* 22.
  Cf. "He (Edward) also exercised very freely what was called the dispensing power, that is the power to suspend the law in certain cases, and in other ways asserted the royal prerogative as no previous king had done for two hundred years." Cheyney, An Introduction to the Industrial and Social History of England (1916) 137.

[45] *Op. cit.* 290.

[46] *Id.* 293, and 3 Stubbs, *op. cit.* 282.
  Cora L. Scofield, the biographer of Edward, supplies additional evidence which leaves little doubt regarding Edward's domination of his judges: "The day came when Edward disgraced himself by dismissing a man whom he should have rewarded, not punished, for the fearless stand he had taken on behalf of justice and right. Chief Justice Markham's only offense consisted in charging the jury to bring a less severe verdict against Sir Thomas Cook than was desired. . . . he lost his office. Again, the trial of Burdett, Stacy and Blake in 1477 is painful evidence how far it lay within the power of the king to control the courts and to pervert justice to serve his own ends . . . and evidently it was not merely in such important cases as that of Burdett, Stacy and Blake that Edward stooped to interfere." 2 The Life and Reign of Edward the Fourth (1923) 372–3.

[47] "It is, indeed, perhaps not generally known, that crimes of a very ordinary nature, such as would now come before a police magistrate, occupied the attention of the Star Chamber. Charges of robbery, murder, sheep stealing, theft . . . were investigated by Councillors." Dicey, The Privy Council (1887) 105, and *cf.* 56–62.
  "The jurisdiction of the Council was not, however, confined to cases in equity or cases in error. It exercised original jurisdiction over cases which specially concerned the King, or which exceeded the competency of the ordinary courts." Scofield, A Study of the Court of Star Chamber (1900) xxv.

[48] Dicey selects as "the most characteristic feature of the period . . . the inseparable combination in the Council of political and judicial authority." *Op. cit.* 106.

[49] Baldwin, The King's Council in England during the Middle Ages 426.

cision was a compromise intended to propitiate the chancellor, and perhaps the king." [50]

The "will of the king" long provided a sufficient explanation of the conduct of the king's servants. The "new" history, reflecting social and economic evolution, has broadened the range of investigation and secured acceptance of the necessity for dealing with a more varied and complex aggregate of phenomena. Even if the essential technique is the same as that found in the older history, its emphasis upon social and economic data and, more important yet, the concomitant changes in thought which are reflected by this literature, compel us to push the quest further if an explanation which will more adequately satisfy current intellectual requirements is to be had.

III. THE ECONOMIC CONDITIONS

We find, on comparison of the Year Book report with Pollock and Wright's translation of it,[51] which has been generally followed, that two very important parts of the judges' opinions have been ignored. The first is contained in the statement by the chancellor that "This is the case of an alien merchant *who comes here with a safe conduct.*" The portion italicized is omitted by Pollock and Wright. The second passage is the last paragraph in the decision (all of which is omitted by Pollock and Wright), which supplements the above as follows:

> And though it is a felony the goods may not be claimed as waifs, for it appears here that the man who demands the goods here is a foreigner, and the King has granted him "safe and sure conduct for himself and his goods," which is a covenant between him and the King. Hence if a felon takes his goods that is no reason why this foreigner should lose them, leaving him only his right to sue the felon, but he may sue the King on this covenant. And thus it seems that the King himself may not have such goods as waifs, and for the same reason he may not grant them to another person, nor may another person claim them by prescription. And note the case was such that the Sheriff of London claimed these goods as waifs, etc., and alleged a prescription to have waifs, etc.

It appears, also, that it was certain "bales" which were broken into, but the contents of the bales are nowhere stated. The only significant remark was that of Choke J., who said that "the twenty pounds were not bailed to him." Lastly, it is reported that the bales were to be carried to Southampton.

We have, therefore, the following intrinsic, specific information to suggest further exploration, namely, that

> 1. the complainant was an alien merchant;
> 2. he had a covenant with the king which provided safe passage for him and his goods;

[50] 3 H. C. L. 139.
　Cf. ". . . the judges, perhaps to please the king . . . reported to the chancellor . . . that it was felony." 3 Holdsworth, H. E. L. 366.
[51] Possession in the Common Law (1888) 134–7.

3. the property taken is described as being within bales, and as weighing twenty pounds;
4. the defendant was a carrier;
5. and he was to deliver the merchandise at Southampton.

In order to strike the general note which, in a word, characterizes much of the following interpretation, it is necessary to recall that one of the most important movements in all of modern history was taking place during this time, namely, the Renaissance.[52] It is not necessary to decide with reference to the thesis here presented whether the Renaissance was a rebirth of the old learning or whether, on the contrary, it represented a decline from the achievements of mediæval scholarship. In either event, it is the revolutionary changes in social institutions which are significant.

Despite the continuity of historical processes, it is possible to recognize certain periods of accelerated social change, and thus to fix an important point in the early development of the Renaissance at the middle of the fifteenth century. Mediæval Europe was being transformed into a relatively modern Europe. Commerce was undergoing radical change along with the rest of the older culture.[53] Many historians select the capture of Constantinople by the Turks in 1453 as the most apt date for the commencement of modern history, while others emphasize the discovery of America. Although all such specifications are somewhat arbitrary, it is defensible, nevertheless, to contrast the essential character of the mediæval world with that of the modern world, and conclude that there are several reasons "why modern history as distinct from mediæval, begins towards the end of the fifteenth century." [54]

A mass of data supports this view. In England the economy of the middle ages was almost exclusively agricultural and rural.[55] "At the time of the great Survey there were hardly any commercial towns." [56] By the fifteenth century, however, a series of important changes had become manifest.[57] Thus, "in the time of Edward III the wealth of England still consisted mainly in raw products, and her industry was but little advanced, but in the fifteenth century manufacturing was springing up in every town." [58] With the growth of manufacturing in the fifteenth century came marked

---

[52] "One cannot say when the Middle Ages gave way to the Renaissance. Indeed, in some respects, the Middle Ages are not over yet. . . . So, one must not expect to find the Renaissance, or any other important era, inaugurated by a striking event or a violent revolution. Only very gradually did the new dispensation take form and shape." E. M. Hulme, The Renaissance, the Protestant Revolution and the Catholic Reformation in Continental Europe (1914) 3.

[53] "Rational commerce is the field in which quantitative reckoning first appeared, to become dominant finally over the whole extent of economic life. . . .
"The first books on computation usable by merchants come from the 15th century, the older literature, going back to the 13th, not being popular enough." Max Weber, General Economic History (Knight's transl.) 223.

[54] Pollard, op. cit. 31.

[55] "Till nearly the end of the fourteenth century, England was a purely agricultural country. Such manufacturers as it possessed were entirely for consumption within the land; and for goods of the finer qualities it was dependent on importation from abroad. The only articles of export were the raw products of the country, and of these by far the most important was the agricultural product, wool. To understand, therefore, the life of rural England during this period, is to understand nine-tenths of its economic activity." Ashley, An Introduction to English Economic History and Theory (3rd ed. 1894) 5–6.

[56] "Even in a place like Cambridge, which had a fairly advanced municipal life, the burgesses were engaged in rural pursuits . . . the people of the towns were still engaged in agriculture." 1 Cunningham, The Growth of English Industry and Commerce (1910) 3.

[57] "Old institutions of every kind, in town and country, were falling to pieces; new attempts were being made to regulate industry and encourage commerce." Id. 459.

[58] A. Abram, Social England in the Fifteenth Century (1909) 1.

changes in the manorial system and numerous departures from its mediæval form. Came also the decay of serfdom and the rise of a new class of tenants whose rights were gradually recognized by the courts. But most important of all is the fact that during this period the old feudal relationships gave way before a rising middle class which owed its influence to the development of a rapidly expanding industry and trade.[59] For example, in the middle of the fourteenth century there were only 169 important merchants, but at the beginning of the sixteenth century there were more than 3000 merchants engaged in foreign trade alone.[60] We may summarize these tremendously important fifteenth century changes by quoting the scholarly editors of a detailed study on this period:

> It was obviously in the course of the later middle ages, and more particularly in the fifteenth century, that there took place the great transformation from mediæval England, isolated and intensely local, to the England of the Tudor and Stuart age, with its world-wide connections and imperial designs. It was during the same period that most of the forms of international trade characteristic of the middle ages were replaced by methods of commercial organization and regulation, national in scope and at times definitely nationalistic in object, and that a marked movement towards capitalist methods and principles took place in the sphere of domestic trade.[61]

The cumulative effect of the new economic organization of society and the changed political institutions, already described, becomes clear upon the presentation of certain interesting facts. Indeed, so interrelated are the institutions of any period that it would be remarkable if there were no connection between the Crown and the new mercantile class. Our expectations in this regard are more than fulfilled, for we are informed that "Philip de Commines says that Edward IV owed his restoration to the aid of the rich burgesses of London, and however this may be, it is certain that he depended largely upon the support of the traders and merchants, and favored them greatly. . . ." [62] Apparently Edward realized "that Richard (II's) failure to protect English shipping alienated the merchants from his side." [63] Certainly Edward cultivated the business interests assiduously.

It may, however, be objected that the merchant in Carrier's Case was an alien. We are led, therefore, both by the internal evidence in the case and the importance of the question, to an examination of English foreign trade in the fifteenth century.[64]

[59] "Now, the industrial and commercial system of meodern history requires two factors which feudalism did not provide; it requires a middle class and it requires an urban population. Without these two there would have been little to distinguish modern from mediæval history. Without commerce and industry, there can be no middle class; where you had no middle class you had no Renaissance and no Reformation."

"So in one way or another, before the end of the fifteenth century a new middle class, a new social force had been created, and this force is one of the greatest factors in the making of modern history." Pollard, *op. cit.* 41, 48. *Cf.* 1 Cunningham, *op. cit.* 387.

[60] Cheyney, *op. cit.* 162.

[61] Studies in English Trade in the Fifteenth Century (ed. Eileen Power and M. M. Posten, 1933) xvii.

[62] Abram, *op. cit.* 212.

[63] 1 Cunningham, *op. cit.* 409.

". . . the weak Lancastrian sovereign, Henry VI, took little thought of commerce, with the result that in the ensuing Wars of the Roses, London and the other leading commercial cities were on the side of the Yorkists. . . . Thus Edward IV was the first avowedly mercantilist King of England." S. A. Cudmore, History of the World's Commerce (1929) 124.

[64] See Studies in English Trade in the Fifteenth Century (1933, ed. E. Power and M. M. Posten).

As a matter of fact, in the middle of the fifteenth century feeling was very strong against alien merchants. Frequent repressive measures were taken against them. So numerous and skillful were they that local traders felt themselves unable to compete successfully. The complaint was made in 1455 that " 'merchant strangers Italians' bought woolen cloth, wool, wool-fells and tin in every port of the kingdom with ready money, and so made their purchases at reduced prices." [65] Bitter attacks against the foreign traders were common. Hostility rose to the point where riots occurred, stimulated by rival merchants; [66] many Italians were assaulted in 1456 and 1457. This was followed by threatened withdrawal of all relations and a decree of the Italian Senate prohibiting trade with London.[67]

The general insecurity of the times made any transportation hazardous.[68] The special risks to which the alien merchant was subjected gave rise to the royal practice of issuing formally executed covenants of safe conduct through the realm.[69] The extraordinary importance of the covenant of safe conduct is indicated by the holding in Carrier's Case denying the Crown's right to waif—this by the king's judges sitting in the king's court and applying the king's law! In two reports of Carrier's Case, other than the principal one given in the Year Book, emphasis is placed on the safe conduct. Kelyng writes, "a merchant alien, who has the king's *securum e salvum conductum tam in corpore quam in bonis*";[70] and Richard Crompton dwelt upon the fact that "a Merchant Stranger (which) came into England by the King's safe conduct." [71]

The combined force of the hazards of transporting goods and of attacks on alien

---

[65] Quoted by 1 Lipson, *op. cit.* 469–70.

"Regarding Italian merchants the 'libille' complains that they brought in trifles and take away 'oure best chaffore, clothe, wolle, and tynne.' " Quoted by Abram, *op. cit.* 36.

[66] 1 Lipson, *op. cit.* 463.

[67] *Id.* 470.

[68] "Even recognized associations of merchants frequently indulged in practices which can only be characterized as piracy. Commerce, in fact, was deeply imbued with the spirit of lawlessness, and in these circumstances it is probable that the depredations of pirates did not excite the same alarm nor discourage trade in the same degree as would be the case in more law-abiding times." 2 Traill, Social England 337–8.

[69] "The merchants of Venice complained that they dare not avail themselves of the permission to resort to England, unless they had a special safe-conduct as well. The existence of a commercial treaty, therefore, was no guarantee that merchants would be allowed to pursue their calling unmolested." *Id.* 404.

Cf. "The requirements to which these relations gave rise among the merchants, looked first in the direction of personal protection. Occasionally this provision took on a sacerdotal character, the foreign merchant being placed under the protection of the gods or of the chieftain. Another form was the conclusion of safe conduct agreements with the political powers of the reign, as in upper Italy during the middle ages. . . .

"The second great requirement of commerce was legal protection. The merchant was an alien and would not have the same legal opportunities as a member of the nation or tribe, and therefore required special legal arrangements." Weber, *op. cit.* 212.

In England, as long ago as Magna Charta, c. 30, "safe and sure Conduct" was assured to foreign merchants.

[70] 145 Eng. Rep. 92.

[71] Crompton reports further, "And it seemeth by the booke that a Merchant shall not loose the Merchandizes, because hee comes hither with the kings safe conduct *ut supra*, 13 Ed. 4. 9. And it is said there that it was adjudged that notwithstanding the statute which giveth that the safe conduct shall be enrolled, and the number of the Marryners, and the name of the ship, that where safe conduct is, and hath not his due circumstances according to this, yet it shall be allowed, for Aliens say that they are not bound to know our statutes for they come by reason of the Kings privy Seale upon his safe conduct: . . . It is held by the Chancellor in the first case, that a Merchant stranger which comes by safe conduct is not bound to sue by the Law of the Land, to try a thing by twelve men, but that it shall bee determined according to the Law of nature, in the Chancery." Star Chamber Cases, reprinted from the Edition of 1630 or 1641 (Soule and Bugbee, 1881) 51–2.

merchants was unable to stem the tide of foreign trade.[72] Indeed, "the rise in English foreign trade, and the consequent interest in national shipping, distinguishes the fifteenth from any previous century." [73] Numerous commercial treaties were made during this period; [74] and the Merchant Adventurers who had secured their charter in 1407 were already enjoying a large international trade and had become wealthy and influential.[75]

This trade was stimulated by the king's cordiality to foreign traders. Two instances are especially suggestive. First is his relationship to the Hanse. In 1465 Edward accepted from the Hanse "a present of a large sum of money for the renewal of their charter" to deal in wool export.[76] The Crown's usual financial distress made such "loans," as they were called, attractive to Edward and profitable for the Hanse. This did not stop the constant altercations between the Hanseatic League and English merchants which culminated in 1468 in the cessation of all trade and in actual war. Edward's loss of the throne and his subsequent efforts to regain it gave the Hanse the greatest possible opportunity for expanding its commerce. Appraising the situation with excellent business acumen, the Hanse merchants rallied to Edward's support.

> When Edward in his turn began to plan an expedition to England, he was able to do so with the assistance of the Hanse . . . it was on Hanseatic boats and under Hanseatic escort that Edward sailed to England, there to resume the war and to emerge victorious on the battlefield of Barnet. For these services he promised to satisfy the Hanseatic complaints and demands, and these services were alleged as the official motive for the far-reaching concessions made to the Hanse at the conference at Utrecht.[77]

Negotiations between the English Crown and the Hanse were begun in 1472,[78] and in 1474 the Treaty of Utrecht restored full privileges to the Hanseatic traders with the understanding that English merchants would be permitted to trade in the dominions of the League. Accordingly, if the merchant in Carrier's Case was a Hanseatic trader, his case could hardly have been heard at a more favorable time. Edward was under heavy obligations to the Hanse; he needed and desired their goodwill; he had established friendly contacts with them, and he was anxious for the success of the pending negotiations to renew commercial intercourse.

The bales in question were, however, to be carried to Southampton. This city had commanded the trade with the Latin countries for many years. It "was the chief port on the south coast, and the great emporium for imported wines and miscellaneous

[72] "Notwithstanding this drawback, however, there can be no doubt that trading connections increased in number, and that greater uniformity and equality of commercial privileges was the outcome of the numerous commercial treaties between the countries of Europe." 2 Traill, *op. cit.* 404.

[73] Abram, *op. cit.* 31.

[74] 1 Cunningham, *op. cit.* 414.

[75] 2 Traill, *op. cit.* 401.

[76] M. Dobb, Capitalist Enterprise and Social Progress 256.

[77] M. M. Posten, *op. cit.* 136.
   Cf. 1 Lipson, *op. cit.* 497; 1 Cunningham, *op. cit.* 422.

[78] M. M. Posten, *op. cit.* 136.

goods." [79] As far back as 1297 an ordinance had "enjoined that wool and other merchandise should have no passage out of the realm save at the following ports . . . Southampton where collectors of customs were appointed." [80] The likelihood, therefore, that the merchant in Carrier's Case was Italian is further supported by the fact that the Italians concentrated their trade in Southampton. After the riots of 1456 and 1457, the Venetians, Genoese, and Florentines decided to cease trade with London; prior to that, "a Genoese merchant urged upon the king to make Southampton the seat of traffic, and was assassinated through the jealousy of the London traders." [81] Italian merchants and financiers were very numerous in England during this period, and they had become so firmly entrenched [82] that they dominated English finance for centuries.[83] The history of the period is replete with recitals of transactions between the king and the Italian traders.[84] Edward's obligations and his intimacy with them resulted in the grant of many privileges.[85] Accordingly, whether the merchant in Carrier's Case was a Hanseatic trader or, as seems more likely, an Italian (and

---

[79] Abram, *op. cit.* 50.

Cf. 1 Cunningham, *op. cit.* 425–6; and J. S. Davies, A History of Southampton (1883) 250–1, 254, 255.

"The stately vessels of Venice and Genoa, bringing the luxuries of the Mediterranean and of the Far East to the shores of England, there to exchange them for her more homely wares—wool and tin and cloth—deigned not to visit Bristol. In London, in Southampton and in Sandwich they unloaded silks and . . . and there they were privileged to ship staple English goods to southern Europe and the Levant." E. M. Carus Wilson, *The Overseas Trade of Bristol,* in Studies in English Trade in the Fifteenth Century (Power and Posten ed.) 224.

[80] Quoted by 1 Lipson, *op. cit.* 472.

[81] 1 Lipson, *op. cit.* 462–3.

[82] "The Florentine branches (of the Medici) in Bruges and London had from early days been closely connected. As late as 1470 Benedetto Dei says of them: 'They rule these lands, having in their hands the lease of the trade in wool and alum and all the other state revenues, and from thence they do business in exchange with every market in the world, but chiefly with Rome, where they make great gains.' This statement is rather boastful, but we have evidence from other sources as to the continued predominance at this time of the Florentine financiers both in England and the Netherlands." R. Ehrenberg, Capital and Finance in the Age of the Renaissance 196.

[83] Tawney, writing even of the middle of the sixteenth century, states: "But financial business continued to be largely in the hands of Italians. When in 1553, Cecil prepared a programme for controlling the exchanges, what he emphasized most was the necessity of keeping a tight hold on the Italians who 'go to and fro and serve all princes at once . . . work what they list and lick the fat from our beards.' " *Introduction* to Wilson's Discourse upon Usury 64.

[84] "The commercial and political dignity of the family of Medici was now supported by Lorenzo the Magnificent, the grandson of Cosmo. King Edward, who was perpetually in want of money, had now borrowed £5000 from him and his brother Guiliano, together with Thomas Portunary, and others, stiled merchants of Florence, probably agents of the Medici, for which, as usual, he gave an assignment upon the customs to fall due." (692.)

". . . Quanvese, one of Cosmo's agents was the chief instrument in supporting Edward IV by furnishing him at a time above 120,000 crowns. . . . (Portunary) another of Cosmo's agents . . . became security for King Edward to the duke of Burgundy for 50,000 crowns and at another time for 24,000. Comines' hint of the damage sustained by delay of payment is supported by a grant of King Edward, dated 30th November 1466, whereby it appears that £5,254:19:10 of the money lent him by Gerald Camzian (whom Comines calls Quanvese) still remained due for payment of which Edward permitted him to berd, clock and clean, any wool whatsoever, and export it, or any other wool, to the Mediterranean, and also to export woven cloth, in grain or without grain, to any country whatever, and to retain in his own hands all the customs . . . till they should amount to the sum owing to him . . . (Rymer's unpublished records, Edw. IV, vol. 1, 467.) . . . Edward was forever borrowing; and we shall again find him receiving further supplies from the house of Medici." 1 Macpherson, Annals of Commerce (1805) 677–8.

[85] "They enjoyed very special privileges about arrest for debt and in regard to the tribunals before which they should plead." 1 Cunningham, *op. cit.* 425–6.

these two groups were practically the only foreign traders in England at the time),
royal support might well have been forthcoming.

But Edward's interest in commerce was not a purely personal one arising from his
need for financial support; indeed, his greatest reputation lies as much in his intelligent encouragement of trade [86] as in his arbitrary rule. The most important legislation passed during his reign was commercial, and the treaties he concluded to facilitate trade were numerous. It was to be expected that a king who was so definitely
and so greatly indebted to mercantile interests, both native and foreign, would be
sympathetic to these interests; but that he should bring considerable ability to his
participation in the economic life of the country and that he should persistently foster
its development were rare qualities in an English monarch.

There was still another reason, important and unusual, for Edward's close attention to business matters: he was himself a merchant, carrying on many private ven-
tures. The Croyland Chronicle reports his activities in this direction: "Having procured
merchant ships, he put on board of them the finest wools, cloths, tin, and other products of the kingdom, and like one of those who lived by trade, did exchange merchandise for merchandise by means of agents both among Italians and Greeks." [87]
In most of these business transactions, which appear to have been numerous, Edward
employed foreign factors to represent him.[88] Some of the highest officials in the land,
including George Neville, Bishop of Exeter and Chancellor of England, likewise engaged in private foreign trade.[89] However, not Neville but Booth was the solicitous
chancellor in Carrier's Case who argued that the "alien merchant . . . is not bound
to sue according to the law of the land nor await the trial of twelve men nor other
formalities of the law of the land, but should sue here where it will be determined in
chancery according to the law of nature." [90]

A final inquiry, projected from the internal evidence of the case itself, adds considerable weight to the conclusions reached thus far. What, in fact, was the merchandise taken? In none of the reports of the case do we find this stated, probably because
the goods were so common that it was thought unnecessary even to name them. The

[86] "The practical interest of Edward IV in trade is familiar," writes C. K. Kingsford, Prejudice and
Promise in XVth Century England (1925) 124.

[87] Quoted by Vickers, England in the Later Middle Ages 483, who also writes, "Despite the splendour of
his court and his delight in costly trappings, he was the first English King for many a long year to die free
of debt." Ibid.

[88] "In this age it was customary for sovereigns to be concerned in merchandize. . . . But King Edward
went beyond all the contemporary sovereigns in commercial transactions: he owned several vessels, and
like a man whose living depended upon his merchandize, 'exported the finest wool, cloth, tin, and the
other commodities of the kingdom to Italy and Greece, and imported their produce in return by the
agency of factors or supercargoes.' . . . But the trade of these royal merchants, when they carried it to a
great extent, as King Edward actually did, must have been very oppressive to the real merchants, who
could not possibly compete with rivals, who paid no customs, and had the national force to protect their
trading speculations." 1 Macpherson, op. cit. 695.

If we were interested in explaining Carrier's Case in terms of specific events which preceded it, instead
of in terms of the changing institutions of the times, the report of a certain transaction of Edward IV
would be most intriguing, for we are informed "that a carrack sailing from Southampton on 30th April,
1473, carried 114½ sacks and 13 cloves of wool which belonged either to Edward or his mother, whose
attorney Peter de Casasse, made the shipment. . . ." Scofield, op. cit. 411. Here, by a curious turn of
circumstances we have almost all of the facts in Carrier's Case: a foreign merchant (the factor), a shipment of wool, from Southampton, and in 1473.

[89] 2 Scofield, op. cit. 419.

[90] Cf. "Frequently petitioners (foreign merchants) declared that juries had been unfair to them. Francis
Dore, merchant of Genoa, stated that the jurors said they would credit no Lombard." Quoted by Abram,
op. cit. 47, from Early Chancery Proceedings, etc.

Year Book report simply noted "certain bales with etc. and other things." In Choke's opinion, however, we have a clue in the remark that "the twenty pounds were not bailed to him."

The principal articles of trade at this time were wool, cloth, hides and tin. Tin would hardly have been packed in bales; nor is it likely, even from the bit of internal evidence regarding the merchandise taken, that hides were contained therein. A case heard before the King's Council in 1439 [91] is suggestive in this connection. John Forde, the defendant, on examination confessed that he attempted to evade customs duties by disguising his shipment "so that it would be appraised by all as a pack of woolen cloth and not of any wool." Certain similarities in the case are strikingly parallel. Forde had sold the merchandise to a foreign trader and had employed a carrier to deliver it. He described his method of ". . . binding together the said pack all around with linen cloth *after the fashion of packs of woolen (goods)* so that" etc. All this fits in well with the reference to the merchandise in Carrier's Case being in "*bales*," a Norman-French word which might with equal propriety have been translated as "packs." [92] The weight of the goods taken (twenty pounds) lends additional support to this view.

The relevant extrinsic evidence strongly reenforces the conclusion that wool, cloth, or both, were the goods taken from the bales in Carrier's Case. So overwhelming in quantity was the trade in wool and cloth that the probabilities are enormously in this direction. Raw wool was the leading commodity of trade in England since at least Norman times,[93] and English cloth had been exported as early as 1265.[94] The Merchant Adventurers, the principal organization of its type for many years, engaged exclusively in the exportation of woolen cloth.[95] The expansion of the wool industry was by no means uniform; a definite depression started in the early part of the fourteenth century.[96] By the middle of the fifteenth century, however, business had revived,[97] the manufacture of cloth had become well established, and the entire textile industry was expanding very rapidly. "There is abundance of evidence to show that the manufacture of cloth had increased with such extraordinary rapidity, that it had grown to be a very important trade . . . the one industry which was already organized on modern lines was flourishing greatly. . . ." [98] With this development came the familiar concomitants of business enterprise—the use of large amounts of capital and of credit facilities,[99] the appearance of numerous middlemen, a division of labor,

[91] Sel. Soc. Select Cases before the King's Council, 1243–1482 at 103–4.

[92] "Bale, ball, *a pack, a bale.*
"*Ballots, little packs*" Robert Kelham, A Dictionary of the Norman or Old French Language (1779) 27.
"Bale, a Pack, or quantity of Goods or Merchandise, as a *Bale* of Silk, Cloth, etc. the word is used in 16 R. 2 Chap. 1 and still in use." Th. Manley, The Interpreter (of) Words and Terms Etc. (1684), first compiled by Dr. Cowel.

[93] 1 Cunningham, *op. cit.* 2.

[94] 2 Traill, *op. cit.* 399.

[95] *Id.* 401.

[96] 1 Lipson, *op. cit.* 397.

[97] Kingsford, *op. cit.* 124.

[98] 1 Cunningham, *op. cit.* 434, 439.
". . . the conditions of the English cloth trade facilitated the growth of capitalism on a large scale, and opened up a new stage in the evolution of industrial organization." 1 Lipson, *op. cit.* 412.

[99] "A wool-exporting firm, like the Celys in the fifteenth century, bought from the growers on six months' credit, and paid them when the wool was sold abroad." Tawney, *op. cit.* 46.

the employment of hundreds of persons by single firms, and the growth of industrial urban areas which penetrated into the rural districts.[100]

Of cumulative significance are the records of the export of wool and cloth in very large quantities from Southampton.[101] They show that this city was one of the most important ports for the shipment of these goods. The conclusion that the merchandise taken in Carrier's Case was very probably wool or cloth means no less than that *the interests of the most important industry in England were involved in the case.*

Transportation of merchandise in England developed alongside of the expanding commerce. But the carrying trade was crude and unreliable.[102] The need for regulation and for raising the standards of honesty resulted from the increasing necessity of the merchants to rely upon professional carriers rather than upon their own servants. Entirely apart from any personal pressure brought by the Crown, the interests of English and foreign merchants were identical in so far as security of transportation of goods was concerned.

IV. THE CONJUNCTION OF LEGAL SANCTIONS WITH POLITICAL AND ECONOMIC CONDITIONS

There is reason to believe, indeed, that a foreign merchant stood in an especially favorable legal position. For, during this period, as we have seen, except for the emerging rule regarding theft by a servant (based upon his having mere custody), the common law recognized no criminality in a person who came legally into posession of property and later converted it. Apparently it was thought that the owner should have protected himself by selecting a trustworthy person. Since, presumably, this could readily be done, the owner must have been negligent if he delivered his property to a person who absconded with it. An alien merchant, however, would obviously be handicapped in his selection of a carrier whom he did not know, but with whom he was compelled to deal nonetheless. The situation made the application of the common law rule a hardship, and this may have suggested the chancellor's observation that a foreign merchant "is not bound to sue according to the law of the land. . . ."[103] Moreover, the civil liability of a carrier in the early common law was absolute.[104] He was virtually held to be liable as though he were an insurer, and this principle of stringent civil liability might have operated to extend criminal liability.

---

[100] 2 Traill, *op. cit.* 399.

[101] See *Tables of Enrolled Customs and Subsidy Accounts 1399 to 1482,* Power and Posten, *op. cit.* 356–8.

[102] "This last letter Makyn sent by the Oxford carrier (about 1465) by whom he desired Marchall to send back 40s. However, he was not too trustful of such a conveyance, so he bade Marchall 'buy a pound of powdered pepper to carry the money privily or else two pounds of rice, for that makes great bulk.'" Quoted by Kingsford, *op. cit.* 33.

[103] "The chancellor, who seems to have had regard rather to the position of the owner of the goods than to the criminality of the carrier, seems to have wished to make the matter turn upon the moral character of the act of misappropriation." 3 Stephen, H. C. L. 139–40.

[104] "The extraordinary liability of a common carrier of goods is an anomaly in our law." Joseph Beale, *The Carrier's Liability: Its History* (1897) 11 Harv. L. Rev. 158–68; *cf.* Holmes, The Common Law, Lecture V; and G. M. Fletcher, The Carrier's Liability (1932) esp. 2, 13, 21, 25–6.

"One outstanding feature of bailment as soon as English law emerged from the realm of speculation was the absolute liability of a bailee to answer to the bailor for the thing bailed. This feature was common to all forms of bailment, and its existence in the period of the Norman Conquest is generally assumed. It is more doubtful whether the rule had any clear continuous history throughout the 13th, 14th and 15th centuries." Fletcher, *op. cit.* 2.

In any event, the fact that the carrier followed a public calling would stimulate efforts to penalize him.

The state of the common law in 1473 explains the direction in which the departure from precedent was made. In the absence of any other even remotely relevant sanction in the criminal law, the only choice was—guilty of larceny or not guilty of any offense.

But it may be a matter of some wonder why the change in law did not come from the legislature rather than from a court which was compelled to disguise its decision in fictitious terms in order to save the face of the existing doctrine. The respective roles of court and legislature in the creation of new law will be discussed later. Here it must suffice to recall first, that Edward rarely summoned Parliament; second, that the sharp distinctions we are accustomed to draw regarding a division of powers cannot be applied accurately to the political instrumentalities of fifteenth century England; and, lastly, that the method actually used was, because of the relationship between the Crown and the Star Chamber, by far the simplest.

We are now in a position to visualize the case and the problem presented to the judges as a result of the legal, political, and economic conditions described above. On the one hand, the criminal law at the time is clear. On the other hand, the whole complex aggregate of political and economic conditions described above thrusts itself upon the court. The more powerful forces prevailed—that happened which in due course must have happened under the circumstances. The most powerful forces of the time were interrelated very intimately and at many points: the New Monarchy and the *nouveau riche*—the mercantile class; the business interests of both and the consequent need for a secure carrying trade; the wool and textile industry, the most valuable, by far, in all the realm; wool and cloth, the most important exports; these exports and the foreign trade; this trade and Southampton, chief trading city with the Latin countries for centuries; the numerous and very influential Italian merchants who bought English wool and cloth inland and shipped them from Southampton. The great forces of an emerging modern world, represented in the above phenomena, necessitated the elimination of a formula which had outgrown its usefulness. A new set of major institutions required a new rule. The law, lagging behind the needs of the times, was brought into more harmonious relationship with the other institutions by the decision rendered in the Carrier's Case.

3. The Law of Vagrancy *
William J. Chambliss

With the outstanding exception of Jerome Hall's analysis of theft [1] there has been a severe shortage of sociologically relevant analyses of the relationship between particular laws and the social setting in which these laws emerge, are interpreted, and

SOURCE: "A Sociological Analysis of the Law of Vagrancy," *Social Problems*, vol. 12, pp. 67–77, Summer, 1964. By permission of the author and publisher.

* For a more complete listing of most of the statutes dealt with in this report the reader is referred to Burn, *The History of the Poor Laws*. Citations of English statutes should be read as follows: 3 Ed. 1. c. 1. refers to the third act of Edward the first, chapter one, etc.

[1] Hall, J., *Theft, Law and Society*, Bobbs-Merrill, 1939. See also, Lindesmith, Alfred R., "Federal Law and Drug Addiction," *Social Problems*, vol. 7, No. 1, 1959, p. 48.

take form. The paucity of such studies is somewhat surprising in view of widespread agreement that such studies are not only desirable but absolutely essential to the development of a mature sociology of law.[2] A fruitful method of establishing the direction and pattern of this mutual influence is to systematically analyze particular legal categories, to observe the changes which take place in the categories and to explain how these changes are themselves related to and stimulate changes in the society. This paper is an attempt to provide such an analysis of the law of vagrancy in Anglo-American Law.

LEGAL INNOVATION: THE EMERGENCE OF THE LAW OF VAGRANCY IN ENGLAND

There is general agreement among legal scholars that the first full fledged vagrancy statute was passed in England in 1349. As is generally the case with legislative innovations, however, this statute was preceded by earlier laws which established a climate favorable to such change. The most significant forerunner to the 1349 vagrancy statute was in 1274 when it was provided:

> Because that abbies and houses of religion have been overcharged and sore grieved, by the resort of great men and other, so that their goods have not been sufficient for themselves, whereby they have been greatly hindered and impoverished, that they cannot maintain themselves, nor such charity as they have been accustomed to do; it is provided, that none shall come to eat or lodge in any house of religion, or any other's foundation than of his own, at the costs of the house, unless he be required by the governor of the house before his coming hither.[3]

Unlike the vagrancy statutes this statute does not intend to curtail the movement of persons from one place to another, but is solely designed to provide the religious houses with some financial relief from the burden of providing food and shelter to travelers.

The philosophy that the religious houses were to give alms to the poor and to the sick and feeble was, however, to undergo drastic change in the next fifty years. The result of this changed attitude was the establishment of the first vagrancy statute in 1349 which made it a crime to give alms to any who were unemployed while being of sound mind and body. To wit:

> Because that many valiant beggars, as long as they may live of begging, do refuse to labor, giving themselves to idleness and vice, and sometimes to theft and other abominations; it is ordained, that none, upon pain of imprisonment shall, under the colour of pity or alms, give anything to such which may labour, or presume to favour them towards their desires; so that thereby they may be compelled to labour for their necessary living.[4]

---

[2] See, for example, Rose, A., "Some Suggestions for Research in the Sociology of Law," *Social Problems* Vol. 9, No. 3, 1962, pp. 281–283, and Geis, G., "Sociology, Criminology, and Criminal Law," *Social Problems*, vol. 7, No. 1, 1959, pp. 40–47.

[3] 3 Ed. 1. c. 1.

[4] 35 Ed. 1. c. 1.

It was further provided by this statute that:

> . . . every man and woman, of what condition he be, free or bond,
> able in body, and within the age of threescore years, not living in mer-
> chandize nor exercising any craft, nor having of his own whereon to
> live, nor proper land whereon to occupy himself, and not serving any
> other, if he in convenient service (his estate considered) be required
> to serve, shall be bounded to serve him which shall him require. . . .
> And if any refuse, he shall on conviction by two true men, . . . be
> commited to gaol till he find surety to serve.
>
> And if any workman or servant, of what estate or condition he be,
> retained in any man's service, do depart from the said service without
> reasonable cause or license, before the term agreed on, he shall have
> pain of imprisonment.[5]

There was also in this statute the stipulation that the workers should receive a standard wage. In 1351 this statute was strengthened by the stipulation:

> An none shall go out of the town where he dwelled in winter, to serve
> the summer, if he may serve in the same town.[6]

By 34 Ed 3 (1360) the punishment for these acts became imprisonment for fifteen
days and if they "do not justify themselves by the end of that time, to be sent to gaol
till they do."

A change in official policy so drastic as this did not, of course, occur simply as a
matter of whim. The vagrancy statutes emerged as a result of changes in other parts
of the social structure. The prime-mover for this legislative innovation was the Black
Death which struck England about 1348. Among the many disastrous consequences
this had upon the social structure was the fact that it decimated the labor force. It
is estimated that by the time the pestilence had run its course at least fifty per cent
of the population of England had died from the plague. This decimation of the labor
force would necessitate rather drastic innovations in any society but its impact was
heightened in England where, at this time, the economy was highly dependent upon
a ready supply of cheap labor.

Even before the pestilence, however, the availability of an adequate supply of
cheap labor was becoming a problem for the landowners. The crusades and various
wars had made money necessary to the lords and, as a result, the lords frequently
agreed to sell the serfs their freedom in order to obtain the needed funds. The serfs,
for their part, were desirous of obtaining their freedom (by "fair means" or "foul")
because the larger towns which were becoming more industrialized during this period
could offer the serf greater personal freedom as well as a higher standard of living.
This process is nicely summarized by Bradshaw:

> By the middle of the 14th century the outward uniformity of the
> manorial system had become in practice considerably varied . . . for
> the peasant had begun to drift to the towns and it was unlikely that
> the old village life in its unpleasant aspects should not be resented.
> Moreover the constant wars against France and Scotland were fought

---

[5] 23 Ed. 3.

[6] 25 Ed. 3 (1351).

> mainly with mercenaries after Henry III's time and most villages con-
> tributed to the new armies. The bolder serfs either joined the armies or
> fled to the towns, and even in the villages the free men who held by
> villein tenure were as eager to commute their services as the serfs were
> to escape. Only the amount of "free" labor available enabled the lord
> to work his demense in many places.[7]

And he says regarding the effect of the Black Death:

> . . . in 1348 the Black Death reached England and the vast mortality
> that ensued destroyed that reserve of labour which alone had made the
> manorial system even nominally possible.[8]

The immediate result of these events was of course no surprise: Wages for the "free"
man rose considerably and this increased, on the one hand, the landowner's problems and, on the other hand, the plight of the unfree tenant. For although wages increased for the personally free laborers, it of course did not necessarily add to the
standard of living of the serf; if anything it made his position worse because the landowner would be hard pressed to pay for the personally free labor which he needed
and would thus find it more and more difficult to maintain the standard of living for
the serf which he had heretofore supplied. Thus the serf had no alternative but flight
if he chose to better his position. Furthermore, flight generally meant both freedom
and better conditions since the possibility of work in the new weaving industry was
great and the chance of being caught small.[9]

It was under these conditions that we find the first vagrancy statutes emerging.
There is little question but that these statutes were designed for one express purpose:
to force laborers (whether personally free or unfree) to accept employment at a low
wage in order to insure the landowner an adequate supply of labor at a price he could
afford to pay. Caleb Foote concurs with this interpretation when he notes:

> The anti-migratory policy behind vagrancy legislation began as an es-
> sential complement of the wage stabilization legislation which accom-
> panied the breakup of feudalism and the depopulation caused by the
> Black Death. By the Statutes of Labourers in 1349–1351, every able-
> bodied person without other means of support was required to work
> for wages fixed at the level preceding the Black Death; it was unlaw-
> ful to accept more, or to refuse an offer to work, or to flee from one
> county to another to avoid offers of work or to seek higher wages, or
> go give alms to able-bodied beggars who refused to work.[10]

In short, as Foote says in another place, this was an "attempt to make the vagrancy
statutes a substitute for serfdom." [11] This same conclusion is equally apparent from
the wording of the statute where it is stated:

> Because great part of the people, and especially of workmen and ser-
> vants, late died in pestilence; many seeing the necessity of masters, and

[7] Bradshaw, F., *A Social History of England*, p. 54.

[8] *Ibid.*

[9] *Ibid.*, p. 57.

[10] Foote, C., "Vagrancy-type Law and Its Administration," *Univ. of Pennsylvania Law Review* (104),
1956, p. 615.

[11] *Ibid.*

> great scarcity of servants, will not serve without excessive wages, and
> some rather willing to beg in idleness than by labour to get their living:
> it is ordained, that every man and woman, of what condition he be,
> free or bond, able in body and within the age of threescore years, not
> living in merchandize, (etc.) be required to serve. . . .

The innovation in the law, then, was a direct result of the afore-mentioned changes
which had occurred in the social setting. In this case these changes were located for
the most part in the economic institution of the society. The vagrancy laws were designed to alleviate a condition defined by the lawmakers as undesirable. The solution
was to attempt to force a reversal, as it were, of a social process which was well
underway; that is, to curtail mobility of laborers in such a way that labor would not
become a commodity for which the landowners would have to compete.

Statutory Dormancy: A Legal Vestige. In time, of course, the curtailment of the geographical mobility of laborers was no longer requisite. One might well expect that
when the function served by the statute was no longer an important one for the society, the statutes would be eliminated from the law. In fact, this has not occurred.
The vagrancy statutes have remained in effect since 1349. Furthermore, as we shall
see in some detail later, they were taken over by the colonies and have remained in
effect in the United States as well.

The substance of the vagrancy statutes changed very little for some time after the
first ones in 1349–1351 although there was a tendency to make punishments more
harsh than originally. For example, in 1360 it was provided that violators of the statute should be imprisoned for fifteen days [12] and in 1388 the punishment was to put
the offender in the stocks and to keep him there until "he find surety to return to his
service." [13] That there was still, at this time, the intention of providing the landowner
with labor is apparent from the fact that this statute provides:

> . . . and he or she which use to labour at the plough and cart, or other
> labour and service of husbandry, till they be of the age of 12 years,
> from thenceforth shall abide at the same labour without being put to
> any mistery or handicraft: and any covenant of apprenticeship to the
> contrary shall be void. [14]

The next alteration in the statutes occurs in 1495 and is restricted to an increase in
punishment. Here it is provided that vagrants shall be "set in stocks, there to remain
by the space of three days and three nights, and there to have none other sustenance
but bread and water; and after the said three days and nights, to be had out and
set at large, and then to be commanded to avoid the town." [15]

The tendency to increase the severity of punishment during this period seems to
be the result of a general tendency to make finer distinctions in the criminal law.
During this period the vagrancy statutes appear to have been fairly inconsequential
in either their effect as a control mechanism or as a generally enforced statute. [16] The

[12] 34 Ed. 3 (1360).

[13] 12 R. 2 (1388).

[14] *Ibid.*

[15] 11 H. & C. 2 (1495).

[16] As evidence for this note the expectation that "the common gaols of every shire are likely to be greatly
pestered with more numbers of prisoners than heretofore . . ." when the statutes were changed by the
statute of 14 Ed. c. 5 (1571).

processes of social change in the culture generally and the trend away from serfdom and into a "free" economy obviated the utility of these statutes. The result was not unexpected. The judiciary did not apply the law and the legislators did not take it upon themselves to change the law. In short, we have here a period of dormancy in which the statute is neither applied nor altered significantly.

A SHIFT IN FOCAL CONCERN

Following the squelching of the Peasants' Revolt in 1381, the services of the serfs to the lord "tended to become less and less exacted, although in certain forms they lingered on till the seventeenth century. . . . By the sixteenth century few knew that there were any bondmen in England . . . and in 1575 Queen Elizabeth listened to the prayers of almost the last serfs in England . . . and granted them manumission." [17]

In view of this change we would expect corresponding changes in the vagrancy laws. Beginning with the lessening of punishment in the statute of 1503 we find these changes. However, instead of remaining dormant (or becoming more so) or being negated altogether, the vagrancy statutes experienced a shift in focal concern. With this shift the statutes served a new and equally important function for the social order of England. The first statute which indicates this change was in 1530. In this statute (22 H.8.c. 12 1530) it was stated:

> If any person, being whole and mighty in body, and able to labour, be taken in begging, or be vagrant and can give no reckoning how he lawfully gets his living; . . . and all other idle persons going about, some of them using divers and subtle crafty and unlawful games and plays, and some of them feigning themselves to have knowledge of . . . crafty sciences . . . shall be punished as provided.

What is most siginificant about this statute is the shift from an earlier concern with laborers to a concern with *criminal* activities. To be sure, the stipulation of persons "being whole and mighty in body, and able to labour, be taken in begging, or be vagrant" sounds very much like the concerns of the earlier statutes. Some important differences are apparent however when the rest of the statute includes those who "can give no reckoning how he lawfully gets his living"; "some of them using divers subtil and unlawful games and plays." This is the first statute which specifically focuses upon these kinds of criteria for adjudging someone a vagrant.

It is significant that in this statute the severity of punishment is increased so as to be greater not only than provided by the 1503 statute but the punishment is more severe than that which had been provided by *any* of the pre-1503 statutes as well. For someone who is merely idle and gives no reckoning of how he makes his living the offender shall be:

> . . . had to the next market town, or other place where they [the constables] shall think most convenient, and there to be tied to the end of a cart naked, and to be beaten with whips throughout the same market town or other place, till his body be bloody by reason of such whipping.[18]

17 Bradshaw, *op. cit.,* p. 61.

18 22 H. 8. c. 12 (1530).

But, for those who use "divers and subtil crafty and unlawful games and plays," etc., the punishment is "whipping at two days together in manner aforesaid." [19] For the second offense, such persons are:

> . . . scourged two days, and the third day to be put upon the pillory from nine of the clock till eleven before noon of the same day and to have one of his ears cut off.[20]

And if he offend the third time "to have like punishment with whipping, standing on the pillory and to have his other ear cut off."

This statute (1) makes a distinction between types of offenders and applies the more severe punishment to those who are clearly engaged in "criminal" activities, (2) mentions a specific concern with categories of "unlawful" behavior, and (3) applies a type of punishment (cutting off the ear) which is generally reserved for offenders who are defined as likely to be a fairly serious criminal.

Only five years later we find for the first time that the punishment of death is applied to the crime of vagrancy. We also note a change in terminology in the statute:

> . . . and if any ruffians . . . after having been once apprehended . . . shall wander, loiter, or idle use themselves and play the vagabonds . . . shall be eftfoons not only whipped again, but shall have the gristle of his right ear clean cut off. And if he shall again offend, he shall be committed to gaol till the next sessions; and being there convicted upon indictment, he shall have judgment to suffer pains and execution of death, as a felon, as an enemy of the commonwealth.[21]

It is significant that the statute now makes persons who repeat the crime of vagrancy a felon. During this period then, the focal concern of the vagrancy statutes becomes a concern for the control of felons and is no longer primarily concerned with the movement of laborers.

These statutory changes were a direct response to changes taking place in England's social structure during this period. We have already pointed out that feudalism was decaying rapidly. Concomitant with the breakup of feudalism was an increased emphasis upon commerce and industry. The commercial emphasis in England at the turn of the sixteenth century is of particular importance in the development of vagrancy laws. With commercialism came considerable traffic bearing valuable items. Where there were 169 important merchants in the middle of the fourteenth century, there were 3,000 merchants engaged in foreign trade alone at the beginning of the sixteenth century.[22] England became highly dependent upon commerce for its economic support. Italians conducted a great deal of the commerce of England during this early period and were held in low repute by the populace. As a result, they were subject to attacks by citizens and, more important, were frequently robbed of their goods while transporting them. "The general insecurity of the times made any transportation hazardous. The special risks to which the alien merchant was subjected gave rise to the royal practice of issuing formally executed covenants of safe conduct through the realm." [23]

[19] *Ibid.*

[20] *Ibid.*

[21] 27 H. 8. c. 25 (1535).

[22] Hall, *op. cit.*, p. 21.

[23] *Ibid.*, p. 23.

Such a situation not only called for the enforcement of existing laws but also called for the creation of new laws which would facilitate the control of persons preying upon merchants transporting goods. The vagrancy statutes were revived in order to fulfill just such a purpose. Persons who had committed no serious felony but who were suspected of being capable of doing so could be apprehended and incapacitated through the application of vagrancy laws once these laws were refocused so as to include "any ruffians . . . [who] shall wander, loiter, or idle use themselves and play the vagabonds. . . ."[24]

The new focal concern is continued in 1 Ed. 6. c. 3 (1547) and in fact is made more general so as to include:

> Whoever man or woman, being not lame, impotent, or so aged or diseased that he or she cannot work, not having whereon to live, shall be lurking in any house, or loitering or idle wandering by the highway side, or in streets, cities, towns, or villages, not applying themselves to some honest labour, and so continuing for three days; or running away from their work; every such person shall be taken for a vagabond. And . . . upon conviction of two witnesses . . . the same loiterer (shall) be marked with a hot iron in the breast with the letter V, and adjudged him to the person bringing him, to be his slave for two years. . . .

Should the vagabond run away, upon conviction, he was to be branded by a hot iron with the letter S on the forehead and to be thenceforth declared a slave forever. And in 1571 there is modification of the punishment to be inflicted, whereby the offender is to be "branded on the chest with the letter V" (for vagabond). And, if he is convicted the second time, the brand is to be made on the forehead. It is worth noting here that this method of punishment, which first appeared in 1530 and is repeated here with somewhat more force, is also an indication of a change in the type of person to whom the law is intended to apply. For it is likely that nothing so permanent as branding would be applied to someone who was wandering but looking for work, or at worst merely idle and not particularly dangerous *per se*. On the other hand, it could well be applied to someone who was likely to be engaged in other criminal activities in connection with being "vagrant."

By 1571 in the statute of 14 El. c. 5 the shift in focal concern is fully developed:

> All rogues, vagabonds, and sturdy beggars shall . . . be committed to the common gaol. . . . he shall be grievously whipped, and burnt thró the gristle of the right ear with a hot iron of the compass of an inch about; . . . And for the second offense, he shall be adjudged a felon, unless some person will take him for two years in to his service. And for the third offense, he shall be adjudged guilty of felony without benefit of clergy.

And there is included a long list of persons who fall within the statute: "proctors, procurators, idle persons going about using subtil, crafty and unlawful games or plays; and some of them feigning themselves to have knowledge of . . . absurd sciences . . . and all fencers, bearwards, common players in interludes, and minstrels . . . all juglers, pedlars, tinkers, petty chapmen . . . and all counterfeiters of licenses, passports and users of the same." The major significance of this statute is

[24] 27 H. 8. c. 25 (1535).

that it includes all the previously defined offenders and adds some more. Significantly, those added are more clearly criminal types, counterfeiters, for example. It is also significant that there is the following qualification of this statute: "Provided also, that this act shall not extend to cookers, or harvest folks, that travel for harvest work, corn or hay."

That the changes in this statute were seen as significant is indicated by the following statement which appears in the statute:

> And whereas by reason of this act, the common gaols of every shire are like to be greatly pestered with more number of prisoners than heretofore hath been, for that the said vagabonds and other lewd persons before recited shall upon their apprehension be committed to the said gaols; it is enacted. . . .[25]

And a provision is made for giving more money for maintaining the gaols. This seems to add credence to the notion that this statute was seen as being significantly more general than those previously.

It is also of importance to note that this is the first time the term *rogue* has been used to refer to persons included in the vagrancy statutes. It seems, *a priori*, that a "rogue" is a different social type than is a "vagrant" or a "vagabond"; the latter terms implying something more equivalent to the idea of a "tramp" whereas the former (rogue) seems to imply a more disorderly and potentially dangerous person.

The emphasis upon the criminalistic aspect of vagrants continues in Chapter 17 of the same statute:

> Whereas divers *licentious* persons wander up and down in all parts of the realm, to countenance their *wicked behavior;* and do continually assemble themselves armed in the highways, and elsewhere in troops, *to the great terror* of her majesty's true subjects, *the impeachment of her laws,* and the disturbance of the peace and tranquility of the realm; and whereas many outrages are daily committed by these dissolute persons, and more are likely to ensue if speedy remedy be not provided. [Italics added.]

With minor variations (*e.g.,* offering a reward for the capture of a vagrant) the statutes remain essentially of this nature until 1743. In 1743 there was once more an expansion of the types of persons included such that "all persons going about as patent gatherers, or gatherers of alms, under pretense of loss by fire or other casualty; or going about as collectors for prisons, gaols, or hospitals; all persons playing of betting at any unlawful games; and all persons who run away and leave their wives or children . . . all person: wandering abroad, and lodging in ale-houses, barns, outhouses, or in the open air, not giving good account of themselves," were types of offenders added to those already included.

By 1743 the vagrancy statutes had apparently been sufficiently reconstructed by the shifts of concern so as to be once more a useful instrument in the creation of social solidarity. This function has apparently continued down to the present day in England. The changes from 1743 to the present have been all in the direction of clarifying or expanding the categories covered but little has been introduced to change either the meaning or the impact of this branch of the law.

[25] 14 Ed. c. 5 (1571).

We can summarize this shift in focal concern by quoting from Halsbury. He has noted that in the vagrancy statutes:

> . . . elaborate provision is made for the relief and incidental control of destitute wayfarers. These latter, however, form but a small portion of the offenders aimed at by what are known as the Vagrancy Laws, . . . many offenders who are in no ordinary sense of the word vagrants, have been brought under the laws relating to vagrancy, and the great number of the offenses coming within the operation of these laws have little or no relation to the subject of poor relief, but are more properly directed towards the prevention of crime, the preservation of good order, and the promotion of social economy.[26]

Before leaving this section it is perhaps pertinent to make a qualifying remark. We have emphasized throughout this section how the vagrancy statutes underwent a shift in focal concern as the social setting changed. The shift in focal concern is not meant to imply that the later focus of the statutes represents a completely new law. It will be recalled that even in the first vagrancy statutes there was reference to those who "do refuse labor, giving themselves to idleness and vice and sometimes to theft and other abominations." Thus the possibility of criminal activities resulting from persons who refuse to labor was recognized even in the earliest statute. The fact remains, however, that the major emphasis in this statute and in the statutes which followed the first one was always upon the "refusal to labor" or "begging." The "criminalistic" aspect of such persons was relatively unimportant. Later, as we have shown, the criminalistic potential becomes of paramount importance. The thread runs back to the earliest statute but the reason for the statutes' existence as well as the focal concern of the statutes is quite different in 1743 than it was in 1349.

VAGRANCY LAWS IN THE UNITED STATES

In general, the vagrancy laws of England, as they stood in the middle eighteenth century, were simply adopted by the states. There were some exceptions to this general trend. For example, Maryland restricted the application of vagrancy laws to "free" Negroes. In addition, for *all* states the vagrancy laws were even more explicitly concerned with the control of criminals and undesirables than had been the case in England. New York, for example, explicitly defines prostitutes as being a category of vagrants during this period. These exceptions do not, however, change the general picture significantly and it is quite appropriate to consider the U.S. vagrancy laws as following from England's of the middle eighteenth century with relatively minor changes. The control of criminals and undesirables was the *raison d'être* of the vagrancy laws in the U.S. This is as true today as it was in 1750. As Caleb Foote's analysis of the application of vagrancy statutes in the Philadelphia court shows, these laws are presently applied indiscriminately to persons considered a "nuisance." Foote suggests that "the chief significance of this branch of the criminal law lies in its quantitative impact and administrative usefulness." [27] Thus it appears that in America the trend begun in England in the sixteenth, seventeenth and eighteenth centuries

[26] Halsbury, Earl of, *The Laws of England*, Butterworth & Co., Bell Yard, Temple Bar, 1912, pp. 606–607.

[27] Foote, *op. cit.*, p. 613. Also see in this connection, Deutscher, Irwin, "The Petty Offender," *Federal Probation*, XIX, June, 1955.

has been carried to its logical extreme and the laws are now used principally as a mechanism for "clearing the streets" of the derelicts who inhabit the "skid rows" and "Bowerys" of our large urban areas.

Since the 1800's there has been an abundant source of prospects to which the vagrancy laws have been applied. These have been primarily those persons deemed by the police and the courts to be either actively involved in criminal activities or at least peripherally involved. In this context, then, the statutes have changed very little. The functions served by the statutes in England of the late eighteenth century are still being served today in both England and the United States. The locale has changed somewhat and it appears that the present day application of vagrancy statutes is focused upon the arrest and confinement of the "down and outers" who inhabit certain sections of our larger cities but the impact has remained constant. The lack of change in the vagrancy statutes, then, can be seen as a reflection of the society's perception of a continuing need to control some of its "suspicious" or "undesirable" members.[28]

A word of caution is in order lest we leave the impression that this administrative purpose is the sole function of vagrancy laws in the U.S. today. Although it is our contention that this is generally true it is worth remembering that during certain periods of our recent history, and to some extent today, these laws have also been used to control the movement of workers. This was particularly the case during the depression years, and California is infamous for its use of vagrancy laws to restrict the admission of migrants from other states.[29] The vagrancy statutes, because of their history, still contain germs within them which make such effects possible. Their main purpose, however, is clearly no longer the control of laborers but rather the control of the undesirable, the criminal and the "nuisance."

DISCUSSION

The foregoing analysis of the vagrancy laws has demonstrated that these laws were a legislative innovation which reflected the socially perceived necessity of providing an abundance of cheap labor to landowners during a period when serfdom was breaking down and when the pool of available labor was depleted. With the eventual breakup of feudalism the need for such laws eventually disappeared and the increased dependence of the economy upon industry and commerce rendered the former use of the vagrancy statutes unnecessary. As a result, for a substantial period the vagrancy statutes were dormant, undergoing only minor changes and, presumably, being applied infrequently. Finally, the vagrancy laws were subjected to considerable alteration through a shift in the focal concern of the statutes. Whereas in their inception the laws focused upon the "idle" and "those refusing to labor" after the turn of the sixteenth century and emphasis came to be upon "rogues," "vagabonds," and others who were suspected of being engaged in criminal activities. During this period the focus was particularly upon "roadmen" who preyed upon citizens who transported goods from one place to another. The increased importance of commerce to England during this period made it necessary that some protection be given persons engaged in this enterprise and the vagrancy statutes provided one source for such protection by refocusing the acts to be included under these statutes.

[28] It is on this point that the vagrancy statutes have been subject to criticism. See for example, Lacey, Forrest W., "Vagrancy and Other Crimes of Personal Condition," *Harvard Law Review* (66), p. 1203.

[29] Edwards vs California. 314 S: 160 (1941).

Comparing the results of this analysis with the findings of Hall's study of theft we see a good deal of correspondence. Of major importance is the fact that both analyses demonstrate the truth of Hall's assertion that "the functioning of courts is significantly related to concomitant cultural needs, and this applies to the law of procedure as well as to substantive law." [30]

Our analysis of the vagrancy laws also indicates that when changed social conditions create a perceived need for legal changes, these alterations will be effected through the revision and refocusing of existing statutes. This process was demonstrated in Hall's analysis of theft as well as in our analysis of vagrancy. In the case of vagrancy, the laws were dormant when the focal concern of the laws was shifted so as to provide control over potential criminals. In the case of theft the laws were re-interpreted (interestingly, by the courts and not by the legislature) so as to include persons who were transporting goods for a merchant but who absconded with the contents of the packages transported.

It also seems probable that when the social conditions change and previously useful laws are no longer useful there will be long periods when these laws will remain dormant. It is less likely that they will be officially negated. During this period of dormancy it is the judiciary which has principal responsibility for *not* applying the statutes. It is possible that one finds statutes being negated only when the judiciary stubbornly applies laws which do not have substantial public support. An example of such laws in contemporary times would be the "Blue Laws." Most states still have laws prohibiting the sale of retail goods on Sunday yet these laws are rarely applied. The laws are very likely to remain but to be dormant unless a recalcitrant judge or a vocal minority of the population insists that the laws be applied. When this happens we can anticipate that the statutes will be negated.[31] Should there arise a perceived need to curtail retail selling under some special circumstances, then it is likely that these laws will undergo a shift in focal concern much like the shift which characterized the vagrancy laws. Lacking such application the laws will simply remain dormant except for rare instances where they will be negated.

This analysis of the vagrancy statutes (and Hall's analysis of theft as well) has demonstrated the importance of "vested interest" groups in the emergence and/or alteration of laws. The vagrancy laws emerged in order to provide the powerful landowners with a ready supply of cheap labor. When this was no longer seen as necessary, and particularly when the landowners were no longer dependent upon cheap labor nor were they a powerful interest group in the society, the laws became dormant. Finally a new interest group emerged and was seen as being of great importance to the society and the laws were then altered so as to afford some protection to this group. These findings are thus in agreement with Weber's contention that "status groups" determine the content of the law.[32] The findings are inconsistent, on the other hand, with the perception of the law as simply a reflection of "public opinion" as is sometimes found in the literature.[33] We should be cautious in concluding, how-

[30] Hall, *op. cit.*, p. XII.

[31] Negation, in this instance, is most likely to come about by the repeal of the statute. More generally, however, negation may occur in several ways including the declaration of a statute as unconstitutional. This later mechanism has been used even for laws which have been "on the books" for long periods of time. Repeal is probably the most common, although not the only, procedure by which a law is negated.

[32] Rheinstein, M., *Max Weber on Law in Economy and Society*, Harvard University Press, 1954.

[33] Friedman, N., *Law in a Changing Society*, Berkeley and Los Angeles: University of California Press, 1959.

ever, that either of these positions are necessarily correct. The careful analysis of other laws, and especially of laws which do not focus so specifically upon the "criminal," are necessary before this question can be finally answered.

4. Federal Law and Drug Addiction
Alfred R. Lindesmith

The popular sovereign remedy for all crime problems is increased penalties. In reecnt years this is nowhere better illustrated than in the case of narcotics laws in the United States. Although Federal anti-drug laws are said to be revenue measures, the penalties for violations at present include the possibility of a death sentence. The average sentence of the Federal offender against these statutes has increased by more than 300 per cent within the last decade, and with the denial of probation and parole many narcotics violators are now being punished more severely than the average murderer. While students of crime and penology generally deplore this popular demand for severity, it should often be regarded as a symptom of a bad law in an advanced stage of deterioration and as the prelude to basic reform. The anti-narcotic laws fall into the category of bad laws because they are basically unjust, inconsistent and irrational.

This paper is an attempt to sketch some of the basic irrationalities and deficiencies in the attitude of the Federal law toward addiction which probably account for its failure to deal effectively with addiction. Since the author is a sociologist who knows less about the law than about addiction, many of the statements made in this paper should be regarded less as definitive assertions than as questions, or as illustrations of the kinds of problems which arise in the mind of a legal layman who observes what is done with drug addicts in the courts.

The basic anti-narcotic statute in the United States is the Harrison Act of 1914 (5). It was passed as a revenue measure and made absolutely no direct mention of addicts or addiction. Its ostensible purpose appeared to be simply to make the entire process of drug distribution within a country a matter of record. The nominal excise tax, the requirement that special forms be used when drugs were transferred, and the requirement that persons and firms handling drugs register and pay fees, all seemed designed to accomplish this purpose. There is no indication of a legislative intention to deny addicts access to legal drugs or to interfere in any way with medical practices in this area. Thus the Act provided that,

> Nothing contained in this chapter shall apply to the dispensing or distribution of any of the drugs . . . to a patient by a physician, dentist, or veterinary surgeon registered . . . in the course of his professional practice only.[1]

This exemption for the doctor-patient relationship became a bone of contention when the Act began to be enforced, for nowhere in the statute or anywhere else was there

SOURCE: "Federal Law and Drug Addiction," *Social Problems*, vol. 7, pp. 48–57, Summer, 1959. By permission of author and publisher.

[1] See sections 1 and 2 of the Act reproduced in (15, pp. 983–984) or (5).

a definition of what constituted legitimate "professional practice" with respect to addicts.

THE EARLY INTERPRETATION OF THE HARRISON ACT

The passing of the Harrison Act in 1914 thus left the status of the addict almost completely indeterminate. The Act did not make addiction illegal and it neither authorized nor forbade doctors to prescribe drugs regularly for addicts. All that it clearly and unequivocally did require was that whatever drugs addicts obtained were to be secured from physicians registered under the Act and that the fact of securing drugs be made a matter of record. While some drug users had obtained supplies from physicians prior to 1914, it was not necessary for them to do so since drugs were available for purchase in pharmacies and even from mail order houses.

In 1915 a Supreme Court decision in the *United States v. Jin Fuey Moy* case (19) took the first important step which ultimately led to the outlawing of the addict when it ruled that possession of smuggled drugs by an addict was a violation of the law. The defense had contended that the section of the Harrison Act, which specifically stated that the possession of drugs by unregistered persons was to create a presumption of guilt, referred only to persons required to register and not to all persons. It was argued that making possession of illegal drugs a crime for anyone had the effect of creating an entire class of criminals with a stroke of the pen. A similar doctrine during the prohibition era would have meant that any person with a glass or a bottle of liquor would have been subject to a prison sentence if he were unable to prove that it was not bootleg liquor. This decision had the effect of forcing the addict to go to the doctor as the only source of legal drugs left to him. This remaining source was shortly eliminated by further court decisions in the doctor cases.

The early Supreme Court rulings concerning the doctor's relationships to addicts were based upon cases involving physicians who had prescribed large quantities of drugs to many addicts in an indiscriminate manner. The Jin Fuey Moy (8), Webb (20), and Behrman (17) Cases were decisive ones of such a nature. In the Webb Case the Court ruled that a prescription of drugs for an addict "not in the course of professional treatment in the attempted cure of the habit, but being issued for the purpose of providing the user with morphine sufficient to keep him comfortable by maintaining his customary use . . ." was not a prescription within the meaning of the law and was not included within the exemption for the doctor-patient situation. The Supreme Court, in reaching this decision, apparently did not bother to consult medical opinion on the matter, for it said that the contrary interpretation "would be so plain a perversion of meaning that no discussion is required." In a later case (8) the Court ruled that a doctor could not legitimately prescribe drugs "to cater to the appetite or satisfy the craving of one addicted to the use of the drug." Treasury Department regulations still use the Webb Case language when they instruct the physician that he may not provide narcotics for a user "to keep him comfortable by maintaining his customary use. . . ." [2]

The Behrman Case in 1922 gave further support to the idea that it was not legitimate for a physician to prescribe drugs for an addict, for in it the court ruled that such prescriptions were illegal regardless of the purpose the doctor may have had.

---

[2] See (12), a pamphlet issued by the Bureau of Narcotics in 1938, and in current circulation.

The decision in this case seemed to deprive physicians of the defense that they had acted in good faith, for Dr. Behrman was convicted despite the fact that the prosecution stipulated that he had prescribed drugs in order to treat and cure addicts.

After the Behrman Case the legal position of the addict seemed quite clear. He was simply denied all access to legal drugs. The rulings by the Supreme Court seemed to be moving toward the idea that the physician could not legally prescribe drugs to relieve the addict's withdrawal distress or to maintain his habit, but could only provide drugs to an addict undergoing institutional withdrawal and then only in diminishing doses. However, criticism of the law from medical sources may have shaken the Court's confidence, for even before the Lindner decision (11) in 1925, a note of doubt crept into some decisions. For example, in the Behrman Case, in which vast quantities of drugs had been prescribed, the Court suggested that a single dose or even a number of doses might not bring a physician within the penalties of the law.

The Supreme Court decisions up to 1922 made it impossible for doctors to treat addicts in any way acceptable to law enforcement officials. The ambulatory method of treatment had been condemned, and since addicts were not accepted in hospitals, the doctor's right to administer diminishing doses during an institutional cure was mainly theoretical. The danger of arrest and prosecution was clearly recognized after 1919 when the first of the important doctor cases had been decided by the Supreme Court. Most doctors simply stopped having anything to do with addicts and the few who did not do this found themselves threatened with prosecution. The illicit traffic burgeoned during these years as addicts who had formerly obtained legal supplies turned to it in increasing numbers.

If the legal situation created by court decisions on the doctor cases had been left as it was in 1922, the addict's legal status and his relationship to the medical profession would at least have been relatively clear. A definite rule prohibiting medical prescriptions for users except under extremely restricted circumstances seemed to be in the process of emerging from a series of court decisions which were reasonably unambiguous and consistent with each other. The Treasury Department, entrusted with the enforcement of the law because it was a tax measure, had drawn up regulations which were based upon these early decisions. These regulations instructed doctors as to when they might give drugs to addicts and when not to and advised them to consult the police for advice in doubtful cases. The whole theory implicit in them was that addiction is not a disease at all but a willful indulgence meriting punishment rather than medical treatment. Regular administration of drugs to addicts was declared to be legal only in the case of aged and infirm addicts in whom withdrawal might cause death and in the case of persons afflicted with such diseases as incurable cancer. Current regulations of the Federal Bureau of Narcotics are still substantially the same with respect to these points (9).

THE LINDNER CASE (11)

Unlike the doctors in the earlier cases, Dr. Lindner, a Seattle practitioner, provided only four tablets of drugs for one addict. The addict, a woman, came to his office in a state of partial withdrawal and he provided her with drugs to be used at her discretion. She was an informer who reported the incident to the police and Dr. Lindner was prosecuted for criminal violation of the law. Judging from the previous court decisions and from the Treasury Department regulations in force at the time, Lindner should have been convicted, and he was. The lower court could hardly have reached any other decision, for Dr. Lindner had obviously given drugs to this user to relieve withdrawal distress and to maintain customary usage and there was no thought of cure.

Nevertheless, after prolonged litigation, which is said to have cost Dr. Lindner $30,000 and caused him to be without a medical license for two years, he was finally exonerated by the Supreme Court. In its opinion, a unanimous one, the Court discussed the earlier doctor cases of Doremus, Jin Fuey Moy, Webb, Balint and Behrman. While it did not specifically repudiate the doctrines drawn from these cases concerning the doctor's right to prescribe for addicts, it did explain that these cases had involved flagrant abuse and that the decisions had to be considered in this context. Reiterating that the Harrison Law was a revenue measure, the Court added the following important statement:

> It (the Act) says nothing of "addicts" and does not undertake to prescribe methods for their medical treatment. They are diseased and proper subjects for such treatment, and we cannot possibly conclude that a physician acted improperly or unwisely or for other than medical purposes solely because he has dispensed to one of them, in the ordinary course and in good faith, four small tablets of morphine or cocaine for relief of conditions incident to addiction. What constitutes bona fide medical practice must be determined upon consideration of evidence and attending circumstances (11, p. 18).

Commenting upon the Webb Case, the interpretation of which it did not accept, the Court commented that the rule therein formulated

> . . . must not be construed as forbidding every prescription for drugs, irrespective of quantity, when designed temporarily to alleviate an addict's pains, although it may have been issued in good faith and without design to defeat the revenues (11, p. 20).

Of the Behrman decision the Court similarly warned:

> The opinion cannot be accepted as authority for holding that a physician who acts bona fide and according to fair medical standards may never give an addict moderate amounts of drugs for self-administration in order to relieve conditions incident to addiction. Enforcement of the tax demands no such drastic rule, and if the Act had such scope it would certainly encounter grave constitutional difficulties (11, p. 22).

The two new elements in this decision are (a) the Court's explicit espousal of the view that addiction is a disease and (b) the rule that a physician acting in good faith and according to fair medical standards may give an addict moderate amounts of drugs to relieve withdrawal distress without necessarily violating the law.

This opinion, which is still the controlling doctrine of the Federal courts, seems to make nonsense of what had gone before, for it said that the addict who had been denied medical care for earlier decisions was a diseased person entitled to such care. More important still it clearly implies that the question of what constitutes proper medical care is a medical issue and therefore, presumably, one to be settled, not by legislators, judges, juries or policemen, but by the medical profession itself. Certainly the Federal courts in particular cannot legally tell doctors what to do with addicts if addiction is viewed as a disease.

The logical consequences which seem to follow from the acceptance of the Lindner opinion were spelled out as follows by Federal Judge Yankwich in 1936:

> I am satisfied therefore, that the Lindner case, and the cases which interpret it, lay down the rule definitely that the statute does not say what drugs a physician may prescribe to an addict. Nor does it say the quantity which a physician may or may not prescribe. Nor does it regulate the frequency of prescription. Any attempt to so interpret the statute, by an administrative interpretation, whether that administrative interpretation be oral, in writing, or by an officer or by a regulation of the department, would be not only contrary to the law, but would also make the law unconstitutional as being clearly a regulation of the practice of medicine (16, p. 553).

The references to administrative interpretation and regulation in this statement refer to Treasury Department regulations already referred to, which do in fact instruct physicians as to when they may and may not prescribe drugs for addicts. If this opinion is correct, the conclusion is inescapable that the present punitive system of dealing with addicts and the Treasury Department regulations on which it is based are in direct violation of Federal law and based upon an unconstitutional interpretation of the Harrison Act.

If the Lindner Case dictum that addiction is a disease had been taken literally, a rational procedure which might have been adopted is suggested by what was done in Britain when the same disagreement arose between enforcement authorities and British physicians concerning the physician's right to prescribe regularly for addicts.[3] The Government was asked to set up a committee of medical men to investigate the question. The Rolleston Committee was the result. After extensive hearings in which this committee listened especially to the testimony of medical men with special knowledge and experience of the subject, the committee reported that doctors might prescribe drugs regularly for addicts and specified the conditions under which this might be done and the precautions which should be observed. This report, published in 1926, then became the official interpretation of the Dangerous Drug Laws of 1920 which were very much like the Harrison Act in all respects except that they were not called tax measures.

No similar appeal to the medical profession was made in the United States where the courts themselves have tried to formulate the relevant rules. The only recourse to medical advice has been through the use of expert testimony in the usual pattern, with prosecution experts supporting the prosecution's view, defense experts opposing

[3] See (10).

them, and the jury choosing between the conflicting views. This makes a jury of laymen the arbiters of a technical medical dispute and in practice means that the courts intervene in a medical controversy on the side of the faction which supports the Government's enforcement program.

OTHER INTERPRETATIONS OF THE LINDNER CASE

As far as enforcement policies are concerned, the Lindner Case has had practically no effect and remains a ceremonial gesture of no practical significance for either addicts or physicians. Most assistant prosecutors acquiring trial experience in narcotics cases, and most police officers, probably do not know of its existence, for there is no reference to it in most of the literature issued by the Federal Bureau of Narcotics. The risk of arrest remains as before for physicians who attempt to treat addicts as diseased persons and addicts still find that the doors of the hospital and the doctor's office are closed to them.

There are a number of reasons for the impotence of the Lindner doctrine and prominent among them is the legal confusion in the subsequent cases. After the Lindner decision appeared in 1925, the Supreme Court has not had the opportunity to expand and clarify it by ruling on other similar cases. Reasons for this lack of opportunity are probably that few reputable physicians care to play Russian roulette with their careers by challenging existing enforcement practices, and secondly, that the Government probably avoids taking certain types of cases to the Supreme Court so as not to give that body a chance to expand and emphasize the precedent of the Lindner Case.

The lower Federal courts were no doubt reluctant to follow the logical implications of the Lindner Case, for this would have meant upsetting an established enforcement policy vigorously supported by police propaganda and to some extent by popular opinion and by part of the medical profession. In 1925 this policy had been in operation for a decade. Apathy in the medical and legal professions, based in large part upon the facts of the addict's low social status, his lack of funds, and that he is a difficult and troublesome person, contributed heavily to the reluctance to change the status quo.

A legal device favoring this conservative position was to interpret the rule of the Lindner Case as one which supplemented rather than replaced the older ones. Thus the Circuit Court of Appeals of the 10th Circuit in the *Strader v. United States* Case (14) reversed the conviction of a doctor and stated:

> The statute does not prescribe the diseases for which morphine may be supplied. Regulation 85 (of the Federal Bureau of Narcotics) issued under its provisions *forbids the giving of a prescription to an addict, or habitual user of narcotics, not in the course of professional treatment, but for the purpose of providing him with a sufficient quantity to keep him comfortable by maintaining his customary use. Neither the statute nor the regulations preclude a physician from giving an addict a moderate amount of drugs in order to relieve a condition incident to addiction* (withdrawal distress), if the physician acts in good faith and in accord with fair medical standards (14, p. 589).[4]

4 Italics added. See also the much later case of *United States v. Brandenberg* (18).

The italicized statements formulate two mutually incompatible rules. The first is that of the Webb Case; the second, that of Lindner. A doctor who provides an addict with drugs to relieve withdrawal distress necessarily also keeps him comfortable by maintaining customary use. No medical person acquainted with addiction would ever have been guilty of making this absurd statement which makes a distinction without a difference. Since both of these rules apply simultaneously to the reputable physician who treats an addict, there is no way of knowing whether he should be convicted under the first or exonerated under the second.

Without analyzing in detail other specific post-Lindner cases, the following general points may be made concerning them and their implications: (1) the courts have not relinquished their right to rule on the good faith of the physician or to submit this question to the jury, and since no definite rules defining good faith have ever been formulated, the physician can only discover whether he acted legitimately *after* a criminal trial; (2) a physician's sincere conviction that the oath of his profession and his ethical duty to relieve human suffering and to give first importance to the welfare of his patient obligate him to provide addicts with drugs, has not been an effective legal defense; (3) physicians of admitted integrity and sound professional reputation have continued to be arrested, indicted and convicted; (4) medical experts of national reputation in the field of addiction whose opinions of the proper treatment of addicts would ordinarily be regarded as of decisive significance in defining legitimate medical practice have been indicted, tried and convicted for acting in accordance with their beliefs; (5) the Federal courts have done next to nothing to restrict their jurisdiction in narcotic cases in a manner consistent with their own doctrine that addiction is a disease.

In connection with point (4), two additional cases should be mentioned, those of *United States v. Anthony* (16) and *Carey v. United States* (3). These two cases involved three physicians, Carey, Williams, and Anthony, who were asked by the City of Los Angeles, at the behest of the Los Angeles Medical Association, to take over the treatment of addicts who were former patients in that city's narcotics clinic. All were convicted in Federal Court for violations of the narcotic laws. The conviction of Anthony was reversed in an appeals court, but the appeals of Carey and Williams were rejected on technical grounds and their convictions stand.[5] Of the three, E. H. Williams was a prominent author included in *Who's Who,* a former associate editor of the *Encyclopaedia Britannica,* and a nationally known expert on narcotic addiction whose writings are still read and respected. The conviction of Williams epitomizes the inconsistency of the legal attitudes in this field, and underlines the risks which lesser figures in the medical field assume when they attempt to treat addiction as a disease.

The irony involved in the conviction of E. H. Williams is emphasized by the fact that in his trial, the stool pigeon who testified in court against him admitted that he was under the influence of drugs supplied to him by Government agents and that he had previously been so supplied. In most of the other doctor cases, drug-using stool pigeons were also used, as the records indicate. The courts have deplored this practice but have tolerated it as a necessary expedient in law enforcement, thus

---

[5] This case is angrily and extensively commented upon by H. S. Williams, brother of the defendant Williams, in (21; 22). Another prominent medical authority on addiction, Dr. E. S. Bishop, was indicted in 1920. Both Williams and Bishop were critics of the Government's enforcement program and it is suspected by some that they may have been prosecuted for that reason.

sanctioning the provision of drugs to addicts by the police while denying the same right to physicians.

THE NARCOTIC BUREAU'S VIEW OF THE LINDNER CASE

That the Lindner Case is an embarrassment to the Federal Bureau of Narcotics is strongly suggested by the consistent failure of this Bureau to call attention to it. In a recent publication, the Bureau disputes the usual interpretaitons and argues that the Lindner decision is explained by a defect in the indictment which did not allege that Dr. Lindner acted in an unprofessional manner:

> It seems, therefore, that the substance of the holding was that, in the absence of an averment in the indictment that the sale was not in the course of professional practice only, the Court could not find as a matter of law that the sale of the tablets by Dr. Lindner "necessarily transcended" the limits of professional practice.
>
> We submit that the Lindner Case did not lay down the rule that a doctor acting in good faith and guided by proper standards of medical practice may give an addict moderate amounts of drugs in order to relieve conditions incident to addiction. What the Court stated in the Lindner Case was that the opinion (in the Behrman Case) "cannot be accepted as authority for holding that a physician, who acts bona fide and according to fair medical standards, may never give an addict moderate amounts of drugs for self-administration in order to relieve conditions incident to addiction." This is not an affirmative declaration that a physician may continue to dispense narcotic drugs to an addict to gratify addiction (4, p. 160).

The Bureau then goes on to call attention to the fact that many doctors have been convicted subsequent to the Lindner Case for supplying drugs to addicts and that in at least ten instances these convictions were upheld by United States Courts of Appeals.

The Bureau in this statement, which is one of the exceedingly rare occasions in which it takes any note whatever of the Lindner Case, makes no mention of the doctrine of the Federal courts that addiction is a disease. Regardless of the merits of the Bureau's position from a legal or a logical point of view, it is this interpretation upon which its regulations are based and it is these regulations, rather than the decisions of the courts or the statutes themselves, which directly guide enforcement policy. The Bureau's interpretation clearly leaves the determination of legitimate medical handling of addicts within the police domain and justifies, however shaky the reasoning may seem, the continued prosecution of physicians whether reputable or not.

OFFICIAL INCONSISTENCY

As already pointed out, while the courts and enforcement officials have shown zealous concern in preventing doctors from keeping drug users "comfortable," the police have been permitted to keep drug-using stool pigeons comfortable while working for the Government. More than that, the police regularly use the withdrawal distress of the addict as a built-in third degree to force addicts to provide information and to act as stool pigeons. They withhold drugs as punishment and provide drugs as a reward in order to secure desired cooperation and testimony.

In addition to these practices of the police, it is of interest to note that Public Health Service officials at the Lexington institution sometimes provide regular supplies of drugs to addicts over a period of time preliminary to complete withdrawal.[6] This is recognized by experienced practitioners as a desirable practice because it permits the addict's health to be built up and it allows for a period of needed psychological preparation for the ordeal of withdrawal. Outside of an institution this practice has the added virtue of removing the user from the control of the underworld drug peddler. Nevertheless, current enforcement practices effectively deny the ordinary physician the right to do this.

Other Lexington practices have even more drastic implications. For example, in experimentation with human subjects in that institution to which users are presumably sent for cure, non-using inmates have on repeated occasions deliberately been given drugs to establish addiction.[7] This has been justified on the grounds that the subjects were volunteers and were addicts of long standing, implying that it is not a crime to provide an addict with drugs if that is what he wants and if he is an incurable addict anyway! If it is a crime to establish active addiction in a non-using person outside of Lexington it is difficult to understand how any conceivable legal authority could make it non-criminal in Lexington. The argument here is, not that the Lexington physicians should have less latitude, but that others should have more.

THE TAX THEORY

It is probably pointless to indicate that the theory that the narcotics laws are merely revenue measures rather than police measures strains the imagination and is not taken seriously. For example, on this theory the police officers who forcibly pumped out the contents of a drug peddler's stomach in the Rochin Case (13) were interested only in the infinitesimal unpaid tax on the drugs found in his stomach. While the courts invalidated this technique, they have more recently approved of a similar forcible search of a drug peddler's rectum on the grounds that probable cause existed for believing that a quantity of drugs was there concealed (2). The penalties provided for violators also clearly do not make sense as tax collection devices.

Apart from the many obvious absurdities of the tax law theory, this view may have contributed to the fact that the narcotics laws make no distinction in principle between the perpetrator of the crime and the victim of it. Under the tax theory it is possible to argue that the addict aids and abets the peddler in the evasion of the tax by buying and possessing illicit drugs. Under this theory the rational solution which would facilitate the collection of the tax would be to give the user access to legal drugs from registered physicians.

If the peddler's crime is regarded as something other than a tax matter, it must be conceded that the harm done by him is mainly upon the addict or the potential addict. This would seem to imply that the function of the law is to protect addicts from peddlers—an obvious absurdity. It is even possible to argue, since the relief of

[6] See the testimony of Dr. Himmelsboch in (6, p. 1481).

[7] See, for example, (7).

withdrawal distress is a medical function and a humanitarian service for the diseased addict whose life may be placed in jeopardy by repeated unattended withdrawals and whose health certainly is, that the peddler substitutes for the doctor and performs a quasi-medical function. Under current conditions the peddler is the only source from which the user can obtain relief from his suffering; without him the addict is forced to undergo withdrawal without medical attention, unless the police will give him relief in violation of law.

The reason for the lack of distinction in the statutes between addict and peddler again represents a sacrifice of principle for expediency. The original formulation in 1915 of the theory that mere possession of illicit drugs by an addict was an offense may well have reflected pressure from enforcement sources which have always complained of the difficulty involved in proving sale. The possession doctrine makes it easier to convict peddlers; it makes it even easier to convict addicts. Placing the victim of the peddler under the same penalties as those provided for peddlers serves another extremely vital enforcement function by providing the leverage to force addicts to cooperate with the police in trapping higher sources of supply. All of this makes sense from the enforcement viewpoint, but it does not make sense if the addict is viewed as a diseased person, for it subjects him to exploitation not only by peddlers but also by the police, and it causes him to be sent to jail or prison solely because he is addicted or because he refuses to become an informer.

In practice the injustice involved is enhanced by the relative ease with which addicts are apprehended and the great difficulty in apprehending important illicit traffickers. The head of the Federal Narcotics Bureau has propounded the remarkable suggestion that the incarceration of users is an effective line of attack upon the peddler:

> From the practical standpoint it is fundamental that a business, legal or illegal, would be bound to fail if deprived of customers, and the peddler of narcotic drugs is no exception. If the peddler were deprived of a market for his illegal wares, he would cease to exist. As long as the addict is at liberty to come and go, the peddler has a steady customer (1, p. 161).

CONCLUSIONS

It has been pointed out that the present system of dealing with addicts is irrational and inconsistent and that it was not established by legislative intention or by court decisions but rather by administrative action within the Treasury Department. Legal confusion as exemplified in court decisions and general indifference on the part of the legal and medical professions form an important part of the background which has permitted the early line which enforcement took to continue in the face of apparently adverse court decisions.

The inefficiency of the narcotics laws is indicated by the relatively enormous extent of the problem and by the many evils which have come to be peculiarly associated with addiction in this country. This inefficiency probably arises from the basic inappropriateness and injustice of the laws as presently interpreted and enforced; more specifically, it arises from encroachments by police and courts upon the medical domain involving the extension of the criminal law beyond its reasonable limits.

In the long run it is fortunate that the narcotics laws have been ineffective, for unjust and inappropriate laws ought to fail. Public hysteria and popular demands for severe penalties played little part in the establishment of current practices and should be considered as effects, rather than causes of the basic legal situation.

Present confusion regarding the nature and purposes of anti-narcotics legislation is so great and so deeply imbedded in popular opinion and in the legal records that it is highly improbable that the situation can be corrected by future court decisions or by any measure short of repeal of the Harrison Act. As penalties have been progressively increased beyond the bounds of reason, as the addict has been progressively reduced in status and stripped of his rights until he has become an outlaw, and as the demand for even more severe penalties has continued, professional opinion has increasingly recognized these trends as symptoms of the need for basic reform. Opposition to the law has grown proportionately with the increase in the penalties. It seems reasonable to believe that legislatures will not for long be able to ignore this drift of opinion.

REFERENCES

1. ANSLINGER, H. J. and W. F. TOMPKINS, *The Traffic in Narcotics* (New York: Funk and Wagnalls, 1953).
2. *Blackford v. United States,* 247 F. 2d 745 (9th Cir., 1957).
3. *Carey v. United States,* 86 F. 2d 461 (9th Cir., 1936).
4. *Comments on Narcotic Drugs: Interim Report of the Joint Committee of the American Bar Association and the American Medical Association on Narcotic Drugs by Advisory Committee to the Federal Bureau of Narcotics,* U.S. Treasury Department, Bureau of Narcotics, 1959.
5. The *Harrison Act,* 38 Stat. 785 (1914) as amended 26 U.S.C.
6. *Hearings before the Subcommittee on Improvements in the Federal Criminal Code of the Committee on the Judiciary, United States Senate,* U.S. Government Printing Office, 1956.
7. ISBELL, H., A. WIKLER, N. B. EDDY, J. L. WILSON and C. F. MORAN, "Tolerance and Addiction Liability of 6-Dimethylamino-4-4–Diphenylheptanone-3 (Methadon)," *Journal of the A.M.A.,* 135 (December 6, 1947), 888–894.
8. *Jin Fuey Moy v. United States,* 254 U.S. 189 (1920).
9. KING, R., "Law and Enforcement Policies," *Law and Contemporary Problems,* 22 (Winter, 1957), 113–131.
10. LINDESMITH, A. R., "The British System of Narcotics Control," *Law and Contemporary Problems,* 22 (Winter, 1957), 138–154.
11. *Lindner v. United States,* 268 U.S. 5 (1925).
12. Pamphlet No. 56, revised, U.S. Treasury Department, Bureau of Narcotics, July, 1938.
13. *Rochin v. California,* 342 U.S. 165 (1952).
14. *Strader v. United States,* 72 F. 2d 589 (10th Cir., 1934).
15. TERRY, C., and M. PELLENS, *The Opium Problem* (New York: Bureau of Social Hygiene, 1928).
16. *United States v. Anthony,* 15 F. Supp. 533 (1936).
17. *United States v. Behrman,* 258 U.S. 280 (1922).
18. *United States v. Brandenberg,* 155 F. 2d 110 (1946).
19. *United States v. Jin Fuey Moy,* 241 U.S. 394 (1915).
20. *Webb v. United States,* 249 U.S. 96 (1919).
21. WILLIAMS, H. S., *Drugs against Man* (New York: McBride, 1935).
22. WILLIAMS, H. S., *Drug Addicts Are Human Beings* (Washington, D.C.: Shaw, 1938).

5. The Diffusion of Sexual Psychopath Laws

Edwin H. Sutherland

This paper is an analysis of the diffusion of sexual psychopath laws from the point of view of collective behavior. Since 1937 twelve states and the District of Columbia have enacted sexual psychopath laws. With minor variations they provide that a person who is diagnosed as a sexual psychopath may be confined for an indefinite period in a state hospital for the insane. This confinement is not ordered by a criminal court as a punishment for crime but by a probate court for the protection of society against persons who are believed to have irresistible sexual impulses.[1]

Implicit in these laws is a series of propositions which have been made explicit in an extensive popular literature, namely, that the present danger to women and children from serious sex crimes is very great, for the number of sex crimes is large and is increasing more rapidly than any other crime; that most sex crimes are committed by "sexual degenerates," "sex fiends," or "sexual psychopaths" and that these persons persist in their sexual crimes throughout life; that they always give warning that they are dangerous by first committing minor offenses; that any psychiatrist can diagnose them with a high degree of precision at an early age, before they have committed serious sex crimes; and that sexual psychopaths who are diagnosed and identified should be confined as irresponsible persons until they are pronounced by psychiatrists to be completely and permanently cured of their malady.[2]

Most of these propositions can be demonstrated to be false and the others questionable. More particularly, the concept of the "sexual psychopath" is so vague that it cannot be used for judicial and administrative purposes without the danger that the law may injure the society more than do the sex crimes which it is designed to correct. Moreover, the states which have enacted such laws make little or no use of them. And there is no difference in the trend in rates of serious sex crimes, so far as it can be determined, between the states which enact such laws and adjoining states which do not.[3]

These dangerous and futile laws are being diffused with considerable rapidity in the United States. Michigan first enacted such a law in 1937.[4] Illinois followed in 1938, and California and Minnesota in 1939. Thus four states have had these laws

SOURCE: "The Diffusion of Sexual Psychopath Laws," *American Journal of Sociology*, pp. 142–148, September, 1950. By permission of the publisher.

[1] In some states conviction of a sex crime is a prerequisite to the operation of this law. Even in this case the significant characteristic of the law is that it takes the criminal out of the realm of ordinary punishment and treats him as a patient with a mental malady.

[2] J. Edgar Hoover, "How Safe Is Your Daughter?" *American Magazine*, CXLIV (July, 1947), 32–33; David G. Wittels, "What Can We Do about Sex Crimes?" *Saturday Evening Post*, CCXXI (December 11, 1948), 30 ff.; C. J. Dutton, "Can We End Sex Crimes?" *Christian Century*, XLIV (December 22, 1937), 1594–95; F. C. Waldrup, "Murder as a Sex Practice," *American Mercury* (February, 1948), 144–58; Charles Harris, "A New Report on Sex Crimes," *Coronet* (October, 1947), 3–9; Howard Whitman, "Terror in Our Cities: No. I, Detroit," *Collier's*, November 19, 1949, pp. 13–15, 64–66.

[3] These appraisals of the sexual psychopath laws have been elaborated in my paper in the *Journal of Criminal Law and Criminology*, XL (January–February, 1950), 534–54.

[4] This law was declared unconstitutional, but a revised law was enacted in 1939.

for ten years. In 1943 Vermont passed a sexual psychopath law; in 1945 Ohio; in 1947 Massachusetts, Washington, and Wisconsin; in 1948 the District of Columbia; and in 1949 Indiana, New Hampshire, and New Jersey. They continue to spread, with no indication of abatement. What is the explanation of this diffusion of laws which have little or no merit?

First, these laws are customarily enacted after a state of fear has been aroused in a community by a few serious sex crimes committed in quick succession. This is illustrated in Indiana, where a law was passed following three or four sexual attacks in Indianapolis, with murder in two. Heads of families bought guns and watchdogs, and the supply of locks and chains in the hardware stores of the city was completely exhausted.[5]

The sex murders of children are most effective in producing hysteria. Speaking of New York City in 1937, after four girls had been murdered in connection with sexual attacks, Austin H. MacCormick says:

> For a while it was utterly unsafe to speak to a child on the street unless one was well-dressed and well-known in the neighborhood. To try to help a lost child, with tears streaming down its face, to find its way home would in some neighborhoods cause a mob to form and violence to be threatened.[6]

The hysteria produced by child murders is due in part to the fact that the ordinary citizen cannot understand a sex attack on a child. The ordinary citizen can understand fornication or even forcible rape of a woman, but he concludes that a sexual attack on an infant or a girl of six years must be the act of a fiend or maniac. Fear is the greater because the behavior is so incomprehensible.

A protracted man-hunt following a sex attack arouses additional fear. The newspapers report daily on the progress of the chase, and every real or imagined sex attack, from near and far, is given prominence. In the case of Fred Stroble in Los Angeles in November, 1949, three days elapsed between the discovery of the mutilated body of his victim and his capture. A description of the crime and of the suspected criminal was sent to all adjoining cities and counties, and blockades were set up along the Mexican border. Watches were set at hotels, motels, bus stations, railway stations, and saloons. Hundreds of reports came to the police from Los Angeles and from other cities. Timid old men were pulled off streetcars and taken to police stations for identification, and every grandfather was subject to suspicion. The body of a drowned man, recovered from the ocean, was at first reported to be Stroble. The history of Stroble's molestations of other girls was reported. A detailed description of seven other cases of sex murders of girls in Los Angeles since 1924 was published. At the end of the week, twenty-five other cases of molestations of girls in Los Angeles had been reported to the Los Angeles police.[7] After three days it appeared that Stroble had gone to Ocean Park, on the edge of Los Angeles, and had stayed in hotels there. He then returned to Los Angeles with the intention of surrendering to the police. He went into a bar after alighting from a bus and was recognized and pointed out to a policeman. The picture of the policeman who made the arrest was

---

[5] *Time,* November 24, 1947, pp. 29–30.

[6] "New York's Present Problem," *Mental Hygiene,* XX (January, 1938), 4–5.

[7] "Molestation" is a weasel word and can refer to anything from rape to whistling at a girl.

published in scores of newspapers over the United States as the "capturer of the sex fiend." After his capture, other details of the case and of related cases kept the community in a state of tension. As soon as the district attorney secured from Stroble an account of the manner of the murder, he went to the assembled reporters and repeated the story, "with beads of sweat standing on his face and neck." The psychiatrist's diagnosis of Stroble was published: he loved this little girl because he was a timid and weak old man, insufficiently aggressive to approach grown women; the murder of the girl was merely an incident due to fear of being caught and punished.

Fear is seldom or never related to statistical trends in sex crimes. New York City's terror in 1937 was at its height in August, although that was not the month when sex crimes reached their peak. The number of sex crimes known to the police of New York City was 175 in April, 211 in May, 159 in August, and 177 in September.[8] Ordinarily, from two to four spectacular sex crimes in a few weeks are sufficient to evoke the phrase "sex crime wave."

Fear is produced more readily in the modern community than it was earlier in our history because of the increased publicity regarding sex crimes. Any spectacular sex crime is picked up by the press associations and is distributed to practically all the newspapers in the nation; in addition, it is often described in news broadcasts. Then weekly and monthly journals publish general articles on sex crimes. All this produces a widespread uneasiness which, given a few local incidents, readily bursts into hysteria.

Although this condition of fear has been found in all the states prior to the enactment of their sexual psychopath laws, it is not a sufficient explanation of the laws. For generations communities have been frightened by sex crimes and have not enacted sexual psychopath laws. In the present generation the states which have not enacted sexual psychopath laws have had similar fears.

A second element in the process of developing sexual psychopath laws is the agitated activity of the community in connection with the fear. The attention of the community is focused on sex crimes, and people in the most varied situations envisage dangers and see the need of and possibility for their control. When a news broadcaster, in connection with the Stroble case, expressed the belief over the radio that something should be done, he received more than two hundred telegrams agreeing with him. The mother of the murdered girl demanded punishment for the daughter of Stroble, who had harbored him without notifying the parents of girls in the neighborhood that he was a dangerous criminal. A woman spoke in condemnation of striptease and other lewd shows as stimulating sex fiends and demanded that they be closed. Letters to the editors demanded that sex criminals be castrated; others recommended whipping. The City Council of Los Angeles adopted a resolution demanding that the legislature of the state be called in special session to enact laws which would punish sex crimes more severely and would make sex criminals ineligible for parole. The attorney-general of the state sent a bulletin to all sheriffs and police chiefs urging them to enforce strictly the laws which required registration of all sex criminals. The judiciary committee of the state legislature appointed a subcommittee to study the problem of sex crimes and to make recommendations to a special session of the legislature. The superintendent of city schools urged, among other things, that sex offenders who loitered around the schools should be prosecuted. The grand

---

[8] Citizens' Committee for the Control of Crime in New York, "Sex Crimes in New York City," quoted in *Journal of Criminal Law and Criminology*, XXIX (May, 1938), 143–44.

jury met and started a general investigation of sex crimes. The Juvenile Protective Committee urged an appropriation of $50,000 for medical and clinical treatment of sex offenders, and the County Probation Department energetically requested the authorizing of a psychiatric clinic for the study and supervision of sex offenders. It was reported that some psychiatrists in the city opposed these suggestions for psychiatric clinics as "socialized medicine" and "statism."

In the meantime, organization developed in other directions. The sheriff's office set up a special detail on sex offenses, with a staff to co-ordinate all police activities on sex offenses in the county. The Parent-Teacher Association sponsored mass meetings, with blanks on which interested persons could enrol as members of an organization which would continue its efforts until effective action for control of sex crimes was taken. At the first mass meeting, attended by about eight hundred people, speakers were scheduled to explain the existing laws and procedures and to suggest programs for improvement. The news of the Stroble crime and of subsequent events was carried over the nation by the press associations and produced national reactions. J. Edgar Hoover was quoted as calling for an all-out war against sex criminals. The Associated Press's science editor wrote a syndicated column on the views of leaders in the nation regarding methods of controlling sex crimes.

The third phase in the development of these sexual psychopath laws has been the appointment of a committee. The committee gathers the many conflicting recommendations of persons and groups of persons, attempts to determine "facts," studies procedures in other states, and makes recommendations, which generally include bills for the legislature. Although the general fear usually subsides within a few days, a committee has the formal duty of following through until positive action is taken. Terror which does not result in a committee is much less likely to result in a law. The appointment of a committee is a conventional method of dealing with any problem. Even during the recent agitations in California and Michigan, which have had sexual psychopath laws for ten years, committees have been appointed to study sex crimes and to make recommendations.

These committees deal with emergencies, and their investigations are relatively superficial. Even so, the community sometimes becomes impatient. Before a committee appointed by the Massachusetts legislature had had time for even a superficial investigation, the impatient legislature enacted a sexual psychopath law. The committee report several months later recommended that the statute which had just been enacted should be repealed on the ground that sex crimes should not be considered apart from the general correctional system of the state.[9] Similarly, the legislature of New Jersey enacted a sexual psychopath law in 1949 and also appointed a committee to investigate sex crimes and to suggest a policy. In New York City, on the other hand, the mayor took certain emergency actions in 1937 and did not appoint a committee until several months after the crisis. This committee made a very thorough study of all sex crimes in New York City in the decade 1930–39 and did not report for two or three years. The result was that New York State did not enact a sexual psychopath law; and, in fact, the committee was divided in its recommendation that such a law should be enacted.

In some states, at the committee stage of the development of a sexual psychopath law, psychiatrists have played an important part. The psychiatrists, more than any

[9] Massachusetts, "Report of the Commission for Investigation of the Prevalence of Sex Crimes," *House Reports,* Nos. 1169 and 2169, 1948.

others, have been the interest group back of the laws. A committee of psychiatrists and neurologists in Chicago wrote the bill which became the sexual psychopath law of Illinois; the bill was sponsored by the Chicago Bar Association and by the state's attorney of Cook County and was enacted with little opposition in the next session of the state legislature.[10] In Minnesota all of the members of the governor's committee except one were psychiatrists. In Wisconsin the Milwaukee Neuropsychiatric Society shared in pressing the Milwaukee Crime Commission for the enactment of a law. In Indiana the attorney-general's committee received from the American Psychiatric Association copies of all of the sexual psychopath laws which had been enacted in other states.

Such actions by psychiatrists are consistent in some respects with their general views. Most psychiatrists assert that serious sex crimes are the result of mental pathology, although few of them would make such unqualified statements as that attributed to Dr. A. A. Brill at the time of the panic in New York City in 1937: "Sex crimes are committed only by people of defective mentality. All mental defectives have either actual or potential sex abnormalities." [11] Also, psychiatrists almost without exception favor the view that criminals should be treated as patients. Moreover, since the sexual psychopath laws usually specify that the diagnosis for the court shall be made by psychiatrists, they have an economic interest in the extension of this procedure.

While psychiatrists have often played an important part in the promotion of sexual psychopath laws, many prominent psychiatrists have been forthright in their opposition to them. They know that the sexual psychopath cannot be defined or identified. Probably most of the psychiatrists in the nation have been indifferent to legislation; they have exerted themselves neither to promote nor to oppose enactment.

The function of the committee is to organize information. The committee, dealing with emergency conditions, customarily takes the information which is available. Much of this has been distributed through popular literature, which contains the series of propositions outlined above. The latter are customarily accepted without firsthand investigation by the committee and are presented to the legislature and the public as "science." Although these propositions are all false or questionable, they have nevertheless been very effective in the diffusion of the laws. Bills are presented to the legislature with the explanation that these are the most enlightened and effective methods of dealing with the problem of sex crimes and that the states which have sexual psychopath laws have found them effective. Very little discussion occurs in the legislature. When the bill for the District of Columbia was presented in Congress, the only question asked was whether this bill, if enacted, would weaken or strengthen the sex laws; the questioner was satisfied with a categorical reply that the bill would strengthen them.[12]

The law is similarly presented to the public as the most enlightened and effective method of dealing with sex offenders. After the sexual psychopath bill had been drafted in Indiana, the *Indianapolis Star* had the following editorial:

[10] W. S. Stewart, "Concerning Proposed Legislation for the Commitment of Sex Offenders," *John Marshall Law Quarterly*, III (March, 1938), 407–21; W. H. Haines, H. R. Hoffman, and H. A. Esser, "Commitments under the Criminal Sexual Psychopath Law in the Criminal Court of Cook County, Illinois," *American Journal of Psychiatry*, CV (November, 1948), 422.

[11] Quoted in *Time*, August 23, 1937, pp. 42–44. If the Kinsey Report is trustworthy, all males, whether defective or not, "have either actual or potential sex abnormalities."

[12] *Congressional Record*, XCIV (April 26, 1948), 4886.

Indiana today is one step nearer an enlightened approach to the growing menace of sex crimes. A proposed new law to institutionalize sexual psychopathics until pronounced permanently recovered has been drafted by a special state citizens' committee which helped the attorney general's office to study the problem. . . . Such a law should become a realistic, practical answer to the sex crime problem. This type of legislation has succeeded elsewhere and is long overdue in Indiana.[13]

The diffusion of sexual psychopath laws, consequently, has occurred under the following conditions: a state of fear developed, to some extent, by a general, nationwide popular literature and made explicit by a few spectacular sex crimes; a series of scattered and conflicting reactions by many individuals and groups within the community; the appointment of a committee, which in some cases has been guided by psychiatrists, which organizes existing information regarding sex crimes and the precedents for their control and which presents a sexual psychopath law to the legislature and to the public as the most scientific and enlightened method of protecting society against dangerous sex criminals. The organization of information in the name of science and without critical appraisal seems to be more invariably related to the emergence of a sexual psychopath law than is any other part of this genetic process.

The most significant reason for the specific content of the proposals of these committees—treatment of the sex criminal as a patient—is that it is consistent with a general social movement.[14] For a century or more two rival policies have been used in criminal justice. One is the punitive policy; the other is the treatment policy. The treatment policy is evidenced by probation, parole, the indeterminate sentence, the juvenile court, the court clinic, and the facilities in correctional institutions for education, recreation, and religion. The treatment policy has been gaining, and the punitive policy has been losing, ground.

The trend toward treatment and away from punishment is based on cultural changes in the society. The trend away from punishment in criminal justice is consistent with the trend away from punishment in the home, the school, and the church. The trend toward treatment is consistent with a general trend toward scientific procedures in other fields, as illustrated by medicine, with its techniques of diagnosis and with treatment and prevention based on scientific knowledge of the causes of disease. The trend away from punishment toward treatment is not, however, based on a demonstration that treatment is more effective than punishment in protecting society against crime, for no such demonstration is available. Also, the fact that the trend in punishment is consistent with trends in other aspects of culture is not an adequate explanation of the trend in punishment. A general theory of social change must include more than a showing that one part of a culture changes consistently with other parts of a culture.

Not only has there been a trend toward individualization in treatment of offenders, but there has been a trend also toward psychiatric policies. Treatment tends to be organized on the assumption that the criminal is a socially sick person; deviant traits of personality, regarded as relatively permanent and generic, are regarded as the

---

[13] December 8, 1948.

[14] See Herbert Blumer, "Social Movements," chap. xxiii in *New Outline of the Principles of Sociology,* edited by A. M. Lee (New York: Barnes & Noble, 1946).

causes of crime. Since the time of Lombroso, at least, the logic of the typological schools of criminology has remained constant, while the specific trait used as the explanation of criminal behavior has changed from time to time. The first school held that criminals constitute a physical type, either epileptoid or degenerate in character; the second, that they are feeble-minded; the third, and current, school holds that criminals are emotionally unstable. All hold that crime can be caused only by a mental pathology of some type. The professionally trained persons other than lawyers who are employed in the field of criminal justice, whether as social workers, psychologists, psychiatrists, or sociologists, tend toward the belief that emotional traits are the explanation of crime. This conclusion likewise has not been demonstrated, and the body of evidence in conflict with the conclusion is increasing.

A specific aspect of this trend toward treatment of offenders as patients is the provision for psychotic and feeble-minded criminals. When such persons do the things prohibited by criminal law, they may be held to be irresponsible from the legal point of view and may still be ordered to confinement in institutions for the protection of society. All the states have some provision for psychotic criminals, and several have provisions for feeble-minded criminals. In some European nations the provisions for psychotic and feeble-minded criminals have been expanded and generalized under the name of "social security" laws: some have included sexual criminals under their social security measures, and the latter are the direct precedents for the sexual psychopath laws of the United States.

One of the questions in criminal law has been the criterion of responsibility. The courts have generally held that "knowledge of right and wrong" is the most satisfactory criterion. The psychiatrists have generally opposed this; they have argued that 90 per cent of the inmates of state hospitals for the insane can distinguish right from wrong but are, nevertheless, legally irresponsible. The important consideration, they argue, is that the psychotic person has impulses which he cannot control and that "irresistible impulse" should be substituted for "knowledge of right and wrong" as the criterion. The psychiatrists, however, have not been able to make their criterion clear cut for practical purposes.

The trend away from punishment and toward treatment of criminals as patients is to some extent a "paper" trend. Laws are enacted which provide for treatment rather than punishment; but the treatment goes on within a framework of punishment, and in many respects the punitive policies continue, despite changes in legislation. Probation, for instance, is upheld from the constitutional poit of view as a suspension of punishment rather than as a method co-ordinate with punishment and is regarded by some persons as effective primarily because of the threat implied in it that punishment will follow violation of probation.

The sexual psychopath laws are consistent with this general social movement toward treatment of criminals as patients. Some laws define sexual psychopaths as "patients"; they provide for institutional care similar to that already provided for psychotic and feeble-minded criminals; they substitute the criterion of "irresistible impulse" for the criterion of "knowledge of right and wrong"; and they reflect the belief that sex criminals are psychopathic. The consistency with a general social movement provides a part of the explanation of the diffusion of sexual psychopath laws.

In the United States the connection between the enactment of sexual psychopath laws and the development of treatment policies is, at best, vague and loose. This is obvious from a consideration of the distribution of the laws. Three New England states, one Middle Atlantic state, and two Pacific Coast states have passed such laws; but the remainder—half of all the states with sexual psychopath laws—are in the North Central region. These laws, in fact, have been enacted in a solid block of North Central states: Ohio, Indiana, Illinois, Michigan, Wisconsin, and Minnesota. On the other hand, no state in the southern, South Central, or Mountain regions has a sexual psychopath law. These regions also are less committed to treatment policies than are the regions which have sexual psychopath laws. While this association may be found when large regions are compared, it is not found when specific states are compared; New York State, for instance, has had an extensive development of treatment policies but no sexual psychopath law. Similarly, the states which have sexual psychopath laws are not differentiated clearly from states which do not have such laws by any statistical variable which has been discovered: they are not differentiated by the rate of rape, by the racial composition of the population, by the proportion of immigrants in the population, by the sex ratio in the population, or by the extent of industrialization or urbanization.

PART TWO

THE ADMINISTRATION
of CRIMINAL LAW

PART TWO

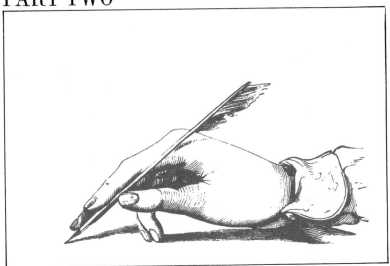

INTRODUCTION

The analysis in Part I of the emergence of legal norms has shown that by a combination of interest-group activity and the taking over of conventional morality the legal order develops its own distinctive shape and content. In every society organizations with specific roles have emerged as the agencies with primary responsibility for seeing that the legal prescriptions and proscriptions are enforced. In Anglo-American law the police, the prosecutor, and the judiciary are the principal administrative agencies responsible for enforcing the law. If we are to understand the law as a living entity then we must understand how these organizations go about accomplishing their jobs. This, in turn, will be best understood by viewing the enforcement agencies as organizations that take a particular form as a result of the dynamics of interaction with their social milieu as they attempt to perform their assigned tasks.

Every organization exists in a social context in which the organization and the individuals who occupy positions within it will find some activities and policies rewarding and others productive of strain. The most salient characteristic of organizational behavior is that the ongoing policies and activities are those designed to maximize rewards and minimize strains for the organization. The activities and policies of law-enforcement agencies, which sometimes appear irrational or whimsical to outside observers, are in fact quite rational (albeit not necessarily desirable) activities which are designed to have the consequences of maximizing organizational rewards and minimizing organizational strain. This general principle is reflected in the fact that in the administration of the criminal law *those persons are arrested, tried, and sentenced who can offer the fewest rewards for nonenforcement of the laws and who can be processed without creating any undue strain* for the organizations which comprise the legal system. The remainder of this introduction and the research studies which follow are an elaboration of this general principle.

The Social Context of American Criminal Law

One can imagine a legal system within which decisions are automatic and where the acts that are supposed to put in motion the legal machinery are clear-cut, unambiguous acts, the desirability of which is in no way open to question. But one can really only *imagine* such a system. Laws are written in language, and language is inherently ambiguous, so that no one has a copyright on *the* interpretation of what a word, much less a string of words, means. To complicate matters even further, in the Anglo-American political process those prescriptions and proscriptions which are enacted into the criminal law are usually enacted precisely because there is sufficient ambiguity so that a large number of legislators can agree to vote in favor of passage.

More complicating still is the fact that in American society the legal system must reckon with a pluralistic value system. As was pointed out in Part I, it is simply mythological to suppose that there is *one* set of values in America upon which there is consensus. Although it may be true that there is consensus with respect to certain legal proscriptions, such as those prohibiting murder, forcible rape, and various kinds of theft, these acts are but a small segment of legal concern. On matters that occupy the bulk of legal activities and which have the greatest impact on the system, such as gambling, prostitution, homosexuality, drunkenness, and drug use, there is considerable disagreement and open debate.

Even where laws may express values that at least some segment of the citizenry are in accord with, the areas of ambiguity are likely to be great indeed. Is a youth "truant" if he slips out of study hall to have a soda? Or is he truant if he accompanies his mother to a concert when he is supposed to be in school? Has a man committed a crime when he is "under the influence of alcohol" and walking down the street, or must he be lying drunk in the gutter? Formally, these issues are left to the court to decide, but in fact each of the processing agencies must make decisions in these ambiguous areas, for it makes little sense for the police constantly to arrest persons whom the prosecutor refuses to prosecute, and it makes little sense for the prosecutor to bring charges when the judges will not try the case.

Then, too, laws are notoriously resistant to change, and this is reflected in the large numbers of laws which are "on the books" at any point in time but which clearly run counter to the prevailing mores. Laws prohibiting the sale of retail merchandise on Sunday abound in the states but are rarely enforced. Laws exist which prohibit a man and his wife from having sexual intercourse on Sunday, and there are laws which declare it a delinquent act for a person under the age of eighteen to smoke or talk back to his parents. Any law-enforcement agency attempting to enforce these rules would be likely to bring forth the wrath, not the praise, of the persons whose values it is presumably protecting.

What all these dilemmas come down to in practice is that *the adminis-*

tration of the criminal law is a highly selective process and involves the use of a wide range of discretion by the agencies responsible for enforcing the law.[1] At every step of the law-enforcement process, from deciding where to send patrolmen to look for crime to determining how many years a man should be sent to prison, the organizations that are responsible for enforcing the law make decisions which have the net effect of determining what types of offenses will come to the notice of officials, what kinds of offenses and offenders will be processed, and precisely how far this processing will go. It is in the day-to-day practices and policies of the processing agencies that the law is put into effect, and *it is out of the struggle to perform their tasks in ways which maximize rewards and minimize strains for the organization and the individuals involved that the legal processing agencies shape the law.*

With a few exceptions, which are detailed below, the rewards which can be offered for nonenforcement of the law and the amount of trouble a suspected offender can create for the legal system are closely linked to the individual's social-class position. Although law-enforcement agencies will generally be rewarded for their conscientious and systematic processing of skid-row drunkards for "public intoxication," nothing but organizational strain and trouble is likely to emerge from efforts to process "respectable" middle-class persons for the same offense. Similarly, whereas the legal system will find public support for the arrest of gamblers who handle policy numbers in the Negro ghettos, they will be rewarded only with trouble for enforcing antigambling laws against a middle-class group that plays poker every Friday night.

A consequence of the unequal ability of members of different social classes to reward the legal system is that at every step of the legal process the lower-class person is more likely to feel the sting of the law-enforcement process. The lower-class person is (1) more likely to be scrutinized and therefore to be observed in any violation of the law, (2) more likely to be arrested if discovered under suspicious circumstances, (3) more likely to spend the time between arrest and trial in jail, (4) more likely to come to trial, (5) more likely to be found guilty, and (6) if found guilty, more likely to receive harsh punishment than his middle- or upper-class counterpart. Even after sentence is passed, the built-in biases continue— among those sentenced to death for murder, lower-class persons are more likely to be executed than are the others.

That this systematic bias in law enforcement is not intentional should be perfectly obvious. But, as Irving Piliavin and Scott Briar's findings suggest, even in so elementary a thing as assessing the meaning of the demeanor of an arrested youth, the police and other law-enforcement personnel invariably give "the break" to people who possess middle-class symbols and middle-class ways of doing things. A "tough" or "cool" demeanor on the part of a youth is likely to be interpreted as meaning that the youth is a more serious and recalcitrant delinquent than is a

[1] For an insightful discussion of police discretion see Joseph Goldstein, "Police Discretion Not to Invoke the Criminal Process: Low-visibility Decisions in the Administration of Justice," *Yale Law Journal,* vol. 69, pp. 543–589, March, 1960.

youth who appears concerned, contrite, and penitent. Yet one could certainly argue on sociological grounds that such an assumption is not at all justified. The urban Negro culture, for example, certainly encourages the expression of a cool posture for the male irrespective of his involvement in illegal behavior.[2] The middle-class culture, by contrast, encourages at least a show of respect for authority and an appearance of compliance with middle-class values. These differences in demeanor, then, mean in effect that a lower-class youth, especially a Negro lower-class youth, is considerably more likely to be processed than is a middle-class youth.

Furthermore, the transgressions of lower-class persons are much more *visible* than the transgressions of middle-class persons. Crowded living conditions create an environment in which most behavior, even that which occurs in one's own home, is susceptible to screening by the neighbors and by law-enforcement officials. Domestic disputes, drinking to excess, and other quasi-illegal acts are much more likely to be seen in the lower classes than in the middle classes. Even the delinquent acts of juveniles are more visible among lower-class persons than among middle-class persons. Middle-class adolescents generally have access to automobiles —many of them have their own cars. And the automobile provides an avenue of escape from the scrutiny of the law enforcers: Drinking can be done in out-of-the-way places; delinquent acts can be committed in neighboring communities rather than near one's own home. The lower-class adolescent, by contrast, will find such mobility difficult to manage. If he drinks, he must do so in an alley; if he gambles, he is not protected by the security of his parents' home; indeed, for the urban lower-class adolescent even so private an act as sexual relations is likely to be carried out in relatively more public arenas than is the case for the middle-class adolescent who has the privacy at least of his car.[3]

Gambling is an excellent example of the difference in visibility for adults as well as for adolescents. In a large house a group of middle-class men wishing to gamble can easily find a room where other members of the family will not be disturbed by the game. In a small apartment with a large number of people, the lower-class male will have less opportunity to gamble in his own home. He is more likely to find an alleyway or the back room of a public place a more convenient place to gamble. But the middle-class person is protected from scrutiny by the police in the privacy of his own home,[4] whereas the lower-class gambler is exposing himself to the sanctions of the legal system by gambling in public.

The deviance of the poor is more visible in a diversity of subtle ways.

[2] See Charles Keil, *Urban Blues,* Bloomington, Ind.: Indiana University Press, 1965, and *The Autobiography of Malcolm X,* New York: Grove Press, Inc., 1963.

[3] The importance of visibility in determining the likelihood that delinquent acts will become public knowledge is detailed in William J. Chambliss, "Two Gangs: A Study of Societal Responses to Deviance and Deviant Careers" (unpublished manuscript).

[4] For a discussion of privacy and the law, see Arthur Stinchcombe, "Institutions of Privacy in the Determination of Police Administrative Practices," *American Journal of Sociology,* vol. 69, pp. 150–160, September, 1963.

Being more frequently involved with governmental agencies, such as those that dispense welfare, vastly increases the possibility of deviance being officially discovered. In their study of a police department's morals detail, Skolnick and Woodworth found that the discovery of statutory-rape cases by the police was largely dependent on referrals from welfare agencies: [5]

> The influence of poverty on the discovery of statutory rapes is obvious: the largest single source of reports is from the family support division (40%). At the time of the study ADC aid could be given to a mother only if her real property was worth less than $5,000 and her personal property less than $600. One social worker reported that most applicants possessed no real property; those who had originally owned such property had exhausted its value prior to applying for aid. Thus, *statutory rape is punished mainly among the poor who become visible by applying for maternity aid from welfare authorities.* [Italics supplied.]

Official statistics are generally interpreted as evidence that problems with drinking, fighting, and gambling are concentrated in lower-class areas. Yet these statistics do not tell a story of differences in the frequency or seriousness of these acts; they simply reflect the fact that middle-class affluence affords a shield against public scrutiny which is not enjoyed by members of the lower class. The weight of the evidence indicates that to a significant degree the legal system's processing of law violators involves the arrest and prosecution of lower-class persons for doing in public what middle- and upper-class persons do in private.

Stinchcombe has argued that the institution of privacy is an effective barrier to legal intervention because it is a strongly held value in America. [6] But there is more involved in the differential application of the statutes than compliance with an institutional norm protecting privacy. Law-enforcement agencies do not hesitate to violate this and a host of other norms when such violation is organizationally rewarding. Thus we find the police violating the privacy of slum dwellers with considerable regularity; we find law-enforcement agents resorting to the illegal use of violence against politically impotent offenders; and we find a patterned and widespread use of violence by police to obtain confessions. Law-enforcement agencies systematically violate strongly held norms of behavior when it is in their best interests to do so. The failure of the legal system to exploit the potential source of offenses that is offered by middle- and upper-class law violators does not derive from the strength of the institution of privacy; it derives instead from the very rational choice on the part of the legal system to pursue those violators that the community will reward them for pursuing and to ignore those violators who have the capability of causing trouble for the agencies.

But the ways in which the legal system and crime interact to create exceptions to this general maxim of social-class discrimination are as

[5] Jerome H. Skolnick and J. Richard Woodworth, "Bureaucracy, Information and Social Control: A Study of a Morals Detail" in David J. Bordua (ed.), *The Police,* New York: John Wiley & Sons, Inc., 1967, p. 109.

[6] Stinchcombe, *op. cit.*

important sociologically as is the general pattern. First, of course, a middle- or upper-class citizen may commit an act sufficiently heinous so that he loses his power to interfere with the smooth running of the law-enforcement machinery. A well-to-do offender will, nevertheless, receive the benefit of mercy at every step of the criminal-legal process. The arresting officer will be courteous, the prosecutor will inform the offender of his legal rights, and the judge and jury will be understanding and lenient in the sentence. But if the offense is serious enough, the legal system will generally be rewarded for having brought the guilty party to trial. Indeed, the risk of not getting a guilty conviction may be greater than when a bum is involved, but the rewards are greater as well. The public, the news media, and colleagues will be much readier to praise the officers, prosecutors, and judges who find a wealthy person guilty of committing a serious offense than they will the officer who has arrested the same alcoholic who has been in and out of jail a hundred times.

From the standpoint of the administration of criminal law a far more important exception to the general maxim that the law is enforced against lower- but not middle- and upper-class persons is the special relationship which emerges between organized and professional criminals and the legal system. Despite the fact that organized and professional criminals operate in, and are members of, the lower class, these groups generally enjoy considerable immunity from the imposition of legal sanctions.

The Law and Professional Criminals: A Study in Symbiosis [7]

At first glance it would seem that the professional criminal (be he a thief, gambler, prostitute, or hustler) would have very little to offer the law-enforcement agencies. It therefore seems unlikely that a set of mutually advantageous relationships should emerge between law-enforcement agencies and professional criminals. As a matter of fact, just the reverse is true. Given the criteria by which law-enforcement agencies are judged and the conflicting cross-pressures they are subjected to, it is virtually impossible for a law-enforcement system to operate effectively and efficiently without developing policies and practices which are mutually advantageous to professional criminals *and* the legal system.

One of the principal criteria by which the police are judged is the number of arrests that they make in comparison with the number of offenses reported to them. Although the simplest technique for making these two statistics correspond is simply to lie, this has many intrinsic dangers since the records of offenses and arrests are public documents. A much safer practice is to agree to provide special favors to professional thieves if they will in turn admit that they committed a large number of offenses. This practice is called "clearing the books" and is used by police departments everywhere as a mechanism for "solving" crimes. The professional thief, for his part, will not agree to clear the books simply out of the kindness of his heart; thus the police must in turn put in a good word

---

[7] This discussion is based on the author's own four-year study of the relationship between professional crime and the legal system in a large American city.

to the prosecuting attorney and suggest that this man, because of his cooperative attitude, be charged with a lesser crime (for example, petty instead of grand larceny). This is but one of many ways in which the law-enforcement agencies find it advantageous to provide special favors to professional criminals in return for special favors from them. The police are occasionally called upon to recover stolen property for an influential and powerful member of the community. The public image of the police is likely to be very dependent on their ability to recover such stolen property. But the people most likely to know who stole what and where it can be retrieved are those who are themselves professional criminals —especially persons who buy and sell stolen goods. If the police have good working relations with persons who buy and sell stolen property, then when there is a hue and cry over a theft, the police can in all likelihood locate the stolen items in a short period of time. If, on the other hand, the police have arrested and prosecuted every receiver of stolen goods they have ever contacted, then they will thereby have cut off one important source of information when they need to recover an item. Needless to say, professional receivers will not be cooperative with the police unless the police in turn agree to let them work without constant harassment and fear of prosecution.

Persons who sell and distribute drugs are particularly difficult for the law-enforcement agencies to apprehend. To accomplish the goal of apprehending drug sellers it is most efficient if the police can use drug users as informants. But drug users could not be paid money in large enough sums to get them to inform; they might agree to inform, however, if the payment were in drugs or if the payment took the form of allowing them access to drugs without fear of prosecution.[8]

Professional gamblers, prostitutes, and hustlers perform similar services for the law-enforcement agencies, and typically these groups of professional criminals develop a special kind of relationship with law-enforcement agencies. To understand this relationship we must first understand some things about the laws prohibiting gambling, prostitution, homosexuality, and other "morality" offenses.

Laws prohibiting gambling, prostitution, drug use, homosexuality, and other minor sexual deviances are unique in that there is a conspicuous lack of community consensus as to whether or not there should even be laws prohibiting such things in the first place. There is little question in most persons' minds that rape, murder, aggravated assault, and theft are acts which should be punished by the law, but the consensus ends abruptly when one turns to the laws controlling other types of conduct. Furthermore, even among persons who agree that these types of behavior are the right and proper sphere for legal action, there is considerable disagreement as to what the "right-and-proper" legal action should

[8] The former head of the Federal Bureau of Narcotics mentions using these practices in Harry J. Anslinger and William F. Tompkins, *The Traffic in Narcotics,* New York: Funk & Wagnalls Company, 1953. These practices are also mentioned in Alfred R. Lindesmith, *The Addict and the Law,* Bloomington, Ind.: Indiana University Press, 1965, and in Jerome Skolnick, *Justice without Trial,* New York: John Wiley & Sons, Inc., 1966.

be—should persons found guilty of committing such acts be imprisoned or counseled? Finally and perhaps most importantly, there are large groups of people (some with considerable power in the community) who insist on their right to enjoy these "pleasures" without interference from law enforcers. And, of course, there is an equally important group of persons who are willing to provide these services for the right price.

The law-enforcement agencies are thus placed squarely in the middle of two essentially conflicting demands—on the one hand it is their job to enforce the law, albeit with discretion, but at the same time there is considerable disagreement as to whether or not some acts should really be considered against the law. The conflict is heightened by the fact that there are some persons of influence in the community who insist that all laws be rigorously enforced, whereas other influential persons demand that some laws *not* be enforced, at least not against themselves.

Faced with such a dilemma and such an ambivalent situation, the law-enforcement agencies are likely to do what any well-managed organization would do under similar circumstances: they follow the line of least resistance. They resolve the problem by establishing procedures which minimize organizational strains and which provide the greatest promise of rewards for the organization and the individuals involved. Typically what this means is that the law enforcers adopt a "tolerance policy" toward the vices and selectively enforce pertinent laws only when it is to their advantage to do so. Since the persons demanding enforcement are generally middle-class persons who rarely go into the less prosperous sections of the city, then by controlling the ecological location where the vices are most visible, the enforcers can minimize complaints. The law enforcers can, then, control the visibility of such things as sexual deviance, gambling, and prostitution and thereby appease those persons who demand the enforcement of the applicable laws. At the same time, since controlling visibility does not eliminate access for persons sufficiently interested to ferret out the tolerated vice areas, then those who demand these services will also be appeased.

Another advantage deriving from such a policy is that the legal system will be in a position to exercise considerable control over potential sources of "real trouble." Violence which may accompany gambling can be controlled by having the cooperation of the gamblers. Sexual deviants who may be inclined toward violence or even toward making a nuisance of themselves (such as exhibitionists and voyeurs) are likely to have been previously identified as they watched the back-room peep shows. Since gambling and prostitution are profitable, there will be competition among persons who want to provide those services. This competition is apt to become violent, and if the legal system is not in control of who is running the vices, competing groups may well go to war to obtain dominance over the rackets. If, however, the legal system cooperates with one group, then there is a sufficient concentration of power to avoid these uprisings. Prostitution can be kept "clean" if the law enforcers cooperate with the prostitutes; the law enforcers can minimize the chance, for example, that a prostitute will steal money from a customer. In these and many other ways, then, the law-enforcement system maximizes its effectiveness by developing a symbiotic relationship with certain types of criminals.

If these were the only consequences of this relationship one might be inclined to argue that the spirit, if not the letter, of the law is best served by the adoption of such a policy. Indeed, this set of practices represents an intriguing illustration of how an organization goes about accomplishing its primary goal (controlling crime) by actually encouraging the existence and persistence of the various types of behavior it is supposed to be suppressing. But, as is typical of social relations, there are some hidden consequences which derive from this symbiotic relationship between professional criminals and the legal system. These consequences, in turn, tend to corrupt the primary goals of the law because the legal order becomes as dependent on the vice organizations as the vice organizations do on them. Ultimately, then, an arrangement for controlling the vices culminates in a set of interdependent relations such that *the legal order is both controlling and controlled by the organizations which provide the vices.*[9]

Since those who supply services such as gambling and prostitution are in a profit-making enterprise, they are generally in a position to see to it that among the many other advantages enjoyed by the law enforcers in return for tolerating these activities is the added incentive of financial remuneration. From the perspective of the law enforcers, since the entire enterprise must be done surreptitiously and since it is clearly in the community's best interests to have the police control the vices in this way, accepting payments from gamblers and prostitutes is not really antithetical to the best interests of law enforcement.[10]

Not all the persons involved in the law-enforcement process will be seduced by the logic of this argument, but some will be and *some* is all that is necessary for such practices to have the ultimate effect of reducing the effectiveness of the law-enforcement agencies in reaching their goal of controlling crime. Once persons in positions of power accept the offer of the vice organizations to share in the profit, then they are, of course, vulnerable. The fact that the "vice lords" are themselves vulnerable means the law enforcers can bargain, but it does not mean that they can disregard what the vice leaders demand. Special favors that are beyond the pale of merely tolerating vice will need to be considered, if not always granted; furthermore, the existence of the cooperative relationship must be kept from public view, and certain other illegal steps become necessary to ensure that disclosure does not take place.

Some of the extralegal mechanisms which law-enforcement officials have been a party to in one community in an effort to avoid public disclosure of widespread graft between a vice syndicate and the legal agen-

[9] This is reminiscent of George Orwell's observations about who is controlled by the colonies. See Lewis Coser (ed.), *Sociology through Literature,* Englewood Cliffs, N.J.: Prentice-Hall, Inc., 1963, pp. 84–89.

[10] For an illustration of how the individual policeman gets caught up in the logic of this process see Mort Stern, "What Makes a Policeman Go Wrong?," *Sunday Denver Post,* Oct. 8, 1961.

cies involved the following: A radio broadcaster agreed on the air to take "any and all phone calls" from people who knew anything about gambling and corruption in the city. With the apparent knowledge and complicity of the police, this broadcaster was shot at on his way home from work. He subsequently cancelled his previous offer. A university professor who was investigating the relationship between the legal system and various types of professional criminals had his office and home telephones "bugged" and was tailed by a plainclothesman. A man who had at one time been part of the vice operation in the city tried to publicize the existence of graft; he was shot at, his property was destroyed, and he was assaulted. His own efforts to bring charges were thwarted by the prosecutor's refusal to prosecute.

In recent years, however, the relatively "strong-arm" techniques have been used less and less. The favored method of controlling the publicity likely to come from disclosure is to get information on prospective informants which makes them vulnerable. In the same city in which the cases cited above occurred this technique was used with great success in bringing a difficult sheriff into line. After this particular sheriff was elected, he refused to cooperate with the racketeers. Since the wire services so crucial to the numbers and bookmaking operations were located in the county, this unyielding stance on the sheriff's part threatened to disrupt the entire vice business. The police, however, were able to get pictures of the sheriff in a motel room with a woman other than his wife. These pictures were then used as blackmail and were most effective in accomplishing their purpose.

Since a legal system will often be effective in concealing the presence of a symbiotic relationship between crime and the legal order, it is fairly difficult to establish the extent to which such a phenomenon characterizes the American legal system. The fact, however, that fairly widespread scandals occur with alarming frequency in the large cities of the United States is reason to suspect that such a relationship is the rule rather than the exception. In recent years, for example, scandals have occurred in Boston, Chicago, Denver, New York, Burlington (Vermont), Reading (Pennsylvania), and Detroit.[11] According to the President's Commission on Law Enforcement, large blocks of states in the United States comprise areas in which core groups of organized criminals reside and are active (see the map on page 94).[12] Other evidence of corruption is the ease with which professional thieves are able to obtain a "fix" in any city in the country.

One man of the author's acquaintance had been a professional thief specializing in safe cracking for some forty years. He estimated that he had been arrested over three hundred times. By employing the fix, he had been able to avoid going to prison for all but five of these offenses.

[11] The first four cities are mentioned in James Q. Wilson, "The Police and Their Problems: A Theory," *Public Policy,* vol. 12, 1963. Scandals have appeared in the other cities since Wilson's paper was published.

[12] *The Challenge of Crime in a Free Society,* Washington: U.S. Government Printing Office, 1967, p. 7.

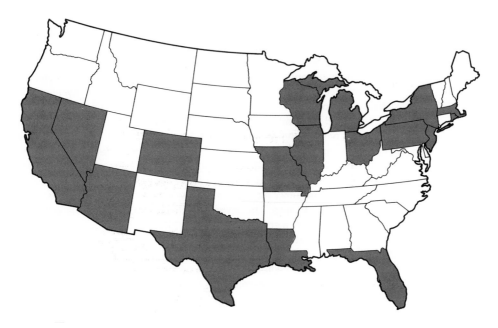

States in which organized-crime core-group members both reside and operate.

Since the fix almost always requires payment in favor or money to law-enforcement officials, this is presumptive evidence of corruption.

The consequences of an ongoing symbiotic relationship between crime and the legal system are far-ranging. Virtually every aspect of the legal process is affected by this relationship, and where it is fully developed, the legal process is likely to exhibit all the worst characteristics attributed to law-enforcement agencies by critics. One legal scholar, Johannes Andenaes, states flatly: "Laxity and corruption in law enforcement in its turn is bound to reduce the general preventive effects of criminal law." [13]

One reason for this reduction in the general preventive effects of a corrupt legal system is the lowering of personal and professional respect resulting from the ongoing cooperation between the legal system and professional criminals. As James Wilson has observed:

> The existence of large-scale corruption is a . . . source of demor-
> alization for any policeman not part of the system and thus not sharing
> in the proceeds. Such corruption affects the entire department by
> bringing formal rules into contempt, providing a powerful inducement
> for participating in the system, and encouraging the officer to view the
> public as cynical and hypocritical.[14]

[13] Johannes Andenaes, "The General Preventive Effects of Punishment," *University of Pennsylvania Law Review,* vol. 114, p. 960, 1965–66.

[14] Wilson, *op. cit.,* p. 189.

Where corruption is widespread one generally finds a tendency for the police to be violent and for the prosecutor's office to be unusually harsh in its request for stern punishment of relatively minor offenders. It is as though the law enforcers felt that by overzealous and harsh handling of other types of crime they made up for the crimes they themselves were committing and those they were overlooking. In one of the cities studied the sheriff's department was relatively free from corruption, and the police were thoroughly involved in a symbiotic relationship with vice. In general, the law-enforcement agents in the sheriff's department took pride in their work and viewed their job with respect. The police appeared to have little respect either for their job or for their work. Observations of the attitudes of juvenile gangs toward these two policing agencies disclosed that the juveniles generally looked upon the officers in the sheriff's department as fair and upon their authority as legitimate but looked upon the police with complete disdain.

The Law and Petty Deviants

Gambling, prostitution, and professional theft provide the clearest illustrations of the mutual advantages to be had by law enforcers and law violators through the establishment of a working relationship. The same is true for virtually any of the illegal acts in this never-never land of enforcing public morality.

Since no one profits very greatly economically from homosexuality, there is not much of an economic exchange between the legal system and the homosexual community. What exchange there is is generally limited to the hiring of off-duty policemen (at generous rates) by homosexual bars and clubs; these policemen are expected to keep out "tourists," to protect the anonymity of the bar, and, if necessary, to keep peace among the patrons.

A more important reward for the legal system is that cooperation keeps homosexuality "under control." As one police chief in a city studied expressed it, "This way we know where the perverts are and we can keep an eye on them. Otherwise we would constantly be bothered by their causing trouble in the wrong places."

Since many of the homosexuals in any community command respect by virtue of their status in the community, processing such persons is always a potential source of trouble for the law enforcers. By cooperating with them this source of potential trouble is neutralized.

The legal system's handling of drug traffic poses an interesting contrast with the handling of some of the other vices. To begin with, traffic in drugs such as heroin, morphine, and cocaine is economically highly rewarding, as are gambling and prostitution. But community sentiment is likely to be much more opposed to allowing persons to traffic in drugs, especially where heroin or any of the opiates is involved. Interestingly, it appears to be the case that law enforcers generally attempt to enforce antidrug-use laws even in communities where there is a well-integrated and mutually dependent relationship between the legal system and other forms of vice. This fact is exceedingly important since it suggests that profit alone is *not* a sufficient explanation for the mutual cooperation of law enforcers and law violators.

Marijuana use is in a different category. Here consensus is once again lacking, and profits may be high. From what data there are available it appears that law-enforcement agencies have generally been much more tolerant of, and cooperative with, the distributors and users of marijuana than they have been with the persons involved in the "hard" drug traffic.

The use of LSD is in still another category. Here community consensus is lacking, but unlike marijuana and opiates, the distribution of LSD offers very little profit. This is largely because of the relative ease with which it can be produced. Although there has been some question as to how the legal system would treat this new vice, the tendency is clearly *not* to tolerate it. Certainly the creation of a federal agency to control dangerous drugs following on the heels of widespread adverse publicity concerning LSD suggests that this vice will be rather seriously dealt with.

There are other types of conduct generally condemned as immoral by the community where the participants can offer few rewards to the legal system for nonenforcement. Where this is true, the legal agencies are likely to enforce the law. The prototypes of this category are the "down-and-outers" who inhabit the skid rows of our cities. These persons, who are frequently vagrants and sometimes drunks, offer no reward to the legal system for nonenforcement. Since they do not have a real voice in the community, processing these offenders causes no trouble for the legal system; furthermore, there is something to be gained by processing them, for their prosecution bespeaks the diligence and watchfulness of the law. The fact that approximately 50 percent of the arrests every year are for offenses such as drunkenness, vagrancy, and "suspicion" suggests the extent to which these types of offenders furnish fodder to keep the bureaucracy operative.

When all the above-detailed relationships between the legal system and the social classes, organized criminals, professional thieves, and sexual deviants are fully developed, the organizations which administer the criminal law maximize the rewards they receive from their environment and they minimize the strains which potentially plague bureaucracies. Much of the organizational effort of the legal system must go into keeping the system functioning smoothly once the necessary relationships have been worked out. Older policemen must socialize newer recruits into the system so that they will not disrupt the processes.[15] Judges will reprimand policemen from the bench for bringing cases to court that violate established procedures.[16] Prosecutors select the cases they will prosecute and thereby communicate to the police what types of offenses to look for.

But errors occur even in the most efficiently organized systems. Not infrequently the legal system breaks down because someone fails to

---

[15] Stern, *op. cit.*

[16] Albert J. Reiss, Jr., and David Bordua, "Environment and Organization: A Perspective on the Police," in Bordua, *op. cit.*, pp. 25–56.

realize a potential source of trouble in a given suspect.[17] For example, the arrest of Margot Fonteyn and Rudolf Nureyev for disorderly conduct while they were attending a party in the hippie section of San Francisco probably would not have taken place had the arresting officers realized whom they were arresting. Few policemen are ballet patrons, so the error was quite understandable.

Highly sophisticated techniques emerge in the law-enforcement agencies to cope with potential sources of disruption. Extensive public relations programs are instituted in order to educate the public about problems of law enforcement and, it is hoped, thereby to reduce public criticism of the law-enforcement agencies. Newspapers are "co-opted" in various ways in order to reduce the chances that reporters will uncover illegal or shoddy law-enforcement practices. The most effective means of obtaining support from the press is to offer ready access to valued information (that is, material that will make good copy) to those reporters who report "sympathetically" on police activities and to exclude from this valued information any and all reporters who are critical of police activities. In some cases the co-optation is more direct. In one city studied by the author, the editor of the newspaper was paid a monthly sum by the county prosecutor to see to it that no unfavorable news about the law-enforcement agencies was printed. This plan was apparently quite successful. In this particular community the police and the prosecutor as well as some members of the city council were engaged in an extensive vice operation which was carried on with very little effort at concealment, a major reason being that the newspapers would not publish anything detrimental to the police, and no one else had an effective mechanism available to bring the existing circumstances to public notice.

Where a symbiotic relationship exists between the legal system and criminal organizations, the potential for severe disruption of the on-going process is omnipresent. Much of the criminal-law effort must therefore be devoted to protecting the system against outsiders' becoming aware of such a relationship. Since the only really reliable information about the system must ultimately come from persons who are themselves involved, considerable protection is automatically afforded. However, new personnel may come in, especially where officials are elected, and their potential disruptive force is great indeed. A sheriff may be elected who refuses to cooperate with the organization and who thereby threatens the entire relationship. A reporter or a sociologist may discover what is taking place and threaten to make the information public.

Conclusion

It must be realized that the events and practices that shape the law are not out of design but are instead the outgrowth of the social processes taking place between the legal order and its social setting. The legal system, and certainly not the law officers, did not make the world in

[17] William J. Chambliss and John T. Liell, "The Legal Process in the Community Setting: A Study of Local Law Enforcement," *Crime and Delinquency*, pp. 310–317, October, 1966.

which public morality is systematically biased against the poor and favors the more well-to-do. But given the problems of operating the law-enforcement system, it is no surprise to find that law-enforcement officials select for prosecution those persons who can be processed without causing any trouble for the organization but who, on the contrary, provide proof of the importance and quality of the legal order.

The studies which follow provide evidence for the theory of the law-enforcement process suggested above. It is not surprising that there is a hiatus between the idea and the reality of the law, but the extent of the gap suggests the necessity for some rather basic and thoroughgoing alterations if we are in fact to have a legal system which in action corresponds to any reasonable degree to the law as it appears in the idealized blueprint.

ARREST

INTRODUCTION

Police decisions and practices doubtless have a greater effect on the shape of the legal system than those of any other agency involved in the administration of the law. Even apparently insignificant and obvious decisions may have profound consequences in determining specifically who is processed through the legal system and more generally what the law in action really means.

The relatively minor and apparently very simple decision of how to distribute the available police manpower has important consequences. Obviously, even in police-state societies, there are not enough police to permit the constant surveillance of every citizen or even of every square mile of territory. Where then, should the police be distributed so that they will be likely to detect crime? The answer is as simple as the question: where the most crime occurs. But the answer to the question of where the most crime occurs may not be as simple as it looks. Generally, the evidence for where the most crimes occur consists in past records. If the central district of a city has had the highest crime rates in years past, then that is where the police must focus their attention today. But behind this simple logic is a potentially dangerous cycle: it is possible that the only reason the central section, or any other section, has shown a higher crime rate in the past is because police were there to look for it. Thus it is quite possible that the police, by this apparently simple decision with an obvious direction implied, may well contribute to the maintenance of a self-fulfilling prophecy which finds crime prevalent where we look for it, not because of the inherent criminality of the areas surveyed, but merely because crime is sufficiently widespread so that any area that was inundated by policemen would show a correspondingly high crime rate.

Weight is added to this interpretation when it is realized that a "high crime rate" for an area does not mean simply that there are large numbers of rapes, murders, assaults, and robberies. Most, probably more than 80 percent, of the crime effort by law enforcers consists in arresting and processing persons accused of very minor offenses: drunkenness, vagrancy, streetwalking, and the like. For example, in 1965 the police in the United States reported making 4,955,047 arrests of which only 834,296 (approximately 20 percent) were for "Type I," or what the Federal Bureau of Investigation considers "major," crimes.[1] There is good reason to question the degree to which even this proportion of the total arrests might not be an overestimate of the number of serious offenses occurring in view of the fact that two categories of major crimes include offenses that are relatively inconsequential. Over 10 percent (101,763) of the major crimes were accounted for by auto theft. Yet the vast majority (over 90 percent) of the auto thefts are more accurately described as joyrides and usually involve an adolescent's taking an automobile for a short period of time and going for a ride with it.[2] In most of these cases the automobile is found within twenty-four hours where it has been abandoned by the thieves. Another category which characteristically includes a number of offenses whose seriousness is questionable is the category of larceny over $50. Thirty or forty years ago it might have been the case that to steal something valued at over $50 required the theft of a rather expensive commodity, but this is certainly no longer true. Indeed, one hubcap from most new automobiles is valued at over $50. To place such offenses in the same category as crimes against the person and burglary is to give a distorted view of the seriousness of such offenses. Much of the

[1] *Uniform Crime Reports,* United States Government Printing Office, 1965. These offenses include murder, rape, aggravated assault, burglary, larceny over $50, and auto theft.

[2] See Jerome Hall, *Theft, Law and Society,* Indianapolis: The Bobbs-Merrill Company, Inc., 1935, chap. 6.

alleged increase in serious crimes in recent years is attributable to an increase in the number of autos taken for a joyride rather than to an increase in other, more serious types of offenses.

Furthermore, even among the major crimes, the bulk of these (roughly 80 percent) are crimes against property, a fact which contrasts rather sharply with the widespread belief that most police activities center on crimes against the person, such as assault, murder, and rape.

These facts suggest, then, that the arrest rate in any area is largely a function of the police making arrests for relatively minor offenses. Although the data are not available for an accurate assessment, casual observation would suggest that the frequency of drunkenness, gambling, and numerous other offenses is probably as great in the middle-class respectable neighborhoods as it is in the lower-class slums. The middle-class transgressions, however, are "invisible," not just because the police do not as thoroughly survey the areas in search of transgressions but also because middle-class wrongdoings (as defined by law) typically take place in private. As was pointed out earlier, privacy is a very effective barrier to scrutiny. James Wilson defines this point and the essence of its implications as follows:

> In a slum neighborhood, personal and family privacy is at a premium. The doors, walls, windows, and locks which provide for most of us the legally-defined privacy which it is the policeman's duty to protect are much less meaningful to people who must share their rooms with other persons and their apartments with other families. Particularly in warm weather, such people move outside, sit on their front steps, lean out their windows, and loiter in the streets. The street is, in effect, every man's front room.[3]

In a word, all types of behavior, including transgressions of varying degrees of seriousness, are much more visible in the slums than anywhere else in the city. This fact is what moves the police to scrutinize with considerably more care the activities which take place. And scrutinizing, they find. Thus is perpetuated the self-fulfilling prophecy of high crime rates' being concentrated in slum areas.

In one city where there is a densely populated area inhabited by Japanese as well as by the more typical urban Negro, the degree of visibility of deviant acts affects the impact of this visibility on the legal process. The official statistics show that Negro youth have the highest delinquency rate of any racial group in the city; the whites have the next highest; and the Japanese have virtually no delinquency at all, as judged by official statistics. The police believe, as do most of the people in the community who are in any way connected with youth and youth problems, that the Japanese youth are of a different cut than most groups; families are more solidary; the adults form a more homogeneous and tight-knit community; and as a consequence, youthful involvement in delinquency is exceedingly rare. Believing this, the police devote little time to surveying the Japanese community. Patrolmen are assigned in large numbers to the

[3] James Q. Wilson, "The Police and Their Problems: A Theory," *Public Policy,* vol. 12, p. 195, 1963.

Negro ghetto and to the skid-row area, but few are assigned to survey the area encompassing the Japanese community. Furthermore, the Japanese socioeconomic level is considerably higher than that of the Negroes; consequently, the residences are more likely to be "private" in the way that conventional middle-class residences are private, thus affording an added barrier to the visibility of transgressions.

Richard Nagasawa, utilizing a self-reported delinquency index, obtained responses on involvement in delinquency from a sample of Japanese, Negro, and white youth attending high school in the area with the highest delinquency rates of the city.[4] His findings (see Table 1) suggest that while the Japanese youth do have a somewhat lower rate of involvement in delinquency than white or Negro youths, they are scarcely "delinquency-free," as is generally assumed. The really striking contrast which emerges between the official rates (as measured by police statistics) and the self-reported rates of the three groups can be explained by differences in the visibility of the acts but certainly not by differences in the propensity of the youths in the various groups to commit transgressions, as judged by their self-reported involvement.

TABLE 1

Comparison of Arrests (for 1963) and Self-reported Delinquency Involvement by Racial Groups

	Percent of Each Group Arrested during 1963	Percent of Each Group Classified as High Delinquent Involvement on the Basis of Self-reported Delinquency *
White	11	53
Negro	36	52
Japanese	2	36

* A self-reported delinquency scale was developed, and the respondents were divided so that 50 percent of the sample was categorized as having high and 50 percent as having low delinquent involvement.
SOURCE: Based on data from Richard H. Nagasawa, "Delinquency and Nondelinquency: A Study of Status Problems and Perceived Opportunity," unpublished master's thesis, University of Washington, Seattle, 1965, p. 35.

The general point to be made here is that police decisions have a good deal of a "self-fulfilling" quality. Precisely how many more offenses would be observed in areas of more sparse and more affluent populations it is impossible to guess. But we should look rather carefully at the assumption that previous crime rates are an adequate index of the propensity of one group to commit more crimes as compared with some other group. Statistics and legal action concerning even apparently obvious offenses such as murder and rape are likely to be very biased against lower-class areas for much the same reason that statistics on minor

[4] Richard H. Nagasawa, "Delinquency and Non-delinquency: A Study of Status Problems and Perceived Opportunity," unpublished master's thesis, University of Washington, Seattle, 1965.

offenses are. Murder is one of the more difficult crimes to hide, yet it is proportionately more difficult for someone in a lower-class area to hide than it is for someone in a middle-class area. In addition, the police are understandably more reluctant to bring charges of murder against a respectable member of the community than they are against someone who is viewed as being suspect.

Data on rape may well be similarly biased. Doubtless many more rapes occur than are reported because of the unwillingness of victims to have it publicly known that the rape took place. If the rape occurs in an auto-mobile or in the privacy of a home, then the likelihood of the event's becoming public is totally dependent on the victim's taking action. If, on the other hand, the rape occurs in an alley or in an apartment where shouts are easily heard by neighbors, then the fact of the rape is far more likely to become public. Indeed, rather than acting as a source of shame, a rape under these circumstances may make the offended person feel compelled to file a complaint in order to demonstrate publicly that she was not a willing partner. Where the event occurs out of public view there is considerably less incentive for making an official report.

The police also contribute to the high incidence of crime in certain areas by adopting poilcies which encourage the concentration of toler-ated but criminal activities in certain ecological areas of the city. Thus, as was pointed out earlier, the fact that the police tolerate gambling, prostitution, homosexual bars, and the distribution of pornography only in the poorer, more run-down sections of the city ensures that these sections will have a higher incidence of crime (at least with respect to the above-mentioned crimes). It also increases the likelihood that assaults, drinking, and the like will occur since in American culture these are frequently concomitants of enjoying the vices.

Once the policeman goes out on the beat (or into a patrol car) the process continues. Even if one is committed to arresting all violators of the law (which virtually no policeman can do) considerable discretion is called for. How does a policeman decide, for example, that something is amiss and should be looked into? Where policemen are assigned the same beat for some period of time, one of the most often-used techniques for making such a decision is to search for "unusual" events. To the uninitiated, things which appear to be unusual events may not be so at all. A policeman may, for example, ignore the fact that a woman comes running from her house screaming that someone is going to kill her. If this has happened every Friday night at approximately the same time for a year, then the policeman may well have decided that it is not significant. Or, if the same shopkeeper is always engaged in an apparently violent argument with the same customer every week, the policeman may well continue on his appointed rounds without so much as even a second look into the store. In fact, what may stand out in his routine as an unusual event is the absence of a shouting argument or the absence of a drunk from a street corner. This weighing of events is a highly selective pro-cedure and is yet another in a series of sociologically significant events which shape the legal process.

6. Wincanton: The Politics of Corruption

John A. Gardiner, with the assistance of
David J. Olson

INTRODUCTION [1]

This study focuses upon the politics of vice and corruption in a town we have chosen to call Wincanton, U.S.A. Although the facts and events of this report are true, every attempt has been made to hide the identity of actual people by the use of fictitious names, descriptions and dates.

Following a brief description of the people of Wincanton and the structure of its government and law enforcement agencies, a section outlines the structure of the Wincanton gambling syndicate and the system of protection under which it operated. A second section looks at the corrupt activities of Wincanton officials apart from the protection of vice and gambling.

The latter part of this report considers gambling and corruption as social forces and as political issues. First, they are analyzed in terms of their functions in the community—satisfying social and psychological needs declared by the State to be improper; supplementing the income of the participants, including underpaid city officials and policemen, and of related legitimate businesses; providing speed and certainty in the transaction of municipal business. Second, popular attitudes toward gambling and corruption are studied, as manifested in both local elections and a survey of a cross-section of the city's population. Finally, an attempt will be made to explain why Wincanton, more than other cities, has had this marked history of law-breaking and official malfeasance, and several suggestions will be made regarding legal changes that might make its continuation more difficult.

WINCANTON

In general, Wincanton represents a city that has toyed with the problem of corruption for many years. No mayor in the history of the city of Wincanton has ever succeeded himself in office. Some mayors have been corrupt and have allowed the city to become a wide-open center for gambling and prostitution; Wincanton voters

SOURCE: *Task Force on Organized Crime,* The President's Commission on Law Enforcement and Administration of Justice, U.S. Government Printing Office, 1967. By permission of the author and publisher.

[1] This study, part of a larger investigation of the politics of law enforcement and corruption, was financed by a grant from the Russell Sage Foundation. All responsibility for the contents of this report remains with the senior author. The authors wish gratefully to acknowledge the assistance of the people and officials of Wincanton who will, at their request, remain anonymous. The authors wish particularly to acknowledge the assistance of the newspapers of Wincanton; Prof. Harry Sharp and the staff of the Wisconsin Survey Research Laboratory; Henry S. Ruth, Jr., Lloyd E. Ohlin, and Charles H. Rogovin of the President's Commission on Law Enforcement and Administration of Justice; and many National, State, and local law enforcement personnel. The authors shared equally in the research upon which this report is based; because of the teaching duties of Mr. Olson, Mr. Gardiner assumed the primary role in writing this report. Joel Margolis and Keith Billingsley, graduate students in the Department of Political Science, University of Wisconsin, assisted in the preparation of the data used in this report.

have regularly rejected those corrupt mayors who dared to seek reelection. Some mayors have been scrupulously honest and have closed down all vice operations in the city; these men have been generally disliked for being too straitlaced. Other mayors, fearing one form of resentment or the other, have chosen quietly to retire from public life. The questions of official corruption and policy toward vice and gambling, it seems, have been paramount issues in Wincanton elections since the days of Prohibition. Any mayor who is known to be controlled by the gambling syndicates will lose office, but so will any mayor who tries completely to clean up the city. The people of Wincanton apparently want both easily accessible gambling and freedom from racket domination.

Probably more than most cities in the United States, Wincanton has known a high degree of gambling, vice (sexual immorality, including prostitution), and corruption (official malfeasance, misfeasance and nonfeasance of duties). With the exception of two reform administrations, one in the early 1950's and the one elected in the early 1960's, Wincanton has been wide open since the 1920's. Bookies taking bets on horses took in several millions of dollars each year. With writers at most newsstands, cigar counters, and corner grocery stores, a numbers bank did an annual business in excess of $1,300,000 during some years. Over 200 pinball machines, equipped to pay off like slot machines, bore $250 Federal gambling stamps. A high stakes dice game attracted professional gamblers from more than 100 miles away; $25,000 was found on the table during one Federal raid. For a short period of time in the 1950's (until raided by U.S. Treasury Department agents), a still, capable of manufacturing $4 million in illegal alcohol each year, operated on the banks of the Wincanton River. Finally, prostitution flourished openly in the city, with at least 5 large houses (about 10 girls apiece) and countless smaller houses catering to men from a large portion of the State.

As in all cities in which gambling and vice had flourished openly, these illegal activities were protected by local officials. Mayors, police chiefs, and many lesser officials were on the payroll of the gambling syndicate, while others received periodic "gifts" or aid during political campaigns. A number of Wincanton officials added to their revenue from the syndicate by extorting kickbacks on the sale or purchase of city equipment or by selling licenses, permits, zoning variances, etc. As the city officials made possible the operations of the racketeers, so frequently the racketeers facilitated the corrupt endeavors of officials by providing liaison men to arrange the deals or "enforcers" to insure that the deals were carried out.

The visitor to Wincanton is struck by the beauty of the surrounding countryside and the drabness of a tired, old central city. Looking down on the city from Mount Prospect, the city seems packed in upon itself, with long streets of red brick row houses pushing up against old railroad yards and factories; 93 per cent of the housing units were built before 1940.

Wincanton had its largest population in 1930 and has been losing residents slowly ever since.[2] The people who remained—those who didn't move to the suburbs or to the other parts of the United States—are the lower middle class, the less well educated; they seem old and often have an Old World feeling about them. The median age in Wincanton is 37 years (compared with a national median of 29 years). While unemployment is low (2.5 per cent of the labor force in April 1965), there are few

[2] To preserve the anonymity of the city, it will only be stated that Wincanton's 1960 population was between 75,000 and 200,000.

professional or white collar workers; only 11 per cent of the families had incomes over $10,000, and the median family income was $5,453. As is common in many cities with an older, largely working class population, the level of education is low—only 27 per cent of the adults have completed high school, and the median number of school years completed is 8.9.

While most migration into Wincanton took place before 1930, the various nationality groups in Wincanton seem to have retained their separate identities. The Germans, the Poles, the Italians, and the Negroes each have their own neighborhoods, stores, restaurants, clubs and politicans. Having immigrated earlier, the Germans are more assimilated into the middle and upper middle classes; the other groups still frequently live in the neighborhoods in which they first settled; and Italian and Polish politicians openly appeal to Old World loyalties. Club life adds to the ethnic groupings by giving a definite neighborhood quality to various parts of the city and their politics; every politician is expected to visit the ethnic associations, ward clubs, and voluntary firemen's associations during campaign time—buying a round of drinks for all present and leaving money with the club stewards to hire poll watchers to advertise the candidates and guard the voting booths.

In part, the flight from Wincanton of the young and the more educated can be explained by the character of the local economy. While there have been no serious depressions in Wincanton during the last 30 years, there has been little growth either, and most of the factories in the city were built 30 to 50 years ago and rely primarily upon semiskilled workers. A few textile mills have moved out of the region, to be balanced by the construction in the last 5 years of several electronics assembly plants. No one employer dominates the economy, although seven employed more than 1,000 persons. Major industries today include steel fabrication and heavy machinery, textiles and food products.

With the exception of 2 years (one in the early 1950's the other 12 years later) in which investigations of corruption led to the election of Republican reformers, Wincanton politics have been heavily Democratic in recent years. Registered Democrats in the city outnumber Republicans by a margin of 2 to 1; in Alsace County as a whole, including the heavily Republican middle class suburbs, the Democratic margin is reduced to 3 to 2. Despite this margin of cont:ol, or possibly because of it, Democratic politics in Wincanton have always been somewhat chaotic—candidates appeal to the ethnic groups, clubs, and neighborhoods, and no machine or organization has been able to dominate the party for very long (although a few men have been able to build a personal following lasting for 10 years or so). Incumbent mayors have been defeated in the primaries by other Democrats, and voting in city council sessions has crossed party lines more often than it has respected them.

To a great extent, party voting in Wincanton follows a business-labor cleavage. Two newspapers (both owned by a group of local businessmen) and the Chamber of Commerce support Republican candidates; the unions usually endorse Democrats. It would be unwise, however, to overestimate either the solidarity or the interest in local politics of Wincanton business and labor groups. Frequently two or more union leaders may be opposing each other in a Democratic primary (the steelworkers frequently endorse liberal or reform candidates, while the retail clerks have been more tied to "organization" men); or ethnic allegiances and hostilities may cause union members to vote for Republicans, or simply sit on their hands. Furthermore, both business and labor leaders express greater interest in State and National issues—

taxation, wage and hour laws, collective bargaining policies, etc.—than in local issues. (The attitude of both business and labor toward Wincanton gambling and corruption will be examined in detail later.)

Many people feel that, apart from the perennial issue of corruption there really are not any issues in Wincanton politics and that personalities are the only things that matter in city elections. Officials assume that the voters are generally opposed to a high level of public services. Houses are tidy, but the city has no public trash collection, or fire protection either, for that matter. While the city buys firetrucks and pays their drivers, firefighting is done solely by volunteers—in a city with more than 75,000 residents. (Fortunately, most of the houses are built of brick or stone.) Urban renewal has been slow, master planning nonexistent, and a major railroad line still crosses the heart of the shopping district, bringing traffic to a halt as trains grind past. Some people complain, but no mayor has ever been able to do anything about it. For years, people have been talking about rebuilding City Hall (constructed as a high school 75 years ago), modernizing mass transportation, and ending pollution of the Wincanton River, but nothing much has been done about any of these issues, or even seriously considered. Some people explain this by saying that Wincantonites are interested in everything—up to and including, but not extending beyond, their front porch.

If the voters of Wincanton were to prefer an active rather than passive city government, they would find the municipal structure well equipped to frustrate their desires. Many governmental functions are handled by independent boards and commissions, each able to veto proposals of the mayor and councilmen. Until about 10 years ago, State law required all middle-sized cities to operate under a modification of the commission form of government. (In the early 1960's, Wincanton voters narrowly— by a margin of 16 votes out of 30,000—rejected a proposal to set up a council-manager plan.) The city council is composed of five men—a mayor and four councilmen. Every odd-numbered year, two councilmen are elected to 4-year terms. The mayor also has a 4-year term of office, but has a few powers not held by the councilmen; he presides at council sessions but has no veto power over council legislation. State law requires that city affairs be divided among five named departments, each to be headed by a member of the council, but the council members are free to decide among themselves what functions will be handled by which departments (with the proviso that the mayor must control the police department). Thus the city's work can be split equally among five men, or a three-man majority can control all important posts. In a not atypical recent occurrence, one councilman, disliked by his colleagues, found himself supervising only garbage collection and the Main Street comfort station! Each department head (mayor and councilmen) has almost complete control over his own department. Until 1960, when a $2,500 raise became effective, the mayor received an annual salary of $7,000, and each councilman received $6,000. The mayor and city councilmen have traditionally been permitted to hold other jobs while in office.

To understand law enforcement in Wincanton, it is necessary to look at the activities of local, county, State, and Federal agencies. State law requires that each mayor select his police chief and officers "from the force" and "exercise a constant supervision and control over their conduct." Applicants for the police force are chosen on the basis of a civil service examination and have tenure "during good behavior," but promotions and demotions are entirely at the discretion of the mayor and council.

Each new administration in Wincanton has made wholesale changes in police ranks —patrolmen have been named chief, and former chiefs have been reduced to walking a beat. (When one period of reform came to an end in the mid-1950's, the incoming mayor summoned the old chief into his office. "You can stay on as an officer," the mayor said, "but you'll have to go along with my policies regarding gambling." "Mr. Mayor," the chief said, "I'm going to keep on arresting gamblers no matter where you put me." The mayor assigned the former chief to the position of "Keeper of the Lockup," permanently stationed in the basement of police headquarters.) Promotions must be made from within the department. This policy has continued even though the present reform mayor created the post of police commissioner and brought in an outsider to take command. For cities of its size, Wincanton police salaries have been quite low—the top pay for patrolmen was $4,856—in the lowest quartile of middle-sized cities in the Nation. Since 1964 the commissioner has received $10,200 and patrolmen $5,400 each year.

While the police department is the prime law enforcement agency within Wincanton, it receives help (and occasional embarrassment) from other groups. Three county detectives work under the district attorney, primarily in rural parts of Alsace County, but they are occasionally called upon to assist in city investigations. The State Police, working out of a barracks in suburban Wincanton Hills, have generally taken a "hands off" or "local option" attitude toward city crime, working only in rural areas unless invited into a city by the mayor, district attorney, or county judge. Reform mayors have welcomed the superior manpower and investigative powers of the State officers; corrupt mayors have usually been able to thumb their noses at State policemen trying to uncover Wincanton gambling. Agents of the State's Alcoholic Beverages Commission suffer from no such limitations and enter Wincanton at will in search of liquor violations. They have seldom been a serious threat to Wincanton corruption, however, since their numbers are quite limited (and thus the agents are dependent upon the local police for information and assistance in making arrests). Their mandate extends to gambling and prostitution only when encountered in the course of a liquor investigation.

Under most circumstances, the operative level of law enforcement in Wincanton has been set by local political decisions, and the local police (acting under instructions from the mayor) have been able to determine whether or not Wincanton should have open gambling and prostitution. The State Police, with their "hands off" policy, have simply reenforced the local decision. From time to time, however, Federal agencies have become interested in conditions in Wincanton and, as will be seen throughout this study, have played as important a role as the local police in cleaning up the city. Internal Revenue Service agents have succeeded in prosecuting Wincanton gamblers for failure to hold gambling occupation stamps, pay the special excise taxes on gambling receipts, or report income. Federal Bureau of Investigation agents have acted against violations of the Federal laws against extortion and interstate gambling. Finally, special attorneys from the Organized Crime and Racketeering Section of the Justice Department were able to convict leading members of the syndicate controlling Wincanton gambling. While Federal prosecutions in Wincanton have often been spectacular, it should also be noted that they have been somewhat sporadic and limited in scope. The Internal Revenue Service, for example, was quite successful in seizing gaming devices and gamblers lacking the Federal gambling occupation stamps, but it was helpless after Wincantonites began to purchase the stamps, since local officials refused to prosecute them for violations of the State antigambling laws.

The court system in Wincanton, as in all cities in the State, still has many of the 18th century features which have been rejected in other States. At the lowest level, elected magistrates (without legal training) hear petty civil and criminal cases in each ward of the city. The magistrates also issue warrants and decide whether persons arrested by the police shall be held for trial. Magistrates are paid only by fees, usually at the expense of convicted defendants. All serious criminal cases, and all contested petty cases, are tried in the county court. The three judges of the Alsace County court are elected (on a partisan ballot) for 10-year terms, and receive an annual salary of $25,000.

GAMBLING AND CORRUPTION: THE INSIDERS

The Stern Empire

The history of Wincanton gambling and corruption since World War II centers around the career of Irving Stern. Stern is an immigrant who came to the United States and settled in Wincanton at the turn of the century. He started as a fruit peddler, but when Prohibition came along, Stern became a bootlegger for Heinz Glickman, then the beer baron of the State. When Glickman was murdered in the waning days of Prohibition, Stern took over Glickman's business and continued to sell untaxed liquor after repeal of Prohibition in 1933. Several times during the 1930's, Stern was convicted in Federal court on liquor charges and spent over a year in Federal prison.

Around 1940, Stern announced to the world that he had reformed and went into his family's wholesale produce business. While Stern was in fact leaving the bootlegging trade, he was also moving into the field of gambling, for even at that time Wincanton had a "wide-open" reputation, and the police were ignoring gamblers. With the technical assistance of his bootlegging friends, Stern started with a numbers bank and soon added horse betting, a dice game, and slot machines to his organization. During World War II, officers from a nearby Army training base insisted that all brothels be closed, but this did not affect Stern. He had already concluded that public hostility and violence, caused by the houses, were, as a side effect, threatening his more profitable gambling operations. Although Irv Stern controlled the lion's share of Wincanton gambling throughout the 1940's, he had to share the slot machine trade with Klaus Braun. Braun, unlike Stern, was a Wincanton native and a Gentile, and thus had easier access to the frequently anti-Semitic club stewards, restaurant owners, and bartenders who decided which machines would be placed in their buildings. Legislative investigations in the early 1950's estimated that Wincanton gambling was an industry with gross receipts of $5 million each year; at that time Stern was receiving $40,000 per week from bookmaking, and Braun took in $75,000 to $100,000 per year from slot machines alone.

Irv Stern's empire in Wincanton collapsed abruptly when legislative investigations brought about the election of a reform Republican administration. Mayor Hal Craig decided to seek what he termed "pearl gray purity"—to tolerate isolated prostitutes, bookies, and numbers writers—but to drive out all forms of organized crime, all activities lucrative enough to make it worth someone's while to try bribing Craig's police officials. Within 6 weeks after taking office, Craig and District Attorney Henry Weiss had raided enough of Stern's gambling parlors and seized enough of Braun's slot machines to convince both men that business was over—for 4 years at least. The Internal Revenue Service was able to convict Braun and Stern's nephew, Dave Feinman, on tax evasion charges; both were sent to jail. From 1952 to 1955 it was still possible to place a bet or find a girl. But you had to know someone to do it, and no one was getting very rich in the process.

By 1955 it was apparent to everyone that reform sentiment was dead and that the Democrats would soon be back in office. In the summer of that year, Stern met with representatives of the east coast syndicates and arranged for the rebuilding of his empire. He decided to change his method of operations in several ways; one way was by centralizing all Wincanton vice and gambling under his control. But he also decided to turn the actual operation of most enterprises over to others. From the mid-1950's until the next wave of reform hit Wincanton after elections in the early 1960's, Irv Stern generally succeeded in reaching these goals.

The financial keystone of Stern's gambling empire was numbers betting. Records seized by the Internal Revenue Service in the late 1950's and early 1960's indicated that gross receipts from numbers amounted to more than $100,000 each month, or $1.3 million annually. Since the numbers are a poor man's form of gambling (bets range from a penny to a dime or quarter), a large number of men and a high degree of organization are required. The organizational goals are three: have the maximum possible number of men on the streets seeking bettors, be sure that they are reporting honestly, and yet strive so to decentralize the organization that no one, if arrested, will be able to identify many of the others. During the "pearl gray purity" of Hal Craig, numbers writing was completely unorganized—many isolated writers took bets from their friends and frequently had to renege if an unusually popular number came up; no one writer was big enough to guard against such possibilities. When a new mayor took office in the mid-1950's, however, Stern's lieutenants notified each of the small writers that they were now working for Stern—or else. Those who objected were "persuaded" by Stern's men, or else arrested by the police, as were any of the others who were suspected of holding out on their receipts. Few objected for very long. After Stern completed the reorganization of the numbers business, its structure was roughly something like this: 11 subbanks reported to Stern's central accounting office. Each subbank employed from 5 to 30 numbers writers. Thirty-five per cent of the gross receipts went to the writers. After deducting for winnings and expenses (mostly protection payoffs), Stern divided the net profits equally with the operators of the subbanks. In return for his cut, Stern provided protection from the police and "laid off" the subbanks, covering winnings whenever a popular number "broke" one of the smaller operators.

Stern also shared with out-of-State syndicates in the profits and operation of two enterprises—a large dice game and the largest still found by the Treasury Department since Prohibition. The dice game employed over 50 men—drivers to "lug" players into town from as far as 100 miles away, doormen to check players' identities, loan sharks who "faded" the losers, croupiers, food servers, guards, etc. The 1960 payroll for these employees was over $350,000. While no estimate of the gross receipts from the game is available, some indication of its size can be obtained from the fact that $50,000 was found on the tables and in the safe when the FBI raided the game in

1962. Over 100 players were arrested during the raid; one businessman had lost over $75,000 at the tables. Stern received a share of the game's profits plus a $1,000 weekly fee to provide protection from the police.

Stern also provided protection (for a fee) and shared in the profits of a still, erected in an old warehouse on the banks of the Wincanton River and tied into the city's water and sewer systems. Stern arranged for clearance by the city council and provided protection from the local police after the $200,000 worth of equipment was set up. The still was capable of producing $4 million worth of alcohol each year, and served a five-State area, until Treasury agents raided it after it had been in operation for less than 1 year.

The dice game and the still raise questions regarding the relationship of Irv Stern to out-of-State syndicates. Republican politicians in Wincanton frequently claimed that Stern was simply the local agent of the Cosa Nostra. While Stern was regularly sending money to the syndicates, the evidence suggests that Stern was much more than an agent for outsiders. It would be more accurate to regard these payments as profit sharing with coinvestors and as charges for services rendered. The east coasters provided technical services in the operation of the dice game and still and "enforcement" service for the Wincanton gambling operation. When deviants had to be persuaded to accept Stern's domination, Stern called upon outsiders for "muscle"—strong-arm men who could not be traced by local police if the victim chose to protest. In the early 1940's, for example, Stern asked for help in destroying a competing dice game; six gunmen came in and held it up, robbing and terrifying the players. While a few murders took place in the struggle for supremacy in the 1930's and 1940's, only a few people were roughed up in the 1950's and no one was killed.

After the mid-1950's, Irv Stern controlled prostitution and several forms of gambling on a "franchise" basis. Stern took no part in the conduct of these businesses and received no share of the profits, but exacted a fee for protection from the police. Several horse books, for example, operated regularly; the largest of these paid Stern $600 per week. While slot machines had permanently disappeared from the Wincanton scene after the legislative investigations of the early 1950's, a number of men began to distribute pinball machines, which paid off players for games won. As was the case with numbers writers, these pinball distributors had been unorganized during the Craig administration. When Democratic Mayor Gene Donnelly succeeded Craig, he immediately announced that all pinball machines were illegal and would be confiscated by the police. A Stern agent then contacted the pinball distributors and notified them that if they employed Dave Feinman (Irv Stern's nephew) as a "public relations consultant," there would be no interference from the police. Several rebellious distributors formed an Alsace County Amusement Operators Association, only to see Feinman appear with two thugs from New York. After the association president was roughed up, all resistance collapsed, and Feinman collected $2,000 each week to promote the "public relations" of the distributors. (Stern, of course, was able to offer no protection against Federal action. After the Internal Revenue Service began seizing the pinball machines in 1956, the owners were forced to purchase the $250 Federal gambling stamps as well as paying Feinman. Over 200 Wincanton machines bore these stamps in the early 1960's, and thus were secure from Federal as well as local action.)

After the period of reform in the early 1950's, Irv Stern was able to establish a centralized empire in which he alone determined which rackets would operate and who would operate them (he never, it might be noted, permitted narcotics traffic in the city while he controlled it). What were the bases of his control within the criminal world? Basically, they were three: First, as a business matter, Stern controlled access to several very lucrative operations, and could quickly deprive an uncooperative gambler or numbers writer of his source of income. Second, since he controlled the police department he could arrest any gamblers or bookies who were not paying tribute. (Some of the local gambling and prostitution arrests which took place during the Stern era served another purpose—to placate newspaper demands for a crackdown. As one police chief from this era phrased it, "Hollywood should have given us an Oscar for some of our performances when we had to pull a phony raid to keep the papers happy.") Finally, if the mechanisms of fear of financial loss and fear of police arrest failed to command obedience, Stern was always able to keep alive a fear of physical violence. As we have seen, numbers writers, pinball distributors, and competing gamblers were brought into line after outside enforcers put in an appearance. Stern's regular collection agent, a local tough who had been convicted of murder in the 1940's, was a constant reminder of the virtues of cooperation. Several witnesses who told grand juries or Federal agents of extortion attempts by Stern, received visits from Stern enforcers and tended to "forget" when called to testify against the boss.

Protection. An essential ingredient in Irv Stern's Wincanton operations was protection against law enforcement agencies. While he was never able to arrange freedom from Federal intervention (although, as in the case of purchasing excise stamps for the pinball machines, he was occasionally able to satisfy Federal requirements without disrupting his activities), Stern was able in the 1940's and again from the mid-1950's through the early 1960's to secure freedom from State and local action. The precise extent of Stern's network of protection payments is unknown, but the method of operations can be reconstructed.

Two basic principles were involved in the Wincanton protection system—pay top personnel as much as necessary to keep them happy (and quiet), and pay something to as many others as possible to implicate them in the system and to keep them from talking. The range of payoffs thus went from a weekly salary for some public officials to a Christmas turkey for the patrolman on the beat. Records from the numbers bank listed payments totaling $2,400 each week to some local elected officials, State legislators, the police chief, a captain in charge of detectives, and persons mysteriously labeled "county" and "State." While the list of persons to be paid remained fairly constant, the amounts paid varied according to the gambling activities in operation at the time; payoff figures dropped sharply when the FBI put the dice game out of business. When the dice game was running, one official was receiving $750 per week, the chief $100, and a few captains, lieutenants, and detectives lesser amounts.

While the number of officials receiving regular "salary" payoffs was quite restricted (only 15 names were on the payroll found at the numbers bank), many other officials were paid off in different ways. (Some men were also silenced without charge—low-ranking policemen, for example, kept quiet after they learned that men who reported gambling or prostitution were ignored or transferred to the midnight shift; they didn't have to be paid.) Stern was a major (if undisclosed) contributor during political campaigns—sometimes giving money to all candidates, not caring who won, sometimes supporting a "regular" to defeat a possible reformer, sometimes paying a candidate not to oppose a preferred man. Since there were few legitimate sources of large contributions for Democratic candidates, Stern's money was frequently regarded as essential for victory, for the costs of buying radio and television time and paying pollwatchers were high. When popular sentiment was running strongly in favor of reform, however, even Stern's contributions could not guarantee victory. Bob Walasek, later to be as corrupt as any Wincanton mayor, ran as a reform candidate in the Democratic primary and defeated Stern-financed incumbent Gene Donnelly. Never a man to bear grudges, Stern financed Walasek in the general election that year and put him on the "payroll" when he took office.

Even when local officials were not on the regular payroll, Stern was careful to remind them of his friendship (and their debts). A legislative investigating committee found that Stern had given mortgage loans to a police lieutenant and the police chief's son. County Court Judge Ralph Vaughan recalled that shortly after being elected (with Stern support), he received a call from Dave Feinman, Stern's nephew. "Congratulations, judge. When do you think you and your wife would like a vacation in Florida?"

"Florida? Why on earth would I want to go there?"

"But all the other judges and the guys in City Hall—Irv takes them all to Florida whenever they want to get away."

"Thanks anyway, but I'm not interested."

"Well, how about a mink coat instead. What size coat does your wife wear? . . ."

In another instance an assistant district attorney told of Feinman's arriving at his front door with a large basket from Stern's supermarket just before Christmas. "My minister suggested a needy family that could use the food," the assistant district attorney recalled, "but I returned the liquor to Feinman. How could I ask a minister if he knew someone that could use three bottles of scotch?"

Campaign contributions, regular payments to higher officials, holiday and birthday gifts—these were the bases of the system by which Irv Stern bought protection from the law. The campaign contributions usually ensured that complacent mayors, councilmen, district attorneys and judges were elected; payoffs in some instances usually kept their loyalty. In a number of ways, Stern was also able to reward the corrupt officials at no financial cost to himself. Just as the officials, being in control of the instruments of law enforcement, were able to facilitate Stern's gambling enterprises, so Stern, in control of a network of men operating outside the law, was able to facilitate the officials' corrupt enterprises. As will be seen later, many local officials were not satisfied with their legal salaries from the city and their illegal salaries from Stern and decided to demand payments from prostitutes, kickbacks from salesmen, etc. Stern, while seldom receiving any money from these transactions, became a broker: bringing politicians into contact with salesmen, merchants, and lawyers willing to offer bribes to get city business; setting up middlemen who could handle the money without jeopardizing the officials' reputations; and providing enforcers who could bring delinquents into line.

From the corrupt activities of Wincanton officials, Irv Stern received little in contrast to his receipts from his gambling operations. Why then did he get involved in them? The major virtue, from Stern's point of view, of the system of extortion that flourished in Wincanton was that it kept down the officials' demands for payoffs directly from Stern. If a councilman was able to pick up $1,000 on the purchase of city equipment, he would demand a lower payment for the protection of gambling. Furthermore, since Stern knew the facts of extortion in each instance, the officials would be further implicated in the system and less able to back out on the arrangements regarding gambling. Finally, as Stern discovered to his chagrin, it became necessary to supervise official extortion to protect the officials against their own stupidity. Mayor Gene Donnelly was cooperative and remained satisfied with his regular "salary." Bob Walasek, however, was a greedy man, and seized every opportunity to profit from a city contract. Soon Stern found himself supervising many of Walasek's deals to keep the mayor from blowing the whole arrangement wide open. When Walasek tried to double the "take" on a purchase of parking meters, Stern had to step in and set the contract price, provide an untraceable middleman, and see the deal through to completion. "I told Irv," Police Chief Phillips later testified, "that Walasek wanted $12 on each meter instead of the $6 we got on the last meter deal. He became furious. He said, 'Walasek is going to fool around and wind up in jail. You come and see me. I'll tell Walasek what he's going to buy.'"

Protection, it was stated earlier, was an essential ingredient in Irv Stern's gambling empire. In the end, Stern's downfall came not from a flaw in the organization of the gambling enterprises but from public exposure of the corruption of Mayor Walasek and other officials. In the early 1960's Stern was sent to jail for 4 years on tax evasion charges, but the gambling empire continued to operate smoothly in his absence. A year later, however, Chief Phillips was caught perjuring himself in grand jury testimony concerning kickbacks on city towing contracts. Phillips "blew the whistle" on Stern, Walasek, and members of the city council, and a reform administration was swept into office. Irv Stern's gambling empire had been worth several million dollars each year; kickbacks on the towing contracts brought Bob Walasek a paltry $50 to $75 each week.

OFFICIAL CORRUPTION

Textbooks on municipal corporation law speak of at least three varieties of official corruption. The major categories are nonfeasance (failing to perform a required duty at all), malfeasance (the commission of some act which is positively unlawful), and misfeasance (the improper performance of some act which a man may properly do). During the years in which Irv Stern was running his gambling operations, Wincanton officials were guilty of all of these. Some residents say that Bob Walasek came to regard the mayor's office as a brokerage, levying a tariff on every item that came across his desk. Sometimes a request for simple municipal services turned into a game of cat and mouse, with Walasek sitting on the request, waiting to see how much would be offered, and the petitioner waiting to see if he could obtain his rights without having to pay for them. Corruption was not as lucrative an enterprise as gambling, but it offered a tempting supplement to low official salaries.

Nonfeasance

As was detailed earlier, Irv Stern saw to it that Wincanton officials would ignore at least one of their statutory duties, enforcement of the State's gambling laws. Bob Walasek and his cohorts also agreed to overlook other illegal activities. Stern, we noted earlier, preferred not to get directly involved in prostitution; Walasek and Police Chief Dave Phillips tolerated all prostitutes who kept up their protection payments. One madam, controlling more than 20 girls, gave Phillips et al. $500 each week; one woman employing only one girl paid $75 each week that she was in business. Operators of a carnival in rural Alsace County paid a public official $5,000 for the privilege of operating gambling tents for 5 nights each summer. A burlesque theater manager, under attack by high school teachers, was ordered to pay $25 each week for the privilege of keeping his strip show open.

Many other city and county officials must be termed guilty of nonfeasance, although there is no evidence that they received payoffs, and although they could present reasonable excuses for their inaction. Most policemen, as we have noted earlier, began to ignore prostitution and gambling completely after their reports of offenses were ignored or superior officers told them to mind their own business. State policemen, well informed about city vice and gambling conditions, did nothing unless called upon to act by local officials. Finally, the judges of the Alsace County Court failed to exercise their power to call for State Police investigations. In 1957, following Federal raids on horse bookies, the judges did request an investigation by the State Attorney General, but refused to approve his suggestion that a grand jury be convened to continue the investigation. For each of these instances of inaction, a tenable excuse might be offered—the beat patrolman should not be expected to endure harassment from his superior officers, State police gambling raids in a hostile city might jeopardize State-local cooperation on more serious crimes, and a grand jury problem might easily be turned into a "whitewash" in the hands of a corrupt district attorney. In any event, powers available to these law enforcement agencies for the prevention of gambling and corruption were not utilized.

Malfeasance

In fixing parking and speeding tickets, Wincanton politicians and policemen committed malfeasance, or committed an act they were forbidden to do, by illegally compromising valid civil and criminal actions. Similarly, while State law provides no particular standards by which the mayor is to make promotions within his police department, it was obviously improper for Mayor Walasek to demand a "political contribution" of $10,000 from Dave Phillips before he was appointed chief in 1960.

The term "political contribution" raises a serious legal and analytical problem in classifying the malfeasance of Wincanton officials, and indeed of politicians in many cities. Political campaigns cost money; citizens have a right to support the candidates of their choice; and officials have a right to appoint their backers to noncivil service positions. At some point, however, threats or oppression convert legitimate requests for political contributions into extortion. Shortly after taking office in the mid-1950's, Mayor Gene Donnelly notified city hall employees that they would be expected "voluntarily" to contribute 2 per cent of their salary to the Democratic Party. (It might be noted that Donnelly never forwarded any of these "political contributions" to the party treasurer.) A number of salesmen doing business with the city were notified that companies which had supported the party would receive favored treatment; Donnelly notified one salesman that in light of a proposed $81,000 contract for the purchase of fire engines, a "political contribution" of $2,000 might not be inappropriate. While neither the city hall employees nor the salesmen had rights to their positions or their contracts, the "voluntary" quality of their contributions seems questionable.

One final, in the end almost ludicrous, example of malfeasance came with Mayor

Donnelly's abortive "War on the Press." Following a series of gambling raids by the Internal Revenue Service, the newspapers began asking why the local police had not participated in the raids. The mayor lost his temper and threw a reporter in jail. Policemen were instructed to harass newspaper delivery trucks, and 73 tickets were written over a 48-hour period for supposed parking and traffic violations. Donnelly soon backed down after national news services picked up the story, since press coverage made him look ridiculous. Charges against the reporter were dropped, and the newspapers continued to expose gambling and corruption.

Misfeasance

Misfeasance in office, says the common law, is the improper performance of some act which a man may properly do. City officials must buy and sell equipment, contract for services, and allocate licenses, privileges, etc. These actions can be improperly performed if either the results are improper (e.g., if a building inspector were to approve a home with defective wiring or a zoning board to authorize a variance which had no justification in terms of land usage) or a result is achieved by improper procedures (e.g., if the city purchased an acceptable automobile in consideration of a bribe paid to the purchasing agent). In the latter case, we can usually assume an improper result as well—while the automobile will be satisfactory, the bribe giver will probably have inflated the sale price to cover the costs of the bribe.

In Wincanton, it was rather easy for city officials to demand kickbacks, for State law frequently does not demand competitive bidding or permits the city to ignore the lowest bid. The city council is not required to advertise or take bids on purchases under $1,000, contracts for maintenance of streets and other public works, personal or professional services, or patented or copyrighted products. Even when bids must be sought, the council is only required to award the contract to the lowest responsible bidder. Given these permissive provisions, it was relatively easy for council members to justify or disguise contracts in fact based upon bribes. The exemption for patented products facilitated bribe taking on the purchase of two emergency trucks for the police department (with a $500 campaign contribution on a $7,500 deal), three fire engines ($2,000 was allegedly paid on an $81,000 contract), and 1,500 parking meters (involving payments of $10,500 plus an $880 clock for Mayor Walasek's home). Similar fees were allegedly exacted in connection with the purchase of a city fire alarm system and police uniforms and firearms. A former mayor and other officials also profited on the sale of city property, allegedly dividing $500 on the sale of a crane and $20,000 for approving the sale, for $22,000, of a piece of land immediately resold for $75,000.

When contracts involved services to the city, the provisions in the State law regarding the lowest responsible bidder and excluding "professional services" from competitive bidding provided convenient loopholes. One internationally known engineering firm refused to agree to kickback in order to secure a contract to design a $4.5 million sewage disposal plant for the city; a local firm was then appointed, which paid $10,700 of its $225,000 fee to an associate of Irv Stern and Mayor Donnelly as a "finder's fee." Since the State law also excludes public works maintenance contracts from the competitive bidding requirements, many city paving and street repair contracts during the Donnelly-Walasek era were given to a contributor to the Democratic Party. Finally, the franchise for towing illegally parked cars and cars involved in accidents was awarded to two garages which were then required to kickback $1 for each car towed.

The handling of graft on the towing contracts illustrates the way in which minor violence and the "lowest responsible bidder" clause could be used to keep bribe payers in line. After Federal investigators began to look into Wincanton corruption, the owner of one of the garages with a towing franchise testified before the grand jury. Mayor Walasek immediately withdrew his franchise, citing "health violations" at the garage. The garageman was also "encouraged" not to testify by a series of "accidents"—wheels would fall off towtrucks on the highway, steering cables were cut, and so forth. Newspaper satirization of the "health violations" forced the restoration of the towing franchise, and the "accidents" ceased.

Lest the reader infer that the "lowest responsible bidder" clause was used as an escape valve only for corrupt purposes, one incident might be noted which took place under the present reform administration. In 1964, the Wincanton School Board sought bids for the renovation of an athletic field. The lowest bid came from a construction company owned by Dave Phillips, the corrupt police chief who had served formerly under Mayor Walasek. While the company was presumably competent to carry out the assignment, the board rejected Phillips' bid "because of a question as to his moral responsibility." The board did not specify whether this referred to his prior corruption as chief or his present status as an informer in testifying against Walasek and Stern.

One final area of city power, which was abused by Walasek et al., covered discretionary acts, such as granting permits and allowing zoning variances. On taking office, Walasek took the unusual step of asking that the bureaus of building and plumbing inspection be put under the mayor's control. With this power to approve or deny building permits, Walasek "sat on" applications, waiting until the petitioner contributed $50 or $75, or threatened to sue to get his permit. Some building designs were not approved until a favored architect was retained as a "consultant." (It is not known whether this involved kickbacks to Walasek or simply patronage for a friend.) At least three instances are known in which developers were forced to pay for zoning variances before apartment buildings or supermarkets could be erected. Businessmen who wanted to encourage rapid turnover of the curb space in front of their stores were told to pay a police sergeant to erect "10-minute parking" signs. To repeat a caveat stated earlier, it is impossible to tell whether these kickbacks were demanded to expedite legitimate requests or to approve improper demands, such as a variance that would hurt a neighborhood or a certificate approving improper electrical work.

All of the activities detailed thus far involve fairly clear violations of the law. To complete the picture of the abuse of office by Wincanton officials, we might briefly mention "honest graft." This term was best defined by one of its earlier practitioners, State Senator George Washington Plunkitt who loyally served Tammany Hall at the turn of the century.

> There's all the difference in the world between [honest and dishonest graft]. Yes, many of our men have grown rich in politics. I have myself.
>
> I've made a big fortune out of the game, and I'm gettin' richer every day, but I've not gone in for dishonest graft—blackmailin' gam-

blers, saloonkeepers, disorderly people, etc.—and neither has any of the men who have made big fortunes in politics.

There's an honest graft, and I'm an example of how it works. I might sum up the whole thing by sayin': "I seen my opportunities and I took 'em."

Let me explain my examples. My party's in power in the city, and it's goin' to undertake a lot of public improvements. Well, I'm tipped off, say, that they're going to lay out a new park at a certain place.

I see my opportunity and I take it. I go to that place, and I buy up all the land I can in the neighborhood. Then the board of this or that makes its plan public, and there is a rush to get my land, which nobody cared particular for before.

Ain't it perfectly honest to charge a good price and make a profit on my investment and foresight? Of course, it is. Well, that's honest graft.[3]

While there was little in the way of land purchasing—either honest or dishonest—going on in Wincanton during this period, several officials who carried on their own businesses while in office were able to pick up some "honest graft." One city councilman with an accounting office served as bookkeeper for Irv Stern and the major bookies and prostitutes in the city.

Police Chief Phillips' construction firm received a contract to remodel the exterior of the largest brothel in town. Finally one councilman serving in the present reform administration received a contract to construct all gasoline stations built in the city by a major petroleum company; skeptics say that the contract was the quid pro quo for the councilman's vote to give the company the contract to sell gasoline to the city. *How Far Did It Go?* This cataloging of acts of nonfeasance, malfeasance, and misfeasance by Wincanton officials raises a danger of confusing variety with universality, of assuming that every employee of the city was either engaged in corrupt activities or was being paid to ignore the corruption of others. On the contrary, both official investigations and private research lead to the conclusion that there is no reason whatsoever to question the honesty of the vast majority of the employees of the city of Wincanton. Certainly no more than 10 of the 155 members of the Wincanton police force were on Irv Stern's payroll (although as many as half of them may have accepted petty Christmas presents—turkeys or liquor). In each department, there were a few employees who objected actively to the misdeeds of their superiors, and the only charge that can justly be leveled against the mass of employees is that they were unwilling to jeopardize their employment by publicly exposing what was going on. When Federal investigators showed that an honest (and possibly successful) attempt was being made to expose Stern-Walasek corruption, a number of city employees cooperated with the grand jury in aggregating evidence which could be used to convict the corrupt officials.

Before these Federal investigations began, however, it could reasonably appear to an individual employee that the entire machinery of law enforcement in the city was controlled by Stern, Walasek, et al., and that an individual protest would be silenced quickly. This can be illustrated by the momentary crusade conducted by First Assistant District Attorney Phil Roper in the summer of 1962. When the district attor-

[3] William L. Riordan, "Plunkitt of Tammany Hall" (New York: E. P. Dutton, 1963), p. 3.

ney left for a short vacation, Roper decided to act against the gamblers and madams in the city. With the help of the State Police, Roper raided several large brothels. Apprehending on the street the city's largest distributor of punchboards and lotteries, Roper effected a citizen's arrest and drove him to police headquarters for proper detention and questioning. "I'm sorry, Mr. Roper," said the desk sergeant, "we're under orders not to arrest persons brought in by you." Roper was forced to call upon the State Police for aid in confining the gambler. When the district attorney returned from his vacation, he quickly fired Roper "for introducing politics into the district attorney's office."

If it is incorrect to say that Wincanton corruption extended very far vertically—into the rank and file of the various departments of the city—how far did it extend horizontally? How many branches and levels of government were affected? With the exception of the local Congressman and the city treasurer, it seems that a few personnel at each level (city, county, and State) and in most offices in city hall can be identified either with Stern or with some form of free-lance corruption. A number of local judges received campaign financing from Stern, although there is no evidence that they were on his payroll after they were elected. Several State legislators were on Stern's payroll, and one Republican councilman charged that a high-ranking State Democratic official promised Stern first choice of all Alsace County patronage. The county chairman, he claimed, was only to receive the jobs that Stern did not want. While they were later to play an active role in disrupting Wincanton gambling, the district attorney in Hal Craig's reform administration feared that the State Police were on Stern's payroll, and thus refused to use them in city gambling raids.

Within the city administration, the evidence is fairly clear that some mayors and councilmen received regular payments from Stern and divided kickbacks on city purchases and sales. Some key subcouncil personnel frequently shared in payoffs affecting their particular departments—the police chief shared in the gambling and prostitution payoffs and received $300 of the $10,500 kickback on parking meter purchases. A councilman controlling one department, for example, might get a higher percentage of kickbacks than the other councilmen in contracts involving that department.

Legal Protection Against Corruption

Later in this report, Wincanton's gambling and corruption will be tied into a context of social and political attitudes. At this point, however, concluding the study of official corruption, it might be appropriate to consider legal reforms which might make future corruption more difficult. Many of the corrupt activities of Wincanton officials are already covered sufficiently by State law—it is clearly spelled out, for example, that city officials must enforce State gambling and prostitution laws, and no further legislation is needed to clarify this duty. The legal mandate of the State Police to enforce State laws in all parts of the State is equally clear, but it has been nullified by their informal practice of entering cities only when invited; this policy only facilitates local corruption.

The first major reform that might minimize corruption would involve a drastic increase in the salaries of public officials and law enforcement personnel. During the 1950's Wincanton police salaries were in the lowest quartile for middle-sized cities in the Nation, and were well below the median family income ($5,453) in the city.

City councilmen then were receiving only slightly more than the median. Since that time, police salaries have been raised to $5,400 (only slightly below the median) and council salaries to $8,500. Under these circumstances, many honest officials and employees were forced to "moonlight" with second jobs; potentially dishonest men were likely to view Stern payoffs or extortionate kickbacks as a simpler means of improving their financial status. Raising police salaries to $7,000 or $8,000 would attract men of higher quality, permit them to forego second jobs, and make corrupt payoffs seem less tempting. The same considerations apply to a recommendation that the salaries of elected officials be increased to levels similar to those received in private industry. A recent budget for the city of Wincanton called for expenditures of $6 million; no private corporation of that size would be headed by a chief executive whose salary was $9,500 per year.

A second type of recommendation would reduce the opportunities available to officials to extort illegal payoffs or conceal corruption. First, the civil service system should be expanded. At the time this report was written, Wincanton policemen could not be discharged from the force unless formal charges were brought, but they could be demoted from command positions or transferred to "punishment" details at the discretion of the chief or mayor. The latter option is probably a proper disciplinary tool, but the former invites policemen to seek alliances with political leaders and to avoid unpopular actions. Promotions within the force (with the possible exception of the chief's position) should be made by competitive examination, and demotions should be made only for proven cause. (While research for this report was being conducted, a full 18 months before the next local election, police officers reported that politicking had already begun. Men on the force had already begun making friends with possible candidates for the 1967 elections, and police discipline was beginning to slip. Command officers reported that the sergeants were becoming unwilling to criticize or discipline patrolmen. "How can I tell someone off?" one captain asked. "I'll probably be walking a beat when the Democrats come back into power, and he may be my boss.") A comprehensive civil service system would also give command officers control over informal rewards and punishments, so that they could encourage "hustlers" and harass slackers, but formal review of promotions and demotions is essential to guard against the politicking which has been characteristic of the Wincanton police force.

Second, opportunities for corruption could be reduced by closing the loopholes in State laws on bidding for municipal contracts. While a city should be free to disregard a low bid received from a company judged financially or technically unable to perform a contract, the phrase "lowest responsible bidder" simply opens the door to misfeasance—either to accepting under-the-table kickbacks or to rewarding political friends. In this regard, the decision to ignore the bid of former Police Chief Phillips is just as reprehensible as the decision to give paving contracts to a major party contributor. Furthermore, there is no reason why service contracts should be excluded from the competitive bidding; while the professions regard it as undignified to compete for clients, there is no reason why road repair or building maintenance contracts could not be judged on the basis of bids (with a proviso regarding some level of competence). Finally, the exclusion of "patented or copyrighted products" is untenable—it is well known that distributors of say, automobiles, vary widely in their profit margins, or allowances for trade-ins, etc. City officials should be forced therefore to seek the best possible deal.

One mechanism, which is often suggested to guard against official misconduct, is an annual audit of city books by a higher governmental agency, such as those conducted of local agencies (e.g., urban renewal authorities) administering Federal programs. The evidence in Wincanton, however, seems to indicate that even while official corruption was taking place, the city's books were in perfect order. When a kickback was received on a city purchase, for example, the minutes of council meetings would indicate that X was the "lowest responsible bidder," if bids were required, and X would slip the payoff money to a "bagman," or contactman, on a dark street corner. The books looked proper and auditors would have had no authority to force acceptance of other bids. It would seem that revision of the bidding laws would be more significant than an outside audit.

Finally, the problem of campaign contributions must be considered. As was stressed earlier, contributions to political candidates are regarded in this country as both a manifestation of free speech and the best alternative to government sponsorship of campaigns. The use of political contributions as a disguise for extortion and bribery could be curtailed, however, by active enforcement of the "full reporting of receipts" provision of State campaign laws (in Wincanton, candidates filed reports of receipts, but, of course, neglected to mention the money received from Irv Stern). Second, city hall employees should be protected against the type of voluntary assessment imposed by Mayor Donnelly. Third, State and local laws might more clearly prohibit contributions, from persons doing business with the city, which can be identified as payoffs for past or future preferment on city contracts. (Tightening of bidding requirements, of course, would make such activities less profitable to the contractors.)[4]

GAMBLING AND CORRUPTION: THE GENERAL PUBLIC

The Latent Functions of Gambling and Corruption

> I feel as though I am sending Santa Claus to jail. Although this man dealt in gambling devices, it appears that he is a religious man having no bad habits and is an unmeasurably charitable man.
>
> —*a Federal judge sentencing slot machine king Klaus Braun to jail in 1948.*

> When I was a kid, the man in the corner grocery wrote numbers. His salary was about $20 a week and he made $25 more on book.
>
> —*a reform candidate for the Wincanton City Council, early 1960's.*

The instances of wrongdoing cataloged in earlier sections seem to paint an easily censurable picture. Irv Stern, Gene Donnelly, Bob Walasek—these names conjure up an image of such total iniquity that one wonders why they were ever allowed to operate as they did. While gambling and corruption are easy to judge in the abstract, however, they, like sin, are never encountered in the abstract—they are encountered

4 See the excellent discussion of political campaign contributions in Alexander Heard, "The Costs of Democracy" (Chapel Hill: University of North Carolina Press, 1960), and Herbert Alexander, "Regulation of Political Finance" (Berkeley: Institute of Governmental Studies, and Princeton: Citizens' Research Foundation, 1966).

in the form of a slot machine which is helping to pay off your club's mortgage, or a chance to fix your son's speeding ticket, or an opportunity to hasten the completion of your new building by "overlooking" a few violations of the building code. In these forms, the choices seem less clear. Furthermore, to obtain a final appraisal of what took place in Wincanton one must weigh the manifest functions served—providing income for the participants, recreation for the consumers of vice and gambling, etc. —against the latent functions, the unintended or unrecognized consequences of these events.[5] The automobile, as Thorstein Veblen noted, has both a manifest function, transportation, and a latent function, affirming the owner's social status. To balance the picture presented in earlier sections, and thus to give a partial explanation of why Wincanton has had its unusual history, this section explores the latent functions, the unintended and unexpected consequences, of gambling and corruption.

Latent Social Functions. The social life of Wincanton is organized around clubs, lodges, and other voluntary associations. Labor unions have union halls. Businessmen have luncheon groups, country clubs, and service organizations, such as the Rotary, Kiwanis, the Lions, etc. Each nationality group has its own meetinghouse—the Ancient Order of Hibernians, the Liederkranz, the Colored Political Club, the Cristoforo Colombo Society, etc. In each neighborhood, a PTA-type group is organized around the local playground. Each fireball is the nightly gathering place of a volunteer firemen's association. Each church has the usual assortment of men's, women's, and children's groups.

A large proportion of these groups profited in one way or another from some form of gambling. Churches sponsored lotteries, bingo, and "Las Vegas nights." Weekly bingo games sponsored by the playground associations paid for new equipment, Little League uniforms, etc. Business groups would use lotteries to advertise "Downtown Wincanton Days." Finally, depending upon the current policy of law enforcement agencies, most of the clubs had slot machines, payoff pinball machines, punchboards, lotteries, bingo, poker games, etc. For many of these groups, profits from gambling meant the difference between financial success and failure. Clubs with large and affluent membership lists could survive with only fees and profits from meals and drinks served. Clubs with few or impecunious members, however, had to rely on other sources of revenue, and gambling was both lucrative and attractive to non-members.

The clubs therefore welcomed slots, pinball machines, punchboards, and so forth, both to entertain members and to bring in outside funds. The clubs usually divided gambling profits equally with machine distributors such as Stern or Klaus Braun. Some clubs owed even more to gamblers; if Braun heard that a group of men wanted to start a new volunteer firemen's association, he would lend them mortgage money simply for the opportunity to put his slot machines in the firehall. It is not surprising, therefore, to find that the clubs actively defended Stern, Braun, and the political candidates who favored open gambling.

Gambling in Wincanton also provided direct and indirect benefits to churches and other charitable organizations. First, like the other private groups, a number of these churches and charities sponsored bingo, lotteries, etc., and shared in the profits. Second, leading gamblers and racketeers have been generous supporters of Wincanton charities. Klaus Braun gave away literally most of his gambling income, aiding

---

[5] See the classic examination of manifest and latent functions in Robert K. Merton, "Social Theory and Social Structures," revised edition (New York: Free Press, 1957), pp. 19–87.

churches, hospitals, and the underprivileged. In the late 1940's, Braun provided 7,000 Christmas turkeys to the poor, and frequently chartered buses to take slum children to ball games. Braun's Prospect Mountain Park offered free rides and games for local children (while their parents were in other tents patronizing the slot machines). Irv Stern gave a $10,000 stained glass window to his synagogue, and aided welfare groups and hospitals in Wincanton and other cities. (Since the residents of Wincanton refuse to be cared for in the room that Stern gave to Community Hospital, it is now used only for the storage of bandages.) When Stern came into Federal court in the early 1960's to be sentenced on tax evasion charges, he was given character references by Protestant, Catholic, and Jewish clergy, and by the staff of two hospitals and a home for the aged. Critics charge that Stern never gave away a dime that wasn't well publicized; nevertheless, his contributions benefited worthwhile community institutions.

(Lest this description of the direct and indirect benefits of gambling be misleading, it should also be stressed that many ministers protested violently against gambling and corruption, led reform movements and launched pulpit tirades against Stern, Walasek, et al.)

One final social function of Wincanton gambling might be termed the moderation of the demands of the criminal law. Bluntly stated, Irv Stern was providing the people with what at least a large portion of them wanted, whether or not State lawmakers felt they should want it. It is, of course, axiomatic that no one has the right to disobey the law, but in fairness to local officials it should be remembered that they were generally only tolerating what most residents of the city had grown up with—easily accessible numbers, horsebetting, and bingo. When reform mayor Ed Whitton ordered bingo parlors closed in 1964, he was ending the standard form of evening recreation of literally thousands of elderly men and women. One housewife interviewed recently expressed relief that her mother had died before Whitton's edict took effect; "It would have killed her to live without bingo," she said.

In another sense, Wincanton law enforcement was also moderated by the aid that the gambling syndicates gave, at no cost to the public, to persons arrested by the police for gambling activity. Stern provided bail and legal counsel during trials, and often supported families of men sent to jail. A large portion of the payments that Stern sent to the east coast syndicates (as discussed earlier) was earmarked for pensions to the widows of men who had earlier served in the Stern organization. In light of the present interest in the quality of legal services available to the poor, this aspect of Wincanton gambling must be regarded as a worthy social function.

In these ways, Wincanton gambling provided the financial basis for a network of private groups, filling social, service, and quasi-governmental functions. Leading the list of latent functions of gambling, therefore, we must put the support of neighborhood and other group social life and the provision of such important services as recreation and fire protection. Providing these services through private rather than public mechanisms not only reduced tax burdens but also integrated the services into the social structure of the neighborhood served. While it is hard to give profits from gambling sole credit for maintaining these clubs, it must be noted that a number of firemen's and political associations were forced to close their doors when law enforcement agencies seized slot and pinball machines.

Latent Economic Functions. Just as the proceeds from gambling made possible, or at least less expensive, an extensive series of social relationships and quasi-public services, so also did gambling and corruption affect the local economy, aiding some businesses while hindering others. Their manifest function, of course, was to increase the incomes of the providers of illicit services (members of the Stern syndicate, individual numbers writers and pinball machine distributors, madams, prostitutes, etc.), the recipients of payoffs (elected officials and policemen, for whom these payments were a welcome addition to low salaries), and the businessmen who secured unwarranted contracts, permits, variances, etc. On the other hand, these arrangements provided entertainment for the consumers of gambling and prostitution.

In describing the latent functions of Wincanton illegality, we can begin with two broad phenomena. First, gambling permitted a number of outmoded businesses to survive technological change. As a quotation at the beginning of this chapter indicated, a "mom and pop" grocery store or a candy or cigar store could make more from writing numbers or taking horse bets than they did from their nominal source of support. When reform mayors cracked down on betting, many of these marginal shops went out of business, not being able to compete with the larger, more efficient operations solely on the basis of sales. Second, the system provided an alternate ladder of social mobility for persons who lacked the educational or status prerequisites for success in the legitimate world. Irv Stern came to this country as a fruit peddler's son and is believed by the Internal Revenue Service to be worth several millions of dollars. Gene Donnelly was a bartender's son; Bob Walasek grew up in a slum, although he was able to attend college on an athletic scholarship. Many Wincantonites believe that each of these men collected at least a quarter of a million dollars during his 4 years in city hall. As Daniel Bell has pointed out,[6] and as these men illustrate, organized crime in America has provided a quick route out of the slums, a means of realizing the Horatio Alger dream.

A number of legitimate enterprises in Wincanton profited directly or indirectly when gambling was wide open. Eight or ten major bingo halls provided a large nighttime business for the local bus company. In one year, for example, 272,000 persons paid to play bingo, and most of them were elderly men and women who were brought to the games on regular or chartered buses. Prizes for the bingo games were purchased locally; one department store executive admitted that bingo gift certificates brought "a sizable amount" of business into his store. Several drugstores sold large quantities of cosmetics to the prostitutes. As in Las Vegas, one Wincanton hotel offered special weekend rates for the gamblers at the dice game, who would gamble at night and sleep during the daytime. Finally, several landlords rented space to Stern for his bookie parlors and accounting offices. Worried that legislative investigations might terminate a profitable arrangement, one landlord asked the investigating committee, "Who else would pay $150 a month for that basement?" Being the center of gambling and prostitution for a wide area also meant increased business for the city's restaurants, bars, and theaters. One man declared that business at his Main Street restaurant was never as good as when gamblers and bingo players were flocking to the downtown area. (Many of these restaurants and bars, of course, provided gambling as well as food and drink for their customers.)

Corruption, like gambling, offered some businessmen opportunities to increase sales and profits. If minor building code violations could be overlooked, houses and office buildings could be erected more cheaply. Zoning variances, secured for a price,

---

[6] Daniel Bell, *The End of Ideology* (New York: Free Press, 1960), ch. 7, "Crime as an American Way of Life."

opened up new areas in which developers could build high-rise apartment buildings and shopping centers. In selling to the city, businessmen could increase profits either by selling inferior goods or by charging high prices on standard goods when bidding was rigged or avoided. Finally, corruptible officials could aid profits simply by speeding up decisions on city contracts, or by forcing rapid turnover of city-owned curb space through either "10-minute parking" signs or strict enforcement of parking laws. (Owners of large stores, however, sought to maximize profits by asking the police to ignore parking violations, feeling that customers who worried about their meters would be less likely to stay and buy.)

This listing of the latent benefits of gambling and corruption must be juxtaposed against the fact that many Wincanton businessmen were injured by the Stern-Walasek method of operations and fought vigorously against it. Leaders of the Wincanton business community—the bankers, industrialists, Chamber of Commerce, etc.—fought Walasek and Stern, refusing to kickback on anything, and regularly called upon State and Federal agencies to investigate local corruption.

It is somewhat misleading, however, to use the single term "business" in analyzing responses to corruption. It will be more fruitful to classify businesses according to the nature of their contact with the city of Wincanton. Some industries had a national market, and only called upon the city for labor and basic services—water, sewage, police and fire protection, etc. Other companies such as sales agencies or construction firms did business directly with City Hall and thus were intimately concerned with the terms upon which the city government did business. Because of the looseness of State bidding procedures, these businesses had to be careful, however, not to alienate officials. A third group, while not doing business with the city, had primarily a local clientele. Under these conditions, businesses in this group were frequently interested in corruption and gambling policies.

Official corruption affected each of these groups differently. Businesses whose markets lay primarily outside the city usually had to be concerned only with the possibility that Walasek might force them to pay for building permits. Companies dealing with City Hall, however, were exposed to every extortionate demand that the mayor might impose. As an example, agencies usually able to underbid their competitors were ignored if they refused to abide by the unofficial "conditions" added to contracts. Businessmen in the third category were in an intermediate position, both in terms of their freedom to act against the system and in terms of the impact that it had upon them. Like the others, they suffered when forced to pay for permits or variances. Legitimate businesses, such as liquor stores, taverns, and restaurants, whose functions paralleled those of the clubs, lost revenue when the clubs were licensed to have gambling and slot machines. Those businesses, such as banks, whose success depended upon community growth, suffered when the community's reputation for corruption and gambling drove away potential investors and developers. (Interestingly, businessmen disagree as to whether it is the reputation for corruption or for gambling that discourages new industry. Several Wincanton bankers stated that no investor would run the risk of having to bribe officials to have building plans approved, permits issued, and so forth. One architect, however, argued that businessmen assume municipal corruption, but will not move into a "sin town," for their employees will not want to raise children in such circumstances.)

The last detrimental aspect of gambling and corruption seems trivial in comparison with the factors already mentioned, but it was cited by most of the business leaders interviewed. Simply stated, it was embarrassing to have one's hometown known throughout the country for its vice and corruption. "I'd go to a convention on the west coast," one textile manufacturer recalled, "and everyone I'd meet would say, 'You're from Wincanton? Boy, have I heard stories about that place!' I would try to talk about textiles or opportunities for industrial development, but they'd keep asking about the girls and the gambling." An Air Force veteran recalled being ridiculed about his hometown while in boot camp. Finally, some insiders feel that a Wincanton judge was persuaded to act against Irv Stern when he found that his daughter was being laughed at by her college friends for being related to a Wincanton official.

PUBLIC ATTITUDES TOWARD GAMBLING AND CORRUPTION

A clean city, a city free of gambling, vice, and corruption, requires at least two things—active law enforcement and elected officials who oppose organized crime. Over the last 20 years, Federal agents have been successful in prosecuting most of the leaders of Wincanton gambling operations. Slot machine king Klaus Braun was twice sent to jail for income tax evasion. Federal agents were also able to secure convictions against Irv Stern for income tax evasion (a 4-year sentence), gambling tax evasion (a 2-year sentence running concurrently with the income tax sentence), and extortion on a city contract to purchase parking meters (a 30-day concurrent sentence). Federal men also sent to jail lesser members of the Stern syndicate and closed down a still and an interstate dice game.

These Federal actions, however, had very little effect upon Wincanton gambling. Lieutenants carried on while Stern was in jail, and local police, at the direction of city officials, continued to ignore numbers writers, bookies, and prostitutes. As one Federal agent put it, "Even though we were able to apprehend and convict the chief racketeers, we were never able to solve the political problem—city officials were always against us." On the two occasions when Wincanton voters did solve the political problem by electing reform officials, however, organized crime was quickly put out of business. Mayor Hal Craig chose to tolerate isolated bookies, numbers writers, and prostitutes, but Stern and Braun were effectively silenced. Mayor Ed Whitton, in office since the early 1960's, has gone even further, and the only gamblers and prostitutes still operating in Wincanton are those whom the police have been unable to catch for reasons of limited manpower, lack of evidence, etc. The American Social Hygiene Association reported after a recent study that Wincanton has fewer prostitutes today than at any time since the 1930's. The police acknowledge that there are still a few gamblers and prostitutes in town, but they have been driven underground, and a potential patron must have a contact before he can do business.

If the level of law enforcement in a community is so directly tied to local voting patterns, we must look more closely at the attitudes and values of Wincanton residents. First, how much did residents know about what was going on? Were the events which have been discussed previously matters of common knowledge or were they perceived by only a few residents? Second, were they voting for open gambling and corruption; were they being duped by seemingly honest candidates who became corrupt after taking office; or were these issues irrelevant to the average voter, who was thinking about other issues entirely? Our conclusions about these questions will indicate whether long-range reform can be attained through legal changes (closing loopholes in the city's bidding practices, expanding civil service in the police department, ending the "home rule" policy of the State Police, etc.) or whether reform must await a change in popular mores.

Public Awareness of Gambling and Corruption

In a survey of Wincanton residents conducted recently,[7] 90 per cent of the respondents were able correctly to identify the present mayor, 63 per cent recognized the name of their Congressman, and 36 per cent knew the Alsace County district attorney. Seventy per cent identified Irv Stern correctly, and 62 per cent admitted that they did recognize the name of the largest madam in town. But how much did the people of Wincanton know about what had been going on—the extent and organization of Irv Stern's empire, the payoffs to city hall and the police, or the malfeasance and misfeasance of Bob Walasek and other city officials? Instead of thinking about simply "knowing" or "not knowing," we might subdivide public awareness into several categories—a general awareness that gambling and prostitution were present in the city, some perception that city officials were protecting these enterprises, and finally a specific knowledge that officials X and Y were being paid off. These categories vary, it will be noticed, in the specificity of knowledge and in the linkage between the result (e.g., presence of gambling or corruption) and an official's action.

While there is no way of knowing exactly how many Wincantonites had access to each type of knowledge about gambling and corruption during the period they were taking place, we can form some ideas on the basis of the newspaper coverage they received and the geographical distribution of each form of illegality. The dice game, for example, was in only one location (hidden and shifted periodically to escape Federal attention) and relied primarily on out-of-town gamblers. The newspapers said little about it, and it was probably safe to say that few residents knew of its existence until it was raided by the FBI in the early 1960's.

Prostitutes were generally found only in two four-block areas in the city—semi-slum areas that no outsider was likely to visit unless he was specifically looking for the girls. The newspapers, however, gave extensive coverage to every prostitution arrest and every report by the American Social Hygiene Association which detailed the extent of prostitution and venereal disease in the city. A series of newspaper articles, with photographs, forced the police to close (for a short period of time) several of the larger brothels. With regard to prostitution, therefore, it is likely that a majority of the adult population knew of the existence of commercialized vice; but, apart from innuendoes in the papers, there was little awareness of payoffs to the police. It was not until after the election of a reform administration, that Stern and Walasek were indicted for extorting payments from a madam.

In contrast to the dice games and prostitution, public awareness of the existence of pinball machines, horsebooks, and numbers writing must have been far more widespread. These mass-consumption forms of gambling depended upon accessibility to large numbers of persons. Bets could be placed in most corner grocery stores,

[7] This survey was conducted by eight female interviewers from the Wisconsin Survey Research Laboratory, using a schedule of questions requiring 45 to 75 minutes to complete. Respondents were selected from among the adults residing in housing units selected at random from the Wincanton "City Directory." One hundred eighty-three completed interviews were obtained.

candy shops, and cigar counters; payoff pinball machines were placed in most clubs and firehalls, as well as in bars and restaurants. Apart from knowing that these things were openly available, and thus not subject to police interference, there was no way for the average citizen to know specifically that Irv Stern was paying to protect these gambling interests until Police Chief Phillips began to testify—again after the election of reformer Whitton.

Public awareness of wrongdoing was probably least widespread in regard to corruption—kickbacks on contracts, extortion, etc. Direct involvement was generally limited to officials and businessmen, and probably few of them knew anything other than that they personally had been asked to pay. Either from shame or from fear of being prosecuted on bribery charges or out of unwillingness to jeopardize a profitable contract, those who did pay did not want to talk. Those who refused to pay usually were unable to substantiate charges made against bribes so that exposure of the attempt led only to libel suits or official harassment. As we have seen, the newspapers and one garage with a towing contract did talk about what was going on. The garageman lost his franchise and suffered a series of "accidents"; the newspapers found a reporter in jail and their trucks harassed by the police. Peter French, the district attorney under Walasek and Donnelly, won a libel suit (since reversed on appeal and dismissed) against the papers after they stated that he was protecting gamblers. Except for an unsuccessful citizen suit in the mid-1950's seeking to void the purchase of fire trucks (for the purchase of which Donnelly received a $2,000 "political contribution") and a newspaper article in the early 1960's implying that Donnelly and his council had received $500 on the sale of a city crane, no evidence —no specific facts—of corruption was available to the public until Phillips was indicted several years later for perjury in connection with the towing contracts.

Returning then to the three categories of public knowledge, we can say that even at the lowest level—general perception of some form of wrongdoing—awareness was quite limited (except among the businessmen, most of whom, as we noted in the "Introduction," live and vote in the suburbs). Specific knowledge—this official received this much to approve that contract—was only available after legislative hearings in the early 1950's and the indictment of Phillips in the early 1960's; on both occasions the voters turned to reform candidates.

If, therefore, it is unlikely that many residents of Wincanton had the second or third type of knowledge about local gambling or corruption (while many more had the first type) during the time it was taking place, how much do they know now— after several years of reform and a series of trials—all well-covered in the newspapers revealing the nature of Stern-Donnelly-Walasek operations? To test the extent of specific knowledge about local officials and events, respondents in a recent survey were asked to identify past and present officials and racketeers and to compare the Walasek and Whitton administrations on a number of points.

Earlier, we noted that 90 per cent of the 183 respondents recognized the name of the present mayor, 63 per cent knew their Congressman (who had been in office more than 10 years), and 36 per cent knew the district attorney. How many members of the Stern organization were known to the public? Seventy per cent recognized Stern's name, 63 per cent knew the head of the numbers bank, 40 per cent identified the "bagman" or collector for Stern, and 31 per cent knew the operator of the largest horsebook in town. With regard to many of these questions, it must be kept in mind that since many respondents may subconsciously have felt that to admit recognition of a name would have implied personal contact with or sympathy for a criminal or a criminal act, these results probably understate the extent of public knowledge. When 100 of the respondents were asked "What things did Mr. Walasek do that were illegal?" 59 mentioned extortion regarding vice and gambling, 2 mentioned extortion on city contracts, 7 stated that he stole from the city, 8 that he fixed parking and speeding tickets, 4 that he was "controlled by rackets," and 20 simply stated that Walasek was corrupt, not listing specific acts.

Even if Wincantonites do not remember too many specific misdeeds, they clearly perceive that the present Whitton administration has run a cleaner town than did Walasek or Donnelly. When asked to comment on the statement, "Some people say that the present city administration under Mayor Whitton is about the same as when Mayor Walasek was in office," 10 per cent said it was the same, 74 per cent said it was different, and 14 per cent didn't know. When asked why, 75 respondents cited "better law enforcement" and the end of corruption; only 7 of 183 felt that the city had been better run by Walasek. Fifty-eight per cent felt the police force was better now, 22 per cent thought that it was about the same as when Walasek controlled the force, and only 7 per cent thought it was worse now. Those who felt that the police department was better run now stressed "honesty" and "better law enforcement," or thought that it was valuable to have an outsider as commissioner. Those who thought it was worse now cited "inefficiency," "loafing," or "unfriendliness." It was impossible to tell whether the comments of "unfriendliness" refer simply to the present refusal to tolerate gambling or whether they signify a more remote police-public contact resulting from the "professionalism" of the commissioner. (In this regard, we might note that a number of policemen and lawyers felt that it had been easier to secure information regarding major crimes when prostitution and gambling were tolerated. As one former captain put it, "If I found out that some gangster was in town that I didn't know about, I raised hell with the prostitutes for not telling me.")

Comparing perceptions of the present and former district attorneys, we also find a clear preference for the present man, Thomas Hendricks, over Peter French, but there is a surprising increase in "Don't knows." Thirty-five per cent felt the district attorney's office is run "differently" now, 13 per cent said it is run in the same way, but 50 per cent did not know. Paralleling this lack of attitudes toward the office, we can recall that only 36 per cent of the respondents were able to identify the present incumbent's name, while 55 per cent knew his more flamboyant predecessor. Of those respondents who saw a difference between the two men, 51 per cent cited "better law enforcement" and "no more rackets control over law enforcement."

In addition to recognizing these differences between past and present officials, the respondents in the recent survey felt that there were clear differences in the extent of corruption and gambling. Sixty-nine per cent disagreed with the statement, "Underworld elements and racketeers had very little say in what the Wincanton city government did when Mr. Walasek was mayor"; only 13 per cent disagreed with the same statement as applied to reform Mayor Whitton. When asked, "As compared with 5 years ago, do you think it's easier now, about the same, or harder to find a dice game in Wincanton?" only one respondent felt it was easier, 8 per cent felt it was about the same, 56 per cent felt it was harder, and 34 per cent didn't know. The respondents were almost as sure that Whitton had closed down horse betting; 51 per cent felt it was harder to bet on horses now than it was 5 years ago, 11 per cent felt it was about the same, and three respondents thought it was easier now than before. Again, 34 per cent did not know.

Public Attitudes Toward Crime and Law Enforcement

Earlier, we asked whether Wincanton's long history of gambling and corruption was based on a few bad officials and formal, structural defects such as the absence of civil service or low pay scales, or whether it was rooted in the values of the populace. The evidence on "public awareness" indicates that most Wincantonites probably knew of the existence of widespread gambling, but they probably had little idea of the payoffs involved. When we turn to public attitudes, we find a similar split—many citizens wanted to consume the services offered by Irv Stern, but they were against official corruption; few residents think that one produces the other. But in thinking about "public attitudes," several problems of definition arise. For one thing, "attitudes" depend on the way in which a question is phrased—a respondent would be likely to answer "no" if he were asked, "Are you in favor of gambling?" but he might also answer "yes" if he were asked whether it was all right to flip a coin to see who would buy the next round of drinks. As we will shortly see, it is very difficult to conclude that because a Wincantonite voted for candidate X, he was voting "for corruption"—in his mind, he might have been voting for a fellow Pole, or a workingman, or an athletic hero, etc., and the decision did not involve "corruption" or "reform."

Second, we have to ask whether "attitude," in the sense of a conscious preference for X over Y, is an appropriate concept. We must keep in mind that for Wincantonites, "reform" has been the exception rather than the rule. The vast majority of local citizens have lived with wide-open gambling all their lives, and the reform administrations of Craig and Whitton add up to only 7 of the last 40 years. As one lawyer said, "When I was a little kid, my dad would lift me up so I could put a dime in the slot machine at his club. We never saw anything wrong in it." In addition to knowing about gambling in Wincanton, the residents knew of other cities in the State in which gambling was equally wide open, and they believe that Wincanton is similar to most cities in the country. Fifty-four per cent of the respondents in the survey agreed with the statement, "There is not much difference between politics in Wincanton and politics in other American cities." (Nineteen per cent were undecided and only 25 per cent disagreed.) Because of this specific history of gambling and this general perception that Wincanton is like other cities, it may be more accurate to speak of latent acceptance of gambling and petty corruption as "facts of life" rather than thinking of conscious choices, e.g., "I prefer gambling and corruption to a clean city and honest officials." Under most circumstances, the question has not come up.

In a series of questions included in the recent attitude survey, Wincantonites indicated a general approval or tolerance of gambling, but they frequently distinguished between organized and unorganized operations. Eighty per cent felt that the State legislature should legalize bingo. Fifty-eight per cent felt that a State-operated lottery would be a good idea. Fifty-four per cent agreed with the general statement, "The State should legalize gambling." When asked *why* the State should legalize gambling, 42 per cent of those favoring the idea felt that gambling was harmless or that people would gamble anyway; 44 per cent thought that the State should control it and receive the profits; 8 per cent felt that legalization would keep out racketeers. Forty-nine per cent agreed that "gambling is all right so long as local people, not outsiders, run the game"; 35 per cent disagreed; and 11 per cent were uncertain. Forty-six per cent felt that "the police should not break up a friendly poker game, even if there is betting." Here, 37 per cent disagreed and 14 per cent were uncertain.

If Wincanton residents are tolerant of gambling, they show little tolerance of official corruption: 72 per cent of the respondents disagreed with a statement that, "A city official who receives $10 in cash from a company that does business with the city should not be prosecuted;" only 13 per cent agreed. Sixty-one per cent were unwilling to agree that, "It's all right for the mayor of a city to make a profit when the city buys some land so long as only a fair price is charged." Thirty-four per cent agreed that, "It's all right for a city official to accept presents from companies so long as the taxpayers don't suffer," but 47 per cent disagreed and 13 per cent were undecided. Fifty-four per cent did not believe that, "The mayor and police chief should be able to cancel parking and speeding tickets in some cases," but 36 per cent thought it might be a good idea.

The intensity of feelings against corruption was brought out most strongly when the respondents were asked about the 30-day jail sentences imposed on Irv Stern and Bob Walasek for extorting $10,500 on city purchases of parking meters. Eighty-six per cent felt that the sentences were too light; seven respondents felt that they were too severe, generally feeling that publicity arising from the trial had hurt Walasek's family. When asked why they felt as they did, 32 per cent felt that Walasek had "betrayed a public trust"; 18 per cent gave an answer such as, "If it had been a little guy like me instead of a guy with pull like Walasek, I'd still be in jail."

In light of the mixed feelings about gambling and corruption, we might wonder whether Wincantonites are hostile toward the police department's present antigambling policy. This does not appear to be the case: 55 per cent of the respondents disagreed with the statement, "The Wincanton police today are concentrating on gambling too much"; only 17 per cent agreed, and 21 per cent were undecided. Further support for the local police was indicated by the respondents when asked to comment on the statement, "If there is any gambling going on in Wincanton, it should be handled by the local police rather than the FBI"; 57 per cent agreed and 19 per cent disagreed. The preference for local action was slightly stronger—58 per cent—when the question stated ". . . the local police rather than State Police."

We have frequently mentioned that Walasek and Stern were convicted on the basis of testimony given by former Police Chief Dave Phillips. Phillips was given immunity from Federal prosecution, and perjury charges against him were dropped. What was the public response to Phillips' having testified? Was he regarded as a "fink" or a hero? Fifty-nine per cent of the respondents felt that it was right for Phillips to testify. Only 15 per cent felt that he should have received immunity, 40 per cent felt the grant of immunity was wrong, and 40 per cent did not know whether it was right or wrong. The most common reaction was that Phillips was as guilty as the others, or "he only testified to save his own skin."

Finally, to ascertain how much citizens know about law enforcement agencies, the survey respondents were asked, first, "As you remember it, who was it who decided that bingo should not be played in Wincanton?" Five per cent attributed the ban to the legislature. Forty-three per cent correctly stated that a joint decision of Mayor Whitton and District Attorney Hendricks (declaring that the State gambling law included bingo) had led to the current crackdown. Thirty-four per cent didn't know. Ironically, 13 respondents believed that Walasek, Donnelly, Police Chief Phillips, or

District Attorney French had ended bingo (all had been out of office for at least 6 months and opposed the ban)!

Second, respondents [8] were asked, "Which of the Federal investigative agencies would you say was primarily responsible for most of the prosecutions of Wincanton people in the past 10 years?" Thirty-one per cent correctly cited the Internal Revenue Service, 20 per cent mentioned the Federal Bureau of Investigation (whose only major involvement had been in raiding the dice game), and 46 per cent did not know. *The Politics of Reform.* In every local election in Wincanton, it seems that some candidates are running on "reform" platforms, charging their opponents with corruption or at least tolerating gamblers and prostitutes. Usually, we see Republicans attacking Democratic corruption. But Democratic primary candidates also attack the records of Democratic incumbents, and in 1955, Democrats promised the voters that they would rid the town of the prostitutes and bookies that "pearl gray" Hal Craig had tolerated. Frequently, officials have become corrupt after they were elected, but Wincanton voters have never returned a known criminal to office. Following legislative investigations in the early 1950's, Mayor Watts lost the general election, receiving only 39 per cent of the vote. After the Federal indictment of Police Chief Phillips in the early 1960's, Bob Walasek was defeated in the Democratic primary, running a poor third, with only 19 per cent of the vote. Even with Walasek out of the running, the voters selected Republican Whitton over his Democratic opponent, a councilman in the Walasek administration. While the Republicans were able to elect councilmen in two elections, they were unable to make inroads in the off-year council elections despite wholesale Federal gambling raids in the months just prior to the elections in these years.

Looking at these voting figures, two questions arise—why corruption and why reform? As we have seen, Wincantonites have never voted for corruption, although they may have voted for men tolerant of the gambling citizens demanded. While the newspapers and the reformers have warned of the necessary connection between gambling and corruption, their impact has been deadened by repetition—Wincanton voters have acquired a "ho-hum" attitude, saying to themselves, "That's just the Gazette sounding off again" or "The Republicans are 'crying wolf' just like they did 4 years ago." As Lord Bryce said of Americans 80 years ago:

> The people see little and they believe less. True, the party newspapers accuse their opponents of such offenses, but the newspapers are always reviling somebody; and it is because the words are so strong that the tale has little meaning. . . .
>
> The habit of hearing charges promiscuously bandied to and fro, but seldom probed to the bottom, makes men heedless.[9]

If the Democrats have dominated Wincanton elections so consistently, why did they lose in two important elections? Those years were different because official corruption was being documented by Federal investigators; in other years investigations were only showing widespread gambling, and only newspaper inferences suggested that officials were being paid off. It is equally, perhaps more, significant to note that Federal investigations attracted national attention—instead of seeing allusions of cor-

[8] This question was inserted in the schedule after the survey was underway; only 87 respondents were asked this question.

[9] James Bryce, "The American Commonwealth," vol. II (London: MacMillan, 1889), p. 204.

ruption in the Wincanton Gazette, city voters were beginning to read about themselves and their city in *The New York Times* and the papers of the larger cities within
the State. Just as national media coverage of the "War on the Press" may have forced
Mayor Donnelly to back down, so the national interest during the two elections may
have shamed local voters into deserting the Democratic Party. The years when the
Republicans won were different because the voters were forced to recognize the conflict between their norms (honesty in government, no corruption, etc.) and the actions of local Democratic officials. Their "active sense of outrage" [10] produced a crisis
leading to a readjustment of their normal patterns of behavior. Furthermore, even
though the voters had been willing to tolerate petty corruption on the part of past
officials, the national investigations indicated that officials were now going too far.
As Irv Stern had predicted, Bob Walasek, unlike his predecessor, got "greedy," and
pushed the voters too far, tolerating too much vice and gambling and demanding
kickbacks on too many contracts and licenses. For the voters, the "price" of Democratic control had gotten too high.[11]

> A city where the government has for its subjects acquaintances, whose
> interests and passions it knows and can at pleasure thwart or forward,
> can hardly expect a neutral government.
>
> —*Sir Ernest Barker,*
> *"Greek Political Theory"* [12]

The Future of Reform in Wincanton

When Wincantonites are asked what kind of law enforcement they want, they are
likely to say that it is all right to tolerate petty gambling and prostitution, but that
"you've got to keep out racketeers and corrupt politicians." Whenever they come to
feel that the city is being controlled by these racketeers, they "throw the rascals out."
This policy of "throwing the rascals out," however, illustrates the dilemma facing
reformers in Wincanton. Irv Stern, recently released from Federal prison, has probably, in fact, retired from the rackets; he is ill and plans to move to Arizona. Bob
Walasek, having been twice convicted on extortion charges, is finished politically.
Therefore? Therefore, the people of Wincanton firmly believe that "the problem" has
been solved—"the rascals" have been thrown out. When asked, recently, what issues
would be important in the next local elections, only 9 of 183 respondents felt that
clean government or keeping out vice and gambling might be an issue. (Fifty-five
per cent had no opinion, 15 per cent felt that the ban on bingo might be an issue,
and 12 per cent cited urban renewal, a subject frequently mentioned in the papers
preceding the survey.) Since, under Ed Whitton, the city is being honestly run and
is free from gambling and prostitution, there is no problem to worry about.

On balance, it seems far more likely to conclude that gambling and corruption will
soon return to Wincanton (although possibly in less blatant forms) for two reasons—
first, a significant number of people want to be able to gamble or make improper
deals with the city government. (This assumes, of course, that racketeers will be available to provide gambling if a complacent city administration permits it.) Second,

---

10 Arnold A. Rogow and Harold D. Lasswell, "Power, Corruption, and Rectitude" (Englewood Cliffs: Prentice-Hall, 1963), p. 72.

11 Cf. Eric L. McKitrick, "The Study of Corruption," 72 Political Science Quarterly 507 (December 1957):

12 Sir Ernest Barker, "Greek Political Theory" (London: Methuen, 1918), p. 13.

and numerically far more important, most voters think that the problem has been permanently solved, and thus they will not be choosing candidates based on these issues, in future elections.

Throughout this report, a number of specific recommendations have been made to minimize opportunities for wide-open gambling and corruption—active State Police intervention in city affairs, modification of the city's contract bidding policies, extending civil service protection to police officers, etc. On balance, we could probably also state that the commission form of government has been a hindrance to progressive government; a "strong mayor" form of government would probably handle the city's affairs more efficiently. Fundamentally, however, all of these suggestions are irrelevant. When the voters have called for clean government, they have gotten it, in spite of loose bidding laws, limited civil service, etc. The critical factor has been voter preference. Until the voters of Wincanton come to believe that illegal gambling produces the corruption they have known, the type of government we have documented will continue. Four-year periods of reform do little to change the habits instilled over 40 years of gambling and corruption.

RESEARCH ON THE POLITICS OF CORRUPTION [13]

Reviewing the literature on the politics of corruption, one is tempted to conclude that while everyone is writing about it, no one is saying very much about it. Most of the material in the field can be classified as simple reports of wrongdoing or official investigations. Both tend to come in waves coinciding with popular interest in reform,[14] and are written with a strongly moralistic bias. The classic exposés of municipal corruption are, of course, the works of the muckrakers—Steffens, Sinclair, Tarbell, etc.—written at the turn of the century.[15] More recently, issues of the "National Civic Review" (known as the "National Municipal Review" until 1958), have presented reports of specific cases of corruption, graft, or bribery; titles such as "Indianapolis Mayor Faces Jail Sentence," "Election Frauds in Philadelphia," and "Eliminating California Bosses" indicate the specific and reforming quality of most "Review" articles. Their authors generally view the world in black and white terms—a conflict between the good guys (the average, basically honest but put-upon citizenry) and the bad guys ("politicians" and "bosses"). The typical "Review" solution to the problem of corruption calls for both structural changes—nonpartisan elections, city manager government, etc.—and citizen action—the uprising of an alert, informed, and indignant public against evil machines. Local politics is represented as a morality play; an example is the story of municipal reform in Des Moines in the 1920's:

> A remarkable story . . . one in which taxpayers were arrayed against
> politicians, prosecuting attorneys against slick lawyers, and municipal

[13] Joel Margolis, a graduate student in the Department of Political Science, University of Wisconsin, performed the research upon which this review of the literature is based.

[14] Ironically, there has been a strong interest in corruption in the years since World War II, even though ethics in government has probably been at a higher level than at most other periods in our history. For a brief overview of American corruption which puts recent misdeeds in their proper historical perspective, see Sidney Warren, "Corruption in Politics," 22 Current History 65–69, 211–215, 285–289, and 348–354 (1962).

[15] The ideas and work of the major muckrakers are summarized in David Mark Chalmers, "The Social and Political Ideas of the Muckrakers" (New York: Citadel Press, 1964).

> graft against good government. It is the story of how an American city cleaned house, lodged a number of public servants . . . in the State's penal institutions . . . placed an increased value on its tax dollar, and put its public affairs on a plane of decency and efficiency all in the last two years. . . .
>
> The people . . . who have been looted see the dawn of a new day in popular self-government.[16]

The official investigations of political corruption display a similar degree of specificity and simplicity. Both Federal (e.g., the Wickersham Commission and the Kefauver and McClellan committee hearings) and State (e.g., the Massachusetts Crime Commission and the Illinois Crime Investigating Commission reports) agencies hold hearings, report that crime and corruption were found in city X or department Y, and then call for prosecutions and new legislation to correct these situations. Little time or space is devoted to analysis of the social or political causes of the events portrayed.

In contrast with these numerous but superficial journalistic and official investigations and reports, social scientists have had an infrequent but somewhat more analytical interest in corruption. Corruption has seldom been the direct focus of their work, but has often been discussed in connection with other phenomena. Generally using the "functional" approach [17] applied earlier in this report, students of political parties, for example, have argued that corruption can serve as an important supplement to legal patronage [18] as a means of financing and holding together a political machine.[19] More broadly, it has been argued that corrupt practices may be necessary to overcome the decentralization of government brought about by the separation of executive, legislative, and judicial processes, the creation of independent boards and commissions, etc.[20] Finally, corrupt distribution of governmental jobs and services has been viewed as a mechanism for instilling a feeling of national identity in new immigrant populations, as well as providing for their social welfare.[21]

From another point of view, political corruption has been considered functional to the business community in offering protection against aggressive competition, speed in finalizing contracts with government, and freedom from cumbersome codes and regulations.[22] In underdeveloped nations, Nathaniel Leff feels that corruption can be a vital catalyst in inclining political leaders toward economic development, mobilizing the state bureaucracy to aid entrepreneurs, and paying off the existing "power elite" to tolerate economic and social change.[23] The benefits that corruption offers to legiti-

[16] Merze Marvin, "Des Moines Cleans House," 14 National Municipal Review 539 (September, 1925).

[17] See Robert K. Merton, "Social Theory and Social Structure," revised edition (New York: Free Press, 1957), pp. 19–87; Eric L. McKitrick, "The Study of Corruption," 72 Political Science Quarterly 502–514 (December, 1967); Don Martindale, editor, "Functionalism in the Social Sciences" (Philadelphia: American Academy of Political and Social Sciences, 1965).

[18] On the role of patronage in the party system, see V. O. Key, Jr., "Politics, Parties and Pressure Groups," 4th ed. (New York: Thomas Y. Crowell, 1958), ch. 13; and James Q. Wilson, "The Economy of Patronage," 69 Journal of Political Economy 369–380 (August, 1961).

[19] For a general description of city machines, see Edward C. Banfield and James Q. Wilson, "City Politics" (Cambridge: Harvard University Press, 1963), ch. 9. Literature on some of our more famous city bosses is listed in Charles R. Adrian, "Governing Urban America" (New York: McGraw-Hill, 1961) pp. 498–499.

[20] Henry Jones Ford, "Municipal Corruption," 19 Political Science Quarterly 673–686 (1904).

[21] V. O. Key, Jr., "The Techniques of Political Graft in the United States," unpublished Ph.D. dissertation, Department of Political Science, University of Chicago, 1934.

[22] Ibid.; McKitrick, op. cit. supra, n. 5.

[23] Nathaniel H. Leff, "Economic Development through Bureaucratic Corruption," 8 American Behavioral Scientist 8–14 (November, 1964).

mate businessmen accrue also to illegitimate enterprises; as we have seen in Win-canton, corruptly procured protection allowed Irv Stern to stabilize the gambling industry and assign contracts with the city, while landowners and businessmen were able to buy immunity from building and zoning regulations.

A third group of studies has served to break down any false notions that corruption and criminality are sharply distinct from the values and way of life of "law-abiding" members of society. A number of studies have shown that to a certain extent criminal careers mirror the approved values of seeking social advancement, prestige, and having one's own business; furthermore, gamblers and racketeers are frequently respected and emulated members of immigrant and lower class social groups.[24] Finally, as law enforcement officers know all too well, some members of all social classes condone or approve gambling and corruption, although many citizens may also, either ambivalently or hypocritically, demand strict law enforcement.[25] Because of these conflicts between legal norms and actual popular attitudes, several political scientists have concluded that corruption can perform the valuable function of permitting the continued existence of the society. Instead of a direct confrontation between the norm and the fact, corrupt enforcement of the laws can permit quiet fulfillment of both sets of values, e.g., through a territorial arrangement in which "good neighborhoods" are kept free of gambling and prostitution while other areas of the city or metropolitan area are "wide open." [26] Until legal norms coincide with popular values, these corruptly induced adjustments allow the society to run more smoothly.[27]

7. The Police on Skid-row: A Study of Peace Keeping *

Egon Bittner

The prototype of modern police organization, the Metropolitan Police of London, was created to replace an antiquated and corrupt system of law enforcement. The early planners were motivated by the mixture of hardheaded business rationality and humane sentiment that characterized liberal British thought of the first half of the

[24] Daniel Bell, "Crime as an American Way of Life," in "The End of Ideology" (New York: Free Press, 1960); William Foote Whyte, "Street Corner Society" (Chicago: University of Chicago Press, 1943), pp. 111–193; David Matza, "Delinquency and Drift" (New York: John Wiley, 1964); Donald R. Cressey, "The Functions and Structure of Criminal Syndicates," a report to the President's Commission on Law Enforcement and Administration of Justice, 1966.

[25] Charles E. Merriam, "Chicago: A More Intimate View of Urban Politics" (New York: MacMillan, 1929), pp. 54–60; Virgil W. Peterson, "Obstacles to Enforcement of Gambling Laws," 269 Annals 9–20 (May, 1950).

[26] Merriam, op. cit. supra, n. 13.

[27] Harold D. Lasswell, "Bribery," 2 Encyclopedia of the Social Sciences 690–692 (New York: MacMillan, 1930); M. McMullan, "A Theory of Corruption," 9 Sociological Review 181-201 (July 1961); Key, op. cit. supra, n. 9.

SOURCE: "The Police on Skid-row: A Study of Peace Keeping," American Sociological Review, vol. 32, pp. 699–715, October, 1967. By permission of the author and publisher.

° This research was supported in part by Grant 64–1–35 from the California Department of Mental Hygiene. I gratefully acknowledge the help I received from Fred Davis, Sheldon Messinger, Leonard Schatzman, and Anselm Strauss in the preparation of this paper.

nineteenth century.[1] Partly to meet the objections of a parliamentary committee, which which was opposed to the establishment of the police in England, and partly because it was in line with their own thinking, the planners sought to produce an instrument that could not readily be used in the play of internal power politics but which would, instead, advance and protect conditions favorable to industry and commerce and to urban civil life in general. These intentions were not very specific and had to be reconciled with the existing structures of governing, administering justice, and keeping the peace. Consequently, the locus and mandate of the police in the modern polity were ill-defined at the outset. On the one hand, the new institution was to be a part of the executive branch of government, organized, funded, and staffed in accordance with standards that were typical for the entire system of the executive. On the other hand, the duties that were given to the police organization brought it under direct control of the judiciary in its day-to-day operation.

The dual patronage of the police by the executive and the judiciary is characteristic for all democratically governed countries. Moreover, it is generally the case, or at least it is deemed desirable, that judges *rather than* executive officials have control over police use and procedure.[2] This preference is based on two considerations. First, in the tenets of the democratic creed, the possibility of direct control of the police by a government in power is repugnant.[3] Even when the specter of the police state in its more ominous forms is not a concern, close ties between those who govern and those who police are viewed as a sign of political corruption.[4] Hence, mayors, governors, and cabinet officers—although the nominal superiors of the police—tend to maintain, or to pretend, a hands-off policy. Second, it is commonly understood that the main function of the police is the control of crime. Since the concept of crime belongs wholly to the law, and its treatment is exhaustively based on considerations of legality, police procedure automatically stands under the same system of review that controls the administration of justice in general.

By nature, judicial control encompasses only those aspects of police activity that are directly related to full-dress legal prosecution of offenders. The judiciary has neither the authority nor the means to direct, supervise, and review those activities of the police that do not result in prosecution. Yet such other activities are unavoidable, frequent, and largely within the realm of public expectations. It might be assumed that in this domain of practice the police are under executive control. This

---

[1] The bill for a Metropolitan Police was actually enacted under the sponsorship of Robert Peel, the Home Secretary in the Tory Government of the Duke of Wellington. There is, however, no doubt that it was one of the several reform tendencies that Peel assimilated into Tory politics in his long career. Cf. J. L. Lyman, "The Metropolitan Police Act of 1829," *Journal of Criminal Law, Criminology and Police Science*, 55 (1964), 141–154.

[2] Jerome Hall, "Police and Law in a Democratic Society," *Indiana Law Journal*, 28 (1953), 133–177. Though other authors are less emphatic on this point, judicial control is generally taken for granted. The point has been made, however, that in modern times judicial control over the police has been asserted mainly because of the default of any other general controlling authority, cf. E. L. Barrett, Jr., "Police Practice and the Law," *California Law Review*, 50 (1962), 11–55.

[3] A. C. German, F. D. Day and R. R. J. Gallati, *Introduction to Law Enforcement*, Springfield, Ill.: C. C. Thomas, 1966; "One concept, in particular, should be kept in mind. A dictatorship can never exist unless the police system of the country is under the absolute control of the dictator. There is no other way to uphold a dictatorship except by terror, and the instrument of this total terror is the secret police, whatever its name. In every country where freedom has been lost, law enforcement has been a dominant instrument in destroying it" (p. 80).

[4] The point is frequently made; cf. Raymond B. Fosdick, *American Police Systems*, New York: Century Company, 1920; Bruce Smith, *Police Systems in the United States*, 2nd rev. ed., New York: Harper, 1960.

is not the case, however, except in a marginal sense.[5] Not only are police departments generally free to determine what need be done and how, but aside from informal pressures they are given scant direction in these matters. Thus, there appear to exist two relatively independent domains of police activity. In one, their methods are constrained by the prospect of the future disposition of a case in the courts; in the other, they operate under some other consideration and largely with no structured and continuous outside constraint. Following the terminology suggested by Michael Banton, they may be said to function in the first instance as "law officers" and in the second instance as "peace officers." [6] It must be emphasized that the designation "peace officer" is a residual term, with only some vaguely presumptive content. The role, as Banton speaks of it, is supposed to encompass all occupational routines not directly related to making arrests, without, however, specifying what determines the limits of competence and availability of the police in such actions.

Efforts to characterize a large domain of activities of an important public agency have so far yielded only negative definitions. We know that they do not involve arrests; we also know that they do not stand under judicial control, and that they are not, in any important sense, determined by specific executive or legislative mandates. In police textbooks and manuals, these activities receive only casual attention, and the role of the "peace officer" is typically stated in terms suggesting that his work is governed mainly by the individual officer's personal wisdom, integrity, and altruism.[7] Police departments generally keep no records of procedures that do not involve making arrests. Policemen, when asked, insist that they merely use common sense when acting as "peace officers," though they tend to emphasize the elements of experience and practice in discharging the role adequately. All this ambiguity is the more remarkable for the fact that peace keeping tasks, i.e., procedures not involving the formal legal remedy of arrest, were explicitly built into the program of the modern police from the outset.[8] The early executives of the London police saw with great clarity that their organization had a dual function. While it was to be an arm of the administration of justice, in respect of which it developed certain techniques for bringing offenders to trial, it was also expected to function apart from, and at times in lieu of, the employment of full-dress legal procedure. Despite its early origin, despite a great deal of public knowledge about it, despite the fact that it is routinely done by policemen, no one can say with any clarity what it means to do a good job of keeping the peace. To be sure, there is vague consensus that when policemen direct, aid, inform, pacify, warn, discipline, roust, and do whatever else they do without making arrests, they do this with some reference to the circumstances of the occasion and, thus, somehow contribute to the maintenance of the peace and order. Peace keeping appears to be a solution to an unknown problem arrived at by unknown means.

The following is an attempt to clarify conceptually the mandate and the practice of keeping the peace. The effort will be directed not to the formulation of a compre-

[5] The executive margin of control is set mainly in terms of budgetary determinations and the mapping of some formal aspects of the organization of departments.

[6] Michael Banton, *The Policeman in the Community,* New York: Basic Books, 1964, pp. 6–7 and 127 ff.

[7] R. Bruce Holmgren, *Primary Police Functions,* New York: William C. Copp, 1962.

[8] Cf. Lyman, *op. cit.,* p. 153; F. C. Mather, *Public Order in the Age of the Chartists,* Manchester: Manchester University Press, 1959, chapter IV. See also Robert H. Bremer, "Police, Penal and Parole Policies in Cleveland and Toledo," *American Journal of Economics and Sociology,* 14 (1955), 387–398, for similar recognition in the United States at about the turn of this century.

hensive solution of the problem but to a detailed consideration of some aspects of it. Only in order to place the particular into the overall domain to which it belongs will the structural determinants of keeping the peace in general be discussed. By structural determinants are meant the typical situations that policemen perceive as *demand conditions* for action without arrest. This will be followed by a description of peace keeping in skid-row districts, with the object of identifying those aspects of it that constitute a *practical skill*.

Since the major object of this paper is to elucidate peace keeping practice as a skilled performance, it is necessary to make clear how the use of the term is intended.

Practical skill will be used to refer to those methods of doing certain things, and to the information that underlies the use of the methods, that *practitioners themselves* view as proper and efficient. Skill is, therefore, a stable orientation to work tasks that is relatively independent of the personal feelings and judgments of those who employ it. Whether the exercise of this skilled performance is desirable or not, and whether it is based on correct information or not, are specifically outside the scope of interest of this presentation. The following is deliberately confined to a description of what police patrolmen consider to be the reality of their work circumstances, what they do, and what they feel they must do to do a good job. That the practice is thought to be determined by normative standards of skill minimizes but does not eliminate the factors of personal interest or inclination. Moreover, the distribution of skill varies among practitioners in the very standards they set for themselves. For example, we will show that patrolmen view a measure of rough informality as good practice vis-a-vis skid-row inhabitants. By this standard, patrolmen who are "not rough enough," or who are "too rough," or whose roughness is determined by personal feelings rather than by situational exigencies, are judged to be poor craftsmen.

The description and analysis are based on twelve months of field work with the police departments of two large cities west of the Mississippi. Eleven weeks of this time were spent in skid-row and skid-row-like districts. The observations were augmented by approximately one hundred interviews with police officers of all ranks. The formulations that will be proposed were discussed in these interviews. They were recognized by the respondents as elements of standard practice. The respondents' recognition was often accompanied by remarks indicating that they had never thought about things in this way and that they were not aware how standardized police work was.

STRUCTURAL DEMAND CONDITIONS OF PEACE KEEPING

There exist at least five types of relatively distinct circumstances that produce police activities that do not involve invoking the law and that are only in a trivial sense determined by those considerations of legality that determine law enforcement. This does not mean that these activities are illegal but merely that there is no legal directive that informs the acting policeman whether what he does must be done or how it is to be done. In these circumstances, policemen act as all-purpose and terminal remedial agents, and the confronted problem is solved in the field. If these practices stand under any kind of review at all, and typically they do not, it is only through internal police department control.

1. Although the executive branch of government generally refrains from exercising a controlling influence over the direction of police interest, it manages to extract certain performances from it. Two important examples of this are the supervision of certain licensed services and premises and the regulation of traffic.[9] With respect to the first, the police tend to concentrate on what might be called the moral aspects of establishments rather than on questions relating to the technical adequacy of the service. This orientation is based on the assumption that certain types of businesses lend themselves to exploitation for undesirable and illegal purposes. Since this tendency cannot be fully controlled, it is only natural that the police will be inclined to favor licensees who are at least cooperative. This, however, transforms the task from the mere scrutiny of credentials and the passing of judgments, to the creation and maintenance of a network of connections that conveys influence, pressure, and information. The duty to inspect is the background of this network, but the resulting contacts acquire tenders, shopkeepers, and hotel clerks become, for patrolmen, a resource that must be continuously serviced by visits and exchanges of favors. While it is apparent that this condition lends itself to corrupt exploitation by individual officers, even the most flawlessly honest policeman must participate in this network of exchanges if he is to function adequately. Thus, engaging in such exchanges becomes an occupational task that demands attention and time.

Regulation of traffic is considerably less complex. More than anything else, traffic control symbolizes the autonomous authority of policemen. Their commands generally are met with unquestioned compliance. Even when they issue citations, which seemingly refer the case to the courts, it is common practice for the accused to view the allegation as a finding against him and to pay the fine. Police officials emphasize that it is more important to be circumspect than legalistic in traffic control. Officers are often reminded that a large segment of the public has no other contacts with the police, and that the field lends itself to public relations work by the line personnel.[10]

2. Policemen often do not arrest persons who have committed minor offenses in circumstances in which the arrest is technically possible. This practice has recently received considerable attention in legal and sociological literature. The studies were motivated by the realization that "police decisions not to invoke the criminal process determine the outer limits of law enforcement." [11] From these researches, it was learned that the police tend to impose more stringent criteria of law enforcement on certain segments of the community than on others.[12]

[9] Smith, *op. cit.*, pp. 15 ff.

[10] Orlando W. Wilson, "Police Authority in a Free Society," *Journal of Criminal Law, Criminology and Police Science*, 54 (1964), 175–177.

[11] Joseph Goldstein, "Police Discretion Not to Invoke the Criminal Process," *Yale Law Journal*, 69 (1960), 543.

[12] Jerome Skolnick, *Justice without Trial*, New York: Wiley, 1966.

It was also learned that, from the perspective of the administration of justice, the decisions not to make arrests often are based on compelling reasons.[13] It is less well appreciated that policemen often not only refrain from invoking the law formally but also employ alternative sanctions. For example, it is standard practice that violators are warned not to repeat the offense. This often leads to patrolmen's "keeping an eye" on certain persons. Less frequent, though not unusual, is the practice of direct disciplining of offenders, especially when they are juveniles, which occasionally involves inducing them to repair the damage occasioned by their misconduct.[14]

The power to arrest and the freedom not to arrest can be used in cases that do not involve patent offenses. An officer can say to a person whose behavior he wishes to control, "I'll let you go this time!" without indicating to him that he could not have been arrested in any case. Nor is this always deliberate misrepresentation, for in many cases the law is sufficiently ambiguous to allow alternative interpretations. In short, not to make an arrest is rarely, if ever, merely a decision not to act; it is most often a decision to act alternatively. In the case of minor offenses, to make an arrest often is merely one of several possible proper actions.

3. There exists a public demand for police intervention in matters that contain no criminal and often no legal aspects.[15] For example, it is commonly assumed that officers will be available to arbitrate quarrels, to pacify the unruly, and to help in keeping order. They are supposed also to aid people in trouble, and there is scarcely a human predicament imaginable for which police aid has not been solicited and obtained at one time or another. Most authors writing about the police consider such activities only marginally related to the police mandate. This view fails to reckon with the fact that the availability of these performances is taken for granted and the police assign a substantial amount of their resources to such work. Although this work cannot be subsumed under the concept of legal action, it does involve the exercise of a form of authority that most people associate with the police. In fact, no matter how trivial the occasion, the device of "calling the cops" transforms any problem. It implies that a situation is, or is getting, out of hand. Police responses to public demands are always oriented to this implication, and the risk of proliferation of troubles makes every call a potentially serious matter.[16]

4. Certain mass phenomena of either a regular or a spontaneous na-

[13] Wayne LaFave, "The Police and Nonenforcement of the Law," *Wisconsin Law Review* (1962), 104–137 and 179–239.

[14] Nathan Goldman, *The Differential Selection of Juvenile Offenders for Court Appearance,* National Research and Information Center, National Council on Crime and Delinquency, 1963, pp. 114 ff.

[15] Elaine Cumming, Ian Cumming and Laura Edell, "Policeman as Philosopher, Guide and Friend," *Social Problems,* 12 (1965), 276–286.

[16] There is little doubt that many requests for service are turned down by the police, especially when they are made over the telephone or by mail, cf. LaFave, *op. cit.,* p. 212, n. 124. The uniformed patrolman, however, finds it virtually impossible to leave the scene without becoming involved in some way or another.

ture require direct monitoring. Most important is the controlling of crowds in incipient stages of disorder. The specter of mob violence frequently calls for measures that involve coercion, including the use of physical force. Legal theory allows, of course, that public officials are empowered to use coercion in situations of imminent danger.[17] Unfortunately, the doctrine is not sufficiently specific to be of much help as a rule of practice. It is based on the assumption of the adventitiousness of danger, and thus does not lend itself readily to elaborations that could direct the routines of early detection and prevention of untoward developments. It is interesting that the objective of preventing riots by informal means posed one of the central organizational problems for the police in England during the era of the Chartists.[18]

5. The police have certain special duties with respect to persons who are viewed as less than fully accountable for their actions. Examples of those eligible for special consideration are those who are under age [19] and those who are mentally ill.[20] Although it is virtually never acknowledged explicitly, those receiving special treatment include people who do not lead "normal" lives and who occupy a pariah status in society. This group includes residents of ethnic ghettos, certain types of bohemians and vagabonds, and persons of known criminal background. The special treatment of children and of sick persons is permissively sanctioned by the law, but the special treatment of others is, in principle, opposed by the leading theme of legality and the tenets of the democratic faith.[21] The important point is not that such persons are arrested more often than others, which is quite true, but that they are perceived by the police as producing a special problem that necessitates continuous attention and the use of special procedures.

The five types of demand conditions do not exclude the possibility of invoking the criminal process. Indeed, arrests do occur quite frequently in all these circumstances. But the concerns generated in these areas cause activities that usually do not terminate in an arrest. When arrests are made, there exist, at least in the ideal, certain criteria by reference to which the arrest can be judged as having been made more or less properly, and there are some persons who, in the natural course of events, actually judge the performance.[22] But for actions not resulting in arrest there are no such criteria and no such judges. How, then, can one speak of such actions as necessary and proper? Since there does not exist any official answer to this query, and

[17] Hans Kelsen, *General Theory of Law and State*, New York: Russell & Russell, 1961, pp. 278–279; H. L. A. Hart, *The Concept of Law*, Oxford: Clarendon Press, 1961, pp. 20–21.

[18] Mather, *op. cit.*; see also, Jenifer Hart, "Reform of the Borough Police, 1835–1856," *English History Review*, 70 (1955), 411–427.

[19] Francis A. Allen, *The Borderland of Criminal Justice*, Chicago: University of Chicago Press, 1964.

[20] Egon Bittner, "Police Discretion in Emergency Apprehension of Mentally Ill Persons," *Social Problems*, 14 (1967), 278–292.

[21] It bears mentioning, however, that differential treatment is not unique with the police, but is also in many ways representative for the administration of justice in general; cf. J. E. Carlin, Jan Howard and S. L. Messinger, "Civil Justice and the Poor," *Law and Society*, 1 (1966), 9–89; Jacobus tenBroek (ed.) *The Law of the Poor*, San Francisco: Chandler Publishing Co., 1966.

[22] This is, however, true only in the ideal. It is well known that a substantial number of persons who are arrested are subsequently released without ever being charged and tried, cf. Barrett, *op. cit.*

since policemen act in the role of "peace officers" pretty much without external direction or constraint, the question comes down to asking how the policeman himself knows whether he has any business with a person he does not arrest, and if so, what that business might be. Furthermore, if there exists a domain of concerns and activities that is largely independent of the law enforcement mandate, it is reasonable to assume that it will exercise some degree of influence on how and to what ends the law is invoked in cases of arrests.

Skid-row presents one excellent opportunity to study these problems. The area contains a heavy concentration of persons who do not live "normal" lives in terms of prevailing standards of middle-class morality. Since the police respond to this situation by intensive patrolling, the structure of peace keeping should be readily observable. Needless to say, the findings and conclusions will not be necessarily generalizable to other types of demand conditions.

THE PROBLEM OF KEEPING THE PEACE IN SKID–ROW

Skid-row has always occupied a special place among the various forms of urban life. While other areas are perceived as being different in many ways, skid-row is seen as completely different. Though it is located in the heart of civilization, it is viewed as containing aspects of the primordial jungle, calling for missionary activities and offering opportunities for exotic adventure. While each inhabitant individually can be seen as tragically linked to the vicissitudes of "normal" life, allowing others to say "here but for the Grace of God go I," those who live there are believed to have repudiated the entire role-casting scheme of the majority and to live apart from normalcy. Accordingly, the traditional attitude of civic-mindedness toward skid-row has been dominated by the desire to contain it and to salvage souls from its clutches.[23] The specific task of containment has been left to the police. That this task pressed upon the police some rather special duties has never come under explicit consideration, either from the government that expects control or from the police departments that implement it. Instead, the prevailing method of carrying out the task is to assign patrolmen to the area on a fairly permanent basis and to allow them to work out their own ways of running things. External influence is confined largely to the supply of support and facilities, on the one hand, and to occasional expressions of criticism about the overall conditions, on the other. Within the limits of available resources and general expectations, patrolmen are supposed to know what to do and are free to do it.[24]

Patrolmen who are more or less permanently assigned to skid-row districts tend to develop a conception of the nature of their "domain" that is surprisingly uniform. Individual officers differ in many aspects of practice, emphasize different concerns, and

[23] The literature on skid-row is voluminous. The classic in the field is Nels Anderson, *The Hobo,* Chicago: University of Chicago Press, 1923. Samuel E. Wallace, *Skid-Row as a Way of Life,* Totowa, New Jersey: The Bedminster Press, 1965, is a more recent descriptive account and contains a useful bibliography. Donald A. Bogue, *Skid-Row in American Cities,* Chicago: Community and Family Center, University of Chicago, 1963, contains an exhaustive quantitative survey of Chicago skid-row.

[24] One of the two cities described in this paper also employed the procedure of the "round-up" of drunks. In this, the police van toured the skid-row area twice daily, during the mid-afternoon and early evening hours, and the officers who manned it picked up drunks they sighted. A similar procedure is used in New York's Bowery and the officers who do it are called "condition men." Cf. *Bowery Project,* Bureau of Applied Social Research, Columbia University, Summary Report of a Study Undertaken under Contract Approved by the Board of Estimates, 1963, mimeo., p. 11.

maintain different contacts, but they are in fundamental agreement about the structure of skid-row life. This relatively uniform conception includes an implicit formulation of the problem of keeping the peace in skid-row.

In the view of experienced patrolmen, life on skid-row is fundamentally different
from life in other parts of society. To be sure, they say, around its geographic limits
the area tends to blend into the surrounding environment, and its population always
encompasses some persons who are only transitionally associated with it. Basically,
however, skid-row is perceived as the natural habitat of people who lack the capaci-
ties and commitments to live "normal" lives on a sustained basis. The presence of
these people defines the nature of social reality in the area. In general, and especially
in casual encounters, the presumption of incompetence and of the disinclination to
be "normal" is the leading theme for the interpretation of all actions and relations.
Not only do people approach one another in this manner, but presumably they also
expect to be approached in this way, and they conduct themselves accordingly.

In practice, the restriction of interactional possibilities that is based on the patrolman's stereotyped conception of skid-row residents is always subject to revision and
modification toward particular individuals. Thus, it is entirely possible, and not
unusual, for patrolmen to view certain skid-row inhabitants in terms that involve non-
skid-row aspects of normality. Instances of such approaches and relationships invariably involve personal acquaintance and the knowledge of a good deal of individually
qualifying information. Such instances are seen, despite their relative frequency, as
exceptions to the rule. The awareness of the possibility of breakdown, frustration,
and betrayal is ever-present, basic wariness is never wholly dissipated, and undaunted
trust can never be fully reconciled with presence on skid-row.

What patrolmen view as normal on skid-row—and what they also think is taken
for granted as "life as usual" by the inhabitants—is not easily summarized. It seems
to focus on the idea that the dominant consideration governing all enterprise and
association is directed to the occasion of the moment. Nothing is thought of as having
a background that might have led up to the present in terms of some compelling
moral or practical necessity. There are some exceptions to this rule, of course: the
police themselves, and those who run certain establishments, are perceived as engaged in important and necessary activities. But in order to carry them out they, too,
must be geared to the overall atmosphere of fortuitousness. In this atmosphere, the
range of control that persons have over one another is exceedingly narrow. Good
faith, even where it is valued, is seen merely as a personal matter. Its violations are
the victim's own hard luck, rather than demonstrable violations of property. There
is only a private sense of irony at having been victimized. The overall air is not so
much one of active distrust as it is one of irrelevance of trust; as patrolmen often
emphasize, the situation does not necessarily cause all relations to be predatory, but
the possibility of exploitation is not checked by the expectation that it will not
happen.

Just as the past is seen by the policeman as having only the most attenuated relevance to the present, so the future implications of present situations are said to be
generally devoid of prospective coherence. No venture, especially no joint venture,
can be said to have a strongly predictable future in line with its initial objectives. It
is a matter of adventitious circumstance whether or not matters go as anticipated.
That which is not within the grasp of momentary control is outside of practical social
reality.

Though patrolmen see the temporal framework of the occasion of the moment mainly as a lack of trustworthiness, they also recognize that it involves more than merely the personal motives of individuals. In addition to the fact that everybody *feels* that things matter only at the moment, irresponsibility takes an *objectified* form on skid-row. The places the residents occupy, the social relations they entertain, and the activities that engage them are not meaningfully connected over time. Thus, for example, address, occupation, marital status, etc., matter much less on skid-row than in any other part of society. The fact that present whereabouts, activities, and affiliations imply neither continuity nor direction means that life on skid-row lacks a socially structured background of accountability. Of course, everybody's life contains some sequential incongruities, but in the life of a skid-row inhabitant every moment is an accident. That a man has no "address" in the future that could be in some way inferred from where he is and what he does makes him a person of *radically reduced visibility*. If he disappears from sight and one wishes to locate him, it is virtually impossible to systematize the search. All one can know with relative certainty is that he will be somewhere on some skid-row and the only thing one can do is to trace the factual contiguities of his whereabouts.

It is commonly known that the police are expert in finding people and that they have developed an exquisite technology involving special facilities and procedures of sleuthing. It is less well appreciated that all this technology builds upon those socially structured features of everyday life that render persons findable in the first place.

Under ordinary conditions, the query as to where a person is can be addressed, from the outset, to a restricted realm of possibilities that can be further narrowed by looking into certain places and asking certain persons. The map of whereabouts that normally competent persons use whenever they wish to locate someone is constituted by the basic facts of membership in society. Insofar as membership consists of status incumbencies, each of which has an adumbrated future that substantially reduces unpredictability, it is itself a guarantee of the order within which it is quite difficult to get lost. Membership is thus visible not only now but also as its own projection into the future. It is in terms of this prospective availability that the skid-row inhabitant is a person of reduced visibility. His membership is viewed as extraordinary because its extension into the future is *not* reduced to a restricted realm of possibilities. Neither his subjective dispositions, nor his circumstances, indicate that he is oriented to any particular long-range interests. But, as he may claim every contingent opportunity, his claims are always seen as based on slight merit or right, at least to the extent that interfering with them does not constitute a substantial denial of his freedom.

This, then, constitutes the problem of keeping the peace on skid-row. Considerations of momentary expediency are seen as having unqualified priority as maxims of conduct; consequently, the controlling influences of the pursuit of sustained interests are presumed to be absent.

THE PRACTICES OF KEEPING THE PEACE IN SKID-ROW

From the perspective of society as a whole, skid-row inhabitants appear troublesome in a variety of ways. The uncommitted life attributed to them is perceived as inherently offensive; its very existence arouses indignation and contempt. More important, however, is the feeling that persons who have repudiated the entire role-status casting system of society, persons whose lives forever collapse into a succession of random moments, are seen as constituting a practical risk. As they have nothing to foresake, nothing is thought safe from them.[25]

The skid-row patrolman's concept of his mandate includes an awareness of this presumed risk. He is constantly attuned to the possibility of violence, and he is convinced that things to which the inhabitants have free access are as good as lost. But his concern is directed toward the continuous condition of peril *in the area* rather than *for society in general*. While he is obviously conscious of the presence of many persons who have committed crimes outside of skid-row and will arrest them when they come to his attention, this is a peripheral part of his routine activities. In general, the skid-row patrolman and his superiors take for granted that his main business is to keep the peace and enforce the laws *on skid-row*, and that he is involved only incidentally in protecting society at large. Thus, his task is formulated basically as the protection of putative predators from one another. The maintenance of peace and safety is difficult because everyday life on skid-row is viewed as an open field for reciprocal exploitation. As the lives of the inhabitants lack the prospective coherence associated with status incumbency, the realization of self-interest does not produce order. Hence, mechanisms that control risk must work primarily from without.

External containment, to be effective, must be oriented to the realities of existence. Thus, the skid-row patrolman employs an approach that he views as appropriate to the *ad hoc* nature of skid-row life. The following are the three most prominent elements of this approach. First, the seasoned patrolman seeks to acquire a richly particularized knowledge of people and places in the area. Second, he gives the consideration of strict culpability a subordinate status among grounds for remedial sanction. Third, his use and choice of coercive interventions is determined mainly by exigencies of situations and with little regard for possible long range effects on individual persons.

The Particularization of Knowledge. The patrolman's orientation to people on skid-row is structured basically by the presupposition that if he does not know a man personally there is very little that he can assume about him. This rule determines his interaction with people who live on skid-row. Since the area also contains other types of persons, however, its applicability is not universal. To some such persons it does not apply at all, and it has a somewhat mitigated significance with certain others. For example, some persons encountered on skid-row can be recognized immediately as outsiders. Among them are workers who are employed in commercial and industrial enterprises that abut the area, persons who come for the purpose of adventurous "slumming," and some patrons of second-hand stores and pawn shops. Even with very little experience, it is relatively easy to identify these people by appearance, demeanor, and the time and place of their presence. The patrolman maintains an impersonal attitude toward them, and they are, under ordinary circumstances, not the objects of his attention.[26]

[25] An illuminating parallel to the perception of skid-row can be found in the more traditional concept of vagabondage. Cf. Alexandre Vexliard, *Introduction à la Sociologie du Vagabondage,* Paris: Libraire Marcel Rivière, 1956, and "La Disparition du Vagabondage comme Fleau Social Universel," *Revue de L'Institut de Sociologie* (1963), 53–79. The classic account of English conditions up to the 19th century is C. J. Ribton-Turner, *A History of Vagrants and Vagrancy and Beggars and Begging,* London: Chapman and Hall, 1887.

[26] Several patrolmen complained about the influx of "tourists" into skid-row. Since such "tourists" are perceived as seeking illicit adventure, they receive little sympathy from patrolmen when they complain about being victimized.

Clearly set off from these outsiders are the residents and the entire corps of personnel that services skid-row. It would be fair to say that one of the main routine activities of patrolmen is the establishment and maintenance of familiar relationships with individual members of these groups. Officers emphasize their interest in this, and they maintain that their grasp of and control over skid-row is precisely commensurate with the extent to which they "know the people." By this they do not mean having a quasi-theoretical understanding of human nature but rather the common practice of individualized and reciprocal recognition. As this group encompasses both those who render services on skid-row and those who are serviced, individualized interest is not always based on the desire to overcome uncertainty. Instead, relations with service personnel become absorbed into the network of particularized attention. Ties between patrolmen, on the one hand, and businessmen, managers, and workers, on the other hand, are often defined in terms of shared or similar interests. It bears mentioning that many persons live *and* work on skid-row. Thus, the distinction between those who service and those who are serviced is not a clearcut dichotomy but a spectrum of affiliations.

As a general rule, the skid-row patrolman possesses an immensely detailed factual knowledge of his beat. He knows, and knows a great deal about, a large number of residents. He is likely to know every person who manages or works in the local bars, hotels, shops, stores, and missions. Moreover, he probably knows every public and private place inside and out. Finally, he ordinarily remembers countless events of the past which he can recount by citing names, dates and places with remarkable precision. Though there are always some threads missing in the fabric of information, it is continuously woven and mended even as it is being used. New facts, however, are added to the texture, not in terms of structured categories but in terms of adjoining known realities. In other words, the content and organization of the patrolman's knowledge is primarily ideographic and only vestigially, if at all, nomothetic.

Individual patrolmen vary in the extent to which they make themselves available or actively pursue personal acquaintances. But even the most aloof are continuously greeted and engaged in conversations that indicate a background of individualistic associations. While this scarcely has the appearance of work, because of its casual character, patrolmen do not view it as an optional activity. In the course of making their rounds, patrolmen seem to have access to every place, and their entry causes no surprise or consternation. Instead, the entry tends to lead to informal exchanges of small talk. At times the rounds include entering hotels and gaining access to rooms or dormitories, often for no other purpose than asking the occupants how things are going. In all this, patrolmen address innumerable persons by name and are in turn addressed by name. The conversational style that characterizes these exchanges is casual to an extent that by non-skid-row standards might suggest intimacy. Not only does the officer himself avoid all terms of deference and respect but he does not seem to expect or demand them. For example, a patrolman said to a man radiating an alcoholic glow on the street, "You've got enough of a heat on now; I'll give you ten minutes to get your ass off the street!" Without stopping, the man answered, "Oh, why don't you go and piss in your own pot!" The officer's only response was, "All right, in ten minutes you're either in bed or on your way to the can."

This kind of expressive freedom is an intricately limited privilege. Persons of acquaintance are entitled to it and appear to exercise it mainly in routinized encounters. But strangers, too, can use it with impunity. The safe way of gaining the privilege is to respond to the patrolman in ways that do not challenge his right to ask questions and issue commands. Once the concession is made that the officer is entitled to inquire into a man's background, business, and intentions, and that he is entitled to obedience, there opens a field of colloquial license. A patrolman seems to grant expressive freedom in recognition of a person's acceptance of his access to areas of life ordinarily defined as private and subject to coercive control only under special circumstances. While patrolmen accept and seemingly even cultivate the rough *quid pro quo* of informality, and while they do not expect sincerity, candor, or obedience in their dealings with the inhabitants, they do not allow the rejection of their approach.

The explicit refusal to answer questions of a personal nature and the demand to know why the questions are asked significantly enhances a person's chances of being arrested on some minor charge. While most patrolmen tend to be personally indignant about this kind of response and use the arrest to compose their own hurt feelings, this is merely a case of affect being in line with the method. There are other officers who proceed in the same manner without taking offense, or even with feelings of regret. Such patrolmen often maintain that their colleagues' affective involvement is a corruption of an essentially valid technique. The technique is oriented to the goal of maintaining operational control. The patrolman's conception of this goal places him hierarchically above whomever he approaches, and makes him the sole judge of the propriety of the occasion. As he alone is oriented to this goal, and as he seeks to attain it by means of individualized access to persons, those who frustrate him are seen as motivated at best by the desire to "give him a hard time" and at worst by some darkly devious purpose.

Officers are quite aware that the directness of their approach and the demands they make are difficult to reconcile with the doctrines of civil liberties, but they maintain that they are in accord with the general freedom of access that persons living on skid-row normally grant one another. That is, they believe that the imposition of personalized and far-reaching control is in tune with standard expectancies. In terms of these expectancies, people are not so much denied the right to privacy as they are seen as not having any privacy. Thus, officers seek to install themselves in the center of people's lives and let the consciousness of their presence play the part of conscience.

When talking about the practical necessity of an aggressively personal approach, officers do not refer merely to the need for maintaining control over lives that are open in the direction of the untoward. They also see it as the basis for the supply of certain valued services to inhabitants of skid-row. The coerced or conceded access to persons often imposes on the patrolman tasks that are, in the main, in line with these persons' expressed or implied interest. In asserting this connection, patrolmen note that they frequently help people to obtain meals, lodging, employment, that they direct them to welfare and health services, and that they aid them in various other ways. Though patrolmen tend to describe such services mainly as the product of their own altruism, they also say that their colleagues who avoid them are simply doing a poor job of patrolling. The acceptance of the need to help people is based on the realization that the hungry, the sick, and the troubled are a potential source of problems. Moreover, that patrolmen will help people is part of the background expectancies of life on skid-row. Hotel clerks normally call policemen when someone gets so sick as to need attention; merchants expect to be taxed, in a manner of speaking, to meet the pressing needs of certain persons; and the inhabitants do not hesitate to accept, solicit, and demand every kind of aid. The domain of the patrolman's service activity is virtually limitless, and it is no exaggeration to say that the solution of every conceivable problem has at one time or another been attempted by a police officer. In one observed instance, a patrolman unceremoniously entered the room of a man he had never seen before. The man, who gave no indication that he regarded the officer's entry and questions as anything but part of life as usual, related a story of having had his dentures stolen by his wife. In the course of the subsequent rounds, the patrolman sought to locate the woman and the dentures. This did not become the evening's project but was attended to while doing other things. In the densely matted activities of the patrolman, the questioning became one more strand, not so much to be pursued to its solution as a theme that organized the memory of one more man known individually. In all this, the officer followed the precept formulated by a somewhat more articulate patrolman: "If I want to be in control of my work and keep the street relatively peaceful, I have to know the people. To know them I must gain their trust, which means that I have to be involved in their lives. But I can't be soft like a social worker because unlike him I cannot call the cops when things go wrong. I am the cops!" [27]

The Restricted Relevance of Culpability. It is well known that policemen exercise discretionary freedom in invoking the law. It is also conceded that, in some measure, the practice is unavoidable. This being so, the outstanding problem is whether or not the decisions are in line with the intent of the law. On skid-row, patrolmen often make decisions based on reasons that the law probably does not recognize as valid. The problem can best be introduced by citing an example.

A man in a relatively mild state of intoxication (by skid-row standards) approached a patrolman to tell him that he had a room in a hotel, to which the officer responded by urging him to go to bed instead of getting drunk. As the man walked off, the officer related the following thoughts: Here is a completely lost soul. Though he probably is no more than thirty-five years old, he looks to be in his fifties. He never works and he hardly ever has a place to stay. He has been on the street for several years and is known as "Dakota." During the past few days, "Dakota" has been seen in the company of "Big Jim." The latter is an invalid living on some sort of pension with which he pays for a room in the hotel to which "Dakota" referred and for four weekly meal tickets in one of the restaurants on the street. Whatever is left he spends on wine and beer. Occasionally, "Big Jim" goes on drinking sprees in the company of someone like "Dakota." Leaving aside the consideration that there is probably a homosexual background to the association, and that it is not right that "Big Jim" should have to support the drinking habit of someone else, there is the more important risk that if "Dakota" moves in with "Big Jim" he will very likely walk off with whatever the latter keeps in his room. "Big Jim" would never dream of reporting the theft; he would just beat the hell out of "Dakota" after he sobered up. When asked what could be done to prevent the theft and the subsequent recriminations, the patrolman proposed that in this particular case he would throw "Big Jim" into jail if he found him tonight and then tell the hotel clerk to throw "Dakota" out of the room. When asked why he did not arrest "Dakota," who was, after all, drunk enough

---

[27] The same officer commented further, "If a man looks for something, I might help him. But I don't stay with him till he finds what he is looking for. If I did, I would never get to do anything else. In the last analysis, I really never solve any problems. The best I can hope for is to keep things from getting worse."

to warrant an arrest, the officer explained that this would not solve anything. While "Dakota" was in jail "Big Jim" would continue drinking and would either strike up another liaison or embrace his old buddy after he had been released. The only thing to do was to get "Big Jim" to sober up, and the only sure way of doing this was to arrest him.

As it turned out, "Big Jim" was not located that evening. But had he been located and arrested on a drunk charge, the fact that he was intoxicated would not have been the real reason for proceeding against him, but merely the pretext. The point of the example is not that it illustrates the tendency of skid-row patrolmen to arrest persons who would not be arrested under conditions of full respect for their legal rights. To be sure, this too happens. In the majority of minor arrest cases, however, the criteria the law specifies are met. But it is the rare exception that the law is invoked merely because the specifications of the law are met. That is, compliance with the law is merely the outward appearance of an intervention that is actually based on altogether different considerations. Thus, it could be said that patrolmen do not really enforce the law, even when they do invoke it, but merely use it as a resource to solve certain pressing practical problems in keeping the peace. This observation goes beyond the conclusion that many of the lesser norms of the criminal law are treated as defeasible in police work. It is patently not the case that skid-row patrolmen apply the legal norms while recognizing many exceptions to their applicability. Instead, the observation leads to the conclusion that in keeping the peace on skid-row, patrolmen encounter certain matters they attend to by means of coercive action, e.g., arrests. In doing this, they invoke legal norms that are available, and with some regard for substantive appropriateness. Hence, the problem patrolmen confront is not which drunks, beggars, or disturbers of the peace should be arrested and which can be let go as exceptions to the rule. Rather, the problem is whether, when someone "needs" to be arrested, he should be charged with drunkenness, begging, or disturbing the peace. Speculating further, one is almost compelled to infer that virtually any set of norms could be used in this manner, provided that they sanction relatively common forms of behavior.

The reduced relevance of culpability in peace keeping practice on skid-row is not readily visible. As mentioned, most arrested persons were actually found in the act, or in the state, alleged in the arrest record. It becomes partly visible when one views the treatment of persons who are not arrested even though all the legal grounds for an arrest are present. Whenever such persons are encountered and can be induced to leave, or taken to some shelter, or remanded to someone's care, then patrolmen feel, or at least maintain, that an arrest would serve no useful purpose. That is, whenever there exist means for controlling the troublesome aspects of some person's presence in some way alternative to an arrest, such means are preferentially employed, provided, of course, that the case at hand involves only a minor offense.[28]

The attenuation of the relevance of culpability is most visible when the presence of legal grounds for an arrest could be questioned, i.e., in cases that sometimes are euphemistically called "preventive arrests." In one observed instance, a man who

---

[28] When evidence is present to indicate that a serious crime has been committed, considerations of culpability acquire a position of priority. Two such arrests were observed, both involving checkpassers. The first offender was caught in flagrante delicto. In the second instance, the suspect attracted the attention of the patrolman because of his sickly appearance. In the ensuing conversation the man made some remarks that led the officer to place a call with the Warrant Division of his department. According to the information that was obtained by checking records, the man was a wanted checkpasser and was immediately arrested.

attempted to trade a pocket knife came to the attention of a patrolman. The initial encounter was attended by a good deal of levity and the man willingly responded to the officer's inquiries about his identity and business. The man laughingly acknowledged that he needed some money to get drunk. In the course of the exchange it came to light that he had just arrived in town, traveling in his automobile. When confronted with the demand to lead the officer to the car, the man's expression became serious and he pointedly stated that he would not comply because this was none of the officer's business. After a bit more prodding, which the patrolman initially kept in the light mood, the man was arrested on a charge involving begging. In subsequent conversation the patrolman acknowledged that the charge was only speciously appropriate and mainly a pretext. Having committed himself to demanding information he could not accept defeat. When this incident was discussed with another patrolman, the second officer found fault not with the fact that the arrest was made on a pretext but with the first officer's own contribution to the creation of conditions that made it unavoidable. "You see," he continued, "there is always the risk that the man is testing you and you must let him know what is what. The best among us can usually keep the upper hand in such situations without making arrests. But when it comes down to the wire, then you can't let them get away with it."

Finally, it must be mentioned that the reduction of the significance of culpability is built into the normal order of skid-row life, as patrolmen see it. Officers almost unfailingly say, pointing to some particular person, "I know that he knows that I know that some of the things he 'owns' are stolen, and that nothing can be done about it." In saying this, they often claim to have knowledge of such a degree of certainty as would normally be sufficient for virtually any kind of action except legal proceedings. Against this background, patrolmen adopt the view that the law is not merely imperfect and difficult to implement, but that on skid-row, at least, the association between delict and sanction is distinctly occasional. Thus, to implement the law naïvely, i.e., to arrest someone *merely* because he committed some minor offense, is perceived as containing elements of injustice.

Moreover, patrolmen often deal with situations in which questions of culpability are profoundly ambiguous. For example, an officer was called to help in settling a violent dispute in a hotel room. The object of the quarrel was a supposedly stolen pair of trousers. As the story unfolded in the conflicting versions of the participants, it was not possible to decide who was the complainant and who was alleged to be the thief, nor did it come to light who occupied the room in which the fracas took place, or whether the trousers were taken from the room or to the room. Though the officer did ask some questions, it seemed, and was confirmed in later conversation, that he was there not to solve the puzzle of the missing trousers but to keep the situation from getting out of hand. In the end, the exhausted participants dispersed, and this was the conclusion of the case. The patrolman maintained that no one could unravel mysteries of this sort because "these people take things from each other so often that no one could tell what 'belongs' to whom." In fact, he suggested, the terms owning, stealing, and swindling, in their strict sense, do not really belong on skid-row, and all efforts to distribute guilt and innocence according to some rational formula of justice are doomed to failure.

It could be said that the term "curb-stone justice" that is sometimes applied to the procedures of patrolmen in skid-rows contains a double irony. Not only is the procedure not legally authorized, which is the intended irony in the expression, but it does not even pretend to distribute deserts. The best among the patrolmen, according to their own standards, use the law to keep skid-row inhabitants from sinking deeper into the misery they already experience. The worst, in terms of these same standards, exploit the practice for personal aggrandizement or gain. Leaving motives aside, however, it is easy to see that if culpability is not the salient consideration leading to an arrest in cases where it is patently obvious, then the practical patrolman may not view it as being wholly out of line to make arrests lacking in formal legal justification. Conversely, he will come to view minor offense arrests made solely because legal standards are met as poor craftsmanship.

The Background of Ad Hoc *Decision Making.* When skid-row patrolmen are pressed to explain their reasons for minor offense arrests, they most often mention that it is done for the protection of the arrested person. This, they maintain, is the case in virtually all drunk arrests, in the majority of arrests involving begging and other nuisance offenses, and in many cases involving acts of violence. When they are asked to explain further such arrests as the one cited earlier involving the man attempting to sell the pocket knife, who was certainly not arrested for his own protection, they cite the consideration that belligerent persons constitute a much greater menace on skid-row than any place else in the city. The reasons for this are twofold. First, many of the inhabitants are old, feeble, and not too smart, all of which makes them relatively defenseless. Second, many of the inhabitants are involved in illegal activities and are known as persons of bad character, which does not make them credible victims or witnesses. Potential predators realize that the resources society has mobilized to minimize the risk of criminal victimization do not protect the predator himself. Thus, reciprocal exploitation constitutes a preferred risk. The high vulnerability of everybody on skid-row is public knowledge and causes every seemingly aggressive act to be seen as a potentially grave risk.

When, in response to all this, patrolmen are confronted with the observation that many minor offense arrests they make do not seem to involve a careful evaluation of facts before acting, they give the following explanations: First, the two reasons of protection and prevention represent a global background, and in individual cases it may sometimes not be possible to produce adequate justification on these grounds. Nor is it thought to be a problem of great moment to estimate precisely whether someone is more likely to come to grief or to cause grief when the objective is to prevent the proliferation of troubles. Second, patrolmen maintain that some of the seemingly spur-of-the-moment decisions are actually made against a background of knowledge of facts that are not readily apparent in the situations. Since experience not only contains this information but also causes it to come to mind, patrolmen claim to have developed a special sensitivity for qualities of appearances that allow an intuitive grasp of probable tendencies. In this context, little things are said to have high informational value and lead to conclusions without the intervention of explicitly reasoned chains of inferences. Third, patrolmen readily admit that they do not adhere to high standards of adequacy of justification. They do not seek to defend the adequacy of their method against some abstract criteria of merit. Instead, when questioned, they assess their methods against the background of a whole system of *ad hoc* decision making, a system that encompasses the courts, correction facilities, the welfare establishment, and medical services. In fact, policemen generally maintain that their own procedures not only measure up to the workings of this system but exceed them in the attitude of carefulness.

In addition to these recognized reasons, there are two additional background factors that play a significant part in decisions to employ coercion. One has to do with the relevance of situational factors, and the other with the evaluation of coercion as relatively insignificant in the lives of the inhabitants.

There is no doubt that the nature of the circumstances often has decisive influence on what will be done. For example, the same patrolman who arrested the man trying to sell his pocket knife was observed dealing with a young couple. Though the officer was clearly angered by what he perceived as insolence and threatened the man with arrest, he merely ordered him and his companion to leave the street. He saw them walking away in a deliberately slow manner and when he noticed them a while later, still standing only a short distance away from the place of encounter, he did not respond to their presence. The difference between the two cases was that in the first there was a crowd of amused bystanders, while the latter case was not witnessed by anyone. In another instance, the patrolman was directed to a hotel and found a father and son fighting about money. The father occupied a room in the hotel and the son occasionally shared his quarters. There were two other men present, and they made it clear that their sympathies were with the older man. The son was whisked off to jail without much study of the relative merits of the conflicting claims. In yet another case, a middle-aged woman was forcefully evacuated from a bar even after the bartender explained that her loud behavior was merely a response to goading by some foul-mouth youth.

In all such circumstances, coercive control is exercised as a means of coming to grips with situational exigencies. Force is used against particular persons but is incidental to the task. An ideal of "economy of intervention" dictates in these and similar cases that the person whose presence is most likely to perpetuate the troublesome development be removed. Moreover, the decision as to who is to be removed is arrived at very quickly. Officers feel considerable pressure to act unhesitatingly, and many give accounts of situations that got out of hand because of desires to handle cases with careful consideration. However, even when there is no apparent risk of rapid proliferation of trouble, the tactic of removing one or two persons is used to control an undesirable situation. Thus, when a patrolman ran into a group of four men sharing a bottle of wine in an alley, he emptied the remaining contents of the bottle into the gutter, arrested one man—who was no more and no less drunk than the others—and let the others disperse in various directions.

The exigential nature of control is also evident in the handling of isolated drunks. Men are arrested because of where they happen to be encountered. In this, it matters not only whether a man is found in a conspicuous place or not, but also how far away he is from his domicile. The further away he is, the less likely it is that he will make it to his room, and the more likely the arrest. Sometimes drunk arrests are made mainly because the police van is available. In one case a patrolman summoned the van to pick up an arrested man. As the van was pulling away from the curb the officer stopped the driver because he sighted another drunk stumbling across the street. The second man protested saying that he "wasn't even half drunk yet." The patrolman's response was "OK, I'll owe you half a drunk." In sum, the basic routine of keeping the peace on skid-row involves a process of matching the resources of control with situational exigencies. The overall objective is to reduce the total amount of risk in the area. In this, practicality plays a considerably more important role than legal norms. Precisely because patrolmen see legal reasons for coercive action much more widely distributed on skid-row than could ever be matched by interventions, they intervene not in the interest of law enforcement but in the interest of producing relative tranquility and order on the street.

Taking the perspective of the victim of coercive measures, one could ask why he, in particular, has to bear the cost of keeping the aggregate of troubles down while others, who are equally or perhaps even more implicated, go scot-free. Patrolmen maintain that the *ad hoc* selection of persons for attention must be viewed in the light of the following consideration: Arresting a person on skid-row on some minor charge may save him and others a lot of trouble, but it does not work any real hardships on the arrested person. It is difficult to overestimate the skid-row patrolman's feeling of certainty that his coercive and disciplinary actions toward the inhabitants have but the most passing significance in their lives. Sending a man to jail on some charge that will hold him for a couple of days is seen as a matter of such slight importance to the affected person that it could hardly give rise to scruples. Thus, every indication that a coercive measure should be taken is accompanied by the realization "I might as well, for all it matters to him." Certain realities of life on skid-row furnish the context for this belief in the attenuated relevance of coercion in the lives of the inhabitants. Foremost among them is that the use of police authority is seen as totally unremarkable by everybody on skid-row. Persons who live or work there are continuously exposed to it and take its existence for granted. Shopkeepers, hotel clerks, and bartenders call patrolmen to rid themselves of unwanted and troublesome patrons. Residents expect patrolmen to arbitrate their quarrels authoritatively. Men who receive orders, whether they obey them or not, treat them as part of life as usual. Moreover, patrolmen find that disciplinary and coercive actions apparently do not affect their friendly relations with the persons against whom these actions are taken. Those who greet and chat with them are the very same men who have been disciplined, arrested, and ordered around in the past, and who expect to be thus treated again in the future. From all this, officers gather that though the people on skid-row seek to evade police authority, they do not really object to it. Indeed, it happens quite frequently that officers encounter men who welcome being arrested and even actively ask for it. Finally, officers point out that sending someone to jail from skid-row does not upset his relatives or his family life, does not cause him to miss work or lose a job, does not lead to his being reproached by friends and associates, does not lead to failure to meet commitments or protect investments, and does not conflict with any but the most passing intentions of the arrested person. Seasoned patrolmen are not oblivious to the irony of the fact that measures intended as mechanisms for distributing deserts can be used freely because these measures are relatively impotent in their effects.

SUMMARY AND CONCLUSIONS

It was the purpose of this paper to render an account of a domain of police practice that does not seem subject to any system of external control. Following the terminology suggested by Michael Banton, this practice was called keeping the peace. The procedures employed in keeping the peace are not determined by legal mandates but are, instead, responses to certain demand conditions. From among several demand conditions, we concentrated on the one produced by the concentration of certain types of persons in districts known as skid-row. Patrolmen maintain that the lives of the inhabitants of the area are lacking in prospective coherence. The consequent reduction in the temporal horizon of predictability constitutes the main problem of keeping the peace on skid-row.

Peace keeping procedure on skid-row consists of three elements. Patrolmen seek to acquire a rich body of concrete knowledge about people by cultivating personal acquaintance with as many residents as possible. They tend to proceed against persons mainly on the basis of perceived risk, rather than on the basis of culpability. And they are more interested in reducing the aggregate total of troubles in the area than in evaluating individual cases according to merit.

There may seem to be a discrepancy between the skid-row patrolman's objective of preventing disorder and his efforts to maintain personal acquaintance with as many persons as possible. But these efforts are principally a tactical device. By knowing someone individually the patrolman reduces ambiguity, extends trust and favors, but does not grant immunity. The informality of interaction on skid-row always contains some indications of the hierarchical superiority of the patrolman and the reality of his potential power lurks in the background of every encounter.

Though our interest was focused initially on those police procedures that did not involve invoking the law, we found that the two cannot be separated. The reason for the connection is not given in the circumstance that the roles of the "law officer" and of the "peace officer" are enacted by the same person and thus are contiguous. According to our observations, patrolmen do not act alternatively as one or the other, with certain actions being determined by the intended objective of keeping the peace and others being determined by the duty to enforce the law. Instead, we have found that *peace keeping occasionally acquires the external aspects of law enforcement.* This makes it specious to inquire whether or not police discretion in invoking the law conforms with the intention of some specific legal formula. The real reason behind an arrest is virtually always the actual state of particular social situations, or of the skid-row area in general.

We have concentrated on those procedures and considerations that skid-row patrolmen regard as necessary, proper, and efficient relative to the circumstances in which they are employed. In this way, we attempted to disclose the conception of the mandate to which the police feel summoned. It was entirely outside the scope of the presentation to review the merits of this conception and of the methods used to meet it. Only insofar as patrolmen themselves recognized instances and patterns of malpractice did we take note of them. Most of the criticism voiced by officers had to do with the use of undue harshness and with the indiscriminate use of arrest powers when these were based on personal feelings rather than the requirements of the situation. According to prevailing opinion, patrolmen guilty of such abuses make life unnecessarily difficult for themselves and for their co-workers. Despite disapproval of harshness, officers tend to be defensive about it. For example, one sergeant who was outspokenly critical of brutality, said that though in general brutal men create more problems than they solve, "they do a good job in some situations for which the better men have no stomach." Moreover, supervisory personnel exhibit a strong reluctance to direct their subordinates in the particulars of their work performance. According to our observations, control is exercised mainly through consultation with superiors, and directives take the form of requests rather than orders. In the background of all this is the belief that patrol work on skid-row requires a great deal of discretionary freedom. In the words of the same sergeant quoted above, "a good man has things worked out in his own ways on his beat and he doesn't need anybody to tell him what to do."

The virtual absence of disciplinary control and the demand for discretionary freedom are related to the idea that patrol work involves "playing by ear." For if it is true that peace keeping cannot be systematically generalized, then, of course, it cannot be organizationally constrained. What the seasoned patrolman means, however, in saying that he "plays by ear" is that he is making his decisions while being attuned to the realities of complex situations about which he has immensely detailed knowledge. This studied aspect of peace keeping generally is not made explicit, nor is the tyro or the outsider made aware of it. Quite to the contrary, the ability to discharge the duties associated with keeping the peace is viewed as a reflection of an innate talent of "getting along with people." Thus, the same demands are made of barely initiated officers as are made of experienced practitioners. Correspondingly, beginners tend to think that they can do as well as their more knowledgeable peers. As this leads to inevitable frustrations, they find themselves in a situation that is conducive to the development of a particular sense of "touchiness." Personal dispositions of individual officers are, of course, of great relevance. But the license of discretionary freedom and the expectation of success under conditions of autonomy, without any indication that the work of the successful craftsman is based on an acquired preparedness for the task, is ready-made for failure and malpractice. Moreover, it leads to slipshod practices of patrol that also infect the standards of the careful craftsman.

The uniformed patrol, and especially the foot patrol, has a low preferential value in the division of labor of police work. This is, in part, at least, due to the belief that "anyone could do it." In fact, this belief is thoroughly mistaken. At present, however, the recognition that the practice requires preparation, and the process of obtaining the preparation itself, is left entirely to the practitioner.

8. Violence and the Police [1]

William A. Westley

Brutality and the third degree have been identified with the municipal police of the United States since their inauguration in 1844. These aspects of police activity have been subject to exaggeration, repeated exposure, and virulent criticism. Since they are a breach of the law by the law-enforcement agents, they constitute a serious social, but intriguing sociological, problem. Yet there is little information about or understanding of the process through which such activity arises or of the purposes which it serves.

SOURCE: "Violence and the Police," *American Journal of Sociology*, vol. 59, pp. 34–41, July, 1953. By permission of the author and publisher.

[1] The writer is indebted to Joseph D. Lohman for his assistance in making contact with the police and for many excellent suggestions as to research procedure and insights into the organization of the police.

This paper presents part of a larger study of the police by the writer. For the complete study see William A. Westley, "The Police: A Sociological Study of Law, Custom, and Morality" (unpublished Ph.D. dissertation, University of Chicago, Department of Sociology, 1951).

This paper is concerned with the genesis and function of the illegal use of violence by the police and presents an explanation based on an interpretative understanding of the experience of the police as an occupational group.[2] It shows that (*a*) the police accept and morally justify their illegal use of violence; (*b*) such acceptance and justification arise through their occupational experience; and (*c*) its use is functionally related to the collective occupational, as well as to the legal, ends of the police.

The analysis which follows offers both an occupational perspective on the use of violence by the police and an explanation of policing as an occupation, from the perspective of the illegal use of violence. Thus the meaning of this use of violence is derived by relating it to the general behavior of policemen as policemen, and occupations in general are illuminated through the delineation of the manner in which a particular occupation handles one aspect of its work.

The technical demands of a man's work tend to specify the kinds of social relationships in which he will be involved and to select the groups with whom these relationships are to be maintained. The social definition of the occupation invests its members with a common prestige position. Thus, a man's occupation is a major determining factor of his conduct and social identity. This being so, it involves more than man's work, and one must go beyond the technical in the explanation of work behavior. One must discover the occupationally derived definitions of self and conduct which arise in the involvements of technical demands, social relationships between colleagues and with the public, status, and self-conception. To understand these definitions, one must track them back to the occupational problems in which they have their genesis.[3]

The policeman finds his most pressing problems in his relationships to the public. His is a service occupation but of an incongruous kind, since he must discipline those whom he serves. He is regarded as corrupt and inefficient by, and meets with hostility and criticism from, the public. He regards the public as his enemy, feels his occupation to be in conflict with the community, and regards himself to be a pariah. The experience and the feeling give rise to a collective emphasis on secrecy, an attempt to coerce respect from the public, and a belief that almost any means are legitimate in completing an important arrest. These are for the policeman basic occupational values. They arise from his experience, take precedence over his legal responsibilities, are central to an understanding of his conduct, and form the occupational contexts within which violence gains its meaning. This then is the background for our analysis.[4]

The materials which follow are drawn from a case study of a municipal police department in an industrial city of approximately one hundred and fifty thousand inhabitants. This study included participation in all types of police activities, ranging from walking the beat and cruising with policemen in a squad car to the observation of raids, interrogations, and the police school. It included intensive interviews with over half the men in the department who were representative as to rank, time in service, race, religion, and specific type of police job.

[2] Interpretative understanding is here used as defined by Max Weber (see *The Theory of Social and Economic Organization*, trans. Talcott Parsons [New York: Oxford University Press, 1947], p. 88).

[3] The ideas are not original. I am indebted for many of them to Everett C. Hughes, although he is in no way responsible for their present formulation (see E. C. Hughes, "Work and the Self" in Rohrer and Sherif, *Social Psychology at the Crossroads* [New York: Harper & Bros., 1951]).

[4] The background material will be developed in subsequent papers which will analyze the occupational experience of the police and give a full description of police norms.

DUTY AND VIOLENCE

In the United States the use of violence by the police is both an occupational pre-rogative and a necessity. Police powers include the use of violence, for to them, within civil society, has been delegated the monopoly of the legitimate means of violence possessed by the state. Police are obliged by their duties to use violence as the only measure adequate to control and apprehension in the presence of counter-violence.

Violence in the form of the club and the gun is for the police a means of persuasion. Violence from the criminal, the drunk, the quarreling family, and the rioter arises in the course of police duty. The fighting drunk who is damaging property or assailing his fellows and who looks upon the policeman as a malicious intruder justifies for the policeman his use of force in restoring order. The armed criminal who has demon-strated a casual regard for the lives of others and a general hatred of the policeman forces the use of violence by the police in the pursuit of duty. Every policeman has some such experiences, and they proliferate in police lore. They constitute a common-sense and legal justification for the use of violence by the police and for training policemen in the skills of violence. Thus from experience in the pursuit of their legally prescribed duties, the police develop a justification for the use of violence. They come to see it as good, as useful, and as their own. Furthermore, although legally their use of violence is limited to the requirements of the arrest and the protection of them-selves and the community, the contingencies of their occupation lead them to enlarge the area in which violence may be used. Two kinds of experience—that with respect to the conviction of the felon and that with respect to the control of sexual conduct —will illustrate how and why the illegal use of violence arises.

1. *The Conviction of the Felon.* The apprehension and conviction of the felon is, for the policeman, the essence of police work. It is the source of prestige both within and outside police circles, it has career implications, and it is a major source of justi-fication for the existence of the police before a critical and often hostile public. Out of these conditions a legitimation for the illegal use of violence is wrought.

The career and prestige implication of the "good pinch" [5] elevate it to a major end in the conduct of the policeman. It is an end which is justified both legally and through public opinion as one which should be of great concern to the police. There-fore it takes precedence over other duties and tends to justify strong means. Both trickery and violence are such means. The "third degree" has been criticized for many years, and extensive administrative controls have been devised in an effort to eliminate it. Police persistence in the face of that attitude suggests that the illegal use of vio-lence is regarded as functional to their work. It also indicates a tendency to regard the third degree as a legitimate means for obtaining the conviction of the felon. How-ever, to understand the strength of this legitimation, one must include other factors: the competition between patrolman and detective and the publicity value of con-victions for the police department.

The patrolman has less access to cases that might result in the "good pinch" than the detective. Such cases are assigned to the detective, and for their solution he will

---

[5] Policemen, in the case studied, use this term to mean an arrest which (*a*) is politically clear and (*b*) likely to bring them esteem. Generally it refers to felonies, but in the case of a "real" vice drive it may include the arrest and *conviction* of an important bookie.

reap the credit. Even where the patrolman first detects the crime, or actually apprehends the possible offender, the case is likely to be turned over to the detective. Therefore patrolmen are eager to obtain evidence and make the arrest before the arrival of the detectives. Intimidation and actual violence frequently come into play under these conditions. This is illustrated in the following case recounted by a young patrolman when he was questioned as to the situations in which he felt that the use of force was necessary:

> One time Joe and I found three guys in a car, and we found that they had a gun down between the seats. We wanted to find out who owned that gun before the dicks arrived so that we could make a good pinch. They told us.

Patrolmen feel that little credit is forthcoming from a clean beat (a crimeless beat), while a number of good arrests really stands out on the record. To a great extent this is actually the case, since a good arrest results in good newspaper publicity, and the policeman who has made many "good pinches" has prestige among his colleagues.

A further justification for the illegal use of violence arises from the fact that almost every police department is under continuous criticism from the community, which tends to assign its own moral responsibilities to the police. The police are therefore faced with the task of justifying themselves to the public, both as individuals and as a group. They feel that the solution of major criminal cases serves this function. This is illustrated in the following statement:

> There is a case I remember of four Negroes who held up a filling station. We got a description of them and picked them up. Then we took them down to the station and really worked them over. I guess that everybody that came into the station that night had a hand in it, and they were in pretty bad shape. Do you think that sounds cruel? Well, you know what we got out of it? We broke a big case in ————. There was a mob of twenty guys, burglars and stick-up men, and eighteen of them are in the pen now. Sometimes you have to get rough with them, see. The way I figure it is, if you can get a clue that a man is a pro and if he won't co-operate, tell you what you want to know, it is justified to rough him up a little, up to a point. You know how it is. You feel that the end justifies the means.

It is easier for the police to justify themselves to the community through the dramatic solution of big crimes than through orderly and responsible completion of their routine duties. Although they may be criticized for failures in routine areas, the criticism for the failure to solve big crimes is more intense and sets off a criticism of their work in noncriminal areas. The pressure to solve important cases therefore becomes strong. The following statement, made in reference to the use of violence in interrogations, demonstrates the point:

> If it's a big case and there is a lot of pressure on you and they tell you you can't go home until the case is finished, then naturally you are going to lose patience.

The policeman's response to this pressure is to extend the use of violence to its illegal utilization in interrogations. The apprehension of the felon or the "good pinch" thus constitutes a basis for justifying the illegal use of violence.

2. *Control of Sexual Conduct.* The police are responsible for the enforcement of laws regulating sexual conduct. This includes the suppression of sexual deviation and the protection of the public from advances and attacks of persons of deviant sexual tendencies. Here the police face a difficult task. The victims of such deviants are notoriously unwilling to cooperate, since popular curiosity and gossip about sexual crimes and the sanctions against the open discussion of sexual activities make it embarrassing for the victim to admit or describe a deviant sexual advance or attack and cause him to feel that he gains a kind of guilt by association from such admissions. Thus the police find that frequently the victims will refuse to identify or testify against the deviant.

These difficulties are intensified by the fact that, once the community becomes aware of sexual depredations, the reports of such activity multiply well beyond reasonable expectations. Since the bulk of these reports will be false, they add to the confusion of the police and consequently to the elusiveness of the offender.

The difficulties of the police are further aggravated by extreme public demand for the apprehension of the offender. The hysteria and alarm generated by reports of a peeping Tom, a rapist, or an exhibitionist result in great public pressure on the police; and, should the activities continue, the public becomes violently critical of police efficiency. The police, who feel insecure in their relationship to the public, are extremely sensitive to this criticism and feel that they must act in response to the demands made by the political and moral leaders of the community.

Thus the police find themselves caught in a dilemma. Apprehension is extremely difficult because of the confusion created by public hysteria and the scarcity of witnesses, but the police are compelled to action by extremely public demands. They dissolve this dilemma through the illegal utilization of violence.

A statement of this "misuse" of police powers is represented in the remarks of a patrolman:

> Now in my own case when I catch a guy like that I just pick him up and take him into the woods and beat him until he can't crawl. I have had seventeen cases like that in the last couple of years. I tell that guy that if I catch him doing that again I will take him out to those woods and I will shoot him. I tell him that I carry a second gun on me just in case I find guys like him and that I will plant it in his hand and say that he tried to kill and that no jury will convict me.

This statement is extreme and is not representative of policemen in general. In many instances the policeman is likely to act in a different fashion. This is illustrated in the following statement of a rookie who described what happened when he and his partner investigated a parked car which had aroused their suspicions:

> He [the partner] went up there and pretty soon he called me, and there were a couple of fellows in the car with their pants open. I couldn't understand it. I kept looking around for where the woman would be. They were both pretty plastered. One was a young kid about eighteen years old, and the other was an older man. We decided, with

> the kid so drunk, that bringing him in would only really ruin his reputation, and we told him to go home. Otherwise we would have pinched them. During the time we were talking to them they offered us twenty-eight dollars, and I was going to pinch them when they showed the money, but my partner said, "Never mind, let them go."

Nevertheless, most policemen would apply no sanctions against a colleague who took the more extreme view of the right to use violence and would openly support some milder form of illegal coercion. This is illustrated in the statement of another rookie:

> They feel that it's okay to rough a man up in the case of sex crimes. One of the older men advised me that if the courts didn't punish a man we should. He told me about a sex crime, the story about it, and then said that the law says the policeman has the right to use the amount of force necessary to make an arrest and that in that kind of a crime you can use just a little more force. They feel definitely, for example, in extreme cases like rape, that if a man was guilty he ought to be punished even if you could not get any evidence on him. My feeling is that all the men on the force feel that way, at least from what they have told me.

Furthermore, the police believe, and with some justification it seems, that the community supports their definition of the situation and that they are operating in terms of an implicit directive.

The point of this discussion is that the control of sexual conduct is so difficult and the demand for it so incessant that the police come to sanction the illegal use of violence in obtaining that control. This does not imply that all policemen treat all sex deviants brutally, for, as the above quotations indicate, such is not the case. Rather, it indicates that this use of violence is permitted and condoned by the police and that they come to think of it as a resource more extensive than is included in the legal definition.

LEGITIMATION OF VIOLENCE

The preceding discussion has indicated two ways in which the experience of the police encourages them to use violence as a general resource in the achievement of their occupational ends and thus to sanction its illegal use. The experience, thus, makes violence acceptable to the policeman as a generalized means. We now wish to indicate the particular basis on which this general resource is legitimated. In particular we wish to point out the extent to which the policeman tends to transfer violence from a legal resource to a personal resource, one which he uses to further his own ends.

Seventy-three policemen, drawn from all ranks and constituting approximately 50 per cent of the patrolmen, were asked, "When do you think a policeman is justified in roughing a man up?" The intent of the question was to get them to legitimate the use of violence. Their replies are summarized in Table 8-1.

An inspection of the types and distribution of the responses indicates (1) that violence is legitimated by illegal ends (A, C, E, F, G) in 69 per cent of the cases;

TABLE 8-1 *

Bases for the Use of Force Named by 73 Policemen

Type of Response	Frequency	Percentage
(A) Disrespect for police	27	37
(B) When impossible to avoid	17	23
(C) To obtain information	14	19
(D) To make an arrest	6	8
(E) For the hardened criminal	5	7
(F) When you know man is guilty	2	3
(G) For sex criminals	2	3
TOTAL	73	100

* Many respondents described more than one type of situation which they felt called for the use of violence. The "reason" which was either (a) given most heatedly and at greatest length and/or (b) given first was used to characterize the respondent's answer to the question. However, this table is exhaustive of the types of replies which were given.

(2) that violence is legitimated in terms of purely personal or group ends (A) in 37 per cent of the cases (this is important, since it is the largest single reason for the use of violence given); and (3) that legal ends are the bases for legitimation in 31 per cent of the cases (B and D). However, this probably represents a distortion of the true feelings of some of these men, since both the police chief and the community had been severely critical of the use of violence by the men and the respondents had a tendency to be very cautious with the interviewer, whom some of them never fully trusted. Furthermore, since all the men were conscious of the chief's policy and of public criticism, it seems likely that those who did justify the use of violence for illegal and personal ends no longer recognized the illegality involved. They probably believed that such ends fully represented a moral legitimation for their use of violence.

The most significant finding is that at least 37 per cent of the men believed that it was legitimate to use violence to coerce respect. This suggests that policemen use the resource of violence to persuade their audience (the public) to respect their occupational status. In terms of the policeman's definition of the situation, the individual who lacks respect for the police, the "wise guy" who talks back, or any individual who acts or talks in a disrespectful way, deserves brutality. This idea is epitomized in admonitions given to the rookies such as, "You gotta make them respect you" and "You gotta act tough." Examples of some of the responses to the preceding question that fall into the "disrespect for the police" category follow:

> Well, there are cases. For example, when you stop a fellow for a routine questioning, say a wise guy, and he starts talking back to you and telling you you are no good and that sort of thing. You know you can take a man in on a disorderly conduct charge, but you can practically never make it stick. So what you do in a case like that is to egg the guy on until he makes a remark where you can justifiably slap him and, then, if he fights back, you can call it resisting arrest.
>
> Well, it varies in different cases. Most of the police use punishment if the fellow gives them any trouble. Usually you can judge a man who

will give you trouble though. *If there is any slight resistance,* you can go all out on him. You shouldn't do it in the street though. Wait until you are in the squad car, because, even if you are in the right and a guy takes a poke at you, just when you are hitting back somebody's just likely to come around the corner, and what he will say is that you are beating the guy with your club.

Well, a prisoner deserves to be hit when he goes to the point where he tries to put you below him.

You gotta get rough when a man's language becomes very bad, when he is trying to make a fool of you in front of everybody else. I think most policemen try to treat people in a nice way, but usually you have to talk pretty rough. That's the only way to set a man down, to make him show a little respect.

If a fellow called a policeman a filthy name, a slap in the mouth would be a good thing, especially if it was out in the public where calling a policeman a bad name would look bad for the police.

There was the incident of a fellow I picked up. I was on the beat, and I was taking him down to the station. There were people following us. He kept saying that I wasn't in the army. Well, he kept going on like that, and I finally had to bust him one. I had to do it. The people would have thought I was afraid otherwise.

These results suggest (1) that the police believe that these private or group ends constitute a moral legitimation for violence which is equal *or superior* to the legitimation derived from the law and (2) that the monopoly of violence delegated to the police, by the state, to enforce the ends of the state has been appropriated by the police as a personal resource to be used for personal and group ends.

THE USE OF VIOLENCE

The sanctions for the use of violence arising from occupational experience and the fact that policemen morally justify even its illegal use may suggest that violence is employed with great frequency and little provocation. Such an impression would be erroneous, for the actual use of violence is limited by other considerations, such as individual inclinations, the threat of detection, and a sensitivity to public reactions.

Individual policemen vary of course in psychological disposition and past experience. All have been drawn from the larger community which tends to condemn the use of violence and therefore have internalized with varying degrees of intensity this other definition of violence. Their experience as policemen creates a new dimension to their self-conceptions and gives them a new perspective on the use of violence. But individual men vary in the degree to which they assimilate this new conception of self. Therefore, the amount of violence which is used and the frequency with which it is employed will vary among policemen according to their individual propensities. However, policemen cannot and do not employ sanctions against their colleagues for using violence,[6] and individual men who personally condemn the use of violence

---

[6] The emphasis on secrecy among the police prevents them from using legal sanctions against their colleagues.

and avoid it whenever possible [7] refuse openly to condemn acts of violence by other men on the force. Thus, the collective sanction for the use of violence permits those men who are inclined to its use to employ it without fear.

All policemen, however, are conscious of the dangers of the illegal use of violence. If detected, they may be subject to a lawsuit and possibly dismissal from the force. Therefore, they limit its use to what they think they can get away with. Thus, they recognize that, if a man is guilty of a serious crime, it is easy to "cover up" for their brutality by accusing him of resisting arrest, and the extent to which they believe a man guilty tends to act as a precondition to the use of violence.[8]

The policeman, in common with members of other occupations, is sensitive to the evaluation of his occupation by the public. A man's work is an important aspect of his status, and to the extent that he is identified with his work (by himself and/or the community) he finds that his self-esteem requires the justification and social elevation of his work. Since policemen are low in the occupational prestige scale, subject to continuous criticism, and in constant contact with this criticizing and evaluating public, they are profoundly involved in justifying their work and its tactics to the public and to themselves. The way in which the police emphasize the solution of big crimes and their violent solution to the problem of the control of sexual conduct illustrate this concern. However, different portions of the public have differing definitions of conduct and are of differential importance to the policeman, and the way in which the police define different portions of the public has an effect on whether or not they will use violence.

The police believe that certain groups of persons will respond only to fear and rough treatment. In the city studied they defined both Negroes and slum dwellers in this category. The following statements, each by a different man, typify the manner in which they discriminate the public:

> In the good districts you appeal to people's judgment and explain the law to them. In the South Side the only way is to appear like you are the boss.
>
> You can't ask them a question and get an answer that is not a lie. In the South Side the only way to walk into a tavern is to walk in swaggering as if you own the place and if somebody is standing in your way give him an elbow and push him aside.
>
> The colored people understand one thing. The policeman is the law, and he is going to treat you rough and that's the way you have to treat them. Personally, I don't think the colored are trying to help themselves one bit. If you don't treat them rough, they will sit right on top of your head.

Discriminations with respect to the public are largely based on the political power of the group, the degree to which the police believe that the group is potentially criminal, and the type of treatment which the police believe will elicit respect from it.

Variations in the administration and community setting of the police will introduce variations in their use of violence. Thus, a thoroughly corrupt police department will

---

[7] Many men who held jobs in the police station rather than on beats indicated to the interviewer that their reason for choosing a desk job was to avoid the use of violence.

[8] In addition, the policeman is aware that the courts are highly critical of confessions obtained by violence and that, if violence is detected, it will "spoil his case."

use violence in supporting the ends of this corruption, while a carefully administrated nonpolitical department can go a long way toward reducing the illegal use of violence. However, wherever the basic conditions here described are present, it will be very difficult to eradicate the illegal use of violence.

Given these conditions, violence will be used when necessary to the pursuit of duty or when basic occupational values are threatened. Thus a threat to the respect with which the policeman believes his occupation should be regarded or the opportunity to make a "good pinch" will tend to evoke its use.

CONCLUSIONS

This paper sets forth an explanation of the illegal use of violence by the police based on an interpretative understanding of their occupational experience. Therefore, it contains a description and analysis of *their* interpretation of *their* experience.

The policeman uses violence illegally because such usage is seen as just, acceptable, and, at times, expected by his colleague group and because it constitutes an effective means for solving problems in obtaining status and self-esteem which policemen as policemen have in common. Since the ends for which violence is illegally used are conceived to be both just and important, they function to justify, to the policeman, the illegal use of violence as a general means. Since "brutality" is strongly criticized by the larger community, the policeman must devise a defense of his brutality to himself and the community, and the defense in turn gives a deeper and more lasting justification to the "misuse of violence." This process then results in a transfer in property from the state to the colleague group. The means of violence which were originally a property of the state, in loan to its law-enforcement agent, the police, are in a psychological sense confiscated by the police, to be conceived of as a personal property to be used at their discretion. This, then, is the explanation of the illegal use of violence by the police which results from viewing it in terms of the police as an occupational group.

The explanation of the illegal use of violence by the police offers an illuminating perspective on the social nature of their occupation. The analysis of their use of brutality in dealing with sexual deviants and felons shows that it is a result of their desire to defend and improve their social status in the absence of effective legal means. This desire in turn is directly related to and makes sense in terms of the low status of the police in the community, which results in a driving need on the part of policemen to assert and improve their status. Their general legitimation of the use of violence *primarily* in terms of coercing respect and making a "good pinch" clearly points out the existence of occupational goals, which are independent of and take precedence over their legal mandate. The existence of such goals and patterns of conduct indicates that the policeman has made of his occupation a preoccupation and invested in it a large aspect of his self.

9. Police Encounters with Juveniles

Irving Piliavin and Scott Briar

As the first of a series of decisions made in the channeling of youthful offenders through the agencies concerned with juvenile justice and corrections, the disposition decisions made by police officers have potentially profound consequences for apprehended juveniles.[1] Thus arrest, the most severe of the dispositions available to police, may not only lead to confinement of the suspected offender but also bring him loss of social status, restriction of educational and employment opportunities, and future harassment by law-enforcement personnel.[2] According to some criminologists, the stigmatization resulting from police apprehension, arrest, and detention actually reinforces deviant behavior.[3] Other authorities have suggested, in fact, that this stigmatization serves as the catalytic agent initiating delinquent careers.[4] Despite their presumed significance, however, little empirical analysis has been reported regarding the factors influencing, or consequences resulting from, police actions with juvenile offenders. Furthermore, while some studies of police encounters with adult offenders have been reported, the extent to which the findings of these investigations pertain to law-enforcement practices with youthful offenders is not known.[5]

The above considerations have led the writers to undertake a longitudinal study of the conditions influencing, and consequences flowing from, police actions with juveniles. In the present paper findings will be presented indicating the influence of certain factors on police actions. Research data consist primarily of notes and records based on nine months' observation of all juvenile officers in one police department.[6] The officers were observed in the course of their regular tours of duty.[7] While these

SOURCE: "Police Encounters with Juveniles," *American Journal of Sociology*, vol. 70, pp. 206–214, September, 1964. By permission of the author and publisher.

[1] This study was supported by Grant MH-06328-02, National Institute of Mental Health, United States Public Health Service.

[2] Richard D. Schwartz and Jerome H. Skolnick, "Two Studies of Legal Stigma," *Social Problems*, X (April, 1962), 133–42; Sol Rubin, *Crime and Juvenile Delinquency* (New York: Oceana Publications, 1958); B. F. McSally, "Finding Jobs for Released Offenders," *Federal Probation*, XXIV (June, 1960), 12–17; Harold D. Lasswell and Richard C. Donnelly, "The Continuing Debate over Responsibility: An Introduction to Isolating the Condemnation Sanction," *Yale Law Journal*, LXVIII (April, 1959), 869–99.

[3] Richard A. Cloward and Lloyd E. Ohlin, *Delinquency and Opportunity* (Glencoe, Ill.: Free Press, 1960), pp. 124–30.

[4] Frank Tannenbaum, *Crime and the Community* (New York: Columbia University Press, 1936), pp. 17–20; Howard S. Becker, *Outsiders: Studies in the Sociology of Deviance* (New York: Free Press of Glencoe, 1963), chaps. i and ii.

[5] For a detailed accounting of police discretionary practices, see Joseph Goldstein, "Police Discretion Not to Invoke the Criminal Process: Low-visibility Decisions in the Administration of Justice," *Yale Law Journal*, LXIX (1960), 543–94; Wayne R. LaFave, "The Police and Non-enforcement of the Law—Part I," *Wisconsin Law Review*, January, 1962, pp. 104–37; S. H. Kadish, "Legal Norms and Discretion in the Police and Sentencing Processes," *Harvard Law Review*, LXXV (March, 1962), 904–31.

[6] Approximately thirty officers were assigned to the Juvenile Bureau in the department studied. While we had an opportunity to observe all officers in the Bureau during the study, our observations were concentrated on those who had been working in the Bureau for one or two years at least. Although two of the officers in the Juvenile Bureau were Negro, we observed these officers on only a few occasions.

[7] Although observations were not confined to specific days or work shifts, more observations were made during evenings and weekends because police activity was greatest during these periods.

data do not lend themselves to quantitative assessments of reliability and validity, the candor shown by the officers in their interviews with the investigators and their use of officially frowned-upon practices while under observation provide some assurance that the materials presented below accurately reflect the typical operations and attitudes of the law-enforcement personnel studied.

The setting for the research, a metropolitan police department serving an industrial city with approximately 450,000 inhabitants, was noted within the community it served and among law-enforcement officials elsewhere for the honesty and superior quality of its personnel. Incidents involving criminal activity or brutality by members of the department had been extremely rare during the ten years preceding this study; personnel standards were comparatively high; and an extensive training program was provided to both new and experienced personnel. Juvenile Bureau members, the primary subjects of this investigation, differed somewhat from other members of the department in that they were responsible for delinquency prevention as well as law enforcement, that is, juvenile officers were expected to be knowledgeable about conditions leading to crime and delinquency and to be able to work with community agencies serving known or potential juvenile offenders. Accordingly, in the assignment of personnel to the Juvenile Bureau, consideration was given not only to an officer's devotion to and reliability in law enforcement but also to his commitment to delinquency prevention. Aessignment to the Bureau was of advantage to policemen seeking promotions. Consequently, many officers requested transfer to this unit, and its personnel comprised a highly select group of officers.

In the field, juvenile officers operated essentially as patrol officers. They cruised assigned beats and, although concerned primarily with juvenile offenders, frequently had occasion to apprehend and arrest adults. Confrontations between the officers and juveniles occurred in one of the following three ways, in order of increasing frequency: (1) encounters resulting from officers' spotting officially "wanted" youths; (2) encounters taking place at or near the scene of offenses reported to police headquarters; and (3) encounters occurring as the result of officers' directly observing youths either committing offenses or in "suspicious circumstances." However, the probability that a confrontation would take place between officer and juvenile, or that a particular disposition of an identified offender would be made, was only in part determined by the knowledge that an offense had occurred or that a particular juvenile had committed an offense. The bases for and utilization of non-offense related criteria by police in accosting and disposing of juveniles are the focuses of the following discussion.

SANCTIONS FOR DISCRETION

In each encounter with juveniles, with the minor exception of officially "wanted" youths,[8] a central task confronting the officer was to decide what official action to take against the boys involved. In making these disposition decisions, officers could select any one of five discrete alternatives:

1. Outright release
2. Release and submission of a "field interrogation report" briefly de-

8 "Wanted" juveniles usually were placed under arrest or in protective custody, a practice which in effect relieved officers of the responsibility for deciding what to do with these youths.

scribing the circumstances initiating the police-juvenile confrontation

3. "Official reprimand" and release to parents or guardian

4. Citation to juvenile court

5. Arrest and confinement in juvenile hall

Dispositions 3, 4, and 5 differed from the others in two basic respects. First, with rare exceptions, when an officer chose to reprimand, cite, or arrest a boy, he took the youth to the police station. Second, the reprimanded, cited, or arrested boy acquired an official police "record," that is, his name was officially recorded in Bureau files as a juvenile violator.

Analysis of the distribution of police disposition decisions about juveniles revealed that in virtually every category of offense the full range of official disposition alternatives available to officers was employed. This wide range of discretion resulted primarily from two conditions. First, it reflected the reluctance of officers to expose certain youths to the stigmatization presumed to be associated with official police action. Few juvenile officers believed that correctional agencies serving the community could effectively help delinquents. For some officers this attitude reflected a lack of confidence in rehabilitation techniques; for others, a belief that high case loads and lack of professional training among correctional workers vitiated their efforts at treatment. All officers were agreed, however, that juvenile justice and correctional processes were essentially concerned with apprehension and punishment rather than treatment. Furthermore, all officers believed that some aspects of these processes (e.g., judicial definition of youths as delinquents and removal of delinquents from the community), as well as some of the possible consequences of these processes (e.g., intimate institutional contact with "hard-core" delinquents, as well as parental, school, and conventional peer disapproval or rejection), could reinforce what previously might have been only a tentative proclivity toward delinquent values and behavior. Consequently, when officers found reason to doubt that a youth being confronted was highly committed toward deviance, they were inclined to treat him with leniency.

Second, and more important, the practice of discretion was sanctioned by police-department policy. Training manuals and departmental bulletins stressed that the disposition of each juvenile offender was not to be based solely on the type of infraction he committed. Thus, while it was departmental policy to "arrest and confine all juveniles who have committed a felony or misdemeanor involving theft, sex offense, battery, possession of dangerous weapons, prowling, peeping, intoxication, incorrigibility, and disturbance of the peace," it was acknowledged that "such considerations as age, attitude and prior criminal record might indicate that a different disposition would be more appropriate." [9] The official justification for discretion in processing juvenile offenders, based on the preventive aims of the Juvenile Bureau, was that each juvenile violator should be dealt with solely on the basis of what was best for him.[10] Unofficially, administrative legitimation of discretion was further justified on the grounds that strict enforcement practices would overcrowd court calendars and detention facilities, as well as dramatically increase juvenile crime rates—conse-

---

[9] Quoted from a training manual issued by the police department studied in this research.

[10] Presumably this also implied that police action with juveniles was to be determined partly by the offenders' need for correctional services.

quences to be avoided because they would expose the police department to community criticism.[11]

In practice, the official policy justifying use of discretion served as a demand that discretion be exercised. As such, it posed three problems for juvenile officers. First, it represented a departure from the traditional police practice with which the juvenile officers themselves were identified, in the sense that they were expected to justify their juvenile disposition decisions not simply by evidence proving a youth had committed a crime—grounds on which police were officially expected to base their dispositions of non-juvenile offenders [12]—but in the *character* of the youth. Second, in disposing of juvenile offenders, officers were expected, in effect, to make judicial rather than ministerial decisions.[13] Third, the shift from the offense to the offender as the basis for determining the appropriate disposition substantially increased the uncertainty and ambiguity for officers in the situation of apprehension because no explicit rules existed for determining which disposition different types of youths should receive. Despite these problems, officers were constrained to base disposition decisions on the character of the apprehended youth, not only because they wanted to be fair, but because persistent failure to do so could result in judicial criticism, departmental censure, and, they believed, loss of authority with juveniles.[14]

DISPOSITION CRITERIA

Assessing the character of apprehended offenders posed relatively few difficulties for officers in the case of youths who had committed serious crimes such as robbery, homicide, aggravated assault, grand theft, auto theft, rape, and arson. Officials generally regarded these juveniles as confirmed delinquents simply by virtue of their involvement in offenses of this magnitude.[15] However, the infraction committed did not always suffice to determine the appropriate disposition for some serious offenders; [16] and, in the case of minor offenders, who comprised over 90 per cent of the youths against whom police took action, the violation per se generally played an insignificant role in the choice of disposition. While a number of minor offenders were seen as serious delinquents deserving arrest, many others were perceived either as "good" boys whose offenses were atypical of their customary behavior, as pawns of undesirable associates or, in any case, as boys for whom arrest was regarded as an unwarranted and possibly harmful punishment. Thus, for nearly all minor violators and for some serious delinquents, the assessment of character—the distinction between serious delinquents, "good" boys, misguided youths, and so on—and the

[11] This was reported by beat officers as well as supervisory and administrative personnel of the juvenile bureau.

[12] In actual practice, of course, disposition decisions regarding adult offenders also were influenced by many factors extraneous to the offense per se.

[13] For example, in dealing with adult violators, officers had no disposition alternative comparable to the reprimand-and-release category, a disposition which contained elements of punishment but did not involve mediation by the court.

[14] The concern of officers over possible loss of authority stemmed from their belief that court failure to support arrests by appropriate action would cause policemen to "lose face" in the eyes of juveniles.

[15] It is also likely that the possibility of negative publicity resulting from the failure to arrest such violators —particularly if they became involved in further serious crime—brought about strong administrative pressure for their arrest.

[16] For example, in the year preceding this research, over 30 per cent of the juveniles involved in burglaries and 12 per cent of the juveniles committing auto theft received dispositions other than arrest.

dispositions which followed from these assessments were based on the youths' personal characteristics and not their offenses.

Despite this dependence of disposition decisions on the personal characteristics of these youths, however, police officers actually had access only to very limited information about boys at the time they had to decide what to do with them. In the field, officers typically had no data concerning the past offense records, school performance, family situation, or personal adjustment of apprehended youths.[17] Furthermore, files at police headquarters provided data only about each boy's prior offense record. Thus both the decision made in the field—whether or not to bring the boy in—and the decision made at the station—which disposition to invoke—were based largely on cues which emerged from the interaction between the officer and the youth, cues from which the officer inferred the youth's character. These cues included the youth's group affiliations, age, race, grooming, dress, and demeanor. Older juveniles, members of known delinquent gangs, Negroes, youths with well-oiled hair, black jackets, and soiled denims or jeans (the presumed uniform of "tough" boys), and boys who in their interactions with officers did not manifest what were considered to be appropriate signs of respect tended to receive the more severe dispositions. Other than prior record, the most important of the above cues was a youth's *demeanor*. In the opinion of juvenile patrolmen themselves the demeanor of apprehended juveniles was a major determinant of their decisions for 50–60 per cent of the juvenile cases they processed.[18] A less subjective indication of the association between a youth's demeanor and police disposition is provided by Table 9-1, which presents the police

TABLE 9-1

Severity of Police Disposition by Youth's Demeanor

Severity of Police Disposition	Youth's Demeanor		Total
	Co-operative	Unco-operative	
Arrest (most severe)	2	14	16
Citation or official reprimand	4	5	9
Informal reprimand	15	1	16
Admonish and release (least severe)	24	1	25
TOTAL	45	21	66

dispositions for sixty-six youths whose encounters with police were observed in the course of this study.[19] For purposes of this analysis, each youth's demeanor in the

[17] On occasion, officers apprehended youths whom they personally knew to be prior offenders. This did not occur frequently, however, for several reasons. First, approximately 75 per cent of apprehended youths had no prior official records; second, officers periodically exchanged patrol areas, thus limiting their exposure to, and knowledge about, these areas; and third, patrolmen seldom spent more than three or four years in the juvenile division.

[18] While reliable subgroup estimates were impossible to obtain through observation because of the relatively small number of incidents observed, the importance of demeanor in disposition decisions appeared to be much less significant with known prior offenders.

[19] Systematic data were collected on police encounters with seventy-six juveniles. In ten of these encounters the police concluded that their suspicions were groundless, and consequently the juveniles involved were exonerated; these ten cases were eliminated from this analysis of demeanor. (The total number of encounters observed was considerably more than seventy-six, but systematic data-collection procedures were not instituted until several months after observations began.)

encounter was classified as either co-operative or unco-operative.[20] The results clearly reveal a marked association between youth demeanor and the severity of police dispositions.

The cues used by police to assess demeanor were fairly simple. Juveniles who were contrite about their infractions, respectful to officers, and fearful of the sanctions that might be employed against them tended to be viewed by patrolmen as basically law-abiding or at least "salvageable." For these youths it was usually assumed that informal or formal reprimand would suffice to guarantee their future conformity. In contrast, youthful offenders who were fractious, obdurate, or who appeared nonchalant in their encounters with patrolmen were likely to be viewed as "would-be tough guys" or "punks" who fully deserved the most severe sanction: arrest. The following excerpts from observation notes illustrate the importance attached to demeanor by police in making disposition decisions.

> 1. The interrogation of "A" (an 18-year-old upper-lower-class white male accused of statutory rape) was assigned to a police sergeant with long experience on the force. As I sat in his office while we waited for the youth to arrive for questioning, the sergeant expressed his uncertainty as to what he should do with this young man. On the one hand, he could not ignore the fact that an offense had been committed; he had been informed, in fact, that the youth was prepared to confess to the offense. Nor could he overlook the continued pressure from the girl's father (an important political figure) for the police to take severe action against the youth. On the other hand, the sergeant had formed a low opinion of the girl's moral character, and he considered it unfair to charge "A" with statutory rape when the girl was a willing partner to the offense and might even have been the instigator of it. However, his sense of injustice concerning "A" was tempered by his image of the youth as a "punk," based, he explained, on information he had received that the youth belonged to a certain gang, the members of which were well known to, and disliked by, the police. Nevertheless, as we prepared to leave his office to interview "A," the sergeant was still in doubt as to what he should do with him.
>
> As we walked down the corridor to the interrogation room, the sergeant was stopped by a reporter from the local newspaper. In an excited tone of voice, the reporter explained that his editor was pressing him to get further information about this case. The newspaper had printed some of the facts about the girl's disappearance, and as a consequence the girl's father was threatening suit against the paper for defamation of the girl's character. It would strengthen the newspaper's position, the reporter explained, if the police had information indicating that the girl's associates, particularly the youth the sergeant was about to interrogate, were persons of disreputable character. This stimulus seemed to resolve the sergeant's uncertainty. He told the

[20] The data used for the classification of demeanor were the written records of observations made by the authors. The classifications were made by an independent judge not associated with this study. In classifying a youth's demeanor as co-operative or unco-operative, particular attention was paid to: (1) the youth's responses to police officers' questions and requests; (2) the respect and deference—or lack of these qualities —shown by the youth toward police officers; and (3) police officers' assessments of the youth's demeanor.

reporter, "unofficially," that the youth was known to be an undesirable person, citing as evidence his membership in the delinquent gang. Furthermore, the sergeant added that he had evidence that this youth had been intimate with the girl over a period of many months. When the reporter asked if the police were planning to do anything to the youth, the sergeant answered that he intended to charge the youth with statutory rape.

In the interrogation, however, three points quickly emerged which profoundly affected the sergeant's judgment of the youth. First, the youth was polite and co-operative; he consistently addressed the officer as "sir," answered all questions quietly, and signed a statement implicating himself in numerous counts of statutory rape. Second, the youth's intentions toward the girl appeared to have been honorable; for example, he said that he wanted to marry her eventually. Third, the youth was not in fact a member of the gang in question. The sergeant's attitude became increasingly sympathetic, and after we left the interrogation room he announced his intention to "get 'A' off the hook," meaning that he wanted to have the charges against "A" reduced or, if possible, dropped.

2. Officers "X" and "Y" brought into the police station a seventeen-year-old white boy who, along with two older companions, had been found in a home having sex relations with a fifteen-year-old girl. The boy responded to police officers' queries slowly and with obvious disregard. It was apparent that his lack of deference toward the officers and his failure to evidence concern about his situation were irritating his questioners. Finally, one of the officers turned to me and, obviously angry, commented that in his view the boy was simply a "stud" interested only in sex, eating, and sleeping. The policemen conjectured that the boy "probably already had knocked up half a dozen girls." The boy ignored these remarks, except for an occasional impassive stare at the patrolmen. Turning to the boy, the officer remarked, "What the hell am I going to do with you?" And again the boy simply returned the officer's gaze. The latter then said, "Well, I guess we'll just have to put you away for a while." An arrest report was then made out and the boy was taken to Juvenile Hall.

Although anger and disgust frequently characterized officers' attitudes toward recalcitrant and impassive juvenile offenders, their manner while processing these youths was typically routine, restrained, and without rancor. While the officers' restraint may have been due in part to their desire to avoid accusation and censure, it also seemed to reflect their inurement to a frequent experience. By and large, only their occasional "needling" or insulting of a boy gave any hint of the underlying resentment and dislike they felt toward many of these youths.[21]

[21] Officers' animosity toward recalcitrant or aloof offenders appeared to stem from two sources: moral indignation that these juveniles were self-righteous and indifferent about their transgressions, and resentment that these youths failed to accord police the respect they believed they deserved. Since the patrolmen perceived themselves as honestly and impartially performing a vital community function, warranting respect and deference from the community at large, they attributed the lack of respect shown them by these juveniles to the latter's immorality.

PREJUDICE IN APPREHENSION AND
DISPOSITION DECISIONS

Compared to other youths, Negroes and boys whose appearance matched the delinquent stereotype were more frequently stopped and interrogated by patrolmen —often even in the absence of evidence that an offense had been committed [22]—and usually were given more severe dispositions for the same violations. Our data suggest, however, that these selective apprehension and disposition practices resulted not only from the intrusion of long-held prejudices of individual police officers but also from certain job-related experiences of law-enforcement personnel. First, the tendency for police to give more severe dispositions to Negroes and to youths whose appearance corresponded to that which police associated with delinquents partly reflected the fact, observed in this study, that these youths also were much more likely than were other types of boys to exhibit the sort of recalcitrant demeanor which police construed as a sign of the confirmed delinquent. Further, officers assumed, partly on the basis of departmental statistics, that Negroes and juveniles who "look tough" (e.g., who wear chinos, leather jackets, boots, etc.) commit crimes more frequently than do other types of youths.[23] In this sense, the police justified their selective treatment of these youths along epidemiological lines: that is, they were concentrating their attention on those youths whom they believed were most likely to commit delinquent acts. In the words of one highly placed official in the department:

> If you know that the bulk of your delinquent problem comes from kids who, say, are from 12 to 14 years of age, when you're out on patrol you are much more likely to be sensitive to the activities of juveniles in this age bracket than older or younger groups. This would be good law enforcement practice. The logic in our case is the same except that our delinquency problem is largely found in the Negro community and it is these youths toward whom we are sensitized.

As regards prejudice per se, eighteen of twenty-seven officers interviewed openly admitted a dislike for Negroes. However, they attributed their dislike to experiences they had, as policemen, with youths from this minority group. The officers reported that Negro boys were much more likely than non-Negroes to "give us a hard time," be unco-operative, and show no remorse for their transgressions. Recurrent exposure to such attitudes among Negro youth, the officers claimed, generated their antipathy

22 The clearest evidence for this assertion is provided by the over-representation of Negroes among "innocent" juveniles accosted by the police. As noted, of the seventy-six juveniles on whom systematic data were collected, ten were exonerated and released without suspicion. Seven, or two-thirds of these ten "innocent" juveniles were Negro, in contrast to the allegedly "guilty" youths, less than one-third of whom were Negro. The following incident illustrates the operation of this bias: One officer, observing a youth walking along the street, commented that the youth "looks suspicious" and promptly stopped and questioned him. Asked later to explain what aroused his suspicion, the officer explained, "He was a Negro wearing dark glasses at midnight."

23 While police statistics did not permit an analysis of crime rates by appearance, they strongly supported officers' contentions concerning the delinquency rate among Negroes. Of all male juveniles processed by the police department in 1961, for example, 40.2 per cent were Negro and 33.9 per cent were white. These two groups comprised at that time, respectively, about 22.7 per cent and 73.6 per cent of the population in the community studied.

toward Negroes. The following excerpt is typical of the views expressed by these officers:

> They (Negroes) have no regard for the law or for the police. They just don't seem to give a damn. Few of them are interested in school or getting ahead. The girls start having illegitimate kids before they are 16 years old and the boys are always "out for kicks." Furthermore, many of these kids try to run you down. They say the damnedest things to you and they seem to have absolutely no respect for you as an adult. I admit I am prejudiced now, but frankly I don't think I was when I began police work.

IMPLICATIONS

It is apparent from the findings presented above that the police officers studied in this research were permitted and even encouraged to exercise immense latitude in disposing of the juveniles they encountered. That is, it was within the officer's discretionary authority, except in extreme limiting cases, to decide which juveniles were to come to the attention of the courts and correctional agencies and thereby be identified officially as delinquents. In exercising this discretion policemen were strongly guided by the demeanor of those who were apprehended, a practice which ultimately led, as seen above, to certain youths' (particularly Negroes [24] and boys dressed in the style of "toughs") being treated more severely than other juveniles for comparable offenses.

But the relevance of demeanor was not limited only to police disposition practices. Thus, for example, in conjunction with police crime statistics the criterion of demeanor led police to concentrate their surveillance activities in areas frequented or inhabited by Negroes. Furthermore, these youths were accosted more often than others by officers on patrol simply because their skin color identified them as potential troublemakers. These discriminatory practices—and it is important to note that they are discriminatory, even if based on accurate statistical information—may well have self-fulfilling consequences. Thus it is not unlikely that frequent encounters with police, particularly those involving youths innocent of wrongdoing, will increase the hostility of these juveniles toward law-enforcement personnel. It is also not unlikely that the frequency of such encounters will in time reduce their significance in the eyes of apprehended juveniles, thereby leading these youths to regard them as "routine." Such responses to police encounters, however, are those which law-enforcement personnel perceive as indicators of the serious delinquent. They thus serve to vindicate and reinforce officers' prejudices, leading to closer surveillance of Negro districts, more frequent encounters with Negro youths, and so on in a vicious circle. Moreover, the consequences of this chain of events are reflected in police statistics showing a disproportionately high percentage of Negroes among juvenile offenders, thereby providing "objective" justification for concentrating police attention on Negro youths.

To a substantial extent, as we have implied earlier, the discretion practiced by juvenile officers is simply an extension of the juvenile-court philosophy, which holds

---

[24] An unco-operative demeanor was presented by more than one-third of the Negro youths but by only one-sixth of the white youths encountered by the police in the course of our observations.

that in making legal decisions regarding juveniles, more weight should be given to the juvenile's character and life-situation than to his actual offending behavior. The juvenile officer's disposition decisions—and the information he uses as a basis for them—are more akin to the discriminations made by probation officers and other correctional workers than they are to decisions of police officers dealing with non-juvenile offenders. The problem is that such clinical-type decisions are not restrained by mechanisms comparable to the principles of due process and the rules of procedure governing police decisions regarding adult offenders. Consequently, prejudicial practices by police officers can escape notice more easily in their dealings with juveniles than with adults.

The observations made in this study serve to underscore the fact that the official delinquent, as distinguished from the juvenile who simply commits a delinquent act, is the product of a social judgment, in this case a judgment made by the police. He is a delinquent because someone in authority has defined him as one, often on the basis of the public face he has presented to officials rather than of the kind of offense he has committed.

10. Shoplifters Who Become "Data"

Mary Owen Cameron

The present study presents an analysis (largely from statistical evidence) of two main samples of the "knowable" class of shoplifters. The first segment of data consists of a sample (called the "Store" sample) of one out of four of the shoplifters arrested by detectives of one department store in the eight year period 1943–1950. The department store from which this sample of arrests is used will be referred to as the Store (capital "S") or Lakeside Co. (Department stores are naturally reluctant to have this punitive phase of their activity become the subject of public discussion, but the validity of the results is in no way affected by the anonymity of the Store. Disguising the name, as is done in this case, is no different in principle from the usual practice of eliminating or disguising names in case history reports.)

The second major sample of shoplifting arrests used in this study (called the "Women's court" sample) is composed of the adult women who were seen, arrested, and *formally charged* with "petty larceny, shoplifting" by all the stores in the city of Chicago for the three year period 1948–1950. Some data on men arrested for shoplifting and prosecuted in the Municipal Court were also obtained, and some information taken from police arrest records of shoplifters is given.

Although these data, coming as they do from specific (and available) sources, cannot be taken as representative of the total group of shoplifters, they nevertheless form the most adequate data so far available on shoplifting.

Since one of the major objectives of this study will be the analysis of factors which bias the statistical records of both "Store" and "court" samples (an objective which can best be realized as the records are themselves presented), there will be little

SOURCE: *The Booster and the Snitch*, New York: The Free Press of Glencoe, 1964. By permission of the author and publisher.

attempt to discuss biasing factors prior to the presentation of the data. It seems useful, however, to make an exception in regard to the "place bias" already touched upon (those shoplifters who happen to steal at stores employing detectives are almost the only ones arrested) and to emphasize the range and variety of selective factors that bring about the arrest of a shoplifter and perhaps bring him to official attention.

Aside from stealing at a store in which arrests are made by managers, proprietors, or private police, in order to be apprehended, the shoplifter must also come under the direct observation of the arresting person. Even when closed-circuit television is used, the person who steals one object and is observed on the television screen must usually be followed by a detective until he steals another article while under the direct observation of the detective. (Although, as noted above, the laws of arrest differ markedly in different States.) The risk to store management of being deliberately "framed" into a "false" arrest by the thief is always present. The risk to the store varies in accordance with the social status of the offender. The apparent marks of social status (dress, grooming, age, race, etc.) influence the detectives or store managers who must file the formal charge of arrest.

Detectives must see the act of shoplifting take place in order to make an arrest, and detectives cannot be equally observant of all persons in the store. (In some department stores, Lakeside Co. among them, sales clerks are rewarded by the management for "tips" to detectives on thieves, but the proportion of shoplifters arrested as a result of such tips is low—12 per cent for Lakeside Co. Actually, the chief objective of the tip procedure is not to detect shoplifters but to use employees to detect fellow employees who commit violations of trust, including stealing merchandise.)

Shoplifters arrested by store detectives, then, are usually persons who are deliberately watched or those the detectives "just happen" to see. Since the detectives' methods of operation determine who will be arrested, the question of the types of person they are "likely to see" is of considerable importance.

In department stores the detectives are mainly women. On duty they wear hats and coats, carry handbags and try to look like typical shoppers. Detectives are distributed one or two to a floor or section in the large stores (except for sections that are devoted to furniture, carpets, yard goods, and other relatively "non-shopliftable" merchandise).

Detectives frequently have duties to perform that involve the safety of staff and customers as well as the protection of merchandise; they are not engaged solely for the detection of shoplifters. If a lighted match is carelessly or deliberately thrown into a trash bin and a fire results, the store protection person is summoned by the sales clerk. If an elevator fails to function or an escalator becomes jammed, the first person on the scene will usually be "store protection." If a heart attack, fainting spell, or epileptic seizure occurs, among customers or employees, the call goes to store protection immediately. Or when customers quarrel and fight over a bargain, "I saw it first," store protection enters the scene to calm upset tempers. The efficient store detective, too, knows that any one of these emergencies may have been created for the purpose of taking him away from what could soon be the scene of a crime. An immediate call for help goes to the central office to bring other store detectives to the spot.

The chief "first floor" operator in a large urban store stated that in one month she and her assistants encountered alcoholics and narcotics addicts dashing in to steal merchandise. They also helped a person who had wandered into the the store and collapsed as a result of a concussion following an automobile accident outside the store. A man was seen indecently exposing himself. And a fatal heart attack occurred. Along with these events, shoplifting, purse-snatching, and pocket-picking continued.

Store detectives are somewhat free to move about and to station themselves wherever experience has shown they will be most successful in their multitudinous assignments. On a floor where costume jewelry is displayed, for example, a detective frequently stands at the counter. While apparently just another customer also trying on jewelry, she is actually watching for someone to "pocket" or to put on and wear something away. She will be particularly attentive when merchandise falls or is pushed onto the floor, for this is done intentionally by thieves so that they can be concealed from the clerks while hiding merchandise in a shopping bag or a handbag. When a shoplifter is seen concealing merchandise or leaving the counter with it, he (or she) will be followed from the department and perhaps from the store before being arrested. For relatively inexpensive items, the thief will probably not be arrested then but will be followed. If a single object of small value is the only theft, the thief may even be allowed to leave the store without being arrested. The danger of error in arrest, and the hazards of deliberate enticement into making false arrests, are comparatively too great to risk arresting a person who has stolen only an inexpensive piece of merchandise.

A man, for example, was observed by the writer and a store detective pocketing a snakeskin billfold valued at $24.00. The store detective, who observed the man acting very suspiciously and conspicuously, did not arrest him. She had observed that he wore a "trench coat" which undoubtedly had doublepocket openings leading to his suit pockets or to the floor. She assumed, correctly it appeared later, that the thief's motivation was to be arrested after having "thrown" the merchandise (kicked the billfold into an inconspicuous corner). Perhaps he would have resisted arrest and forced the detective to injure him (such cases have occurred before) in the arrest proceedings. He might even have stationed seemingly reputable witnesses in strategic locations to observe the damage inflicted upon him. He could therefore become the plaintiff in a suit for large damages from the store. In this particular case, at least, the store detective pointed out that the thief had indeed "thrown" the stolen billfold by the simple expedient of placing it between his sets of pockets and allowing it to fall to the floor. If captured, there would be no evidence of stolen merchandise on his person: he would have seemed to be an innocent victim of an overenthusiastic store detective and the store would have been the victim of a cleverly arranged suit for false arrest.

An experienced store detective made the interesting observation that most thieves once they are outside of the store and believe themselves beyond the range of observation of store detectives remove the stolen merchandise from parcels or pockets and examine it. When this examination takes place on a street corner or on a public conveyance, as it frequently does, the detective who has followed the thief then makes his arrest. If the thief proceeds to the privacy of his own home without showing incriminating evidence, he has less likelihood of being caught.

In sections of a department store where the technique is applicable, and especially for the "gift" departments during the Christmas season, one-way mirrors and peep holes (through which, in either case, the operator can see without being seen) may make up a part of the ornamentation. The usefulness of this technique, however, is limited, as is closed-circuit television. In order to arrest a shoplifter who has been seen stealing merchandise, the operator behind the mirror must either have some way of signaling to another on the floor, or the operator must let the shoplifter out of his sight for the period of time it takes him to get from his hiding place to the shoplifter. This is undesirable since the thief may, during this time, have changed his mind, or passed the merchandise to a confederate or may deliberately have "thrown" the merchandise to invite false arrest.

In departments where especially valuable items are displayed: fur coats, silver, cameras, luggage, etc., operators may be especially stationed to guard these things. There they often function best by looking, to the initiated, conspicuously like plain clothes detectives or they may even wear uniforms. One detective to whom I was introduced—she looked like an unflattering stereotype of a prison matron or a female "cop"—said that she had been "in furs" for six years. "No," she said, "I've never arrested anyone. I just come here every day and either sit where people can see me or just walk around and look at people suspiciously. The insurance company requires a guard, and I'm it."

Many stores station uniformed police at exits. Again their service is prevention and assistance in arrest rather than detection.

Aside from watching merchandise being handled by customers, operators follow and observe "likely" suspects. They develop, they believe, after years of experience on their job, a "sixth sense" for people who are intending to steal. Certain mannerisms of the shoplifter are sometimes clues. The typical shopper looks at merchandise and ignores other people in the store; the shoplifter constantly watches people in order to know whether or not he is being observed or followed. When the store detective observes a "customer" looking at people rather than merchandise, he may follow the person, unobtrusively of course, through the store. Among other specific clues that the store detectives look for are shopping bags, knitting bags, brief cases, large purses, etc., within which merchandise may be concealed. Large bags with the store label (hat bags and the like) that appear to be crinkled or to have been folded and refolded may have been acquired by shoplifters and kept for shoplifting tours. Persons with such "luggage" are carefully observed. Detectives also look for signs of tension and strain.

Another group of people considered "likely" suspects and watched by most department store detectives are unaccompanied adolescents. In many stores adolescent groups are under almost constant observation, and this practice, according to detectives, proves worth while. It is also a distorting factor in statistical generalizations that involve frequency of arrest.

Negro people are also kept under much closer observation than whites. It is clear that here, too, the selective observations of store detectives constitute a source for distortion of arrest statistics. One cannot measure this bias nor the bias against adolescents and evaluate its importance by any objective standard, but it is unquestionably present and is a factor of some significance in influencing the selection of persons to be arrested. Racial bias is general and not especially characteristic of any particular store. Operators who have worked in several stores and in different cities have the same outlook and the same prejudices. Shoplifters who blend into the dominant group of shoppers are less likely to be noticed. The woman shoplifter who appears to be well-to-do and carries herself with poise and assurance is least likely to be observed, or apprehended even if she is observed. A detective must be very sure of his evidence before he risks the arrest of someone he believes to have no prior criminal record, or possibly may have connections in high places, and be able to obtain first-rate legal counsel.

To summarize: the distorting factors in arrest statistics that have been touched on so far have included five points: Some stores employ detectives empowered to make arrests and others do not; the stationing and operating methods of detectives employed by stores influence what they see being stolen; the anti-Negro attitude of many detectives increases the chance of their seeing Negro shoplifters; adolescents are more frequently under observation than adults; and finally, the caution the store detective feels he must exercise in arresting anyone is enhanced when the suspected thief appears to be "respectable."

These distorting factors probably apply generally to all stores as well as department stores. They operate to select out of the general run of shoplifters those who will have any action taken against them. They are, in a sense, accidental or unconscious selective factors. But in the step which occurs between store arrest, once made, and court procedure, selective screening is deliberately and consciously introduced.

When inventory shrinkage is particularly high, store officials announce, sometimes stridently, that all apprehended shoplifters will be prosecuted. They may even post signs to this effect. They believe that "word gets around" and that shoplifters will go elsewhere. These assertions are not, however, to be taken at face value.

Store police cannot formally charge all persons who are arrested. Since testimony in court takes up the time of store detectives, department store staff generally wish to prosecute as few arrested persons as possible. The problem is much the same for stores everywhere.

> It will surprise people to learn that one important London store lost between £15,000 and £20,000 last year through petty pilfering. . . . Arrests are made but few thieves are charged, for when a summons is issued the head of the department involved and at least one of his assistants, must attend the court, which means the staff is shorthanded for several days. An average of twenty thieves are caught weekly in a large department store, and were all charged the directors would be faced with a total of at least 1,040 court cases a year. Suppose it were decided to proceed in all these cases and suppose an average of two witnesses were needed on each charge, and suppose in each case only two days were needed on each charge, and suppose in each case only two witnesses were needed, the firm would still lose 4,160 working days in the year. It is obvious that under these circumstances no firm can afford to push a campaign against the shoplifter.[1]

In the Chicago Municipal Court, a misdemeanant court, procedures are somewhat less time consuming than in the British court described by Cecil Bishop. But if the defendant demands, as he may, a jury trial, or if he obtains continuances of his case, several man-days of detectives' time may be wasted, from the store viewpoint, in court. Even a routine case requires at least half a day of detectives' time.

All large stores, then, face the problem of who among those who have been caught is to be prosecuted. The actual method of selection, however, is, in some degree, arbitrary and "intuitional." The store protection official who is judge of this process

[1] Bishop, Cecil, *Women and Crime.* (London, 1931), p. 6–7.

acts on an individual basis and without following any necessary rules of precedence. A social worker at the Chicago Municipal Court said that after twenty years' experience of seeing shoplifters being tried, she had yet to discover any principles underlying what appeared to be "sheer caprice" on the part of department store staffs. "Sometimes," she said, "one store will have its detectives in court testifying every day of the week. And another time only a few well-known professionals will be brought in."

Although "sheer caprice" may have some hand in the selective screening procedure, some general principles operate also. Individuals are screened within a context which makes it desirable to prosecute as few persons as possible and still to protect merchandise from theft and the store from suits for false arrest. In determining whether or not a person is to be formally charged or released without charge, store officials look at two different problems: they wish to prosecute thieves who are shoplifting commercially, and they need to obtain a conviction in court.

If the arrested shoplifter is likely to be a person stealing merchandise in order to sell it or to return it for refund of the "purchase" price, he is almost certain to be formally charged. The evidence pointing toward "commercial" theft that interrogators look for includes a catalogue of items such as inadequate or inaccurate personal identification. A thief may carry a driver's license or other identifying documents belonging to someone whose pocket he has picked earlier in the day. Failure of the thief to live up to all aspects of his "identification" is cause for further interrogation at the very least. The thief who gives an out-of-town address or a hotel address may well be a *professional* thief. Pawn tickets, keys to public lockers, and the like are sure to be followed through by a thorough search of the places indicated before the shoplifter is allowed to walk out of the store. The nature and value of the stolen merchandise and special equipment for stealing or concealing merchandise is considered in determining whether the detective is confronted with commercial theft. Store detectives also observe the thief's behavior during the time he is being followed. They know that an experienced thief, having stolen merchandise of value will often go *up* an escalator rather than immediately *down* and out of the store. The thief will discover in this way whether or not he is being followed. He will also try to find a place where he can conceal himself and remove price tags or other incriminating labels. Staircases, rest rooms, and telephone booths are usually the most available places; hence they are watched with some care. Store detectives also look for narcotics addiction as evidenced by behavior, by needle marks, or by the possession of narcotics.

While it is clearly in the interest of department stores to prosecute commercial shoplifters, they must also have a voluntary statement or a court finding of guilt for every arrested person. Those who refuse to sign a confession and a waiver of suit against the store must be prosecuted in the court. Only when a shoplifter has signed a confession of guilt—or has been found guilty by the court—is the store free from suit for false arrest. Although a shoplifter may be an obvious novice, he must still be prosecuted if he refuses to absolve the store from guilt in apprehending him.

Aside from protective and financial considerations, other factors sometimes influence the decision to prosecute or release. Occasionally, for instance, prosecution is used as a means of getting a severely disturbed neurotic or psychotic person to a source of adequate medical care. The court can, and sometimes does, refer arrested persons to the psychiatric division.

The overall number of formal charges made by a particular store may be subject to considerable variation. The formal arrest rate will increase, for instance, if the store management becomes worried about the problem of inventory shrinkage and adopts a "get tough" policy for a period of time. There are also variations between stores. Store officials differ in the proportion of persons they feel it desirable to charge formally. "Sheer caprice" may play a part. Since knowledge of prosecution policy is not something store officials desire to make public, they discuss the problems involved with an outsider only with the understanding that they will not be quoted. Enough information was gathered in interviews with protection officials of stores in several cities, however, to make it seem likely that, among department stores, "class" stores generally prefer charges against a smaller proportion of arrested persons than do "mass" stores. Store detectives who have worked in both types of stores agreed with this generalization. Prosecution policy of "mass" stores requires less emphasis on screening. Persons who shoplift in "mass" stores are already somewhat self-selected for lower social class status, and the likelihood of a prominent individual or his wife entering a "not guilty" plea and being found so by the court is therefore not as great as in the "class" stores. . . .

RESIDENCE AND BECOMING "DATA"

In order to compare the areas of concentration of Store and Court arrests, the residential addresses of arrested persons were spotted on maps according to census area. Rate maps were constructed on the basis of the 1950 census reports of the population of these areas. The Court cases show the characteristic concentration at the center of the city of the rate of arrested women per 1,000 female population (Map 10-1, p. 181). The rate declines as one approaches the middle and peripheral areas. (The rate is "accidently" high in certain peripheral areas where the population base is very low.) Altogether this rate-map of shoplifters resembles closely the residential maps of persons arrested for other types of crimes, or, indeed, indices of almost all other sociopathic phenomena. The rate at the first quartile of census areas is approximately 7.5 times the rate of the third quartile of census areas.

The rates by census areas of persons arrested for shoplifting at Lakeside Co., however, (Map 10-2, p. 182) show no such concentration at the center of the city. The dispersion is slightly greater ($Q_1 = 6Q_3$) and the areas with the highest rates are not concentrated at the center of the city but extend along the entire shore of Lake Michigan from the 9500 block South to the 6400 block North and follow the major transportation lines. The area includes prosperous neighborhoods and communities as well as deteriorated ones. There is little or no relationship (coefficient of mean square contingency .013) between the rate of Court cases and the rate of Store arrests in the census areas of Chicago, the index of correlation being but .01.

If the residential distribution of the persons *arrested* by Lakeside Co. is different from the residential distribution of persons charged in the Municipal Court with shoplifting, is the distribution of the persons Lakeside Co. *formally charged* with shoplifting likewise different from the Municipal Court cases? Since Lakeside Co. prosecuted only 13 per cent of all adults arrested, there were too few cases to construct a rate map with these data alone. A spot map, however, showed in general the distribution of cases formally charged in the Municipal Court (Branch 40) by

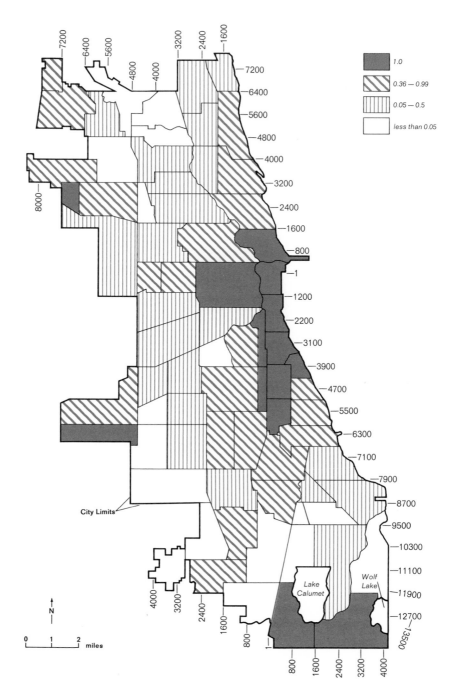

MAP 10-1 Residential addresses of women charged with shoplifting, 1948–1950. Rate per 1,000 Chicago 1950 female population. *N*-633. (Women's Court data.)

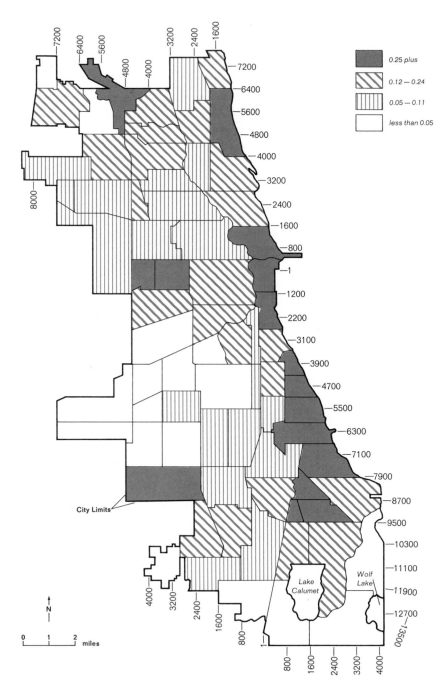

MAP 10-2 Residential addresses of all persons in sample arrested for shoplifting, 1943–1950. Rate per 1,000 Chicago 1950 population. *N*-626. (Lakeside Co. Data.)

Lakeside Co. to be quite similar to that of all court cases and dissimilar to the Lakeside Co. arrest cases. Six of the seven areas with the highest number of court cases in the map of Lakeside Co. court cases are the same as the areas with the highest number of cases in Women's Court. Only three of these seven were among the top seven areas for actual Lakeside Co. arrests.

In addition to the records of Lakeside Co. obtained from the Store data, the data of the Municipal Court contained (for the three years studied) another sample of women (all the cases prosecuted in three years) charged with shoplifting by Lakeside Co. Since only 8.3 per cent of these cases duplicated the records of Lakeside Co. used in the Store data, the two samples could be combined to give a larger sample of the residential addresses of offenders prosecuted on the complaint of the Store. The two samples were thus combined and a map showing the rate of prosecuted women shoplifters per 1,000 female population (Map 10-3, p. 183) was constructed. This map combines as much data as it was possible to accumulate to show the residential distribution of women prosecuted for shoplifting by Lakeside Co.

When Map 10-3 (p. 183) is compared with the map of Court cases (Map 10-1, p. 181), and with the map for Store arrests (Map 10-2, p. 182), it is clearly shown that Lakeside Co. shoplifters who were *formally charged* with shoplifting are distributed more in accordance with all formal official arrests in Chicago than with Lakeside Co. store arrests. Moreover, other maps showing the distribution of the Lakeside Co. arrests of white women and all Store prosecutions of white women, show similar dispersion and similar failure to concentrate noticeably in any areas of the city.

Decisions as to which people will be released with an admonition and which people will be formally charged with larceny are made, as has been pointed out, by members of store protection staffs. A number of factors enter into such decisions (discussed in the first chapters) and among other factors, decisions reflect the biases and prejudices of these staffs. The residential maps constructed from data on prosecutions initiated by the Store staff show clearly that one important factor influencing the decision to prosecute is the race of the offender, for prosecutions were most frequent in the "ghetto" areas of Chicago where the inhabitants were almost totally Negro. In Store data, 6.5 per cent of all adults arrested were Negroes and 24 per cent of all prosecutions were of Negroes. Whereas the Store formally charged 10.9 per cent of all arrested non-Negroes with larceny, 58 per cent of all Negroes who were arrested were so charged. Of white women arrested 8.85 per cent were charged with larceny, and of Negro women, 42 per cent were formally charged.

Did the disproportionate charging of Negroes with larceny occur because the Negroes were "more criminal" than the whites? The median and mean values of merchandise which each group was recorded as having stolen was examined. Measured either by the median (since the distribution was skewed toward the upper values) or by the mean, Negro men and women arrested in the Store stole less valuable articles than white men and women so charged. It is clear that the magnitude of the crime was not the distinguishing factor. Roughly the same proportion of Negro and white women who were prosecuted had prior records (3/13 or 23 per cent of Negro women and 11/60 or 18 per cent of white women).

For Negro and white women in the Court sample, the differences between the number of objects stolen are very small at all age levels, and in no case is there statistical probability of a true difference.

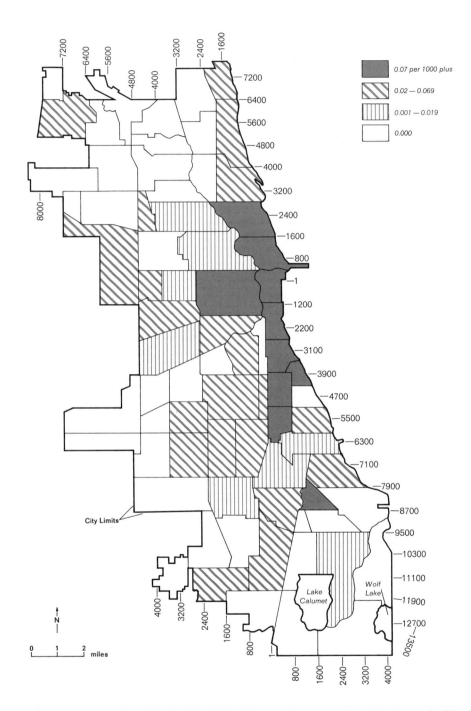

MAP 10-3 Residential addresses of women formally charged with shoplifting. Rate per 1,000 Chicago 1950 female population. *N*-126. (Lakeside Co. data.)

TABLE 10-1

Average Value in Dollars of Stolen Merchandise Found in the Possession of Adults Formally Charged, by Race and Sex (Lakeside Co. Data)

	Men	
	White	Negro
Mean	71.00	32.70
Median	43.32	25.03
	Women	
Mean	46.86	25.03
Median	26.34	11.69

Since being Negro was mainly equivalent at the time of this study in Chicago to residence in a "ghetto" area, the evidence thus indicates that a disproportionate number of people from these areas are brought to official attention through formal charges of larceny being place against them. The same social forces, in other words, that operate to segregate people into the "ghettos," also operate to bring them to police and court attention. The Store arrest rate for shoplifting is much higher in many "good" residential areas than in deteriorated areas, but the proportion of people from these "good" residential areas who come to official attention is so small and the proportion of Negro "ghetto" dwellers brought to official attention so large that the reverse picture is seen in the Store cases which become part of official criminal statistics.

Moreover there is reason to believe that the reversal of proportions is true not only for the Lakeside Co. store arrests, but for all department store arrests. Store protection, as already noted, is a trade, and the practices which characterize this trade in one department store characterize it in others. If the selective processes are similar for all stores, and it seems probable that they are, an interesting figure can be derived which, *if* correct (and it is purely a hypothetical figure), could show the degree to which discrimination against Negro women affects the official criminal statistics on shoplifting by women.

For the Lakeside Co. data, the proportion of Negroes among women prosecuted is about 4 times the proportion found in women apprehended. Of Negro women, 13/31 or 42 per cent are prosecuted and 60/678 or 9 per cent of white women. Table 10-2 (p. 186) shows the number of Negro and white women officially charged with shoplifting for each of the Chicago stores which made official charges. The stores that would be expected to have the highest proportion of Negro women shoppers, i.e., stores carrying less expensive lines of merchandise, have a higher proportion of Negro women in their court prosecutions (Mandel, Fair, Sears, Wards, Goldblatts, Lerner) than do the "class" stores (Carson, Pirie, Scott; Marshall Fields; C. H. Stevens). Of Negro women, 349 were prosecuted, and 524 white women were prosecuted. If the proportion of white women arrested but not formally charged is four times the proportion of Negro women arrested but not charged as it is in the Lakeside Co. data then the relationship in store arrests is 4 × 524 or 2096 white women apprehended in store arrests to 349 Negro women. Thus 349/2445 or 14.2 per cent of all department store arrests of women, hypothetically, would be of Negro women.

TABLE 10-2

Relation of Numbers of Negro and White Women Prosecutions for Shoplifting (Women's Court Data)

Store	Negro		White	Total
	Number	*Per cent*	*White*	*Total*
Carson, Pirie, Scott	46	22.2	161	207
Mandel	72	49.6	73	145
Fair	46	63.9	26	72
Sears	26	48.2	28	54
Montgomery Ward	31	32.7	64	95
Marshall Field	11	15.5	60	71
Goldblatts	26	45.6	31	57
Lerner Shop	30	68.2	14	44
Robert Hall	10	71.2	4	14
Madigan	0	——	9	9
Wiebolts	0	——	3	3
C. H. Stevens	3	18.8	13	16
Lane Bryant	0	——	2	2
Spiegel	0	——	3	3
Boston	3	33.3	6	9
Other Clothing	31	78.4	9	40
Drug Stores	1	33.3	2	3
Variety Stores	8	66.7	4	12
Grocery Stores	5	29.4	12	17
TOTAL	349	40.0	524	873

Since 7.9 per cent of the women 20 years of age and over in Chicago were, at the time of this study, Negro women, this would mean that Negro women were probably arrested in department stores about 1.8 times their proportion in the population instead of 4.5 times their proportion as appears in the official figures. It would also mean that the apparent concentration of cases of shoplifting in Negro "ghetto" areas was largely a direct result of minority group discrimination and not the result of a *real* rate of criminality among the people resident in those areas that much exceeds the rate in the nearby white residential areas.

The rate of arrest of Negro women is, even with the allowance for the screening procedures of stores, 1.8 times the rate for white women. It would seem probable that if an additional allowance could be calculated for the bias entering into the initial selection for arrest by store detectives, this proportion would be further reduced. An actual ratio of *crime* of 1:1 would not seem at all unlikely.

This study, presenting as it does, two sets of data ("official" and "private") on arrests for shoplifting gives an unusual opportunity to present a numerical analysis of racial bias and discrimination. The question has, of course, been raised many times before, but without answer. Sutherland, for example, states:

> The question which has been raised most persistently, perhaps, is whether the arrests or juvenile court appearances do not give a biased measure of delinquencies because of the poverty of the families in the areas which are reported as having the highest delinquency rates. Wealth and social position, to be sure, do provide a certain degree of

immunity against arrest. Also, certain national or religious groups maintain welfare agencies which take problem cases that would otherwise be referred to the police or to the juvenile court, while other national and religious groups have no agencies of this nature. *Even when allowance is made for these variables,* the concentration seems to remain, and this concentration is in accordance with the experience of people who suffer from delinquencies. [Italics added.] [2]

Sutherland's statement that "even when allowance is made for these variables . . ." unfortunately gives no clue as to how much allowance should be made. The allowance which these department store data seem to indicate would, in fact, remove the extremely high concentration. Indeed a "reasonable" allowance removes any concentration at all.

Does this discrimination factor apply only to shoplifting? In this study there are no data on other types of crimes, but since the judgment of whether or not a person is to be officially charged with a crime has to be made by *someone* (private detective, employer, citizen, or policeman) in most types of crime, it is probable that a very considerable allowance should be made for the existence of racial prejudice in reporting other types of crime as well as shoplifting and hence white and Negro actual crime rates for larceny by women at least are probably much closer than has been thought.

DISPOSITION OF CASES: STORE AND COURT

Store Cases. After store officials have made the decision for disposition of a case, shoplifters are either "escorted" from the door with a warning never to return to the store, or they are formally charged and conveyed by the city police in a patrol wagon to the "lockup." Those that are to be prosecuted are usually sent to jail for the night and "booked"; when they can furnish or obtain bond, they are released on bail until trial.

The typical trial averages 5 to 10 minutes and unless the defendant has some sophistication in legal matters, the trial is likely to be over before he realizes that it has begun. In Women's Court especially, confused defendants were—as I observed—propelled away from the judge's bench by court aides or by their attorneys as they asked in a bewildered way what was going to happen to them. And what does happen to the shoplifter who is found guilty seemingly depends on the sex, race, and prior record of the shoplifter, and on the individual predilections of the judge who sits on the bench.

Of the 110 *adults* from the Store sample who were formally charged with larceny, the outcome of court action is known for 99. Of these 99, 43 per cent were sentenced to jail for periods of from five days to one year; six per cent were fined; 29 per cent were placed on probation; 21 per cent were given token sentences ($1.00 considered paid and one day considered served); and one was discharged without prosecution. None was found "not guilty." But the overall figures conceal the differences found in court action between sentences given to men and to women; to Negro and to white shoplifters. Thirteen per cent of the white women who were tried on the complaint of Lakeside Co., for example, were sentenced to jail, 33 per cent of the Negro

[2] Sutherland, Edwin H. *Principles of Criminology.* (Philadelphia, 1939), p. 139.

women. Thus the likelihood of a Negro woman arrested in the store serving a jail sentence is about six times the likelihood of a white woman (and keep in mind the similar mean and median value of stolen merchandise as between Negro women and white women). In proportion to their numbers at time of apprehension, four times as many Negro women as white women were formally charged, and of those formally charged, twice as many Negro women were sentenced to jail.

Seventy per cent of white men tried were sentenced to jail and 75 per cent of Negro men. Men, as noted before, stole merchandise of greater value than women. They were also, in larger number than women, probably commercial thieves.

Court Cases. In the "Court sample" of women, differentials similar to those of the Store cases were found in sentences by racial group. Differences are especially striking in the proportions of Negro and white women not found guilty on the one hand, and those actually sentenced to jail on the other. Of white women 16.2 per cent were not found guilty and of Negro women 3.7 per cent (*C.R.* 6.7). Of white women, 4.1 per cent, and of Negro women 21.8 per cent were sentenced to jail (*C.R.* 7.46). Of the 21 white women sentenced to jail, 2 (9.5 per cent) were sentenced to 30 days or more. Of the 76 Negro women, 20 (26.3 per cent) were sentenced for 30 days or more (*C.R.* 2.07). The differences in the proportion of jail sentences handed down to Negro and white women might have resulted from a greater proportion of commercial shoplifters or "occupational criminals" among Negro women. But, in the small sample of women whose prior court records were ascertained through Police Department records, of 15 white women sentenced to jail, 8 had prior records of arrest, and of 20 Negro women sentenced to jail, 10 had prior records.

The sentences imposed on women shoplifters by different municipal court judges showed considerable variation. Among eight judges who sat at the Women's Court in three years, the range in the proportion of women found "not guilty" ran from 5.0 per cent for one judge to 19.5 per cent for another. Women given "token sentences" by judges ranged from 0 for one judge to 58.4 per cent for another; probation from 10.5 per cent to 62.4 per cent and jail sentences ranged from 3.3 per cent to 31.2 per cent. The idiosyncrasies of judges rotating in the same court have been studied with similar conclusions by others.[3]

11. The Narcotics Enforcement Pattern
Jerome H. Skolnick

ROUTINE ACTIVITY AND THE PETTY INFORMANT

In a municipal police department, vice control officers, like all plainclothesmen, spend a portion of their working hours on surveillance, simply riding in unmarked cars on street patrol. But vice control men spend much less time in this fashion than

---

[3] Smith, R. H. and H. B. Ehrmann. *"The Criminal Courts," Cleveland Survey of Criminal Justice.* Part 1, pp. 76–80. Also, Gaudet, F. J., G. S. Harris, and C. W. St. John. "Individual Differences in the Sentencing Tendencies of Judges," *Journal of Criminal Law, Criminology and Police Science.* 23: 811–818, January, 1933.

SOURCE: *Justice without Trial: Law Enforcement in Democratic Society,* New York: John Wiley & Sons, Inc., 1966. By permission of the author and publisher.

patrol division detectives, since they frequently are able to "create" crimes through the leads of informants, while patrol division detectives must await the report of a felony before they can take action. Thus, the patrol detective—who rides alone, while vice control men team up in pairs—may find boredom a major enemy. Entire evenings may pass when patrolling detectives do nothing other than drive a car slowly around a city for eight hours. After a while, the detective may feel gratitude for the felon who provides him with activity.

Much of the generative activity in enforcing narcotics crimes takes place within the police station. This is not because narcotics police are lazy but because the nature of narcotics crime requires that invocation of activity be based upon receipt of messages.[1] Thus, all detectives, but especially narcotics detectives, do a lot of work on the telephone. Many of the informants (some of whom are transients) do not have telephones of their own, and others prefer not to be called at home by a policeman. As a result, the narcotics policeman is continually being called to the telephone.

Not all informing, however, takes place over the telephone. Petty informants seem to enjoy wandering into the separate quarters of the vice control squad, and narcotics officers must be available to greet and chat with them. Indeed, due to their constant need for information, narcotics officers encourage informants to "drop in." To this end, the Westville vice control squad is not only quartered separately from the rest of the police department but it even has a special entrance through which informants can pass unobserved by other policemen.

During the evening being described, Sergeant Harris was visited by a long-time addict and regular informant for the vice control squad, who was a mercenary, paid for his information. Members of the vice control squad suspected him of "dealing a little methedrine" himself and had another addict-informant keeping an eye on him. Actually, each addict-informant accused the other of dealing methedrine, but the vice control squad had been unable to convict either.

The informant, especially one who seems odd or eccentric, is in an advantageous position, since he can gain a fairly accurate idea of the physical location of members of the narcotics detail by the simple expedient of telephoning them. Narcotics officers, however, are alert to deceptive techniques used by informants and take care to counteract these whenever possible. From the officers' point of view, the least serious is the petty informant dealer who, for instance, drops around to the police station to impress the officers that he is "working" in their interest. There are evidently two reasons for the policeman's indulgent response to the maneuvers of an informant of this type. First, although the policeman sees through his artifices, such an informant may sometimes produce useful information and is consequently tolerated. Indeed, the policeman may feel genuinely sorry for such a man. In my experience, most policemen can empathize somewhat with the petty addict-informant. I have several times heard various vice squad detectives express the notion that such-and-such an informant "could have been somebody if he hadn't gotten hooked on that stuff. It's terrible what it does to you." In addition, the petty informant is typically not a symbolic assailant but is perceived as something of a pitiful figure, rather like a punch-drunk prizefighter.

[1] If the idea that policemen are slow to arrive at the scene of a crime is true, the cause is typically overwork rather than laziness. Policemen seem inclined toward physical activity, provided it occurs in an authoritative context. They do not care to be sent on errands and above all dislike paper work. They seem to enjoy most of all, the processes of investigation: talking, telephoning, going "out on the street." These activities are of course the ones where their authority is most evident and exercised.

Perhaps the more important reason, however, is instrumental. An informant would at most risk using "only" a so-called dangerous drug when visiting the narcotics detail, since such use constitutes a misdemeanor rather than a felony. Consequently, in the narcotics officer's scale of values, the user simply does not constitute a "good pinch." In practice, therefore, although such an informant does not have a "license" to operate, neither do the narcotics police strive to bring about his apprehension. Of course, if he were to be caught selling drugs illegally, he would surely be arrested (even if only to be released again in return for information).

Police take most seriously deceptive techniques whereby informants attempt to use their working relations with law enforcement officers for positive personal gain. This situation poses the gravest dilemma for detectives by suspending them between the ideals of morality and the demands of efficiency. For example, when informant A says that B is in possession of an illegal object, there is often reason to suspect A's motives. Within the system, the morally acceptable motive is to extricate oneself from a difficult situation. It is not that such motivation is positively countenanced either by the police or by the informants themselves. But if the situation of the informant is perceived as an equilibrium with a set of minuses on one side and pluses on the other, it is seen as understandable for a man in a minus situation to bring himself back to normal. Thus, when the petty informant gives information in exchange for money to purchase drugs, or to avoid a penal sanction, his motives are acceptable, and the police feel no hesitancy in engaging his services.

However, the police do not consider it morally acceptable for a man to inform to gain positive benefits. Policemen may not personally like the idea, but they sometimes find themselves in a position of having to use information given by people who are vengeful, or worse yet, who will gain some unlawful benefit from the arrest of another, such as freedom to take over another seller's clientele if he is sent to jail or the opportunity to strip clean of resalable articles the premises of a man who has been arrested. What troubles police most is the "set-up," the "planting," for instance, of a good supply of narcotics in addict A's house by B to take A "out of the scene." Suspicious of being deceived, police usually check carefully an informant's story if the context makes it appear the informant is somehow being positively rewarded. Policemen have few, if any, moral reservations about setting a trap for a suspected felon on their own initiative. What hurts both pride and morality is to permit a false trap to be set by one "criminal" for another.

SETTING UP A "GOOD PINCH"

In what follows, the events of the "good pinch" evening are described. They are also interpreted in light of how organizational commitments of the police influence their capacity to observe the rule of law.

> Shortly after the petty informant left, a telephone call came in from another addict-informant, Charlie, who was scheduled for preliminary hearing on a charge of possession for sale with one prior conviction. Charlie reported that a couple of addicts had stolen a large supply of drugs from a warehouse or drugstore, and had "split up the loot" in his "pad." He could not provide the address of the thieves, although he had visited one of them and thought he might be able to find his

way there again. (According to the police, "hypes" find it difficult to remember addresses. Thus, an uninformed narcotics officer might believe an addict to be lying when he claimed to be unable to remember a friend's address.)

Charlie also reported a rumor that one of the thieves, Dave, had been robbed by another addict, Bill. Charlie didn't know where Bill lived either, but he knew a close friend of Bill's who was living in Cedarville. Charlie reasoned that if Bill had any "stuff," it would be likely that Bill's friend, Archie, would also have gotten some.

On the strength of Charlie's tip, Sergeant Harris decided it would be worthwhile to try to locate Archie, since he was well known to the police as an addict. Archie's address was on file, and some checking revealed Archie to be living in the Bismarck Hotel in Cedarville. Before we left, the Sergeant called the Cedarville vice control squad (consisting of two men), explaining that this was his way of maintaining good relations with adjacent police departments. In addition, the Sergeant notified the State of California narcotics agents, who are invited by the Westville police department to make use of the office space and equipment of the Westville vice control.

The Westville Police Department, especially the vice control squad, is proud of its relations with other law enforcement agencies. This working relationship is important for the efficient enforcement of the narcotics laws, since state agents and the local police provide each other with complementary services. The Westville vice control squad has three resources that state agents lack: they possess greater knowledge of local conditions, have the services of a well-developed network of local informants, and are allowed to arrest for "marks" alone—tiny red bruises that indicate recent use of narcotics. (Using narcotics or "being under the influence" is itself a misdemeanor under Section 11721 of the penal code.) [2] State agents typically do not arrest for "marks," since their chief interest is to uncover large sources of illegal narcotics. The arrest for "marks," however, is an added value in the vice control officer's resources in bargaining for information and thus enables the Westville vice control squad to initiate cases more effectively than can state police. Finally, the Westville squad can call for the services of the local patrol police when "extra bodies" are required.

The state agents are better equipped than the local vice control squad to follow through on cases, especially those involving large quantities of narcotics. Since they have statewide jurisdiction, state police can take a plane from, for instance, San Francisco to Los Angeles to investigate a lead on a supplier in the other city. Furthermore, large amounts of money are sometimes required to make incriminating purchases of opiates or heroin, especially in transactions coming over the border from Mexico. Westville police have neither the funds nor the jurisdiction to handle this type of law enforcement operation. Therefore, local and state police complement each other, the local police by initiating small arrests and the state police by having the resources to track down the bigger "pinches." As will be shown, narcotics arrests

[2] Until 1962, one could be arrested in Westville for *being* an addict. However, that was declared unconstitutional in *Robinson v. California,* 370 U.S. 660 (1962).

are seen as a series of increasingly larger steps up a ladder, at the top of which is the narcotics officer's prize: the "source."

CREATING AN INFORMANT

We left Westville in two cars—four state agents in a flashy-looking hard top convertible, and the Sergeant, and another state agent and I in the 1963 blue Plymouth sedan well known to addicts in the area. As we drove up to the hotel in Cedarville, we spotted the two local vice control men, looking like two professional football players on their way to a Friday night movie. One of the state agents recognized a car that seemed to be Archie's, which of course suggested that Archie was either in his room or nearby. Three state agents stayed outside while two of the state agents, the Cedarville vice control man, Sergeant Harris and I entered the hotel.

Inside the hotel, the chief state agent approached the desk clerk and asked whether Archie was in the hotel. The clerk said he thought he was, but that he might well be in another (Dominick's) room. Three policemen and I went to Dominick's room on the third floor, and two went to Archie's second-floor room with a key they obtained from the clerk. Approaching Dominick's room on tiptoe, we heard several men's voices. One policeman suggested that somebody ought to go upstairs and tell the other policemen that Dominick's room was occupied. I volunteered, because I wanted to see what the other policemen were doing in the meantime.

When I arrived they were searching Archie's room. (I relayed the message to the policemen upstairs.) The room served as a painting studio for Archie, and most of the space was crammed with paints, bottles, and canvasses at different stages of completion in an apparently haphazard disarray. The officers, who by my observation were skilled at searching without changing the appearance of the room, had been looking mainly through drawers. They rearranged the little they had upset and the three of us went downstairs.

Legally, the police are not permitted to enter a room and make a search without a warrant, except "incident" to an arrest of some person in the room. Thus, they cannot search an empty room without a warrant, even if they see marihuana on the table through a window. In California, unless a search has some reasonable relationship to an arrest, it becomes an unlawful exploratory search.[3] The practice of making an unlawful exploratory search of the room of a suspected criminal is, so far as I could tell on several occasions, accepted by both the Westville police and the state police. As one policeman commented:

> "Of course, it's not exactly legal to take a peek beforehand. It's not one of the things you usually talk about as a police technique. But if you

---

[3] See Rex Collings, Jr., "Toward Workable Rules of Search and Seizure—an Amicus Curiae Brief," *California Law Review*, 50 (1962), 443 [citing *People v. Molarius*, 146 Cal. App. 2d 129, 303 P. 2d 350 (1956)].

find something, you back off and figure out how you can do it legal. And if you don't find anything, you don't have to waste a lot of time."

The policeman does not feel legally constrained in conducting an exploratory examination of suspicious premises. Even less does he feel *morally* at fault in conducting a prior search of a known addict's room for narcotics.

The process by which the policeman justifies his unlawful exploratory search is similar to that by which many criminals justify theirs. Thus, the policeman distinguishes between *legality* and *morality,* just as the criminal does, and as we all do to a certain extent. The prostitute, for example, justifies her activity by asserting that she engages in an enterprise her "trick" desires. The confidence man rationalizes his deceptions with the belief that "there is a bit of larceny in the soul of every man" and that his motives are no different from his victims'. The civil-rights "sit-in" justifies his "trespass" on grounds of a higher morality. Similarly, the policeman countenances *his* unlawful exploration by pointing to the difficulties of his job and asserting that his activity has no adverse effect upon the person whose property is unlawfully searched, *provided* that person is not a criminal. Thus, the policeman typically alleges that unless he conducts unlawful searches, for example, dangerous addicts might escape capture; furthermore, he maintains that innocent persons have no cause for complaint.

> When the group reassembled, it was decided to break into Dominick's room, but without kicking the door in. The following strategy was used: one of the Cedarville vice control men knocked on Dominick's door, and said, "Phone," imitating the Spanish accent of the desk clerk. From inside the door, Dominick said, "What?" and the officer repeated, "Phone." Dominick opened the door slightly, and as he did, several policemen pushed inside.
>
> At this point, it was important for the narcotics officer to keep talking in a friendly, calm tone. "Well, hello, Archie," Sergeant Harris said, "just relax and everybody stay where they are and everything is going to be okay." Archie and Dominick began to protest that they hadn't done anything wrong, and it wasn't nice of the police to "just come busting into" the room this way.

The denial of guilt in this case was important for the police because it implied that the suspect would not mind having his arms examined. Had the suspect refused to answer, and ordered the police out in the absence of a warrant, the police would again have been on shaky legal ground. So far, their suspicion of Archie was based on a reliable informant's word that Archie probably had some "stuff," since he was a friend of an addict who, the informant had heard, was "dealing." This vague, hearsay information was also insufficient legally to establish probable cause for a frisk and an examination of his body.[4] What the policeman required was a tactic to circumvent the legal restrictions.

By denying his guilt, the suspect gives the policeman an opening wedge. He can say, as Sergeant Harris did, "Okay, Archie, you know it's my job to check you out," simultaneously grabbing Archie's arm and pulling up the shirtsleeve. Before Archie

---

4 See Frank J. Remington, "The Law Relating to 'On the Street' Detention, Questioning, and Frisking," *Journal of Criminal Law, Criminology and Police Science,* 51 (December, 1960), 386–394.

had an opportunity to emit the words suggested by the look of protest on his face, the Sergeant had his fingers on a pair of tiny red "marks" in the crook of the elbow. By finding the marks in the way he had, the Sergeant had introduced new elements into the legal situation. First, he could reasonably claim that Archie had "volunteered" to show his arms and that no physical coercion was used. More important, from the Sergeant's point of view, by finding marks, he had established reasonable cause for arresting Archie as a man "under the influence" of narcotics. In addition, the legality of the arrest further established a basis for a thorough search, after the exploratory "peek," although it is arguable whether the means of entry would be upheld by an appellate court.

We might ask why the suspect did not assert his legal rights and demand a search warrant as soon as the door was opened. There were several reasons. First, he was physically coerced (albeit by indirection, since no actual violence was used). Five physically well-constituted, armed men (plus one middle-sized unarmed professor) broke in unexpectedly and stood around with no-nonsense looks on their faces. At that moment, it would have taken an act of heroism to order them out.

Second, these men did represent authority. To a certain extent, the suspect must interpret the policeman's behavior as being proper, for the policeman represents the state. His very being conveys an impression of legitimacy to this type of addict, an occupant of a cheap hotel room, a user of narcotics, a struggling painter. In addition to being surprised and upset, the suspect may not be entirely aware of his legal rights, and the police in this situation did not advise him of his rights.

Furthermore, Archie was, after all, a known addict and had previous experiences with the police. Consequently, there was on his part an anticipation of future encounters. If he acted like a "wise-guy" this time (by ordering the police to leave), he could have "the book thrown at him" the next. One narcotics detective reported that no known addict had ever refused him permission to make an examination for "marks," even though there was no legal justification for a search. I have seen a detective pull to the curb and ask a man how things are going, adding, "You wouldn't happen to be dirty, would you?" The detective may look, or just wish the man well and leave.

Finally, there is for the suspect in a room, as for the man stopped by the police on the street, the genuine possibility of innocence combined with the mildness of the request. The police are, after all, making a seemingly innocuous request, permission to glance at the crook of an elbow. Objectively, its fulfillment demands no more exertion than the common courtesy of giving a match or the correct time to a stranger. In a nonlegal context, it might almost be insulting to refuse. In the situation, however, we might think the insulted party would be the suspect; it is far more degrading to be suspected of being an addict than to be asked for a match. But for the already convicted user, most of the stigma has already been manifested. Having once been proved culpable, the suspect can hardly claim to be shocked by the suspicion of use. All of these factors combine to impede assertion of legal rights. Furthermore, if the addict is innocent, the police leave, with the suspect disturbed but not substantially harmed.

The failure to consider such facts by appellate courts and civil liberties lawyers puzzles and annoys the policeman. He claims that he would never do this sort of thing to a respectable citizen, and that the law should somehow recognize the difference in its search-and-seizure rules between respectable citizens and known criminals. Since the search-and-seizure rules are based on concepts of probability, a degree of irrationality in ignoring probabilities associated with an individual's past *status* as an addict cannot be denied. The policeman is far less interested in questions of constutionality than in the reasonableness of a *working* system.

The criminal law, however, largely because it is so heavily influenced by constitutional requirements, is not necessarily administratively rational. Indeed the principle of legality often stands in oppsition to the principle of administrative rationalty. Like the policeman, the addict typically does not perceive interactions against a background of higher legal requirements. He operates according to the normative assumptions of everyday life, emphasizing the factual. He knows he is an addict, that he will sometimes be in possession of narcotics and, fearing that he will be discovered, he is not going to unduly antagonize the police. Of all types of "criminality," addiction is undoubtedly the most difficult, because the addict must anticipate continual and relatively uncontrolled participation in the forbidden activity, and, therefore, repeated contact with police.

Moreover, the experienced addict knows much about how police operate and what they are after. He knows they are not interested in a "vag" addict who possesses only a supply of drugs sufficient for immediate personal use. On the other side, the policeman is confident that his behavior is not going to be the subject of an appellate court decision. If no incriminating evidence has been found, it is hardly likely the addict will sue in tort, or even lodge a complaint with the police department, partly because of the practical ineffectiveness of such remedies, but mainly because the addict has an expectation of continuing relations with the police.

The policeman's encounter with the addict is a game with a twist. Each playing is influenced by the anticipation of future games. As a result, it is difficult to describe, in any single instance, the values held by the competing parties, since these are modified by each party's subjective assessment of what his opponent's strength will be in future encounters. Thus, the addict would not sue in tort, nor would he complain to the police department about a narcotics officer's behavior, because this would be taken as an affront by the policeman. Such aggressive behavior on the part of the addict toward the policeman would doubtless lead to another sort of game situation in the future where the addict would be defined as an enemy. Outcomes of games played between superordinates and subordinates are going to vary greatly depending on the conception the authority has of his antagonist. Typically, when no incriminating evidence is discovered, the addict is happy to forget the affair. By the same token, when incriminating evidence is discovered, the policeman expects the addict to "cop out" (confess) sometime during the adjudicative process. In the present case, the copping out occurred early, exactly as anticipated.

> The sergeant, the supervising state agent, and the suspect went back upstairs to the suspect's room for interrogation. The purpose was to convince Archie to purchase narcotics from Bill under surveillance. When we reached his room, the state agent opened the conversation by saying, "Look, Archie, you know the score. Tell us how much stuff you've got—and you know you'd better tell us the truth, because we're going to search anyway." Archie showed the agent a "fit" (eyedropper and hypodermic needle) and some pills in the bathroom. The agent found other pills that Archie claimed were vitamins. Additional ques-

tions revealed that Archie had been purchasing his drugs from Bill. Archie also said that Bill had quite a lot and that he understood Bill had gotten his supply by "burning" (stealing from) a third person whom Archie didn't know.

Since Archie's story was consistent with the one the police had gotten from the original informant, Charlie, they offered Archie a deal. In return for his "cooperation" (calling Bill and making a "connection" with him that night), they would overlook his "marks" (thus saving him a probable period of ninety days in the county jail). Archie hesitated and tried to argue his way out, but it was perfectly evident that he understood the futility of his argument, especially since he had informed for them in the past. Within a span of ten minutes, Archie agreed to "cooperate." He said, however, that he owed Bill fourteen dollars and couldn't "make a buy from him" unless he could say he would pay him the "bread." The police offered to provide the money, and Archie called Bill, who, according to Archie, had agreed to a sale.

TRIAL BY POLICE

At this point, any lingering doubt the police might have had as to Bill's guilt was erased. They had been only slightly uncertain after the original informant, Charlie, had called and told them that he had personally seen Dave and another addict divide up the spoils of a theft of narcotics and dangerous drugs and that Dave had in turn been robbed by Bill. Now that Archie had "testified" to the effect that Bill was dealing narcotics, any remaining residue of "reasonable doubt" was obliterated.

The use of legal terminology emphasizes the similarity between the reasoning processes of the policeman and those employed by the formal evidentiary standards governing determinations of guilt or innocence. An eyewitness had established that a crime had been committed, and knew the identity of one of the culprits. In addition, he had given hearsay testimony (not admissible in a courtroom) that one of the original culprits had been robbed by a third party, Bill. Although no eyewitness observed this robbery, another witness testified to its effects: Archie not only gave hearsay testimony that Bill "had plenty of stuff," but in addition said that he, Archie, had personally purchased narcotics from Bill. The evidence in this "case" was circumstantial, but strong (depending on the weight conferred on the testimony of the chief witnesses). Moreover, the testimony was given against a background of police experience with the typical behavior patterns of addicts. The stories told by the informants not only fit together, thereby reinforcing the validity of each, but conformed generally to the policeman's conception of usual addict behavior. Therefore, so far as the police were concerned, reliable witnesses had provided circumstantial evidence and eyewitness testimony sufficient to convict Bill.

The standards used by the police to assess Bill's guilt were not unlike those employed by the trial court. (Of course, only one side of the case was stated, since Bill had been given no opportunity to testify or bring witnesses on his own behalf; but for the police this omission was irrelevant.) The evidentiary standards employed by the police in this case are obvious and are those to which reasonable men seem naturally to gravitate. For instance, African tribal judges, as described by Gluckman, employed reasoning similar to that the policeman uses to assess the addict's guilt and to that English and American jurists would likely employ if placed in the social situation of the policeman. Gluckman says:

> Judges work not only with standards of reasonable behaviour for upright incumbents of particular social positions, but also with standards of behaviour which are reasonably interpreted as those of particular kinds of wrongdoers. There are social stereotypes of how thieves, adulterers, and other malefactors act. If the witnessed actions of a defendant assemble into one of these stereotypes, he is found guilty, though the judges prefer direct evidence to convict.[5]

In effect, the behavior reported about Bill fit the stereotype of the guilty addict-seller, although guilt had by no means been judicially established. Consequently, for the police, the job now was not to convince themselves of the suspect's guilt, but to demonstrate it in a fashion that would satisfy two closely related requirements: the maintenance of the informer system, and the standard of evidence sufficient to convict in court.

It is instructive to consider the probable legal outcome if at this time the police had decided to arrest Bill on the strength of the evidence presented. In court, Charlie's testimony about Bill's activities would be objected to and upheld as irrelevant, immaterial, and hearsay. Charlie did not see Bill rob Dave of narcotics but had merely heard of this through the addict grapevine. Although Archie's testimony would be admissible, he would be the sole prosecution witness, and any competent defense attorney could destroy Archie's credibility by bringing out that he was a narcotics addict who had been offered a deal in return for testimony. Thus, the case would turn on the testimony of a single vulnerable prosecution witness. By practical courtroom standards, the State at this point had no case against Bill, although by police standards Bill was guilty beyond a reasonable doubt.

Therefore, the police needed Archie's agreement to purchase narcotics from Bill to satisfy judicial criteria for conviction. The primary reason for requiring Archie to "make a buy," however, was not to establish probable cause, but to determine the location of the narcotics and establish that the suspect possessed narcotics, either on his person or "constructively" in his home, or his car or even on the person of a female companion.[6] Because Bill was a user-dealer and therefore likely to have his supply close at hand, his apprehension would be relatively easy. By contrast, if he had been a nonuser-dealer, it would have been much more difficult for the police to capture him successfully, since nonuser-dealers do not generally care whether the narcotics are close at hand. Indeed, from his familiarity with the law about possession, the nonaddict-dealer is likely to have a "stash" or a "stash pad" somewhere removed from his own residence, perhaps at the home of a girl friend, or even in any of the

---

[5] Max Gluckman, *The Judicial Process Among the Barotse of Northern Rhodesia* (Glencoe, New York: The Free Press, 1955), p. 359.

[6] A person is in possession of a narcotic when it is under his dominion and control, and, to his knowledge, either is carried on his person or in his presence, the possession thereof is immediate, accessible, and exclusive to him, provided, however, that two or more persons may have joint possession and the possession may be individual, through an agent or joint with another. *People v. Bigelow*, 104 Cal. App. 2d 380, 388. Cited by Fricke, *California Criminal Law*, 8th ed., 1961, p. 395.

numerous places in the public domain that can serve as "stashes," [7] such as trees, directional signs, the undersides of benches and so forth.

There is an important law enforcement distinction to be drawn between popularly reported *transport stashes*—false heels, false bottomed suitcases, diaphragms—and *storage stashes*. Although it is difficult to deceive police in a search of one's self and immediate effects, it is equally difficult for the police to prove a legal connection between an individual and a stash of narcotics stuffed behind the stairway carpeting of an open apartment house. Thus a "buy" is often required to ascertain the location of the narcotics. In the present case, for example, Bill might have had a "stash" half a block away, in a neighbor's backyard. Archie's job was to trigger Bill into getting his supply, not so much for the police to see where it was, as where it was not.

> The police conducted an extended interrogation of Archie about how much "stuff" Bill had, how long he had it, how much he had on hand, and where he kept it. Archie said he thought Bill had gotten the "stuff" about two weeks earlier and had been "shooting and dealing" during this period, but that he wasn't sure exactly how much Bill had on hand, and he certainly didn't know where Bill kept it. Consequently, the police drove to Bill's place in Westville, after Archie had called Bill and told him he had the "bread" he owed him. The police watched Archie enter. He came out more quickly than expected and drove to an appointed spot for a rendezvous. There Archie explained that Bill said he wasn't dressed and didn't want to sell anything tonight, but that he'd give him something in the morning.

The question the police had to resolve was whether they should break into Bill's that night, or wait until morning for Archie to make a buy. After some discussion, it was decided for two reasons to break in immediately. First, it was felt that the longer the wait before breaking in on the suspect, the less likely he would be caught with a sizable amount (large enough to warrant a charge of possession for sale rather than mere possession) or, worst of all, from the policeman's view, they would merely be able to charge him with being "under the influence." When an addict has a large supply over a period of time, he is likely to have built up his habit with the free access. This, coupled with the knowledge that Bill had already sold a portion of his original holdings, made the police reluctant to wait longer.

Second, Bill was on parole, and was required to take the Nalline test weekly. In 1957 the California legislature authorized the court to require the Nalline test as a condition of probation, if the court has reason to believe that the probationer is a narcotics user.[8] The easily administered test involves reading the size of the subject's pupil, followed by an injection of the drug. According to the developer, prior use of an opiate will cause the diameter of the pupil to enlarge, the size of the increase being related to the amount used. Occasional use results in practically no change in

---

[7] For a discussion of stashes in an institutional setting, see Erving Goffman, *Asylums* (Garden City, New York: Anchor Books, 1961), pp. 248 ff.

[8] The use of Nalline (a Merck & Co., Inc., trademark for the narcotic, N-allynormorphine) for the diagnosis of addiction was first explored by Dr. Harris Isbell and his associates at the United States Public Health Service Hospital in Lexington, Kentucky, and was further developed by Dr. James Terry, Medical Officer on the Sheriff's staff of the Alameda County, California, Rehabilitation Center. It is now used as a means of controlling addiction in several California counties.

pupillary diameter, while absence of narcotics is revealed by reduction of the diameter of the pupil.[9]

If the addict is taking the Nalline test, he will therefore usually be a probationer or a parolee. Even though the test is technically "voluntary" in that the addict signs an "Authorization and Waiver" form, addicts do not generally like it, and submit only as an alternative to jail or State prison. For example, a petty user (a so-called "vag" addict) [10] may receive a sentence of ninety days in the county jail with judgment suspended for as long as three years, provided he takes and passes the Nalline test during this time. He is thus liable for the entire period of suspended judgment to examination for use of narcotics [11] by his probation or parole officer, who often delegates his authority to the police.

Relations between probation officers and police are apt to be difficult, especially when the probationer is a narcotics addict. In this situation, it is mainly the probation officer who is placed in an ambiguous position between therapist and policeman.[12] The policeman's goal is, by contrast, much more clearly defined. His immediate task is to make narcotics arrests using every resource at his command. One of his prime resources is the addict. To the extent, however, that policemen make use of addict-probationers, probation officers fear that the addict will be reintroduced into the world of criminality from which he has so recently emerged, interfering with his potential rehabilitation.

The relations between probation officers and police vary from jurisdiction to jurisdiction. In some, they may be hostile. Westville vice control officers were proud of their cordial relations with the probation department and with parole officers. In general, the police have led the probation officers to believe that whenever a probationer-addict is used as an informant, the probation officer will routinely be informed. Indeed, the police department has one man assigned to the Nalline testing program, who also acts as liaison to the probation department. Meetings between the two departments are held weekly and telephone conversations may occur many times each day. Actually, the police do not routinely disclose the names of their informants to the probation officers but do supply them with information about their probationers' behavior, especially when the behavior seems to be illegal. In return for this information, probation officers (and parole officers) will cooperate with police by giving information, and more importantly by authorizing police to make an arrest as a violation of probation or parole when the police require such authorization.

The police were already apprised of Bill's failure to present himself for the Nalline

[9] For additional information on the technical, administrative, medical, and legal aspects of the Nalline test, see the following: Harris Isbell, "Nalline—A Specific Narcotic Antagonist: Clinical and Pharmacologic Observations," *The Merck Report*, 62 (April, 1953), 23–26; J. G. Terry, "Nalline: An Aid to Detecting Narcotics Users," *California Medicine*, 85 (November, 1956), 299–301; A. Wikler, H. F. Fraser, and Harris Isbell, "N-allynormorphine: Effects of Single Doses and Precipitation of Acute Abstinence Syndromes during Addiction to Morphine, Methadone, or Heroin in Man (Post Addicts)," *Journal of Pharmacology and Experimental Therapy*, 109 (September, 1953), 8–20; Stewart Weinberg, "Nalline as an Aid in the Detection and Control of Users of Narcotics," *California Law Review*, 48 (1960), 282–294; Thorvald T. Brown, Chapter IX, "The Nalline Test," in *The Enigma of Drug Addiction* (Springfield, Illinois: Charles C Thomas, 1961), pp. 287–334; and Ernest B. Smith, *Nalline Examinations of Narcotic Addicts: Analysis of Deterrent Effects*, unpublished M.A. thesis, Department of Criminology, University of California, Berkeley, 1960.

[10] The term stems from the days when police used to arrest users under the vagrancy laws. Presently, Sec. 11721 of the Penal Code serves the same purpose.

[11] It has happened, but rarely, that a vag addict chooses ninety days in jail over three years of Nalline.

[12] Lloyd E. Ohlin, Herman Piven, and Donnell M. Pappenfort, "Major Dilemmas of the Social Worker in Probation and Parole," *National Probation and Parole Association Journal*, 2 (July, 1956), 211–225.

test the preceding week, and as a result suspected he had been using narcotics. The Sergeant was on friendly terms with Bill's parole officer, and counted on him for support in an arrest of Bill for parole violation. That is, although the parole officer had not specifically requested that Bill be arrested, the Sergeant depended upon the parole officer's willingness to affirm he had so requested should the issue arise. As in many systems of so-called rational procedure, the actual practice depends on independently created strategies for avoiding the sanctions of regulation, rather than on formal delegation of authority.

The problem for the police then became how to break into Bill's apartment. Especially in vice control, police frequently must kick doors in sharply and quickly, without giving advance notice of their intentions to the suspect. The purpose of such violent entries is evident: to counteract the speed with which the suspect may destroy or hide incriminating evidence. Thus, a floating crap game can take on the appearance of a discussion group in seconds. Similarly, narcotics are easily flushed down a toilet, and most addicts will stash their supply near one. Even the word "supply," however, is misleading because it connotes a substantial amount of matter, when actually large quantities of narcotics are measured in ounces. As a result, the policeman must be able to control the suspect's behavior before a brush of his hand destroys his cache.

> In this case, the police questioned Archie on the layout of Bill's apartment. Archie thought it would be difficult for the police to find incriminating evidence on Bill. He explained the house had a front and rear door, with a heavy chain and bolt on the front door, and creaky stairs in the rear. It would be, the police figured, a "tough pad to crack." Finally, Sergeant Harris constructed what turned out to be an effective plan. He called for a "beat car" with flashing red light and uniformed patrolmen to pull up in the street in front of the house, and instructed the patrolmen to make a lot of noise. They were to pound on the front door, demand admission, and if not admitted immediately, kick the door in. In the meantime, he detailed three men up the back stairs while the beat car was driving up front, correctly anticipating that Bill's attention would be riveted on the front of the house when he saw the flashing red light and the beat car outside. This gave the three plainclothesmen sufficient time to station themselves outside the rear door, without being heard going upstairs.
>
> As assumed, Bill panicked when he saw the patrolmen heading for the front door and ran across the length of the apartment to the kitchen in the rear. The top half of the rear door was made of glass and the plainclothesmen stationed outside could see Bill run in and attempt to hide a package of white powder under the refrigerator. Whether they kicked the door in before, after, or simultaneously with Bill's attempt to dispose of the heroin, I cannot say, since I was at the front door behind the uniformed policemen. The fact is, however, that Bill was caught in the act.

The case described above was a "good pinch." It resulted in a charge and conviction of possession for sale upon the defendant's plea of guilty. Because of his youth, the seller was given a relatively light six-month term in the county jail, and his wife was given thirty days. Some time later, I interviewed the wife in the county jail, quite by accident, in connection with part of the study concerning defendants' perceptions of the criminal process. It was clear she did not recall this "Dr. Skolnick" who was interviewing her as one of the "policeman" involved in her arrest. (I was visible throughout the arrest proceedings and the subsequent interrogation, but this new context offered a new identity.) She was pleased with the way her case had gone and felt that both she and her husband had "gotten off" lightly. They each felt, she reported, that they had committed a serious crime, the police had treated them well, the judge had been understanding and the defense attorney, a public defender, competent. Whatever resentment she held was toward the unknown "fink" who had "ratted" on them to the police. The police, however, were perceived as men doing their jobs, an impression they convey well.

THE BIG CASE

Cases like the one now discussed occur so rarely that no special term, other than "big case" or "big one," develops to describe them. This case yielded the largest amount of narcotics confiscated in three years by the Westville department. Since there was much secrecy, it was fortunate that the apprehension took place after rapport had been established with the Westville vice control squad. A member of this squad informed me of developments and invited me (via an unexpected telephone call to my home one evening) to observe the proceedings when "the caper was scheduled to go down."

A major difference between the ordinary "good pinch" and the big narcotics case is whether the ultimate source has been tapped. In the typical "good pinch," narcotics officers make every effort to apprehend a larger dealer. Since Bill had stolen his narcotics from a drugstore, he was himself the ultimate source, and the police could make no further arrests. Most of the time, narcotics officers are not able to arrest important men in the dealership hierarchy, nor are they able to confiscate more than a small proportion of the annual narcotics traffic. In the State of California, a man offering to sell a pound of heroin was regarded by narcotics agents at the federal, state and local levels whom I interviewed as being about "as big as they come." Such a man, of course, purchases his narcotics from another dealer who usually is foreign and therefore may be outside the jurisdiction of federal agents. Since the flow of narcotics is part of an international traffic, even federal agents are usually unable to reach high into ultimate sources of supply.[13]

The analysis of this "big case" illustrates two principles: first, how its enforcement pattern affords the police more leeway in complying with legal rules; and second, how such cases aid the police to acquire the commodities they need to carry out the enforcement of middle-sized cases. In this case, the Westville narcotics detail apprehended a nonuser-dealer whose activities they had been following for almost two years. The nonuser-dealer, the straight businessman in narcotics, is more difficult to apprehend than the man who sells and also takes narcotics. When the "heat is on," or when he perceives it to be "on," the nonuser-dealer can keep away from his source

---

[13] Official Treasury Department figures indicate that in 1961, 40.26 kilograms of heroin and 20.25 kilograms of other narcotics drugs were seized or purchased by federal authorities; in 1962, 87.80 kilograms of heroin and 21.55 kilograms of other narcotics were seized or purchased by federal agents. The Treasury Department Bureau of Narcotics makes no official estimate of the amount of heroin used annually in the United States, but agents interviewed agreed that the amount confiscated is a small percentage of the amount used. (The figures cited above are given in the Bureau of Narcotics report *Traffic in Opium and Other Dangerous Drugs,* Washington, D.C.: Government Printing Office, 1963, p. 66.)

of supply more easily than the addict-dealer. As long as the narcotics are hidden in a neutral stash, the dealer need not be concerned about police apprehension. All involved—the police, the addict, the dealer—are well aware of the implications attached to possession, and perhaps more importantly, to nonpossession of narcotics. Thus, the police always fear that when they set up a "buy," the seller will not show up with the "stuff" on his person.[14]

The apprehension of the nonuser-dealer involved the use of several petty informants, plus diligent and patient police work. The police finally took a room where they were able to keep him under constant surveillance and caught him selling several "balloons" of heroin. When apprehended, nonuser-dealers do not usually agree to serve as informants, since they are themselves exceptionally "good pinches," and are more "reliable businessmen" than addicts. In this case, however, partly because of the persuasive abilities of the police, but largely because there was bigger game in the offing, it was possible, through the cooperation of the district attorney's office, to offer a substantial reduction in charges.

Cooperation here meant more and was more dangerous than the cooperation demanded of Archie. Archie merely had to "make a buy." In this case, however, the strategy was to have a state agent make a series of purchases. Where nonuser-dealers are involved, speed of apprehension is not as important as is patience. Unlike the user-dealer, the nonuser is unlikely to consume his supply. The aim is not to catch him quickly but to bring him to the point where he purchases quantities as large as the abundance of his source will permit him to offer. To bring him to this point, he must come to trust his purchaser. Accordingly, the strategy of the narcotics police required the local dealer to make several purchases and to introduce another "buyer" provided by the state police.

The advantage of this strategy is that it allows the purchaser to risk exposure through public testimony. The informant who performs the introduction is still under suspicion, but he can always claim that the state agent was introduced to him by a third party, just as he introduced the agent to the source. In the Pirandello-like setting of a narcotics investigation, it is difficult for an accused party to sort out the actual identities and loyalties of those with whom he has been involved. If the accused chooses to go to trial, however, the true identity of the man who testifies that he purchased narcotics from the accused is revealed. Where the State's witness is a narcotics officer, law enforcement need not be concerned about disclosing identity and, furthermore, can rely on him to testify persuasively. (Police, in my experience, make excellent witnesses.) The only drawback for the police arises from a concern for police resources; each time a policeman participates in such a maneuver he too is partly "burned" and loses some of his value as an undercover agent. Given budgetary limitations, the police can afford to use narcotics agents only in the bigger cases. It is also true that the speed of apprehension typically required in smaller cases normally does not permit police to be used as *agent provocateurs*. Thus, in the "good pinch" described above, a police agent could not have been substituted for Archie since by

---

[14] A shrewd nonuser-dealer had the Westville narcotics police completely stymied at the time of this writing. His mode of operation was based on a skillful combination of use of assistants and of negotiation to take advantage of protections afforded the defendant in the criminal process. He personally handled neither cash nor heroin, and never associated himself with a direct exchange of one for the other. He would have the buyer give his assistant the money for the heroin and would telephone the buyer the next day giving the location of the stash. Furthermore, he had developed a reputation for trustworthiness among his customers; so much so that the head of the Westville narcotics detail ruefully acknowledged, "He gives good quantity and good quality. The only way we'll ever get him is through a conspiracy charge."

the time the necessary introductions and purchases could have been made, the *corpus delecti* would have been consumed.

In that "good pinch" only one purchase was made. Here there were four, each large. The state agent was introduced to the sellers, the Gomez brothers, by the informant who represented the agent as a friend "dealing" in the northwestern United States, and able to dispose of large amounts of heroin. The agent was first introduced to the dealer's younger brother, Arthur, who was a partner, but evidently did not personally have the "connections." The agent was especially skillful in using his knowledge of narcotics and his demeanor to impress the younger Gomez that he was an "old-time Mexican dealer" rather than a flashy newcomer. The younger Gomez agreed to let the agent have three ounces of heroin in exchange for cash, and also two ounces on "consignment."

About two weeks later, after payment had been made for the consignment purchase, several recorded telephone calls were made over a four-day period to the older brother Charles. He continued to promise delivery of heroin to the agent, but on each day "backed off," claiming to be unable to locate his "connection." The agent also made a recorded telephone call to the dealer's girl friend during which she told him that Charles was trying to contact the "connection." A week later the agent recorded two telephone calls to Charles arranging for the delivery of heroin to Westville. It was agreed that Charles and Arthur would fly to the local airport, to be met by the agent. On the appointed day, the agent purchased five ounces of heroin [15] from the brothers for close to twenty-one hundred dollars. There was no recording of the actual transaction, but several state agents and members of the Westville narcotics detail observed it from a distance.

At this point, the police saw their next move as luring the defendants to a place where a transaction could be "bugged" by a concealed microphone. Accordingly, the state agent telephoned Charles Gomez and told him he was fearful of the "heat" at the airport, and had arranged for the next deal to take place in a Westville motel room. Two days later, the dealer and his girl friend appeared at the motel, where the agent purchased approximately ten ounces of heroin for twenty-eight hundred dollars. Several other narcotics police were observing near the motel and a hidden camera took a photograph of the dealer entering the motel room. The purchase went off smoothly, however, and any suspicions Gomez might have held were evidently allayed.

A week later the agent called the brothers and made arrangements to purchase as much as twenty-two ounces of narcotics later in the week, in the same Westville motel room. This was to be the setting for the "big pinch," the exchange of five thousand dollars for at least a pound of heroin, with, presumably, the remainder on consignment. The younger Gomez agreed to come and the events leading to arrest were initiated. It was decided that the agent would give the money to the younger Gomez, who was scheduled to arrive with the heroin at eight in the evening. Following the transfer, the younger Gomez was expected to call his older brother and tell him that everything "had come off okay" and that he would arrive home in the morning. After this phone call, the police planned for the agent to call the elder Gomez and to indicate that there was a "panic" [16] on, and that if the brother could come up that night with another dozen or so ounces of heroin, the agent could pay for it.

[15] An ounce of heroin is not necessarily an ounce of pure heroin. Usually what is purchased has already been "cut." Most of the heroin sold by the Gomez brothers was about 6 per cent pure.

[16] When an area runs dry of narcotics, addicts in that area, because of their pressing need, will be enormously anxious to the point of panic, and hence the term.

Anticipation of a "big case" arouses much anxiety in the police. With each successful purchase, the stakes become higher. There already was enough evidence to arrest and, in all likelihood, to convict the Gomez brothers. But the aim of the police was, at this point, to implicate the brothers as fully and as clearly as possible. Indeed, at a certain point the big case becomes almost an aesthetic matter, and style, defined by the personal satisfactions of the narcotics policeman, counts for almost as much as results. Unfortunately, from the policeman's viewpoint, the expectation of a "big case" not only arouses personal anxiety, but also requires unusual cooperation among law enforcement organizations. This increases the number of men involved, the personal tensions of each, and thus the possibility that the charade will be revealed to the offender.

In the present case these factors resulted in several mishaps that destroyed the aesthetic of this night's work, but which also, against the background of prior incriminating encounters with the offenders, made little legal difference. First, the younger Gomez failed to arrive on schedule. When he did arrive somewhat unexpectedly, the state agent was in conversation with three Westville police officers. Gomez, the state agent later reported, had asked him what was going on, and the agent replied that he was asking directions from these strangers about where to meet the helicopter. (One of the police commented, "This guy Gomez must really be stupid. Any one of our nickel-and-dime dealers here in Westville would have smelled the heat a mile away.") At the time, however, the state agent did not know whether the dealer had caught on to the trap. He could not be certain at how to interpret the dealer's lateness. It might have been, as Gomez explained, that he had difficulty getting the heroin from his connection. But the agent also was concerned that Gomez had become suspicious, arrived early, had hidden the heroin, then returned to the airport. Without the heroin, the evening's plan would be a failure. Nor could the agent be sure that Gomez was not armed; a report that he might be had been received from police in another part of the state.

Under these circumstances, it is not surprising that the usually cool state agent missed the highway turnoff to the motel and arrived twenty minutes late. In the meantime, the police at the motel were becoming increasingly fidgety. Two policemen (and the writer) were stationed in the room next to where the "buy" was to take place, to record the conversation and to be available for assistance should the dealer be armed. Five policemen were in the motel manager's office with equipment for recording the expected telephone conversation with Charles Gomez, and another policeman (along with a newspaperman) was stationed across the courtyard as an additional check on Gomez's movements.

Gomez and the state agent arrived in the room at about 10:30 P.M. In the adjoining room the recording equipment had failed, which not only meant the loss of a recorded conversation of the narcotics purchase, but also heightened concern for the agent's safety and caused partial inability to keep track of Gomez. Presumably, if he left the room, the agent across the courtyard would see him and notify the police in the manager's office via the walkie-talkies with which each of the three police locations were equipped. About fifteen minutes after Gomez arrived, we in the adjoining room were informed by walkie-talkie that Gomez had telephoned his brother to say that everything was okay. We were also told that the detectives in the office had evidently recorded this conversation, but that they were going to listen to the record to make sure. So far everything was proceeding as planned. Fifteen minutes later we were told that Gomez was in custody in the manager's office.

This is what had happened. Gomez decided after his telephone call to go to the lobby to buy a soft drink. When he left, the walkie-talkie in the surveillance room did not respond. The agent become so flustered he forgot to use the telephone to warn the other officers of Gomez's impending arrival. Gomez entered the lobby from a side entrance, because it was a shorter distance from the room, and literally walked into a bevy of policemen listening intently to the recording of Arthur Gomez speaking to Charles. Whether the policemen or the dealer was more surprised, I cannot say. At that point, however, it was incumbent that the police arrest Arthur.

Shortly after Arthur was taken into custody, he was brought out into the court-yard and photographed by the newsmen. The problem for the police at this point was to convince Arthur Gomez to call his brother Charles and to persuade him to come to Westville with additional narcotics. Arthur finally complied about two hours later when, in my opinion, he believed his brother would know that something had gone wrong. In any event, Charles did not arrive the next morning, but was arrested at his home by the state and local police of his area. Both men finally pleaded guilty to two counts of possession for sale and were sentenced to three years in San Quentin prison. The sentence of the younger Gomez was suspended (partly on the recommendation of the police for his "cooperation" in making the telephone call), but he was required to serve the first year of his suspended sentence in the county jail.

The following day a story appeared in the local Westville newspaper with an eight-column headline and front-page pictures reporting that a one-and-a-half-million dollar "dope ring" had been "smashed." The size of the dope ring was reported in the newspaper headline according to the ultimate possible price of the narcotics on the illicit retail market. Actually, the "pound" of narcotics confiscated contained only 6 per cent pure heroin. Such a quantity does go a long way on the retail market, but not nearly as far as the newspaper story suggested.

Such stories serve several functions for the narcotics police. This sort of report gives the policeman public recognition as a reward for his services. In this case, however, the police did not personally feel that they deserved as much recognition as they received. Although the case had yielded an acceptable outcome, it did not "come off" with the smoothness which they regard as the fundamental satisfaction of narcotics work. This is not to say that the police were dissatisfied; rather events had spoiled an unusual opportunity for a masterful arrest and transformed it into a less than craftsmanlike occasion.

Another purpose served by exaggerated newspaper treatment of narcotics cases is to indicate to the public that "dope rings" are in common operation, but that the police are able to "smash" them. To a certain extent, however, the "dope ring" referred to in the newspaper article was itself "created" by the narcotics police. This is not to say that Charles Gomez was not a criminal purveyor of narcotics; but when law enforcement agencies themselves become major purchasers of narcotics, they make someone like Gomez a much more important-appearing dealer than he would have been had not close to twelve thousand dollars worth of narcotics been purchased from him by the State. In this sense, then, in the "big case," narcotics police inevitably are part of the "dope rings" they themselves help to create.

Finally, newspaper stories of this kind serve the more important function of giving the narcotics police support in their campaign for increasingly severe penalties against those trafficking in narcotics. These penalties, as we indicated, provide the police with greater commodities to maintain the information system enabling "good pinches."

SUMMARY AND CONCLUSION

This chapter has described the work of the narcotics officer at three levels: his routine activities, especially with petty informants; the "good pinch"; and "the big case." These levels were shown to be interrelated, since narcotics enforcement typically involves the apprehension of a hierarchy of offenders. Therefore, for that reason, because the ordinary addict is a criminal, actually and symbolically, and also in conformity to a belief that the way to destroy the narcotics traffic is to rid the community of customers, the police pursue the petty user.[17]

In those instances where a petty user has enough narcotics in his possession to lay the basis for a felony charge, his arrest is considered a "good pinch." The apprehension of a petty user affords a degree of satisfaction to the police, but not nearly so much as participation in a "big case," especially when a nonuser-dealer is caught. The latter is considered part of the organized narcotics traffic; bringing about his conviction is therefore regarded as especially meritorious.

Beyond these reasons for the policeman's preference of the "big case" arrest over the "good pinch" is another important consideration. The "big case" provides the policeman with the conditions under which conventional and constitutional standards of legality may best be met. Thus, a typical difference in conditions underlying the two types of arrests is the amount of time the police have: little in the "good pinch," much in the "big case." Greater time permits the police to obtain warrants, allows the offender to make several observed infractions of the law, and enables the police to make more adequate records of infractions.

The main reason the police are able to keep more adequate records in the "big case" revolves around the most important condition distinguishing these two types of arrests. In the "good pinch," the informant is typically an addict, while in the "big case," the informant is typically a narcotics officer. This difference is also related to the amount of time available; since the police must move quickly in the "good pinch," they usually have insufficient time to establish a new identity for the policeman, whereas the addict comes equipped with his own.

Not only is the policeman a better record keeper than the addict-informant but he is also a more persuasive witness during the trial. Even if the informant were able to give convincing testimony, he would be asked to take the stand only in rare instances, since the policeman is usually obliged to protect the informer's criminal status. It is therefore ironic that the cases in which the policeman least prefers to participate arise as test cases to restrict the limits of his behavior. In the narcotics area, a "big case" is rarely the subject of an appellate judicial decision for the simple reason that the "big case" provides the policeman with the conditions under which constitutional standards of legality may best be met.[18] From the policeman's point of view, meeting these standards is preferable to not meeting them, but he is not so concerned about the standards in the abstract. The meeting of constitutional requirements is primarily a way to demonstrate his ability to do his job well; that is the principal concern of the detective.

---

[17] See generally the panel on "Law Enforcement and Controls" and especially the statement by John C. Cross in *Proceedings of the White House Conference on Narcotic and Drug Abuse* (Washington, D.C.: Government Printing Office, 1962), pp. 23–65.

[18] One recent important case—which was indeed a "good pinch"—was the case of *People v. Ker*, 374 U.S. 23 (1963). Although this decision in some respects limits the policemen's actions, it also recognizes the special circumstances under which narcotics police perform their duties.

PROSECUTION

INTRODUCTION

No one really knows how much crime occurs, but one thing is clear from a survey of the crimes processed through the courts: there is a great deal more crime than the processing agencies are equipped to handle. The prosecutor's office typically has two overriding problems: to appear efficient and effective by maintaining a record of convictions and to sift through the plethora of available cases and prosecute some and not others. This latter problem is a simple and direct function of the fact that there are many more cases than the courts and prosecutor's office can possibly process. The former problem is a direct function of the fact that the prosecutor is usually an elected officer, and his public image will directly affect his reelection. His public image, in turn, is dependent on how well he performs his task of seeing that criminals are punished.

With limited resources and a virtually unlimited supply of potential cases, how does the prosecutor go about deciding who shall be processed and who shall not? Many of the institutionalized (patterned) mechanisms developed to cope with this issue have been detailed above. In addition, the prosecutor typically develops other techniques as well. Of these, none is more important nor more effective than the use of "bargain justice." Donald Newman's article on this subject makes it very clear how the mechanism of bargaining works: the prosecutor agrees to a lesser charge or some other concession to the offender in exchange for a plea of guilty. Guilty pleas, of course, eliminate the necessity for a jury trial (except in first-degree murder trials, where a jury is mandatory), and the entire legal process is expedited.

Bargaining is the rule rather than the exception among prosecutors across the nation. In a survey conducted by the editors of the *University of Pennsylvania Law Review,* 86 percent of the prosecutors responding to their questionnaire answered yes to the question, "Is it the practice of your office to make arrangements with criminal defendants (or their counsel), when appropriate, in order to obtain a plea of guilty?" [1] The same survey disclosed that three general categories of bargains were made by the prosecutor: promises of sentence recommendation to the court, acceptance of pleas to lesser included offenses, and dismissals of court or other indictments. Ninety-five percent of the prosecutors indicated use of lesser charges, eighty-six percent indicated use of dismissal of indictments, and fifty-eight percent indicated use of promises of sentence recommendation to court.

Since by far the least advantageous agreement from the standpoint of the offender is the promise to recommend a light sentence, the fact that this category is the least-often used suggests that the prosecutor is unable to strike this bargain with any regularity. Once again we see operating in the relationship between the criminal and the legal system a process of exchange wherein the criminal or the accused has something to offer the representatives of the law and the representatives of the law must bend or perhaps totally break the legal yardstick to effect a resolution of the bargain which is to their advantage. That this resolution may not be to the advantage of the law or society generally is a point on which there would be considerable disagreement. Certainly one must realize that the prosecutors do not engage in bargaining because of an inherent personal corruptness, nor should one interpret the development of cooperation between professional gamblers and the police as evidence of the inherent corruptibility of policemen. Rather, both these events should be understood as manifestations of the operating principle that an organization must come to grips with the facts of the world it is given and must work out a solution in everyday practices which takes that world into account. Bargaining for punishments with accused is one such device for working out the problems involved in appearing effective and handling large numbers of complaints.

The prosecutor's office must also deal directly with persons filing complaints against presumed offenders. These complaints are rarely rewarding for a prosecutor's office. Most of the complaints involve extremely trivial occurrences (from the standpoint of the prosecutor); more important, the accused person is not someone who needs to be "taught a lesson" and is rarely a real "criminal." Therefore, the prosecutor's office seeks to minimize the time and effort devoted to citizen complaints. In large metropolitan areas the most effective technique is to put up bureaucratic barriers. A person wishing to file a complaint is likely to be met with an endless string of referrals to various persons and divisions in the prosecutor's office. If the complainant persists long enough (which few of them do), then as a last resort an official is likely to tell him (1) that the evidence he presents is insufficient to bring the case to court and (2) that if he insists on bringing it to court he himself may be sanctioned because he was not totally uninvolved in what took place (this is particu-

---

[1] "Guilty Plea Bargaining: Compromises by Prosecutors to Secure Guilty Pleas," *University of Pennsylvania Law Review,* vol. 112, April, 1964, pp. 896–908.

larly effective in dealing with assault-and-battery cases); or the prosecutor will point out that the accused may sue the complainant for false accusations. By this time only the very determined will have survived, and as a consequence the prosecutor's office handles very few cases which begin with a citizen's complaint.

Precisely what the total impact of these and similar administrative decisions is on the processing of persons through the legal system is not altogether clear. There are undoubtedly systematic biases built into such a system which parallel the biases against lower-class persons, minority-group members, and persons who lack the aura of respectability. There is, in addition, the fact that the professional criminal can offer the system compensations for leniency and is therefore in a much stronger bargaining position than the amateur or occasional thief. It would therefore seem likely that we would typically fill our corrective institutions (penitentiaries and jails) with a predominantly youthful, quasi-criminal group while the more systematic and sophisticated offenders would be relatively unimpaired by the law. Interestingly, this does in fact seem to be the case even where there is a public-defender system (at least insofar as the findings from David Sudnow's study can be generalized). For the public defender is faced with many of the same problems that plague the prosecuting attorney's office, and the most readily available solution to these administrative problems is to cooperate with the prosecutor's office.

The prosecutor's office, then, shares many of the problems of the police department: it must constantly be on guard against public scrutiny and it must continuously cope with some contradictory goals and means built into the system. That the solution is to avoid the strict letter of the law is no surprise; whether anything remains which is even a faint shadow of what the law was intended to be is yet another question.

12. Pleading Guilty for Considerations: A Study of Bargain Justice

Donald J. Newman

One of the major problems faced by social scientists interested in studying criminal behavior involves obtaining samples of offenders to be used as units of research. Ordinarily such samples are drawn from prisons or probation files because the study of unapprehended criminals is extremely difficult. Conviction by a court or authorized agency is, therefore, the usual basis of sample selection.[1] Virtually all sociologists admit the inadequacy of such a technique and qualify their samples as non-representative of any kind of a criminal universe. At the same time, the conviction record

SOURCE: "Pleading Guilty for Considerations: A Study of Bargain Justice," *Journal of Criminal Law, Criminology and Police Science*, vol. 46, pp. 780–790, March–April, 1956. By permission of author and publisher.

[1] See Paul Tappan, *Who Is the Criminal?* in: Amer. Sociol. Rev., vol. 12, no. 1, pp. 96–102 and Donald R. Cressey, *Criminological Research and the Definitions of Crimes*, Amer. Jour. of Sociol., vol. 57, May, 1951, pp. 546–551.

of the offenders who are selected for study from prisons and courts is used as the basis for typing the offenders and for various statistical computations. In general, the man's conviction record is assumed to be a quasi-automatic legal stamp which defines those activities which make him a criminal.

Of course very few researchers would treat a person such as Al Capone as merely an income tax violator, but this is because they would know, or think that they know that such an individual had committed other offenses or had different patterns of criminal behavior than those for which he was sentenced. In less notorious cases, however, the type of offense and the severity of the sentence, remain the pivotal points around which research is pursued and prison classification systems are built.

This does not mean that sociologists naïvely accept conviction on a specific charge as definitive nor that they have little interest in the mechanics of justice. The reverse, of course, is more accurate. But the emphasis of both sociological exposition and research has been on the *gross* misuse of justice, on methods used by criminals, political officials and the business elite to avoid conviction. It is also true that some sociological interest has been shown in procedural variation, particularly brutal, and in many cases, illegal, arrest and interrogation methods. The police particularly have come under sociological scrutiny.[2] Nevertheless, apart from the "fix" and the "third degree," the conviction process has generally been neglected in research as of minor importance in the complicated process of defining "criminal" as the basic unit of research.

METHODS OF STUDYING THE CONVICTION PROCESS

In order to bring to light some of the less apparent factors influencing the procedural steps by which society labels the criminal, a sample of men, all convicted of "conventional" felonies in one court district was interviewed in regard to the processes involved in their own convictions. Men from a single county were selected in order to keep formal legal procedures and court and prosecuting officials constant for each case. The lawyers and judges of this district had been interviewed previously by the author,[3] so that information was available about conviction processes from the legal participants' viewpoints. The county was located in the mid-west (Wisconsin) and was of "medium" size, neither rural nor metropolitan. The county seat had a population of approximately 100,000 persons. Furthermore, the district was politically clean, having no widespread organized crime or vice nor a tradition of "fixing" criminal cases by bribery or intimidation. Supposedly in such a setting, felony convictions would follow a quasi-automatic, "combat" theory of criminal justice, involving a jury trial or at least an unconditional plea of guilty.

MOST CONVICTIONS THE RESULT OF GUILTY PLEAS

The felons who were interviewed, a group of ninety-seven representing all men from the district under active sentence, had all been convicted of felonies ranging from non-support to murder. There were no white-collar criminals in the group,

---

[2] William Westley, *Violence and the Police* (in: Amer. Jour. of Sociol., July, 1953), pp. 34–41 and Ernest J. Hopkins, *Our Lawless Police* (New York: Viking Press, 1931).

[3] This study took place in 1951 and 1952 as part of the American Bar Association's study entitled *Criminal Law and Litigation*.

except for three clerks serving sentence for embezzlements, nor were there any racketeers or professional criminals such as confidence men, and no individuals sentenced from Juvenile Court were included. The men were serving sentences under the following conditions:

State prison	34
State reformatory	6
Parole	9
Probation	48
TOTAL	97

Most of the convictions (93.8 percent) were not convictions in a combative, trial-by-jury sense, but merely involved sentencing after a plea of guilty had been entered. On the surface this might lend support to the contention that most convictions are mere rubber stamps of the court applied to the particular illegal behavior involved in each case.

On closer analysis, however, it was seen that over a third (38.1 percent) of the men had originally entered a not guilty plea, changing to guilty only at a later procedural stage short of an actual trial. The question immediately arose, why did these men change their minds? Was it because of a promise of leniency or some such bargain as suggested by the Wickersham report, Moley and other writers of a decade ago? [4] A second question followed. Did the men who pleaded guilty immediately do so unconditionally to the charge as contained in the complaint or was there any evidence of informal "arranging" of the sentence so widely alleged in criminology texts?

TABLE 12-1

Type of Plea by Retention of Counsel

	Type of Plea		
		Changed Not Guilty	
Retention of Counsel	*Guilty*	*to Guilty*	*Total*
Offenders with lawyers	21	24	45
	(23.2)	(26.3)	(49.5)
Offenders without lawyers	39	7	46
	(42.7)	(7.8)	(50.5)
TOTAL	60	31	91*
Percent	(65.9)	(34.1)	(100.0)

* Offenders pleading not guilty and retaining this plea through a jury trial were eliminated. All, however, had counsel.

$x^2 = 14{,}713$, d.f. $= 1$, significant at the 5 percent level. Yules Q $= -.728$ indicating a negative correlation between initial admission of guilt and the retention of counsel.

[4] National Commission on Law Observance and Enforcement, *Report on Prosecution,* Bulletin 4 (Washington, D.C.: Government Printing Office, 1931); and Raymond Moley, *Our Criminal Courts* (New York: Minton, Balch Co., 1930) and *Politics and Criminal Prosecution* (New York: Minton, Balch Co., 1929). See also Newman F. Baker and Earl H. DeLong, *The Prosecuting Attorney: Powers and Duties in Criminal Prosecution* (in: Jour. of Crim. L. and Criminol., vol. 24, no. 6, March–April, 1934) and Newman F. Baker, *The Prosecutor–Initiation of Prosecution* (in: Jour. of Crim. L. and Criminol., vol. 23, no. 5, September, 1933).

Pursuing these lines of inquiry, an interesting difference between the two groups of men was seen. Men entering an initial plea of not guilty were significantly more often represented by defense attorneys than the men pleading guilty immediately. On all other demographic characteristics, age, gross type of offense for which sentenced (personal, property, sex, and miscellaneous violations such as carrying a concealed weapon), education, occupation, residence and so on, the groups showed no significant differences. Furthermore, on the eventual disposition of the cases, e.g., whether sent to prison or placed on probation, the groups did not differ. In fact, only one other difference besides the retention of counsel was noted. It was found that the men who initially pleaded guilty and who more often than not did not hire or request counsel were recidivists, whereas the men with lawyers, who at first pleaded innocent, were more often experiencing their first conviction.

This phenomenon is rather curious when it is recalled that the groups showed no differences in the frequency of being placed on probation. It might logically be expected, in the light of current sentencing practices, that first offenders would more likely receive probation than men with previous convictions, particularly if, as was the case, there was no significant variation in the types of crimes for which they were sentenced. The implications of this lack of difference in sentences for the role of the lawyer in the conviction process was so great that the men were further analyzed by dividing them into two groups, one characterized by the retention of counsel, the other comprising men who pleaded without an attorney.

TABLE 12-2

Expected Punishment by Retention of Counsel

Punishment Expected at Time of Arrest	Retention of Counsel		Total
	Offenders with Lawyers	Offenders without Lawyers	
Expected same as actual or didn't know what to expect	3 (3.2)	10 (10.3)	13 (13.5)
Expected less severe than actual	11 (11.3)	11 (11.3)	22 (22.6)
Expected more severe than actual	37 (38.1)	25 (25.8)	62 (63.9)
TOTAL	51	46	97
Percent	(52.6)	(47.4)	(100.0)

$\chi^2 = 5.827$, d.f. $= 2$, not significant at 5 percent level.

The outcome of the conviction process from the point of view of the offender is satisfactory or unsatisfactory depending upon the actual sentence he receives compared to his expectations of punishment at the time he is arrested. It might be supposed that a violator who expected a severe sentence would seek legal advice. However, an analysis of the responses of the men showed that their expectations were not the determining factor in their decisions to retain counsel or to plead without counsel.

TABLE 12-3

Non-represented Offenders' Reasons for Not Retaining Counsel

	Percent
Obviously guilty, hoped for mercy from the court	19.5
Made deal for concurrent sentence or had charges dropped	30.4
Made deal for lesser charge or a light sentence	23.9
Don't trust lawyers	4.4
Had no money, didn't know about court-assigned lawyers	13.0
Other*	4.4
Not ascertained	4.4
TOTAL	100.0

* These cases claimed that they were subjected to long and arduous questioning and "confessed" to "get it over with" and thus had neither the time nor the inclination to get a lawyer.

REASONS FOR PLEADING GUILTY WITHOUT A LAWYER

The reasons given for claiming or for disdaining counsel varied from confessions of "obvious" guilt and a hope for mercy from the court to poverty coupled with ignorance of provisions for state-paid defense attorneys. The chief reason, however, appeared to be an expedient one, related to the factor of past experience in going through the conviction process. The recidivists were both conviction wise and conviction susceptible in the dual sense that they knew of the possibility of bargaining a guilty plea for a light sentence and at the same time were vulnerable, because of their records, to threats of the prosecutor to "throw the book" at them unless they confessed. Over half (54.3 percent) of the men claimed that they had bargained for their sentences, and 84 percent of these men had been convicted previously. A number of factors, all interrelated, seem to account for this. First, a general fear expressed by multiple offenders of facing a jury or of antagonizing sentencing officials was revealed in most cases. Some felt that their records would be held against them by a jury (actually the admission in court of the offender's previous criminal record is closely regulated by law to assure a fair trial on the current charge). They felt conviction would be more certain because in the public mind they were "ex-cons." A more general fear, however, was that the judge would be especially severe in sentencing if they did decide to fight and then lost. They felt that pleading not guilty and hiring a lawyer would only irritate the various officials, particularly the prosecutor, whose recommendation at the time of sentencing is an important consideration of the court. One of the men said:

> When the day comes to go and the D.A. stands up and says you're a dirty rat and a menace to society and should be locked up and have the key thrown away—then look out! You're going away for a few years.

These fears, whether justified or not, undoubtedly make these men more amenable to an informal "settling" of their cases.

A second factor making for bargaining and the rejection of counsel was the experience of these men gained in previous convictions. Many of the recidivists, particularly those with two or more convictions, knew the sentencing judges and some of the prosecutors quite well and all of the offenders knew most of the police. They were on a first name basis with many of these men and could bargain in a friendly or even a jocular manner. One man (on probation) said:

> Old _____ told me he was going to throw the book at me. I told him he didn't have a damn thing on me. He said I'd get five to ten. I told him he couldn't even book me, that's how little he had. I knew he was riding me; he didn't mean a thing by it. I've known him for years. He just likes to act tough.

Men who had been convicted in other states or in other counties but never before in this district were quite conscious of this "friendship" factor in the bargaining processes. Each of them expressed the belief that had he been a "local" he would have fared better.

Previous sentences served in institutions also seemed to be relevant to bargaining without a lawyer. Former inmates were more legal-wise; their conceptions of their offenses were not primarily in terms of guilt or innocence but contained more references to evidence and its relation to the outcome of the conviction process. They referred to how much the prosecutor "had on me" and the ability of the prosecution to make a charge stick. One of the men expressed it this way:

> The D.A. needed my help. His evidence was all circumstances (sic). He knew I done it but he couldn't ever prove it. But I couldn't go to court and take a chance with my record. When I saw he was going to stick me with something, I was willing to make the best deal.

Not only does a quasi-legal knowledge evidently develop in incarceration (most of these men knew the statute numbers of their offenses and all knew such terms as "preliminary hearing," "arraignment" and "pre-sentence investigation") but those men seemed better able to recognize a good bargain when they saw one. Although all offenders recognized probation as the best break, of course, and many knew the possible length of sentence for their particular crime, recidivists knew customary sentences (and court district variations) for their offenses. In short, they recognized a "good-as-compared-to-other-guys-I-know" sentence when they faced it.

OFFENDERS WHO RETAIN COUNSEL

Over half (52.6%) of the men in the total sample retained lawyers and proceeded through more of the formal stages of the conviction process (preliminary hearing, arraignment) than those men who pleaded without attorneys. As anticipated from the analysis of the group of non-represented offenders, the factor of recidivism with its accompanying implication of bargaining skills learned from past experience was almost completely absent from this group. As one of these men expressed it:

> I'd never been in trouble before. I didn't know which end was up. I thought sure I was going to prison. It seemed as if they had a million laws I'd broken. The only thing I could think of was calling my wife to get me a lawyer.

These men with their lawyers, either privately hired or court assigned, significantly more often pleaded not guilty when first apprehended, changing their pleas only later in the process. On the surface, this observation might lead to one of two conflicting conclusions. The fact that the retention of counsel correlated with a change of plea to guilty might mean that the lawyers, having a better grasp of the legal worth of the evidence against their clients, advised them to plead guilty and that the clients followed their advice. Or, it could with equal validity indicate that perhaps the lawyers, through informal bargaining skills similar to the non-represented recidivists, had arranged satisfactory charges or more lenient sentences than originally expected by their clients. The latter would seem to be the most convincing in view of the offenders' responses. When asked their lawyer's advice in regard to pleading, 75 percent of those first pleading not guilty and then guilty, responded that their counsel's advice was to maintain a not guilty plea "until something can be arranged." This they did. The remainder were advised to plead guilty without promise of any arrangement, although bargaining is not thus ruled out.

Only fifteen of the represented offenders said that their convictions were the result of unconditional pleas of guilty. The remainder, including not only the offenders whose lawyers' advice was to hold off pleading guilty until settlement was made, but twelve of the men who entered initial guilty pleas as well, claimed to have received some consideration in the nature of the charge or type and length of sentence in exchange for their admissions of guilt.

TYPES OF BARGAINING WHERE ATTORNEY HAS BEEN RETAINED

While the frequency of claimed bargaining does not differ significantly between the groups of offenders without lawyers and with lawyers, there is some difference in the frequencies of the various types reported. Men without attorneys significantly more often mentioned as the consideration they received in exchange for a guilty plea either the reduction of the charge or the promise of a suitable, fixed sentence.

TABLE 12-4

Offenders Pleading Guilty after Bargaining over Charge or Sentence

| | Offenders Pleading Guilty | | |
Retention of Counsel	Pleaded Guilty for Consideration	Pleaded Guilty without Bargaining	Total
Offenders with lawyers	30	15	45
	(33.0)	(16.5)	(49.5)
Offenders without lawyers	25	21	46
	(27.4)	(23.1)	(50.5)
TOTAL	55	36	91
Percent	(60.4)	(39.6)	(100.0)

$\chi^2 = 1.443$, d.f. $= 1$, not significant at 5 percent level.

TABLE 12-5

Frequency of Types of Bargaining by Retention of Counsel *

	Offenders with Lawyers	Offenders without Lawyers	Total
1. Pleading to a lesser charge	8 (14.5)	3 (5.5)	11 (20.0)
2. Pleading for a light sentence	17 (30.9)	8 (14.6)	25 (45.5)
3. Pleading for concurrent sentences	3 (5.5)	9 (16.3)	12 (21.8)
4. Pleading for the dismissal of charges	2 (3.6)	5 (9.1)	7 (12.7)
TOTAL	30	25	55
Percent	(54.5)	(45.5)	(100.0)

* Combining the first two types (lesser charge, light sentence) and comparing them with the last two (concurrent sentence, charge dismissed) a significant difference between types of bargaining and retention of counsel is seen. $\chi^2 = 23.72$, d.f. $= 1$, significant at 5 percent level. Yules $= -.732$ indicating a negative correlation between retention of lawyer and pleading guilty for considerations of concurrent sentences of dismissed charges.

It would seem from this that lawyers are more likely to be retained by offenders who fear a severe punishment or in cases involving a disputable charge whereas violators with many charges against them "cop a plea" directly from the prosecution or the court without a lawyer as intermediary. This would also seem to substantiate the evidence from the unrepresented defendants that the function of the lawyer in bargaining is not essential for all offenders, and that men experienced in the conviction process can informally and successfully arrange their own legal fate.

TYPES OF INFORMAL CONVICTION AGREEMENTS

The considerations received by the offenders in exchange for their guilty pleas were of four general types:

> **1.** *Bargain concerning the charge.* A plea of guilty was entered by the offenders in exchange for a reduction of the charge from the one alleged in the complaint. This ordinarily occurred in cases where the offense in question carried statutory degrees of severity such as homicide, assault, and sex offenses. This type was mentioned as a major issue in twenty percent of the cases in which bargaining occurred. The majority of offenders in these instances were represented by lawyers.
>
> **2.** *Bargain concerning the sentence.* A plea of guilty was entered by the offenders in exchange for a promise of leniency in sentencing. The most commonly accepted consideration was a promise that the offender would be placed on probation, although a less-than-maximum prison term was the basis in certain instances. All offenses except murder,

serious assault, and robbery were represented in this type of bargaining process. This was by far the most frequent consideration given in exchange for guilty pleas, occurring in almost half (45.5 percent) of the cases in which any bargaining occurred. Again, most of these offenders were represented by attorneys.

3. *Bargain for concurrent charges.* This type of informal process occurred chiefly among offenders pleading without counsel. These men exchanged guilty pleas for the concurrent pressing of multiple charges, generally numerous counts of the same offense or related violations such as breaking and entering and larceny. This method, of course, has much the same effect as pleading for consideration in the sentence. The offender with concurrent convictions, however, may not be serving a reduced sentence; he is merely serving one sentence for many crimes. Altogether, concurrent convictions were reported by 21.8 percent of the men who were convicted by informal methods.

4. *Bargain for dropped charges.* This variation occurred in about an eighth of the cases who reported bargaining. It involved an agreement on the part of the prosecution not to press formally one or more charges against the offender if he in turn pleaded guilty to (usually) the major offense. The offenses dropped were extraneous law violations contained in, or accompanying, the offense alleged in the complaint such as auto theft accompanying armed robbery and violation of probation where a new crime had been committed. This informal method, like bargaining for concurrent charges, was reported chiefly by offenders without lawyers. It occurred in 12.6 percent of cases in which bargaining was claimed.

The various types of informal conviction agreements were described in the majority of the cases and, as mentioned, only six members of the sample went to jury trial. The remainder of the sample (37.1 percent) pleaded guilty, they said, without any considerations. It is possible, however, that in those 15 instances where the men had counsel, the attorney had bargained, or had attempted to bargain, without the knowledge of the offender.

In instances where informal methods were used, the roles of the various participants were cooperative rather than combative. Central to the entire process were the roles of offender and prosecutor; the defense attorney played a significant part chiefly in cases of first offenders and in instances where the nature of the charge was in dispute. The judge sometimes played an informal role in cases involving a fixed sentence, but even here the prosecutor's role dominated because of the common practice in the court whereby the judge asks for, and generally follows, the prosecutor's recommendation as to sentence in cases pleading guilty.

THE BARGAIN THEORY OF CRIMINAL JUSTICE

The most significant general finding of the study was that the majority of the felony convictions in the district studied were not the result of the formal, combative theory of criminal law involving in effect a legal battle between prosecution and defense, but were compromise convictions, the result of bargaining between defense and prosecution. Such informal conviction processes were observed in over half of the cases studied.

In the informal process the accused, directly or through his attorney, offered to plead guilty to the offense for which he was arrested, providing it was reduced in kind or degree, or in exchange for a given type or length of sentence. The prosecutor benefitted from such a bargain in that he was assured of a conviction, yet did not have to spend the time and effort to prepare a trial case. He also avoided the ever-present risk of losing even a clear-cut case should the accused have gone before a jury. The court, too, benefitted. Court calendars were, and are, crowded and the entire court system would be admittedly inadequate to cope with criminal trials should all, or even a fraction of the felony arrests decide to go to trial. This, coupled with a generally favorable attitude toward bargaining processes on the part of the lawyers, civil and criminal, in the local bar, made informal methods of conviction almost inevitable.

Instead of proceeding through all the formal stages of conviction such as hearing before a magistrate, preliminary hearing, arraignment, etc., the majority of the offenders waived most of these procedures and because of informal promises of leniency or threats of long sentences, entered guilty pleas and were sentenced. About half (50.5 percent) of the sample went to preliminary hearings of their cases but only 6.2 percent proceeded through a jury trial.

CONCLUSIONS: SIGNIFICANCE OF INFORMAL CONVICTION PROCESSES TO CRIMINOLOGY

Criminological research has generally ignored methods of conviction in conventional felony cases except the illegal "fix" and brutal "third-degree" as primarily legal steps automatically defining the unit to be studied. The automatism of conviction has here been challenged, and within the limits of the present research, inter-action processes of sociological interest in themselves, have been outlined.

It was felt in conducting this research that, if informal methods of convictions were discovered, they would be of a nature to negate the use of conviction records in many types of research and correctional administration. In the typology of criminals, in prison classification, and in other applied fields such as parole prediction, bargaining techniques would rule out the accuracy of the "paper" conviction as an index of the offender's actual patterns of criminality. In spite of the high incidence (56.7 percent) of admitted bargaining in the sample, however, only a very small proportion of cases admitted guilt to offenses grossly different from those alleged in the complaint, and only a small proportion had offenses dismissed so that they did not appear at all on the offenders' records. In other words, the informal conviction processes tended to result in guilty pleas to the same or very similar offenses, so that the offenses for which convicted did not usually deviate greatly from the crime actually committed. The greater proportion of the bargaining was concerned with directly gaining a lighter sentence regardless of the offense, rather than indirectly by pleading to a lesser charge.

One of the most important implications of the informal methods is the effect of these processes on selection for probation. A promise of the prosecutor's recommendation for probation was one of the most common values given in exchange for a guilty plea. This occurred in 34.5 percent of the cases reporting bargaining. With such informal tactics, selection for placement on probation is determined by the skill of the offender or his lawyer in bargaining, rather than on factors of the case which would have more relevance to successful rehabilitation by field rather than institutional placement.

The existence of informal methods also has broader significance to law and law enforcement as well as to criminology and related areas. The use of such methods involves a differential implementation of the law comparable to the discrepancies noted by Reckless in his "categoric risk" of conviction and Sutherland in his conceptions of white collar crime.[5] An analysis of the sample of offenders showed no clear-cut categories separating bargaining from non-bargaining convictions, yet the fact that some offenders, without going to trial, pleaded guilty without any considerations in the charge or in sentencing while others "settled" their cases informally, raises again the sociological, and presumably the moral, problems of criminal justice.

Evidently the criminal law is not only differentially enforced in general, but as far as this study shows, this also occurs within groups of offenders convicted of the ordinary (or conventional) felonies of robbery, homicide, burglary, larceny and sex offenses. Certain proportions of these violators (56.7 percent in this sample), without resorting to bribery or other methods of the professional "fix," can modify the nature of the charge against them or the length or type of their sentences in much the same manner as the white collar offender.

Whether bargaining is legal, that is, whether men convicted as the result of bargaining are convicted by due process of law, is a difficult question to answer without referring the decision to a specific case. Likewise, whether bargaining is ethical cannot be summarily answered. Certainly in cases where bargaining is misused, where the accused is exploited or the community subjected to danger, the issue is clear. Under these conditions bargaining is not only unethical but would probably be held unconstitutional, as a violation of the "due process" clauses of the Constitution.

When compromise is used, however, to gain a certain conviction of a surely guilty offender, the question is not so clear. Defense lawyers, prosecutors, and criminal court judges interviewed in an earlier study overwhelmingly favored bargain-justice where judiciously used. They felt it to be the most expedient way of gaining justice. Likewise the offenders who bargained successfully were well satisfied with this process. It was the men who went to trial or who failed to bargain successfully who more often claimed injustice in their cases.

As the lawyers said, bargaining appears to be an expedient method of answering numerous problems of the administration of justice. Our criminal procedure is cumbersome. Legal defense is expensive both for the state and the accused. Court calendars are crowded and would not be able to cope with the number of trials which would ensue if all arrestees pleaded not guilty. Furthermore, no conviction is ever a sure thing, no matter how overwhelming the evidence, if the case goes before a jury. Prosecutors, who need convictions to be successful, know this. For these reasons, "bargain-justice" appears the natural answer to lawyers and court officials and, of course, to offenders who are guilty. For these reasons, too, the problem of bargaining cannot easily be corrected, if it should be corrected at all. Bargain-justice appears as a natural, expedient outgrowth of deficiencies in the administration of our "trial-

---

[5] See Walter Reckless, *The Crime Problem*, 2nd edition (New York: Appleton-Century-Crofts, Inc., 1955), pp. 26–42; and Edwin H. Sutherland, *White Collar Crime* (New York: Dryden Press, 1949), pp. 3–14.

by-combat" theory of justice. It is supported by both the attitudes of offenders who see justice as a purely personal thing, how well they fare in sentencing, and by the attitudes of lawyers and court officials who can only "get things done" in this way.

While bargain-justice may thus be an expedient and at present even a necessary and legitimate legal phenomenon in certain cases, some broader implications of bargaining should be mentioned. Cases of conventional felonies that are "settled" may well result in strengthening attitudes which favor a general disregard for law and for justice, in much the same way as does the differential legal treatment of business and political violators. If conviction on a charge is to be determined in great part by skill of the offender in bargaining with the court or in hiring a lawyer to bargain for him, then our concept of impartial justice based upon facts and rules of evidence becomes meaningless. Furthermore, the fact that opportunities and techniques for bargaining exist in our system can have an adverse effect upon attempts to rehabilitate offenders and generally to decrease crime rates. What happens, for example, when one man, merely because he is unsophisticated, does not know of bargaining techniques nor of the right lawyer to contact, is sentenced to prison while another more sophisticated offender, a recidivist who commits the same offense, arranges a sentence to be served on probation? Certainly the rationalizations of the man sentenced to prison to the effect that he is a "fall guy," and his conception of himself gained from serving prison time, make rehabilitation far more complex if not impossible. The way bargaining now works, the more experienced criminals can manipulate legal processes to obtain light sentences and better official records while the less experienced, occasional offenders receive more harsh treatment. Under these conditions the effectiveness of law as a means of social control is seriously jeopardized and any long range attempts to build respect for the law and law abiding attitudes will prove extremely difficult.

13. The Practice of Law as Confidence Game: Organizational Cooptation of a Profession

Abraham S. Blumberg

A recurring theme in the growing dialogue between sociology and law has been the great need for a joint effort of the two disciplines to illuminate urgent social and legal issues. Having uttered fervent public pronouncements in this vein, however, the respective practitioners often go their separate ways. Academic spokesmen for the legal profession are somewhat critical of sociologists of law because of what they perceive as the sociologist's preoccupation with the application of theory and methodology to the examination of legal phenomena, without regard to the solution of legal problems. Further, it is felt that "contemporary writing in the sociology of law . . . betrays the existence of painfully unsophisticated notions about the day-to-day oper-

SOURCE: "The Practice of Law as Confidence Game: Organizational Cooptation of a Profession," *Law and Society Review*, vol. 1, pp. 15–39, June, 1967. By permission of the author and publisher.

ations of courts, legislatures and law offices." [1] Regardless of the merit of such criticism, scant attention—apart from explorations of the legal profession itself—has been given to the sociological examination of legal institutions, or their supporting ideological assumptions. Thus, for example, very little sociological effort is expended to ascertain the validity and viability of important court decisions, which may rest on wholly erroneous assumptions about the contextual realities of social structure. A particular decision may rest upon a legally impeccable rationale; at the same time it may be rendered nugatory or self-defeating by contingencies imposed by aspects of social reality of which the lawmakers are themselves unaware.

Within this context, I wish to question the impact of three recent landmark decisions of the United States Supreme Court; each hailed as destined to effect profound changes in the future of criminal law administration and enforcement in America. The first of these, *Gideon v. Wainwright*, 372 U.S. 335 (1963) required states and localities henceforth to furnish counsel in the case of indigent persons charged with a felony.[2] The Gideon ruling left several major issues unsettled, among them the vital question: What is the precise point in time at which a suspect is entitled to counsel? [3] The answer came relatively quickly in *Escobedo v. Illinois*, 378 U.S. 478 (1964), which has aroused a storm of controversy. Danny Escobedo confessed to the murder of his brother-in-law after the police had refused to permit retained counsel to see him, although his lawyer was present in the station house and asked to confer with his client. In a 5–4 decision, the court asserted that counsel must be permitted when the process of police investigative effort shifts from merely investigatory to that of accusatory: "when its focus is on the accused and its purpose is to elicit a confession—our adversary system begins to operate, and, under the circumstances here, the accused must be permitted to consult with his lawyer."

As a consequence, Escobedo's confession was rendered inadmissible. The decision triggered a national debate among police, district attorneys, judges, lawyers, and

[1] H. W. Jones, *A View From the Bridge*, Law and Society: Supplement to Summer, 1965 Issue of Social Problems 42 (1965). See G. Geis, *Sociology, Criminology, and Criminal Law*, 7 Social Problems 40–47 (1959); N. S. Timasheff, *Growth and Scope of Sociology of Law*, in *Modern Sociological Theory in Continuity and Change* 424–49 (H. Becker & A. Boskoff, eds. 1957), for further evaluation of the strained relations between sociology and law.

[2] This decision represented the climax of a line of cases which had begun to chip away at the notion that the Sixth Amendment of the Constitution (right to assistance of counsel) applied only to the federal government, and could not be held to run against the states through the Fourteenth Amendment. An exhaustive historical analysis of the Fourteenth Amendment and the Bill of Rights will be found in C. Fairman, *Does the Fourteenth Amendment Incorporate the Bill of Rights? The Original Understanding*, 2 Stan. L. Rev. 5–139 (1949). Since the Gideon decision, there is already evidence that its effect will ultimately extend to indigent persons charged with misdemeanors—and perhaps ultimately even traffic cases and other minor offenses. For a popular account of this important development in connection with the right to assistance of counsel, see A. Lewis, *Gideon's Trumpet* (1964). For a scholarly historical analysis of the right to counsel see W. M. Beaney, *The Right to Counsel in American Courts* (1955). For a more recent comprehensive review and discussion of the right to counsel and its development, see Note, *Counsel at Interrogation*, 73 Yale L.J. 1000–57 (1964).

With the passage of the Criminal Justice Act of 1964, indigent accused persons in the federal courts will be defended by federally paid legal counsel. For a general discussion of the nature and extent of public and private legal aid in the United States prior to the Gideon case, see E. A. Brownell, *Legal Aid in the United States* (1961); also R. B. von Mehren, et al., *Equal Justice for the Accused* (1959).

[3] In the case of federal defendants the issue is clear. In *Mallory v. United States*, 354 U.S. 449 (1957), the Supreme Court unequivocally indicated that a person under federal arrest must be taken "without any unnecessary delay" before a U.S. commissioner where he will receive information as to his rights to remain silent and to assistance of counsel which will be furnished, in the event he is indigent, under the Criminal Justice Act of 1964. For a most interesting and richly documented work in connection with the general area of the Bill of Rights, see C. R. Sowle, *Police Power and Individual Freedom* (1962).

other law enforcement officials, which continues unabated, as to the value and propriety of confessions in criminal cases.[4] On June 13, 1966, the Supreme Court in a 5–4 decision underscored the principle enunciated in *Escobedo* in the case of *Miranda v. Arizona*.[5] Police interrogation of any suspect in custody, without his consent, unless a defense attorney is present, is prohibited by the self-incrimination provision of the Fifth Amendment. Regardless of the relative merit of the various shades of opinion about the role of counsel in criminal cases, the issues generated thereby will be in part resolved as additional cases move toward decision in the Supreme Court in the near future. They are of peripheral interest and not of immediate concern in this paper. However, the *Gideon, Escobedo,* and *Miranda* cases pose interesting general questions. In all three decisions, the Supreme Court reiterates the traditional legal conception of a defense lawyer based on the ideological perception of a criminal case as an *adversary, combative* proceeding, in which counsel for the defense assiduously musters all the admittedly limited resources at his command to *defend* the accused.[6] The fundamental question remains to be answered: Does the Supreme Court's conception of the role of counsel in a criminal case square with social reality?

The task of this paper is to furnish some preliminary evidence toward the illumination of that question. Little empirical understanding of the function of defense counsel exists; only some ideologically oriented generalizations and commitments. This paper is based upon observations made by the writer during many years of legal practice in the criminal courts of a large metropolitan area. No claim is made as to its methodological rigor, although it does reflect a conscious and sustained effort for participant observation.

COURT STRUCTURE DEFINES ROLE OF DEFENSE LAWYER

The overwhelming majority of convictions in criminal cases (usually over 90 per cent) are not the product of a combative, trial-by-jury process at all, but instead merely involve the sentencing of the individual after a negotiated, bargained-for plea of guilty has been entered.[7] Although more recently the overzealous role of police

---

[4] See N.Y. Times, Nov. 20, 1965, p. 1, for Justice Nathan R. Sobel's statement to the effect that based on his study of 1,000 indictments in Brooklyn, N.Y., from February–April, 1965, fewer than 10% involved confessions. Sobel's detailed analysis will be found in six articles which appeared in the New York Law Journal, beginning November 15, 1965, through November 21, 1965, titled *The Exclusionary Rules in the Law of Confessions: A Legal Perspective—A Practical Perspective.* Most law enforcement officials believe that the majority of convictions in criminal cases are based upon confessions obtained by police. For example, the District Attorney of New York County (a jurisdiction which has the largest volume of cases in the United States), Frank S. Hogan, reports that confessions are crucial and indicates "if a suspect is entitled to have a lawyer during preliminary questioning . . . any lawyer worth his fee will tell him to keep his mouth shut," N.Y. Times, Dec. 2, 1965, p. 1. Concise discussions of the issue are to be found in D. Robinson, Jr., *Massiah, Escobedo and Rationales for the Exclusion of Confessions,* 56 J. Crim. L. C. & P.S. 412–31 (1965); D. C. Dowling, *Escobedo and Beyond: The Need for a Fourteenth Amendment Code of Criminal Procedure,* 56 J. Crim. L. C. & P.S. 143–57 (1965).

[5] *Miranda v. Arizona,* 384 U.S. 436 (1966).

[6] Even under optimal circumstances a criminal case is a very much one-sided affair, the parties to the "contest" being decidedly unequal in strength and resources. See A. S. Goldstein, *The State and the Accused: Balance of Advantage in Criminal Procedure,* 69 Yale L.J. 1149–99 (1960).

[7] F. J. Davis et al., *Society and the Law: New Meanings for an Old Profession* 301 (1962); L. Orfield, *Criminal Procedure from Arrest to Appeal* 297 (1947).

D. J. Newman, *Pleading Guilty for Considerations: A Study of Bargain Justice,* 46 J. Crim. L. C. & P.S.

and prosecutors in producing pretrial confessions and admissions has achieved a good deal of notoriety, scant attention has been paid to the organizational structure and personnel of the criminal court itself. Indeed, the extremely high conviction rate produced without the features of an adversary trial in our courts would tend to suggest that the "trial" becomes a perfunctory reiteration and validation of the pretrial interrogation and investigation.[8]

The institutional setting of the court defines a role for the defense counsel in a criminal case radically different from the one traditionally depicted.[9] Sociologists and others have focused their attention on the deprivations and social disabilities of such variables as race, ethnicity, and social class as being the source of an accused person's defeat in a criminal court. Largely overlooked is the variable of the court organization itself, which possesses a thrust, purpose, and direction of its own. It is grounded in pragmatic values, bureaucratic priorities, and administrative instruments. These exalt maximum production and the particularistic career designs of organizational incumbents, whose occupational and career commitments tend to generate a set of priorities. These priorities exert a higher claim than the stated ideological goals of "due process of law," and are often inconsistent with them.

Organizational goals and discipline impose a set of demands and conditions of practice on the respective professions in the criminal court, to which they respond by abandoning their ideological and professional commitments to the accused client, in the service of these higher claims of the court organization. All court personnel, including the accused's own lawyer, tend to be coopted to become agent-mediators [10] who help the accused redefine his situation and restructure his perceptions concomitant with a plea of guilty.

Of all the occupational roles in the court the only private individual who is officially recognized as having a special status and concomitant obligations is the lawyer. His legal status is that of "an officer of the court" and he is held to a standard of ethical performance and duty to his client as well as to the court. This obligation is thought to be far higher than that expected of ordinary individuals occupying the various occupational statuses in the court community. However, lawyers, whether privately retained or of the legal-aid, public defender variety, have close and continuing relations with the prosecuting office and the court itself through discreet relations with the judges via their law secretaries or "confidential" assistants. Indeed,

---

780–90 (1954). Newman's data covered only one year, 1954, in a midwestern community, however, it is in general confirmed by my own data drawn from a far more populous area, and from what is one of the major criminal courts in the country, for a period of fifteen years from 1950 to 1964 inclusive. The English experience tends also to confirm American data, see N. Walker, *Crime and Punishment in Britain: An Analysis of the Penal System* (1965). See also D. J. Newman, *Conviction: The Determination of Guilt or Innocence Without Trial* (1966), for a comprehensive legalistic study of the guilty plea sponsored by the American Bar Foundation. The criminal court as a social system, an analysis of "bargaining" and its functions in the criminal court's organizational structure, are examined in my forthcoming book, *The Criminal Court: A Sociological Perspective*, to be published by Quadrangle Books, Chicago.

[8] G. Feifer, *Justice in Moscow* (1965). The Soviet trial has been termed "an appeal from the pretrial investigation" and Feifer notes that the Soviet "trial" is simply a recapitulation of the data collected by the pretrial investigator. The notions of a trial being a "tabula rasa" and presumptions of innocence are wholly alien to Soviet notions of justice. ". . . the closer the investigation resembles the finished script, the better. . . ." *Id.* at 86.

[9] For a concise statement of the constitutional and economic aspects of the right to legal assistance, see M. G. Paulsen, *Equal Justice for the Poor Man* (1964); for a brief traditional description of the legal profession see P. A. Freund, *The Legal Profession*, Daedalus 689–700 (1963).

[10] I use the concept in the general sense that Erving Goffman employed it in his *Asylums: Essays on the Social Situation of Mental Patients and Other Inmates* (1961).

lines of communication, influence and contact with those offices, as well as with the Office of the Clerk of the court, Probation Division, and with the press, are essential to present and prospective requirements of criminal law practice. Similarly, the subtle involvement of the press and other mass media in the court's organizational network is not readily discernible to the casual observer. Accused persons come and go in the court system schema, but the structure and its occupational incumbents remain to carry on their respective career, occupational and organizational enterprises. The individual stridencies, tensions, and conflicts a given accused person's case may present to all the participants are overcome, because the formal and informal relations of all the groups in the court setting require it. The probability of continued future relations and interaction must be preserved at all costs.

This is particularly true of the "lawyer regulars" i.e., those defense lawyers, who by virtue of their continuous appearances in behalf of defendants, tend to represent the bulk of a criminal court's non-indigent case workload, and those lawyers who are not "regulars," who appear almost casually in behalf of an occasional client. Some of the "lawyer regulars" are highly visible as one moves about the major urban centers of the nation, their offices line the back streets of the courthouses, at times sharing space with bondsmen. Their political "visibility" in terms of local club house ties, reaching into the judge's chambers and prosecutor's office, are also deemed essential to successful practitioners. Previous research has indicated that the "lawyer regulars" make no effort to conceal their dependence upon police, bondsmen, jail personnel. Nor do they conceal the necessity for maintaining intimate relations with all levels of personnel in the court setting as a means of obtaining, maintaining, and building their practice. These informal relations are the *sine qua non* not only of retaining a practice, but also in the negotiation of pleas and sentences.[11]

The client, then, is a secondary figure in the court system as in certain other bureaucratic settings.[12] He becomes a means to other ends of the organization's incumbents. He may present doubts, contingencies, and pressures which challenge existing informal arrangements or disrupt them; but these tend to be resolved in favor of the continuance of the organization and its relations as before. There is a greater community of interest among all the principal organizational structures and their incumbents than exists elsewhere in other settings. The accused's lawyer has far greater professional, economic, intellectual and other ties to the various elements of the court system than he does to his own client. In short, the court is a closed community.

This is more than just the case of the usual "secrets" of bureaucracy which are fanatically defended from an outside view. Even all elements of the press are zealously determined to report on that which will not offend the board of judges, the prosecutor, probation, legal-aid, or other officials, in return for privileges and courtesies granted in the past and to be granted in the future. Rather than any view of

---

[11] A. L. Wood, *Informal Relations in the Practice of Criminal Law,* 62 Am. J. Soc. 48–55 (1956); J. E. Carlin, *Lawyers on Their Own* 105–109 (1962); R. Goldfarb, *Ransom—A Critique of the American Bail System* 114–15 (1965). Relatively recent data as to recruitment to the legal profession, and variables involved in the type of practice engaged in, will be found in J. Ladinsky, *Careers of Lawyers, Law Practice, and Legal Institutions,* 28 Am. Soc. Rev. 47–54 (1963). See also S. Warkov & J. Zelan, *Lawyers in the Making* (1965).

[12] There is a real question to be raised as to whether in certain organizational settings, a complete reversal of the bureaucratic-ideal has not occurred. That is, it would seem, in some instances the organization appears to exist to serve the needs of its various occupational incumbents, rather than its clients. A. Etzioni, *Modern Organizations* 94–104 (1964).

the matter in terms of some variation of a "conspiracy" hypothesis, the simple explanation is one of an ongoing system handling delicate tensions, managing the trauma
produced by law enforcement and administration, and requiring almost pathological
distrust of "outsiders" bordering on group paranoia.

The hostile attitude toward "outsiders" is in large measure engendered by a defensiveness itself produced by the inherent deficiencies of assembly line justice, so
characteristic of our major criminal courts. Intolerably large caseloads of defendants
which must be disposed of in an organizational context of limited resources and personnel, potentially subject the participants in the court community to harsh scrutiny
from appellate courts, and other public and private sources of condemnation. As a
consequence, an almost irreconcilable conflict is posed in terms of intense pressures
to process large numbers of cases on the one hand, and the stringent ideological and
legal requirements of "due process of law," on the other hand. A rather tenuous resolution of the dilemma has emerged in the shape of a large variety of bureaucratically
ordained and controlled "work crimes," short cuts, deviations, and outright rule violations adopted as court practice in order to meet production norms. Fearfully antici-
pating criticism on ethical as well as legal grounds, all the significant participants in
the court's social structure are bound into an organized system of complicity. This
consists of a work arrangement in which the patterned, covert, informal breaches,
and evasions of "due process" are institutionalized, but are, nevertheless, denied to
exist.

These institutionalized evasions will be found to occur to some degree, in all
criminal courts. Their nature, scope and complexity are largely determined by the
size of the court, and the character of the community in which it is located, e.g.,
whether it is a large, urban institution, or a relatively small rural county court. In
addition, idiosyncratic, local conditions may contribute to a unique flavor in the
character and quality of the criminal law's administration in a particular community.
However, in most instances a variety of stratagems are employed—some subtle, some
crude, in effectively disposing of what are often too large caseloads. A wide variety
of coercive devices are employed against an accused-client, couched in a deperson-
alized, instrumental, bureaucratic version of due process of law, and which are in
reality a perfunctory obeisance to the ideology of due process. These include some
very explicit pressures which are exerted in some measure by all court personnel,
including judges, to plead guilty and avoid trial. In many instances the sanction of
a potentially harsh sentence is utilized as the visible alternative to pleading guilty,
in the case of recalcitrants. Probation and psychiatric reports are "tailored" to organizational needs, or are at least responsive to the court organization's requirements for
the refurbishment of a defendant's social biography, consonant with his new status.
A resourceful judge can, through his subtle domination of the proceedings, impose
his will on the final outcome of a trial. Stenographers and clerks, in their function as
record keepers, are on occasion pressed into service in support of a judicial need
to "rewrite" the record of a courtroom event. Bail practices are usually employed for
purposes other than simply assuring a defendant's presence on the date of a hearing
in connection with his case. Too often, the discretionary power as to bail is part of
the arsenal of weapons available to collapse the resistance of an accused person. The
foregoing is a most cursory examination of some of the more prominent "short cuts"
available to any court organization. There are numerous other procedural strategies
constituting due process deviations, which tend to become the work style artifacts of

a court's personnel. Thus, only court "regulars" who are "bound in" are really accepted; others are treated routinely and in almost a coldly correct manner.

The defense attorneys, therefore, whether of the legal-aid, public defender variety, or privately retained, although operating in terms of pressures specific to their respective role and organizational obligations, ultimately are concerned with strategies which tend to lead to a plea. It is the rational, impersonal elements involving economies of time, labor, expense and a superior commitment of the defense counsel to these rationalistic values of maximum production [13] of court organization that prevail, in his relationship with a client. The lawyer "regulars" are frequently former staff members of the prosecutor's office and utilize the prestige, know-how and contacts of their former affiliation as part of their stock in trade. Close and continuing relations between the lawyer "regular" and his former colleagues in the prosecutor's office generally overshadow the relationship between the regular and his client. The continuing colleagueship of supposedly adversary counsel rests on real professional and organizational needs of a *quid pro quo*, which goes beyond the limits of an accommodation or *modus vivendi* one might ordinarily expect under the circumstances of an otherwise seemingly adversary relationship. Indeed, the adversary features which are manifest are for the most part muted and exist even in their attenuated form largely for external consumption. The principals, lawyer and assistant district attorney, rely upon one another's cooperation for their continued professional existence, and so the bargaining between them tends usually to be "reasonable" rather than fierce.

FEE COLLECTION AND FIXING

The real key to understanding the role of defense counsel in a criminal case is to be found in the area of the fixing of the fee to be charged and its collection. The problem of fixing and collecting the fee tends to influence to a significant degree the criminal court process itself, and not just the relationship of the lawyer and his client. In essence, a lawyer-client "confidence game" is played. A true confidence game is unlike the case of the emperor's new clothes wherein that monarch's nakedness was a result of inordinate gullibility and credulity. In a genuine confidence game, the perpetrator manipulates the basic dishonesty of his partner, the victim or mark, toward his own (the confidence operator's) ends. Thus, "the victim of a con scheme must have some larceny in his heart." [14]

Legal service lends itself particularly well to confidence games. Usually, a plumber will be able to demonstrate empirically that he has performed a service by clearing up the stuffed drain, repairing the leaky faucet or pipe—and therefore merits his

[13] Three relatively recent items reported in the New York Times, tend to underscore this point as it has manifested itself in one of the major criminal courts. In one instance the Bronx County Bar Association condemned "mass assembly-line justice," which "was rushing defendants into pleas of guilty and into convictions, in violation of their legal rights." N.Y. Times, March 10, 1965, p. 51. Another item, appearing somewhat later that year reports a judge criticizing his own court system (the New York Criminal Court), that "pressure to set statistical records in disposing of cases had hurt the administration of justice." N.Y. Times, Nov. 4, 1965, p. 49. A third, and most unusual recent public discussion in the press was a statement by a leading New York appellate judge decrying "instant justice" which is employed to reduce court calendar congestion "converting our courthouses into counting houses . . . , as in most big cities where the volume of business tends to overpower court facilities." N.Y. Times, Feb. 5, 1966, p. 58.

[14] R. L. Gasser, *The Confidence Game*, 27 Fed. Prob. 47 (1963).

fee. He has rendered, when summoned, a visible, tangible boon for his client in return for the requested fee. A physician, who has not performed some visible surgery or otherwise engaged in some readily discernible procedure in connection with a patient, may be deemed by the patient to have "done nothing" for him. As a consequence, medical practitioners may simply prescribe or administer by injection a placebo to overcome a patient's potential reluctance or dissatisfaction in paying a requested fee, "for nothing."

In the practice of law there is a special problem in this regard, no matter what the level of the practitioner or his place in the hierarchy of prestige. Much legal work is intangible either because it is simply a few words of advice, some preventive action, a telephone call, negotiation of some kind, a form filled out and filed, a hurried conference with another attorney or an official of a government agency, a letter or opinion written, or a countless variety of seemingly innocuous, and even prosaic procedures and actions. These are the basic activities, apart from any possible court appearance, of almost all lawyers, at all levels of practice. Much of the activity is not in the nature of the exercise of the traditional, precise professional skills of the attorney such as library research and oral argument in connection with appellate briefs, court motions, trial work, drafting of opinions, memoranda, contracts, and other complex documents and agreements. Instead, much legal activity, whether it is at the lowest or highest "white shoe" law firm levels, is of the brokerage, agent, sales representative, lobbyist type of activity, in which the lawyer acts for someone else in pursuing the latter's interests and designs. The service is intangible.[15]

The large scale law firm may not speak as openly of their "contacts," their "fixing" abilities, as does the lower level lawyer. They trade instead upon a facade of thick carpeting, walnut panelling, genteel low pressure, and superficialities of traditional legal professionalism. There are occasions when even the large firm is on the defensive in connection with the fees they charge because the services rendered or results obtained do not appear to merit the fee asked.[16] Therefore, there is a recurrent problem in the legal profession in fixing the amount of fee, and in justifying the basis for the requested fee.

Although the fee at times amounts to what the traffic and the conscience of the lawyer will bear, one further observation must be made with regard to the size of the fee and its collection. The defendant in a criminal case and the material gain he may have acquired during the course of his illicit activities are soon parted. Not infrequently the ill gotten fruits of the various modes of larceny are sequestered by a defense lawyer in payment of his fee. Inexorably, the amount of the fee is a function of the dollar value of the crime committed, and is frequently set with meticulous precision at a sum which bears an uncanny relationship to that of the net proceeds of the particular offense involved. On occasion, defendants have been known to commit additional offenses while at liberty on bail, in order to secure the requisite funds with which to meet their obligations for payment of legal fees. Defense lawyers condition even the most obtuse clients to recognize that there is a firm interconnection between fee payment and the zealous exercise of professional expertise, secret knowledge, and organizational "connections" in their behalf. Lawyers, therefore, seek to keep their clients in a proper state of tension, and to arouse in them the precise edge of anxiety which is calculated to encourage prompt fee payment. Consequently, the

[15] C. W. Mills, *White Collar* 121–29 (1951); J. E. Carlin, *supra*, note 11.

[16] E. O. Smigel, *The Wall Street Lawyer* (New York: The Free Press of Glencoe, 1964), p. 309.

client attitude in the relationship between defense counsel and an accused is in many instances a precarious admixture of hostility, mistrust, dependence, and sycophancy. By keeping his client's anxieties aroused to the proper pitch, and establishing a seemingly causal relationship between a requested fee and the accused's ultimate extrication from his onerous difficulties, the lawyer will have established the necessary preliminary groundwork to assure a minimum of haggling over the fee and its eventual payment.

In varying degrees, as a consequence, all law practice involves a manipulation of the client and a stage management of the lawyer-client relationship so that at least an *appearance* of help and service will be forthcoming. This is accomplished in a variety of ways, often exercised in combination with each other. At the outset, the lawyer-professional employs with suitable variation a measure of sales-puff which may range from an air of unbounding self-confidence, adequacy, and dominion over events, to that of complete arrogance. This will be supplemented by the affectation of a studied, faultless mode of personal attire. In the larger firms, the furnishings and office trappings will serve as the backdrop to help in impression management and client intimidation. In all firms, solo or large scale, an access to secret knowledge, and to the seats of power and influence is inferred, or presumed to a varying degree as the basic vendible commodity of the practitioners.

The lack of visible end product offers a special complication in the course of the professional life of the criminal court lawyer with respect to his fee and in his relations with his client. The plain fact is that an accused in a criminal case always "loses" even when he has been exonerated by an acquittal, discharge, or dismissal of his case. The hostility of an accused which follows as a consequence of his arrest, incarceration, possible loss of job, expense and other traumas connected with his case is directed, by means of displacement, toward his lawyer. It is in this sense that it may be said that a criminal lawyer never really "wins" a case. The really satisfied client is rare, since in the very nature of the situation even an accused's vindication leaves him with some degree of dissatisfaction and hostility. It is this state of affairs that makes for a lawyer-client relationship in the criminal court which tends to be a somewhat exaggerated version of the usual lawyer-client confidence game.

At the outset, because there are great risks of nonpayment of the fee, due to the impecuniousness of his clients, and the fact that a man who is sentenced to jail may be a singularly unappreciative client, the criminal lawyer collects his fee *in advance*. Often, because the lawyer and the accused both have questionable designs of their own upon each other, the confidence game can be played. The criminal lawyer must serve three major functions, or stated another way, he must solve three problems. First, he must arrange for his fee; second, he must prepare and then, if necessary, "cool out" his client in case of defeat [17] (a highly likely contingency); third, he must satisfy the court organization that he has performed adequately in the process of negotiating the plea, so as to preclude the possibility of any sort of embarrassing incident which may serve to invite "outside" scrutiny.

[17] Talcott Parsons indicates that the social role and function of the lawyer can be therapeutic, helping his client psychologically in giving him necessary emotional support at critical times. The lawyer is also said to be acting as an agent of social control in the counseling of his client and in the influencing of his course of conduct. See T. Parsons, *Essays in Sociological Theory*, 382 et seq. (1954); E. Goffman, *On Cooling the Mark Out: Some Aspects of Adaptation to Failure*, in *Human Behavior and Social Processes* 482–505 (A. Rose ed., 1962). Goffman's "cooling out" analysis is especially relevant in the lawyer-accused client relationship.

In assuring the attainment of one of his primary objectives, his fee, the criminal lawyer will very often enter into negotiations with the accused's kin, including collateral relatives. In many instances, the accused himself is unable to pay any sort of fee or anything more than a token fee. It then becomes important to involve as many of the accused's kin as possible in the situation. This is especially so if the attorney hopes to collect a significant part of a proposed substantial fee. It is not uncommon for several relatives to contribute toward the fee. The larger the group, the greater the possibility that the lawyer will collect a sizable fee by getting contributions from each.

A fee for a felony case which ultimately results in a plea, rather than a trial, may ordinarily range anywhere from $500 to $1,500. Should the case go to trial, the fee will be proportionately larger, depending upon the length of the trial. But the larger the fee the lawyer wishes to exact, the more impressive his performance must be, in terms of his stage managed image as a personage of great influence and power in the court organization. Court personnel are keenly aware of the extent to which a lawyer's stock in trade involves the precarious stage management of an image which goes beyond the usual professional flamboyance, and for this reason alone the lawyer is "bound in" to the authority system of the court's organizational discipline. Therefore, to some extent, court personnel will aid the lawyer in the creation and maintenance of that impression. There is a tacit commitment to the lawyer by the court organization, apart from formal etiquette, to aid him in this. Such augmentation of the lawyer's stage managed image as this affords, is the partial basis for the *quid pro quo* which exists between the lawyer and the court organization. It tends to serve as the continuing basis for the higher loyalty of the lawyer to the organization; his relationship with his client, in contrast, is transient, ephemeral and often superficial.

DEFENSE LAWYER AS DOUBLE AGENT

The lawyer has often been accused of stirring up unnecessary litigation, especially in the field of negligence. He is said to acquire a vested interest in a cause of action or claim which was initially his client's. The strong incentive of possible fee motivates the lawyer to promote litigation which would otherwise never have developed. However, the criminal lawyer develops a vested interest of an entirely different nature in his client's case: to limit its scope and duration rather than do battle. Only in this way can a case be "profitable." Thus, he enlists the aid of relatives not only to assure payment of his fee, but he will also rely on these persons to help him in his agent-mediator role of convincing the accused to plead guilty, and ultimately to help in "cooling out" the accused if necessary.

It is at this point that an accused-defendant may experience his first sense of "betrayal." While he had perhaps perceived the police and prosecutor to be adversaries, or possibly even the judge, the accused is wholly unprepared for his counsel's role performance as an agent-mediator. In the same vein, it is even less likely to occur to an accused that members of his own family or other kin may become agents, albeit at the behest and urging of other agents or mediators, acting on the principle that they are in reality helping an accused negotiate the best possible plea arrangement under the circumstances. Usually, it will be the lawyer who will activate next of kin in this role, his ostensible motive being to arrange for his fee. But soon latent and unstated motives will assert themselves, with entreaties by counsel to the accused's next of kin, to appeal to the accused to "help himself" by pleading. *Gemeinschaft* sentiments are to this extent exploited by a defense lawyer (or even at times by a district attorney) to achieve specific secular ends, that is, of concluding a particular matter with all possible dispatch.

The fee is often collected in stages, each installment usually payable prior to a necessary court appearance required during the course of an accused's career journey. At each stage, in his interviews and communications with the accused, or in addition, with members of his family, if they are helping with the fee payment, the lawyer employs an air of professional confidence and "inside-dopesterism" in order to assuage anxieties on all sides. He makes the necessary bland assurances, and in effect manipulates his client, who is usually willing to do and say the things, true or not, which will help his attorney extricate him. Since the dimensions of what he is essentially selling, organizational influence and expertise, are not technically and precisely measurable, the lawyer can make extravagant claims of influence and secret knowledge with impunity. Thus, lawyers frequently claim to have inside knowledge in connection with information in the hands of the D.A., police, probation officials or to have access to these functionaries. Factually, they often do, and need only to exaggerate the nature of their relationships with them to obtain the desired effective impression upon the client. But, as in the genuine confidence game, the victim who has participated is loath to do anything which will upset the lesser plea which his lawyer has "conned" him into accepting.[18]

In effect, in his role as double agent, the criminal lawyer performs an extremely vital and delicate mission for the court organization and the accused. Both principals are anxious to terminate the litigation with a minimum of expense and damage to each other. There is no other personage or role incumbent in the total court structure more strategically located, who by training and in terms of his own requirements, is more ideally suited to do so than the lawyer. In recognition of this, judges will cooperate with attorneys in many important ways. For example, they will adjourn the case of an accused in jail awaiting plea or sentence if the attorney requests such action. While explicitly this may be done for some innocuous and seemingly valid reason, the tacit purpose is that pressure is being applied by the attorney for the collection of his fee, which he knows will probably not be forthcoming if the case is concluded. Judges are aware of this tactic on the part of lawyers, who, by requesting an adjournment, keep an accused incarcerated awhile longer as a not too subtle method of dunning a client for payment. However, the judges will go along with this, on the ground that important ends are being served. Often, the only end served is to protect a lawyer's fee.

The judge will help an accused's lawyer in still another way. He will lend the official aura of his office and courtroom so that a lawyer can stage manage an impres-

---

[18] The question has never been raised as to whether "bargain justice," "copping a plea," or justice by negotiation is a constitutional process. Although it has become the most central aspect of the process of criminal law administration, it has received virtually no close scrutiny by the appellate courts. As a consequence, it is relatively free of legal control and supervision. But, apart from any questions of the legality of bargaining, in terms of the pressures and devices that are employed which tend to violate due process of law, there remain ethical and practical questions. The system of bargain-counter justice is like the proverbial iceberg, much of its danger is concealed in secret negotiations and its least alarming feature, the final plea, being the one presented to public view. See A. S. Trebach, *The Rationing of Justice* 74–94 (1964); Note, *Guilty Plea Bargaining: Compromises by Prosecutors to Secure Guilty Pleas*, 112 U. Pa. L. Rev. 865–95 (1964).

sion of an "all out" performance for the accused in justification of his fee. The judge and other court personnel will serve as a backdrop for a scene charged with dramatic fire, in which the accused's lawyer makes a stirring appeal in his behalf. With a show of restrained passion, the lawyer will intone the virtues of the accused and recite the social deprivations which have reduced him to his present state. The speech varies somewhat, depending on whether the accused has been convicted after trial or has pleaded guilty. In the main, however, the incongruity, superficiality, and ritualistic character of the total performance is underscored by a visibly impassive, almost bored reaction on the part of the judge and other members of the court retinue.

Afterward, there is a hearty exchange of pleasantries between the lawyer and district attorney, wholly out of context in terms of the supposed adversary nature of the preceding events. The fiery passion in defense of his client is gone, and the lawyers for both sides resume their offstage relations, chatting amiably and perhaps including the judge in their restrained banter. No other aspect of their visible conduct so effectively serves to put even a casual observer on notice, that these individuals have claims upon each other. These seemingly innocuous actions are indicative of continuing organizational and informal relations, which, in their intricacy and depth, range far beyond any priorities or claims a particular defendant may have.[19]

Criminal law practice is a unique form of private law practice since it really only appears to be private practice.[20] Actually it is bureaucratic practice, because of the legal practitioner's enmeshment in the authority, discipline, and perspectives of the court organization. Private practice, supposedly, in a professional sense, involves the maintenance of an organized, disciplined body of knowledge and learning; the individual practitioners are imbued with a spirit of autonomy and service, the earning of a livelihood being incidental. In the sense that the lawyer in the criminal court serves as a double agent, serving higher organizational rather than professional ends, he may be deemed to be engaged in bureaucratic rather than private practice. To some extent the lawyer-client "confidence game," in addition to its other functions, serves to conceal this fact.

THE CLIENT'S PERCEPTION

The "cop-out" ceremony, in which the court process culminates, is not only invaluable for redefining the accused's perspectives of himself, but also in reiterating publicly in a formally structured ritual the accused person's guilt for the benefit of

---

[19] For a conventional summary statement of some of the inevitable conflicting loyalties encountered in the practice of law, see E. E. Cheatham, *Cases and Materials on the Legal Profession* 70–79 (2d ed., 1955).

[20] Some lawyers at either end of the continuum of law practice appear to have grave doubts as to whether it is indeed a profession at all. J. E. Carlin, *op. cit.*, *supra*, note 11, at 192; E. O. Smigel, *supra*, note 16, at 304–305. Increasingly, it is perceived as a business with widespread evasion of the Canons of Ethics, duplicity and chicanery being practiced in an effort to get and keep business. The poet, Carl Sandburg, epitomized this notion in the following vignette: "Have you a criminal lawyer in this burg?" "We think so but we haven't been able to prove it on him." C. Sandburg, *The People, Yes* 154 (1936).

Thus, while there is a considerable amount of dishonesty present in law practice involving fee splitting, thefts from clients, influence peddling, fixing, questionable use of favors and gifts to obtain business or influence others, this sort of activity is most often attributed to the "solo," private practice lawyer. See A. L. Wood, *Professional Ethics Among Criminal Lawyers*, Social Problems 70–83 (1959). However, to some degree, large scale "downtown" elite firms also engage in these dubious activities. The difference is that the latter firms enjoy a good deal of immunity from these harsh charges because of their institutional and organizational advantages, in terms of near monopoly over more desirable types of practice, as well as exerting great influence in the political, economic and professional realms of power.

significant "others" who are observing. The accused not only is made to assert publicly his guilt of a specific crime, but also a complete recital of its details. He is further made to indicate that he is entering his plea of guilt freely, willingly, and voluntarily, and that he is not doing so because of any promises or in consideration of any commitments that may have been made to him by anyone. This last is intended as a blanket statement to shield the participants from any possible charges of "coercion" or undue influence that may have been exerted in violation of due process requirements. Its function is to preclude any later review by an appellate court on these grounds, and also to obviate any second thoughts an accused may develop in connection with his plea.

However, for the accused, the conception of self as a guilty person is in large measure a temporary role adaptation. His career socialization as an accused, if it is successful, eventuates in his acceptance and redefinition of himself as a guilty person.[21] However, the transformation is ephemeral, in that he will, in private, quickly reassert his innocence. Of importance is that he accept his defeat, publicly proclaim it, and find some measure of pacification in it.[22] Almost immediately after his plea, a defendant will generally be interviewed by a representative of the probation division in connection with a presentence report which is to be prepared. The very first question to be asked of him by the probation officer is: "Are you guilty of the crime to which you pleaded?" This is by way of double affirmation of the defendant's guilt. Should the defendant now begin to make bold assertions of his innocence, despite his plea of guilty, he will be asked to withdraw his plea and stand trial on the original charges. Such a threatened possibility is, in most instances, sufficient to cause an accused to let the plea stand and to request the probation officer to overlook his exclamations of innocence. The table that follows is a breakdown of the categorized responses of a random sample of male defendants in Metropolitan Court [23] during 1962, 1963, and 1964 in connection with their statements during presentence probation interviews following their plea of guilty.

It would be well to observe at the outset, that of the 724 defendants who pleaded

---

[21] This does not mean that most of those who plead guilty are innocent of any crime. Indeed, in many instances those who have been able to negotiate a lesser plea, have done so willingly and even eagerly. The system of justice-by-negotiation, without trial, probably tends to better serve the interests and requirements of guilty persons, who are thereby presented with formal alternatives of "half a loaf," in terms of, at worst, possibilities of a lesser plea and a concomitant shorter sentence as compensation for their acquiescence and participation. Having observed the prescriptive etiquette in compliance with the defendant role expectancies in this setting, he is rewarded. An innocent person, on the other hand, is confronted with the same set of role prescriptions, structures and legal alternatives, and in any event, for him this mode of justice is often an ineluctable bind.

[22] "Any communicative network between persons whereby the public identity of an actor is transformed into something looked on as lower in the local scheme of social types will be called a 'status degradation ceremony.'" H. Garfinkel, *Conditions of Successful Degradation Ceremonies*, 61 Am. J. Soc. 420–24 (1956). But contrary to the conception of the "cop out" as a "status degradation ceremony," is the fact that it is in reality a charade, during the course of which an accused must project an appropriate and acceptable amount of guilt, penitence and remorse. Having adequately feigned the role of the "guilty person," his hearers will engage in the fantasy that he is contrite, and thereby merits a lesser plea. It is one of the essential functions of the criminal lawyer that he coach and direct his accused-client in that role performance. Thus, what is actually involved is not a "degradation" process at all, but is instead, a highly structured system of exchange cloaked in the rituals of legalism and public professions of guilt and repentance.

[23] The name is of course fictitious. However, the actual court which served as the universe from which the data were drawn, is one of the largest criminal courts in the United States, dealing with felonies only. Female defendants in the years 1950 through 1964 constituted from 7–10% of the totals for each year.

guilty before trial, only 43 (5.94 per cent) of the total group had confessed prior to their indictment. Thus, the ultimate judicial process was predicated upon evidence independent of any confession of the accused.[24]

As the data indicate, only a relatively small number (95) out of the total number of defendants actually will even admit their guilt, following the "cop-out" ceremony.

TABLE 13-1

Defendant Responses as to Guilt or Innocence after Pleading Guilty

N = 724   Years — 1962, 1963, 1964

Nature of Response		N of Defendants
INNOCENT (Manipulated)	"The lawyer or judge, police or D.A. 'conned me' "	86
INNOCENT (Pragmatic)	"Wanted to get it over with" "You can't beat the system" "They have you over a barrel when you have a record"	147
INNOCENT (Advice of counsel)	"Followed my lawyer's advice"	92
INNOCENT (Defiant)	"Framed"— Betrayed by "Complainant," "Police," "Squealers," "Lawyer," "Friends," "Wife," "Girlfriend"	33
INNOCENT (Adverse social data)	Blames probation officer or psychiatrist for "Bad Report," in cases where there was pre-pleading investigation	15
GUILTY	"But I should have gotten a better deal" Blames Lawyer, D.A., Police, Judge	74
GUILTY	Won't say anything further	21
FATALISTIC (Doesn't press his "Innocence," won't admit "Guilt")	"I did it for convenience" "My lawyer told me it was only thing I could do" "I did it because it was the best way out"	248
NO RESPONSE		8
TOTAL		724

[24] My own data in this connection would appear to support Sobel's conclusion (see note 4 *supra*), and appears to be at variance with the prevalent view, which stresses the importance of confessions in law enforcement and prosecution. All the persons in my sample were originally charged with felonies ranging from homicide to forgery; in most instances the original felony charges were reduced to misdemeanors by way of a negotiated lesser plea. The vast range of crime categories which are available, facilitates the patterned court process of plea reduction to a lesser offense, which is also usually a socially less opprobrious crime. For an illustration of this feature of the bargaining process in a court utilizing a public defender office, see D. Sudnow, *Normal Crimes: Sociological Features of the Penal Code in a Public Defender Office*, 12 Social Problems 255–76 (1964).

However, even though they have affirmed their guilt, many of these defendants felt that they should have been able to negotiate a more favorable plea. The largest aggregate of defendants (373) were those who reasserted their "innocence" following their public profession of guilt during the "cop-out" ceremony. These defendants employed differential degrees of fervor, solemnity and credibility, ranging from really mild, wavering assertions of innocence which were embroidered with a variety of stock explanations and rationalizations, to those of an adamant, "framed" nature. Thus, the "Innocent" group, for the most part, were largely concerned with underscoring for their probation interviewer their essential "goodness" and "worthiness," despite their formal plea of guilty. Assertion of his innocence at the post-plea stage, resurrects a more respectable and acceptable self concept for the accused defendant who has pleaded guilty. A recital of the structural exigencies which precipitated his plea of guilt, serves to embellish a newly proffered claim of innocence, which many defendants mistakenly feel will stand them in good stead at the time of sentence, or ultimately with probation or parole authorities.

Relatively few (33) maintained their innocence in terms of having been "framed" by some person or agent-mediator, although a larger number (86) indicated that they had been manipulated or "conned" by an agent-mediator to plead guilty, but as indicated, their assertions of innocence were relatively mild.

A rather substantial group (147) preferred to stress the pragmatic aspects of their plea of guilty. They would only perfunctorily assert their innocence and would in general refer to some adverse aspect of their situation which they believed tended to negatively affect their bargaining leverage, including in some instances a prior criminal record.

One group of defendants (92), while maintaining their innocence, simply employed some variation of a theme of following "the advice of counsel" as a covering response, to explain their guilty plea in the light of their new affirmation of innocence.

The largest single group of defendants (248) were basically fatalistic. They often verbalized weak suggestions of their innocence in rather halting terms, wholly without conviction. By the same token, they would not admit guilt readily and were generally evasive as to guilt or innocence, preferring to stress aspects of their stoic submission in their decision to plead. This sizable group of defendants appeared to perceive the total court process as being caught up in a monstrous organizational apparatus, in which the defendant role expectancies were not clearly defined. Reluctant to offend anyone in authority, fearful that clear-cut statements on their part as to their guilt or innocence would be negatively construed, they adopted a stance of passivity, resignation and acceptance. Interestingly, they would in most instances invoke their lawyer as being the one who crystallized the available alternatives for them, and who was therefore the critical element in their decision-making process.

In order to determine which agent-mediator was most influential in altering the accused's perspectives as to his decision to plead or go to trial (regardless of the proposed basis of the plea), the same sample of defendants were asked to indicate the person who first suggested to them that they plead guilty. They were also asked to indicate which of the persons or officials who made such suggestion, was most influential in affecting their final decision to plead.

The following table indicates the breakdown of the responses to the two questions:

TABLE 13-2

Role of Agent-mediators in Defendant's Guilty Plea

Person or Official	First Suggested Plea of Guilty	Influenced the Accused Most in His Final Decision to Plead
JUDGE	4	26
DISTRICT ATTORNEY	67	116
DEFENSE COUNSEL	407	411
PROBATION OFFICER	14	3
PSYCHIATRIST	8	1
WIFE	34	120
FRIENDS AND KIN	21	14
POLICE	14	4
FELLOW INMATES	119	14
OTHERS	28	5
NO RESPONSE	8	10
TOTAL	724	724

It is popularly assumed that the police, through forced confessions, and the district attorney, employing still other pressures, are most instrumental in the inducement of an accused to plead guilty.[25] As Table 13-2 indicates, it is actually the defendant's own counsel who is most effective in this role. Further, this phenomenon tends to reinforce the extremely rational nature of criminal law administration, for an organization could not rely upon the sort of idiosyncratic measures employed by the police to induce confessions and maintain its efficiency, high production and overall rational-legal character. The defense counsel becomes the ideal agent-mediator since, as "officer of the court" and confidant of the accused and his kin, he lives astride both worlds and can serve the ends of the two as well as his own.[26]

While an accused's wife, for example, may be influential in making him more amenable to a plea, her agent-mediator role has, nevertheless, usually been sparked and initiated by defense counsel. Further, although a number of first suggestions of a plea came from an accused's fellow jail inmates, he tended to rely largely on his counsel as an ultimate source of influence in his final decision. The defense counsel, being a crucial figure in the total organizational scheme in constituting a new set of perspectives for the accused, the same sample of defendants were asked to indicate at which stage of their contact with counsel was the suggestion of a plea made. There

[25] Failures, shortcomings and oppressive features of our system of criminal justice have been attributed to a variety of sources including "lawless" police, overzealous district attorneys, "hanging" juries, corruption and political connivance, incompetent judges, inadequacy or lack of counsel, and poverty or other social disabilities of the defendant. See A. Barth, *Law Enforcement versus the Law* (1963), for a journalist's account embodying this point of view; J. H. Skolnick, *Justice without Trial: Law Enforcement in Democratic Society* (1966), for a sociologist's study of the role of the police in criminal law administration. For a somewhat more detailed, albeit legalistic and somewhat technical discussion of American police procedures, see W. R. LaFave, *Arrest: The Decision to Take a Suspect into Custody* (1965).

[26] Aspects of the lawyer's ambivalences with regard to the expectancies of the various groups who have claims upon him, are discussed in H. J. O'Gorman, *The Ambivalence of Lawyers,* paper presented at the Eastern Sociological Association meetings, April 10, 1965.

are three basic kinds of defense counsel available in Metropolitan Court: Legal-aid, privately retained counsel, and counsel assigned by the court (but may eventually be privately retained by the accused).

The overwhelming majority of accused persons, regardless of type of counsel, re- lated a specific incident which indicated an urging or suggestion, either during the course of the first or second contact, that they plead guilty to a lesser charge if this could be arranged. Of all the agent-mediators, it is the lawyer who is most effective in manipulating an accused's perspectives, notwithstanding pressures that may have been previously applied by police, district attorney, judge or any of the agent- mediators that may have been activated by them. Legal-aid and assigned counsel would apparently be more likely to suggest a possible plea at the point of initial interview as response to pressures of time. In the case of the assigned counsel, the strong possibility that there is no fee involved, may be an added impetus to such a suggestion at the first contact.

In addition, there is some further evidence in Table 13-3 of the perfunctory, minis- terial character of the system in Metropolitan Court and similar criminal courts. There

TABLE 13-3

Stage at Which Counsel Suggested Accused to Plead

N = 724

Contact	Counsel Type							
	Privately Retained		Legal-aid		Assigned		Total	
	N	%	N	%	N	%	N	%
FIRST	66	35	237	49	28	60	331	46
SECOND	83	44	142	29	8	17	233	32
THIRD	29	15	63	13	4	9	96	13
FOURTH OR MORE	12	6	31	7	5	11	48	7
NO RESPONSE	0	0	14	3	2	4	16	2
TOTAL	190	100	487	101*	47	101*	724	100

* Rounded percentage.

is little real effort to individualize, and the lawyer's role as agent-mediator may be seen as unique in that he is in effect a double agent. Although, as "officer of the court" he mediates between the court organization and the defendant, his roles with respect to each are rent by conflicts of interest. Too often these must be resolved in favor of the organization which provides him with the means for his professional existence. Consequently, in order to reduce the strains and conflicts imposed in what is ultimately an overdemanding role obligation for him, the lawyer engages in the lawyer-client "confidence game" so as to structure more favorably an otherwise onerous role system.[27]

[27] W. J. Goode, *A Theory of Role Strain*, 25 Am. Soc. Rev. 483–96 (1960); J. D. Snoek, *Role Strain in Diversified Role Sets*, 71 Am. J. Soc. 363–72 (1966).

CONCLUSION

Recent decisions of the Supreme Court, in the area of criminal law administration and defendant's rights, fail to take into account three crucial aspects of social structure which may tend to render the more libertarian rules as nugatory. The decisions overlook (1) the nature of courts as formal organization; (2) the relationship that the lawyer-regular *actually* has with the court organization; and (3) the character of the lawyer-client relationship in the criminal court (the routine relationships, not those unusual ones that are described in "heroic" terms in novels, movies, and TV).

Courts, like many other modern large-scale organizations possess a monstrous appetite for the cooptation of entire professional groups as well as individuals.[28] Almost all those who come within the ambit of organizational authority, find that their definitions, perceptions and values have been refurbished, largely in terms favorable to the particular organization and its goals. As a result, recent Supreme Court decisions may have a long range effect which is radically different from that intended or anticipated. The more libertarian rules will tend to produce the rather ironic end result of augmenting the *existing* organizational arrangements, enriching court organizations with more personnel and elaborate structure, which in turn will maximize organizational goals of "efficiency" and production. Thus, many defendants will find that courts will possess an even more sophisticated apparatus for processing them toward a guilty plea!

14. Normal Crimes: Sociological Features of the Penal Code in a Public Defender Office *

David Sudnow

Two stances toward the utility of official classificatory schema for criminological research have been debated for years. One position, which might be termed that of the "revisionist" school, has it that the categories of the criminal law, e.g., "burglary,"

28 Some of the resources which have become an integral part of our courts, *e.g.*, psychiatry, social work and probation, were originally intended as part of an ameliorative, therapeutic effort to individualize offenders. However, there is some evidence that a quite different result obtains, than the one originally intended. The ameliorative instruments have been coopted by the court in order to more "efficiently" deal with a court's caseload, often to the legal disadvantage of an accused person. See F. A. Allen, *The Borderland of Criminal Justice* (1964); T. S. Szasz, *Law, Liberty and Psychiatry* (1963) and also Szasz's most recent, *Psychiatric Justice* (1965); L. Diana, *The Rights of Juvenile Delinquents: An Appraisal of Juvenile Court Procedures,* 47 J. Crim. L. C. & P.S. 561–69 (1957).

° This investigation is based on field observations of a Public Defender Office in a metropolitan California community. The research was conducted while the author was associated with the Center for the Study of Law and Society, University of California, Berkeley. I am grateful to the Center for financial support. Erving Goffman, Sheldon Messinger, Harvey Sacks, and Emanuel Schegloff contributed valuable suggestions and criticisms to an earlier draft.

SOURCE: "Normal Crimes: Sociological Features of the Penal Code in a Public Defender Office," *Social Problems,* vol. 12, pp. 255–276, Winter, 1965. By permission of the author and publisher.

"petty theft," "homicide," etc., are not "homogeneous in respect to causation." [1] From an inspection of penal code descriptions of crimes, it is argued that the way persons seem to be assembled under the auspices of criminal law procedure is such as to produce classes of criminals who are, at least on theoretical grounds, as dissimilar in their social backgrounds and styles of activity as they are similar. The entries in the penal code, this school argues, require revision if sociological use is to be made of categories of crime and a classificatory scheme of etiological relevance is to be developed. Common attempts at such revision have included notions such as *"white collar* crime," and *"systematic* check forger," these conceptions constituting attempts to institute sociologically meaningful specifications which the operations of criminal law procedure and statutory legislation "fail" to achieve.

The other major perspective toward the sociologist's use of official categories and the criminal statistics compiled under their heading derives less from a concern with etiologically useful schema than from an interest in understanding the actual operations of the administrative legal system. Here, the categories of the criminal law are not regarded as useful or not, as objects to be either adopted, adapted, or ignored; rather, they are seen as constituting the basic conceptual equipment with which such people as judges, lawyers, policemen, and probation workers organize their everyday activities. The study of the actual use of official classification systems by actually employed administrative personnel regards the penal code as data, to be preserved intact; its use, both in organizing the work of legal representation, accusation, adjudication, and prognostication, and in compiling tallies of legal occurrences, is to be examined as one would examine any social activity. By sociologically regarding, rather than criticizing, rates of statistics and the categories employed to assemble them, one learns, it is promised, about the "rate producing agencies" and the assembling process. [2]

While the former perspective, the "revisionist" position, has yielded several fruitful products, the latter stance (commonly identified with what is rather loosely known as the "labelling" perspective), has been on the whole more promissory than productive, more programmatic than empirical. The present report will examine the operations of a Public Defender system in an effort to assess the warrant for the continued theoretical and empirical development of the position argued by Kitsuse and Cicourel. It will address the question: what of import for the sociological analysis of legal administration can be learned by describing the actual way the penal code is employed in the daily activities of legal representation? First, I shall consider the "guilty plea" as a way of handling criminal cases, focusing on some features of the penal code as a description of a population of defendants. Then I shall describe the Public Defender operation with special attention to the way defendants are represented. The place of the guilty plea and penal code in this representation will be examined. Lastly, I shall briefly analyze the fashion in which the Public Defender

---

[1] D. R. Cressey, "Criminological Research and the Definition of Crimes," *American Journal of Sociology*, vol. 61 (no. 6), 1951, p. 548. See also, J. Hall, *Theft, Law and Society*, second edition, Indianapolis: Bobbs-Merrill, 1952; and E. Sutherland, *Principles of Criminology*, revised, New York: Lippincott, 1947, p. 218. An extensive review of "typological developments" is available in D. C. Gibbons and D. L. Garrity, "Some Suggestions for the Development of Etiological and Treatment Theory in Criminology," *Social Forces*, vol. 38 (no. 1), 1959.

[2] The most thorough statement of this position, borrowing from the writings of Harold Garfinkel, can be found in the recent critical article by J. I. Kitsuse and A. V. Cicourel, "A Note on the Official Use of Statistics," *Social Problems*, vol. 11, no. 2 (Fall, 1963), pp. 131–139.

prepares and conducts a "defense." The latter section will attempt to indicate the connection between certain prominent organizational features of the Public Defender system and the penal code's place in the routine operation of that system.

GUILTY PLEAS, INCLUSION, AND NORMAL CRIMES

It is a commonly noted fact about the criminal court system generally, that the greatest proportion of cases are "settled" by a guilty plea.[3] In the county from which the following material is drawn, over 80 per cent of all cases "never go to trial." To describe the method of obtaining a guilty plea disposition, essential for the discussion to follow, I must distinguish between what shall be termed "necessarily-included-lesser-offenses" and "situationally-included-lesser-offenses." Of two offenses designated in the penal code, the lesser is considered to be that for which the length of required incarceration is the shorter period of time. *Inclusion* refers to the relation between two or more offenses. The "necessarily-included-lesser-offense" is a strictly legal notion:

> Whether a lesser offense is included in the crime charged is a question of law to be determined solely from the definition and corpus delicti of the offense charged and of the lesser offense. . . . If all the elements of the corpus delicti of a lesser crime can be found in a list of all the elements of the offense charged, then only is the lesser included in the greater.[4]

Stated alternatively:

> The test in this state of necessarily included offenses is simply that where an offense cannot be committed without necessarily committing another offense, the latter is a necessarily included offense.[5]

The implied negative is put: could Smith have committed A and not B? If the answer is yes, then B is not necessarily included in A. If the answer is no, B is necessarily included. While in a given case a battery might be committed in the course of a robbery, battery is not necessarily included in robbery. Petty theft is necessarily included in robbery but not in burglary. Burglary primarily involves the "intent" to acquire another's goods illegally (e.g., by breaking and entering); the consummation of the act need not occur for burglary to be committed. Theft, like robbery, requires that some item be stolen.

I shall call *lesser* offenses that are not necessarily but "only" *actually* included, "situationally-included-lesser-offenses." By statutory definition, necessarily included offenses are "actually" included. By actual here, I refer to the "way it occurs as a course of action." In the instance of necessary inclusion, the "way it occurs" is irrelevant. With situational inclusion, the "way it occurs" is definitive. In the former case, no particular course of action is referred to. In the latter, the scene and progress of the criminal activity would be analyzed.

[3] See D. J. Newman, "Pleading Guilty for Considerations," 46 *J. Crim. L. C. and P.S.* Also, M. Schwartz, *Cases and Materials on Professional Responsibility and the Administration of Criminal Justice*, San Francisco: Matthew Bender and Co., 1961, esp. pp. 79–105.

[4] C. W. Fricke, *California Criminal Law*, Los Angeles: The Legal Book Store, 1961, p. 41.

[5] *People v. Greer*, 30 Cal. 2d, 589.

The issue of necessary inclusion has special relevance for two procedural matters:

> A. A man cannot be charged and/or convicted of two or more crimes any one of which is necessarily included in the others, unless the several crimes occur on separate occasions.

If a murder occurs, the defendant cannot be charged and/or convicted of both "homicide" and "intent to commit a murder," the latter of which is necessarily included in first degree murder. If, however, a defendant "intends to commit a homicide" against one person and commits a "homicide" against another, both offenses may be properly charged. While it is an extremely complex question as to the scope and definition of "in the course of," in most instances the rule is easily applied.

> B. The judge cannot instruct the jury to consider as alternative crimes of which to find a defendant guilty, crimes that are not necessarily included in the charged crime or crimes.

If a man is charged with "statutory rape" the judge may instruct the jury to consider as a possible alternative conviction "contributing to the delinquency of a minor," as this offense is necessarily included in "statutory rape." He cannot however suggest that the alternative "intent to commit murder" be considered and the jury cannot find the defendant guilty of this latter crime, unless it is charged as a distinct offense in the complaint.

It is crucial to note that these restrictions apply only to (a) the relation between several charged offenses in a formal allegation, and (b) the alternatives allowable in a jury instruction. At any time before a case "goes to trial," alterations in the charging complaint may be made by the district attorney. The issue of necessary inclusion has no required bearing on (a) what offense(s) will be charged initially by the prosecutor, (b) what the relation is between the charge initially made and "what happened," or (c) what modifications may be made after the initial charge and the relation between initially charged offenses and those charged in modified complaints. It is this latter operation, the modification of the complaint, that is central to the guilty plea disposition.

Complaint alterations are made when a defendant agrees to plead guilty to an offense and thereby avoid a trial. The alteration occurs in the context of a "deal" consisting of an offer from the district attorney to alter the original charge in such a fashion that a lighter sentence will be incurred with a guilty plea than would be the case if the defendant were sentenced on the original charge. In return for this manipulation, the defendant agrees to plead guilty. The arrangement is proposed in the following format: "if you plead guilty to this new lesser offense, you will get less time in prison than if you plead not guilty to the original, greater charge and lose the trial." The decision must then be made whether or not the chances of obtaining complete acquittal at trial are great enough to warrant the risk of a loss and higher sentence if found guilty on the original charge. As we shall see below, it is a major job of the Public Defender, who mediates between the district attorney and the defendant, to convince his "client" that the chances of acquittal are too slight to warrant this risk.

If a man is charged with "drunkenness" and the Public Defender and Public Prosecutor (hereafter P.D. and D.A.) prefer not to have a trial, they seek to have the defendant agree to plead guilty. While it is occasionally possible, particularly with first offenders, for the P.D. to convince the defendant to plead guilty to the originally charged offense, most often it is felt that some "exchange" or "considera-tion" should be offered, i.e., a lesser offense charged.

To what offense can "drunkenness" be reduced? There is no statutorily designated crime that is necessarily included in the crime of "drunkenness." That is, if any of the statutorily required components of drunk behavior (its corpus delicti) are absent, there remains no offense of which the resultant description is a definition. For drunk-enness there is, however, an offense that while not necessarily included is "typically-situationally-included," i.e., "typically" occurs as a feature of the way drunk persons are seen to behave—"disturbing the peace." The range of possible sentences is such that, of the two offenses, "disturbing the peace" cannot call for as long a prison sen-tence as "drunkenness." If, in the course of going on a binge, a person does so in such a fashion that "disturbing the peace" may be employed to describe some of his behavior, it would be considered as an alternative offense to offer in return for a guilty plea. A central question for the following analysis will be: in what fashion would he have to behave so that disturbing the peace would be considered a suitable reduction?

If a man is charged with "molesting a minor," there are not any necessarily in-cluded lesser offenses with which to charge him. Yet an alternative charge—"loitering around a schoolyard"—is often used as a reduction. As above, and central to our analysis the question is: what would the defendant's behavior be such that "loitering around a schoolyard" would constitute an appropriate alternative?

If a person is charged with "burglary," "petty theft" is not necessarily included. Routinely, however, "petty theft" is employed for reducing the charge of burglary. Again, we shall ask: what is the relation between burglary and petty theft and the *manner in which the former occurs* that warrants this reduction?

Offenses are regularly reduced to other offenses the latter of which are not neces-sarily or situationally included in the former. As I have already said the determination of whether or not offense X was situationally included in Y involves an analysis of the course of action that constitutes the criminal behavior. I must now turn to examine this mode of behavioral analysis.

When encountering a defendant who is charged with "assault with a deadly weapon," the P.D. asks: "what can this offense be reduced to so as to arrange for a guilty plea?" As the reduction is only to be proposed by the P.D. and accepted or not by the D.A., his question becomes "what reduction will be allowable?" (As shall be seen below, the P.D. and D.A. have institutionalized a common orientation to allowable reductions.) The method of reduction involves, as a general feature, the fact that the particular case in question is scrutinized to decide its membership in a class of similar cases. But *the penal code does not provide the reference for deciding the correspondence between the instant event and the general case; that is, it does not define the classes of offense types.* To decide, for purposes of finding a suitable reduction, if the instant case involves a "burglary," reference is not made to the statutory definition of "burglary." To decide what the situationally included offenses are in the instant case, the instant case is not analyzed as a *statutorily* referable course of action; rather, reference is made to a *non-statutorily* conceived class, burglary, and offenses that are typically situationally included in it, taken as a class of be-havioral events. Stated again: in searching an instant case to decide what to *reduce it to,* there is no analysis of the statutorily referable elements of the instant case; instead, its membership in a class of events, the features of which cannot be described by the penal code, must be decided. An example will be useful. If a defendant is charged with burglary and the P.D. is concerned to propose a reduction to a lesser offense, he might search the elements of the burglary at hand to decide what other offenses were committed. The other offenses he might "discover" would be of two sorts: those necessarily and those situationally included. In attempting to decide those other offenses situationally included in the instant event, the instant event might be analyzed as a statutorily referable course of action. Or, as is the case with the P.D., the instant case might be analyzed to decide if it is a "burglary" in common with other "burglaries" conceived of in terms other than those provided by the statute.

Buglaries are routinely reduced to petty theft. If we were to analyze the way burglaries typically occur, petty theft is neither situationally nor necessarily included; when a burglary is committed, money or other goods are seldom illegally removed from some person's body. If we therefore analyzed burglaries, employing the penal code as our reference, and then searched the P.D.'s records to see how burglaries are reduced in the guilty plea, we could not establish a rule that would describe the transformation between the burglary cases statutorily described and the reductions routinely made (i.e., to "petty theft"). The rule must be sought elsewhere, in the character of the non-statutorily defined class of "burglaries," which I shall term *normal burglaries*.

NORMAL CRIMES

In the course of routinely encountering persons charged with "petty theft," "burglary," "assault with a deadly weapon," "rape," "possession of marijuana," etc., the Public Defender (P.D.) gains knowledge of the typical manner in which offenses of given classes are committed, the social characteristics of the persons who regularly commit them, the features of the settings in which they occur, the types of victims often involved, and the like. He learns to speak knowledgeably of "burglars," "petty thieves," "drunks," "rapists," "narcos," etc., and to attribute to them personal biographies, modes of usual criminal activity, criminal histories, psychological characteristics, and social backgrounds. The following characterizations are illustrative:

> Most ADWs (assault with deadly weapon) start with fights over some girl.
>
> These sex fiends (child molestation cases) usually hang around parks or schoolyards. But we often get fathers charged with these crimes. Usually the old man is out of work and stays at home when the wife goes to work and he plays around with his little daughter or something. A lot of these cases start when there is some marital trouble and the woman gets mad.
>
> I don't know why most of them don't rob the big stores. They usually break into some cheap department store and steal some crummy item like a $9.95 record player you know.
>
> Kids who start taking this stuff (narcotics) usually start out when some buddy gives them a cigarette and they smoke it for kicks. For some reason they always get caught in their cars, for speeding or something.

They can anticipate that point when persons are likely to get into trouble:

> Dope addicts do O.K. until they lose a job or something and get back on the streets and, you know, meet the old boys. Someone tells them where to get some and there they are.
>
> In the springtime, that's when we get all these sex crimes. You know, these kids play out in the schoolyard all day and these old men sit around and watch them jumping up and down. They get their ideas.

The P.D. learns that some kinds of offenders are likely to repeat the same offense while others are not repeat violators or, if they do commit crimes frequently, the crimes vary from occasion to occasion:

> You almost never see a check man get caught for anything but checks —only an occasional drunk charge.
>
> Burglars are usually multiple offenders, most times just burglaries or petty thefts.
>
> Petty thefts get started for almost anything—joy riding, drinking, all kinds of little things.
>
> These narcos are usually through after the second violation or so. After the first time some stop, but when they start on the heavy stuff, they've had it.

I shall call *normal crimes* those occurrences whose typical features, e.g., the ways they usually occur and the characteristics of persons who commit them (as well as the typical victims and typical scenes), are known and attended to by the P.D. For any of a series of offense types the P.D. can provide some form of proverbial characterization. For example, *burglary* is seen as involving regular violators, no weapons, low-priced items, little property damage, lower class establishments, largely Negro defendants, independent operators, and a nonprofessional orientation to the crime. *Child molesting* is seen as typically entailing middle-aged strangers or lower class middle-aged fathers (few women), no actual physical penetration or severe tissue damage, mild fondling, petting, and stimulation, bad marriage circumstances, multiple offenders with the same offense repeatedly committed, a child complainant, via the mother, etc. *Narcotics* defendants are usually Negroes, not syndicated, persons who start by using small stuff, hostile with police officers, caught by some form of entrapment technique, etc. *Petty thefts* are about 50-50 Negro-white, unplanned offenses, generally committed on lower class persons and don't get much money, don't often employ weapons, don't make living from thievery, usually younger defendants with long juvenile assaultive records, etc. *Drunkenness* offenders are lower class white and Negro, get drunk on wine and beer, have long histories of repeated drunkenness, don't hold down jobs, are usually arrested on the streets, seldom violate other penal code sections, etc.

Some general features of the normal crime as a way of attending to a category of persons and events may be mentioned:

> 1. The focus, in these characterizations, is not on particular individuals, but offense types. If asked "What are burglars like?" or "How are burglaries usually committed?" the P.D. does not feel obliged to

refer to particular burglars and burglaries as the material for his answer.

2. The features attributed to offenders and offenses are often not of import for the statutory conception. In burglary, it is "irrelevant" for the statutory determination whether or not much damage was done to the premises (except where, for example, explosives were employed and a new statute could be invoked). Whether a defendant breaks a window or not, destroys property within the house or not, etc., does not affect his statutory classification as a burglar. While for robbery the presence or absence of a weapon sets the degree, whether the weapon is a machine gun or pocket knife is "immaterial." Whether the residence or business establishment in a burglary is located in a higher income area of the city is of no issue for the code requirements. And, generally, the defendant's race, class position, criminal history (in most offenses), personal attributes, and particular style of committing offenses are features specifically not definitive of crimes under the auspices of the penal code. For deciding "Is this a 'burglary' case I have before me," however, the P.D.'s reference to this range of non-statutorily referable personal and social attributes, modes of operation, etc., is crucial for the arrangement of a guilty plea bargain.

3. The features attributed to offenders and offenses are, in their content, specific to the community in which the P.D. works. In other communities and historical periods the lists would presumably differ. Narcotics violators in certain areas, for example, are syndicated in dope rackets or engage in systematic robbery as professional criminals, features which are not commonly encountered (or, at least, evidence for which is not systematically sought) in this community. Burglary in some cities will more often occur at large industrial plants, banking establishments, warehouses, etc. The P.D. refers to the population of defendants in the county as "our defendants" and qualifies his prototypical portrayals and knowledge of the typically operative social structures, "for our county." An older P.D., remembering the "old days," commented:

> We used to have a lot more rapes than we do now, and they used to be much more violent. Things are duller now in. . . .

4. Offenses whose normal features are readily attended to are those which are routinely encountered in the courtroom. This feature is related to the last point. For embezzlement, bank robbery, gambling, prostitution, murder, arson, and some other uncommon offenses, the P.D. cannot readily supply anecdotal and proverbial characterizations. While there is some change in the frequencies of offense-type convictions over time, certain offenses are continually more common and others remain stably infrequent. The troubles created for the P.D. when offenses whose features are not readily known occur, and whose typicality is not easily constructed, will be discussed in some detail below.

5. Offenses are ecologically specified and attended to as normal or not according to the locales within which they are committed. The P.D.

learns that burglaries usually occur in such and such areas of the city, petty thefts around this or that park, ADWs in these bars. Ecological patterns are seen as related to socio-economic variables and these in turn to typical modes of criminal and noncriminal activities. Knowing where an offense took place is thus, for the P.D., knowledge of the likely persons involved, the kind of scene in which the offense occurred, and the pattern of activity characteristic of such a place:

> Almost all of our ADWs are in the same half a dozen bars. These places are Negro bars where laborers come after hanging around the union halls trying to get some work. Nobody has any money and they drink too much. Tempers are high and almost anything can start happening.

6. One further important feature can be noted at this point. Its elaboration will be the task of a later section. As shall be seen, the P.D. office consists of a staff of twelve full time attorneys. Knowledge of the properties of offense types of offenders, i.e., their normal, typical, or familiar attributes, constitutes the mark of any given attorney's competence. A major task in socializing the new P.D. deputy attorney consists in teaching him to recognize these attributes and to come to do so naturally. The achievement of competence as a P.D. is signalled by the gradual acquisition of professional command not simply of local penal code peculiarities and courtroom folklore, but, as importantly, of relevant features of the social structure and criminological wisdom. His grasp of that knowledge over the course of time is a key indication of his expertise. Below, in our brief account of some relevant organizational properties of the P.D. system, we shall have occasion to re-emphasize the competence-attesting aspects of the attorney's proper use of established sociological knowledge. Let us return to the mechanics of the guilty plea procedure as an example of the operation of the notion of normal crimes.

Over the course of their interaction and repeated "bargaining" discussions, the P.D. and D.A. have developed a set of unstated recipes for reducing original charges to lesser offenses. These recipes are specifically appropriate for use in instances of normal crimes and in such instances alone. "Typical" burglaries are reduced to petty theft, "typical" ADWs to simple assault, "typical" child molestation to loitering around a schoolyard, etc. The character of these recipes deserves attention.

The specific content of any reduction, i.e., what particular offense class X offenses will be reduced to, is such that the reduced offense may bear no obvious relation (neither situationally nor necessarily included) to the originally charged offense. The reduction of burglary to petty theft is an example. The important relation between the reduced offense and the original charge is such that the reduction from one to the other is considered "reasonable." At this point we shall only state what seems to be the general principle involved in deciding this reasonableness. The underlying premises cannot be explored at the present time, as that would involve a political analysis beyond the scope of the present report.

Both P.D. and D.A. are concerned to obtain a guilty plea wherever possible and thereby avoid a trial. At the same time, each party is concerned that the defendant "receive his due." The reduction of offense X to Y must be of such a character that the new sentence will depart from the anticipated sentence for the original charge to such a degree that the defendant is likely to plead guilty to the new charge and, at the same time, not so great that the defendant does not "get his due."

In a homicide, while battery is a necessarily included offense, it will not be considered as a possible reduction. For a conviction of second degree murder a defendant could receive a life sentence in the penitentiary. For a battery conviction he would spend no more than six months in the county jail. In a homicide, however, "felony manslaughter," or "assault with a deadly weapon," whatever their relation to homicide as regards inclusion, would more closely approximate the sentence outcome that could be expected on a trial conviction of second degree murder. These alternatives would be considered. For burglary, a typically situationally included offense might be "disturbing the peace," "breaking and entering" or "destroying public property." "Petty theft," however, constitutes a reasonable lesser alternative to burglary as the sentence for petty theft will often range between six months and one year in the county jail and burglary regularly does not carry higher than two years in the state prison. "Disturbing the peace" would be a thirty-day sentence offense.

While the present purposes make the exposition of this calculus unnecessary, it can be noted and stressed that the particular content of the reduction does not necessarily correspond to a relation between the original and altered charge that could be described in either the terms of necessary or situational inclusion. Whatever the relation between the original and reduced charge, its essential feature resides in the spread between sentence likelihoods and the reasonableness of that spread, i.e., the balance it strikes between the defendant "getting his due" and at the same time "getting something less than he might so that he will plead guilty."

The procedure we want to clarify now, at the risk of some repetition, is the manner in which an instant case is examined to decide its membership in a class of "crimes such as this" (the category *normal crimes*). Let us start with an obvious case, burglary. As the typical reduction for burglary is petty theft and as petty theft is neither situationally nor necessarily included in burglary, the examination of the instant case is clearly not undertaken to decide whether petty theft is an appropriate statutory description. The concern is to establish the relation between the instant burglary and the normal category "burglaries" and, having decided a "sufficient correspondence," to now employ petty theft as the proposed reduction.

In scrutinizing the present burglary case, the P.D. seeks to establish that "this is a burglary just like any other." If that correspondence is not established, regardless of whether or not petty theft in fact was a feature of the way the crime was enacted, the reduction to petty theft would not be proposed. *The propriety of proposing petty theft as a reduction does not derive from its in-fact-existence in the present case, but is warranted or not by the relation of the present burglary to "burglaries," normally conceived.*

In a case of "child molestation" (officially called "lewd conduct with a minor"), the concern is to decide if this is a "typical child molestation case." While "loitering around a schoolyard" is frequently a feature of the way such crimes are instigated, establishing that the present defendant *did in fact loiter around a schoolyard* is secondary to the more general question "Is this a typical child molestation case?" What appears as a contradiction must be clarified by examining the status of "loitering around a schoolyard" as a typical feature of such child molestations. The typical character of "child molesting cases" does not stand or fall on the fact that "loitering around a schoolyard" is a feature of the way they are in fact committed. It is *not* that "loitering around a schoolyard" as a *statutorily referable behavior sequence* is part of typical "child molesting cases" but that "loitering around a schoolyard" as a *socially distinct mode of committing child molestations typifies the way such offenses are enacted.* "Strictly speaking," i.e., under the auspices of the statutory *corpus delicti,* "loitering around a schoolyard," requires *loitering, around,* a *schoolyard;* if one loiters around a ball park or a public recreation area, he "cannot," within a proper reading of the statute, be charged with loitering around a *schoolyard.* Yet "loitering around a schoolyard," as a feature of the typical way such offenses as child molestations are committed, has the status not of a description of the way in *fact (fact,* statutorily decided) it occurred or typically occurs, but "the-kind-of-social-activity-typically-associated-with-such-offenses." It is not its statutorily conceived features but its socially relevant attributes that gives "loitering around a schoolyard" its status as a feature of the class "normal child molestations." Whether the defendant loitered around a schoolyard or a ball park, and whether he loitered or "was passing by," "loitering around a schoolyard" as a reduction will be made if the defendant's activity was such that "he was hanging around some public place or another" and "was the kind of guy who hangs around schoolyards." As a component of the class of normal child molestation cases (of the variety where the victim is a stranger), "loitering around a schoolyard" typifies a mode of committing such offenses, the class of "such persons who do such things as hang around schoolyards and the like." A large variety of actual offenses could thus be nonetheless reduced to "loitering" if, as kinds of social activity, "loitering," conceived of as typifying a way of life, pattern of daily activity, social psychological circumstances, etc., characterized the conduct of the defendant. The young P.D. who would object "You can't reduce it to 'loitering'—he didn't really 'loiter,' " would be reprimanded: "Fella, you don't know how to use that term; he might as well have 'loitered'—it's the same kind of case as the others."

Having outlined the formal mechanics of the guilty plea disposition, I shall now turn to depict the routine of representation that the categories of crime, imbued with elaborate knowledge of the delinquent social structure, provide for. This will entail a brief examination of pertinent organizational features of the P.D. system.

PUBLIC "DEFENSE"

Recently, in many communities, the burden of securing counsel has been taken from the defendant.[6] As the accused is, by law, entitled to the aid of counsel, and as his pocketbook is often empty, numerous cities have felt obliged to establish a public defender system. There has been little resistance to this development by private attorneys among whom it is widely felt that the less time they need spend in the criminal courts, where practice is least prestigeful and lucrative, the better.[7]

Whatever the reasons for its development, we now find, in many urban places,

[6] For general histories of indigent defender systems in the United States, see The Association of the Bar of the City of New York, *Equal Justice for the Accused,* Garden City, New York: 1959; and E. A. Brownell, *Legal Aid in the United States,* Rochester, New York: The Lawyers Cooperative Publishing Company, 1951.

[7] The experience of the Public Defender system is distinctly different in this regard from that of the Legal Aid Societies, which, I am told, have continually met very strong opposition to their establishment by local bar associations.

a public defender occupying a place alongside judge and prosecutor as a regular court employee. In the county studied, the P.D. mans a daily station, like the public prosecutor, and "defends" all who come before him. He appears in court when court begins and his "clientele," composed without regard for his preferences, consists of that residual category of persons who cannot afford to bring their own spokesmen to court. In this county, the "residual" category approximates 65 per cent of the total number of criminal cases. In a given year, the twelve attorneys who comprise the P.D. Office "represent" about 3,000 defendants in the municipal and superior courts of the county.

While the courtroom encounters of private attorneys are brief, businesslike and circumscribed, interactionally and temporally, by the particular cases that bring them there, the P.D. attends to the courtroom as his regular work place and conveys in his demeanor his place as a member of its core personnel.

While private attorneys come and leave court with their clients (who are generally "on bail"), the P.D. arrives in court each morning at nine, takes his station at the defense table, and deposits there the batch of files that he will refer to during the day. When, during morning "calendar," [8] a private attorney's case is called, the P.D. steps back from the defense table, leaving his belongings in place there, and temporarily relinquishes his station. No private attorney has enough defendants in a given court on a given day to claim a right to make a desk of the defense table. If the P.D. needs some information from his central office, he uses the clerk's telephone, a privilege that few private lawyers feel at home enough to take. In the course of calendar work, a lawyer will often have occasion to request a delay or "continuance" of several days until the next stage of his client's proceedings. The private attorney addresses the prosecutor via the judge to request such an alteration; the P.D. talks directly over to the D.A.:

> P.A.: *If the prosecutor finds it convenient your Honor, my client would prefer to have his preliminary hearing on Monday, the 24th.*
> JUDGE: *Is that date suitable to the district attorney?*
> PROS.: *Yes, your Honor.*
> P.A.: *Thank you, your Honor.*
> P.D.: *Bob (D.A.), how about moving Smith's prelim up to the 16th?*
> PROS.: *Well, Jim, we've got Jones on that afternoon.*
> P.D.: *Let's see, how's the 22nd?*
> PROS.: *That's fine, Jim, the 22nd.*

If, during the course of a proceeding, the P.D. has some minor matter to tend to with the D.A., he uses the time when a private attorney is addressing the bench to walk over to the prosecutor's table and whisper his requests, suggestions or questions. The P.D. uses the prosecutor's master calendar to check on an upcoming court date; so does the D.A. with the P.D.'s. The D.A. and P.D. are on a first name basis and throughout the course of a routine day interact as a team of co-workers.

While the central focus of the private attorney's attention is his client, the courtroom and affairs of court constitute the locus of involvements for the P.D. The public defender and public prosecutor, each representatives of their respective offices, jointly handle the greatest bulk of the court's daily activity.

[8] "Calendar part" consists of that portion of the court day, typically in the mornings, when all matters other than trials are heard, e.g., arraignments, motions, continuances, sentencing, probation reports, etc.

The P.D. office, rather than assign its attorneys to clients, employs the arrangement of stationing attorneys in different courts to "represent" all those who come
before that station. As defendants are moved about from courtroom to courtroom
throughout the course of their proceedings (both from municipal to superior courtrooms for felony cases, and from one municipal courtroom to another when there is
a specialization of courts, e.g., jury, non-jury, arraignment, etc.), the P.D. sees
defendants only at those places in their paths when they appear in the court he is
manning. A given defendant may be "represented" by one P.D. at arraignment,
another at preliminary hearing, a third at trial and a fourth when sentenced.

At the first interview with a client (initial interviews occur in the jail where
attorneys go, *en masse*, to "pick up new defendants" in the afternoons) a file is
prepared on the defendant. In each file is recorded the charge brought against
the defendant and, among other things, his next court date. Each evening attorneys
return new files to the central office where secretaries prepare court books for each
courtroom that list the defendants due to appear in a given court on a given day. In
the mornings, attorneys take the court books from the office and remove from
the central file the files of those defendants due to appear in "their court" that
day.

There is little communication between P.D. and client. After the first interview,
the defendant's encounters with the P.D. are primarily in court. Only under special
circumstances (to be discussed below) are there contacts between lawyers and defendants in the jail before and after appearances in court. The bulk of "preparation
for court" (either trials or non-trial matters) occurs at the first interview. The attorney on station, the "attending attorney," is thus a stranger to "his client," and vice
versa. Over the course of his proceedings, a defendant will have several attorneys
(in one instance a man was "represented" by eight P.D.'s on a charge of simple
assault). Defendants who come to court find a lawyer they don't know conducting
their trials, entering their motions, making their pleas, and the rest. Often there is
no introduction of P.D. to defendant; defendants are prepared to expect a strange
face:

> Don't be surprised when you see another P.D. in court with you on
> Tuesday. You just do what he tells you to. He'll know all about your
> case.

P.D.'s seldom talk about particular defendants among themselves. When they
converse about trials, the facts of cases, etc., they do so not so much for briefing,
e.g., "This is what I think you should do when you 'get him,'" but rather as small
talk, as "What have you got going today." The P.D. does not rely on the information
about a case he received from a previous attending attorney in order to know how
to manage his "representation." Rather, the file is relied upon to furnish all the
information essential for making an "appearance." These appearances range from
morning calendar work (e.g., arraignments, motions, continuances, etc.) to trials
on offenses from drunkenness to assault with a deadly weapon. In the course of a
routine day, the P.D. will receive his batch of files in the morning and, seeing them
for the first time that day, conduct numerous trials, preliminary hearings, calendar
appearances, sentencing proceedings, etc. They do not study files overnight.
Attorneys will often only look over a file a half hour or so before the jury trial
begins.

THE FIRST INTERVIEW

As the first interview is often the only interview and as the file prepared there is central for the continuing "representation" of the defendant by other attorneys, it is important to examine these interviews and the file's contents. From the outset, the P.D. attends to establishing the typical character of the case before him and thereby instituting routinely employed reduction arrangements. The defendant's appearance, e.g., his race, demeanor, age, style of talk, way of attending to the occasion of his incarceration, etc., provides the P.D. with an initial sense of his place in the social structure. Knowing only that the defendant is charged with section 459 (burglary) of the penal code, the P.D. employs his conception of typical burglars against which the character of the present defendant is assessed.

> He had me fooled for a while. With that accent of his and those Parliaments he was smoking I thought something was strange. It turned out to be just another burglary. You heard him tell about New York and the way he had a hold on him there that he was running away from. I just guess N.Y. is a funny place, you can never tell what kinds of people get involved in crimes there.

The initial fact of the defendant's "putting in a request to see the P.D." establishes his lower position in the class structure of the community:

> We just never get wealthier people here. They usually don't stay in jail overnight and then they call a private attorney. The P.D. gets everything at the bottom of the pile.

Searching over the criminal history (past convictions and arrests) the defendant provides when preliminary face sheet data is recorded in the file, the P.D. gets a sense of the man's typical pattern of criminal activity. It is not the particular offenses for which he is charged that are crucial, but the constellation of prior offenses and the sequential pattern they take:

> I could tell as soon as he told me he had four prior drunk charges that he was just another of these skid row bums. You could look at him and tell.
>
> When you see a whole string of forgery counts in the past you pretty much know what kind of case you're dealing with. You either get those who commit an occasional forgery, or those that do nothing but. . . . With a whole bunch of prior checks (prior forgery convictions) you can bet that he cashes little ones. I didn't even have to ask for the amount you know. I seldom come across one over a hundred bucks.
>
> From the looks of him and the way he said "I wasn't doing anything, just playing with her," you know, it's the usual kind of thing, just a little diddling or something. We can try to get it out on a simple assault.

When a P.D. puts questions to the defendant he is less concerned with recording nuances of the instant event (e.g., how many feet from the bar were you when the cops came in, did you break into the back gate or the front door), than with establishing its similarity with "events of this sort." That similarity is established, not by discovering statutorily relevant events of the present case, but by locating the event in a sociologically constructed class of "such cases." The first questions directed to the defendant are of the character that answers to them either confirm or throw into question the assumed typicality. First questions with ADWs are of the order: "How long had you been drinking before this all started?" with "child molestation cases": "How long were you hanging around before this began?" with "forgery" cases: "Was this the second or third check you cashed in the same place?"

We shall present three short excerpts from three first interviews. They all begin with the first question asked after preliminary background data is gathered. The first is with a 288 (child molestation), the second with a 459 (burglary) and the last with a 11530 (possession of marijuana). Each interview was conducted by a different Public Defender. In each case the P.D. had no information about the defendant or this particular crime other than that provided by the penal code number:

288

P.D.: *O.K., why don't you start out by telling me how this thing got started?*

DEF.: *Well, I was at the park and all I did was to ask this little girl if she wanted to sit on my lap for awhile and you know, just sit on my lap. Well, about twenty minutes later I'm walkin' down the street about a block away from the park and this cop pulls up and there the same little girl is, you know, sitting in the back seat with some dame. The cop asks me to stick my head in the back seat and he asks the kid if I was the one and she says yes. So he puts me in the car and takes a statement from me and here I am in the joint. All I was doin' was playin' with her a little. . . .*

P.D.: (interrupting) *. . . O.K. I get the story, let's see what we can do. If I can get this charge reduced to a misdemeanor then I would advise you to plead guilty, particularly since you have a record and that wouldn't look too well in court with a jury.*

(The interview proceeded for another two or three minutes and the decision to plead guilty was made.)

459

P.D.: *Why don't you start by telling me where this place was that you broke into?*

DEF.: *I don't know for sure . . . I think it was on 13th street or something like that.*

P.D.: *Had you ever been there before?*

DEF.: *I hang around that neighborhood you know, so I guess I've been in the place before, yeah.*

P.D.: *What were you going after?*

DEF.: *I don't know, whatever there was so's I could get a little cash. Man, I was pretty broke that night.*

P.D.: *Was anyone with you?*

DEF.: *No, I was by myself.*

P.D.: *How much did you break up the place?*

DEF.: *I didn't do nothing. The back window was open a little bit see and I just put my hand in there and opened the door. I was just walking in when I heard police comin' so I turn around and start to run. And, they saw me down the block and that was that.*

P.D.:   *Were you drunk at the time?*

DEF.:   *I wasn't drunk, no, I maybe had a drink or two that evening but I wasn't drunk or anything like that.*
11530

P.D.:   *Well, Smith, why don't you tell me where they found it (the mari-juana)?*

DEF.:   *I was driving home from the drugstore with my friend and this cop car pulls me up to the side. Two guys get out, one of them was wearing a uniform and the other was a plain clothes man. They told us to get out of the car and then they searched me and then my friend. Then this guy without the uniform he looked over into the car and picked up this thing from the back floor and said something to the other one. Then he asked me if I had any more of the stuff and I said I didn't know what he was talking about. So he wrote something down on a piece of paper and made me sign it. Then he told my friend to go home and they took me down here to the station and booked me on possession of marijuana. I swear I didn't have no marijuana.*

P.D.:   *You told me you were convicted of possession in 1959.*

DEF.:   *Yeah, but I haven't touched any of the stuff since then. I don't know what it was doing in my car, but I haven't touched the stuff since that last time.*

P.D.:   *You ought to know it doesn't make any difference whether or not they catch you using, just so as they find it on your possession or in a car, or in your house, or something.*

DEF.:   *Man, I swear I don't know how it got there. Somebody must have planted it there.*

P.D.:   *Look, you know as well as I do that with your prior conviction and this charge now that you could go away from here for five years or so. So just calm down a minute and let's look at this thing reasonably. If you go to trial and lose the trial, you're stuck. You'll be in the joint until you're 28 years old. If you plead to this one charge without the priors then we can get you into jail maybe, or a year or two at the most in the joint. If you wait until the preliminary hearing and then they charge the priors, boy you've had it, it's too late.*

DEF.:   *Well how about a trial?*
(After ten minutes, the defendant decided to plead guilty to one charge of possession, before the date of the preliminary hearing.)

Let us consider, in light of the previous discussion, some of the features of these interviews.

1. In each case the information sought is not "data" for organizing the particular facts of the case for deciding proper penal code designa-tions (or with a view toward undermining the assignment of a desig-nation in an anticipated trial). In the 288 instance, the P.D. inter-

rupted when he had enough information to confirm his sense of the case's typicality and construct a typifying portrayal of the present defendant. The character of the information supplied by the defendant was such that it was specifically lacking detail about the particular occurrences, e.g., the time, place, what was said to the girl, what precisely did the defendant do or not do, his "state of mind," etc. The defendant's appearance and prior record (in this case the defendant was a fifty-five year old white, unemployed, unskilled laborer, with about ten prior drunk arrests, seven convictions, and two prior sex offense violations) was relied upon to provide the sense of the present occasion. The P.D. straight-forwardly approached the D.A. and arranged for a "contributing to the delinquency of a minor" reduction. In the burglary case, the question, "Had you ever been there before?" was intended to elicit what was received, e.g., that the place was a familiar one to the defendant. Knowing that the place was in the defendant's neighborhood establishes its character as a skid row area business; that the First Federal Bank was not entered has been confirmed. "What were you going after?" also irrelevant to the 459 section of the penal code, provides him with information that there was no special motive for entering this establishment. The question, "Was anyone with you?" when answered negatively, placed the event in the typical class of "burglaries" as solitary, non-coordinated activities. The remaining questions were directed as well to confirming the typical character of the event, and the adequacy of the defendant's account is not decided by whether or not the P.D. can now decide whether the statutory definition of the contemplated reduction or the original charge is satisfied. Its adequacy is determined by the ability with which the P.D. can detect its normal character. The accounts provided thus may have the character of anecdotes, sketches, phrases, etc. In the first instance, with the 288, the prior record and the defendant's appearance, demeanor and style of talking about the event was enough to warrant his typical treatment.

2. The most important feature of the P.D.'s questioning is the presupposition of guilt that makes his proposed questions legitimate and answerable at the outset. To pose the question, "Why don't you start by telling me where this place was that you broke into?" as a lead question, the P.D. takes it that the defendant is guilty of a crime and that the crime for which he is charged probably describes what essentially occurred.

The P.D.'s activity is seldom geared to securing acquittals for clients. He and the D.A., as co-workers in the same courts, take it for granted that the persons who come before the courts are guilty of crimes and are to be treated accordingly:

> Most of them have records as you can see. Almost all of them have been through our courts before. And the police just don't make mistakes in this town. That's one thing about———, we've got the best police force in the state.

As we shall argue below, the way defendants are "represented," (the station manning rather than assignment of counselors to clients), the way trials are conducted, the way interviews are held and the penal code employed—all of the P.D.'s work is premised on the supposition that people charged with crimes have committed crimes.

This presupposition makes such first questions as "Why don't you start by telling me where this place was . . ." reasonable questions. When the answer comes: "What place? I don't know what you are talking about," the defendant is taken to be a phony, making an "innocent pitch." The conceivable first question: "Did you do it?" is not asked because it is felt that this gives the defendant the notion that he can try an "innocent pitch:"

> I never ask them, "did you do it?" because on one hand I know they did and mainly because then they think that they can play games with us. We can always check their records and usually they have a string of offenses. You don't have to, though, because in a day or two they change their story and plead guilty. Except for the stubborn ones.

Of the possible answers to an opening question, bewilderment, the inability to answer or silence are taken to indicate that the defendant is putting the P.D. on. For defendants who refuse to admit anything, the P.D. threatens:

> Look, if you don't want to talk, that's your business. I can't help you. All I can say is that if you go to trial on this beef you're going to spend a long time in the joint. When you get ready to tell me the story straight, then we can see what can be done.

If the puzzlement comes because the wrong question is asked, e.g., "There wasn't any fight—that's not the way it happened," the defendant will start to fill in the story. The P.D. awaits to see if, how far, and in what ways the instant case is deviant. If the defendant is charged with burglary and a middle class establishment was burglarized, windows shattered, a large payroll sought after and a gun used, then the reduction to petty theft, generally employed for "normal burglaries," would be more difficult to arrange.

Generally, the P.D. doesn't have to discover the atypical kinds of cases through questioning. Rather, the D.A., in writing the original complaint, provides the P.D. with clues that the typical recipe, given the way the event occurred, will not be allowable. Where the way it occurs is such that it does not resemble normal burglaries and the routinely used penalty would reduce it *too far* commensurate with the way the crime occurred, the D.A. frequently charges various situationally included offenses, indicating to the P.D. that the procedure to employ here is to suggest "dropping" some of the charges, leaving the originally charged greatest offense as it stands.

In the general case he doesn't charge all those offenses that he legally might. He might charge "child molesting" and "loitering around a schoolyard" but typically only the greater charge is made. The D.A. does so so as to provide for a later reduction that will appear particularly lenient in that it seemingly involves a *change* in the charge. Were he to charge both molesting and loitering, he would be obliged, moreover, should the case come to trial, to introduce evidence for both offenses. The D.A. is thus always constrained not to set overly high charges or not situationally included multiple offenses by the possibility that the defendant will not plead guilty to a lesser offense and the case will go to trial. Of primary importance is that he doesn't charge multiple offenses so that the P.D. will be in the best position vis-a-vis the defendant. He thus charges the first complaint so as to provide for a "setup."

The alteration of charges must be made in open court. The P.D. requests to have a new plea entered:

> P.D.: *Your Honor, in the interests of justice, my client would like to change his plea of not guilty to the charge of burglary and enter a plea of guilty to the charge of petty theft.*
>
> JUDGE: *Is this new plea acceptable to the prosecution?*
>
> D.A.: *Yes, your Honor.*

The prosecutor knows beforehand that the request will be made, and has agreed in advance to allow it.

I asked a P.D. how they felt about making such requests in open court, i.e., asking for a reduction from one offense to another when the latter is obviously not necessarily included and often (as is the case in burglary-to-petty theft) not situationally included. He summarized the office's feeling:

> In the old days, ten or so years ago, we didn't like to do it in front of the judge. What we used to do when we made a deal was that the D.A. would dismiss the original charge and write up a new complaint altogether. That took a lot of time. We had to re-arraign him all over again back in the muni court and everything. Besides, in the same courtroom, everyone used to know what was going on anyway. Now we just ask for a change of plea to the lesser charge regardless of whether it's included or not. Nobody thinks twice about asking for petty theft on burglary, or drunkenness on car theft, or something like that. It's just the way it's done.

Some restrictions are felt. Assaultive crimes (e.g., ADW, simple assault, attempted murder, etc.) will not be reduced to or from "money offenses" (burglary, robbery, theft) unless the latter involve weapons or some violence. Also, victimless crimes (narcotics, drunkenness) are not reduced to or from assaultive or "money offenses," unless theer is some factual relation, e.g., drunkenness with a fight might turn out to be simple assault reduced to drunkenness.

For most cases that come before their courts, the P.D. and D.A. are able to employ reductions that are formulated for handling typical cases. While some burglaries, rapes, narcotics violations and petty thefts, are instigated in strange ways and involve atypical facts, some manipulation in the way the initial charge is made can be used to set up a procedure to replace the simple charge-alteration form of reducing.

RECALCITRANT DEFENDANTS

Most of the P.D.'s cases that "have to go to trial" are those where the P.D. is not able to sell the defendant on the "bargain." These are cases for which reductions are available, reductions that are constructed on the basis of the typicality of the offense and allowable by the D.A. These are normal crimes committed by "stubborn" defendants.

So-called "stubborn" defendants will be distinguished from a second class of offenders, those who commit *crimes which are atypical in their character (for this community, at this time, etc.) or who commit crimes which while typical (recurrent for this community, this time, etc.) are committed atypically.* The manner in which the P.D. and D.A. must conduct the representation and prosecution of these defendants is radically different. To characterize the special problems the P.D. has with each class of defendants, it is first necessary to point out a general feature of the P.D.'s orientation to the work of the courts that has hitherto not been made explicit. This orientation will be merely sketched here.

As we noticed, the defendant's guilt is not attended to. That is to say, the presupposition of guilt, as a *presupposition*, does not say "You are guilty" with a pointing accusatory finger, but "You are guilty, you know it, I know it, so let's get down to the business of deciding what to do with you." When a defendant agrees to plead guilty, he is not *admitting* his guilt; when asked to plead guilty, he is not being asked, "Come on, admit it, you know you were *wrong*," but rather, "Why don't you be sensible about this thing?" What is sought is not a *confession*, but reasonableness.

The presupposition of guilt as a way of attending to the treatment of defendants has its counterpart in the way the P.D. attends to the entire court process, prosecuting machinery, law enforcement techniques, and the community.

For P.D. and D.A. it is a routinely encountered phenomenon that persons in the community regularly commit criminal offenses, are regularly brought before the courts, and are regularly transported to the state and county penal institutions. To confront a "criminal" is, for D.A. and P.D., no special experience, nothing to tell their wives about, nothing to record as outstanding in the happenings of the day. Before "their court" scores of "criminals" pass each day.

The morality of the courts is taken for granted. The P.D. assumes that the D.A., the police, judge, the narcotics agents and others all conduct their business as it must be conducted and in a proper fashion. That the police may hide out to deceive petty violators; that narcotics agents may regularly employ illicit entrapment procedures to find suspects; that investigators may routinely arrest suspects before they have sufficient grounds and only later uncover warrantable evidence for a formal booking; that the police may beat suspects; that judges may be "tough" because they are looking to support for higher office elections; that some laws may be specifically prejudicial against certain classes of persons—whatever may be the actual course of charging and convicting defendants—all of this is taken, as one P.D. put it, "as part of the system and the way it has to be." And the P.D. is part of the team.

While it is common to overhear private attorneys call judges "bastards," policemen "hoodlums" and prosecutors "sadists," the P.D., in the presence of such talk, remains silent. When the P.D. "loses" a case—and we shall see that *losing* is an adequate description only for some circumstances—he is likely to say "I knew *he* couldn't win." Private attorneys, on the other hand, will not hesitate to remark, as one did in a recent case, "You haven't got a fucking chance in front of that son-of-a-bitch dictator." In the P.D. office, there is a total absence of such condemnation.

The P.D. takes it for granted and attends to the courts in accord with the view that "what goes on in this business is what goes on and what goes on is the way it should be." It is rare to hear a public defender voice protest against a particular law, procedure, or official. One of the attorneys mentioned that he felt the new narcotics law (which makes it mandatory that a high minimum sentence be served for "possession or sale of narcotics") wasn't too severe "considering that they wanted to give them the chair." Another indicated that the more rigid statute "will probably cure a lot of them because they'll be in for so long." One P.D. feels that wiretapping would be a useful adjunct to police procedure. It is generally said, by everyone in the office, that ". . . is one of the best cities in the state when it comes to police."

In the P.D.'s interviews, the defendant's guilt only becomes a topic when the defendant himself attempts to direct attention to his innocence. Such attempts are never taken seriously by the P.D. but are seen as "innocent pitches," as "being wise," as "not knowing what is good for him." Defendants who make "innocent pitches" often find themselves able to convince the P.D. to have trials. The P.D. is in a professional and organizational bind in that he requires that his "clients" agree with whatever action he takes "on their behalf":

> Can you imagine what might happen if we went straight to the D.A. with a deal to which the client later refused to agree? Can you see him in court screaming how the P.D. sold him out? As it is, we get plenty of letters purporting to show why we don't do our job. Judges are swamped with letters condemning the P.D. Plenty of appeals get started this way.

Some defendants don't buy the offer of less time as constituting sufficient grounds for avoiding a trial. To others, it appears that "copping out" is worse than having a trial regardless of the consequences for the length of sentence. The following remarks, taken from P.D. files, illustrate the terms in which such "stubborn" defendants are conceived:

> Def wants a trial, but he is dead. In lieu of a possible 995, D.A. agreed to put note in his file recommending a deal. This should be explored and encouraged as big break for Def.
>
> Chance of successful defense negligible. Def realizes this but says he ain't going to cop to no strong-arm. See if we can set him straight.
>
> Dead case. Too many witnesses and . . . used in two of the transactions. However, Def is a very squirmy jailhouse lawyer and refuses to face facts.
>
> Possibly the D.A. in Sup/Ct could be persuaded into cutting her loose if she took the 211 and one of the narco counts. If not, the Def, who is somewhat recalcitrant and stubborn, will probably demand a JT (jury trial).

The routine trial, generated as it is by the defendant's refusal to make a lesser plea, is the "defendant's fault":

> What the hell are we supposed to do with them? If they can't listen to good reason and take a bargain, then it's their tough luck. If they go to prison, well, they're the ones who are losing the trials, not us.

When the P.D. enters the courtroom, he takes it that he is going to lose, e.g., the defendant is going to prison. When he "prepares" for trial, he doesn't prepare to "win." There is no attention given to "how am I going to construct a defense in order that I can get this defendant free of the charges against him." In fact, he doesn't "prepare for trial" in any "ordinary" sense (I use the term *ordinary* with hesitation; what *preparation for trial* might in fact involve with other than P.D. lawyers has not, to my knowledge, been investigated.)

For the P.D., "preparation for trial" involves, essentially, learning what "burglary cases" are like, what "rape cases" are like, what "assaults" are like. The P.D.'s main concern is to conduct his part of the proceedings in accord with complete respect for proper legal procedure. He raises objections to improper testimony; introduces motions whenever they seem called for; demands his "client's rights" to access to the prosecution's evidence before trial (through so-called "discovery proceedings"); cross examines all witnesses; does not introduce evidence that he expects will not be allowable; asks all those questions of all those people that he must in order to have addressed himself to the task of insuring that the *corpus delicti* has been established; carefully summarizes the evidence that has been presented in making a closing argument. Throughout, at every point, he conducts his "defense" in such a manner that no one can say of him "He has been negligent, there are grounds for appeal here." He systematically provides, in accord with the prescriptions of due process and the fourteenth amendment, a completely proper, "adequate legal representation."

At the same time, the district attorney, and the county which employs them both, can rely on the P.D. not to attempt to morally degrade police officers in cross examination; not to impeach the state's witnesses by trickery; not to attempt an exposition of the entrapment methods of narcotics agents; not to condemn the community for the "racial prejudice that produces our criminals" (the phrase of a private attorney during closing argument); not to challenge the prosecution of "these women who are trying to raise a family without a husband" (the statement of another private attorney during closing argument on a welfare fraud case); in sum, not to make an issue of the moral character of the administrative machinery of the local courts, the community or the police. He will not cause any serious trouble for the routine motion of the court conviction process. Laws will not be challenged, cases will not be tried to test the constitutionality of procedures and statutes, judges will not be personally degraded, police will be free from scrutiny to decide the legitimacy of their operations, and the community will not be condemned for its segregative practices against Negroes. The P.D.'s defense is completely proper, in accord with correct legal procedure, and specifically amoral in its import, manner of delivery, and perceived implications for the propriety of the prosecution enterprise.

In "return" for all this, the district attorney treats the defendant's guilt in a matter-of-fact fashion, doesn't get hostile in the course of the proceedings, doesn't insist that the jury or judge "throw the book," but rather "puts on a trial" (in their way of referring to their daily tasks) in order to, with a minimum of strain, properly place the defendant behind bars. Both prosecutor and public defender thus protect the moral character of the other's charges from exposure. Should the P.D. attend to demonstrating the innocence of his client by attempting to undermine the legitimate character of police operations, the prosecutor might feel obliged in return to employ devices to degrade the moral character of the P.D.'s client. Should the D.A. attack defendants in court, by pointing to the specifically immoral character of their activities, the P.D. might feel obligated, in response, to raise into relief the moral texture of the D.A.'s and police's and community's operations. Wherever possible, each holds the other in check. But the "check" need not be continuously held in place, or even attended to self consciously, for both P.D. and D.A. trust one another implicitly. The D.A. knows, with certainty, that the P.D. will not make a closing argument that resembles the following by a private attorney, from which I have paraphrased key excerpts:

> If it hadn't been for all the publicity that this case had in our wonderful local newspapers, you wouldn't want to throw the book at these men.
>
> If you'd clear up your problems with the Negro in . . . maybe you wouldn't have cases like this in your courts.
>
> (after sentence was pronounced) Your Honor, I just would like to say one thing—that I've never heard or seen such a display of injustice as I've seen here in this court today. It's a sad commentary on the state of our community if people like yourself pay more attention to the local political machines than to the lives of our defendants. I think you are guilty of that, your Honor.

(At this last statement, one of the P.D.'s who was in the courtroom turned to me and said, "He sure is looking for a contempt charge.")

The P.D. knows how to conduct his trials because he knows how to conduct "assault with deadly weapons" trials, "burglary" trials, "rape" trials, and the rest. The *corpus delicti here* provides him with a basis for asking "proper questions," making the "proper" cross examinations, and pointing out the "proper" things to jurors about "reasonable doubt." He need not extensively gather information about the specific facts of the instant case. Whatever is needed in the way of "facts of the case" arise in the course of the D.A.'s presentation. He employs the "strategy" of directing the same questions to the witness as were put by the D.A. with added emphasis on the question mark, or an inserted "Did you really see . . . ?" His "defense" consists of attempting to "bring out" slightly variant aspects of the D.A.'s story by questioning his own witnesses (whom he seldom interviews before beginning trial but who are interviewed by the Office's two "investigators") and the defendant.

With little variation the same questions are put to all defendants charged with the same crimes. The P.D. learns with experience what to expect as the "facts of the case." These facts, in their general structure, portray social circumstances that he can anticipate by virtue of his knowledge of the normal features of offense categories and types of offenders. The "details" of the instant case are "discovered" over the course of hearing them in court. In this regard, the "information" that "comes out" is often as new to him as to the jury.

Employing a common sense conception of what criminal lawyers behave like in cross examination and argument, and the popular portrayal of their demeanor and style of addressing adversary witnesses, the onlooker comes away with the sense of having witnessed not a trial at all, but a set of motions, a perfunctorily carried off event. A sociological analysis of this sense would require a systematic attempt to describe the features of adversary trial conduct.

A NOTE ON SPECIAL CASES

To conduct trials with "stubborn" defendants, so-called, is no special trouble. Here trials are viewed as a "waste of time." Murders, embezzlements, multiple rape cases (several defendants with one victim), large scale robberies, dope ring operations, those cases that arouse public attention and receive special notice in the papers—these are cases whose normal features are not constructed and for which, even were a guilty plea available, both parties feel uncomfortably obliged to bring issues of moral character into the courtroom. The privacy of the P.D.–D.A. conviction machinery through the use of the guilty plea can no longer be preserved. Only "normal defendants" are accorded this privacy. The pressure for a public hearing, in the sense of "bringing the public in to see and monitor the character of the proceedings," must be allowed to culminate in a full blown jury trial. There is a general preference in the P.D. office to handle routine cases without a jury, if it must go to trial at all. In the special case the jury must be employed and with them a large audience of onlookers, newspaper men, and daily paper coverage must be tolerated.

To put on a fight is a discomforting task for persons who regularly work together as a team. Every effort is made to bind off the event of a special case by heightened interaction outside the courtroom. In the routine case, with no jury or at least no press coverage, the whole trial can be handled as a backstage operation. With special cases there can be no byplay conversation in the courtroom between D.A. and P.D., and no leaving court together, arm in arm. Metaphorically, two persons who regularly dance together must now appear, with the lights turned on, to be fighting.

The P.D. Office reserves several of its attorneys to handle such cases. By keeping the regular personnel away from particular courtrooms, their routine interactions with the D.A. can be properly maintained. An older, more experienced attorney, from each side, comes to court to put on the show. The device of so handling the assignment of attorneys to cases serves to mark off the event as a special occasion, to set it outside the regular ordering of relationships that must resume when the special, and dreaded, case becomes a statistic in the penal institution records.

With the special cases, the client-attorney assignment procedure is instituted. The head of the P.D. Office, along with a coterie of older attorneys, goes to the first interview in the jail, and these same attorneys, or some of them, take over the case and stay with it, handling its development with kid gloves. The concern to provide "adequate legal representation" may be relegated to a back seat. Both P.D. and D.A. must temporarily step outside their typical modes of mutual conduct and yet, at the same time, not permanently jeopardize the stability of their usual teamlike relationship.

SOME CONCLUSIONS

An examination of the use of the penal code by actually practicing attorneys has revealed that categories of crime, rather than being "unsuited" to sociological analysis, are so employed as to make their analysis crucial to empirical understanding. What categories of crime are, i.e., who is assembled under this one or that, what constitute the behaviors inspected for deciding such matters, what "etiologically significant" matters are incorporated within their scope, is not, the present findings indicate, to be decided on the basis of an *a priori* inspection of their formally available definitions. The sociologist who regards the category "theft" with penal code in hand and proposes necessary, "theoretically relevant" revisions, is constructing an imagined use of the penal code as the basis for his criticism. For in their actual use, categories of crime, as we have reiterated continuously above, are, at least for this legal establishment, the shorthand reference terms for that knowledge of the social structure and its criminal events upon which the task of practically organizing the work of "representation" is premised. That knowledge includes, embodied within what burglary, petty theft, narcotics violations, child molestation and the rest *actually stand for*, knowledge of modes of criminal activity, ecological characteristics of the community, patterns of daily slum life, psychological and social biographies of offenders, criminal histories and futures; in sum, practically tested criminological wisdom. The operations of the Public Defender system, and it is clear that upon comparative analysis with other legal "firms" it would be somewhat distinctive in character, are routinely maintained via the proper use of categories of crime for everyday decision making. The proprieties of that use are not described in the state criminal code, nor are the operations of reduction, detailed above.

A cautionary word is required. It will appear as obvious that the system of providing "defense" to indigent persons described above is not representative of criminal defense work generally. How the penal code is employed, i.e., how behaviors are scrutinized under its jurisdiction and dispensations made via operations performed on its categories, in other kinds of legal establishments, has not been investigated here. The present case, albeit apparently specialized, was chosen as an example only. It may well be that, in certain forms of legal work, the penal code as a statutory document is accorded a much different and more "rigorous" scrutiny. The legalistic character of some criminal prosecutions leads one to suspect that the "letter of the law" might constitute a key reference point in preparing for a criminal defense, aiming for acquittal, or changing a statutory regulation.

15. The Fix

Edwin H. Sutherland

The profession of theft is organized around the effort to secure money with relative safety. In this respect the profession of theft is similar to other professions and to other permanent groups. For money and safety are values inherent in Western civilization, and the methods which are used to realize these objectives are adjusted to the general culture.

The thief is relatively safe in his thefts for three reasons: First, he selects rackets in which the danger is at a minimum. The shakedown (extortion from homosexuals and certain other violators of law) is safe because the victims, being themselves violators of the law, cannot complain to the police. The confidence game is safe for the same reason, for the victims have entered into collusion with the thieves to defraud someone else and were themselves defrauded in the attempt. Stealing from stores is relatively safe because the stores are reluctant to make accusations of theft against persons who appear to be legitimate customers. Picking pockets is relatively safe because the legal rules of evidence make it almost impossible to convict a pickpocket. The professional thief scrupulously avoids the types of theft which are

SOURCE: *The Professional Thief*, by a professional thief, Chicago: The University of Chicago Press, pp. 217–223, 1937. By permission of the publisher.

attended with great danger and especially those which involve much publicity. The theft of famous art treasures, for instance, is never attempted by professional thieves. It would probably not be especially difficult for them to steal the treasures, but it would be practically impossible, because of the publicity, for them to sell the treasures. It is significant that the two most famous thefts of art treasures in the last century—Gainsborough's "Duchess of Devonshire" and Da Vinci's "Mona Lisa"— were not motivated by the expectation of financial gain.

Second, by training and experience the professional thief develops ingenious methods and ability to control situations. A thief is a specialist in manipulating people and achieves his results by being a good actor. Third, he works on the principle that he can "fix" practically every case in which he may be caught.

Because of the importance of "the fix" for a general interpretation of professional theft, it is elaborated at this point. Cases are fixed in two ways: first, by making restitution to the victim in return for an agreement not to prosecute; second, by securing the assistance of one or more public officials by payment of money or by political order or suggestion. These two methods are generally combined in a particular case.

The victim is almost always willing to accept restitution and drop the prosecution. This is true not only of the individual victim but also of the great insurance companies, which frequently offer rewards for the return of stolen property with an agreement not to prosecute and are thus the best fences for stolen property. The length of time required for the prosecution of a case is one of the reasons for the willingness of the victim to drop the prosecution. At any rate, the victim is more interested in the return of his stolen property than he is in maintaining a solid front of opposition against theft. He tries to get what he can, just as the thief tries to get what he can; neither has much interest in the general social welfare.

The violation of trust by the office-holders is also necessary for the success of the fix. The party machine is an agency for the organization of violation of trust by office-holders. The party machine is for the most part unofficial and exists primarily for its own welfare. It is engaged in predatory control in many places and in many respects. This is best seen in the patronage system, which is generally regarded as beneficial for the party but is certainly injurious to the country. It reaches out, partly by means of the patronage system, to control predaciously all aspects of political life. The muckrakers in the first decade of this century found predatory political organizations in practically all the large cities.[1] The Hofstadter and Seabury Commission in New York City, Merriam in Chicago, and others elsewhere have shown that the system has not changed appreciably since the first decade of the century.[2] Intimate details of the picture are brought out in the autobiographies of office-holders who have made some effort to work for the public interest,[3] and in the biographies of

---

[1] See, esp., Lincoln Steffens, *Autobiography* (New York, 1931).

[2] Samuel Seabury, *Final Report in the Matter of the Investigation of the Magistrates' Courts* (New York, 1932); W. B. Northrup and J. B. Northrup, *Insolence of Office: The Story of the Seabury Investigation* (New York, 1932); Charles E. Merriam, *Chicago* (New York, 1929), pp. 24–69.

[3] See, for instance, Carter H. Harrison, *Stormy Years: Autobiography of Carter H. Harrison* (Indianapolis: Bobbs-Merrill Co., 1935). Harrison states that in the decade of the nineties in Chicago "the control of public affairs was the exclusive appanage of a low-browed, dull-witted, baseminded gang of plug-uglies, with no outstanding characteristic beyond an unquenchable lust for money" [p. 72 (by permission)]. Harrison made the charge in the Democratic National Convention in Baltimore in 1912 that a post of authority under the sergeant of arms in that convention was being held by the proprietor of a Chicago saloon which was a hangout for pickpockets and which was owned by Roger Sullivan, the head of the rival faction of the party in Illinois.

persons who, while holding public office, act as the agents of special interests.[4] The attitudes of the common people are revealed in Caroline F. Ware's illuminating description of Greenwich Village in New York City.[5]

These are samples of the available descriptions of the predatory control in the enacting and blocking of legislation, in voting, in granting franchises, letting contracts, making purchases, depositing public funds in banks, and making appointments to offices. The "badness" is practically always in the form of collusion between those in public offices and others who are not in public offices, and in both groups appears to be a product of natural forces in the social order.

The fixing of criminal cases is a part of this general system of predatory control. And the fixing of cases by professional thieves is a part of the much more general system of fixing cases. A retired police detective made the statement: "Everyone is going to try to get out when arrested. The method that he uses depends on the people he is dealing with rather than on his own moral ideals."

The fixing of traffic tickets is especially prevalent. A judge in Chicago, in charge of the court which had jurisdiction over traffic offences, asserted that 90 per cent of the persons who received citations for traffic violations attempted to fix their cases. The Chicago newspapers in April, 1934, reported that only one-tenth of 1 per cent of the persons who had received such citations during the preceding three months were punished in any way whatsoever. This condition in Chicago is probably typical of most large American cities.

The fixing of cases of violations of laws against gambling, prostitution, and alcohol is more organized than the fixing of traffic tickets. John C. Weston, deputy district-attorney in the Woman's Court in New York City, testified before the Hofstadter Commission in 1931 that he had received $20,000 in bribes from lawyers, policemen, bondsmen, and others for aiding in the discharge of six hundred cases of prostitution in that court, that a ring of twenty-one lawyers participated in this business, and that two police-detectives on the vice squad were included in the organization. This situation, also, could be duplicated in many other large cities and also in smaller cities.

The fixing of cases occurs, also, though probably less frequently, in more violent crimes. Sile Doty, horse thief and burglar in New York, Michigan, and Indiana from 1820 to 1850, stated, "In case I should get overtaken in any of my exploits I had the means to buy my liberty, which I could do of nearly all of the officials." [6] Langdon W. Moore, a professional bank burglar in the last half of the nineteenth century, reported that it was almost always possible for him to secure immunity from punishment for bank burglary by bribing public officials.[7] George M. White, another bank burglar in the same period, reported that members of the police department of New York City who co-operated with the bank burglars were known as the "bank ring," that they received 10 per cent of the proceeds of all bank burglaries committed by the protected burglars, and also gave the burglars information regarding banks that might easily be burglarized; two members of the "bank ring" subsequently became superintendents of police in New York City.[8] Pat Crowe, kidnaper and robber, explained that many of his serious crimes were fixed with the assistance of prominent

---

[4] C. H. Woody, *The Case of Frank L. Smith* (Chicago, 1931).

[5] *Greenwich Village* (Boston, 1935), pp. 267–91.

[6] J. G. W. Colburn, *The Life of Sile Doty* (Toledo, 1880), p. 137.

[7] Langdon W. Moore, *His Own Story of His Eventful Life* (Boston, 1893).

[8] George M. White, *From Boniface to Bank Burglar* (New York, 1907), pp. 278–380, 440–80.

lawyers, including two senators and a national committeeman for the state of Iowa.[9] The Associated Press reports of July 18, 1936, contained testimony that of the $100,000 ransom paid in the Hamm kidnaping, $25,000 went to Thomas Brown, formerly chief of police of St. Paul and at the time assigned to the kidnaping squad, in return for information regarding the police plans for the capture of the kidnapers.

It is in this situation that the professional thief finds ways of making money safely. The situation may be called, generically, "social disorganization." The society is not working harmoniously and smoothly for the suppression of theft. Enough of the office-holders are co-operating with the thief so that he can carry on his occupation with security. Also, the victim who agrees to drop the prosecution in return for the restitution of his stolen property is typical of the individual in modern society: his interests are immediate and personal, and the public welfare means little to him. Because the public welfare means little to the average citizen, we have thieves, corrupt political machines, and inefficient office-holders. The public is not united for its own welfare; that absence of unity is social disorganization.

16. The Differential Selection of Juvenile Offenders for Court Appearance

Nathan Goldman

RESEARCH DESIGN

[This study is an attempt to] test the general hypothesis that there is a differential selection of juvenile offenders for court appearance of such a nature that in the juvenile court there is found a biased sample of the population of juvenile offenders known to the police. This broad hypothesis, based on previous experience, on the research literature, and on observations made during a preliminary study in Chicago, might be tested by a consideration of the differences between a population of juvenile offenders known to the police, and those referred by the same police to a juvenile court. In the following study, the extent to which two such groups differ in types of offenses, racial characteristics, sex composition, and age distribution, will be investigated. Statistical evidence will be adduced to test the hypothesis that only a portion of the juvenile offenders known to the police are referred to the juvenile court. Data will be presented to show how this sample of delinquents referred to the juvenile court varies from community to community. Finally, having indicated the validity of this general hypothesis, the nature of this selection process will be examined by means of information obtained from the police in personal interviews.

The procedure of this study thus falls into two parts. First, quantitative or statistical information is presented with regard to the composition of the juvenile court sample of the population of delinquents known to the police, as obtained from police

[9] Patrick T. Crowe, *Spreading Evil: Autobiography, as Told to Thomas Regan* (New York, 1927).

SOURCE: *The Differential Selection of Juvenile Offenders for Court Appearance*, National Research and Information Center, National Council on Crime and Delinquency, 1963. By permission of the author and publisher.

records. For this purpose statistical data obtained from police records in several municipalities are analyzed. These data are considered from the point of view of the disposition of each case by the police, with respect to the several variables mentioned above, age, race, sex, and nature of the offense. Inter-community comparisons as well as intra-community analysis of the data are attempted.

The second part of the research consists in the analysis of a series of interviews with police officers in a number of communities in Allegheny County outside the city of Pittsburgh, and in several police districts of Pittsburgh. These interviews were aimed at obtaining statements with regard to the policeman's attitude toward those various factors on which the court and non-court populations of juvenile offenders were found to differ. These interviews may be considered as a qualification of the statistical data presented in the previous section.

It was difficult to find many communities in Allegheny County where police records on juveniles were kept and to which access was allowed. Of five such communities which were found out of twenty-two visited, the records of only four could be used. The other data were discarded because it was found that records had been kept only on those cases which the police chief thought might be needed in the future for referral to the juvenile court. Needless to say, such records can be of little use for research purposes.

The municipalities from which police data were available fortunately represented areas of different socio-economic structure. However, one must guard against considering these "typical" of similar communities in the county. The fact that adequate records were kept and made available by the police chief for research purposes would in itself indicate a superior degree of social interest. The selection of such a police chief and subordinate may well be a reflection of community attitudes toward social problems. To preserve the confidential nature of these data, code names will be used to designate the four communities and population figures will be given in round numbers. However, for a better understanding of the problem, some minimal description of the communities involved was deemed necessary. It is hoped that the identity of these municipalities will thus not be made public.

The Juvenile Court Law of Pennsylvania [1] designates as a child any minor under the age of eighteen years. A juvenile delinquent child is defined as:

> 1. A child who has violated any law of the Commonwealth or ordinance of any city, borough or township.
> 2. A child who, by reason of being wayward or habitually disobedient, is uncontrolled by his or her parent, guardian, or custodian or legal representative.
> 3. A child who is habitually truant from school or home.
> 4. A child who habitually so deports himself or herself as to injure or endanger the morals or health of himself, herself or others.

The juvenile courts in Pennsylvania have full and exclusive jurisdiction in all proceedings affecting delinquent children, except in cases of a capital offense. A judge of the juvenile court has, however, the privilege of referring any juvenile between the age of fourteen and eighteen to the district attorney of the county for disposition, at his discretion.

[1] Lillian P. Strauss and Edwin P. Rome, *The Child and the Law in Pennsylvania* (Philadelphia: The Public Charities Association of Pennsylvania, 1943).

Juvenile court proceedings may be initiated upon the petition of any citizen certifying that a given child is neglected, dependent, or delinquent and is in need of care, guidance, and control. The powers of the court may also be exercised upon commitment by a magistrate, alderman, or justice of the peace, of a child arrested for any indictable offense, other than murder, or for the violation of any other laws of the Commonwealth or the ordinance of any city, borough, or township. Preliminary hearings in any cases affecting dependent, delinquent, or neglected children under eighteen years are forbidden by the law. Some question had been raised regarding the authority of magistrates in trying and in imposing fines or other penalities on youths under eighteen in cases such as automobile violations. Such trial and imposition of penalties upon juveniles was considered by the attorney general of the state in 1940 as being contrary to the provisions of the Juvenile Court Act. The Act provides specifically that in Allegheny County any person charged with crime and found to be under eighteen must be "certified" by a magistrate to the juvenile court. The Juvenile Court of Allegheny County was given the power to inquire into all crimes triable in the county wherein the person charged is a child under eighteen.

Juvenile offenders apprehended by police in Allegheny County may be placed in one of five groups:

> **First,** those cases known to the police and not known to the juvenile court.
>
> **Second,** those cases reported to the court by police for the information of the court. This does not constitute an official complaint filed by the police and does not presume official action on the part of the court authorities. Such reports are the result of a cooperative arrangement between the court and the police, instituted by Judge Schramm, to keep the court in touch with juvenile problems in the community.
>
> **Third,** cases in which official action by the court has been initiated by means of a legal "information" filed by a police officer or by a citizen through a justice of the peace, alderman, or magistrate.
>
> **Fourth,** cases referred to the juvenile court on a petition. The police or any citizen may petition the court to the effect that a given child, because of neglect, delinquency, or dependency, is in need of care, guidance, and control. Such a petition may be sent to the court with or without the child. The court, through its intake staff, then decides on the action to be taken.
>
> **Fifth,** juveniles on probation or parole who commit further offenses may be turned over to the probation or parole officer, or they may be again taken to the juvenile court on a new petition or complaint.

In this study we are interested in the distinctions which may obtain between cases known to the court and those known only to the police. We shall, therefore, treat the second, third and fourth of the above groups—that is, those known to the court unofficially and those known officially, as one. The decision with regard to disposition of the case is no longer in the hands of the police at this point.

Through juvenile court personnel a visit was arranged with a police chief who it was felt would be willing to discuss frankly his handling of juvenile offenders and would cooperate to the extent of allowing access to his files on juvenile arrests. The project was explained to him and his cooperation was obtained. He arranged for an interview with a police chief in a neighboring municipality and provided the names of others whom it might be useful to see. Each interviewee was asked to suggest others who might help on the project. In this way I could in each instance introduce myself as having been referred by a police official in another town. Such in-group referral, together with some knowledge of the community and the special problems of the police, generally reduced the defensiveness of the police chief.

Data were obtained directly from the police files in each of the four municipalities in Allegheny County: [Mill Town is a small mill town; Trade City is a trade center; Steel City is an industrial center; and Manor Heights is an upper-class residential area. The social characteristics of these municipalities appear in Table 16-11, page 277]. From these files were recorded the name of the offender, the age, race, sex, home address, nature of the offense, and disposition of the case. A conference was held with the person principally responsible for the records (in one instance the juvenile officer; in the other three, the chief of police) in which all cases were discussed and questionable cases clarified. The records were, in the main, those of boy offenders, with only a scattering of girls. Data from the community labeled Steel City contained no female offenders. No Negro juveniles were arrested in Manor Heights.

In the following discussion, the data will be divided into two categories according to the disposition of the case by the police. We shall compare cases released by the police without referral to the court with those which became known to the juvenile court through the police. Cases reported unofficially for the information of the court will be included in the latter category, together with cases referred by a petition or other form of direct referral. The number of arrests will usually be greater than the number of individuals arrested because of the repetition of offenses.

The problem confronting us in this study is that of comparing certain characteristics of the population of juvenile offenders known to the court with those which are disposed of unofficially by the police and thus remain known only to them. The nature of the process of the selection of juvenile offenders for court appearance may be ascertained from an analysis of these data. The statistical significance of the differences found between the proportions of cases disposed of by the police with court referral, and without court referral, will be estimated by the calculation of the Critical Ratio. Since, in many instances, the number of cases is relatively small it was considered more adequate to obtain an estimate of the variability of the random sampling distribution of the difference between proportions by combining the two groups. A better approximation of the universe standard error will be obtained by this procedure.[2]

The statistical significance of the difference between the observed proportions of offenders disposed of by release or by court referral by the police can be judged in terms of the extent of the deviation of such differences from that which might be expected in the random selection of two samples from the same universe. Assuming the null hypothesis (that the two samples, cases referred to the court and cases released by the police, are drawn from universes where the proportions of these two events are equal), we can then test the extent to which our data deviates from this assumed hypothesis. In the present study a P value of .01, corresponding to a Critical Ratio of 2.6, is used as the criterion for the rejection of the null hypothesis. The Critical Ratio was not computed for data where a cell value was less than 5.

---

[2] Quinn McNemar, *Psychological Statistics* (New York: John Wiley & Sons, Inc., 1949), p. 76; Margaret J. Hagood, *Statistics for Sociologists* (New York: Reynal and Hitchcock, 1941), pp. 438–440.

THE RESEARCH FINDINGS

The data collected from the four municipalities will first be analyzed as a whole. Although the four police organizations operated under the same juvenile delinquency laws and were within the jurisdiction of the same juvenile court, differences in functioning are to be expected. Since the four communities differed in social and economic characteristics it was assumed that these would be reflected in the treatment by police of juvenile violators of the law. Such differences in the handling of cases of delinquent conduct might be masked in the combined data. In order to observe the relations between community variables and the differential reporting of arrests to the court we shall also analyze each community separately.

It must be remembered that the data were not collected for comparable lengths of time for each municipality. Comparisons therefore between the four and computations of annual rates must be corrected for differences in the time factor. In this section of the study we shall be concerned with the proportions of offenders arrested who were referred to court and those treated otherwise by the police. We shall consider the relation of nature of offense, race, sex, and age to this reporting process.

Analysis of the Combined Data

The group of 1,083 individuals had accumulated a total of 1,236 arrests, with an average of 1.14 arrests per individual. The range of number of arrests was from one to six each. Of the total, 89.5 per cent had been recorded only once. Two individuals, as may be seen in Table 16-1, had six arrests each.

TABLE 16-1

Frequency of Arrests per Individual: Combined Data

Frequency of Arrests	Individuals	Total Arrests	Per Cent of Total Individuals
1	969	969	89.5
2	85	170	7.8
3	23	69	2.1
4	4	16	0.4
5	0	0	—
6	2	12	0.2
TOTAL	1,083	1,236	

Average: 1.14 arrests per individual.

Of the 1,083 individuals arrested, 696 or 64.3 per cent were released without court referral. Only 387 or 35.7 per cent of the individuals arrested were referred to court by the police. In Table 16-2 it is indicated that 31.9 per cent of those arrested appeared in court only once, and that 3.8 per cent had more than one court referral. One boy had four court appearances and another had five during the period covered by our records. On the average there were 0.40 court referrals per person arrested and an average of 1.12 court appearances of those children who were referred to court.

TABLE 16-2

Frequency of Court Referrals per Individual: Combined Data

Number of Court Referrals	Individuals	Total Referrals	Per Cent of Total Individuals
0	696	0	64.3
1	346	346	31.9
2	34	68	3.1
3	5	15	0.5
4	1	4	0.1
5	1	5	0.1
TOTAL	1,083	438	

Average: 0.40 court referrals per individual.

The rates of arrests and of court referrals per year were calculated for the combined areas. The data for arrest and for referral for each community, originally obtained for different time periods, were converted into annual figures. These were then summed and divided by the total number of children aged ten to seventeen in the four communities. The annualized rate of arrest for the combined data thus obtained was 32.6 per thousand children. The annualized rate of court referrals was 9.9 per thousand children.

The various offenses are grouped in Tables 16-3 and 16-4 so as to eliminate the small numbers of cases in some categories and to facilitate statistical computation. The arrangement of offenses in seven groups is used in all tables in this and in the following chapter. An attempt was made to group together those offenses which, in the writer's judgment, seem to have a similar behavioral significance. Each group category includes patterns of proscribed behavior, which can be subsumed under the general headings of larceny, burglary, larceny of a motor vehicle, assault, being delinquent and incorrigible, violation of a local ordinance, and mischief. The subcategories included in each of these groupings are judged to be of the same level of misconduct. The offenses for which juveniles were arrested by police are presented in Table 16-3. The reliability of the difference between the proportion of a given offense group referred to the juvenile court and the sum of all the other offenses disposed of in the same manner is indicated by the magnitude of the Critical Ratios.

It appears in Table 16-4 that the largest portion of the total arrests is for the offense of larceny, 22.9 per cent. The next large group of arrests is for the violation of a local ordinance, 12.4 per cent of the total arrests. Following these we find burglary, property damage, and malicious mischief, in decreasing order. These five offense categories include 65.3 per cent of the total number of arrests. A few of the remaining categories include only very few cases. Prowling and the illegal use of the U.S. Army uniform are represented by only one case each. Under assault and under arson we find two cases each. Only three arrests for carrying concealed weapons were found in the records of the 1,236 arrests.

Offenses seem to be differentially treated with respect to court referral. Some offenses were always reported to the court, while others were reported relatively infrequently. It is indicated in Table 16-3 that of the ten cases of robbery, all were

TABLE 16-3

Disposition of Cases by Police: Combined Data

Offense	Total Arrests	Disposition Release	Disposition Court	Percentage to Juvenile Court	Grouped %	Critical Ratio
Larceny	284	178	106	37.3	38.1	1.17*
Receiving Stolen Goods	10	4	6	60.0		
Burglary	138	37	101	73.2	75.0	10.70
Robbery	10	0	10	100.		
Motor Vehicle Larceny	46	4	42	91.3	91.1	8.83
Riding in Stolen Car	10	1	9	90.0		
Assault	2	0	2	100.		
Sex	42	7	35	83.3	82.9	6.80
Carrying Concealed Weapons	3	1	2	66.7		
Incorrigible-Delinquent	42	8	34	80.9	69.5	6.64
Runaway	40	17	23	52.5		
Disorderly	54	35	19	35.2		
Vagrancy	4	3	1	25.0		
Prowling	1	0	1	100.		
Drunkenness	8	7	1	12.5	11.6	10.63
Gambling	31	30	1	3.2		
Trespassing	39	39	0	0.		
Violation Boro Ordinance	153	145	8	5.2		
Motor Law Violation	20	16	4	20.0		
Army Uniform Violation	1	0	1	100.		
Mischief	64	61	3	4.7	10.7	10.90
Malicious Mischief	104	90	14	13.5		
Property Damage	128	114	14	10.9		
Arson	2	1	1	50.0		
TOTAL	1,236	798	438	35.4		

* $P > .08$. All others, $P < .01$.

TABLE 16-4

Proportion of Arrests and Court Referrals for Each Offense: Combined Data

Offense	Arrests	Per Cent of Total Arrests	Per Cent of All Court Referrals
Larceny	284	22.9	24.2
Receiving Stolen Goods	10	0.8	1.4
Burglary	138	11.2	23.1
Robbery	10	0.8	2.3
Motor Vehicle Larceny	46	3.7	9.6
Riding in Stolen Car	10	0.8	2.1
Assault	2	0.2	0.5
Sex	42	3.4	8.0
Carrying Concealed Weapons	3	0.2	0.5
Incorrigible-Delinquent	42	3.4	7.8
Runaway	40	3.2	5.3
Disorderly	54	4.4	4.3
Vagrancy	4	0.3	0.2
Prowling	1	0.1	0.2
Drunkenness	8	0.6	0.2
Gambling	31	2.5	0.2
Trespassing	39	3.2	—
Violation Boro Ordinance	153	12.4	1.8
Motor Law Violation	20	1.6	0.9
Army Uniform Violation	1	0.1	0.2
Mischief	64	5.2	0.7
Malicious Mischief	104	8.4	3.2
Property Damage	128	10.8	3.2
Arson	2	0.2	0.2

referred for official action. Ninety-one per cent of the arrests for the larceny of a motor vehicle and 90 per cent of the arrests for riding in a stolen car were reported to the juvenile court. Eighty-three per cent of the sex offenses and 80.9 per cent of cases in the delinquent and incorrigible group were made known to the court. Some offense categories with 100 per cent referral contain very few cases. On the other hand, the relatively frequent offenses of gambling, violation of a borough ordinance, violation of the motor vehicle code, mischief, property damage, and drunkenness are relatively infrequently made the bases of an official or unofficial report to the court. The proportion of court referrals of cases of larceny and also of the specific charge of disorderly conduct coincided with the mean frequency of all referrals.

Critical Ratio values were computed on the grouped data in Table 16-3. They indicate rather definitely that in each offense group, except in the case of larceny, the proportion of court referrals is significantly different from the proportion referred to the court of all other offenses combined. Some offense groups are usually consistently over-represented, and some under-represented. It may be said, then, that the data indicate with a high degree of statistical significance the differential reporting by police of all offenses except larceny. That is, in terms of frequency of arrest, certain offenses are more, or less, frequently represented in the court sample than would be expected by the operation of chance alone.

For the purpose of further observing the differential treatment of various offenders, comparisons might be made between the portion which a given offense category is of the total number of arrests, and the portion which this same category is of the total of juvenile court referrals. Such comparisons for arrests may be made from Table 16-4. Taking the largest offense groups in order, it may be observed first, that the offense of larceny makes up only a slightly larger proportion of juvenile court referrals than it does of the total number of arrests. Arrests for the violation of a borough ordinance, on the other hand, are very markedly under-represented in the juvenile court sample. The proportion which this particular offense represents of the total arrest column is more than six times as great as its proportion in the juvenile court column. Similarly, the offenses of property damage and malicious mischief are under-represented in the court group. On the other hand, some offenses were reported to the court relatively much more frequently than would be expected on the basis of their representation in the arrest group. Burglary, although comprising 11.2 per cent of the total arrests, makes up twice this proportion of the total court referrals. Automobile theft and riding in a stolen car appear in the court data 2.6 times as frequently as would be expected from the representation of these offenses in the arrest data. Offenders charged with being delinquent and incorrigible, being a runaway, and with sex offense comprise a portion of court referrals more than twice as large as would be expected from the arrest distribution.

Compared to the referral rate of 35.4 per cent of all offenses for the aggregated data, certain offenses seem to be over-reported and others under-reported. Arrests for burglary, robbery, auto theft, riding in a stolen car, assault, and sex offenses are almost always referred to the court. Carrying concealed weapons resulted in two cases out of three in court referral. These offenses seem to have in common some sort of threat of attack or injury to the person. A stolen car in the hands of youth was referred to as a "lethal weapon" and a threat to the lives of citizens. Thus, such cases had to be referred for authoritative handling and, as will be seen later, for the protection of the police against charges of laxness and incompetence.

A high percentage of arrests of children on complaints of being "incorrigible or delinquent" and for being a "runaway from home" were also referred to court. Such behavior was viewed by the police as indicating that somehow parental control in the home was unsuccessful since the complaint originated in most instances from the parents. Running away from home was similarly interpreted in terms of unsatisfying home relations. Referral to the court, in the absence of local social work agencies, was deemed advisable to bring the situation to the attention of the professional court staff.

Violations of regulations concerning public order—disorderly conduct, drunkenness, gambling, motor vehicle regulations, or violations of other municipal rules (loitering, trespassing, etc.)—were considered problems for local rather than county court handling. Not one of the 39 trespassing arrests was referred to the court. Offenses involving some damage to private or public property—mischief, malicious mischief, property damage, arson—were also rarely reported for court action. These were viewed as largely childhood pranks or aberrations which could be handled by the administration of various corrective techniques, either by the police or by the parents. In one community the penalty for such offenses was the loss of use of one's automobile driving license, to be retained by the police chief for a period of time determined in conference with the parents.

Larceny and disorderly conduct correspond, in court referral rates, to the mean of all offenses. This may be a function of the broad coverage of these two categories. Some forms of larceny may be more "serious" than some burglaries. Disorderly conduct in our data covered a wide range of misbehavior, from loitering to the possession of burglar tools. Within such broadly defined categories of conduct one would expect to find police handling comparable to that of a variety of offenses.

It is probable that offenses generally considered "serious" may be more frequently referred to the court than "minor" offenses. Combination of the first four offense groups in Tables 16-3 and 16-4 as "serious" resulted in a total of 545 such offenses. Of these, 313 or 57.4 per cent were referred to the court by the police. Only 125 or 18.1 per cent of the 691 remaining "non-serious" offenses were so reported. The Critical Ratio value of 4.56 suggests the statistical significance of the difference between these two proportions. Dropping the larceny cases from the "serious" classification results in an even greater difference. The police reported to the court 80.1 per cent of such 251 "serious" and 24.1 per cent of the remaining "non-serious" cases. The significance of the difference between these proportions is indicated by a Critical Ratio value of 6.57.

The extent of the differential treatment accorded Negro juveniles arrested may be observed in Table 16-6. It appears that 33.6 per cent of the white arrests were re-

TABLE 16-5

Disposition of "Serious" Offenses: Combined Data

| Offenses | No. | % of Arrests | Disposition | | % to Court | % of Court |
			Release	Court		
Serious	545	44.1	232	313	57.4	71.5
Other	691	55.9	566	125	18.1*	28.5
Serious (excl. Larceny)	251	20.3	50	201	80.1	45.9
Other	985	79.7	748	237	24.1**	54.1
TOTAL	1,236		798	438	35.4	

* C. R. = 4.56, $P < .01$.
** C. R. = 6.57, $P < .01$.

TABLE 16-6

Disposition of Arrests by Race: Combined Data

| Race | No. | % of Arrests | Disposition | | % to Court | % of Court |
			Release	Court		
White	1,165	94.3	773	392	33.6	89.5
Negro	71	5.7	25	46	64.8*	10.5
TOTAL	1,236		798	438	35.4	

* C. R. = 5.35, $P < .01$.

ferred to the juvenile court, while 64.8 per cent of the Negro arrests were given such official recognition. Moreover, although Negro juveniles arrested in the aggregate sample were 5.7 per cent of the total of juvenile arrests, these Negro juveniles made up 10.5 per cent of the total court referrals. On the basis of the Critical Ratio of 5.35 we may say that there is a statistically significant difference between the proportion of Negro juvenile arrests referred to the court and the proportion of arrests of white children so treated. The probability is less than 1 in 1,000 that a difference of this magnitude could have been obtained by chance when no such difference actually exists between the two populations.

The apparent differential treatment of Negro children arrested might be a reflection of the more serious offenses committed by Negro boys and girls. Table 16-7 presents the data for serious and minor offenses by race. There appears to be little difference in the disposition of cases of white and Negro children who were arrested for serious offenses. However, there does appear to be a statistically significant difference in the disposition of minor offenses. A Negro child arrested for a *minor* offense has a greater chance of being taken to the juvenile court than does a white child. It must be remembered, however, that a child who was referred to court on a minor charge might have been previously arrested on a serious law violation.

For our combined sample there seemed to be little differential treatment of boy and girl offenders. Although girls made up 1.9 per cent of the arrests, they composed 3.0 per cent of the court referrals (Table 16-8). However, such a difference between the proportion of boy arrests referred to the court and the girl arrests so handled might possibly have been obtained by chance alone. The Critical Ratio of 1.95 could be obtained in five cases out of one hundred by the operation of chance factors alone. The null hypothesis, therefore, cannot be rejected.

The age distribution in the 1,236 arrests ranged from four to seventeen, with twenty-eight cases in which the age could not be determined. This age distribution is presented in Table 16-9. The modal age for all arrests is sixteen; the median age is ten years four months. The median age is fourteen years three months for court referrals, and thirteen years one month for those not referred to the court.

There appears to be an under-representation in court of arrests below the age of twelve, and an over-representation of arrests in the sixteen- and seventeen-year groups. It is possible, if not probable, that the nature of the offenses of children under age twelve is much less serious than that of the older boys and girls. For a variety of other reasons, however, police are loath to refer younger children to court. Some, referring back to their own early childhood escapades, find justification for the informal rather than official treatment of such children. Other police, referring to court and institution experiences as leading to habituation in the ways of delinquency, use court referral only as a last resort. Some, in terms of their self-conceptions as professional antagonists of the criminal, are embarrassed at having to assume a police role with respect to a young child. They prefer, then, to overlook juvenile offenses.

Critical Ratios in Table 16-9 indicate statistically significant differences in the disposition of cases at ages twelve, sixteen, and seventeen. In the younger age group a higher proportion of offenders were disposed of by police release than would be expected from the proportion of such cases in arrest files. The sixteen- and seventeen-year-old offenders are markedly over-represented in the juvenile court group. Other age groups show no discrimination in referral rates. Further analysis of these data, presented in Table 16-10, reveals that in cases of offenders below age fifteen, and especially below age ten, the police tend to use court referral proportionately less frequently than in the age groups of fifteen and over. The hypothesis of the differential disposition of cases according to age of the offender is thus found to be justified.

TABLE 16-7

Disposition of Arrests for Serious and Minor Offenses by Race: Combined Data

Race	Arrests	Serious (excl. Larceny)					Minor				
		No.	% of Serious	Court	% to Court	% of Court	No.	% of Minor	Court	% to Court	% of Court
White	1,165	227	90.4	180	79.3	89.6	938	95.2	212	22.6	89.5
Negro	71	24	9.6	21	87.5**	10.4	47	4.8	25	53.2*	10.5
TOTAL	1,236	251	100.0	201	80.1	100.0	985	100.0	237	24.1	100.0

** C. R. = 0.96, P > .30.
* C. R. = 4.78, P < .01.

275

TABLE 16-8

Disposition of Arrests by Sex: Combined Data

| Sex | No. | % of Arrests | Disposition | | % to Court | % of Court |
			Release	Court		
Male	1,212	98.1	787	425	35.1	97.0
Female	24	1.9	11	13	54.2*	3.0
TOTAL	1,236		798	438	35.4	

* C. R. = 1.95, P > .05.

TABLE 16-9

Disposition of Arrests by Age: Combined Data

| Age | No. | % of Total Arrests | Disposition | | % to Court | % of Court | Critical Ratio |
			Release	Court			
4	2	0.2	2	0	—	—	—
5	3	0.2	1	2	66.7	0.45	—
6	10	0.8	9	1	10.0	0.22	—
7	10	0.8	7	3	30.0	0.7	—
8	41	3.3	37	4	9.8	0.9	—
9	49	4.0	35	14	28.6	3.2	1.06
10	70	5.7	48	22	31.4	5.0	0.73
11	75	6.1	49	26	34.7	5.9	0.14
12	120	9.7	98	22	18.3	5.0	4.15
13	133	10.8	97	36	27.1	8.2	2.13
14	175	14.2	109	66	37.7	15.1	0.67
15	181	14.6	106	75	41.4	17.1	1.89
16	192	15.5	102	90	46.9	20.5	3.68
17	147	11.9	76	71	48.3	16.2	3.48
Unknown	28	2.3	22	6	21.4	1.4	—

TABLE 16-10

Disposition of Arrests by Age Groups: Combined Data

| Age | No. | % of Arrests | Disposition | | % to Court | % of Court |
			Release	Court		
Below 10	115	9.3	91	24	20.9*	5.5
10–15	573	46.4	401	172	30.0**	39.3
15–18	520	42.1	284	236	45.4***	53.9
Unknown	28	2.3	22	6	21.4	1.4
TOTAL	1,236		798	438	35.4	

* C. R. = 3.40, P < .01.
** C. R. = 3.90, P < .01.
*** C. R. = 6.14, P < .01.

TABLE 16-11

Social Characteristics of Areas Studied *

	Allegheny County	Steel City	Trade City	Manor Heights	Mill Town
Population (1940 census)	1,411,539**	55,000	29,900	20,000	12,700
Population, age 10–17	—	8,117	3,387	2,631	2,070
Land use	—	Industrial	Residential and commercial	Residential	Industrial
Population density (per gross acre)	3.02	25.6	23.1	6.0	18.9
Percentage foreign born (white)	12.71	15.77	7.03	4.84	13.77
Percentage Negro	6.38	3.95	1.58	0.45	3.28
Nationality groups	Italy Br. Isles Poland	Hungary Czech. Br. Isles	Br. Isles Germany Italy	Br. Isles Germany	Italy Poland Austria Br. Isles
Median rental	$28.57	$28.56	$42.06	$81.88	$27.87
Occupations	Clerical-sales operatives	Laborers operatives clerical	Clerical craftsmen foremen	Clerical proprietor managers officials	Laborers clerical operatives
Median school grade completed	8.3	10.7	12.6	14.8	10.5
Percentage completed college	5.5	3.4	10	21.5	3.5

* From Social Facts about Pittsburgh and Allegheny County (Pittsburgh: Federation of Social Agencies, 1945).
** 52.4 per cent living outside Pittsburgh.

Summary

There were found in the police files of the four communities investigated, the records of 1,236 arrests of 1,083 juvenile offenders. Of these 35.7 per cent of the individuals and 35.4 per cent of the arrests were reported to the juvenile court. The rest were released by the police and remained known only to them. On the average, there were 1.14 arrests and 0.40 court referrals per individual; and 1.12 court appearances per individual referred. The most frequent arrests were found to be for the following offenses listed in decreasing order: larceny, violation of a borough ordinance, burglary, property damage, malicious mischief. All the robbery cases were referred to the court. Ninety-one per cent of the cases of larceny of a motor vehicle and 90 per cent of the cases of riding in a stolen car were reported. Eighty-three per cent of the sex offenses were reported to the court. On the other hand, offenses such as larceny, disorderly conduct, gambling, violation of a borough ordinance, etc., were reported only infrequently. The proposition of the differential treatment of various offenses was found statistically justified, except for the offense of larceny. Offenses which might be classed as "serious" are very much more frequently referred to court than are other offenses.

The presence of a pattern of differential treatment of white and Negro children seems to be established. While only 33.6 per cent of the offenses committed by white juveniles were referred to the court, 64.8 per cent of the Negro arrests were disposed of by court referral. Although Negro juvenile arrests constituted only 5.7 per cent of the total arrests, these Negro children contributed 10.5 per cent of the total court population. Moreover, the differential in referral rates seems to be a result of the disproportionate referral of minor rather than serious offenses of Negro children.

There appeared to be no discriminatory treatment of girls with respect to court referral in these aggregated data. With regard to age, there seems to be a statistically reliable difference in the treatment of different age groups, with an under-representation of ages below twelve, and an over-representation of ages fifteen, sixteen, and seventeen in the court sample.

Except for the findings with regard to female juvenile offenders and the offense of larceny, most of the surmises or propositions stated at the beginning of this chapter have been substantiated. However, whereas previous investigators had to be satisfied with guesses, the present investigation of actual police records has provided us with the possibility of basing our inferences on concrete data. Moreover, the conclusions may now be stated in more precise terms than previous investigations would allow. . . .

THE COMMUNITIES COMPARED

[Now let us turn to an analysis of] the data obtained from each of the four communities. It was previously implied that each of the four municipalities studied (Steel City, Trade City, Mill Town, and Manor Heights) might be considered as representative of a specific type of community suggested by its pseudonym. A comparison of the differences in police disposition of cases of juvenile offenders in these four communities might reveal some significant aspects of the differential selection of juvenile offenders for court referral, according to the type of community. Data for making comparisons are grouped together in Table 16-12.

There appear to be marked differences in the rates of juvenile arrests between the four communities in our study. In the combined data we found an annual arrest rate of 32.6 per cent per 1,000 children aged ten to seventeen, with a range from 49.7 to 12.4 per thousand. The highest arrest rate was found in Manor Heights, the municipality with the highest socio-economic rating. The lowest rate of arrests was found in Trade City, the commercial and residential community with a high degree of transiency in population (see Table 16-12).

TABLE 16-12

Summary

	Steel City	Trade City	Mill Town	Manor Heights	Combined Data
Arrests per 1,000 population age 10 to 17*	37.3	12.4	34.8	49.7	32.6
Court referrals per 1,000 population age 10 to 17*	17.1	8.9	5.2	4.1	9.9
Per cent of serious** cases to all arrests	26.9	37.1	6.1	6.7	20.3
Per cent of arrests referred to court	46.1	71.2	14.9	8.6	35.4
Per cent of serious** cases referred to court	80.1	71.4	100.0	96.0	80.2
Per cent of minor arrests referred to court	33.6	71.0	9.3	2.3	24.1
Per cent of Negro cases referred to court	51.2	82.4	84.6	—	64.8
Per cent of female cases referred to court	—	71.4	75.0	—	54.2
Per cent of cases below age 10 to court	26.4	14.3	16.7	5.6	20.9
Per cent of cases age 10 to 15 to court	42.2	67.3	20.4	6.2	30.0
Per cent of cases age 15 to 18 to court	57.1	77.1	7.5	12.6	45.4

* Social Facts about Pittsburgh and Allegheny County.
** Excluding larceny and receiving stolen goods.

There also appears to be a wide variation in the proportion of serious offenses found among the arrests in the different communities. In the combined data it was found that 20.3 per cent of the arrests were for serious offenses such as automobile theft, assault, burglary, sex offenses, etc. Conversely, 79.7 per cent of the arrests were for offenses which are considered for purposes of this study as minor, such as larceny, violating a borough ordinance, mischief, disorderly conduct, etc. The highest proportion of arrests for serious offenses, 37.1 per cent of the arrests, occurred in Trade City. Next in order of frequency came the other large city in our sample, Steel City, with 26.9 per cent of its arrests for serious offenses. There is a very marked drop from the level of these two communities to the proportions of arrest for serious offenses in Manor Heights and Mill Town. The figures for these two towns were 6.7 per cent and 6.1 per cent respectively.

It appears from these data that the community which has the lowest overall arrest rate has the highest proportion of arrests for serious offenses. On the other hand, Manor Heights, with the highest arrest rate has a very small portion of arrests for serious offenses, only very slightly above the lowest, that of Mill Town. It is indicated in Table 16–12 that the relatively high arrest rates in Manor Heights and in Mill Town are a reflection of the large number of arrests for minor rather than serious offenses.

The high arrest rates of Manor Heights and of Mill Town are largely a result of arrests for trespassing, disorderly conduct, mischief, violation of a borough ordinance, property damage, etc. These are offenses which are, to a large extent, usually overlooked by citizens and police in other communities. The police chief in Manor Heights was frequently called by citizens to complain of children who took shortcuts across their lawns, or children who damaged prized shrubbery, or who were annoyingly noisy on the street or in the public buses. On the other hand, Trade City, with the lowest rate of arrest and the highest rate of arrests for serious offenses, had very few recorded arrests for vagrancy, violation of a borough ordinance, mischief, etc.

The rate of court referral per 1,000 population of children aged ten to seventeen was 9.9 for the combined data. The highest rate of such court referrals was found in Steel City, the largest of our four communities. The next lower rate of court referrals was found in Trade City, also next smaller in size. Mill Town and Manor Heights follow with rates of 5.2 and 4.1 per thousand respectively.

Of all arrests, 35.4 per cent resulted in court referral. Trade City had the highest rate of court referral, 71.2 per cent of arrests. In Steel City slightly less than half, 46.1 per cent, of the arrests resulted in court appearance of the offender. Mill Town and Manor Heights had a considerably lower proportion of arrests referred to court, 14.9 per cent and 8.6 per cent respectively.

When seriousness of offense is considered, it appears that most of the arrests result in court appearance. For the combined communities it was found that 80.2 per cent of these arrests were referred to court. All of the arrests for serious offenses in Mill Town and 96 per cent of such arrests in Manor Heights were disposed of by court referral. In Steel City, 80.1 per cent of the arrests on serious charges were referred to court. The lowest rate of court referral for serious offenses was found in Trade City, 71.4 per cent. Thus, in contrast to rates of arrest for all offenses, rates of arrest for serious offenses, and rates of court referral for all offenses, the rates of referral for *serious* offenses are relatively consistent, with little spread.

In the combined sample it was found that 24.1 per cent of the arrests for minor offenses were referred to court. This is in marked contrast to the 80.2 per cent referral of serious offenses. Manor Heights and Mill Town referred relatively few cases of minor offenses to the court, 2.3 per cent and 9.3 per cent respectively. Trade City had the highest rate of referral of arrests for minor offenses, 71.0 per cent. There is thus considerably more variability in the reporting of minor offenses to the court than in the case with serious offenses. It appears that the variation in rates of court referral between different communities is largely a result of local policies with respect to the reporting of *minor* offenses.

In Manor Heights, although 93 per cent of the arrests of apprehended juveniles were for minor offenses, only 2.3 per cent of these became known to the court. Although about 94 per cent of the arrests in Mill Town were for minor offenses only 9.3 per cent were referred to the court. Minor offenses constituted 73 per cent of the arrests in Steel City, but only 34 per cent of these were forwarded for court handling. On the other hand, although minor offenses constituted the reasons for about 63 per cent of the arrests in Trade City, 71 per cent of these arrests were referred to the court. There seems to be a sort of inverse relation between the proportion of arrests for minor offenses and the manner of disposition of such cases. The greater the proportion of arrests for minor offenses, the lower the proportion of such offenses which are referred to the court.

Thus it appears from these data that the communities with the highest rates of arrest have the lowest proportions of arrests referred to the juvenile court. This seems to a large extent to be the result of the differential handling of minor offenses, although there seem to be also some relatively slight differences in the treatment of serious offenses. In Manor Heights and Mill Town, with the highest arrest rates for minor offenses and the lowest court referral rates for these offenses, we have the highest court referral rates for *serious* offenses. This suggests possibly a more critical weighing of the offense on the part of police in Manor Heights and Mill Town than in the other two communities. It seems that in Steel City and in Trade City, the nature of the offense itself, in terms of seriousness may not always be the basic determinant of case disposition.

In the combined data there appears to be a differential disposition of Negro offenders. Although arrests of Negro juveniles comprised only 5.7 per cent of the total arrests, Negro boys and girls made up 10.5 per cent of the court population. In both Steel City and Trade City the proportion of Negro juveniles in the court data is approximately the same as their representation in the arrest data. In Mill Town, on the other hand, although Negro children provided 11.4 per cent of the total arrests they comprised 64.7 per cent of the court sample. No Negro children were arrested in Manor Heights. These data seem to suggest that in our larger communities the fact of race is not in itself a determinant of disposition of a juvenile arrest by police. The interpretation of the data on Negro offenders in our small industrial town is complicated by the fact that all cases of Negro juvenile arrests were referred by the police chief to one of his Negro officers. This man apparently "leaned over backward" in the direction of a formal rather than informal disposition of cases of juvenile offenders of his own race.

The number of female cases in our data is insufficient for any but a very guarded statement regarding the differential disposition of female arrests. The combined data for the four communities showed no statistically significant differences between the handling of cases of boy and girl offenders. Mill Town seems to discriminate against girls, referring to court 75 per cent of the female arrests as opposed to 12.7 per cent of the male arrests. It must be noted, however, that there were only four girls arrested in Mill Town during the nineteen months for which data were available. These girls were all charged with minor offenses. None of the six girls arrested, all for minor offenses, in Manor Heights was referred to court. In Trade City the fourteen girls arrested were referred to court in the same proportions as male cases. These data suggest, within the limits imposed by the small size of the female sample, that there is no discriminatory treatment in our large commercial-residential town, an under-reporting to the court of female arrests in our superior socio-economic residential community, and an over-reporting of girl offenders by the police in the small industrial community.

In the combined data it appears that offenders below age ten are less frequently referred to court than are juveniles between the ages of ten and fifteen. The latter group is, in turn, less frequently reported to court than are the fifteen- to eighteen-year-old offenders. These differences were found to be statistically significant at the .01 level. Steel City records showed some differential court referral of juvenile offenders below age ten and above age fifteen. Trade City showed some under-reporting of offenders below age ten. There appeared to be no significant differences in Manor Heights and in Mill Town with respect to the court referral of children in different age groups. Although there appears to be a general tendency not to refer children below age ten to court, and an over-representation of children fifteen to eighteen years old in the court sample, these observations do not hold for our two smaller communities.

Each of these communities seems to have a discernible pattern of dealing with its arrested juvenile offenders. The differential handling of different offenses, serious and minor, and trends in the dispositions of cases differing on race, sex, and, age characteristics might be observed by comparison with the court referral rate for all offenses in a given community. Such observed differences might be accounted for by reference to some aspects of the community such as size and socio-economic status, and the nature of the relation between the police and the public.

Steel City had a moderately high rate of male juvenile arrests, and a moderately high court referral rate of boys arrested. Serious offenses and children aged fifteen to eighteen seem to be reported at a slightly higher rate than that of the *total* arrests in Steel City. Since age and serious offenses are probably related this association is not surprising. Also, minor offenses and cases of boys under age ten are reported to the court at a lower rate than the rate for all offenses. It appears, then, that there is some selective referral of cases to court on the basis of age and seriousness of the offense in Steel City.

All of the male juvenile arrests in Steel City were handled by a single policeman assigned to that duty. He had no special training in this field of police work, but was sincerely interested in the welfare of youth. He tried to treat each case individually insofar as he could understand the problems of the boy. He visited the home of each boy, talked to the parents, and made an informal study of each case. He carried a number of boys on "unofficial probation," hoping to keep them from a formal court referral. Seriousness of the offense and age of the offender, but not race, were considered as significant factors in the police officer's decision to refer the boy to court. He also attempted to consider the child's personality and family situation.

Trade City had a relatively low rate of juvenile arrests and a high rate of referral of arrests to the court. However, quite unlike the other three communities, there was practically no distinction between this overall rate of court referral and the rate of referral for serious offenses, minor offenses, for females, and for children aged ten to eighteen. There was some slight increase in the referral rate for Negro children, and a marked decrease in the court referrals of children below age ten.

No one man was assigned to juvenile work in Trade City. Decisions with regard to disposition were made by the police chief on the basis of the arresting officer's report. No study was made of the circumstances of the offender or of the offense. All cases were thus handled more or less routinely.

The police in Trade City had to deal with a highly transient population. Many people who did not live there passed through Trade City daily. Moreover, their contacts with the citizens of Trade City were on an objective, instrumental level rather than on a personal primary group level. Also, because of some political differences between the police chief and the city administration, known to juveniles as well as to adults, the prestige of the police was at a low ebb. The result of this lack of personal contact with the community was the rather indiscriminate and formal handling of cases of juveniles brought into the police station.

Manor Heights had the highest arrest rate of the four communities. It had, however, the lowest percentage of arrests referred to court. Although it had a very low percentage of arrests for serious offenses it had a very high rate of court referral of these arrests. Very few of the large number of arrests for minor offenses were referred to court. Except for this distinction on the basis of seriousness of offense there seems to be no selective referral of arrests.

In Manor Heights the police chief handled each juvenile arrest personally. He interviewed the complainant, the child, and his parents and reviewed each case carefully. He had the most adequate set of records on juveniles arrested of any of the communities in this study. He received a large number of complaints of trespassing, property damage, disorderly conduct, etc., from irate property owners. These he solved, to the satisfaction of the citizens, by imposing various penalties on the offenders with the cooperation and approval of their parents. Informal "hearings" were held in his office on Saturday mornings.

Mill Town, the smallest of our communities, had a moderately high arrest rate and a low proportion of arrests referred to court. Although Mill Town had the lowest rate of serious offenses among its arrests it had the highest rate, 100 per cent, of referral of such offenses to court. The rate of referral of minor offenses was very low. There seemed to be some discrimination in the disproportionate referral of arrests of Negro and older children.

The chief of police in Mill Town handled personally all cases of juvenile arrests with the exception of cases of Negro children. These he referred to a Negro officer for disposition. The chief was a native of Mill Town and knew the parents of many of the children who were apprehended by the police, either as school classmates, members of civic and social clubs, or as members of the same church. Thus he disposed of most cases informally, in personal discussion with the child's parents. Serious cases were referred directly to the court while the disposition of minor cases was based on an evaluation of the child and his family situation. . . .

CONCLUSIONS AND DISCUSSION

The following set of conclusions is drawn from the foregoing data, which are based on an analysis of the police records of the four communities, Steel City, Trade City, Mill Town, and Manor Heights, and on a series of interviews with police in the city of Pittsburgh and in twenty-two minor municipalities around Pittsburgh. The problem of this research was to test the general hypothesis of the differential selection, by police, of juvenile offenders for court referral and to investigate this process of selection. These conclusions are presented with the reservation that, since they are based on four individual communities and a sample of policemen in a relatively circumscribed industrial and commercial area, generalizations to other communities may not be justified.

Conclusions

I. There is a wide variation in rates of arrest in different communities.

A. Arrests per 1,000 population aged ten to seventeen ranged from 12.4 to 49.7, with an average rate of 32.6 per thousand.

B. The gross variations in arrest rates may be accounted for principally by variations in arrests for minor offenses.

1. In some communities citizens are more apt to complain about minor offenses such as trespassing, mischief, and disorderly conduct which are disregarded in other communities.

II. Not all children apprehended in law violation are recorded in the juvenile court.

A. Among those apprehended by citizens, few are reported to the police.

B. Among those apprehended by the police, not all are inscribed on police records.

1. It is estimated that about half of the children who come to the attention of the police for law violation are taken to the police station.

C. Among those officially registered on police records, only a small proportion, 35.4 per cent, are referred to the juvenile court for official action.

III. There are wide variations in rates of court appearance of juveniles in various communities.

A. Court appearances per 1,000 population aged ten to seventeen varied from community to community.

1. Rates ranged from 4.1 to 17.1 with an average of 9.9 per thousand.

B. The proportion of arrests referred to the juvenile court varied between communities.

1. Rates ranged from 8.6 per cent to 71.2 per cent with an average of 35.4 per cent.

IV. There is a differential handling by police of arrests, based on the seriousness of the offense.

A. The proportion of arrests for serious offenses varies from community to community.

1. Such offenses range from 6.1 per cent to 37.1 per cent of arrests with an average of 20.3 per cent.

B. Arrests for serious offenses are more frequently referred to court than are arrests for minor offenses.

1. Between 71.4 per cent and 100 per cent with an average of 80.2 per cent of serious offenses were reported to the court.

2. Between 2.3 per cent and 71 per cent with an average of 24.1 per cent of arrests for minor offenses were referred to court.

      C. Differences in the court referral rates are largely a result of the differential handling of minor offenses.

V. There are differentials in court referral rates of Negro and white children arrested for law violation.

      A. Arrests of Negro children are more frequently referred to court than arrests of white children.

          1. 33.6 per cent of the arrests of white children and 64.8 per cent of the arrests of Negro children were referred for juvenile court action.

          2. Although arrests of Negro children were 5.7 per cent of the total juvenile arrests, these cases constituted 10.5 per cent of the total court referrals.

      B. The rate of referral of Negro juvenile offenders to court varies from community to community.

          1. 51.2 per cent to 84.6 per cent of the Negro children arrested in three communities were referred to court.

      C. The differences in rates of referral of arrests of Negro children are largely a result of the more frequent referral of minor offenses of Negro children.

          1. 79.3 per cent of arrests of white children and 87.5 per cent of arrests of Negro children for serious offenses were referred to court.

          2. 22.6 per cent of the arrests of white children and 53.2 per cent of the arrests of Negro children for minor offenses were so referred.

VI. Conclusions regarding the differential disposition of arrests of boys and of girls are not justified because of the small number of female arrests.

      A. It is suggested, however, that girls brought to the attention of the police are more liable to court referral than are boys.

          1. Slightly more than half, 54.2 per cent of the girls arrested, and 35.1 per cent of the boys were referred to court. The differences between these rates, however, are *not statistically significant.*

      B. There appears to be considerable variation in the court referral of girls in different communities.

          1. These referral rates varied from zero to 75 per cent.

VII. The rate of court referrals of arrested children increases with the age of the child.

      A. Offenders below age ten are less frequently referred to court than are older children.

          1. 20.9 per cent of the children below age ten are referred to court.

      B. Children between ages ten and fifteen were more frequently referred to court than were younger children and less frequently so referred than older children.

          1. 30 per cent of children aged ten to fifteen were referred to court after arrest by police.

      C. Offenders between the ages of fifteen and eighteen were more frequently reported to court than were younger children.

         1. 45.4 per cent of these arrests were referred to court.

      D. The increase in the rate of court referral with age is fairly consistent in different communities.

         1. In one of the four communities studied there was a decrease in the rate of referral of offenders aged fifteen to eighteen. This appeared to be a special result of police attitude toward court "leniency."

VIII. There are distinguishable patterns of handling cases of juvenile offenders in different communities. These patterns are as follows:

      A. A low arrest rate coupled with a high court referral rate. Very little differentiation in handling cases. Offense, sex, and race seem of little influence in disposition, with age the only discernible differentiating factor.

      B. A high arrest rate, coupled with a high arrest rate for minor offenses. A very low court referral rate, based on seriousness of offense, sex, and age of the offender.

      C. A moderately high arrest rate with a relatively moderately high court referral rate for all offenses. Differential reporting based on race and age.

      D. A moderately high arrest rate with a low court referral rate. Referral varies with seriousness of the offense, sex, race, and age of the child.

  IX. These patterns are a function of the relations between the police and the community.

      A. In general, police will attempt to reflect what they consider to be the attitudes of the public toward delinquency.

         1. The concern of the public with respect to minor offenses such as shoplifting, trespassing, mischief, disorderly conduct, etc., will determine the police arrests of such offenses.

         2. The desires of the public with regard to official court handling of delinquency problems, as opposed to informal handling of offenses within the community will affect court referral rates.

      B. Where there exists an objective, impersonal relation between the police and the public, court referral rates will be high and there will be little discrimination with respect to seriousness of offense, race, and sex of the offender.

      C. Where there exists a personal face-to-face relation between the police and the public, there will be more discrimination with respect to court referral of an arrested juvenile.

         1. Rates of court referral will be low:

            a. More cases will be carried on an unofficial level.

         2. Disposition will be significantly determined by the seriousness of the offense.

      a. Minor offenses, even though they make up the bulk of
the arrests, will be reported only rarely.

    3. Sex and race of the offender will vary as factors in the referral process.

X. The differential selection of offenders for court by police is determined by the attitudes of the policeman toward the offender, his family, the offense, the juvenile court, his own role as a policeman, and the community attitudes toward delinquency.

    A. *The policeman's attitudes toward the juvenile court.* This may be based on actual experience with the court or on ignorance of court policies. The policeman who feels the court unfair to the police or too lenient with offenders may fail to report cases to the court since, in his opinion, nothing will be gained by such official referral.

    B. *The impact of special individual experiences in the court, or with different racial groups, or with parents of offenders, or with specific offenses, on an individual policeman.* This may condition his future reporting of certain types of offenses or classes of offenders.

    C. *Apprehension about criticism by the court.* Cases which the policeman might prefer, for various reasons, not to report for official action may be reported because of fear that the offense might subsequently come to the attention of the court and result in embarrassment to the police officer.

    D. *Publicity given to certain offenses either in the neighborhood or elsewhere may cause the police to feel that these are too "hot" to handle unofficially and must be referred to the court.* In the discussion of police interviews it was indicated how this factor might operate to bring into court an offense of even a very insignificant nature.

    E. *The necessity for maintaining respect for police authority in the community.* A juvenile who publicly causes damage to the dignity of the police, or who is defiant, refusing the "help" offered by the police, will be considered as needing court supervision, no matter how trivial the offense.

    F. *Various practical problems of policing.* The fact that no witness fees are paid policemen in juvenile court was mentioned by a small number as affecting the policy of some police officers with respect to court referral of juveniles. The distance to the court and the detention home and the availability of police personnel for the trip were likewise indicated as occasionally affecting the decision of the policeman.

    G. *Pressure by political groups or other special interest groups.* Such pressure may determine the line of action a policeman will follow in a given case. He considers it necessary to accede to such pressures in order to retain his job.

    H. *The policeman's attitude toward specific offenses.* The reporting or non-reporting of a juvenile offender may depend on the policeman's own childhood experiences or on attitudes toward specific offenses developed during his police career.

I. *The police officer's impression of the family situation, the degree of family interest in and control of the offender, and the reaction of the parents to the problem of the child's offense.* A child coming from a home where supervision is judged to be lacking, or where the parents—especially the mother—are alcoholic, or one whose parents assume an aggressive or "uncooperative" attitude toward the police officer, is considered in need of supervision by the juvenile court.

J. *The attitude and personality of the boy.* An offender who is well mannered, neat in appearance, and "listens" to the policeman will be considered a good risk for unofficial adjustment in the community. Defiance of the police will usually result in immediate court referral. Athletes and altar boys will rarely be referred to court for their offenses. The minor offenses of feeble-minded or atypical children will usually be overlooked by the police. Maliciousness in a child is considered by the police to indicate need for official court supervision.

K. *The Negro child offender is considered less tractable and needing more authoritarian supervision than a white child.* He is generally considered inherently more criminal than a white offender. Exceptions to this general attitude were found in the upper-class residential area and also among white policemen in the crowded Negro slum area of Pittsburgh. The statistical data, except for the small mill town, do not corroborate these discriminatory attitudes expressed by the police.

L. *The degree of criminal sophistication shown in the offense.* The use of burglar tools, criminal jargon, a gun, or strong-arm methods, or signs of planning or premeditation, are generally taken by the police to indicate a need for immediate court referral.

M. *Juvenile offenders apprehended in a group will generally be treated on an all-or-none basis.* The group must be released or reported as a whole. Some police may attempt to single out individuals in the gang for court referral. Such action, however, exposes the policeman to the censure of the court for failing to report the others involved in the offense.

Discussion

It must be borne in mind that in this study the several variables were artificially isolated. In reality, no one of the factors which have been shown to operate in the determination of which offenders are officially reported to the court by the police can be found to exist alone. There is an interrelationship between the variables which cannot be expressed in statistical terms. Some of the factors discussed above among the conclusions may automatically exclude consideration of other factors. At times the task of the policeman may be akin to that of solving a problem containing a number of variables. At other times, *one* of the considerations mentioned above—such as political pressure—may force the decision of the police officer in a given direction.

The concept of juvenile delinquency is to some extent determined by the policeman in selectively reporting juvenile offenders to the court. As was indicated in the opening chapter of this paper, research in the field of juvenile delinquency has been based primarily on juveniles in a court, clinic, or in an institution. Institutionalized delinquents, and offenders in a juvenile court had been, for the most part, apprehended and officially reported by the police.

This research has shown that the police base their reporting partly on the act of the offender, but also on the policeman's idiosyncratic interpretation of this act, and the degree of pressure applied by the community on the police. The collective pressures mentioned above, the attitudes of the community toward the offense, toward the offender and toward his family, affect the decision of the policeman in his reporting of juvenile offenses. In addition, the policeman's own private attitudes, his special experiences, his concern for status and prestige in the community may be important factors in determining which particular juvenile offender will be referred to the court. Once reported to the court, the child then becomes available for official scrutiny and study. The availability of a juvenile offender for official recording and for research studies on delinquency thus depends ultimately on the responsiveness of the police officer to a series of collective social pressures and personal attitudes. The policeman's interpretation of these pressures serves to select or determine the composition of the sample of those juvenile offenders who will become officially recognized from among all those known to him.

Selection of a sample of the population of offenders on the basis of collective pressures and private attitudes cannot help but result in a marked and unpredictable bias. It is on this biased sample that most of the juvenile delinquency research has been conducted. Generalizations based on such a sample can have only limited validity. For a more adequate understanding of the social and psychological processes involved in juvenile delinquent behavior it is necessary to observe juvenile offenders in the community in their earliest contacts with the police, before they have been selected by differential treatment. There can be no complete study of the etiological factors in juvenile delinquent conduct unless the unpredictable variable of the policeman is removed from the process. An adequate study of juvenile delinquency must begin at a point before the one at which the police officer begins to operate. To provide more valid generalizations, juvenile delinquency must be studied in the community where it occurs, where a relatively unselected sample of juvenile offenders may be observed.

The decision regarding the disposition of a given instance of juvenile law violation, by the policeman, may have some very significant effects on the future conduct of the child. The consequences of any act will significantly affect the behavior of the actor in similar situations in the future. The interaction, or exchange of gestures, between the policeman and the child apprehended in law violation may serve to increase or to decrease the probability of future excursions into delinquency. Thus the behavior of the police toward the child may be a significant determinant of the child's continued participation in delinquent conduct.

An important corollary of these observations is that the police must be provided training in the problems of handling children who come to their attention for law violation. They must be aided in understanding the possible effects of their attempts to "help" the apprehended violator by giving him "another chance," or the possible effects of discrimination with respect to the race of the child. Since he will be, by virtue of his job, in a position where he has to make decisions crucial to the child's welfare, and of great significance for the child's future conduct, it is important that he be supplied with the proper sensitivities and perceptions for making the best decisions for the child and for the community.

TRIAL and SENTENCING

INTRODUCTION

Judges are like professors in that they occupy positions of high esteem in the society, and they are automatically viewed as being learned, knowledgeable, and men of high integrity. It is because of this presumption concerning their character, as well as the fact that their mistakes and misdeeds are exceedingly difficult to see, that judges generally occupy their seats for life, even, as was pointed out earlier, where there is some semblance of an election every once in a while.

Furthermore the judge's role is one that is free from many of the conflicts and incompatibilities inherent in the roles of the police and the prosecutor. Judges, after all, are not evaluated according to how many people they send to prison or how many they let go free. They, again like professors, are assumed competent unless proved otherwise. And since their language is obscure and impressive even to educated people, and since, in addition, judges have staffs which are expert at concealing personal weaknesses, then public disclosure of ineptness or impropriety is likely to be rare.

All this security is quite beneficial in meeting the legal system's requirements in some ways. For one thing, it removes the judge from the kinds of pressures that, as we have seen, play such an important role in undermining the goals of the legal processes at lower levels. Furthermore, this security makes the judgeship a coveted position, and therefore highly talented people can be attracted to a position that is less rewarding in some other ways (principally economic) than readily available alternatives, such as a lucrative law practice.

But the sword of security is two-edged. Such a set of circumstances also means that judges can twist and bend the legal system to their own ends without too much fear of reprisal. It also means that judges may develop an attitude of indifference and unconcern for the opinions of others and thereby express highly personal and idiosyncratic values; indeed, they may force these values on persons who come before the law.[1]

Although we lack evidence on the extent to which highly idiosyncratic acts characterize judicial decisions, we do have a substantial amount of evidence which demonstrates considerable variation in the sentencing practices of different judges.[2] Among judges presiding over the Chicago Women's Court during a three-year period, Mary Owen Cameron found wide variation in their propensity to use different kinds of sanctions for persons brought before the court for shoplifting.[3] The proportion of cases found "not guilty" ranged from 5 percent for one judge to 20 percent of the cases tried by another. One judge gave no "token sentences," while another judge meted out token sentences in 58 percent of the cases he handled over this period. The number of cases receiving probation ranged from a low of 10 percent for one barrister to 62 percent for another. The proportion of defendants receiving jail sentences also varied from a low of 3 percent of the cases tried by one judge to 31 percent of those tried by another.

Edward Green's study of sentencing practices in Philadelphia courts revealed similar differences.[4] Green categorized cases by the seriousness of the crime and compared the sentences received. Green concludes: ". . . at each level of gravity there are statistically significant differences among the judges in the severity of the sentences imposed."

[1] There are, of course, innumerable illustrations of this. One recent example is the case of a California judge who gave a young married woman charged with drunkenness the alternatives of being sterilized or going to jail. On appeal, the judge's decision was reversed.

[2] F. J. Gaudet, G. S. Harris, and C. W. St. John, "Individual Differences in the Sentencing Tendencies of Judges," *Journal of Criminal Law, Criminology and Police Science,* vol. 23, pp. 811–818, January, 1933; Edward Green, "Sentencing Practices of Criminal Court Judges in Philadelphia," *American Journal of Corrections,* pp. 32–35, July–August, 1960; Mary Owen Cameron, *The Booster and the Snitch,* New York: The Free Press of Glencoe, 1965.

[3] Cameron, *ibid.,* pp. 143–144.

[4] Edward Green, *Judicial Attitudes in Sentencing,* London: Macmillan & Co., Ltd., 1961.

Inquiries into judicial decision making have also consistently demonstrated the operation of racial and social-class biases in the decisions of judges. Cameron's findings concerning the sentencing of women for shoplifting illustrate this. Judges found 16 percent of the white women brought before them on charges of shoplifting to be not guilty but found only 4 percent of the Negro women to be so. In addition, 22 percent of the Negro women, as compared with 4 percent of the white women, were sent to jail. Finally, of the twenty-one white women sentenced to jail, only two (10 percent) were sentenced for thirty days or more; of the seventy-six Negro women sentenced to jail, twenty (26 percent) were sentenced for thirty days or more.

Green's Philadelphia study showed similar tendencies of judges to impose sanctions more often and more severely on Negroes than on whites. Green notes, however, that in his sample this differential treatment is obviated when prior criminal record is taken into account. Green interprets this to mean that the differential severity with which Negroes are treated in the courts does not stem from racial discrimination but rather from the fact that Negroes are more likely to have a past criminal record. We have already seen in previous sections that at the time of arrest and arraignment, the organization of law enforcement is such that the Negro is much more likely to have a "record" than is the white person. In view of this, the fact of a past criminal record may indicate no more than persistently biased processing. Nevertheless, if Green's findings are generally applicable, they suggest that at least the sentencing practices of judges are nondiscriminatory. It seems more likely, however, that Philadelphia is unique, since these findings contradict the results of other investigations. We cannot answer this question with a great deal of confidence, however, since the other inquiries into sentencing practices have not controlled for seriousness of offense. We can certainly conclude that Negroes receive harsher treatment before the courts than do whites, but we must await further research before we can adequately assess the influence of race as contrasted with other variables, such as prior arrest records.

The fact of more severe treatment of Negroes than whites continues after sentencing takes place. From 1930 to 1964 there were 3,849 persons executed in the United States. Of these 45 percent (1,743) were white and 54 percent (2,065) were Negro. Negroes constitute less than 13 percent of the population, yet they comprise over 50 percent of the persons executed. Negroes are more often arrested for all kinds of capitally punishable offenses than are whites, and this may account for the higher frequency of executions. For example, in 1965 there were 6,509 arrests for murder and non-negligent manslaughter in the United States, and 57 percent (3,704) of these arrests for murder were Negroes. To what extent these arrests are a function of discrimination against the Negro can only be a guess at this point. It is pertinent to note, however, that many more whites than Negroes are arrested for manslaughter due to negligence: in 1965 there were 1,883 whites arrested for this offense and 541 Negroes. The practice of prosecutors to bargain for guilty pleas suggests that this differential in the proportion of arrests for manslaughter by negligence may in part reflect the propensity of prosecutors to file lesser charges on whites more often than on Negroes.

That such an interpretation is plausible receives indirect support from a study by Marvin Wolfgang, Arlene Kelly, and Hans Nolde, who report that among persons awaiting execution on death row in Pennsylvania, 20 percent of the whites compared with 12 percent of the Negroes had the death sentence commuted. The difference is even greater for felony murders than for nonfelony murders.[5]

It is the Negro felony-murderer more than any other type of offender who will suffer the death penalty. This finding is especially striking when we note that nearly three times more white than Negro felony-murderers have their sentences commuted.

Regional differences are rather striking. In the South a higher proportion of Negroes is convicted and executed than in any other section of the country, and Negroes are convicted for a greater variety of crimes. From 1930 to 1964, 263 persons were executed in North Carolina: 207 for murder, 47 for rape, and 9 for "other offenses."[6] Of the 263 persons executed, 199 were Negroes and 59 whites. Thus 76 percent of the persons executed in North Carolina from 1930 to 1964 were Negro. Execution for rape is an almost exclusively Southern phenomenon: from 1930 to 1964 there were 455 executions for rape and all but 12 of these occurred in the South; 10 of the exceptions took place in Missouri and 2 in Nevada. Of the 455 persons executed for rape, 405 were Negro, 48 were white, and 2 were "other races."

Guilty Pleas and Organizational Efficiency

It is undoubtedly the case that part of the more severe sanctioning of Negroes reflects the pressures on the courts to accept guilty pleas. Justice Henry T. Lummus has stated flatly: ". . . a criminal court can operate only by inducing the great mass of actually guilty defendants to plead guilty, paying in leniency the price for the pleas."[7] Newman has estimated that 90 percent of all criminal convictions are the result of a guilty plea.[8] For the most part these guilty pleas are obtained by promises of less severe sanctioning than the defendant anticipates if he pleads not guilty. More often than not, judges take into account the guilty plea and apply less severe sanctions. The editors of the Yale Law Journal sent questionnaires to 240 federal judges and received responses from 140 of them. Sixty-six percent of the respondents reported that the defendant's plea was "a relevant factor in local sentencing procedure," and the ma-

[5] Marvin E. Wolfgang, Arlene Kelly, and Hans C. Nolde, "Comparison of the Executed and the Commuted among Admissions to Death Row," in Norman Johnston, Leonard Savitz, and Marvin E. Wolfgang (eds.), The Sociology of Punishment and Correction, New York: John Wiley & Sons, Inc., 1962, pp. 63–69.

[6] These statistics are taken from Frank E. Hartung, "Trends in the Use of Capital Punishment," Annals of the American Academy of Political and Social Science, November, 1952, and from National Prisoner Statistics Bulletin, Bureau of Prisons, Washington.

[7] Donald J. Newman, Conviction: The Determination of Guilt or Innocence without Trial, Boston: Little, Brown and Company, 1966, p. 62.

[8] Ibid., p. 3.

jority of the judges rewarded the defendant pleading guilty with a less severe sentence than his counterpart who had trial.

There are any number of reasons why courts and prosecutors look with favor on guilty pleas: in one way or another, all the reasons come down to the fact that these agencies can operate more efficiently and with less strain if the bulk of the offenders processed are handled by guilty pleas. It is probably the case, as the statement by Justice Lummus quoted above implies, that the courts would come to a standstill if all defendants insisted on court trials, for at present the manpower is not available to withstand the onslaught of a 90 percent increase in court cases. Furthermore, even if the personnel were available, trials are expensive, time-consuming, and the outcome is rarely predictable. A guilty plea by the defendant ensures that the case will be handled expeditiously. Little is gained by insisting on a trial merely to impose a more severe penalty.

These practices and policies may be organizationally effective, but they constitute yet another area in which the poor and the minority-group members are discriminated against. Since the guilty plea is obtained by striking a bargain between the defendant and the court, the benefit to the defendant is going to depend on the strength of his bargaining position. The strength of his bargaining position will, in turn, be reflected in his ability to hire private counsel, his knowledge of his legal rights, and his sophistication about the law. Most middle- and upper-class persons arrested for crime are as ignorant of the law as are most lower-class persons, but they can pay for good legal counsel to inform them of their bargaining power. The professional thief is quite sophisticated about the legal system and can also afford legal counsel. It remains for the poor to receive the brunt of the disadvantageous possibilities of bargain justice. Since the Negroes processed in the courts tend to be poor, they will be the ones most likely to receive the short end of a bargain; indeed, the statistics on murder and executions suggest that they may be unable to obtain *any* concessions from the court or the prosecutor in exchange for a guilty plea.

The judge's role in Anglo-American law allows for as much discretion as that of the prosecutor and the police, but it is far less open to scrutiny. In many respects, judges are less encumbered by organizational restrictions than are other agencies in the legal system. The fact remains, however, that in actual practice the judges' decisions are just as likely to be determined by extralegal events as are the decisions of other law-enforcement agencies. The demands for efficient and orderly performance of the court take priority and encourage a propensity to dispose of cases in ways that ensure the continued smooth functioning. The consequence of such a policy is to systematically select certain categories of offenders (specifically the poor and the Negro) for the most severe treatment. Thus, with all the autonomy and independence from public control judges enjoy, the fact remains that their decisions, like those at every other level of the law-enforcement process, are to a much greater extent a function of the organizational requirements of the legal system than they are a function of the blueprint that supposedly guides those decisions.

17. Vagrancy-type Law and Its Administration

Caleb Foote

I. INTRODUCTION

This study combines analysis of the history, theory and purposes of vagrancy-type laws with a report of their administration by the police, magistrates and correctional authorities in Philadelphia. Such a dual approach is essential. Minor offenses are seldom reviewed by higher courts, and the actual limits of vagrancy are set not in the statute but by practices of police and magistrates. Conversely, an intelligent appraisal of these practices requires some historical orientation. The vagrancy laws "might be unintelligible if we did not regard them as a supplement to the old Poor Laws . . ."; [1] they continue to reflect their inception in the fourteenth century when they were "a kind of substitute for the system of villainage and serfdom." [2]

The material on the administration of vagrancy-type laws was obtained by a field study of Philadelphia practices. The basic technique employed was the intermittent observation of hundreds of trials in the magistrates' courts during a period beginning in 1951, supplemented by interviews with a small sample of convicted vagrants at the House of Correction and the compilation of statistical information from police and House of Correction records. This method was time-consuming and in many ways unsatisfactory, but there was no alternative, for no stenographic notes of testimony are made at the trials, and the records maintained by the magistrates were useless for the purpose of this study.

It is impossible, short of a more intensive examination, to determine whether the hundreds of vagrancy, drunkenness and disorderly conduct trials which were observed were exceptional or whether they represent a fair sample of Philadelphia practices. It is believed, however, that the sample is representative. A number of different magistrates conducted the hearings, and while there were differences among them, their general attitude towards and conduct of vagrancy-type cases was remarkably similar. The fact that the observation extended from June, 1951, through March, 1954, and that the more serious abuses in magisterial practice so pervaded all of the observed hearings throughout this period make it reasonable to infer that they are typical of Philadelphia practices.

While the administrative material is drawn solely from Philadelphia, the significance of the study has broader application. No comparable study has been made elsewhere, but it is probable that many Philadelphia practices are widespread.

At a time when there is dispute as to the extent to which latitude should be accorded police and administrative action by easing the procedural and constitutional

SOURCE: "Vagrancy-type Law and Its Administration," *University of Pennsylvania Law Review*, vol. 104, pp. 603–650, 1956. By permission of the publisher.

EDITOR'S NOTE: The historical discussion has for the most part been deleted.

[1] Kenny, *Outlines of the Criminal Law*, 381 (15th ed. 1936).

[2] 3 Stephen, *History of the Criminal Law of England*, 204 (1883).

restrictions imposed by our criminal law,[3] the practices described in this study offer a revealing illustration of what happens when those restrictions are removed. Procedural due process does not penetrate to the world inhabited by the "bums" of Philadelphia, and this description of what occurs in that world is certainly relevant to the problem of how far our criminal law administration should relax constitutional and procedural controls to permit greater administrative police discretion.

II. A VAGRANT'S DAY IN COURT

Because the issues raised by vagrancy-type law can only be understood in the context of the law's everyday administration, examples of typical proceedings in the Philadelphia magistrates' courts are a useful introduction to the problem. The enforcement efforts of the police and magistrates were conducted on a year-round basis, but from time to time during the period of this study the tempo of enforcement was stepped up with a well-publicized "drive" against vagrants. One of the more recent examples was a "cleanup" to make the newly completed Independence Mall "out of bounds for undesirables," [4] the theory apparently being that the publicity would induce vagrants already in the city to depart and would deter "undesirables" who had planned to come to Philadelphia from entering the city. A description of one of these "cleanups" reveals many of the complex factors and motives that underlie vagrancy administration.

On January 31, 1954, the Philadelphia press reported that police had "opened a drive against vagrants and habitual drunkards in the central city area." By February 2, the drive was at its height, and that morning 56 cases were awaiting disposition when the magistrate opened the daily divisional police court for the district which included the "skid row" and the central city area. These cases were the last items on the morning's docket, and the magistrate did not reach them until 11:04 a.m. In one of the cases there was a private prosecutor, and the hearing of evidence consumed five minutes. As court adjourned at 11:24, this left 15 minutes in which to hear the remaining 55 cases. During that time the magistrate discharged 40 defendants and found 15 guilty and sentenced them to three months terms in the House of Correction.

Four of these committed defendants were tried, found guilty and sentenced in the elapsed time of seventeen seconds from the time that the first man's name was called by the magistrate through the pronouncing of sentence upon the fourth defendant. In each of these cases the magistrate merely read off the name of the defendant, took one look at him and said, "Three months in the House of Correction." As the third man was being led out he objected, stating, "But I'm working . . . ," to which the magistrate replied, "Aw, go on."

The magistrate then called the name of one defendant several times and got no answer. Finally he said, "Where are you, Martin?" The defendant raised his hand and answered, "Right here." "You aren't going to be 'right here' for long," the magistrate said. "Three months in Correction." Another defendant was called. The magistrate stated: "I'm going to send you up for a medical examination—three months in the House of Correction."

---

[3] See, e.g., the differences of opinion within the Supreme Court on two recently decided cases: *Stein* v. *New York*, 346 U.S. 156 (1953); *Irvine* v. *California*, 347 U.S. 128 (1954).

[4] *Philadelphia Inquirer*, Aug. 9, 1955, p. 1, col. 1.

A number of defendants were discharged with orders to get out of Philadelphia or to get out of the particular section of Philadelphia where they were arrested. "What are you doing in Philadelphia?" the magistrate asked one of these. "Just passing through." "You get back to Norristown. We've got enough bums here without you." Another defendant whose defense was that he was passing through town added, "I was in the bus station when they arrested me." "Let me see your bus ticket," the magistrate said. "The only thing that's going to save you this morning is if you have that bus ticket. Otherwise you're going to Correction for sure." After considerable fumbling the defendant produced a Philadelphia to New York ticket. "You better get on that bus quick," said the magistrate, "because if you're picked up between here and the bus station, you're a dead duck."

In discharging defendants with out-of-the-central-city addresses, the magistrate made comments such as the following:

> "You stay out in West Philadelphia."
> "Stay up in the fifteenth ward; I'll take care of you up there."
> "What are you doing in this part of town? You stay where you belong; we've got enough bums down here without you."

Near the end of the line the magistrate called a name, and after taking a quick look said, "You're too clean to be here. You're discharged."

The next morning, the *Philadelphia Inquirer* ran an editorial under the title, "Get Bums off the Street and into Prison Cells," [5] which noted with satisfaction that three month sentences were being imposed and that "Chief Magistrate Clothier has threatened them with jail sentences of two years." The editorial felt that "If they have nothing worse to expect from the police than a warm cell to sleep it off for the night, the vagrants will hardly be discouraged. But two years in prison is something else again; only the most hardened bum will take a chance on that." The editorial had no suggestions on how one who was already a "bum" could avoid taking the chance.

The hearings that morning moved even more rapidly; between 50 and 60 defendants were handled between 10:39 and 10:54. Five defendants were committed under the same procedure already noted, the magistrate merely calling their names, taking one look, and then pronouncing sentence. To another he said, "You look like one, three months."

"Three months for you, Tom Harris," he said to a defendant. "I'm working," the defendant replied. "Yes, I know," the magistrate responded, "working on the Bible. Take him away, oh, and take Mr. Gurdy here back with you for another three months."

Three other defendants alleged the defense of working. Two were ignored, but the third kept insisting that he had a job with a packing company. The magistrate asked him under whom he worked, what the first name of his boss was, and finally discharged him.

"Well, what do you want to tell me?" the magistrate said to another defendant. The reply was that he was on his way to Harrisburg. "You keep going to Harrisburg, then, and don't you stop, because if you do, you're a dead duck." Other defendants from Camden and Conshohocken were told to "go back where you belong."

The court room at the 12th and Pine St. police station was jammed at these hearings. Spectators were packed in solidly behind the railing, and the defendants, all of whom were herded out at once, occupied every bit of space between the rail and the bench. The noise and confusion were continuous.

At one of the hearings floodlights were mounted behind the bench and as the defendants were called up one by one, a photographer, crouching just behind the magistrate, took motion pictures of the proceedings. The lights were arranged in such a way that they must have blinded those standing in front of the magistrate; the effect was much like that of a police line-up.[6]

Although the legal effect of "discharged" is that the defendant has been found not guilty and is free to go, this was not the usual result at these hearings. As the "discharged" defendant made his way out of the crowded courtroom, he had to pass an officer who directed him either to the left, which led to the hallway and the street, or to the right, back to the cell block. Most of the acquitted were directed to the right; only those who looked "clean" or were better dressed or obviously physically incapable of any work were freed at once. Some of those sent back to cells objected, but the officer would state: "Oh, go on, some work will do you good." The detained men, whom both police and magistrates called the "goon squad," were kept for a couple of hours to mop and clean the building.

As the hearings progressed through February the court adopted a new technique which governed assignments to the "goon squad." Each defendant was asked how much he had to contribute to the magistrate's "favorite charity." Those who dropped at least a dollar into a collection box for the Heart Fund, which was on the desk, were freed at once. Those who contributed something more than 25¢ were also usually exonerated. Those who were discharged but did not contribute anything or enough were assigned to the squad.

This 1954 winter drive lasted for almost a month. Usually the duration was shorter, and as soon as the newspaper publicity ceased, the atmosphere at the hearings relaxed. With no drive in progress, there were fewer spectators, a higher proportion of discharges, and the magistrates sometimes took longer to hear the cases.

Hearings observed earlier at another court before other magistrates are illustrative of the unpublicized enforcement which went on between drives. At the time the court was observed, it was handling up to 1600 summary cases a month, and of necessity it worked rapidly. One of the magistrates did not even bother to hear the routine drunkenness cases; only aggravated offenders whom the police wished to have committed were brought before him, and the other defendants were automatically discharged without a hearing. The usual practice, however, was for the magistrate to tell an officer, "bring on the boarders," and for the police to herd all the vagrancy-type defendants into the courtroom at one time, a process that was frequently accompanied by general hilarity. The magistrate greeted his favorites with a broad grin; the police joked with the defendants as they shoved them along; and the loafers on the spectator's side of the railing joked about the stench. The officer who sat with the magistrate took the night list of arrests and called the defendants one by one. Some were still so drunk that they could scarcely make it across the room alone, and stood stolidly, with glazed eyes. The emaciated, gaunt, tattered appear-

---

[6] Compare this practice with the American Bar Association's Judicial Canon 35, as amended Sept. 15, 1952, 77 A.B.A. Rep. 110 (1952), and as adopted by the Pennsylvania Bar Association, which bans such photography because it is "calculated to detract from the essential dignity of the proceedings, distract the witness in giving his testimony, degrade the court, and create misconceptions with respect thereto in the mind of the public. . . ." (Italics omitted.)

ance of some indicated both poverty and chronic alcoholism. Many of the defendants were discharged with a brief explanation:

> "George, I feel sorry for you; go on home and quit drinking."
> "I haven't seen you for three weeks—discharged."
> "You work, don't you? I know you. I know every one of you. I'm around here seven days a week, 365 days a year. Now go on and get back to work."

But there were some of the same summary convictions noted above, where as soon as a defendant's name was called, and while he was still making his way forward, the magistrate pronounced: "Three months in the House of Correction," and the police hustled the convicted man back to his cell. Presumably in these cases, listed as "drunk" on the arrest roster but as habitual drunkenness on the commitment sheet, the test of habitualness being applied was that described by several magistrates as: "When you get sick of seeing their faces, you send them to Correction."

Most of the Philadelphians were discharged, but one defendant who gave a Philadelphia address was next asked, "Do you have any proof that you live there?" "No, judge, I don't have anything with me." "Three months in the House of Correction." As another Philadelphian, summarily given the same sentence, was led away, the magistrate remarked to one of the officers, "He doesn't belong in this district. He ought to stay where he belongs."

Different magistrates followed different policies regarding out-of-town transients. Some followed the practice of discharging out-of-town defendants with a warning to leave Philadelphia immediately. Another magistrate's invariable opening gambit was the question, "Where do you live?" If the answer was anything other than a Philadelphia address, usually a three months sentence was immediately imposed.

III. PUNISHMENT BY ANALOGY

Enough has been said to indicate the speed and informality characteristic of Philadephia's vagrancy-type proceedings. Any legal analysis of such cases is handicapped at the outset by the difficulty of determining what law was being applied by a magistrate in any given case. The crimes which form the components of vagrancy-type legislation and which were available to the magistrates as sanctions in these cases involved the following statutes.

1. Vagrancy

At common law a vagrant is an idle person who is without visible means of support and who, although able to work, refuses to do so. The offense is punishable in all American jurisdictions,[7] with many variations from and accretions upon the common-law concept. The Pennsylvania vagrancy statute [8] defines as vagrants persons who

---

[7] By statute in all states except West Virginia, where it is a common-law crime. *City of Huntington v. Salyer*, 135 W.Va. 397, 63 S.E.2d 575 (1951); see *Ex parte* Hudgins, 86 W.Va. 526, 103 S.E. 327 (1920).

[8] Pa. Stat. Ann. tit. 18, § 2032 (Purdon 1945). The penalty provided by this act is not less than 30 days or more than 6 months. *Id.* § 2033.

come from outside the state, follow no labor, are without visible means of support, and are unable to give a "reasonable account of themselves or their business in such place." A vagrant can be tried summarily, *i.e.*, without the necessity for indictment or the right to a jury trial; in Pennsylvania he can be punished with imprisonment up to six months for the first offense and up to two years for certain subsequent offenses.[9]

2. Habitual Drunkenness

This offense, sometimes called "common drunkenness," is punishable in many jurisdictions, frequently as a part of a broad vagrancy statute.[10] It must be distinguished from occasional acts of intoxication, for defendants are punishable only·if subject to a fixed habit of drunkenness, such as that of one who is drunk "one-half of his time."[11] The Pennsylvania law on this point is ambiguous, and under very questionable authority, Philadelphia police and magisterial practice assumes that habitual drunkenness is a crime subject to the same penalty as vagrancy. Pennsylvania explicitly makes criminal only the lesser offense of intoxication, which proscribes a single act of drunkenness and which is punishable by a fine of either 67¢[12] or $5,[13] but not by imprisonment. The only authority for imposing prison sentences for drunkenness is found in the statute establishing the House of Correction, which provides that the institution shall be the place of imprisonment for "all persons, adults or minors, that may hereafter be convicted, according to the laws of this commonwealth . . . as a vagrant, drunkard, or disorderly streetwalker."[14] This statute is merely concerned with the treatment of offenders convicted under other laws and does not purport to create the crime of being a "drunkard."

3. Disorderly Conduct

The Pennsylvania statute is typical: "Whoever wilfully makes or causes to be made any loud, boisterous and unseemly noise or disturbance to the annoyance of the peaceable residents nearby, or near to any public highway [or other public place], whereby the public peace is broken or disturbed or the traveling public annoyed . . ." is guilty of disorderly conduct and is punishable upon conviction in a summary

---

[9] By the House of Correction Act, imprisonment of up to 1 year for a first offender and 2 years for repeaters is provided. *Id.* tit. 61, §§ 672, 681 (Purdon 1930). See also the statute proscribing the offense of tramping. *Id.* tit. 18, § 4617 (Purdon 1945); no use of this statute was observed during this study.

[10] *E.g.*, Ala. Code Ann. tit. 14, § 437 (1940).
Gray) 85 (1855) (reversing conviction for being a common drunkard where proof showed only three instances of intoxication within six months).

[11] *Ludwick v. Commonwealth,* 18 Pa. 172, 175 (1851); see *Commonwealth v. Whitney,* 71 Mass. (5

[12] Pa. Stat. Ann. tit. 18, § 1523 (Purdon 1945).

[13] *Id.* tit. 47, § 722 (Purdon 1952).

[14] The basis of the practice is the House of Correction Act. *Id.* tit. 61, §§ 672, 681 (Purdon 1930). The only authority for punishing anyone as an habitual drunkard, therefore, would be under the statute preserving common-law offenses, *id.* tit. 18, § 5101 (Purdon 1945), which would apply if habitual drunkenness were an offense at common law. This question has never been decided by Pennsylvania courts, but other jurisdictions have held that it is not. *Commonwealth v. O'Connor,* 89 Mass. (7 Allen) 583 (1863); *State v. Munger,* 43 Wyo. 404, 4 P.2d 1094 (1931); see *State v. Hunter,* 106 N.C. 796, 11 S.E. 366 (1890); see also 2 Broom and Hadley, *Commentaries* 446 (Wait ed. 1875) (intoxication not an indictable offense at common law, although common drunkenness sometimes treated as a public nuisance).

proceeding with a fine not exceeding $10, or, in default of payment of the fine, with imprisonment not exceeding thirty days.[15]

Pennsylvania also has a pickpocket statute,[16] which could be used against vagrancy-type defendants, but no prosecutions under this statute were observed. The state has not enacted a "public enemy" law proscribing the association of known criminals for an unlawful purpose.[17] Thus vagrancy, habitual drunkenness and, to a lesser extent, disorderly conduct were the important working tools of the police in the cases observed.

Even within these narrow confines, however, it was not easy to determine which statute was being applied in any given case. The police roster of arrests, which the magistrates used as a docket, listed the charge entered by the arresting officer and also provided a space for the officer to note whether the arrestee was drunk or sober on arrest. In no observed hearing, however, was this charge read to the defendant. Occasionally it was clear that the magistrate was proceeding against a defendant as an habitual drunkard, as where the testimony indicated that he was a repeated offender and no issue of transient status was involved. Sometimes when imposing sentence, the magistrate for the first time would tell the defendant the crime with which he was charged. An example was a case where the police charge was "drunk" and where the trial of the defendant consisted of the following exchange:

MAGISTRATE: *Where do you live?*
DEFENDANT: *Norfolk.*
MAGISTRATE: *What are you doing in Philadelphia?*
DEFENDANT: *Well, I didn't have any work down there, so I came up here to see if I could find . . . .*
MAGISTRATE (who had been shaking his head): *That story's not good enough for me. I'm going to have you investigated. You're a vagrant. Three months in the House of Correction.*

During one month in one police district there were 1125 arrests for summary offenses; 139 of these defendants were sentenced to three months, and five were sentenced to six months. Of these commitments, the police arrest records charged 57 with "habitual drunk," 50 with "drunk," 27 with "vagrancy," five with "drunk and vagrant," two with "drunk and panhandling," two with "disorderly conduct," and one with "drunk and disorderly." Most of these cases were observed, and in many of them it was impossible to determine what crime the magistrate had in mind when the sentence was imposed. Some of those arrested merely as "drunk" were habitual offenders, and some charged with "habitual drunk" had apparently never been in Philadelphia before and therefore could not have been known to the police as habitual anythings. A number of those listed as "drunk" and committed as "habitual drunk" were apparently being punished for something unrelated to their intoxication, the magistrate imposing sentence because the defendant was not "where you belong."

Where conviction can be obtained by sight and smell alone, it makes little prac-

[15] Pa. Stat. Ann. tit. 18, § 4406 (Purdon 1945).

[16] *Id.* § 4821, providing a punishment of not more than 90 days or a peace bond for not more than one year.

[17] *E.g.,* N.J. Stat. Ann. § 2A:170–1 (1953).

tical difference what charge is listed in the records, and it was apparent that police and magistrates frequently used these offenses interchangeably. The definition of vagrancy and the fact of drunkenness are regarded as merely illustrative of a mode of life which is to be suppressed. The vagrancy statute describes what is commonly known as a "bum"; so, by analogy, any bum is punishable, whether or not his acts amount to the legal definition of vagrancy or habitual drunkenness. Add to this the fact that most "vagrants" also appeared to be chronic alcoholics and that most alcoholics meet the generous magisterial definition of vagrancy, and the compounding and confusion of the statutes is understandable.

Such loose administration was not restricted by the technical elements of a crime. Conviction as an habitual drunkard required no proof beyond simple intoxication. Many Philadelphia residents were committed as vagrants under a statute limiting that crime to non-residents who have come "from without the Commonwealth." Many out-of-state vagrancy defendants were not allowed to give an explanation of their presence in Philadelphia, although the statute provides that it shall be a defense. These problems of proof will be considered in more detail below.

Such administration explains two curious anomalies found in police and prison records. One is the fact that in 1950 in Philadelphia there were 1430 commitments of vagrants to the House of Correction, but only 1241 arrests for that offense.[18] As a number of those arrested for vagrancy were discharged—over 40 per cent by one sample tabulation [19]—the discrepancy is substantial. The excess of convictions over arrests doubtless resulted from the method of recruiting the ranks of vagrants in part from those arrested and brought before the magistrates merely as drunks. Second, the records of habitual offenders at the House of Correction frequently showed vagrancy convictions interspersed among commitments as habitual drunkards, which under the Pennsylvania law would be legally impossible. This interchangeable use of the two offenses is illustrated by the record of an inmate interviewed in the summer of 1951:

Committed	Charge	Sentence	Discharged
6/ 4/47	Vagrancy	6 months	12/ 4/47
12/22/47	Vagrancy	3 months	3/ 9/48
4/ 9/48	Vagrancy	3 months	6/25/48
8/ 7/49	Hab. Drunk.	3 months	10/25/49
10/31/49	Hab. Drunk.	3 months	12/30/49
1/ 4/50	Vagrancy	3 months	3/22/50
3/25/50	Hab. Drunk.	6 months	6/21/50
9/ 2/50	Hab. Drunk.	3 months	9/25/50
11/10/50	Vagrancy	3 months	1/26/51
1/31/51	Vagrancy	3 months	4/18/51
5/24/51	Vagrancy	3 months	8/10/51
8/12/51	Vagrancy	3 months	. . . .

[18] Phila. House of Correction, Ann. Rep. 42 (1950); Phila. Bureau of Police, Ann. Rep. table 1 (1950).

[19] Philadelphia 6th Police District, June 1951. Arrests for vagrancy, 46, of whom 20 discharged and 26 committed. Arrests for "drunk and vagrant," 7, of whom 2 discharged and 5 committed. But for drunkenness the proportion of discharges was very high. There were 850 arrests for "drunkenness," of whom 51 were committed; 89 arrests for "habitual drunkenness," of whom 57 were committed; thus a total of 108 out of 939 drunkenness arrests were committed.

IV. POLICY OBJECTIVES OF VAGRANCY LAW ENFORCEMENT

Philadelphia magistrates observed during this study frequently expressed the policies which guided their administration of vagrancy-type law. They viewed their function as a deterrent one to banish "bums" from Philadelphia and keep them out ("After this you stay where you belong"), or as a form of civic sanitation ("I'll clean up this district if I have to stay here until 5 o'clock every afternoon"), or as control of suspicious persons ("There have been a lot of robberies around here. I'm going to have you investigated—three months"), or as humanitarian ("I'm saving his life by sending him where he can't booze").

The wide scope of these policy objectives illustrates the important place of vagrancy-type law in our criminal administration. The acts which are made punishable are petty in terms of social dangerousness, but the chief significance of this branch of the criminal law lies in its quantitative impact and administrative usefulness. More persons are arrested for vagrancy proper than for any of the more serious offenses except possibly larceny and assault,[20] and it is quite likely that more persons are convicted for this offense than for any other.[21] Add the related offenses of drunkenness and disorderly conduct, and vagrancy-type crime accounts for more than one third of all arrests tabulated in the *Uniform Crime Reports*.[22] Then there are the countless additional arrests made for these offenses which are never recorded with the Federal Bureau of Investigation.[23]

Administratively, vagrancy-type statutes are regarded as essential criminal preventives, providing a residual police power to facilitate the arrest, investigation and incarceration of suspicious persons. When the District of Columbia vagrancy law was revised ten years ago, Congress was told by police officials "that one of the principal needs to assist in correcting the existing criminal situation in the District of Columbia is the strengthening of the existing vagrancy law." [24] In most jurisdictions these statutes are sufficiently indefinite to give the police wide scope. They permit arrest without warrant and summary prosecution without jury before a justice of the peace or magistrate, and often simplify the problem of proof by placing on the defendant the burden of at least going forward with evidence of innocence. To the extent that the police actually are hampered by the restrictions of the ordinary law

[20] Arrests for vagrancy between 1940 and 1946 ranged between 5.7% and 8.8% of all arrests tabulated in the *Uniform Crime Reports*. Major categories in 1945 were: drunkenness (22.9%), larceny (9.2%), assault (7.9%), disorderly conduct (7.0%) and vagrancy (6.2%). Of all arrests in that year, 6.6% were for "suspicion," and no other charge was ever made. *Uniform Crime Reports* (U.S. Dept. of Justice) for the years indicated: 1951 at 105; 1950 at 107; 1949 at 112; 1948 at 114; 1947 at 115; 1946 at 116; 1945 at 113; 1944 at 91; 1943 at 87; 1942 at 86; 1941 at 203; 1940 at 204.

[21] This may result because (1) the overwhelming number of those arrested for drunkenness are probably merely discharged, and (2) many persons arrested for vagrancy, including many in Philadelphia, were not tabulated in these reports because they were not fingerprinted.

[22] The combined arrests for vagrancy, disorderly conduct, drunkenness and suspicion constituted the following proportion of all arrests for the years indicated: 1951, 39.4%; 1950, 40.2%; 1949, 41.8%; 1948, 42.8%; 1947, 43.1%; 1946, 42.6%; 1945, 42.7%; 1944, 42.6%; 1943, 45.3%. *Uniform Crime Reports, op. cit. supra* note 20.

[23] Statistics in the *Uniform Crime Reports* are based on fingerprints registered with the F.B.I., and in respect to offenses such as vagrancy and drunkenness, they are incomplete to a degree which cannot be ascertained. In Philadelphia, when this field study was made, such persons were not fingerprinted on arrest, and only a few of those convicted were fingerprinted at the House of Correction; thus the great majority were not included in the F.B.I.'s statistics.

[24] H.R. Rep. No. 1248, 77th Cong., 1st Sess. 1 (1941).

of arrest,[25] by the illegality of arrests on mere suspicion alone,[26] and by the defects and loopholes of substantive criminal law, vagrancy-type statutes facilitate the apprehension, investigation or harassment of suspected criminals. When suspects can be arrested for nothing else, it is often possible to "go and vag them." [27]

This usefulness as a criminal catch-all is not confined to its effectiveness against criminal suspects. Perhaps its principal employment is as a clean-up measure in dealing with the problems of congested urban "skid row" districts. Unwanted drunkards, panhandlers, gamblers, peddlers or paupers are committed or banished, a procedure that is alleged to deter other like persons from entering or remaining in a given locality. Miscellaneous problems in practice are embraced within its broad scope; during the period of this study in Philadelphia, vagrancy convictions were used at least twice to imprison unsuccessful would-be suicides and repeatedly as a means of commitment of mentally ill persons.

It is somewhat incongruous that these modern and peculiarly urban problems are dealt with by statutes created centuries ago to meet the utterly dissimilar problems of a rural England faced with the break-up of feudalism and its resulting economic dislocation. The basic elements of the Pennsylvania vagrancy statute merely repeat legislation enacted 400 years ago in the immediate aftermath of the Black Death. Despite the drastic change in social and economic conditions that has intervened, there is striking similarity between the policy objectives of modern vagrancy law administration and of the pre-Elizabethan Parliaments. . . .

1. Banishment of Unwanted Persons

Philadelphia's Banishment Policy. [The] fifteenth century policy objective of erecting barriers against the wanderings of the poor and of banishment of those who were found where they were not supposed to be retains surprising vitality in present day Philadelphia vagrancy administration. Any migrant, whether a transient en route between jobs, or stopping over to spend the proceeds of one job before moving on to the next, or arriving in a city destitute and planning to stay there while seeking employment, is bait for a vagrancy arrest.[28] He tends to gravitate to the skid row in any city through which he passes, if only because that is where 50¢ beds can be obtained, and he can patronize the bars, walk the streets, or sit on a park bench on a warm summer night. Some, but by no means exclusively the drinkers,[29] get scooped up in the nightly rounds of clean-up arrests. They constituted a small but significant minority of the drunkenness and vagrancy prosecutions observed in this

[25] See Note, *Philadelphia Police Practice and the Law of Arrest,* 100 U. Pa. L. Rev. 1182 (1952).

[26] *Stoutenburgh v. Frazier,* 16 App. D.C. 229, 48 L.R.A. 220 (1900).

[27] *People v. Craig,* 152 Cal. 42, 47, 91 Pac. 997, 1000 (1907).

[28] See *Bower v. State,* 135 N.J.L. 564, 53 A.2d 357 (Sup. Ct. 1947): "It is not an offense to have a dirty face, or to wear blue overalls or to travel by gratuitous rides from Bangor, Maine, to Florida, or to sleep in a truck, or to pick potatoes in one part of the country or, with $14 in pocket, to be temporarily out of employment on the way from completion of one job to the search for another." The conviction of this defendant, arrested under the circumstances described, was reversed; but in vagrancy such a rare appeal may very well indicate arrest practices which continue despite a decision. "Typically, the policemen are given little information about the laws they are required to enforce, and they are usually unaware of appellate decisions that affect the meaning of those laws whose texts they may have read." Note, 59 Yale L.J. 1351, 1357 (1950).

[29] In the 6th police district in June, 1951, 18 of 46 vagrancy arrests were listed as "sober" and 28 "drunk" on arrest.

study. In the magistrates' courts their defense of recent employment or search for employment was viewed with such extreme suspicion that it was very difficult to establish.

Some examples will illustrate the operation of the anti-migratory policy in Philadelphia. On a July morning after one of the hottest nights of the summer, a group of defendants were brought before a Philadelphia magistrate. A police officer checked the record of arrests and said: "These men were arrested sleeping in Reyburn Plaza at 2:20 a.m." The arresting officers were not present, and there were no other witnesses.

The magistrate took them one by one, first asking each one, "Where are you from?" If the answer was Philadelphia, the defendant was discharged with a warning not to sleep outdoors in a park again.

In each case where the defendant's answer revealed an out-of-city residence, even when the defendant tried to say more, the magistrate immediately concluded the hearing with, "You can't sleep in the parks. Three months in the House of Correction." The commitment sheets showed that these men were convicted of vagrancy.

A number of American jurisdictions have emulated the British statute which prohibits what has been called the "scandal" [30] of "sleeping in . . . the open air" by persons "who can give no good account of themselves." [31] Pennsylvania does not have this statutory provision. Thus, its enforcement can only be described as punishment by analogy, and in any case, the "good account" proviso is essential unless the offense is to include boy scouts, naturalists or persons taking a nap under a tree on a hot day. [32]

The convicted defendants were subsequently interviewed in the House of Correction. A and B stated that they were staying in skid row hotels while visiting Philadelphia, and it was so hot that they went out to sit in the park and fell asleep. A declared, "The next thing I knew they were kicking me in the shins and told me to get into the wagon."

A middle aged man, C, reported that he worked nine months a year in a cotton seed oil processing plant in Virginia, where he had a wife and three children, and that during the seasonal shut-down of the plant he worked as an agricultural migrant. He alleged that he had worked on a New Jersey farm on the day of his arrest, came in to visit Philadelphia in the evening on the labor contractor's truck, had some drinks and missed the truck back. He said he went to the bus station to wait for the first early morning bus, but it was so hot there that he retreated to the park and was arrested.

D and E were Negro youths of about 20. D said he was en route from New York, where he had been working, to his home in Mississippi; he arrived in Philadelphia by bus in the evening and wanted to stay over to look around and see a friend. They lounged in the bus station for a while, walked up Market Street, decided against taking in an all night movie, and ended up on the park bench. D had $25 on his

[30] Departmental Committee on Vagrancy, Report 326 (London 1906).

[31] E.g., Conn. Gen. Stat. § 8644 (1949); Del. Code Ann. tit. 11, § 881 (1953); D.C. Code Ann. § 22-3302(6) (Supp. 1949); Mass. Ann. Laws c. 272, § 66 (1933); N.J. Stat. Ann. § 2A:170-4 (1952); N.Y. Pen. Code § 887(6).

[32] But see Conn. Gen. Stat. § 8644 (1949) (vagrants include "all persons camping on the public highway without the consent of the selectmen of the town or on private property without the consent of the owner. . . ."); see also Wis. Stat. § 348.351 (1953), as amended, Wis. Laws 1951, c. 332 (no "good account" exception).

person at the time of his arrest to finance his trip to Mississippi.[33] All of these defendants were listed as "sober" when arrested, and none of them fitted the stereotype of "bum."

Transient types observed during the study included: (1) agricultural migrants, like C in the above example; (2) men who alleged they had just come to Philadelphia hoping to stay and find employment, like the Virginian noted above; (3) men who alleged that they had stopped in Philadelphia to visit friends or "to see the sights" (to one of the latter a magistrate said: "I'll show you some sights—three months in the House of Correction"); and (4) one non-resident seaman. This man was interviewed at the House of Correction. He said he had come off a ship with $175, which he proceeded to spend in a week-long binge. About the third time he appeared before a magistrate, he was committed.

When the transient defendant is allowed to have his say before the magistrate, the defenses he advances are often difficult to substantiate. One who alleges that he has been working in New York and is en route to Baltimore to get a job has no practical way of proving either statement. Nor is it reasonable to expect a defendant who claims that he is seeking work in Philadelphia to produce as witnesses the men who have turned him down for a job. Under the pressure of time and mass production in the magistrates' courts, questions of proof are greatly simplified. One defendant stated that he was from Trenton, New Jersey, and that he was in Philadelphia looking for work. "Why didn't you get work in Trenton?" "I tried. I was registered with the Employment Service there, but I didn't get anything so I came down here." He was then committed. When interviewed later, he said that he had intended to register with the U.S. Employment Service in Philadelphia, but had not had a chance, because he had been arrested within a few hours after his arrival.

One morning two men who had been arrested as intoxicated but whom the magistrate was apparently trying as transients, and therefore for vagrancy, told similar stories. The first claimed that he had come from Richmond en route to New York and had stopped to see a girl friend. The second alleged that he had come from Baltimore to pick up some laundry which he had forgotten to take with him after a previous visit here. There was no prosecution evidence in either case except the fact of arrest. The first man was committed for three months as a vagrant; the second, the magistrate discharged with these words: "You get your laundry and be on your way to Baltimore by two o'clock this afternoon. If you're picked up here again you'll go to Correction."

After the hearing the magistrate distinguished the cases, explaining that after years of experience on the bench one becomes a pretty good judge of men. "Some people, you look at them, you know they're lying." But this simple and time-saving substitute for direct examination, cross-examination and impeachment occasionally backfired. One such case was that of a young man who claimed he both lived and worked in Philadelphia but was without identification. The magistrate gave him a half minute of quizzical study and sentenced him to six months. Half an hour later, as the prisoners were being loaded into the van and the magistrate was picking up his papers, a man who turned out to be the defendant's employer came in and substantiated the defendant's story. The defendant was brought back from the

[33] At the House of Correction it was later confirmed that C had a Virginia residence, wife and children, and that D was from Mississippi. Police records confirmed D's claim to have had $25 on him at the time of his arrest.

van, the magistrate tore up the commitment sheet he had signed and gave a discharge.[34]

A defendant whose employer did not thus seek him out was not so fortunate. He was a 21-year old Indian arrested intoxicated late at night by railroad police in Broad Street Station, and he was found to have a knife concealed on his person.[35] This trial was not observed, but when interviewed the defendant stated that the following proceedings took place: the magistrate asked him where he was from, and he replied with his Philadelphia address. "I mean, where are you from originally." "Oklahoma." "You're a vagrant. One year in the House of Correction." This defendant claimed that he was not allowed to telephone anyone before the hearing commenced, that when he tried to say something more at the hearing he was grabbed by two officers and dragged back to his cell, and that not until he had been at the House of Correction for several days was he allowed to contact anyone. He stated that he had come to Philadelphia a month before, that he was employed in a photographic supply store on Market Street, and that the reason he had a knife (which he said was "nothing but a small penknife") was because he used it in his work. The employer confirmed this man's story, stated that he was a good worker and that when he had learned what had happened, he had gone to see the magistrate who refused to do anything.

The exclusionary policy was often applied in cases of acquittal, with defendants being discharged on the sole condition that they get out of Philadelphia. To one who said he had come to Philadelphia for a week's visit, the magistrate said, "You cut your week short and get out today." A defendant, who said he was from Trenton, declared that he had come to Philadelphia to see a friend. "You were panhandling, too, weren't you?" "Oh no, judge." "Well, let me warn you. Don't come back here again, or you go up to Correction. No more panhandling. Discharged." As the defendant left, the police officer who served as the magistrate's "clerk" called after him: "You go back up to Trenton. You do your panhandling up there, see?"

Some of the cases which have been discussed indicate that magisterial antimigratory policy was not confined to transients but was used to deter intra-city travel. A very small minority of Philadelphians arrested in the skid row district but resident in another part of the city were convicted, the magistrate remarking, "He should stay where he belongs." More often there were discharges with a warning to "keep away from this district."

Even the statutory and administrative release procedures were geared to this policy of banishment. A statute (which was apparently in disuse) provides that upon release of a vagrant, he shall be given a certificate of discharge "which shall exempt him from any further arrest for vagrancy for a period of five days upon condition that he shall forthwith leave the county wherein confined. . . ."[36] Banishment was also enforced as a condition of an informal "parole" given some vagrancy inmates at the House of Correction in 1951. At that time some of the transients who were

---

34 "It shall be unlawful for any magistrate to (a) Review, alter, modify or remit any sentence of fine or imprisonment imposed by him. . . ." Pa. Stat. Ann. tit. 42, § 1144 (Purdon Supp. 1953).

35 *Id.* tit. 18, § 4416 (Purdon 1945) provides that "Whoever carries any . . . deadly weapon, concealed upon his person, *with the intent therewith unlawfully and maliciously to do injury to any other person,* is guilty of a misdemeanor. . . ." (Emphasis added.) This defendant, however, was not charged with this offense and in view of his explanation for carrying the knife (*supra*), it is probable that he could not have been convicted under it.

36 Pa. Stat. Ann. tit. 18, § 2042 (Purdon 1945).

committed as vagrants were visited by a probation officer of the Municipal Court. If their residence claims in other states were confirmed and they either had or could obtain funds to finance a bus ticket home, they were taken before a Municipal Court judge and given parole on condition that they go straight home.[37] The probation officer accompanied them to the bus terminal to make sure that they really left.

One possibly important aspect of anti-migratory policy cannot be evaluated on the information available in this study. It was reported that some vagrant-type defendants were threatened with arrest for vagrancy, but were let off by the police officer with a warning to get out of town. This practice has been recommended as a means whereby vagrancy law could be enforced "at the least possible expense to the taxpayer," [38] but there is no way of testing the frequency with which it occurs.

Validity of Banishment Sanction. In one of the earliest criminal prosecutions on American soil, the penalty inflicted upon Ann Hutchinson in 1637 was to be "banished from out of our jurisdiction as being a woman not fit for our society . . . ," [39] and in 1800, a legislative imposition of banishment was upheld.[40] Whether or not a legislature today has the constitutional power to impose such a punishment may be open to question,[41] but it is agreed that in the absence of express legislative authority, a sentence which includes banishment is void.[42] No Pennsylvania statute authorizes banishment as a punishment for crime. Technically the orders by which magistrates banish defendants in Philadelphia are not sentences, for a discharge is given upon condition that the defendant leave the city or a particular district within the city. The result is the same, however, as the "floating sentence" outlawed in a California case in which a two year sentence was suspended on condition that the defendant leave the county and stay away for two years,[43] and in the New York case where execution of sentence was stayed for 24 hours "to give the defendant a chance to leave Town and not come back." [44] Certainly the policy reasons against banishment which have been stressed by the courts apply in full force to Philadelphia practices. It is no solution to the problem posed by the urban derelict to pass

[37] This type of parole appears to have no statutory authority, and the procedures followed have since been changed.

[38] *Commonwealth v. Dean,* 19 Pa. Dist. 534 (Bradford County C.P. 1909). "In most cases those who are in fact vagrants if notified by officers to leave the vicinity or suffer arrest would immediately take their departure." *Id.* at 537.

[39] Quoted in Douglas, *An Almanac of Liberty,* 135 (1954).

[40] *Cooper v. Telfair,* 4 U.S. (4 Dall.) 14 (1800) upheld a Georgia statute banishing from the state named persons who had sided with England during the Revolution. Justice Cushing said: "The right to confiscate and banish, in the case of an offending citizen, must belong to every government. It is not within the judicial power, as created and regulated by the Constitution of Georgia; and it, naturally, as well as tacitly, belongs to the Legislature." *Id.* at 19.

[41] It has been suggested that today such legislative action might be banned as cruel and unusual punishment. *People v. Wallace,* 124 N.Y.S.2d 201, 204 (Suffolk County Ct. 1953).

[42] In re Scarborough, 76 Cal. App. 2d 648, 173 P.2d 825 (1946); *Ex parte* Baum, 251 Mich. 187, 231 N.W. 95 (1930); *State v. Doughtie,* 237 N.C. 368, 74 S.E.2d 922 (1953); *People v. Wallace, supra* note 41; *State v. Baker,* 58 S.C. 111, 36 S.E. 501 (1900). See *Cooper v. Telfair,* 4 U.S. (4 Dall.) 14, 19 (1800) (dictum); *United States v. Ju Toy,* 198 U.S. 253, 269 (1905) (dissenting opinion). However, it has been held that a pardon conditioned on banishment is valid. *Kavalin v. White,* 44 F.2d 49 (10th Cir. 1930); see Comment, 31 Minn. L. Rev. 742, 743 (1947).

[43] In re Scarborough, 76 Cal. App. 2d 648, 173 P.2d 825 (1946).

[44] *People v. Wallace,* 124 N.Y.S.2d 201, 203 (Suffolk County Ct. 1953).

him back and forth from one jurisdiction to another,[45] and if, as seems highly likely, other jurisdictions are doing the same thing, such a policy is ultimately self-defeating.[46]

A more basic concern is the fact that the anti-migratory policy of vagrancy administration squarely contravenes the right of persons to travel freely from state to state. While the Supreme Court once said in *City of New York v. Miln* that it is "as competent and as necessary for a State to provide precautionary measures against the moral pestilence of paupers, vagabonds, and possibly convicts, as it is to guard against physical pestilence . . . ,"[47] that 1837 decision has little validity in view of *Edwards v. California*.[48] There the Supreme Court held unconstitutional a statute which banned importing indigent persons into a state. The majority rested their decision on the statute's repugnance to the commerce power; three Justices applied the privileges and immunities clause; and one Justice thought the statute void under both clauses.[49] The majority pointed out that "the theory of the Elizabethan poor laws no longer fits the facts" and specifically repudiated *Miln*: "Whatever may have been the notion then prevailing, we do not think that it will be seriously contended that because a person is without employment and without funds he constitutes a 'moral pestilence.' "[50]

Yet a major part of Philadelphia's vagrancy administration rests on just such a contention. Cases were repeatedly observed in which "because a person is without employment and without funds," conviction resulted. However the *Edwards* case is viewed, it clearly bans restrictions against persons whose interstate travel is for any lawful purpose. The inevitable effect of vagrancy statutes is to impede such travel, and Philadelphia practice accentuates this by its conscious effort to deport persons who are chiefly undesirable because of their poverty, and to deter such persons from coming to the city. The Pennsylvania statute is particularly vulnerable under the *Edwards* case because it singles out interstate migrants and limits vagrants to those who have come from without the state.[51] But the Philadelphia practice and the statutes of other jurisdictions which also embrace intrastate migration within vagrancy would also seem to be invalid under the *Edwards* policy. A state cannot allow a migrant to enter but then restrict his freedom of movement; the freedom to

---

[45] In *State v. Doughtie*, 237 N.C. 368, 371, 74 S.E.2d 922, 924 (1953), the court noted that "It is not favorable to him to force him to go for two years into another state, where the state of North Carolina can exercise no restraining influence upon him for purposes of reformation."

[46] Compare the prediction of the Michigan Supreme Court that banishment of criminals "would tend to . . . provoke retaliation." *Ex parte* Baum, 251 Mich. 187, 231 N.W. 95 (1930).

[47] 36 U.S. (11 Pet.) 102, 142 (1837).

[48] 314 U.S. 160 (1941).

[49] Despite the failure of the majority to expressly rule on the privileges and immunities point in *Edwards v. California*, it seems to be well established that the right to enter and reside in any state of one's choice is a right arising "out of the nature and essential character of the national government." *Twining v. New Jersey*, 211 U.S. 78, 97 (1908). Before the fourteenth amendment was adopted, the Court invalidated a Nevada tax on persons leaving that state as inconsistent with the right incident to national citizenship to travel across the country without restriction. *Crandall v. Nevada*, 73 U.S. (6 Wall.) 35 (1867). The Third Circuit sustained an injunction to restrain the police from exporting C.I.O. organizers from Jersey City on the grounds that freedom of movement between states is protected by the privileges and immunities clause. *Hague v. CIO*, 101 F.2d 774 (3d Cir. 1939); see also *Allgeyer v. Louisiana*, 165 U.S. 578, 589 (1897) (fourteenth amendment includes right "to live and work where he will"). "If national citizenship means less than this, it means nothing." *Edwards v. California*, 314 U.S. 160, 183 (1941) (concurring opinion of Justice Jackson).

[50] 314 U.S. at 174, 177.

[51] See note 8 *supra*.

enter the state of one's choice is more than the freedom to be sent to a restricted ghetto.[52]

2. Suspicion

We have seen that in Philadelphia many vagrant-type defendants are banished merely because their poverty—often but not always combined with alcoholism—makes them aesthetically undesirable on the city's streets and parks, a practice which carries out the Poor Law policy that pauperism alone is sufficient reason to compel people to "stay where they belong." There is, however, a second important factor involved in the policy of exclusion, banishment and control of vagrant-type defendants. It has been thought that the circumstances under which vagrant-type defendants are frequently apprehended are sufficiently suspicious to raise a reasonable inference that criminal conduct other than vagrancy or drunkenness is involved. It is important to note that two quite different kinds of suspicion are involved. The alleged vagrant may be suspected of *past criminality*, the arrest for vagrancy offering the opportunity to investigate whether the suspect is wanted in another jurisdiction or has committed other crimes.[53] On the other hand, the suspicion may be of *future criminality*, the inference being that purposeful poverty is likely to lead to other crimes unless the state steps in.

The commonest judicial explanation of vagrancy's place in a penal code is based on the second of these assumptions. The traditional view expressed in cases and texts is that the vagrant mode of life denounced by the statutes is of itself a crime breeder and the vagrant "the chrysalis of every species of criminal." [54] This view appears very early in vagrancy's legislative history,[55] and courts have continued to echo the preamble of a pre-Elizabethan statute that "idleness and vagabondry is the mother and root of all thefts, robberies, and all evil acts, and other mischiefs. . . ." [56] Vagrancy statutes are viewed as "police regulations to prevent crime," [57] to check the spread of "a parasitic disease" [58] which is not only evil in itself but "productive of innumerable vices and crimes of great magnitude." [59] Thus, the arrests are supposed to "check evil in its beginning" [60] and "prevent crime by disrupting and scattering the breeding spot." [61]

This theory that purposeful poverty will lead to other criminality has a certain basis in common sense, for if a man is idle with no means of support, "there is a great

---

[52] "Individuals coming into or going about a city upon their lawful concerns must be allowed free locomotion upon the streets and public places." *Hague v. CIO,* 101 F.2d 774, 780 (3d Cir. 1939).

[53] For a recent example of this, see the following news item: "Tony Labandeira, 35, was released from the Dawes County jail Monday morning after serving a 10-day sentence for vagrancy during which he was questioned about the rape-slaying of Donna Sue Davis in Sioux City, Ia." *Lincoln* (Nebr.) *Star,* July 2, 1955, p. 16, col. 1.

[54] Tiedeman, *Limitations of Police Powers* 117 (1886).

[55] The earliest reference was to vagabonds as "idle, and suspected persons." 11 Hen. 7, c. 2 (1494).

[56] 1 Edw. 6, c. 3 (1547).

[57] *In the Matter of Forbes,* 11 Abb. Pr. 52, 55 (N.Y. Sup. Ct. 1860); see *Commonwealth v. Roth,* 136 Pa. Super. 301, 304, 7 A.2d 145, 146 (1939). "The . . . idea that 'where there is smoke there must be fire' is the reason why vagrancy has been a crime for centuries." Note, 80 U. Pa. L. Rev. 565, 568 (1932).

[58] *State v. Harlow,* 174 Wash. 227, 233, 24 P.2d 601, 603 (1933).

[59] *County of Northampton v. West,* 28 Pa. 173, 175 (1857).

[60] *Levine v. State,* 110 N.J.L. 467, 470, 166 Atl. 300, 302 (Hudson County C.P. 1933).

[61] *People v. Pieri,* 269 N.Y. 315, 323, 199 N.E. 495, 498 (1936).

temptation to steal in order to relieve his hunger." [62] But that statement suggests the rationale's limitations, for if the necessity of self-support is what turns the vagrant to crime, that criminality may be of a very petty nature.[63] The most common example is undoubtedly begging which, although usually proscribed by statute or ordinance,[64] still retains strong public tolerance carried over from religious teaching on giving and the tradition of holy men living upon alms.[65] The sanction against begging has not repressed the practice [66] and is not vigorously enforced, with the result that there are sufficient funds to be coaxed out of the public to meet the demands of those who seek merely a meal, a bed or another drink. A man with such limited objectives is not forced into very serious criminality to obtain gratification.

Nor does it necessarily follow that one who is idle and apparently without means of support will turn to criminality. When completely down and out, he may be able to go on relief or to obtain help from friends or relatives. Many casual workers obtain jobs between periods of unemployment—which last as long as any funds remain—after which they may ship out to sea, go back to migratory agricultural labor or seasonal industrial work or even get a job right in the skid row. A man willing to undergo the very low standard of living of the stereotype vagrant may, like Thoreau in *Walden*, work at odd jobs only to the extent necessary to provide for his limited needs. Men whose stories would place them in each of these categories were interviewed at the House of Correction, and they find occasional recognition in the reported cases.[67]

No adequate studies have been found to correlate the incidence of other criminality among vagrants and thus test the validity of this breeding-ground theory. Probably no such study could be made, for police practices have little relationship to this judicially-created rationale. Even if it could be determined that persons arrested for vagrancy also had a high incidence of other criminality, little light would be thrown on the breeding ground theory, for the police make many arrests for vagrancy without regard to whether or not the arrested person falls into the status of a vagrant.

Such material as is available, however, lends weight to the belief that there is little correlation between pauperism and serious criminality. A study of the prior convic-

[62] *Daniel v. State*, 110 Ga. 915, 916, 36 S.E. 293 (1900).

[63] See notes 68–71 *infra*.

[64] *E.g.*, Colo. Stat. Ann. c. 48, § 281 (1935); Vt. Rev. Stat. § 8444 (1947). In Philadelphia several magistrates informed me that begging is punished as straight vagrancy, although no such cases were observed. Compare the tramp statute, Pa. Stat. Ann. tit. 18, § 4617 (Purdon 1945), which covers begging but which is a misdemeanor.

[65] "[T]here grew up in the course of time the theory of the religious merit of almsgiving. Charity became a means of securing forgiveness of sin to the giver, a means of grace. Almsgiving, no longer the means primarily of helping a fellow-man in need, became fundamentally a method of washing away one's sins.

"With the rise of monasticism in Christendom the religious basis of begging in the cleansing grace of charity was completed in the theory that those were of superior sanctity who forsook all their worldly possessions and depended entirely upon the charity of God's people. Thus, the religious basis of beggary had its roots deep in man's desire to free himself from sin by giving to a beggar, and on the other hand got its justification from the desire to attain salvation by becoming a beggar. From both points of view religion sanctified begging." Gillin, *Vagrancy and Begging*, 35 Am. J. Soc. 425, 426 (1929).

[66] "Excepting prohibition, there is probably no problem in which attempts at control appear to have been a more blatant and universal failure than they have in the case of begging." Gilmore, *The Beggar*, 213 (1940).

[67] *Leonard v. State*, 5 Ga. App. 494, 63 S.E. 530 (1909) (defendant who usually loafed not a vagrant when earning enough to live in meager style); *Lewis v. State*, 3 Ga. App. 322, 59 S.E. 933 (1907); *Senegal v. State*, 112 Tex. Crim. 408, 16 S.W.2d 1070 (1929) (idling around pool halls by the longshoremen with only occasional employment held not vagrancy).

tions of a sample of inmates admitted to the Philadelphia House of Correction reveals fairly high recidivism confined to other vagrancy and habitual drunkenness convictions but a low rate of recidivism for other more serious crimes.[68] Even writers who support the "breeding ground" rationale also state that it does not breed dangerous criminality.[69] The British Vagrancy Committee's exhaustive study in 1906 reported that "the witnesses who have given evidence before us agree that the vagrant class as a whole is not much addicted to the worse forms of crime, but minor offenses are very common," citing petty larcenies from the back doors of houses as an example.[70] Kinberg's study of vagrants in Sweden found a large group of tramps, hobos, vagabonds and intermittent vagrants characterized by an absence of criminality in the usual sense, and he cites other European studies showing many subjects punished innumerable times for vagrancy but with no manifestations of other forms of criminality.[71] This Philadelphia study appears to support these conclusions, for there was no indication by police and magistrates that they regarded the vagrants as dangerous potential criminals. Many, indeed, when in the grip of acute alcoholism, were more an object of pathos than anything else.

In any event this analysis is rendered somewhat academic because the police take a much more pragmatic view of suspicion as a policy behind vagrancy law. The arrests, both in Philadelphia and in other jurisdictions as revealed in reported cases, give little indication that the police are consciously suppressing a mode of life because it may lead to future criminality. Where suspicion of any sort is involved, it is suspicion of past criminality. In Philadelphia, magistrates would sometimes commit with some such explanation as "I'm going to have you investigated; there have been a lot of robberies around here." On a number of occasions one magistrate delivered a "You people may think I'm cruel" speech to the spectators at his hearings, one version of which would continue: "It may seem cruel to send all these people up like this, but you'd be surprised how many are wanted in other jurisdictions. Last month alone 50 of these men were wanted." (The month referred to was June, 1951; according to information supplied the writer at the House of Correction, only one of the commitments for that month was wanted in another jurisdiction.) This is a crude, free-swinging method of trying to solve past crimes, not an attack on a breeding place of potential criminals.

Cases in other jurisdictions indicate that, where suspicious circumstances cause an

---

68 See Hiller & Rector, *Intake and Release Procedures in the House of Correction, Philadelphia, Pa.* (Nat'l Probation & Parole Ass'n 1953) (mimeo). For the recidivism of all 164 inmates studied, see *id.* table I at 94; of 134 males, see *id.* table K at 96–97. Of the cases studied, 61 were defendants serving vagrancy or habitual drunkenness sentences, of whom 24 appeared to be first commitments, 29 had prior commitments for vagrancy or habitual drunkenness, and only 8 had other criminal records, of which several appeared to be for minor criminality only.

69 For an example of this confusion compare the following excerpts from Dawson, *The Vagrancy Problem* (1910):

"Dislike of regular labor makes them tramps, tramping makes them criminals—the two conditions are inseparably connected as cause and effect, for their kinship lies in the very constitution and instincts of human nature. . . ." *Id.* at 37.

"It is not—in the main, at any rate—a dangerous criminal class with which we have to do, but for the most part the weak and aimless characters whose great need is the moral tonic of discipline and compulsion." *Id.* at 72.

70 Departmental Committee on Vagrancy, Report 25 (London 1906). For an optimistic recent British report on the rehabilitative possibilities of tramps and vagrants, see editorial comment, 112 Just. P. 727 (1948).

71 Kinberg, *On So-called Vagrancy; A Medico-sociological Study,* 24 J. Crim. L., C. & P.S. 409, 552 (1933).

arrest for vagrancy, something more specific than status is involved.[72] The charge may be a mere cloak for an arrest that officers have been ordered to make,[73] an arrest for some other offense, as a means of validating what would otherwise be an illegal search.[74] The defendant may be a suspected prostitute [75] or pickpocket,[76] an associate of bootleggers [77] or suspected of participation in the narcotics traffic.[78] He may be acting suspiciously near a saloon [79] or in a car [80] or by peering into store windows,[81] where the facts observed do not amount to an attempt. The charge has been used to support arrests for activities which the police desire to suppress, such as "communistic agitation," [82] or labor organization.[83] The San Francisco police once arrested 375 men at one time, mostly in union halls, and charged them with vagrancy.[84]

A traditional vagrancy statute such as Pennsylvania's is ill-adapted to such police practices. Such elements as idleness and being without visible means of support describe a status and are aimed at a mode of life, not at isolated instances of idleness.[85] If the statutes were correctly construed and applied, such status elements would seriously interfere with what is now one of vagrancy's most convenient aspects from a police standpoint—the authority to arrest without a warrant on view of the offense.[86] Observation of an isolated instance of idleness would not justify an arrest; an officer would have to wait until he had observed "a series of acts extending over a considerable period of time, and only constituting a criminal offense because of their continuance and repetition. . . ." [87]

[72] See generally Note, *Use of Vagrancy-type Laws for the Arrest and Detention of Suspicious Persons,* 59 Yale L.J. 1351 (1950).

[73] *People v. Craig,* 152 Cal. 42, 47, 91 Pac. 997, 1000 (1907).

[74] *Gray v. State,* 243 Wis. 57, 9 N.W.2d 68 (1943).

[75] *Beail v. District of Columbia,* 82 A.2d 765 (D.C. Munic. App. 1951), *rev'd,* 201 F.2d 176 (D.C. Cir. 1952).

[76] *Burns v. District of Columbia,* 34 A.2d 714 (D.C. Munic. App. 1943).
S.W.2d 319 (1937).

[77] *Campbell v. State,* 31 Okla. Crim. 39, 237 Pac. 133 (1925); *Hutchins v. State,* 172 Tenn. 108, 110

[78] *Blakeley v. State,* 78 Ga. App. 516, 51 S.E.2d 598 (1949).

[79] *State v. Carrol,* 129 N.J.L. 416, 30 A.2d 54 (Sup. Ct.), *aff'd per curiam,* 130 N.J.L. 559, 33 A.2d 907 (Ct. Err. & App. 1943).

[80] *People v. Johnaken,* 196 Misc. 1059, 94 N.Y.S.2d 102 (New Rochelle City Ct. 1950).

[81] *McNeilly v. State,* 119 N.J.L. 237, 195 Atl. 725 (Sup. Ct. 1937).

[82] *In the Matter of Cutler,* 1 Cal. App. 2d 273, 36 P.2d 441 (1934); see Ames, *A Reply to "Who Is a Vagrant in California?",* 23 Calif. L. Rev. 616, 618 (1935).

[83] See Note, 59 Yale L.J. 1351, 1357 n.20 (1950), citing a report on interference with labor and civil liberties in Hudson County, N.J.

[84] *People v. Jackson* (Super. Ct. San Francisco 1935) (unreported); see Comment, *Who Is a Vagrant in California?,* 23 Calif. L. Rev. 507 nn.2 & 3 (1935).

[85] *Brooks v. State,* 33 Ala. App. 390, 34 So. 2d 175 (1948). There is little authority on how much of a continuendo is required to establish a vagrant mode of life. *Compare Branch v. State,* 73 Tex. Crim. 471, 165 S.W. 605 (1914) (conviction affirmed where police had watched defendant loaf and dance jigs for 13 days), *with Blakeley v. State,* 78 Ga. App. 516, 51 S.E.2d 598 (1949) (conviction reversed where police watched defendant loaf for 11 days).

[86] This authority is generally assumed and is frequently explicitly provided by statute. E.g., N.J. Rev. Stat. § 2A:169-3 (1951); Me. Rev. Stat. Ann. c. 137, § 37 (1954) (may arrest "upon view of" the offense); see Pa. Stat. Ann. tit. 18, § 2033 (Purdon 1945). Where the power to arrest on sight is not statutory, it has been implied. *People v. Formiscio,* 39 N.Y.S.2d 149 (N.Y. City Ct. Spec. Sess. 1943).

[87] *People v. Craig,* 152 Cal. 42, 46, 91 Pac. 997, 999 (1907).

No cases were observed in this study in which the police gave any indication of trying to get evidence on a defendant's mode of life and making an arrest only after they had observed a sufficient series of acts to add up to the prohibited status. Vagrancy is of use to the police in Philadelphia today as a weapon against suspicious persons only because the law is so loosely and illegally administered that an isolated act is all that is required for conviction. The magistrates were apparently unaware of the proof necessary to establish the status elements which are essential ingredients of the offense; in any event, they never applied them.

This emphasizes the absurdity of utilizing traditional vagrancy as a means of controlling persons suspected of serious criminality. Pauperism and vagrant status are not important indicia of the evils the police are primarily concerned with suppressing. Professional criminals are likely to have "visible means of support," and the attempt to prove they are vagrants runs into the difficulty described by a Chicago municipal court judge in discussing a vagrancy prosecution:

> "In the Winkler case, if there ever was a case where there should have been a conviction, that was the case. They introduced machine guns and everything else, but the jury took the position, as they told one of the bailiffs afterwards, that a man who is a vagrant has no visible means of support, and how could he be a vagrant if he lives on Sheridan Road?" [88]

A number of jurisdictions have tried to deal with this problem by enacting statutes whose elements are believed to be more reliable indicators of professional criminality. Such statutes have had constitutional difficulties as they have strayed from the traditional patterns whose common-law vintage makes them acceptable to the courts.[89] One type of statute makes the key element the consorting of persons who have criminal reputations.[90] So far these have been upheld by the courts,[91] although they raise serious policy and constitutional problems. When compared with traditional vagrancy they have the advantage of making the elements of the offense reflect more reasonable grounds of suspicion under modern conditions than is provided by the status of poverty.

3. Catch-all of the Criminal Law

The third major policy objective which is served by vagrancy law administration in Philadelphia has been almost completely ignored by courts and writers. When a magistrate talked about "cleaning up his district," he was referring to the role of vagrancy-type enforcement as the garbage pail of the criminal law. Prosecutions were carried on in a bewildering variety of other situations which had no relation to the suppression of criminality. These included cleaning "loafers" out of the city

[88] Testimony of Judge Thomas A. Green of Chicago Municipal Court, in *Hearings before a Subcommittee of the Senate Committee on Commerce*, 73d Cong., 2d Sess. 305, 308–09 (1934).

[89] For decisions invalidating such statutes, see *e.g.*, *Lanzetta v. New Jersey*, 306 U.S. 451 (1939); *People v. Belcastro*, 356 Ill. 144, 190 N.E. 301 (1934); *People v. Licavoli*, 264 Mich. 643, 250 N.W. 520 (1934); *St. Louis v. Fitz*, 53 Mo. 582 (1873).

[90] *E.g.*, N.J. Rev. Stat. § 2A:170-1 (1951); N.Y. Pen. Law § 722(11). Illegal intent is also an element of such statutes, but typically this is unimportant because proof of the key elements is prima facie evidence of the required intent.

[91] *E.g.*, *People v. Pieri*, 269 N.Y. 315, 199 N.E. 495 (1936).

center, "mopping up" the drunkards in the skid row, punishing attempted suicides, obliging persons who desired to send unwanted aged relatives to the House of Correction on cooked-up vagrancy charges, convicting mentally ill persons of vagrancy and likewise confining them behind the House of Correction's bars, punishing minor nuisances which do not amount to any crime and vindicating affronts to police dignity. The common ground which brings such a motley assortment of human troubles before the magistrates in vagrancy-type proceedings is the procedural laxity which permits "conviction" for almost any kind of conduct and the existence of the House of Correction as an easy and convenient dumping-ground for problems that appear to have no other immediate solution.

Dressing up the City Center. These efforts were usually supported by editorials urging that:

> "It is about time that these breathing spaces in the heart of the city be taken away from the idlers and the parolees and given back safely to the people." [92]

During an earlier "blitz" it was reported that:

> "[The effectiveness of the drive] . . . prompted the Central YMCA and other organizations yesterday to ask Captain Kronbar to widen the 'no man's land' for vagrants and rout them from other midcity loitering places." [93]

At such times the tempo of activity in magistrates' courts increased, but unpublicized "clean-up" activity goes on continuously. None of the usual motivations of vagrancy apply to such action. There was apparently no suspicion of other criminality involved, and there was no attempt to force people to work. The only reason for the arrests was that the appearance of the victims was not attractive. Usually the evidence fell far short of that necessary to sustain vagrancy or habitual drunkenness, the offense in most instances being, as the newspapers report, no more than "idling and loitering." Pennsylvania has no statute outlawing loitering; indeed, most statutes which have sought to proscribe mere loitering have been held unconstitutional.[94]

Cleaning Up the Skid Row. The principal problem is drunkenness, but loitering is also involved. One magistrate described the clean-up process:

> "About midnight on Saturday night the patrol wagons roll out with a group of officers on each. No call has come in for them; they know what they want. When they come to a certain block they stop, two officers go up one sidewalk and two on the other, and literally scoop them up."

A feature of these clean-ups are the "protective arrests" which occur when the officers find

[92] *Philadelphia Inquirer,* July 13, 1954, p. 12, col. 2.

[93] *Id.,* June 27, 1949, p. 1, col. 8.

[94] *Territory of Hawaii v. Anduha,* 48 F.2d 171 (9th Cir. 1931); *Commonwealth v. Carpenter,* 325 Mass. 519, 91 N.E.2d 666 (1950); *St. Louis v. Gloner,* 210 Mo. 502, 109 S.W. 30 (1908). *But see State v. Jasmin,* 105 Vt. 531, 535, 168 Atl. 545, 546 (1933).

". . . a better-dressed man, perhaps with a nice watch. He doesn't belong there. The police know only one thing can happen, so they pick
him up, too, to protect him, charge him with vagrancy, and then the
next morning the magistrate releases him, or after a few hours the
house sergeant releases him on a Form 80.[95] This helps the police, by saving them from having to look for the man who would
have robbed him, and it helps the man by keeping him from being
robbed."

This process goes on continuously. The drunk cell in a skid row police station is
no sooner emptied by one morning's hearings than new arrests start coming in, grist
for the following day's mill. Anyone familiar with skid row conditions will approach
the problem of the police with understanding. One officer stated, "You find the same
guy lying around night after night. Finally you get fed up, tip the magistrate off, and
at least you know that you won't have to see his face for the next three months." Thus
frequently, when a drunkenness defendant would be called up, a police officer would
interject, "Judge, this man's in here all the time. He's a regular pest." The magistrate
would then impose sentence, and several times stressed to the writer the importance
of such "cooperation" with the police. Many of these defendants were doubtless
chronic alcoholics, and some may have been known as such to the magistrates on
the basis of personal observation, but in not one of the hearings observed was there
competent evidence to sustain the charge of habitual drunkenness.[96] The seriousness
of alcoholism as a national problem and the complicated medical and emotional
disorders which it presents dramatize the fact that radical changes are needed in
procedures for handling the indigent alcoholic. The magistrates are completely un-
equipped to deal with the problem.[97]

Conviction of the Mentally or Physically Ill. The use of a vagrancy conviction as a
means of institutionalizing mentally ill persons was admitted to be illegal by magistrates interviewed but was defended as a necessary humanitarian service. The commitment of the physically ill is probably not intentional but is another by-product of
procedural laxity. This abuse of the criminal process is best illustrated by abstracts
from the medical records at the House of Correction:

A. G., vagrancy, 1/31/51. Had to be carried from the van by other
prisoners, immediately transferred to Philadelphia General Hospital,
where he died within 24 hours. The Medical Officer at Correction protested to the committing magistrate, who claimed that the defendant

[95] See note 150 *infra.* Compare this practice with Mass. Ann. Laws c. 272, § 46 (1933), § 45 (Supp.
1954) (§ 46 provides for release of drunks "upon recovery" on condition that person so released waives
any claim for damages which he might otherwise have had against arresting officer).

[96] See note 11 *supra.* See *Able v. State,* 62 So. 2d 239 (Ala. App. 1953), reversing a conviction as a
common drunkard where there was evidence of only six instances of drunkenness in a year, and imposing
as a test that sobriety must be the exception; compare the following definition from the Pennsylvania Mental
Health Act, Pa. Stat. Ann. tit. 50, § 1072 (Purdon Supp. 1954): "(7) 'Inebriate' shall mean a person who
is so habitually addicted to the use of alcoholic or other intoxicating or narcotic substances as to be unable or unwilling to stop the excessive use of such substances without help. The term shall include . . .
'habitual drunkard.' "

[97] For alternative provisions for dealing with alcoholics, see the Mental Health Act, *id.* § 1161(a)(3) (provision for voluntary admission of inebriate to mental institution); *id.* § 1201(a)(6) (petition for court
commitment). As the institution to which the patient is sent must approve, *id.* § 1203(e), and as institutional facilities are severely limited, the availability of this treatment is limited.

stood before him; the Medical Officer stated this would have been impossible.

H. Y., vagrancy, 2/5/51. Arrested at 4 P. M., he was taken to a hospital, treated for malnutrition, returned to the police station and committed the next morning. He arrived on a stretcher.

F. S., vagrancy, 2/14/51. The defendant was taken to Philadelphia General Hospital by police. At 5:30 A. M. the hospital called police asking them to take him back. He was placed under arrest at 6:10 A. M. for being at the hospital "contrary to law" and was committed that morning. Arriving on a stretcher in serious condition, he was immediately transferred 10 miles back to Philadelphia General Hospital.

J. M., habit. drunk., 4/24/51. Arrived on a stretcher in restraints, answered all questions with whistles, previous mental hospital history.

T. S., vagrancy, 4/26/51. On arrival at House of Correction, immediately transferred to Philadelphia General Hospital, diagnosis possible skull fracture.

H. B., habit. drunk., 5/26/51. Arrived in restraints.

A. K., habit. drunk., 5/28/51. Arrested at 9:30 P. M., at 2:30 A. M. taken to Philadelphia General Hospital, diagnosis alcoholism with suicidal intent. As no bed available, returned to station house, committed, arrived on stretcher.

S. G., vagrancy, 5/29/51. After trying to commit suicide in Reading Terminal, defendant taken by police to hospital, injury dressed, returned to station house and committed next morning. Immediately transferred to Philadelphia General Hospital because of loss of blood, suicidal tendencies.

F. M., habit. drunk., 6/28/51. Arrived on stretcher, semi-stuporous, died 7/1 in Philadelphia General Hospital.

Y. H., habit. drunk., 7/10/51. Arrived in restraints, suicide threats.

P. W., vagrancy, 7/15/51. Arrived on stretcher, immediately transferred to Philadelphia General Hospital in serious condition. In answer to protests, the magistrate admitted that the defendant, a Philadelphia resident, was in bad physical condition when before him, but stated that defendant's son was prosecutor and requested the commitment.

Similar cases were reported the following year during a study of the House of Correction by the National Probation and Parole Association, which observed that "it is unfortunate that so many psychotic or feebleminded inmates are held in the House of Correction for long periods." [98] These cases indicated attempts by the magistrates to find satisfactory solutions of problems for which they had neither the facilities nor the training to handle. The excuse that it was necessary to use a prison for cases of this kind because of the unavailability of other facilities may or may not

[98] Hiller & Rector, *Intake and Release Procedures in the House of Correction, Philadelphia, Pa.* 11 (Nat'l Probation & Parole Ass'n 1953) (mimeo).

have been valid.[99] Even if it was, it does not mitigate the fact that there was no justification for allowing a magistrate, untrained in medicine or law, to determine who should be committed in a summary, vagrancy-type criminal proceeding.

Jail for the Aged. An official at the House of Correction reported a case which typifies this problem. A private agency had been supporting a sixty-four year old alien who was ineligible for relief but wished to get him into the Home for the Indigent until he was eligible for old age assistance. One of the agency's social workers was told by a magistrate that this could be done if she would bring her client before him. When this was done, he was immediately convicted as a vagrant and sentenced to three months. This brought him within a stone's throw of his intended destination, as the House of Correction adjoins the Home for the Indigent on the same grounds; but the social worker was upset even though the magistrate assured her this was "the normal procedure." When the defendant found himself in a gloomy cell behind bars he became very agitated. A director's release and transfer to the Home for the Indigent were arranged. This is typical of the administrative rather than judicial correction of the more flagrant abuses. However, it leaves the defendant with a criminal record as a vagrant, which might have particularly serious consequences for an alien.

Other cases were observed in which daughters or wives of elderly men accused as habitual drunkards appeared to request commitment. The magistrates almost invariable complied and left the question of conviction up to the complainant. In some of these cases it appeared that this was the first time the defendant had ever appeared in court. Here again there may have been evidence which would have justified institutionalization in a home for the aged, but such evidence was not before the magistrates when they made their decisions. The result was a summary decision, based on one party's evidence without any social case work investigation of the circumstances, and a criminal conviction and prison confinement for a "crime" that at most was senility.[100]

Occasionally aged persons were picked up, convicted as vagrants and sent to the House of Correction where, for the first time, it was discovered that they had homes and that their relatives were engaged in a frantic search for them.[101]

Self-commitments. A few cases were observed in which a defendant walked into the police station of his own accord and asked the magistrate to send him up. Such defendants were committed as vagrants. One case at the House of Correction was also observed. As the writer arrived in the morning, the guards were trying to get rid of an inmate who had just been discharged but who was sitting on the sidewalk just outside the entrance. Three hours later he was still sitting, this time 100 yards further down the sidewalk. Two mornings later he was observed arriving in the police van with a three month sentence as a vagrant.

A number of inmates appeared to be of this type, and some had as many as seventy prior commitments to the House of Correction. They were totally unable to take care

---

[99] Compare the experience of Allegheny County, where the same necessity argument was advanced. When the County Board of Prison Inspectors ruled in October, 1953, that mental patients would no longer be accepted in jail, a temporary solution for the supposedly insoluble problem was found within two months. See Janavitz & Bozeman, *Allegheny County Tackles a Mental Health Problem*, Currents in Pennsylvania's *Health & Welfare*, 14, 16 (Pa. Citizen's Ass'n for Health & Welfare, Summer 1954).

[100] For similar cases, see Hiller & Rector, *op. cit. supra* note 98, cases number 2, 7, 9, 31 and 44.

[101] *Id.* case number 14, in which a resident of Atlantic City who owned his own home and had a $2,000 savings bank account was taken from a hospital to a magistrate who committed him as a vagrant at a time when his family was searching for him.

of themselves, and as they advanced in age, they were transferred to the Home for the Indigent.

Abating Nuisances. Disputes within the confines of the home between a landlady and her boarder, between husband and wife or father and daughter, men who refused to pay for meals in restaurants, a man arrested because he entered a restaurant from which he had previously been ejected with orders never to return—these are examples of "annoyance" cases which illustrate the variety of magisterial practice. Usually this type of defendant was charged with disorderly conduct, which carries a maximum penalty of only a $10 fine, or imprisonment up to 30 days in default of payment of the fine.[102] Convictions were observed in all the foregoing cases, although probably none of the convictions would stand up on appeal. Such defendants were punished for nuisances which the complainant, the police, the magistrate and probably many of the public all agree should be punishable.

The most unusual instance of a vagrancy-type conviction being used to abate a nuisance involved a defendant who was convicted as an habitual drunkard, although he was not drunk when arrested and claimed that he did not drink. According to an oral report given to the House of Correction by the social worker of a private agency, the real reason for his commitment was that he was "oversexed." He allegedly requested intercourse with his wife three or four times a night, and neighbors who had overheard his requests testified against him. The social worker reported that he was committed for habitual drunkenness because "the magistrate couldn't think of anything else. What could he do? He had to send him away, he couldn't leave him there with that poor girl."

Affronts to Police Dignity. A problem related to the administration of vagrancy-type laws concerns arrests and prosecutions, usually for disorderly conduct but occasionally for vagrancy, which arise from altercations between the defendant and the police. Depending upon the character of the defendant, these cases may or may not fall within the scope of this study.[103] Frequently disorderly conduct charges of this kind concerned "respectable" defendants; [104] but in a number of instances alleged hostility between a police officer and the defendant was the ground upon which a vagrancy-type arrest was made.

Examples include a defendant described as a "tough guy" who was involved in a run-in with a police captain in plain clothes. Another was a defendant whom police testimony described as "known to be a cop-fighter," who was sitting in a bar making uncomplimentary comments about the police in general. When a plainclothesman who was present told him to stop, he became abusive and police used force to overcome him. A defendant of Mexican ancestry was found guilty for the use of abusive language to an officer who had ordered him to move out of the bus terminal. The

---

[102] Pa. Stat. Ann. tit. 18, § 4406 (Purdon 1945).

[103] Many of the disorderly conduct cases observed are not reported in this study because they are irrelevant to the general problems of vagrancy-type law, *e.g.*, street fights, disturbances in taprooms, boisterous activity in public places. We are concerned with disorderly conduct, however, where it is applied as a vehicle for prosecuting vagrancy-type defendants or to punish by analogy conduct which is not specifically proscribed by statute but is objectionable to police or magistrates.

[104] *E.g.*, a case in which a defendant charged with disorderly conduct tore up a parking ticket in front of the officer who had just handed it to him and allegedly cursed the officer. *Compare Taylor v. Olschafsky*, 35 Delaware County Rep. 393, 395 (Delaware County, Pa., C.P. 1947) (upholding damages for false arrest where, in argument over traffic ticket, the officer "lost his head and, in a police officer, this is not good"), *with Commonwealth v. Savko*, 34 Erie County Rep. 77 (Erie County, Pa., Q.S. 1951) (upholding conviction of disorderly conduct on similar facts).

defendant moved only from one side of the terminal to the other and talked back. As the defendant spoke Spanish, the officer did not understand what he said, but he assumed the words were abusive and made the arrest.

V. PROBLEMS OF PROOF

In a recent case a Washington publisher found he had only 15¢ in his possession when his car stalled in Dover, Delaware. He went to the police station to phone his relatives for money, but while he was there his talk "just didn't ring right" to the police chief, "so we held him overnight on a vagrancy charge." The magistrate who heard the case next day said that the defendant "rambled" and "if he hadn't been so belligerent . . . he could have been released right away." So the defendant spent another twenty-four hours in jail until his relatives persuaded the magistrate that the defendant was in fact the respectable citizen he claimed to be. The magistrate explained, "We didn't want to let the man loose in society without being very sure of his background." [105]

This case epitomizes the manner in which the burden of proof was allocated in Philadelphia practice observed in this study. As a practical matter in many of the cases, the defendant is prima facie guilty, and the burden is placed upon him to give a satisfactory answer to the question, "What have you got to say for yourself?" Despite the "overriding presumption of innocence," [106] vagrancy statutes are so drafted that to a limited extent this magisterial practice can be justified under the law.

On its face the Pennsylvania vagrancy statute requires that five facts must be found before a valid conviction can be returned.[107] The defendant must

1. have come from outside the state, and
2. be found loitering or residing therein, and
3. follow no labor, trade, occupation or business, and
4. have no visible means of subsistence, and
5. be unable to give a reasonable account of himself or his business in the place where he is found.

The first two requirements raise no unusual procedural problems. On its face the third element would appear to be part of the proof which the prosecution must supply, but although the cases are often strangely silent on the point, the indication is that this element creates an implied burden on the defendant to prove that he has employment or has made efforts to obtain it. The fourth element also creates an implied presumption which must be rebutted by the defendant. Although the statute purports to say that, in combination with the other elements, lack of visible means of support is punishable,[108] this construction would lead to ridiculous results where the defendant, although apparently without means of support, in fact could prove that he had sufficient resources. It is clear from the cases that proof of no visible

---

[105] *Wilmington* (Del.) *Morning News*, June 21, 1955, p. 1, col. 3.

[106] *Morissette v. United States*, 342 U.S. 246, 275 (1952).

[107] Pa. Stat. Ann. tit. 18, § 2032 (IV) (Purdon 1945).

[108] An argument that the statute should be given this literal interpretation will be found in *Gentry v. Town of Booneville*, 199 Miss. 1, 5, 24 So. 2d 88, 89–90 (1945) (concurring opinion of Smith, C.J.).

means of subsistence merely creates a prima facie case which the defendant can rebut by showing actual lawful means of support.[109] The fifth element clearly places a burden on the defendant; once guilty appearances have been shown, he must rebut the prima facie case by giving a "reasonable account of himself." Thus once it has been shown that a person who has come from without the state has been found loitering, some burden must be assumed by the defendant if he is to show his innocence.

As there are no relevant Pennsylvania cases, an analysis of the nature of these burdens requires examination of analogous provisions in other jurisdictions. A few vagrancy statutes provide for the allocation of the burden of persuasion, such as a provision that proof of idleness and other appearances of guilt "shall constitute a prima facie presumption that such person is a vagrant, . . ." [110] or mean that "the burden of proof shall be upon the defendant to show that he has sufficient property from which to obtain a support, or sufficient means of maintaining a fair, honest, and reputable livelihood. . . ." [111] A showing of idleness may place upon the defendant the burden "to show reasonable efforts in good faith to secure employment, . . ." [112] and the legislative history of the District of Columbia vagrancy statute shows the congressional intent "that the burden shall be upon the defendant arrested under this legislation to show that he has a lawful employment or has lawful means of support realized from a lawful occupation or source." [113] Without such legislative aid the courts have reached the same result, that "the State has made out its case when these appearances of guilty violation are proven." [114]

A few courts have held that the "prima facie case" made out by such a showing of guilty appearances bursts in the face of uncontradicted rebuttal testimony, and that unless the state then proceeds with additional evidence, a conviction will be reversed.[115] But in most jurisdictions the burden upon the defendant is the burden of persuasion; [116] thus the jury "will not be bound to accept in satisfaction the unsupported statement of the accused although no witness is produced who is able to testify directly to the contrary—this because to hold otherwise would, in many cases, put it in the power of the accused, by his own unsupported assertions, to nullify the statute, and render it of no use." [117] The defendant's income, if not apparent, is "peculiarly within his knowledge and power to bring forward and establish. . . . If he had an employer he might have produced him, or fellow employees; if he had a bank account he might have produced his banker." [118] On this theory a District of

---

[109] See note 108 *supra*, and notes 108, 114, 115 *infra*.

[110] S.D. Code § 13.1424 (1939).

[111] Ala. Code Ann. tit. 14, § 439 (1940).

[112] Iowa Code § 746.2 (1950); see also Va. Code Ann. § 63-339 (1950).

[113] H.R. Rep. No. 1248, 77th Cong., 1st Sess. (1941).

[114] *Hutchins v. State*, 172 Tenn. 108, 112, 110 S.W.2d 319, 321 (1937).

[115] *Blakeley v. State*, 78 Ga. App. 516, 51 S.E.2d 598 (1949); *State v. Oldham*, 224 N.C. 415, 30 S.E.2d 318 (1944); *cf. State v. Hagen*, 130 S.W.2d 250, 252 (Mo. App. 1939); *People v. Sohn*, 269 N.Y. 330, 335, 199 N.E. 501, 503 (1936).

[116] See, *e.g.*, *Wallace v. State*, 16 Ala. App. 85, 75 So. 633 (1917); *Burns v. District of Columbia*, 34 A.2d 714 (D.C. Munic. App. 1943); *State v. Hall*, 25 N.J. Misc. 381 (Essex County Ct. Spec. Sess. 1947); *City of Greenville v. Ward*, 94 S.C. 321, 77 S.E. 1021 (1913).

[117] *Gentry v. Town of Boonville*, 199 Miss. 1, 5, 24 So. 2d 88, 89 (1945).

[118] *Hutchins v. State*, 172 Tenn. 108, 111, 110 S.W.2d 319, 321 (1937).

Columbia pickpocket-vagrancy conviction was sustained although the defendant gave a plausible and unrebutted explanation of the $65 found on his person.[119]

The burden of rebuttal which the courts have thus placed upon the defendant is magnified by the vagueness of the statutory elements. If the defendant wishes to show that he has "visible means of support," and thereby challenge the basic fact on which rests the presumption of no actual means of support, he will find no guidance in Pennsylvania and little in other jurisdictions. Some courts state, without elaboration, that this is "a term well understood" and with "a definite and fixed meaning." [120] Others have stated that, although "difficult of precise definition or measurement," [121] its "long usage" has "fixed" its significance and directed it against the man "who hangs about streets and public places without . . . visible means of support. . . ." [122] Under the parent British law a penny in the pocket may be sufficient; [123] thus when a woman arrested for vagrancy was found on examination to possess 9 shillings 6 pence, the magistrate "had no option but to discharge her." [124] In this country the few decisions range from those following the British rule to cases excluding as irrelevant evidence the fact that the defendant had money on his person at the time of arrest.[125] It is unknown what the law is on this point in Pennsylvania; [126] in the few cases which were observed where the police records showed that the defendant had a considerable sum of money on his person when arrested, the problem was resolved by convicting the defendant so rapidly that he had no chance to raise the defense.

The Pennsylvania statute makes one element of the crime the fact that the accused has no employment. Suppose he is physically unfit or is unemployed and cannot find a job? It has been suggested that "he may be convicted and imprisoned, whether such condition is his misfortune or his fault." [127] Such an interpretation of the statute would unquestionably be rejected today, and it would be a good defense if the defendant could show "good faith" or "due diligence" or "reasonable effort" to obtain employment.[128] We have already seen that the defendant's unsupported testimony may not be credited by the trier of fact and thus may not be sufficient to rebut the prima facie evidence. Must he produce copies of his employment applications or bring into court to testify on his behalf the men who have refused to employ

---

[119] Burns v. District of Columbia, 34 A.2d 714 (D.C. Munic. App. 1943).

[120] Ex parte Taft, 284 Mo. 531, 544, 225 S.W. 457, 461 (1920).

[121] People v. Johnaken, 196 Misc. 1059, 1061, 94 N.Y.2d 102, 104 (New Rochelle City Ct. 1950).

[122] People v. Sohn, 269 N.Y. 330, 334–35, 199 N.E. 501, 502 (1936).

[123] Departmental Committee on Vagrancy, Report (London 1906).

[124] See 95 Just. P. 267 (1931).

[125] Branch v. State, 73 Tex. Crim. 471, 165 S.W. 605 (1914). Money in the pocket may be regarded as no proof because of the "danger" that vagrants will carry money as a subterfuge to avoid arrest. People v. Cramer, 139 Misc. 545, 547, 247 N.Y. Supp. 821, 824 (N.Y. City Ct. Spec. Sess. 1930).

[126] Similarly if the defendant wishes to rebut the presumed fact by showing that he has actual means of support, there is no case authority to guide the courts in determining what amount of money is required. One court has required that a defendant have enough "to support himself reasonably." People v. Cramer, supra note 125, at 825. To the obvious questions, "for how long, and by what standard of living?" there is no answer.

[127] In the Matter of Forbes, 11 Abb. Prac. 52, 55 (N.Y. Sup. Ct. 1860).

[128] Cf. Ex parte Taft, 284 Mo. 531, 545, 225 S.W. 457, 461 (1920), where the ordinance in question required one charged with vagrancy to show "reasonable effort and in good faith" to secure work to rebut a prima facie case. The court held that this was too vague because "each trial tribunal would be making its own ordinance" as to what "amounted to 'reasonable effort.'"

him? An early English statute made it a violation if a man refused an offer to work "for meate and drynke" alone if nothing better could be obtained.[129] American statutes imply that if the basic fact of idleness is to be rebutted, a defendant must not refuse any offer of work, no matter what the wages, working conditions or choice of employment.[130]

The vagueness of the statutory elements and the difficulties of making the rebuttals which the courts have required raise serious constitutional problems which are beyond the scope of this article.[131] At the practical level in Philadelphia, it is clear that most defendants could not possibly meet such a burden of rebuttal. Although a statute applicable to Philadelphia requires that "all persons arrested shall be given the opportunity to communicate promptly with, be interviewed or examined by, such persons as they desire . . . ,"[132] some defendants alleged that they were denied this right following their arrest, and such denials may be common.[133] Even if unrestricted access to the telephone were provided, it would be difficult for a man arrested during the night to marshal the witnesses he needs to carry his burden of proof and have them assembled ready to testify when court convenes at 9 a.m.

Frequently defendants were not permitted to make any rebuttal, being cut off with some such remark as "nothing you say will help," or if rebuttal was permitted, the magistrate indicated that he had already prejudged the case, making remarks such as these:

> "You're a bum. Well, what have you got to say for yourself?"
> "What do you do for a living? Steal a little here and a little there?"

In one case a defendant was charged with disorderly conduct. The complaining witnesses were his ex-girl-friend and her sister, who alleged that he had annoyed them and created a disorderly scene in their home. After an impassioned descrip-

---

[129] 1 Edw. 6, c. 3 (1547).

[130] The only exceptions found are Kan. Gen. Stat. Ann. § 21-2409 (1949) (violation to refuse to work only "when work at fair wages is to be procured in the community"), and Va. Code Ann. § 63-338(2) (1949) (punishes only those who "refuse to work for the usual and common wages given to other laborers in like work in the place where they then are").

[131] In *Mobile, J. & K.C.R.R. v. Turnipseed*, 219 U.S. 35, 43 (1910), the only requirement was that there be "some" rational connection between the fact proved and ultimate fact presumed. But *Turnipseed* was a civil case, and it is doubtful if that rule is correct for criminal cases. It was not even applied in the peonage cases, *Bailey v. Alabama*, 219 U.S. 219 (1911), and *Taylor v. Georgia*, 315 U.S. 25 (1942), and in other cases where the Court purported to find an insufficient rational connection it appears that other factors actually motivated the decisions, *e.g.*, unfairness to the defendant in *Manley v. Georgia*, 279 U.S. 1 (1929), and *Tot v. United States*, 319 U.S. 463 (1943). More useful is Justice Cardozo's examination of the basic fact to see if it carries "a hint of criminality." "For a transfer of the burden, experience must teach that the evidence held to be inculpatory has at least a sinister significance." *Morrison v. California*, 291 U.S. 82, 90 (1934). This test was the one applied in that case and the peonage cases, and is implied in *Casey v. United States*, 276 U.S. 413 (1928) (proof that defendant had possession of narcotics creates immediate suspicion of criminality and presumption therefore valid); *Yee Hem v. United States*, 268 U.S. 178 (1925) (same as to opium); and in the cases cited and distinguished in *Tot v. United States, supra*. By this standard the presumptions implicit in a vagrancy prosecution would fall. "The mere state of being without funds is a neutral fact—constitutionally an irrelevance, like race, creed, or color." *Edwards v. California*, 314 U.S. 160, 185 (1941) (concurring opinion of Jackson, J.). This reasoning would apply to the vagrancy presumptions with even more force, for the basic fact which the state must prove is merely that the defendant *apparently* has no job and means of livelihood.

[132] Pa. Stat. Ann. tit. 42, § 1113 (Purdon Supp. 1954).

[133] See also Note, *Compelling Appearance in Court: Administration of Bail in Philadelphia*, 102 U. Pa. L. Rev. 1031, 1054–55 (1954).

tion of these activities, one of the girls stated that this sort of thing could not go on much longer.

> "Well, you won't have to worry about it for the next three months," said the magistrate. He turned to the defendant for the first time and said, in rapid-fire succession: "Well, what have you got to say for yourself? Why did you do it? Three months in the House of Correction."

On the evidence presented, this defendant probably had a valid defense to the charge of disorderly conduct for which he was ostensibly on trial, *i.e.*, that the disturbance alleged against him was not in public. But as the sentence imposed upon him was greatly in excess of the maximum for disorderly conduct, it is apparent that he was convicted of either habitual drunkenness or vagrancy, although there was no evidence relating to either charge.

VI. SUMMARY PROCEDURE

Like the substantive law, the practice of making vagrancy summarily triable before a magistrate originated early in the fifteenth century in the aftermath of the Black Death and feudalism.[134] This procedure was carried over to the colonies, and, by mechanical application of the rule that limited jury trial to cases for which it existed when the constitution was adopted, it was held that vagrancy-type offenses were summarily triable.[135] Yet a magistrate in a vagrancy case can impose up to one year's imprisonment for the first offense and two years for certain repeaters. In no other category of criminality does Pennsylvania impose so severe a sanction without the right to trial by jury. Some offenses classified as misdemeanors have a lesser sanction than vagrancy,[136] and all other Pennsylvania summary offenses provide for imprisonment only in default of payment of a fine, and then only for 30 days or less.[137]

This denial of jury trial has been rationalized on the grounds that it saves expense to the state and benefits the defendant by avoiding oppressive delay.[138] It is maintained that the defendant is not deprived of any substantial rights, because the summary proceeding must still satisfy due process requirements of a fair hearing.[139] Beyond this, because it is in derogation of the right to jury trial, English writers have taken a "strict view" of summary procedure,[140] a view applied in Pennsylvania.[141] At its minimum the fair hearing required would include the opportunity for the de-

---

[134] 2 Hen. 5, c. 4 (1414).

[135] *Byers & Davis v. Commonwealth,* 42 Pa. 89 (1862).

[136] See Pa. Stat. Ann. tit. 18, § 4511 (Purdon 1945) (keeping disorderly house), *id.* § 4512 (prostitution), *id.* § 4519 (public indecency) and *id.* § 4524 (obscene literature) for offenses classified as misdemeanors with trial by jury but with a maximum penalty of one year, less than vagrancy.

[137] *E.g., id.* § 4406 (disorderly conduct, $10 or 30 days in default); *id.* § 4699.4 (worldly employment on Sunday, $4 or 6 days in default).

[138] *State v. Glenn,* 54 Md. 572, 605 (1880); 4 Stephen, *Commentaries on the Laws of England,* 265 (15th ed. 1908) (summary procedure is "designed for the greater ease of the subject, by doing the offender speedy justice, and by not harassing jurymen with frequent attendances to try every minute offence").

[139] See, *e.g., Palko v. Connecticut,* 302 U.S. 319, 327 (1937): "The hearing, moreover, must be a real one, not a sham."

[140] *E.g.,* 4 Blackstone, *Commentaries* °280–81.

[141] *Commonwealth v. Borden,* 61 Pa. 272 (1869).

fendant to know and plead to the charge against him, that the case against him be by competent evidence, that he have adequate opportunity to make a defense and that there be a record made so that judicial review is possible.[142]

The failure to meet these requirements in all observed cases would suggest that, while undue delay may be oppressive, a procedure that moves so rapidly that a defendant cannot prepare a defense is perhaps even worse. The following conclusions about the way in which summary procedure was administered in the observed cases shows how Philadelphia practice in vagrancy-type prosecutions deprived defendants of the most elementary requirements of a fair hearing.

> **1.** Defendants were rarely informed of the charge against them until the "trial" was completed, and in only one or two instances were they asked to plead guilty or not guilty.
>
> **2.** There was no pretense of proving the crime charged with competent evidence and, with only one exception,[143] there were no competent witnesses for the prosecution. Usually the only testimony was the hearsay statement of a police officer not present at the arrest, who reported to the magistrate what the police records said about the case. Even this was dispensed with in many cases.
>
> The proof in most cases consisted of the mere exhibition of a "bum," with the result that there should have been an acquittal in almost every case. Thus there was no evidence of habitualness in any habitual drunkenness prosecution observed, unless the magistrate's unsubstantiated memory and/or opinion or a policeman's unsworn comments be so considered; and in many vagrancy cases, despite undisputed testimony that the defendants were Pennsylvania residents, convictions were found under a statute that applies only to those who come from "without this Commonwealth."
>
> This suggests that perhaps the primary importance of the right to a jury trial is that it militates, to some degree, against sham hearings.
>
> **3.** Defendants were uncounselled and unaided. While lawyers appeared in a few disorderly conduct cases, in not one observed vagrancy or habitual drunkenness prosecution was the defendant represented by counsel. The Voluntary Defender was not present; and the District Attorney plays no part in these prosecutions.
>
> **4.** All other irregularities were accentuated by the speed of judicial process, referring both to the rapidity with which the "trials" themselves are dispatched [144] and the short interval between arrest and final disposition. A man arrested during the night had usually been tried, convicted and was en route to the House of Correction by eleven

---

[142] For other Pennsylvania citations see, Binns, *Justice* 883–87 (12th ed. 1928). Compare *State v. Labato*, 7 N.J. 137, 150–51, 80 A.2d 617, 623 (1951), to the effect that vagrancy-like crimes are "minor offenses denounced by statute below the grade of misdemeanors, and therefore punishable in a summary manner, yet *quasi*-criminal in essence and subject to the procedural rules governing criminal prosecutions."

[143] In this case, a defendant was apparently charged with panhandling, and although his examination showed him to be within the broad magisterial definition of vagrancy, the particular magistrate sitting that day discharged him because the prosecution witness failed to appear. This was the only vagrancy case observed in which there was any reference to prosecution witnesses.

[144] See text at pp. 269–299 *supra*. One magistrate has described sitting over a weekend and disposing of 66 prisoners in 3 hours on Saturday and 100 in 4 hours on Sunday. Gilbert, *Our Magistrate's Courts*, 6 The Shingle, 68, 71 (1943).

in the morning. We have noted that this minimizes the opportunity to retain a lawyer, contact friends or prepare a defense, even assuming defendants are allowed to contact anyone.

5. No records were kept which are available to magistrates at time of trial to show prior convictions, although the frequency of intoxication arrests is obviously a relevant factor in a determination of whether a defendant is an habitual drunkard. Further, the House of Correction Act rigidly conditions the sentence which a magistrate can lawfully impose upon the number of prior commitments,[145] but this requirement is ignored. At least one magistrate seemed to feel no need for such records, on numerous occasions telling defendants: "All right, don't let me see you here again. I never forget a face. I may not remember your name, but I never forget a face."

6. In the overwhelming majority of cases, the magistrate's court is also in practice the court of last resort. The careful provisions for appeal, certiorari and habeas corpus,[146] which on the statute books look so fair, are almost a dead letter as far as these defendants are concerned.[147] Thus there is given "to the magistrate in [vagrancy law] . . . an almost unchecked opportunity for arbitrary oppression or careless cruelty." [148] The few figures available in other jurisdictions show a similar rarity of appeal.[149]

7. Summary procedure suffers from the absence of the pretrial procedure, which in felony or misdemeanor cases operates to weed out defendants who are innocent or against whom there is insufficient evidence. Such defendants pass through numerous checks: preliminary examination, indictment or information, and preparation of the case leading, perhaps, to a nolle prosequi. All these involve correctives for police errors or abuse, and many cases in practice are dropped at these various levels. The only pretrial procedure in a vagrancy-type case is that of the police house sergeant, who, in perhaps 10 per cent of the drunk arrests, releases the defendant without any appearance before a magistrate.[150] Thus the presumption of innocence has much more

---

[145] Pa. Stat. Ann. tit. 61, § 681 (Purdon 1930).

[146] For discussion of these three methods and the distinctions between them in Philadelphia practice, see Crimes Survey Comm. of the Law Ass'n of Philadelphia, Report 302-09 (1926). All of these methods of review require allowance by the reviewing court, and there is no appeal as of right.

[147] The magistrate who in 1951 was handling the largest number of vagrancy cases informed the writer at that time that he could recall "only two appeals in the last six years." At the same time, the clerk of the Philadelphia Quarter Sessions Court could not recall a single vagrancy appeal.

[148] In the Matter of Forbes, 11 Abb. Prac. 52, 55 (N.Y. Sup. Ct. 1860).

[149] A few studies show less than 1% appeals. See Note, 59 Yale L.J. 1351, 1357 n.21 (1950). Appeal figures for New York City were found for two years, and showed that for vagrancy other than prostitution in 1930 and 1931, there were 3,359 convictions and 1 appeal. City Magistrate's Courts, New York City, Ann. Rep. 20, 56 (1930); id. at 38 (1931).

[150] Under this procedure, when persons whom the police described as respectable were arrested for drunkenness, they were permitted to telephone relatives to come get them. Form 80 of the police department was executed, as follows: "I, ... do hereby accept the responsibility of safely escorting to his home . . . . who has been taken into custody on . . . . at . . . . for his own protection because of intoxication. My relation to him is . . . ." In the 6th Police District in June, 1951, out of 850 drunkenness arrests, there were 81 discharges on Form 80. This practice is probably illegal. See Note, 59 Yale L.J. 1351, 1359 n.28 (1950); Doherty v. Shea, 320 Mass. 173, 68 N.E.2d 707 (1946). But the form might be construed as a waiver of any claims for damages for false imprisonment. Cf. Mass. Ann. Laws c. 272, §§ 45–46 (Supp. 1954).

probative validity in a magistrate's court because of the absence of pretrial discretion, but, paradoxically, it is given much less weight than in the Court of Quarter Sessions.

8. The background and lack of legal training of most of the magistrates is an important factor. As no other lawyers participate in the proceedings, a magistrate who himself is probably untrained in law must administer technically difficult vagrancy laws. This is not the place to assess the magisterial system as a whole, or to review the arguments for and against a lay judiciary.[151] The principal reason advanced for having "local community courts" presided over by a lay judiciary is that this will prevent the development of "a legal formalism." [152] Whether or not such informality is desirable in minor civil controversies,[153] it is precisely the lack of any "legal formalism" which is the primary cause of much of the abuse in vagrancy-type cases. Informality is a dubious goal for proceedings whose outcome may be a sentence of imprisonment of up to two years.

9. As has been noted, the magistrate is crippled by the lack of any of the treatment tools developed by modern criminology. He cannot grant a suspended sentence which includes supervised probation, or commit the obviously ill to a medical institution, or obtain any of the information essential to intelligent disposition of the cases. There is neither the time nor the facilities for obtaining pre-sentence reports or checking with other social agencies for information about the defendants. One woman defendant found walking the streets stated that she had no family and no friends in Philadelphia and lived in rooming houses with temporary work as a typist. She appeared to be mentally ill, and the magistrate was obviously trying to make a more constructive disposition of her case than sentencing her to the House of Correction. He finally discharged her and sent her to the YWCA in a cab, but he had no means of insuring that she would get attention or even that she would go there. A complete gulf separates the magistrates' courts from constructive welfare and treatment facilities.

The explanation of the tolerance by bar and public of such abuse of elementary procedural rights is rooted in one fact: most of the defendants are drawn from skid row—drunks, idlers, loungers, suspected petty criminals, beggars, bench-sleepers. Perhaps most are chronic alcoholics, often incapable of aiding themselves, and many

[151] Compare Ervin, The Magistrates' Courts of Philadelphia, 108–15 (1931) (stressing the necessity of legal training for the discharge of magisterial duties), with Commission Appointed at the Recommendation of the Special Grand Jury of 1935 to Study and Recommend Improvements in the Laws Relating to Magistrates and Magistrates' Courts in the City of Philadelphia, Report. The Commission supported the concept of "local community courts" and rejected proposals which would have required that magistrates be members of the bar. The reasoning of the Commission was directed wholly at civil suitors who "have no clear conception of the legal aspects of their problems. . . . Their need is less for a determination of their technical legal rights, than for a wise adjustment of their difficulties with their neighbors and others."

[152] Ibid.

[153] No study has ever been made examining magisterial practices in their civil jurisdiction, and how the Commission, supra note 151, was able to reach the conclusions it did in the absence of such evidence is not clear from its report. It would certainly seem to be no solution for the problem of untrained and unrepresented litigants to provide that the judge shall be untrained as well. For a study revealing magisterial inadequacy and abuse in another aspect of their jurisdiction—admission to bail, see Note, Compelling Appearance in Court: Administration of Bail in Philadelphia, 102 U. Pa. L. Rev. 1031, 1036–46 (1954).

are transients in a strange city. Economically most are at or near the level of poverty. Many persons interviewed during this study summed up this attitude and explained their lack of concern with what the police and magistrates do by the label they attached to the entire group: "Bums."

VII. CONCLUSION

Some of the abuses which have been outlined can be met by reforms such as (1) extension of the Voluntary Defender system to the magistrates' courts, which would not only provide legal aid where it is urgently needed but would result in an immediate raising of the level of procedural fairness in vagrancy-type proceedings; (2) transfer of jurisdiction over vagrancy-type offenses to the Municipal Court to achieve essential centralization in the handling of the cases and to provide the necessary probation, social service and psychiatric diagnostic and treatment services; (3) development and utilization of other treatment possibilities for indigent alcoholics, with commitment to the House of Correction reserved for use only as a last resort if no other treatment program can be developed.

Beyond such immediate procedural and treatment reforms, however, is the need for re-examination of the whole vagrancy policy of our law. Little can be said in support of the use of vagrancy-type statutes to repress alcoholism, for the recidivism of the confirmed "habitual drunkard" shows that short prison sentences are wholly ineffective as a means of treating what is essentially a medical problem.[154] Nor is there any legal or policy justification for imprisoning people because their poverty or characterization as "bums" makes them vaguely undesirable. The use of vagrancy sanctions to deter such persons from entering Philadelphia and to banish them if they do come is unconstitutional and indefensible. The only reason such administration is tolerated is because the defendants involved are too poor or too weak to assert their obvious rights.

If vagrancy-law administration in Philadelphia involves any socially desirable policy, therefore, it is because its flexibility gives the police a residual discretionary power to control suspicious persons or harass suspected professional criminals. This is an illusory advantage, for the substitution of harassment for the more difficult job of obtaining the evidence necessary to convict criminals of the substantive offenses of which they are guilty encourages superficial and inefficient police work.[155] If the

---

[154] An example of the recidivism is given at p. 312 *supra*. Of 5166 inmates committed to the House of Correction in 1950, 40% had prior commitments to that institution; 6.3% had more than ten prior commitments; and 1.4% more than 30 commitments. Philadelphia House of Correction, Ann. Rep. 50 (1950). Of the cases studied by Hiller & Rector, *op. cit. supra* note 98, many involved repeated recidivism. Compare the report on a 51 year old Seattle alcoholic, who in a 25 year period was arrested 223 times and spent 11 years and 143 days in Seattle City Jail on short sentences for drunkenness. *Seattle Times*, Oct. 17, 1946, p. 10, col. 1. See also *New York Times*, Jan. 26, 1953, p. 14, col. 1 (Brooklyn man arrested 103 times for intoxication and vagrancy since 1925). The cost of such treatment is staggering. In Philadelphia County alone, 1430 vagrants and 1645 habitual drunkards were committed in 1950, at a cost of over $400,000 for House of Correction maintenance alone. Figures compiled from Philadelphia House of Correction, Ann. Rep. (1950), on the basis of an average stay of 58 days per inmate at $2.34 a day. To this must be added the combined value of police services diverted from more important tasks to handle this multitude of cases.

[155] "The underlying purpose [of public enemy vagrancy laws] is to relieve the police of the necessity of proving that criminals have committed or are planning to commit specific crimes." N.Y. Law Revision Commission, Report 591 (1935).

suspect is actually a professional criminal, harassment with a three months vagrancy sentence serves neither the incapacitative nor the deterrent end of the criminal law.[156] At most it may drive a few criminals into another jurisdiction without any net improvement in the control of crime. If the defendant is suspected merely because of his past criminal record, vagrancy-type harassment, like criminal registration ordinances,[157] impedes the rehabilitative end of the criminal law by closing "the doors to reformation, repentance or a new try at life." [158] In fact vagrancy laws of the Pennsylvania type can never be an effective harassment device, for their utility depends upon illegal administration, and the illegality means that any professional criminal with funds at his disposal can gain a speedy release by retaining an attorney to bring habeas corpus.[159] Thus only the paupers and the helpless can be harassed with vagrancy-type commitments to the House of Correction.

Nor is harassment either a necessary or a desirable method of deterring professional criminality. Probationary control over a defendant who has once been convicted offers a more equitable and effective means of supervising persons suspect because of past criminality. Requiring such a probationer to report on his employment, his income and his net worth at periodic intervals would be a far more efficient deterrent against a return to criminality than to permit the police to arrest him at will for consorting or other vaguely suspicious activities.

One cannot escape the conclusion that the administration of vagrancy-type laws serves as an escape hatch to avoid the rigidity imposed by real or imagined defects in criminal law and procedure. To the extent that such rigidity presents a real problem and that the need for a safety valve is not merely the product of inefficiency on the part of police or prosecutors, such a problem should not be dealt with by indirection. If it is necessary to ease the prosecution's burden of proof or to legalize arrests for mere suspicion, then the grave policy and constitutional problems posed by such suggestions should be faced. If present restrictions on the laws of attempts or arrest place too onerous a burden upon the police because of the nature of modern crime, then such propositions should be discussed and resolved on their merits, as, for example, the proposals in the Uniform Arrest Act.[160]

The economic purposes which once gave vagrancy a function no longer exist, and the philosophy and practices of welfare agencies have so changed relief methods that a criminal sanction to enforce an Elizabethan poor law concept is outdated. To try to utilize a feudal statute as a weapon against modern crime and as a means of liberalizing the restrictions of criminal law and procedure is both inefficient

---

[156] Under an Illinois reputation-vagrancy law, "we have harassed and convicted otherwise immune gangsters, kidnapers, gunmen, thugs and racketeers in the persons of Maxie Eisen, 'Machine Gunner' Jack McGurn, 'King of the Bomb Throwers' James Belcastro, 'Two Gun' Louie Alterie, and numerous mad dogs of the west side. . . ." Testimony of Thomas A. Green, in *Hearings, supra* note 88, at 307. This campaign was short-lived, however, as the statute was declared unconstitutional. *People v. Belcastro*, 356 Ill. 144, 190 N.E. 301 (1934). As the maximum penalty was six months, it seems doubtful that such a conviction is much of a solution to the problem posed by a man called "King of the Bomb Throwers."

[157] See Note, *Criminal Registration Ordinances: Police Control of Potential Recidivists*, 103 U. Pa. L. Rev. 60 (1954).

[158] *People v. Pieri*, 269 N.Y. 315, 327, 199 N.E. 495, 499 (1936).

[159] An example was revealed during the hearings of the Kefauver Committee in which Samuel Hoffman, a Philadelphian with a long criminal record, was arrested as he got off the train at 30th Street Station and immediately sentenced to a year as a vagrant. He retained an attorney and was promptly released on habeas corpus. *Philadelphia Evening Bulletin*, March 6, 1951, p. 31, col. 7.

[160] Warner, *The Uniform Arrest Act*, 28 Va. L. Rev. 315, 343–47 (1942).

and an invitation to the kind of abuses which this study has shown to be widespread.

It was to avoid just such abuses that the restrictions of our criminal procedure were developed. If the administrative flexibility gained by the circumvention of that procedure in vagrancy-type cases has resulted in a return of those abuses, perhaps that more than anything else demonstrates the wisdom of our traditional procedural protections.

18. The Law in a Rural Setting

Harry M. Caudill

In her checkered history Kentucky has had four written Constitutions. Beginning with the first in 1792 they were extremely democratic documents, vesting in the voters the power to elect almost every man who governs them or has charge of public affairs. The present Constitution, written in 1890, attempted to preserve undiluted the rough frontier equality whose character had been stamped on the state's people a century before. First of all the Constitutional Convention undertook to reserve all real power at the local level. A host of county and city elective officers was established. In a six-year interval the people in a typical plateau county choose the following officials: the state senator, state representative, circuit judge, Circuit Court clerk, Commonwealth attorney, County Court clerk, county judge, county attorney, tax commissioner, sheriff, coroner, eight justices of the peace, eight constables and five members of the Board of Education. In addition the people in each municipality elect a mayor, a police judge, five or six members of the Common Council, and, in some towns, a city attorney and marshal.

At the state level they elect a governor, lieutenant-governor, secretary of state, auditor of public accounts, treasurer, commissioner of agriculture, attorney-general and seven judges of the Court of Appeals. Most ridiculous of all they elect a clerk of the Court of Appeals. This official keeps a record of the proceedings of the state's highest court and has to earn his modest salary by electioneering among three million people in forty thousand square miles of territory.

But the state officials are a façade. The real power of government is at the base. Except for the judicial officers all this great host of local servants are paid by fees. The amount of their compensation is dependent upon their ability to collect charges from the general public. The state officials lack power to remove any of these "fee grabbers" other than the sheriffs, and there is no practical means by which malfeasance at the local level can be punished. To all intents and purposes the governor is little more than a presiding county judge. His ability to lead depends upon his capacity to persuade, because once a governor has fallen into the disfavor of the courthouse cliques his days are numbered. Dealing with a faceless multitude of county-centered and often illiterate voters, the county officials can propagandize endlessly to the detriment of a state administration, assuring its political doom regard-

SOURCE: *Night Comes to the Cumberlands,* Boston: Little, Brown and Company, 1962. By permission of the publisher.

less of the worthiness of the governor's aims. The courthouses are one hundred and twenty anchors which perpetually hold developments to the political center of the stream at a virtual standstill. At the bottom of this courthouse conservatism is a relentless determination to prevent any change that might replace fees with salaries or dilute the powers of local offices.

And what is the role of the public servant who holds office in such a setting? What kind of people knock at his door and what standards of public service do they demand of him? By what creed do they expect him to serve the holy principles of Liberty and Justice? In this most democratic of all states, how does Democracy fare?

The office of the county judge is the nerve center of the courthouse. In addition to being a judicial official charged with the trial of misdemeanors and minor civil actions, His Honor is the chief executive officer of the county. He presides over the fiscal court, directs the spending of county funds and is generally the chief "contact man" with Frankfort in political matters pertaining to the county.

His office consists of two dingy rooms. The long unpainted walls are peeling and paint hangs in scales from the ceiling. The rays of the sun struggle with small success to pierce the dirty, rain-streaked windowpanes. In the corner of the outer room a tobacco-stained cardboard box serves as a waste can.

The outer room contains the desk of his secretary and a half-dozen chairs are lined up along the walls. No matter how harassed she may be by the constant procession of callers, his secretary never fails to smile ingratiatingly—because even the smallest frown may offend a voter. From 8:30 in the morning when the office opens until 4:30 when the doors are locked, there is seldom a moment when a group of people are not waiting to "see the judge."

A day spent with the county judge in such an office in a plateau county is a revealing experience. It tells a story of the breakdown of Democracy and of the growing dependence and futility of the population. If Democracy is to eventually prevail over totalitarian ideologies the individual citizen must be able to shoulder a multitude of responsibilities and to discharge them out of a sense of duty. To do this he must possess the ability to meet social and economic problems and the willingness to grasp them. Until a generation ago the mountaineer was accustomed to "turn out" for road workings and other undertakings for community betterment. He was not paid and he did not expect to be. His willingness to work on roads and other essential projects was a holdover from the frontier where no government or government largesse existed. However, as government expanded and its benefits multiplied the old sturdiness began to dissolve. Though many frontier modes and outlooks survive and are sharply impressive, the traumas of fifty years have left a lasting imprint on the character of the mountaineer. His forefathers lived by the frontier maxim "root hog or die." They would be astounded if they could return in the spirit to behold their descendants thronging the office of the county judge to implore his assistance in a multitude of situations which, in an earlier time, would have been met by the citizens without its once occurring to them that help from any quarter was either possible or desirable.

A moment after the judge unlocked the door to his office an elderly woman darted in behind him. The judge greeted her with an affable smile and after a moment of smalltalk about her family and community, he inquired her business. She drew a paper from her purse and displayed it to him. On it was scrawled in longhand: *"We the undersigned persons have contributed to help _____ who is sick and has to stay at home."* Below this caption four or five courthouse officeholders and county-seat merchants had written their names. Each of them had noted his contribution of $1.00 to the sufferer. The old lady explained that her son had a family and had been sick for a long time. "The doctors," she said, "can't find out what's the matter with him, and, as fer me, I'm almost certain it's cancer. You know, judge, how we've always voted fer you every time you ever run for anything and will again just as shore as you run. If you can help him out now when he's having such bad luck, we shore will appreciate it."

The judge sighed ruefully, because such pleas are routine, but he added his name to the list and handed the woman a dollar bill.

A moment later the secretary arrived and callers began to fill the chairs in the waiting room. Some said they had just dropped by to shake hands with the judge and had no business in particular, but three very determined gentlemen were ushered into his office. Dressed in mud-spattered overalls, they lived on a creek some eleven miles from the county seat. The state had built a rural highway into the community in 1949 and later hard-surfaced it. But long neglect had allowed the road to deteriorate badly. The spokesman for the group, a tall, raw-boned mountaineer, told their story:

"Judge, you know what kind of a shape our road is in and that it's prac'ly impossible to travel it. The ditch lines are all stopped up and there are holes all over it big enough to set a washtub in. One feller broke an axle right in the middle of the road last week. Now you know our precinct has always been one of the best in the county and you never come up there electioneering in your life that you didn't get a big vote, but if you can't do something for us now we'll sure as hell remember it if you ever run for anything else again. We ain't got no governor or he wouldn't let the roads get in the shape they're in now. We've just got to have the ditch lines cleaned out and the holes filled up."

The judge attempted to mollify his angry visitors, for this was not their first visit to his office on the same business. He pointed out very courteously, however, that funds were short and that a new coat of surfacing was out of the question. He promised to send a scraper to clean out the drainage ditches, and pledged an application of gravel for the worst places in the road. He warned them, however, "The roads all over this county are going to pieces, and we simply don't have the money to keep them up. We are doing everything in our power to maintain the roads, but we just don't have the money to do a decent job."

Somewhat mollified, the men departed—but not before dropping another threat of retribution at the polls if some effective relief did not ensue.

As they left, the county attorney rapped on the door and then entered the judge's private office. The Grand Jury had adjourned the day before and, as their predecessors had done for a good many years, the jurors had blasted the county officials for allowing the courthouse and jail to fall into filthy ruin. In a report to the circuit judge they declared that they had inspected the jail and found that structure wholly "unfit for human occupancy." The walls were cracked and broken, the roof leaked and the cells were inadequately heated. The commodes were without seats and the coal-black mattresses were without sheets. The entire facility reeked of excrement, urine and sweat. They recommended that the jail be closed and not reopened until completely renovated. They found the courthouse in almost equally foul condition, and said so in scathing terms.

The judge and the county attorney went over the report together line by line and agreed with the sentiments expressed in it. The county attorney remarked that it was a good report. "They would have been a lot more helpful, though," he said, "if they had told us where to get the money to do something about it." The judge reminded him that in several mountain counties the question of a bond issue for the construction of a new jail and courthouse had been referred to the people and sternly rejected at the polls. The county attorney opined, "If the same issue was placed on the ballot in this county you wouldn't get three votes for it out of that grand jury panel."

While he and the judge talked, proof of the jury's criticism was manifested by a vile stench which crept into the office from the public toilet in the basement of the courthouse.

When the county attorney was gone one of the county's justices of the peace brought his son-in-law to meet the judge. The justice pointed out that the fiscal court would soon have to add another man to the county road crew, and that his son-in-law desperately needed the job. The judge and justice were political allies, and His Honor agreed that the jobless son-in-law was ideally suited for the position. When this happy accord had been reached his secretary informed the judge that a deputy sheriff had arrested a speeder and that the culprit was awaiting trial. Whereupon the judged walked into the unswept little courtroom near his office and sat down behind the judicial desk.

A middle-aged man and his wife were sitting on the front bench in the section of the courtroom reserved for spectators. Nearby sat a man in overalls and an open-collared, blue workshirt. He wore a baseball player's cap and an enormous star-shaped badge was pinned to the bib of his overalls. Strapped to his side was a German Luger pistol, a memento of some distant battlefield. The judge cleared his throat and asked the officer the nature of the charge against the defendant. The deputy stood up and came forward.

"Judge," he said, "this man was driving in a very reckless way. I got behind 'im and follered 'im about four mile, and I seen his car cross the yaller line at least three times. I want a warrant chargin' 'im with reckless driving."

His Honor turned to the offender and asked what he had to say. He was from New Jersey and was on his way to visit his son in Virginia. He and his wife had decided to turn aside and see the Kentucky mountains, about whose beauty they had heard so much. They had driven neither recklessly nor rapidly, and if their automobile had crossed the center line at any time it had been done inadvertently and on a relatively straight stretch of road where no other vehicles were in view.

It was obvious that the judge was impressed by the "violator's" sincerity and that he believed what he had said. He paused for a long moment and reflected upon the situation and, to one versed in mountain politics, his silent cogitations left a plainly discernible track. He weighed the fact that on the one hand he was dealing with a deputy who voted in the county and whose kinsmen and friends were equipped with razor-sharp votes. He knew that if the motorist paid no fine the deputy would be offended. The officer made his living from the fees collected in cases such as this one. If the New Jersey motorist paid a fine he must also pay the costs, six dollars of which would go into the pocket of the deputy. The guardian of the public peace would take unkindly to a dismissal of the case after he had gone to the trouble to capture the man and bring him three miles to the county seat. Weighed on the other end of the scale was a stranger who would never be here again and who, even if he paid a small fine, perhaps unjustly, would not suffer irreparably. These considerations produced the inevitable conclusion. His Honor decreed the minimum fine allowed under the statute. The total came to eighteen dollars and fifty cents. When justice had thus been meted out the judge did not return to his office but took advantage of the opportunity to escape for lunch. When he returned at 1:00 p.m. the callers had increased in number and their problems had grown even more vexatious.

A fifty-year-old man, his wife and her father had come to tell the judge that the Welfare worker had denied his claim for public assistance. He wanted the judge to talk to her and, if necessary, to go to Frankfort and see if the claim couldn't be straightened out. He said:

"Judge, I just can't work. I can't do nary a thing. I'm sick and I've got a doctor's certificate to prove it. I worked in the mines for twenty-five years before they shut down but you know I got into bad air and ever since then when I git hot or a little bit tired I get so nervous I can't hardly stand it.I don't have a thing in the world to live on and they've turned down my claim, and I know that if you will get onto the people at Frankfort you can get it straightened out. There's a sight of people in this county that ain't as bad off as I am and they didn't have any trouble gettin' it and I'm sure not a-goin' to give up on it without seeing into it a little further."

At this juncture the man's father-in-law, a gentleman of approximately seventy-five, chimed in. He had lived with his daughter and son-in-law for three years and never had known anybody who was a harder worker. He had seen the man work an hour or two in his vegetable garden and get so nervous that he would spill his coffee when he came into the house to rest. He assured the judge that he would be the first to say so if he thought his son-in-law was "putting on."

The judge heard this tale of woe with deep respect and assured his visitors that they had his sympathy and that he would make every effort to help them. He hedged by pointing out that public assistance is administered by a state agency over which he had no control. The Welfare Department had a lot of stubborn people on its staff, some of whom, unfortunately, were quite unreasonable. He remembered that the sick man had always been his friend and had stood by him in bygone years. He summed up his gratitude with the assertion, "You've scratched my back in the past and I'll try to scratch yours now. You know, turn about is fair play."

Highly gratified, the nervous man, his wife and his father-in-law left, after again reminding the judge that they sure would appreciate his help.

The next caller had been drawing State Aid but his check had been discontinued because his children had not been attending school regularly. He explained that his young-'uns had been sick. "Not sick enough to have a doctor, but feelin' bad and I just couldn't make 'em go to school a-feelin' bad. As soon as they got to feelin' better they went right back to school, and I don't know what we'll do if we don't git some help fer 'em again."

He promised that if the judge could prevail upon the Welfare worker to restore his check he would make an affidavit to send his children to school on each day when they were well enough to go.

About 3:30 in the afternoon the county truant officer (known officially by the horrendous title of Director of Pupil Personnel) made his appearance. A warrant had been sworn out charging a father with failing to send his children to school and the trial was set for that hour. The defendant was already present in the little court-room. A few moments later the county attorney appeared to prosecute the case for the state. The truant officer explained that the defendant was the father of six children, all of whom were of elementary school age. They had not been to school in the preceding month despite his pleas that the father keep them in regular attendance. The county attorney asked the Court to impose a fine or jail sentence. The judge asked the defendant why he had not been sending his children to school. The man stalked forward and gazed around him with the uncertainty of a trapped animal. He had dressed in tattered overalls to which many patches had been affixed. He was approximately forty-five years old and it was obvious from his huge hands and stooped shoulders that he had spent many years under the low roof of a coal mine. He pleaded his defense with the eloquence of an able trial lawyer. With powerful conviction he said:

"I agree with everything that's been said. My children have not been going to school and nobody wants them to go any more than I do. I've been out of work now for four years. I've been all over this coalfield and over into Virginia and West Virginia looking for work. I've made trip after trip to Indianny, Ohio and Michigan and I couldn't find a day's work anywhere. I drawed out my unemployment compensation over three years ago and the only income I've had since has been just a day's work now and then doing farm work for somebody. I sold my old car, my shotgun, my radio and even my watch to get money to feed my family. And now I don't have a thing in the world left that anybody would want. I'm dead-broke and about ready to give up. I live over a mile from the schoolhouse and I simply don't have any money to buy my children shoes or clothes to wear. I own a little old four-room shanty of a house and twenty acres of wore-out hillside land. Last spring the coal company that owns the coal augered it and teetotally destroyed the land. I couldn't sell the whole place for five hundred dollars if my life depended on it. Me and my oldest boy have one pair of shoes between us, and that's all. When he wears 'em I don't have any and when I wear 'em he don't have any. If it wasn't for these rations the gover'ment gives us, I guess the whole family would of been starved to death long afore now. If you want to fine me I ain't got a penny to pay it with and I'll have to lay it out in jail. If you think puttin' me in jail will help my young-'uns any, then go ahead and do it and I'll be glad of it. If the county attorney or the truant officer will find me a job where I can work out something for my kids to wear I'll be much abliged to 'em as long as I live."

At the conclusion of this declaration the judged looked uneasily around, eying the county attorney and the truant officer in the hope that some help would come from that quarter. Both gentlemen remained silent. At length the judge plied the defendant with questions. The man had a third-grade education. He had worked in the mines for a total of twenty years and had spent three years as an infantry soldier in the war against Japan. He had been fortunate, however, and had received no wounds. Consequently, he drew no pension or compensation from the Veteran's Administration. The factories to which he had applied for employment had insisted on men with more education than he possessed. They also wanted younger men. Finally the county attorney demanded to know whether he had any skill except mining coal. The answer was an emphatic "No." Then he blurted out:

"Judge, I'm not the only man in this fix on the creek where I live. They's at least a dozen other men who ain't sent their children to school for the same reason mine ain't a-goin'. They can't send 'em cause they can't get hold of any money to send 'em with. Now the county attorney and the truant officer are trying to make an example out of me. They think that if I go to jail for a week or two the rest of 'em will somehow find the money to get their kids into the schoolhouse."

He looked intently at the truant officer and demanded, "Ain't that so?" to which the truant officer hesitantly assented.

The judge mulled the problem over for a moment or two and then "filed away" the warrant. He explained that it was not being dismissed, but was being continued upon the docket indefinitely. "If the case is ever set for trial again I will write you a letter well in advance of the trial date and tell you when to be here," he said. "In the meantime go home and do the best you possibly can to make enough money to educate your children. If they don't go to school they'll never be able to make a living and when they get grown they'll be in just as bad a fix as you are in now."

The defendant thanked the judge, picked up his battered miner's cap and walked to the door. There he paused and looked back at judge, attorney and truant officer for a long moment, as though framing a question. Then he thought better of it and closed the door behind him. His Honor had had enough for one day, and decided to go home. While he was locking the door I glanced at the headlines on the newspaper the morning mail had brought to his desk:

> FEDERAL AID TO EDUCATION BILL DIES IN HOUSE COMMITTEE
>
> BILLIONS APPROVED FOR FOREIGN AID
>
> JOBLESS MINER KILLS SELF IN HARLAN

19. Justice in Moscow: The Average
George Feifer

The room is number 7 in the rear, small and square and shabby; layers of paint have petrified the look of fatigue. Perhaps the merchant's daughters slept in this part of the house, but it is hard now to picture it gay. The walls are faded, the wood is worn, and three bare bulbs harden the stale gloom. Only the portrait masters the drabness—above the dais a smiling-frowning likeness of Lenin, challenging the living. It is the young Lenin, eager and confident, in a stylish suit; probably he had not long before won his law degree from a reluctant tsarist examiner. Grayed chips of plaster reach out from where the nail has been banged into the wall. From the office next door—someone has forgotten to close the door—a telephone jangles unanswered.

"Defendant, we are waiting. The court is waiting to hear how you explain your unsatisfactory performance as a worker."

He is standing in the dock, heavy, rough hands behind his back, shaking his head slowly, looking up plaintively at the disapproving judge, and again at his feet. He does not answer.

"I repeat, how do you explain your record? You misbehaved, you systematically

SOURCE: *Justice in Moscow*, New York: Dell Publishing Co., Inc., 1965. By permission of the publisher.

violated work discipline. Why? You were a burden to the administration and your fellow workers. What prompted you to act that way?"

No answer. He looks away; he does not want to begin.

The judge clears her throat, flips the pages of the record and finds her place with a stout finger. She is prim and plump, a schoolteacherish woman over forty, a matron in shapeless dress, with rimless glasses and hair combed back into a tight bun.

"Have you been reprimanded for truancy at the factory?"

"Yes."

"Absent from work with no good reason—that is your attitude toward your work, toward your responsibilities. And rebukes for appearing drunk in the factory—did you get any of these?"

He does not answer.

"*Did* you?"

"I think . . . well, yes."

"How many?"

"I don't know. I don't remember."

"Four?"

"Maybe. I didn't count. Sometimes it was on a holiday, when everybody was drunk."

"Four reprimands! That's an unheard-of attitude toward work and life in our socialist society. Disgraceful! It started with disinterest in work; then drinking and hooliganism—and led from that to stealing; of course it led to stealing, naturally to stealing—do you understand that? Why were you repeatedly late? Why did you continue to violate work discipline in spite of your warnings? You ignored them. You drank on the job. You were truant. And then you stole. Logical."

"I . . . never drank on the job."

"You came to work drunk; it's the same thing. You knew that you may not appear on the job in a drunken condition. Your attitude is quite clear."

He shakes his head again and looks away, sunk in resignation. But then he glances at a woman in the rear of the room who is nervously clasping a swaddled infant in her arms, and a smile makes quick, deep wrinkles in his cheeks. The woman, apparently his wife, tries to smile back.

"I don't consider myself a bad worker. Not worse than average; I've a decent record. You're just collecting all my sins."

"You have a record of consistent violation of discipline and have had plenty of opportunity to pull yourself together. Evidently you are not interested in leading an honest life as a Soviet worker."

"I admit I was wrong. I'm sorry. But all I did before was to drink sometimes. I admit that; I'm not perfect."

"But don't you see where that drinking led you? And the ignoring of the warnings —your attitude? Do you understand that now? That's what this court wants to know."

In the early stages of the trial the court seeks what it wants to know in this dialogue. Judge and defendant have a talk. The judge works almost singlehandedly; other voices rarely intrude. The other members of the court, known as lay assessors—in this case they are an abstracted, mousy young woman and a tieless, frayed man of middle age—shift uncomfortably in their unaccustomed high-backed chairs. The relatives and spectators, bundled up in overcoats and babushkas in spite of the suffocating heat of the room, look on with noises of protest, resignation or despair.

The pretty young secretary looks at nothing and does not cover her yawns. No prosecutor or defense counsel has appeared; the case is too unimportant and too simple. Eleven persons in all are present, plus two ham-faced policemen in huge blue greatcoats alongside the dock.

As the judge and the defendant have their talk, the story—the plea, the protest, the excuse, the explanation, the denial, the confirmation, the confession, the appeal— spills out in words as simple as the setting.

"You did not intend to take the galoshes? Strange. What *did* you intend? How did they get under your coat?"

"I don't remember, I was drunk. I just know I didn't mean to steal."

"We are not here to listen to what you intended. Are you going to deny now that the galoshes were found concealed under your coat?"

"No. I must have done it. I just don't know why. I never stole anything before in my life."

"Never stole anything, or never was caught? Well, let's start from the beginning again. Exactly what time did you get to work?"

"At about eleven-thirty p.m.; I was on the night shift."

"You arrived drunk?"

"I must have been fairly high."

"So you knowingly, willfully broke the rules, in spite of all previous warnings. . . ."

This was the average of averages. The charge was violation of Article 96: Petty Theft of State Property. A pair of woman's rubber boots; they sold for four rubles and sixty kopeks [1] in the stores.

I saw about fifty such cases in all, and this one was closest to the common denominator among them. The excuses of the defendant, the didacticism of the judge, the slow movement toward an inevitable end, made those two hours typical of those that occupy the People's courts, Monday through Saturday in Moscow. I would like to describe it, therefore, in some detail and as carefully as possible. For this is what I was looking for on the hard wooden benches in those dusty rooms.

An air of informality prevails from the start. The little blue card at the door indicates the trial will start at 1 p.m.; at 1:25 three of the witnesses have not arrived. Those who have come chat distractedly and wait, as Russians are used to waiting. A secretary, lips reddened and young voice already thickened with *burokratism*, bellows the roll; the others pay her no mind. Without the high-backed chairs embellished by crumbling Soviet emblems, they might be waiting for the milk train in a provincial station.

At last, a man in worker's garb—rumpled jacket far too short in the sleeves, faded flannel shirt—is marched down the corridor and into the dock by two booted policemen to the directions of a third. A tall, gaunt, wordless man, probably blond; his features look too large against a shaved head. He sits behind the railing against the wall and looks out the double window.

Some time later the court appears unannounced: three ordinary citizens in ordinary office-drab dress, and before everyone understands that he is to get to his feet they

[1] Sums in rubles will appear often in this account; I have not rendered the dollar equivalents because there is no sure way of doing it. The official exchange—the Soviet government's exchange—is: one ruble = $1.11. International and domestic black markets value the ruble at from one third to one fifth of that. What a ruble is *worth* in Moscow is a tricky business too, because a respectable pair of leather shoes costs 50, and a respectable apartment 8 per month; a skilled worker earns about 100 per month; a fine restaurant meal costs 3 or 4. All in all, I used to think of a ruble as *about* a dollar, remembering that they were much less easy to come by. There are 100 kopeks to the ruble.

are in their places on the dais and the case has started, without a hint of flourish. No costuming or ceremony, no magic words or mystery; the judge slips on her glasses and opens the dossier. "The People's Court of Kropotkinskii District is in session. The case of Kondakov will be heard."

The first few items of routine are quickly completed. The participants are identified, the witnesses are sent to wait their turns in the corridor, and the judge is at her accustomed work.

"Defendant, stand. Your name?"

"Kondakov."

"Christian name and patronymic?"

"Vyacheslav Sergeyevich."

"Date of birth?"

"August 14, 1933."

"Nationality?"

"Russian."

"Education?"

"Eight classes [of primary school]."

"*Partiinost* [Party affiliation]?"

"*Bezpartiinii* [Not a member of the Communist Party]."

"Married?"

"Yes."

"Children?"

"A daughter, five months."

"Occupation and place of work?"

"I'm a stitcher in a factory, the Red Hero."

"You earn?"

"Eighty rubles [per month]."

"Ever convicted before?"

"No."

"No criminal convictions whatsoever?"

"None."

"But you were sentenced for petty hooliganism."

"Yes."

"How many times?"

"Once."

"And that was when?"

"About a year and a half ago."

"May 25, 1961? Drunk and disorderly in the metro?"

"I think so."

"When were you arrested on the present charge?"

"October 12."

"And received a copy of the indictment?"

"I don't remember. A few days ago."

"December 16?"

"Yes."

Soviet trials begin with a short biography of the accused—his "introduction" to the court. A Russian judge would think it silly to deal with Ivan Ivanov, a stranger off the street. Who is this fellow? What is his record at work? In the courts? What about his personal and family background? And so, information about the character and history of the defendant—information which is usually kept secret in English and American courts until guilt or innocence has been decided—is sought and aired at the outset.

"Kondakov, you are the accused in this case. As the accused, you have the right to make explanations concerning the accusation against you, to present evidence, submit petitions, participate in the hearing, challenge the composition of the court, and appeal its actions and decisions. You have, also, the right to the last word. Are these rights clear to you?"

"Clear."

"You entrust the present members of the court to hear your case?"

"Of course."

"Have you any requests at this time?"

"What kind of requests?"

"Anything to ask of the court?"

"I do. I ask the court to call Shisko and Vorabiova. They know me from the factory, they can tell how I worked on the shift. The investigator questioned them, but they're not on the list of witnesses. . . ."

"You saw the list. Why didn't you request this earlier?"

"I didn't think it was important."

"Well, you *ought* to have thought." The judge pauses. "The court will postpone decision until after the other witnesses are heard. If necessary, we will call them later."

The judge has proceeded to a reading of the indictment, and although she reads rapidly, it takes her a full five minutes. For the indictment in Soviet procedure is so detailed and so seemingly accurate and complete—so *long*—that there seems little left to be heard afterward. It is not merely an accusation, but a detailed, repetitious account of the crime as reconstructed by the investigation, a summary of the testimony of each witness called, a résumé of the defendant's "explanation," a description of his personality and the relationship of the crime to his past behavior, and a juridical qualification of the acts charged under the code. The indictment tells the story and sets the tone—and leaves little to the imagination or to suspense.

Stripped to the plot—which it repeats seven times—it is a simple charge. On the night of October 11–12, Kondakov reported for work drunk, behaved suspiciously, excused himself to go to the toilet and was stopped by the guard at the gate with a pair of finished boots stuffed awkwardly under his jacket. The guard called the foreman; the foreman, the police. Kondakov had no excuse.

"Defendant, stand. Do you understand the charges against you?"

"I understand."

"Do you admit your guilt?"

"I . . . suppose so. Yes, I admit my guilt."

"Tell the court exactly what happened that night—everything you know."

"Comrade Judges, what can I say? I don't remember much about it. I guess I took the galoshes, I don't know why. I had too much to drink, I suppose; it was my wife's birthday, we've been married three years. We observed the occasion; had some friends over, you know—a little celebration. I guess we celebrated too much."

"What were you drinking?"

"Vodka. Wine."

"How much?"

"Not very much. I don't remember. A few glasses of vodka, a few of wine."

"I can imagine. Go on, what happened then? Were you very drunk?"

"I didn't think so; a little bit high. But maybe I was. Well, I was at my place, stitching; we were working hard on the winter stuff. Then I had to relieve myself and—well, you know the rest. I don't remember anything about it, I have no idea what the galoshes were doing there. I was on my way to the toilet and the guard took my arm and they found this pair of woman's galoshes I was carrying. I honestly don't know to where. 'What have you got under your coat?' he said; I thought he was joking. Honestly, Comrade Judges. This is very shameful to me; I've never stolen a thing in my life. I ask the court to forgive me, I had no intention at all to steal. It's not true that I resisted efforts to stop me."

"So you admit that you were taking the galoshes out under your coat?"

"Yes, I must have done it."

"Then why did you deny it when you were stopped?"

"I don't know . . . I don't remember. Perhaps I really didn't know they were there."

"Then why did you try to run away?"

"I . . . don't know."

"You don't know? Do you know that it is wrong to take for yourself the fruits of your collective's labor? Do you know that that is stealing?"

"Of course I do."

"And what do you think about it, about the way you behaved?"

"It was very wrong."

"Yes, we agree. Very wrong. With whom were you operating—to steal footwear?"

"Not with anyone. You don't understand, this was a mistake, an accident."

"Are you sure? We have had a lot of trouble lately at the Red Hero; a lot of shoes have been missing." The judge's voice is professionally dry.

"It was absolutely unplanned."

"What did you intend doing with the galoshes afterward?"

"I didn't intend anything. Honest, I'm telling you."

"Then why did you take them? The court wants to hear your explanation."

Kondakov hangs his head; he does not answer. The judge, squinting, peers steadily at him through her glasses. The assessors look faintly ashamed.

"*Why did you steal?*"

"I was drunk, that's all; I didn't know what I was doing."

"Were things difficult for you? Did you live badly?"

"I lived O.K.—like everyone else."

"You earned eighty rubles; not bad. And your wife? Where does she work? What does she earn?"

"About the same—ninety rubles. She's a bookkeeper."

"So you were not suffering. Life was not bad for you. Was it necessary for you to steal? *What did you lack?* Did you lack something? What was your *reason?*"

In this vein, inquisition continues. Not about the galoshes; that is known from the first. About other things—the drinking (one of the neighbors had revealed during the investigation that Kondakov was sometimes tipsy in the apartment); about the affair in the metro eighteen months before; about language (several witnesses had said that he was free with strong words)—about the "whole man."

But one part of the whole is given special attention.

"How long have you worked at the Red Hero?"

"Just over a year."

"And before that?"

"I had a number of jobs."

"A number of jobs? You had four in three years, is that correct?"

"Yes."

"Why such an unsatisfactory record?"

"No reason. I didn't plan it. I just couldn't find a job to suit me."

"That's not right. What about the job at Mosstroi? You were fired from that job, is that correct?"

"Well, technically I was fired. It wasn't my fault."

"What was the reason?"

"My foreman didn't like me. We didn't get along. It was personal."

"Not according to the record. You were fired for drunkenness and absences, isn't that the case? You were warned several times, then fired when you didn't show up for three days."

No answer.

"That was in May 1961. And your next job was at the Red Hero, which you took in September. Is that correct?"

"I think so."

"For four months you were without a job? You did nothing?"

"Well no, not nothing. I had odd jobs. And we had a place in the country—I worked on the vegetable garden."

"Four months without a job. Doing nothing, living off others. A parasite. And that's the way you treat your obligations as a Soviet citizen; no interest at all in your work. A man without a job is a man without a soul. No wonder you stole, it was just another step, with that attitude. Don't you understand that a man needs a steady job—for his own sake, not only for others? Or are you interested only in vodka? Where did you get the money for all that drinking when you had no job?"

"I didn't drink that much, you are exaggerating. You are blowing everything up. I drink average. Not so much at all. Average."

After Kondakov, the witnesses are called. "You must tell the court only the truth. If you give untruthful testimony, you will be criminally responsible; the punishment may be deprivation of freedom. Sign this paper indicating that you have been warned. . . ."

In Anglo-Saxon law, the case would have ended with Kondakov's admission of guilt; in fact, the great majority of such cases end this way. But the great majority of Soviet trials *begin* with "I admit my guilt"; for here it is not a plea, but merely an answer, and it does not relieve the prosecution of the obligation to present further proof. It is a humane rule, for it protects against false confession. And it is an essential one for a court concerned as much with repentance and reform as with retribution.

The witnesses testify from the rickety, three-sided, almost-black wooden box near the center of the room. Their testimony seems superfluous; everyone knows what they will say. The judge knows; the record of the preliminary investigation is in her hands. Kondakov knows; he has read the record. Even the spectators know; they have heard the substance of the testimony in the indictment. Excitement at a Moscow trial is like excitement on a roller coaster: the real suspense is repetition. The witnesses confirm, they do not report. Sometimes a witness forgets, sometimes he adds new details. But rarely—very rarely—does he produce evidence not expected of him.

The defendant was caught in the act. When the old guard spied and stopped him, Kondakov was finished. Everyone saw the galoshes and heard the stammering excuses. Three fellow workers are called, in addition to the watchman and the foreman, to confirm the story.

"Tell us all you know about this case. . . ."

One by one they describe the incident: Kondakov drunk, acting strangely, leaving for the toilet, with the bulge in his coat, denying, admitting, protesting. . . . The evidence is overwhelming; the repetition wearying.

The fourth witness is Polyanskaya, Vera Petrovna, a slight girl in her early twenties who stands easily in the box, with her hands in the pockets of her overcoat.

"What do you remember about this case? Tell the court everything you know."

"What do I remember? Not very much. I remember it happened on the night shift, sometime in early October—"

"The night of October 11–12?"

"That's right. Kondakov"—she glances in his direction and smiles at him—"arrived about twenty minutes late for work. It was quite clear that he had been drinking. He was pretty drunk. He kept on getting up from his table—I worked next to him—and singing the first stanzas of folk songs. And getting up to congratulate us, I don't know for what. Ordinarily he is a quiet sort.

"Well, at about three-thirty he announced loudly that he was going to the bathroom. Of course, I paid no attention. But a few minutes later there was a commotion in the next shop. Everyone ran out—I did too. There he was with the galoshes. He had stuffed them under his coat and the guard noticed it. Well, that's all I know. The police came and took him away. He seemed confused. Embarrassed. He kept saying, 'I never stole a thing in my life.' "

"Did he swear?"

"Not while I was there. He just muttered to himself, sort of."

"Was he stealing shoes before this incident?"

"I don't know, I have no idea. I don't think so."

"Why do you think he committed this act?"

"I haven't the faintest idea. He was quite drunk."

"But not so drunk that he didn't know he was stealing?"

"I can't say. I don't think so."

"Was he often drunk at work?"

"Not often."

"But he *has* been drunk; did you know he was warned about that?"

"Yes, I knew."

"What can you tell us about his character?"

"He was all right. Decent. I never had any unpleasantness with him."

"But you know that he had 'unpleasantness' with the administration."

"Yes."

"Did you know that he was fired from other jobs and arrested for petty hooliganism?"

"No."

"You didn't know that. Perhaps you ought to have interested yourself in your neighbor. Well, what kind of man was he at work? Did you expect that he might steal? What can you say about his working habits?"

"He wasn't a bad worker. Or unusually good, either. He did his share. I'd call him normal."

"You mean that a normal worker is late and absent and drunk on the job?"

"Uh, he worked well—"

"Worked well! He *stole* well. What about the reprimands he kept getting?"

"During the last couple of months, he worked very hard. I don't think he had any reprimands."

"If you don't count thieving."

"I think he was trying to—"

"Such people have got to be taken under control, they have got to be shown. He drinks, he fails to appear at work, he creates scandals—and now look where he ended. The logical end; he didn't want to heed the warnings. Well, we have a job to do: the people of Moscow need shoes and the Red Hero is trying to supply them. We don't have to put up with people who deliberately stand in the way."

The judge puts back her glasses.

"Now is there anything else you would like to add? Can you tell us anything more about his intentions?"

"I don't know anything more. It was a surprise to me."

The judge turns to the assessors. "Have you any questions?"

They shake their heads, No.

"Does the defendant want to question the witness?"

Kondakov has no questions.

There is no defense in the special sense of the word. No one to pick at the flaws in the indictment, to discover the escapes, to suggest that Kondakov had intended to return the galoshes, to ridicule the idea that a man would intentionally take an almost worthless pair of boots, to break down the guard's story, to argue that the procurator had classified the crime under too drastic an article of the code. Even had a lawyer been present, these tactics probably would not have been used, for when facts seem obvious in a Moscow court, they are usually taken as such. In a way, the judge herself represents the defense, for even though most of her questions point in the other direction, she does make clear that Kondakov served honorably for three years in the Soviet Army and that he did social work in his apartment house.

The accused too has a turn at questioning each witness (he may do it even when a lawyer defends him) and Kondakov makes greater use of his right than most defendants.

"Do *you* think I intended to steal? . . . Would *you* call me a bad worker? . . . It isn't true that I deliberately ignored warnings, why do you say that to the court?"

And when the last witness is testifying, there is help from another, unexpected source. A voice in tears breaks into the questioning. "You are twisting everything to the worst. He is a good man, not a thief."

It is Kondakov's wife, round and red-faced, looking ten years older than he, rocking her infant while she sobs. The judge demands silence—"This is a court!"—but when she does not get it, she listens without interrupting. The trial stops for the stricken woman's plea.

"It's not fair. I tell you it's not fair. It is my fault. It was my birthday, I arranged the evening, I poured him his vodka. He didn't mean to get drunk, he didn't mean anything wrong. He is an honest man. He gives me all his wages. And the child—what are we to do now? He is a good man, and you are making of him a thief, an ordinary criminal. Why are you doing that to him?"

The judge waits until the woman, sobbing, ends her plea.

"Defendant, you have heard the testimony. Have you anything to add to it before your last word?" The judge's voice softens again, but remains detached. No play of emotions between confessant and confessor; this is her job, she has handled hundreds of cases like this before, and there is another one scheduled for late afternoon.

"I would like to say that I did not intend to steal, I don't understand myself why I did it. I've tried, at least, to be an honest man."

"An honest man does not put galoshes under his coat. Well, enough. What will you say as your last word?"

There is a short pause which seems long. Kondakov looks up at the judge, but she keeps her gaze now to the record book.

"Comrade Judges, what can I say? I committed a serious crime, of course, I fully understand that now. But I ask the court to remember my family—my daughter. Let me redeem myself! Let me show that I can work honestly and be a useful member of society. This will never happen again. I ask the court not to deprive me of my freedom."

The judge has closed the record book and is on the edge of her chair. "Is that all?"

"Yes."

And the court steps out quickly to deliberate, as unceremoniously as it entered.

The hearing lasted not quite an hour. Then there is half an hour of waiting, of strong cigarettes puffed in resignation rather than anxiety, before the defendant is marched back to his place and the court takes theirs.

"The sentence is announced. In the name of the Russian Soviet Federated Socialist Republic, on December 20, 1962, People's Court, Kropotkinskii District, People's Judge Volochova presiding in association with People's Assessors Kuptsov and Sidorenko, heard the case of Kondakov, Vyacheslav Sergeyevich, twenty-nine, Russian, *Bezpartiinii*, married, with eight years of education, living at. . . ."

The details of identification once more, exaggeratedly precise.

And the story again, too, a final time, hardly changed from the wording of the indictment. Again intoxication, strange behavior, the toilet, the coat, the bulge and discovery, the galoshes, the record of tardiness, absences and drunkenness, the ignoring of warnings . . . "Kondakov denied an intention to steal, but according to witness Markova, who said . . . and Polyanskaya, who testified . . . and T. and Zh., who confirmed. . . . The court considers the accusation fully proved, considers that Kondakov concealed the galoshes intending to steal them, considers the qualification correct under Article Ninety-six, Paragraph One, considers. . . ."

Kondakov, at last, is guilty.

"In determining measures of punishment, the court took into consideration a history of unsatisfactory attitudes toward work and responsibilities as a citizen, and also the absence of previous criminal convictions. . . ."

The sentence is one year in a labor colony.

At the worst moment, Kondakov, still calm and awkward, still somehow impervious to his misfortune, looks at the windows. The judge finishes quickly and does not look at him again, but the assessors cannot refrain from staring.

"Kondakov, is the sentence clear to you?"

"It is clear."

"You have seven days in which to appeal. . . ."

And it is over. The court is through with him; as if in a hurry now, it leaves the dais hastily. Kondakov is again the ward of the police. A year for a pair of galoshes. His wife rushes to him and he kisses her before he is led away; and as he is marched down the corridor from where he came, he orders her not to worry about him.

20. Witch Murder and *Mens Rea:* A Problem of Society under Radical Social Change

Robert B. Seidman

That Africa is a land of extreme contrasts is the hackneyed introduction to every travelogue. One such contrast is between those areas where the indigenous peoples have assimilated the colonialists' mores, and those areas where they have not. Now, in the blazing morn of independence, the new African governments face the task of developing legal, social and economic institutions which will bring the more backward elements of the population into harmony with the demands of twentieth-century industrialized society. To what extent is the criminal law an apt tool to accomplish these changes?

In the last decades of Empire, the colonial courts were presented with this problem in a variety of masks. Perhaps the most persistently nagging cases are those in which the defendant was tried because he killed a supposed witch in imagined self-defense against her diabolical craft. With monotonous regularity, courts have convicted, sentenced the defendant to death, and—in the same breath—recommended executive clemency. Why this ambivalent result? Is there some organizing concept which, tolerably with the pattern of the criminal law, can resolve the seeming contradiction?

To answer this question, we shall examine first the nature of witchcraft belief, the defenses raised in prosecutions for the murder of supposed witches, and the judicial response to them. In an effort to find a satisfactory solution, however, we shall have to explore the conceptual mazes of *mens rea,* which is the analytical concept chiefly at issue.

I

For many Africans, witchcraft belief is an integral part of their *Weltanschauung,* growing out of indigenous theories about the psyche.[1] The Akan (one of the largest West African tribal groupings), for example, postulate man as tripartite. His physical body, a mere shell, encloses two indwelling souls, the *kra,* or life-soul and the *sun-*

SOURCE: "Witch Murder and *Mens Rea:* A Problem of Society under Radical Social Change," *Modern Law Review,* vol. 28, pp. 46–61, January, 1965. By permission of the author and publisher.

[1] Field, *Search for Security* (1960), *passim;* and see Evans-Pritchard, *Witchcraft, Oracles and Magic among the Azande* (1937), p. 21 ("A witch performs no rite, utters no spell, and possesses no medicine. An act of witchcraft is a psychic act").

sum, or personality-soul.[2] A wicked entity, the *obayi,* on occasion seizes dominion of the *sunsum* of a witch. Without her volition, her *sunsum* makes excursions from her earthly body. Free of physical restraint, it attacks the *kra* or *sunsum* of its victim by sucking it forth secretly from its material shell. As the *kra* is devoured, sometimes by degrees, sometimes in a rush, so the physical body of the victim withers. As the *sunsum* is destroyed, so will the victim's hope of worldly success disappear.[3]

Prior to European overlordship, death, usually in some peculiarly horrible form,[4] was the invariable punishment for proven [5] witches. The colonial governments, having but recently abolished equally barbaric measures against witches in the metropole, abolished them in the colonies as well. But superstition nevertheless flourished [6] albeit now shorn of institutional protection.

The African who believes in witchcraft is thus faced by a fearful dilemma. He believes in witches to his bones.[7] He knows that they can destroy his *kra* or *sunsum* in sundry mysterious ways, without chance for defense, so that both his physical being and his hope for earthly success are endangered, as much as by threatened blow of panga or spear or matchet. He sees nothing in the societal order to which he can appeal for protection. His tradition approves of capital punishment for witches.

Faced by such dread forces, bereft of societal shield, terrified by the loss of the values at stake, some Africans not surprisingly have struck back in terror and in self-defense. How have the common law judges [8] treated them when they were charged with murder?

II

The response of the courts has been practically unvarying: such defendants are guilty of murder. But the verdict, with its concomitant death sentence, is in both West [9] and East [10] Africa almost invariably leavened with a judicial prayer that the

[2] Meyrowitz, *The Sacred State of the Akan* (1951), p. 24; Rattray, *Ashanti* (1923), p. 46.

[3] Field, *op. cit.,* note 1 above, p. 36; Debrunner, *Witchcraft in Ghana* (1959) at p. 35 *et seq.*

[4] See Debrunner, *op. cit.,* note 3 above, p. 102; Rattray, *Religion and Art among the Ashanti* (1927), p. 29; Rattray, *Ashanti Law and Constitution* (1929), p. 313. The shocking mode of execution of wizards in Uganda (see Hayden, *Law and Justice in Buganda* (1960), p. 283) was actually used by the defendants in *Fabiano* (1941) 8 E.A.C.A. 96 (Uganda). [Note: place names after E.A.C.A. and W.A.C.A. citations indicate country of origin of the cause.]

[5] Typically, the "proof" was by ordeal. Rattray, *Ashanti Law and Constitution* (1929), pp. 392–395; Kingsley, *Travels in West Africa* (1897), p. 464; Parrinder, *Witchcraft: European and African* (1958), pp. 177, 178. A death arising from such an ordeal was the *actus reus* in *Palumba s/o Fundikila,* 14 E.A.C.A. 96 (Tanganyika) (*held,* since the defendant intended to cause death only if deceased were a witch, and since witches are imaginary, he is not guilty of intentional homicide but only of manslaughter).

[6] In Africa, as in Europe, witchcraft superstition seemingly flourishes in times of social instability, Parrinder, *op. cit.,* note 5 above, p. 205; Debrunner, *op. cit.,* note 3 above, p. 71. Colonialism made African society even more unstable than it had been.

[7] The judges repeatedly find that the defendant genuinely believed that the deceased was a witch who threatened his life. See, *e.g., Galikuwa* (1951) 18 E.A.C.A. 175 (Uganda); *Gadam* (1954) 14 W.A.C.A. 442 (Nigeria). Many Africans are convinced that they are witches; in some of the cases, the deceased has threatened the defendant. See, *e.g., Sitakimatata s/o Kimwage* (1941) 8 E.A.C.A. 57 (Tanganyika). Field, *op. cit.,* note 1 above, is based upon confessions of witches made at anti-witchcraft shrines in Ghana.

[8] All the formerly British African countries have criminal codes embodying, in most essentials, the common law of crimes.

[9] See, *e.g., Maawole Konkomba* (1952) 14 W.A.C.A. 236 (Gold Coast); *Gadam* (1954) 14 W.A.C.A. 442 (Nigeria).

[10] See, *e.g., Sitakimatata s/o Kimwage* (1941) 8 E.A.C.A. 57 (Tanganyika); *Akope s/o Karouon* (1947) 14 E.A.C.A. 105 (Kenya).

executive reverse the decision just made. Such a formalized, indeed institutionalized,[11] reliance upon executive clemency at once negates any supposed deterrent effect of the death penalty and confesses a felt inadequacy for the judicial solutions to the problems posed by these cases.

That judicial solution has been an all but unvarying rejection of the various defenses urged. Whether the claim is nakedly that these defendants lack a guilty mind, or whether an attempt is made to fit them within the conventional categories of self-defense, or defense of others, mistake, insanity or provocation, it has been rejected by the courts.

The evisceral response of any lawyer to the killing of a supposed witch in imagined self-defense is that the superstition negates *mens rea*. That claim was rejected in *Kumwaka Wa Malumbi & 69 Others* (Kenya).[12] Seventy defendants admitted beating to death an old woman they believed to be a witch. The court overruled a plea that the homicide was *ipso facto* excusable: "For courts to adopt any other attitude in such cases, would be to encourage the belief that an aggrieved party may take the law into his own hands, and no belief could well be more mischievous or fraught with greater danger to public peace and tranquillity." [13] Sixty defendants were sentenced to death; ten juveniles were detained.[14]

The more conventional plea of self-defense has not fared better. In *Erika Galikuwa* [15] (Uganda), the defendant was convicted of killing an unscrupulous witch-doctor. The defendant imagined that he heard the witch-doctor's "spirit voice" repeat a demand for ransom on two occasions, at one point with a threat to kill "by sucking your blood." Terrified, the defendant killed "and saved my life." The court, upholding a conviction for murder, pointed out that a plea of self-defense was not tenable, for "it is difficult to see how an act of witchcraft unaccompanied by some physical attack could be brought within the principles of English Common Law." [16]

The defense that the killing was necessary to save the life of another has been equally unavailing. In *Konkomba* (Gold Coast),[17] the defendant's first brother died. He consulted a "juju" man who pointed out the deceased as the guilty witch. Defendant's second brother became ill, and charged deceased with causing his illness by witchcraft. The defendant slew the supposed witch. He was, of course, found guilty of murder.

The case may fairly be contrasted with the familiar *Bourne*.[18] There the defendant, a socially prominent doctor, was charged with committing abortion upon a fifteen-

[11] "In dismissing both appeals, we conclude by observing that in all cases such as this we are aware that the element of witchcraft as a mitigating factor is always taken fully into account by the Governor in Council." *Kajuna s/o Mbake* (1945) 12 E.A.C.A. 104 (Tanganyika).

[12] (1932) 14 K.L.R. 137.

[13] *Ibid.* at p. 139.

[14] *Cf.* Goodhart, *English Law and Moral Law* (1953), p. 93: "Retribution in punishment is an expression of the community's disapproval of crime, and if this retribution is not given recognition then the disapproval may disappear." Which society is expressing its disapproval of crime when a British colonial judge sentences the male population of a Kenya village to death?

[15] (1951) 18 E.A.C.A. 175 (Uganda).

[16] *Ibid.* at p. 178. Presumably, the court meant that the plea is unavailable unless the defendant is pursued to the wall: 1 Hale 481. In *Kasalo* [1914–1946] R.L.R. 110, the deceased taunted the defendant by telling him that he (the deceased) had killed four of defendant's relatives by witchcraft the week before, and was going to kill the defendant. The claim of self-defence was denied, because the defendant had no immediate fear of death. *Accord: Kajuna s/o Mbake* (1945) 12 E.A.C.A. 104 (Tanganyika).

[17] (1952) 14 W.A.C.A. 236 (Gold Coast).

[18] [1939] 1 K.B. 687.

year-old victim of a brutal rape. His defense in part was that he had relied upon advice of a psychiatrist that, if the pregnancy were permitted to continue, severe psychiatric damage to the child might well ensue. The abortion was held justifiable.

The cases are not dissimilar. In each, the defendant honestly believed that what he did was necessary to save another. Each acted upon the advice of an expert in the relevant field. Yet one man was found guilty, and the other exonerated. The only apparent difference is that the tribunal believed in psychiatry, and not in witchcraft.[19]

Seemingly, it is the validity of the belief under which the defendant acted which determines his criminality. Discussion along this line is usually subsumed under the heading of mistake: to what extent will a misapprehension about the true state of affairs exculpate a criminal defendant?

In *Gadam* [20] (Nigeria), defendant was convicted of murder. The Crown's case was that he believed that his wife had been bewitched by the deceased, whom he therefore killed. The defendant relied upon a section of the Nigerian Code, affording a defense for a mistake which is both "honest and reasonable." The court conceded that witchcraft belief was common among ordinary members of the community, but held that "it would be a dangerous precedent to recognize that because a superstition, which may lead to such a terrible result as is disclosed by the facts of this case, is generally prevalent among the community, it is therefore reasonable." [21]

The critical question is, of course, the standard to be used in determining what is "reasonable." The measure adopted has invariably been not the average man of the defendant's community, but the reasonable Englishman.

Att.-Gen. for Nyasaland v. Jackson [22] (Federation) states the rule with unparalleled bluntness. There the court held squarely that the standard of reasonableness of mistake in the killing of a witch in imagined self-defense "is what would appear reasonable to the ordinary man in the street in England. . . . On this basis, and bearing in mind that the law of England is still the law of England even when it is extended to Nyasaland, I do not see how any court, applying the proper test, could hold that

---

[19] No less an authority than Lord Hale once charged a jury: "That there were such creatures as witches he has no doubt at all; for first, the Scriptures affirmed so much; secondly, the wisdom of all nations had provided laws against such persons, which is an argument of their confidence of such a crime. And such hath been the judgment of this kingdom, as appears by the Act of Parliament which hath provided punishments proportionate to the quality of the offence. . . ." *Trial of the Suffolk Witches* (1665) 6 St.Tr. 687 at pp. 700–701. *Accord:* 4 Blackstone, Commentaries, pp. 60–61.

[20] (1954) 14 W.A.C.A. 442.

[21] Quoted by the court from *Ifereonwe*, W.A.C.A. selected judgments for July-October-December 1954, p. 79 (cyclostyled). *Accord: Akope s/o Karvon* (1947) 14 E.A.C.A. 105. ("A mere belief that witchcraft has been or is being exercised may be an honest belief . . . but the suspicions of the person cannot be said to be both honest and reasonable. To hold otherwise would be to supply a secure refuge for every scoundrel with homicidal tendencies.")

[22] [1957] R. & N. 443. *Accord: Mbombela,* [1933] A.D. (S.A.) 269: ("The standard to be adopted in deciding whether mistake of fact is reasonable is the standard of the reasonable man, and the race and idiosyncrasies or the superstitions or the intelligence of the person accused do not enter into the question"); *cf. Ruka Matengula* (1952) 5 L.R.N.R. 148 (four defendants carried a coffin through the village; it "pointed" at a supposed witch, and jumped forward so violently that the witch suffered broken ribs and died. A defense of automatism was rejected; a defense based on native custom was rejected as being against justice, which the court construed as "not being against justice as we people in England see it"). *Contra: Wabwire,* 16 E.A.C.A. 131 at p. 134 (reasonableness of belief judged by community from which defendant comes; dictum). A case is stated in 1 Bishop, *Criminal Law,* 9th ed., pp. 218–219 from Washington Territory (U.S.A.) in which the judge charged: "The law permitted one to kill another to save his wife's life, which the latter [an Indian wizard] was in the act of taking away; and though they would not themselves credit the deceased with the power attributed to him, yet if the defendant in good faith did, and this belief was a reasonable one in *him,* considering his education and surroundings, it would furnish him, under the circumstances proved, a good defense."

a belief in witchcraft was reasonable so as to form the foundation of a defense that the law could recognize." [23]

If mistake has not afforded refuge for these defendants, neither has insanity. In *Philip Muswi s/o Musola* [24] (Kenya), the defendant killed his wife by shooting her with an arrow when she was sitting in her kitchen. There had been continual quarrels between them for some time, and the defendant believed that she was practicing witchcraft against him. A psychiatrist testified that there was a history of madness and epilepsy in the family and that the defendant was probably suffering from a mild depression on the night of the killing. The psychiatrist believed that the defendant knew what he was doing; that he could distinguish right from wrong; that what he was doing was not contrary to tribal law; and that the defendant believed that he was justified in doing what he did. A defense of insanity was overruled, for

> ". . . even if [the defendant] believed that he was justified in killing his wife because she was practicing witchcraft, there is again no evidence that such belief arose from any mental defect; it is a belief sometimes held by entirely sane Africans." [25]

The case which most clearly articulates why witchcraft belief *per se* is not insanity within the M'Naghten Rules, arose, of all unexpected forums, in the Supreme Court of the United States. In *Hotema v. United States*,[26] the defendant killed a supposed witch in obedience of the biblical injunction. The court approved a charge which directed that if the defendant's belief in witches was simply the erroneous conclusion of a sane mind, he was to be convicted; but if as the result of a disordered mind, acquitted. Insanity as a defense exculpates only when the defect is a function of mental disease and not merely of training.[27]

Nor does the defense of partial delusion stand on any better ground. Under the traditional rule, the facts imagined must themselves be sufficient to excuse or justify the killing.[28] Since the accused does not imagine himself physically backed to the wall, the delusion is an insufficient defense.[29]

---

[23] *Ibid*, at p. 447.

[24] (1956) 23 E.A.C.A. 622.

[25] *Ibid.* at p. 625. *Contra: Magata s/o Kachehakana* [1957] E.A.C.A. 330 (High Court, Uganda) (defendant killed his father "because he bewitched my two sons and killed them, he again bewitched my wife and killed her, also he bewitched me and made me impotent. . . . He bewitched my goats and killed them all, he bewitched my cow which is still sick, he bewitched my second wife. . . ." The defendant was medically normal. *Held*, guilty but insane; "an African living far away in the bush may become so obsessed with the idea that he is being bewitched that the balance of his mind may be disturbed to such an extent that it may be described as a disease of the mind.")

[26] 186 U.S. 413; 22 S.Ct. 895; 46 L.Ed. 1225 (1901).

[27] *Cf.*, 2 Stephen's *Hist. Crim. Law*, p. 163: "Anyone would fall into the description in question [*i.e.*, insane] who was deprived by reason of disease affecting the mind of the power of passing a rational judgment on the moral character of the act which he meant to do." Query, whether defendants in the witchcraft cases had the power of passing such a judgment.

[28] *M'Naghten's Case* (1843) 10 Cl. and F. 200 at p. 211; 8 E.R. 718 at p. 723 (Rule IV).

[29] *Skekanja* (1948) 15 E.A.C.A. 158 (Tanganyika) (defendant imagined a devil commanded him to kill a boy; he strangled a half-grown lad and beheaded him at a cross-roads in obedience to the imagined command; *held*, murder). Query, the result under the extraordinary wording of the Criminal Code, 1960 (Ghana), s. 27 (verdict of guilty but insane indicated where the accused "did the act in respect of which he is accused under the influence of an insane delusion of such a nature as to render him, in the opinion of the jury or the court, an unfit subject for punishment of any kind with respect of such an act.") The defense of insanity would probably not be available in the witchcraft cases even under the *Durham* rule (*Durham v. United States*, 214 F. (2d). 862; 45 A.L.R. 1430). (Defendant legally insane if the defendant did the act as a product of mental disease.)

The defense of provocation, with one very narrow exception, has been equally unavailing.[30] In *Fabiano* (Uganda),[31] defendants believed that the deceased was a wizard who had killed members of their families. They discovered the supposed wizard, naked, crawling about their compound at night. The court found that the defendants actually believed that the deceased was then and there practicing witchcraft against them, and allowed a partial defense of provocation.

> "We think that if the facts proved establish that the victim was performing in the actual presence of the accused some act which the accused did genuinely believe, and which an ordinary person of the community did genuinely believe, to be an act of witchcraft against him or another person under his immediate care (which act would be a criminal offence under the Criminal Law (Witchcraft) Ordinance of Uganda . . .) he might be angered to such an extent as to be deprived of the power of self-control and induced to assault the person doing the act of witchcraft. And if this is to be the case a defense of grave and sudden provocation is open to him." [32]

This is merely a special application of the usual rule which reduces to manslaughter a killing done in a provoked passion. The standard is always that of the reasonable man of the community to which the accused belongs.[33] And the killing must actually be done in the heat of passion engendered by the provocation.[34]

The plea has been unavailing in most of the witchcraft cases because there is usually time for passion to cool. But the peculiar nature of witchcraft is that it presents an overhanging, omnipresent threat. Time in such a case does not cool the passions; it inflames them. It was inevitable that provocation like all the other defenses invoked would not be a useful shield for these defendants.

III

No doubt, the received conceptual patterns of the common law could have been manipulated to reach a more equitable result. The reasonableness of the mistake might readily have been measured against the community from which the accused comes, rather than the "man on the Clapham omnibus"; moreover, there is the serious

---

[30] *Mawole Konkomba* (1952) 14 W.A.C.A. 236 at p. 237 (Gold Coast); *Kumataiaruf Mursei* (1939) 16 E.A.C.A. 117; *Sitakimatata s/o Kumwage* (1941) 8 E.A.C.A. 57 (Tanganyika); *Kasalo*, [1944–1946] R.L.R. 110; *Akobe s/o Karuon* (1947) 14 E.A.C.A. 105 (Kenya); *Kajuna s/o Mbake* (1945) 12 E.A.C.A. 104 (Tanganyika); *Kelementi Magnga s/o Ochieng* (1942) 10 E.A.C.A. 49 (Uganda).

[31] (1941) 8 E.A.C.A. 96.

[32] *Ibid.* at p. 101. It is difficult to understand the requirement that the act which causes the provocation be illegal. If a man sees his wife in the act of adultery, the passion engendered is surely not a function of the fact that adultery may be a violation of positive law. So the passion engendered by a witch performing his odious craft might well cause passion to override reason, whether or not a Witchcraft Ordinance prohibits it.

[33] *Mensah* [1946] A.C. 83 (P.C.); *Atta* [1959] G.L.R. 337. (*Held,* insults and a slap by his wife may be provocation for an illiterate Ashanti peasant); *cf. Bedder v. D.P.P.* (1954) 38 C.A.R. 133 (words cannot be provocation). The common law rules are largely embodied in the African codes. See, *e.g.,* Criminal Code, 1960 (Ghana), s. 52.

[34] *Rothwell* (1891) 12 Cox 145; *Thomas*, 7 C. & P. 182; *Hall* (1928) 21 C.A.R. 48; *Mancrus v. D.P.P.* [1942] A.C. 1; 28 C.A.R. 65.

question that the common law requires that the mistake be "reasonable." [35] It might have been possible to treat witchcraft belief as evidence of insanity; so Professor Kenny advocated.[36] The defense of provocation might have been extended by recognizing that belief in witchcraft provides the sort of provocation in which passion may overcome reason even after long brooding. Or, finally, it might be possible to deal with these cases by specific legislation, as Glanville Williams has suggested.[37]

The acceptability of these various solutions might be assessed in terms of the ultimate objectives of criminal law. To one degree or another, they retain some deterrent function; to one degree or another, they identify the defendant as a person who is exceptionally dangerous [38] and hence the subject of rehabilitative or restraining sanctions. But they all suffer from a common vice. These cases are only examples of a broad spectrum of prosecutions in which what is right and proper in indigenous society is criminal at common law.[39] In all these cases the criminal act is intentional, and the defendants cannot, unless the courts ape Procrustes, be fitted to any recognized defense. It is as though England had been conquered by a nation of Hindus,

[35] Williams, *Criminal Law: The General Part* (2nd ed., 1960), pp. 366–368. See also: Hall, *General Principles of Criminal Law* (2nd ed., 1960), pp. 201 *et seq.* (*Mens rea* a function of the defendant's opinion of the facts, whether or not reasonable); Williams, "Homicide and the Supernatural" (1949) 65 L.Q.R. 504 (requirement that mistake be reasonable applies only to crimes of negligence); Lewis, "Outlook for a Devil in the Colonies" [1958] Crim.L.R. 661; Burchell, "Unreasonable Mistake of Fact as a Defense in Criminal Law," 80 S.A.L.J. 46; *Griffin*, 1962 (4) S.A. 495. (Requirement of reasonableness questioned.) In "Homicide and the Supernatural," Williams argues that the true criterion is subjective, not objective. If the defendant intended to kill a non-human being, he cannot be convicted of murder, which requires an intention to kill a human being. Williams concedes that this leads to difficulties: Are witches "old women with magical powers, or on the other hand . . . not old women at all but magical creatures in the shape of old women?" Hence he concludes that "One has to inquire of the accused what are the characteristics of the class to which he believed his victim to belong, and one has to decide whether this class, assuming it to exist, would fall within the legal definition of the class to be protected." This test assumes that tribalized Africans make the distinction that educated persons do between magical and human beings. When an African slays a witch does he believe he is killing the physical shell, the *kra*, the *sunsum*, or perhaps the wicked *obayi*?

[36] Kenny, *Outlines of Criminal Law* (17th ed., 1958), p. 54 ("No belief which now has come to be currently regarded as an obsolete superstition can be treated as a mistake sufficiently reasonable to excuse a crime. . . . It would be more satisfactory if these instances of fantastic superstitious belief could be approached as insane delusions and treated in accordance with the rules applicable thereto.")

[37] *Loc. cit.*, note 35 above, p. 488 ("In the last resort, if a particular superstition is common in a community, it may be best to deal with it by an explicit statute so that those laboring under the superstitious delusion will know that their practices, independently of the truth or falsity of the belief, are punishable.") It may be doubted that legislation provides any notice of illegality, within the context of the African bush.

[38] The defendant in most of these cases *ex hypothesi* is subject to the same superstitions as most of the members of his community, and therefore is not identifiably more dangerous than they are. Query, the extent to which the average man in contemporary indigenous society will resort to killing a supposed witch; for to the extent that he does not, to that extent is the defendant who does kill, identified as more dangerous than the rest of his community. In Ashanti society of olden time, the "power of the knife"—i.e., to inflict capital punishment—inhered in the Asantehene. Rattray, *op. cit.*, note 5 above, pp. 289–290. But there were recognized tribunals before which a charge of witchcraft might be laid, so that an individual who believed that he was being attacked by a witch had some recourse. In Ghana, there are innumerable anti-witchcraft shrines which have sprung up in recent years.

[39] See, *e.g.*, *Alpha Kanu* (1959) 16 W.A.C.A. 90 (Sierra Leone), and *Ufuonye Enweonye* (1959) 15 W.A.C.A. 1 (Nigeria) (whole village co-operating to kill trespassers on "their" section of a river); *Akpunono* (1947) 8 W.A.C.A. 107 (Nigeria) (killing of infant twin); *Zanhibe*, 1954 (3) S.A. 597 (woman horribly burned by witch-doctor who was exorcising a demon); *Lekishon ole Sang' Are* (1956) 23 E.A.C.A. 626 (Kenya) (deceased killed while defending cattle from young initiates who demanded them as tradition dues); *Kofi Antwi* (1955) 1 W.A.L.R. 29 (Gold Coast) (man shot by elders resisting attempt by malcontents to seize the stool, traditional symbol of a chief's authority); *Ukpe* (1938) 4 W.A.C.A. 141 (Nigeria) (a member of one village slain by a member of another; every member of the victim's village swore juju to kill a member of the village of the slayer, presumably to accompany the victim on his funeral voyage).

so that the eating of beef immediately became a high crime.[40] Would the English-man who ate his usual dinner possess a guilty mind? Can it fairly be said that an African under analogous circumstances possesses *mens rea*? [41]

Now there is a sharp dichotomy between our myths about *mens rea,* and the actual requirements of the law. The myth is that the criminal law requires the presence of a "guilty mind" as a pre-condition to guilt,[42] a requirement patently demanded by humanitarian and ethical notions.[43] But the hard-nosed rule of law is that a man is guilty of a crime if he commits it intentionally,[44] and if he is not within one of a very few prescribed categories—self-defense, mistake, insanity, youth, and the like. *Mens rea* in modern law is wholly objective.[45] Its ethical content is at best lim-ited.

The judges' unease at the results which they have reached in the witchcraft cases arises because these defendants seem without *mens rea* in the mythological—*i.e.,* the moral and subjective—sense, although they plainly have *mens rea* in the legal—*i.e.,* the objective—sense. Can the contradiction be resolved? Is it possible perhaps to generalize from the exceptional defenses to find some new exception that will fit all

[40] "The gross absurdity of endeavoring to apply the substance but particularly the forms of our law to the people of India may be best conceived by supposing for a moment 12 Cononogoes, Moreland and Pundits, taking their seats in Westminster Hall, beginning the administration of justice there and gravely assuring the people of England that it was intended merely for their advantage. In the short space of one term every inhabitant of this metropolis would be capitally convicted for eating his ordinary food, and perhaps it would be no more than a just retaliation for the capital conviction of a Gentoo on the Coventry Act or one of the Statutes of Forgery." Statement of A. Macdonald, Counsel for the East India Company, December 26, 1782 (Ms. Home Misc. No. 411, India Office, London; quoted in Michael & Wechsler, *Criminal Law and Its Administration* (1940), p. 285, note 8).

[41] In *Kichingeri,* 3 E.A.L.R. accomplice evidence was accepted although uncorroborated. The court later commented on that case, saying that "It is interesting to note that the exceptional circumstance in the *Kichingeri* case was that because the accomplices bona fide thought they had performed a legal and meri-torious act in putting a suspected witch-doctor to death, the court concluded that their evidence was not tainted . . . because they were not shown to be persons of bad or doubtful character." *Khetsho Neghgi* (1948) 23 K.L.R. 36 at p. 37. Presumably the accomplices, for all that they were not persons of bad or doubtful character, were also found guilty of murder and condemned to death.

[42] "It is true that under the old common law, breaches of the laws of morality and crime were much the same. In a mass of cases *mens rea* involved moral blame, and the result is that people have got into the habit of translating the words *mens rea* as meaning guilty mind, and thinking that a person is not guilty of a penal act unless in doing what he did he had a wicked mind. That to my mind is wrong." *Per* Shear-man J. in *Allard v. Selfridge* [1925] 1 K.B. 129 at p. 137. See also Williams, *op. cit.,* note 35 above, p. 30 ("Any theory of criminal punishment leads to a requirement of *mens rea.* . . . However, the requirement as we have it in the law does not harmonize perfectly with any of these theories.") *Cf.,* Devlin, *loc cit.,* note 44 below (objective definition of *mens rea*) with Devlin. "Enforcement of Morals" (1959) 45 Proc. Brit. Acad. ("I think it clear that criminal law as we know it is based upon moral principles.")

[43] Turner, "The Mental Element in Crimes at Common Law" in Radzinowicz and Turner (eds.), *The Modern Approach to Criminal Law* (1945), p. 195; Williams, *op. cit.,* note 35 above, p. 30; Kenny, *op. cit.,* note 36 above, pp. 10–14; *Russell on Crime* (10th ed., 1950), vol. 12, p. 25 *et seq.*

[44] Turner, *loc cit.,* note 43 above, p. 199; Williams, *op. cit.,* note 35 above, p. 31; Devlin, "Statutory Of-fences" (1958) 4 J. Soc. Pub. Teachers of Law 213. The shift from the moral notion of *mens rea* to an "objective" *mens rea* is frequently supposed to be one with a temporal characteristic. Thus statements such as those in *Fowler v. Padget* (1789) 7 T.R. 514, imply a concept of wickedness which could only have meaning if there was consciousness of moral guilt. This view is supposed to have been overthrown in the modern cases, *e.g.,* Shearman J. in *Allard v. Selfridge,* note 42 above ("The true translation to my mind of *mens rea* is 'criminal intention' or, to put it at greater length, 'the intention to do the act which is made penal by the statute or by common law.' ") See generally Stallybrass, "A Comparison of the Crim-inal Law of England," in *Modern Approach,* note 43 above, p. 406.

[45] "Every man runs the risk that a court may decide that what he has done is a crime or is immoral, but his liability does not depend on his own ability to make that decision; and his risk is just the same whether or not he has any idea that what he is doing is immoral, or a civil wrong, or a crime." Turner, *loc. cit.,* note 43 above, p. 216.

these cases? To find a common denominator, a brief excursion seems required into the psychology which underlies these defenses.

IV

It is commonplace to conceive of the psychology which provides the foundation for the M'Naghten Rules as a constant wrestling match between reason and passion.[46] The same psychology underlies our notions of *mens rea*. An American court once described it as the notion that "there is a separate little man in the top of one's head called reason whose function it is to guide another unruly little man called instinct, emotion or impulse the way he should go." [47]

The role of the criminal law both in Benthamite and neo-classical theory, is to provide, by its sanctions, an incentive to reason to follow the right road.[48] Sanctions must be imposed, therefore, whenever an intentional criminal harm is caused, unless for one of three exceptional causes, reason understandably failed to guide passion along the road of legality. First, reason may be withered by inherent infirmity. Insanity and youth are the chief examples. Secondly, reason in choosing to do the act, may be acting reasonably. Self-defense and mistake fall within the category. Thirdly, reason under all the circumstances of the case may understandably be temporarily overpowered by passion. Provocation is of course the principal sort.

These categories aside, the law punishes a man whose reason does not control his passion. Save perhaps in cases of inherent physical infirmity the test is invariably that of the reasonable man. If a mistake be one that a reasonable man would not have made, it is no excuse. If the error be that the defendant failed to act as carefully as a reasonable man, he is guilty, whether or not he actually perceived the risk.[49] If the issue is whether the defendant foresaw the consequences of his conduct, the test is not whether he actually foresaw, but whether a reasonable man would have foreseen.[50] In short, the law actually punishes if a man's reason fails to control his actions, save where a reasonable man's reason would likewise have failed, or where the defendant is physically incapable of reasoning.[51]

The reasonable man, however, is a normative concept,[52] which hypostatizes not

---

[46] The literature is voluminous. See, *e.g.*, Biggs, *The Guilty Mind* (1955), p. 203 *et seq.* This is, of course, the central target of the medical attack upon the M'Naghten Rules. Zilboorg, "Misconceptions of Legal Insanity" (1939) 9 Am. J. Orthopsychiatry 540 at pp. 552–553; Royal Commission on Capital Punishment 1949–1953, paras. 227–228.

[47] *Holloway v. United States*, 148 F. (2d) 668; certiorari denied, 334 U.S. 852 (1948).

[48] Bentham, *Principles of Penal Law*, Pt. II, Bk. 1, c. 4, in 1 Bentham's *Works* 397 (Bowring ed., 1843).

[49] *Machekequnabe* (1897) 28 Ont. Rep. 309 (the defendant, an Indian, was posted as guard to defend against a Wendigo or man-eating spirit, which had been seen in the area; he shot and killed his foster-father, whom he mistook for the Wendigo; *held*, manslaughter).

[50] *D.P.P. v. Smith* [1961] A.C. 290.

[51] Drunkenness is of course a case of physical disability of the mind. By denying that drunkenness is a defense, the courts punish a man for the sin of drunkenness, but measure the punishment by the appropriate harm committed. The illogic is in the measure of punishment, not the measure of guilt.

The objective standard even applies to factual knowledge. "There have been a number of convictions, and the relevant holdings imply that ignorance of ordinary factual knowledge, possessed by every 'normal' adult in the community, except such eccentrics as these defendants, is no defense. Although mitigation is undoubtedly frequent, it is assumed that the ignorance is 'unreasonable' and the conduct is held criminal." Hall, *op. cit.*, note 35 above, at p. 375.

[52] Williams, "Provocation and the Reasonable Man" [1954] Crim.L.R. 740 at p. 742.

the average man, but the ideal man—*i.e.*, a man with some, but not the grosser, human failings. It is a statement of the judge's notion of a standard of conduct which the average man can fairly be expected to achieve. In the criminal law, the concept of *mens rea* performs a similarly normative function. It is a statement of a standard of conduct for the little man labelled reason. To state that *mens rea* is present, is merely to say that defendant's reason failed to act as would a reasonable man's under the circumstances.

The use of the standard of the reasonable man in defining *mens rea* resolves a pervasive conflict in the criminal law. On the one hand, "objective" *mens rea* ignores the defendant's actual consciousness of guilt. It finds its social justification not in the reformation of individual criminals, but in exemplary deterrence. Holmes, an ardent proponent of the objective theory,[53] once wrote, "If I were having a philosophical talk with a man I was going to have hanged or electrocuted, I should say, I don't doubt that your act was inevitable for you but to make it more avoidable by others we proposed to sacrifice you to the common good. You may regard yourself as a soldier dying for his country if you like. But the law must keep its promises." [54]

This harsh utilitarianism finds its source in society's interest in protecting its individual members. Out of the same regard for human beings arises a countervailing humanitarian or moral consideration. "This moral objection normally would be couched as the insistence that it is *unjust*, or *unfair*, to take someone who has not broken the law or was unable to comply with it, and use him as a mere instrument to protect society and increase its welfare." [55]

This humanitarian consideration, like the utilitarian objective, is partially met by a concept of *mens rea* modelled upon the reasonable man, for "moral wickedness cannot well be imputed to a man who behaved as a reasonable man behaves. . . ." [56] So consideration is extended to the criminal, if not for his own idiosyncratic weaknesses, then at least for those of the reasonable man.

The tension between the utilitarian and humanitarian objective of criminal punishment thus finds one resolution in the concept of objective *mens rea*. That concept simultaneously serves both ends: it furnishes a rationale to punish one who fails to meet objective norms, and an excuse to exonerate one who failed to meet them where most men would likewise have failed. Like many of the germinal legal concepts, it resolves the pervasive antagonism between social expediency and individual right.

The success of objective *mens rea* in resolving this tension obviously turns upon how close a fit there is between the reasonable and the average man. Where they are fairly congruent (as they are in English society), then objective *mens rea* serves its function tolerably well. In most cases, it protects the morally innocent; in some cases, the morally innocent may be criminally guilty, but the result will not be too shocking; and in the few cases where moral innocence is distressingly clear, the

---

[53] See Hall, *op. cit.*, note 35 above, pp. 147–152. Hall, while in general agreement with Holmes' perception of the essential soundness of the objectivity of the penal law, finds its justification not in expediency (as Holmes did), but in a mystique of the "community:" ". . . the valid ground . . . is not expediency, but . . . the correctness of the community's freely derived values, as expressed in penal law. . . ." *Ibid.*, p. 163. Query, in the African context, whether Hall could argue that there was any validity to the imposition of the English law of crimes, since it is hardly an expression of the African community's "freely derived values."

[54] *Holmes-Laski Letters* (Howe ed., 1953), p. 806.

[55] Gardiner, "The Purposes of Criminal Punishment" (1958) 21 M.L.R. 117 at p. 125.

[56] Kenny, *op. cit.*, note 36 above, pp. 11–12.

executive can spring to the rescue. In short, where such congruence exists, there is rarely more than a small difference between the morally and the legally guilty.[57]

A very different state of affairs was obtained, however, when *mens rea* was cut from African cloth, but shaped to British patterns. Then the reasonable man and the average man were continents and in some cases worlds apart. Since the humanitarian function of *mens rea* depends upon the narrowness of the gap (although the function of exemplary deterrence is indifferent to it), the result was that colonial law was devoted almost entirely to the objective of deterrence. Put bluntly, in the final analysis colonial law in these cases selected its victims without regard to moral guilt; it imposed its norms upon the indigenous population by sheer terror. Despite the best intentions of judges and administrators, the use of objective *mens rea* based upon English precedents guaranteed that the law would be concerned only with deterrence by harsh example.[58] *Mens rea,* originally a humanitarian concept, became its very opposite. But the colonial judges were humane men. So they regularly impleaded the executive to save the law from the pit which it had dug.

V

Is it possible to find some organizing principle which would subsume the cases which led to this discussion, and facilitate reaching more defensible results?

One possible solution would be to model *mens rea* more closely upon the community from which the defendant comes. This, I believe, would be unacceptable. The Africans who now control their own countries, educated as they are to the highest standards of European culture, will not accept a pre-scientific standard of knowledge and behavior. Nor could they, for they must build modern industrialized societies, and belief in witchcraft and its equivalents is impermissible.

A second possible solution would be to retain as norm the standard of educated, twentieth-century, rationalist man, but to take into account as a mitigating circumstance on sentence the fact that this particular defendant could not reach that standard and could not have acted otherwise than he did. This is the South African solution, where the practice has always been to treat belief in witchcraft as extenuation.[59]

---

[57] *Cf.* Hall, *op. cit.,* note 35 above, pp. 166–167 (". . . since most defendants are 'reasonable' men both the objective method of fact-finding and the objective standard of liability function accurately and justly in most cases. In other words, although the defendant is directly and verbally held to the objective standard of liability, that standard in most cases also fits the defendant's actual ('subjective') state of mind.")

[58] *Atma Singh s/o Chanda Singh* (1942) 9 E.A.C.A. 69 (Kenya) (the defendant, following Sikh custom, cut off the nose and ears of his unfaithful wife. On appeal from sentence, the court said: "When one further considers that one of the most important objects of punishment is deterrence, our view is that a lesser sentence might be misunderstood. If . . . there still exists among the Sikh or any other Indian community a custom of disfiguring deserting or unfaithful wives in the hideous and barbaric fashion exemplified in this case, then the demand for a heavy sentence for such acts would be all the more necessary"); *Zanhibe,* 1954 (3) S.A. 597 (the defendant, a native doctor, had a woman forcibly restrained over a fire to exorcise a demon; the woman died. The court assumed that moral guilt was absent, but said: "It . . . seems to me that even where moral guilt is absent a court may, in a proper case, where a very large section of the community, especially an unenlightened one, required to be protected against dangerous practices, disregard the existence of that form of mitigation").

[59] *Fundakabi,* 1948 (3) S.A. 810. *Accord (semble) Peter Mukasa* (1944) 11 E.A.C.A. 114 (Uganda) (defendants killed some thieves stealing food crops. "Prior to the advent of British rule the killing of persons caught stealing food crops was held by the Buganda to be justifiable homicide." *Held,* in the light of this, sentences reduced).

A third, possibly more radical solution, seems indicated. The whole doctrine of *mens rea* arises historically. It bottoms itself upon two historically derived conditions. The first is that the felony verdict not so long ago determined not only guilt, but punishment as well—and the punishment was death. Had it been otherwise, moral guilt might have been merely a consideration affecting punishment. Instead, it became the touchstone of legal guilt. The resulting confusion between religious, ethical and legal considerations has plagued the criminal law ever since—as the witchcraft cases here discussed bear witness.

The second historically determined condition for the doctrine of *mens rea* is a system of pseudo-psychology that today is a superstitution to which apparently only judges and lawyers subscribe. Reason and emotion are simply not independent entities. Man's personality is a unity. No doubt, in the interplay between conscious and subconscious, there remains some area in which it is not incorrect to speak of free will; but as one descends into the criminal classes that area becomes progressively more circumscribed by the inevitable. How could a doctrine built on so sandy a psychological foundation be more than accidentally valid?

To abandon the notion of the wrestling match between reason and emotion, however, implies a substantial abandonment of deterrence as an objective of the criminal law.[60] It is at best a largely unachieved objective; speaking of the slaying of supposed witches, a South African court once sadly confessed: "not that great reliance can be placed on the severity of punishment alone to get rid of the evil. . . ."[61]

If the death penalty did not automatically flow from a finding of guilt, and if the objective of exemplary deterrence were abandoned, the solution would become easy enough. The guilty verdict would mean only that the accused was made subject to administrative processes of re-education. The objective of criminal sanction would be to rehabilitate the criminal, not to deter others. There could then be made available to the sentencing authority a whole host of procedures which are foreclosed by an emphasis upon exemplary deterrence: re-education, vocational rehabilitation, family counselling, compulsory attendance at a job, transportation to another part of the country, and the like. The objective of the criminal law would become wholly humanitarian, for no man would be regarded as expendable in the interests of the state. The *actus reus* would become merely the identifying mark of one who needs to be re-educated, not that of the next sacrifice on the altar of deterrence.

CONCLUSION

We have come full circle. The original unease of the judges over their results forced them to call upon the executive for clemency for those just solemnly sentenced. To the extent that such a reaction became institutionalized, both the automatic death penalty and its presumed deterrent effect were negated. The judges themselves thus recognized that the criminal law is a poor instrument of radical social change.

The independent African states, it may be hoped, will also recognize this patent

[60] "Ultimately . . . there is no solution except that of allowing the concept of responsibility to wither away. . . . In this way, and only in this way, can all the contradictions be resolved, and all the unanswerable questions avoided. Forget responsibility, and psychiatrists need no longer masquerade as moralists. . . . Forget responsibility and we can ask not whether an offender *ought* to be punished, but whether . . . he is likely to benefit from punishment." Lady Wootton of Abinger, "Diminished Responsibility: A Layman's View" (1960) 76 L.Q.R. 224 at p. 239.

[61] *Fundakabi*, note 59 above, at p. 819.

fact. For a colonial court to apply law, which, except when relieved by executive clemency, seemed to rule by terror, was bad enough. It would be intolerable if the African nations sought to implement the radical social change now required by the same means.

The solution lies in the abandonment of the concept of objective *mens rea,* a concept which has a specific historical origin and setting, and reaches strange and unworkable results when wrenched out of it. The new African governments base themselves on doctrines of humanism, upon the dignity and worth of the individual personality. To retain the doctrine of *mens rea* in its received form, based upon the norms of rulers but not necessarily of the governed, denies that basic value.

PART THREE

THE IMPACT
of LEGAL SANCTIONS

PART THREE

INTRODUCTION

In the last analysis a legal system must be judged according to the impact it has on the social order. If that impact is largely deleterious to the lives of men, then maintaining the legal system can scarcely be justified. If, on the other hand, the law contributes in some important ways to the goals of society and its members, then there is justification for keeping it. And, of course, if the legal system is useful in certain ways but deleterious in others, then this condition requires changing the system so as to increase its effectiveness while maintaining those aspects which are found to have desirable consequences.

The presumed consequences of the law are not all equally amenable to empirical verification. The idea, for example, that if a person commits a criminal act, the state must punish him for that act because it is the only way to restore the balance of nature to its proper order is not amenable to systematic investigation. Such an idea rests, ultimately, on the purely philosophical assumption that retribution for wrongdoings is intrinsically valuable.

Such vague and ill-defined assertions about the consequences of the law have in recent years been relegated to a much less important place than the more directly demonstrable question of whether or not the presence of laws and the imposition of punishment act as a deterrent to crime.[1] As Richard Schwartz and Jerome Skolnick point out:

> Legal thinking has moved increasingly toward a sociologically meaningful view of the legal system. Sanctions, in particular, have come to be regarded in functional terms. In criminal law, for instance, sanctions

[1] See the discussions in Johannes Andenaes, "The General Preventive Effects of Punishment," *University of Pennsylvania Law Review*, vol. 114, pp. 949–983, May, 1966, and "General Prevention," *Journal of Criminal Law, Criminology, and Police Science*, vol. 43, pp. 176–193, 1942.

are said to be designed to prevent recidivism by rehabilitating, restraining or executing the offender. They are also said to be intended to deter others from the performance of similar acts and, sometimes, to provide a channel for the expression of retaliatory motives.[2]

It is principally with the question of deterrence that the social sciences have been concerned, for it is here that the impact of the legal system is most amenable to empirical and systematic evaluation.[3]

The Deterrent Influence of Capital Punishment

The question of the deterrent influence of capital punishment has occupied the forefront in criminological research for years. The preponderance of the evidence indicates that capital punishment does not act as a deterrent to murder. This general conclusion is based on a number of observations and researches which have demonstrated:

1. The fact that despite trends away from the use of capital punishment the murder rates have remained constant.
2. The fact that within the United States where one state has abolished capital punishment and another has not, the murder rate is no higher in the abolition state than in the death-penalty state.
3. The fact that the possible consequences of the act of murder are apparently not considered by the murderer at the time of the crime.

Some of the evidence substantiating these three conclusions is presented below.

There has been a very clear tendency throughout the Western world to eliminate capital punishment. In the United States this trend away from the use of capital punishment has taken several forms. To begin with, there has been a rapid decline in the number of states where capital punishment is mandatory if an accused is found guilty: in 1924 the death penalty was mandatory in eight states, but by 1964 it was not mandatory in any. There has also been a tendency to impose the death sentence less and less frequently: from 1933 to 1934 of those persons sentenced to death by the court, 80 percent were ultimately executed. From 1940 to 1945 81 percent of those sentenced to death were executed. But from 1960 to 1964, of all the persons sentenced to death by the court, only 34 percent were executed.

There has also been a steady increase in the number of states that have abolished capital punishment for various crimes. In 1920 only six states had abolished capital punishment; by 1957 the number of states that had abolished it had risen to eight, and by 1965 there were thirteen states that had formally abolished capital punishment. Perhaps even more significant is the rapid decline in the number of persons actually

[2] Richard Schwartz and Jerome Skolnick, "Two Studies of Legal Stigma," *Social Problems,* vol. 10, pp. 133–141, Fall, 1962.

[3] Legal writers typically distinguish between general deterrence (the deterrence of potential law violators) and specific deterrence (the deterrence of a violator from commiting further transgressions). Although this distinction may be useful in the abstract, it is difficult to maintain in empirical research and may in fact obscure more than it clarifies. Therefore, in this discussion we shall adopt the more inclusive conception of deterrence without differentiating general and specific consequences.

executed. In 1951 there were 105 executions in the United States; since that time, the number of executions has shown a steady and precipitous decline, with 15 executions in 1964 and 7 in 1965. In 1966 there was only one execution in all fifty states.

Thus we see in the United States a steady and rapid alteration in the propensity to administer capital punishment. From the standpoint of deterrence, the significance of this trend is that during this same period we find *no significant change* in the murder rate (see Table 1). If the presence of capital punishment, either in principle or in fact, were a deterrent to murder, it would seem that the murder rate should have gone up as we have experienced a decline in both the potential and the actual use of capital punishment.

The conclusion that the rate has not gone up emerges when the murder rates in states that have retained the death penalty are compared with those in states that have abolished it.[4] This general conclusion also holds true when one compares contiguous states—states which are presumably relatively homogeneous culturally, but where one state has retained the death penalty and the other has not (see Table 2).

The states that have *abolished* the death penalty do not show an increase in the murder rate compared with states that have retained it. In three out of four pairs of states included in Table 2, the abolition state has a lower murder rate. In one pairing the rates are identical. However, if one compares Michigan (an abolition state) with Indiana instead of with Illinois (both death-penalty states), then the abolition state has a slightly higher murder rate (3.8 for Michigan as opposed to 3.2 for Indiana).

Thus, considering the five possible pairings, three show a lower murder rate for the abolition state, one pair shows no difference between the two states, and one pair shows a higher murder rate for the abolition state. The differences are slight in every instance, and the only safe conclusion to be drawn from these data is that propensity to murder is no greater when capital punishment is not a possibility than when it is. The point is not that abolishing capital punishment decreases the murder rate; rather, the point is that since the murder rate does not increase, we must conclude that capital punishment is not an effective deterrent.

The same conclusion is also suggested in a study by Leonard Savitz of the murder rate in Philadelphia immediately preceding and following particularly well-publicized executions. If executing someone for a capital crime were a deterrent, one would expect its influence to be at a peak when an execution was imminent or had just occurred. But Savitz found no difference in the murder rate immediately prior to, and following, such executions.[5]

Given this preponderance of evidence, it seems safe to conclude that

[4] Karl F. Schuessler, "The Deterrent Influence of the Death Penalty," *Annals of the American Academy of Political and Social Science,* vol. 284, pp. 54–82, November, 1952.

[5] Leonard D. Savitz, "A Study of Capital Punishment," *Journal of Criminal Law, Criminology, and Police Science,* vol. 49, pp. 338–341, November–December, 1958.

capital punishment does not act as an effective deterrent. This does not tell us, however, about punishment generally since, as is well recognized, murder and other capital offenses are generally complicated by a great deal of emotional involvement on the part of the offender; thus one might well expect punishment to be less effective in deterring such crimes precisely because they are less apt to be dictated by "rational" considerations of gain or loss. It would therefore be well to look at different types of offenses and see what the evidence indicates.[6]

TABLE 1

Comparison of Prisoners Executed under Civil Authority and Murder Rate, 1951–1966

Year	Number of Persons Executed	Murder Rate (per 100,000 Population)
1951	105	4.9
1952	83	5.0
1953	62	4.8
1954	81	4.8
1955	76	4.9
1956	65	5.0
1957	65	5.1
1958	49	4.6
1959	49	4.8
1960	56	5.1
1961	42	4.7
1962	47	4.5
1963	21	4.5
1964	15	4.8
1965	7	5.1
1966	1	5.6

TABLE 2

Annual Average Homicide Rates in Selected Contiguous States

	Homicide Rate 1959–1964
Rhode Island *	1.0
Connecticut †	1.4
Michigan *	3.8
Illinois †	4.4
Wisconsin *	1.3
Indiana †	3.2
Minnesota *	1.1
Iowa †	1.1

* Abolition state.

† Death-penalty state.

SOURCE: This table is a revision and updating of the one in Karl F. Schuessler, "The Deterrent Influence of the Death Penalty," *Annals of the American Academy of Political and Social Science,* vol. 284, pp. 54–82, November, 1952.

[6] The importance of looking at types of offenses is noted in Andenaes, *op. cit.*

Drug Addiction and the Law [7]

There is a saying among drug addicts that "once the monkey's on your back you never shake him off." The empirical research on drug addiction strongly supports this contention. In a study of 800 addicts who were followed after treatment, it was found that 81.6 percent of these had relapsed within the first year, 93.9 percent within three years, and 96.7 percent within five years.[8]

The federally run hospitals at Lexington, Kentucky, and Fort Worth, Texas, report similar recidivism rates among persons treated at these hospitals; relapses occur in excess of 90 percent of the persons treated.

Even among persons who are, presumably, the most likely to be rehabilitated through treatment, the recidivism rate is exceedingly high. Synanon, an organization for the treatment of drug addicts in Los Angeles, accepts only those addicts who volunteer for treatment. In addition to volunteering, the addicts must agree to undergo rather severe "hazing" in order to demonstrate the sincerity of their desire to abstain from drug use. Given these conditions, it is reasonable to assume that Synanon treats only those persons whose desire to "kick the habit" is very strong. But even with these persons the number who fail to complete the treatment program at Synanon is in excess of 70 percent of all those who initially apply.[9]

For the question of the deterrent influence of punishment, the significance of these statistics lies in the following: concomitant with this propensity to recidivate has been a constantly increasing effort by the federal government to severely sanction drug users. The Federal Narcotics Bureau has increased its efforts at control, and the formal sanctions have drastically increased in severity to the extent that under certain federal statutes a person who violates the drug laws will be sentenced to prison for six years with no possibility of parole. Thus drug use is one of the most severely punished crimes in the United States.

This evidence, then, suggests that drug addiction, like murder, is relatively unaffected by the threat or the imposition of punishment. But one may still raise the question of whether these findings can be generalized to include all types of offenses. Indeed, at least in one respect, drug addiction and murder share something which is lacking in many other types of offenses: that is, both of these acts are "expressive"—the act is committed because it is an end in and of itself and not because it is a route to some other goal. Let us then turn our attention to more instrumental and, presumably, more "rational" types of offenses.

[7] The following discussion is limited to the use of opiates and its derivatives, principally heroin and morphine; whether other so-called "drugs" would show the same characteristics is as yet unknown.

[8] Reported in Alfred R. Lindesmith, *Opiate Addiction*, Principia Press, 1939.

[9] Rita Volkman and Donald R. Cressey, "Differential Association and the Rehabilitation of Drug Addicts," *American Journal of Sociology*, pp. 129–142, September, 1963.

The Violation of Parking Regulations

If murder and drug addiction are at one extreme in the typology of criminal acts, parking-law violations would be at the other. It is probably the case that no one violates parking laws as an end in itself; rather, persons violate these laws primarily because it is instrumental to the attainment of some other goal. Does the imposition of punishment on parking-law violators have the same effect as is the case for drug addicts and murderers?

Chambliss's study of the violation of parking regulations (see pp. 388–393) disclosed that the propensity to violate these rules is directly related to the likelihood that offenders will be sanctioned. When punishment for violation of the regulations was sporadically and lightly administered, a substantial minority were prone to violate. When, however, the likelihood of the imposition of sanctions was increased, violation of the regulations decreased.[10]

"White-collar" Crimes

Although the data are less systematic than one might wish, studies on the impact of the enforcement of sanctions against business-connected crimes on businessmen suggest effects similar to those of the impact of sanctions on parking-law violators. Where penal sanctions are imposed, there is a decline in the propensity to violate the law. Marshall Clinard summarized the findings from his study of black-market violations during World War II as follows:

> [During the first stage of enforcement] . . . the public and business had been developing an attitude that the OPA did not mean business, that violations would be followed with only minor actions, usually simply a warning letter, and that the penalties described in the regulations were virtually meaningless. New types of violations were rapidly being devised and were spreading from business concern to business concern and from consumer to consumer. . . .
>
> As the economy was rapidly getting out of hand with this slow hit-and-miss method of price control, the government on April 28, 1942, froze the prices on nearly all uncontrolled commodities. . . . This regulation provided "Persons violating any provision of this Regulation are subject to the criminal penalties, civil enforcement actions, and suits for treble damages provided by the Emergency Price Control Act of 1942." . . .
>
> The penalty of imprisonment, even for a short period of time, was the punishment most feared by businessmen, according to their own statements; yet it was seldom invoked as a deterrent for others. A survey of wholesale food dealers' opinions, for example, revealed that they considered imprisonment a far more effective penalty than any other government action, including fines. In fact, some 65 per cent of them made such a statement. They made remarks such as the following about jail sentences: "Jail is the only way; nobody wants to go to jail." "Everybody gets panicky at the thought of a jail sentence." "A

[10] William J. Chambliss, "The Deterrent Influence of Punishment," *Crime and Delinquency*, pp. 70–75, January, 1966.

jail sentence is dishonorable; it jeopardizes the reputation." "It [jail] spoils the offender's reputation and frightens the other fellow." "The thing that puts a man to shame—closing his store and sending him to jail." These expressions are in marked contrast to the attitudes of the same men toward the imposition of fines and other monetary penalties: "They don't hurt anybody." "They're never missed." "People are making enough money nowadays to pay a fine easily." "The violators violate again, so they must not care about paying a fine." "It just comes out of the profits, like a tax." "They make so much in the black market they can afford to pay steep fines."

District enforcement attorneys of the OPA also felt the lack of this element of deterrence for, according to one survey, they reported that where sentences were generally adequate, observance of regulations was best, and that a converse situation existed where sentences were inadequate.

As an example, one concern was found guilty of handling over 300,000 pounds of meat in five months, with over-ceiling side payments of from 7 to 11 cents a pound. The convicted defendants were fined only $250 on each of six counts, and given a suspended sentence of thirty days, to run concurrently on each of the six counts. As a result of this case the OPA district enforcement attorney reported that subsequent efforts of investigators to enforce the regulations were laughed at by businessmen. On the other hand, in one midwestern city two automobile dealers were fined $5,000 apiece, and in addition one was sent to federal penitentiary for fifteen months, for selling used cars above ceiling. After this sentence numerous automobile dealers commented that they were not going to take any chances of facing a sentence such as that imposed on these violators, and better compliance resulted.[11]

At least the expressed reaction of persons sentenced to jail for violation of the Sherman Antitrust Laws suggests a similar impact: George Burens, a General Electric vice-president who was fined $4,000 and given thirty days in jail, said after he was sentenced, "There goes my whole life. Who's going to want to hire a jailbird." [12]

The Snitch and the Booster

Mary Owen Cameron's study of shoplifting throws still more light on the impact of punishment as a deterrent. Cameron points out that there are two types of shoplifters: the snitch and the booster. The booster is a professional thief whose principal form of theft is shoplifting. The snitch (or pilferer), by contrast, is generally a respectable citizen (usually a middle-class housewife) who shoplifts in order to supplement the family income. Cameron was able to check on the recidivism of persons apprehended by careful examination of department-store files. Once a person is apprehended by a store detective, a card is filed with her picture, and every store in the city has access to this file. Thus it is quite likely that if anyone has been apprehended before this will come out. Cameron

---

[11] Marshall B. Clinard, *The Black Market,* New York: Rinehart & Company, Inc., 1952, pp. 58–60.

[12] Apparently someone wanted to hire jailbirds: of the seven men who received jail sentences, all but one were employed at the same or higher levels with either their own companies or similar ones a year later. The one who was not was on the verge of retiring and simply took this opportunity to do so.

found that persons who were professional thieves invariably had prior arrest records in the stores' files but that the snitches almost never did. For a snitch one arrest was almost always sufficient to ensure that she would never be arrested again. It is possible, but quite unlikely, that snitches simply became more careful after having been arrested once. It is more likely, however, that they were in fact deterred from further shoplifting by the experience of being caught:

> Among pilferers who are apprehended and interrogated by the store police but set free without formal charge, there is very little or no recidivism. . . . [O]nce arrested, interrogated, and in their own perspective, perhaps humiliated, pilferers apparently stop pilfering. The rate of recidivism is amazingly low. The reward of shoplifting, whatever it is, is not worth the cost of reputation and self-esteem. . . . [One] woman was observed who, thoroughly shaken as the realization of her predicament began to appear to her, interrupted her protestations of innocence from time to time, overwhelmed at the thought of how some particular person in her "in-group" would react to her arrest. Her conversation with the interrogator ran somewhat as follows: "I didn't intend to take the dress. I just wanted to see it in daylight. [She had stuffed it into a shopping bag and carried it out of the store.] Oh, what will my husband do? I did intend to pay for it. It's all a mistake. Oh, my God, what will my mother say! I'll be glad to pay for it. See, I've got the money with me. Oh, my children! They can't find out I've been arrested! I'd never be able to face them again!" . . .
>
> The contrast in behavior between the pilferer and the recognized and self-admitted thief is striking. The experienced thief either already knows what to do or knows precisely where and how to find out. His emotional reactions may involve anger directed at himself or at features in the situation around him, but he is not at a loss for reactions. He follows the prescribed modes of behavior, and knows, either because of prior experience or through the vicarious experiences of acquaintances, what arrest involves by way of obligations and rights. He has some familiarity with bonding practice and either already has or knows how to find a lawyer who will act for him.[13]

These findings, then, suggest that the amateur shoplifter or snitch will be deterred from further criminality by the imposition of punishment, whereas the professional thief will be little affected by it.

Cameron's findings concerning professional thieves are also corroborated by other investigators. Edwin Lemert's study of the systematic check forger suggests that receiving an occasional jail sentence is merely part of the life of being a professional thief and that it is accepted as one of the "hazards of the business," just as other occupational groups accept certain undesirable characteristics of their work as inevitable hazards.[14] The fact that arrest and jail sentence do not interrupt the ongoing interpersonal relations of professional thieves is undoubtedly an important element in rendering the punishment relatively ineffective.

But this fatalistic acceptance of imprisonment as an inevitability should

[13] Mary O. Cameron, *The Booster and the Snitch,* New York: The Free Press of Glencoe, 1966.

[14] Edwin Lemert, "The Behavior of the Systematic Check Forger," *Social Problems,* pp. 141–149, Fall, 1948.

not be interpreted to mean that the professional thief is wholly unresponsive to the threat of punishment. On the contrary, a much greater proportion of a thief's energy is devoted to avoiding capture and imprisonment than is devoted to stealing. That a thief accepts occasional "bits" without, apparently, being deterred from further crime must be viewed in light of the fact that for a reasonably competent and skillful thief, prison sentences occur relatively infrequently.[15]

A Typology of Crime and Deterrence

The preceding summary of research findings on the deterrent influence of punishment on various types of crimes suggests some interesting contrasts. First is the contrast between acts which are "expressive" and acts which are "instrumental." Murder as an expressive act is relatively unaffected by the threat of punishment, as is drug addiction; on the other hand, instrumental acts, such as the violation of parking regulations and shoplifting by middle-class housewives, are more likely to be influenced by the threat or imposition of punishment.

Another major distinction suggested by the research is that between persons who are highly committed to crime as a way of life and persons whose commitment is low. Cameron discusses this distinction in contrasting the booster and the snitch and argues that this is essentially a difference in the group support perceived by these different categories of offenders for their transgressions. More generally, we could say that persons with a high commitment perceive group support, conceive of themselves as criminal, and pattern their way of life around the fact of their involvement in criminality. Persons with low commitment would, of course, exhibit the reverse of these characteristics.

By combining these two dimensions of criminality and offender, it is possible to construct a typology of criminal acts with clear implications as to how given combinations of offender and offense will respond to punishment by reducing their involvement in crime. The hypothesis is that where a high commitment to crime as a way of life is combined with involvement in an act that is expressive, one finds the greatest resistance to rehabilitation or deterrence through threat of punishment. At the other extreme are violators whose commitment to crime is low and where the act itself is instrumental (such as the snitch, the white-collar criminal, or the parking-law violator), and here we would expect both general and specific deterrence to be maximally effective (see the typology outlined in Table 3).

Although we can assert with some confidence that the remaining two combinations—high-commitment-instrumental and low-commitment-expressive—will fall between the two polar types, it is somewhat more difficult to know which of these types will be most responsive to punishment. It seems likely, however, that the impulsive nature of expressive acts, even when commitment to crime is low, will make such acts less responsive

---

[15] See the autobiography annotated by Edwin H. Sutherland, *The Professional Thief,* Chicago: The University of Chicago Press, 1937.

to punishment than are acts which are instrumental, even though commitment may be high.

We have, then, the following hierarchy of types which can be ranked according to whether or not they are likely to be deterred by punishment or the threat of it:

Most likely to be deterred: Low-commitment-instrumental
                              High-commitment-instrumental
Least likely to be deterred: Low-commitment-expressive
                              High-commitment-expressive

In considering this typology it must be stressed that the sociological types represented do *not* correspond perfectly with legal types. If they did, there would be no reason for developing the typology. For example, the legal category murder is represented in at least three of the four sociological types. Probably in over 90 percent of the cases,[16] murder is an expressive act where the commitment to crime as a way of life is low. Typically, murder occurs during an argument betweeen two people. But there are other types of murder which would fit into the instrumental category of offenses; gangland murders, which constitute only a very small portion of the total number of murders, would of course be such a type. Murdering someone to collect insurance and sundry other profit-making schemes represent instrumental types of offenses where commitment would probably be low.

The above argument can now be used to throw more light on the earlier discussion of the deterrent influence of capital punishment. For if our theory is correct, then those murders which are instrumental and where commitment to crime is low should be deterred by the threat of punishment. The fact that capital punishment does not affect the murder rate therefore must be explained by the fact that most murders are expressive types of offenses.[17]

If this typology has in fact the kind of general utility in predicting the deterrent influence of punishment that research findings suggest it should have, then a truly rational system of justice would be one which would maximize its effectiveness by imposing criminal sanctions where these act as an effective deterrent and which would at the same time develop alternatives to punishment where it is found to be ineffective. The impli-

---

[16] Marvin Wolfgang, *Patterns in Criminal Homicide,* Philadelphia: University of Pennsylvania Press, 1958.

[17] The policy question raised by this argument is a sticky one: Assuming that instrumental-type murders are deterred by capital punishment (a conclusion that is consistent with the preceding argument), then should we continue to impose capital punishment generally for murder in order to achieve that deterrent effect? The answer to this query must of course take into account the costs of such a policy. In the case of murder, the cost of deterring instrumental murderers through capital punishment is to execute persons who would not be deterred by the threat of punishment because their acts are expressive; and in the case of murder, this represents the vast bulk of the offenders. The argument becomes even more complicated when one takes into account the fact that in all likelihood an instrumental murderer faces a lesser possibility of having sanctions imposed, and this fact inevitably flows from the difference in the two types of offenses. We can only raise these issues here and hope that others will help pursue the answers.

cation of the foregoing analysis is that the legal system will have little effect in reducing the frequency of such things as excessive drinking, drug use, most murders, most sex offenses, and aggravated assault. For these types of behavior, alternative mechanisms of social control must be instituted.

TABLE 3

Types of Deviance

Degree of Commitment to Crime as a Way of Life	Type of Act	
	Instrumental	Expressive
High	Professional thief Booster Some check forgers Some murderers	Most drug addicts Some murderers Some sex offenders
Low	Snitch Parking-law violator White-collar criminal Some murderers	Most murderers Some drug addicts Most sex offenders

Ironically, most of the criminal-legal effort is devoted to processing and sanctioning those persons *least* likely to be deterred by legal sanctions. Most of the arrests made by police and most of the persons sentenced in the courts are accused of relatively minor offenses, most of which are unlikely to be deterred by the imposition of sanctions. In 1965, for example, police reporting to the FBI recorded 4,955,047 arrests, of which only 834,296 were for offenses which are categorized by the FBI as "Type I" or "major" crimes.[18] There is even reason to question whether this latter statistic is not an overestimate of the proportion that are major crimes, since 101, 763 of these offenses are accounted for by auto theft, which in over 90 percent of the cases consists in an adolescent's borrowing an automobile for a short period of time and going for a joyride. In any event, well over 80 percent of the arrests made by the police are for relatively minor offenses. Although some of these offenses might be responsive to sanctions, most will not. Drunkenness accounts for a larger share of arrests made than any other single offense: in 1965, 1,535,040 of the arrests were for drunkenness, and this figure represents almost one-third of the total arrests made. Furthermore, when drunkenness-related offenses [19] are added together, then these offenses constitute *almost 50 percent* of all criminal arrests.[20] Finally, when arrests for other offenses unlikely to be deterred are added, such as for drug-law violations (most

[18] *Uniform Crime Reports,* Washington: Federal Bureau of Investigation, 1966.

[19] These include violation of liquor laws, driving while under the influence of alcohol, disorderly conduct, and vagrancy.

[20] Total arrests in 1965 were 4,955,047; arrests for drunkenness-related offenses totaled 2,467,089.

of which are arrests of drug addicts),[21] aggravated assault, vandalism, and sex offenses, then the proportion of the arrests which are for offenses not likely to be deterred by the imposition of sanctions approaches 60 percent.

That arresting persons for drunkenness is not likely to be an effective deterrent is implied by the typology. Indeed, since the bulk of such arrests are of the chronic, skid-row inebriate, such persons fall into the category of offenders least likely to be deterred: those with high commitment to a criminal way of life (in this case, persistent drunkenness) and those whose acts are also expressive. Studies of such offenders bear out this conclusion. In their study of chronic police-court inebriates, David Pittman and Wayne Gordon found that the majority of these offenders were persons who had been through the "revolving door" of the police station and jail innumerable times:

> The results of our investigation negate completely the assumption that incarceration acts as a deterrent to the chronic public inebriate. . . . Of the 1,357 men committed to the Monroe County Penitentiary in 1954 on charges of public intoxication or allied offenses, only 5 were newcomers to prison life. About one-third of these men—455 to be exact—were there for their second to tenth round. Nearly 6 out of 10 (80 men) had been committed from 10 to 25 times to a penal institution, and 96 men had served 25 or more jail terms. Our study group, a random sample of their kind, includes men who have been arrested 81, 90 and 110 times for public intoxication. There is no question about it: jailing has not deterred them from further public drunkenness.[22]

Pittman and Gordon's claims are a little stronger than their data warrant. Although it is true that the persons studied in the county jail were not deterred by penal sanctions, it may well be that many more persons who were no longer in jail but who had been arrested previously were subsequently deterred, which is why they did not appear in the researchers' sample. Thus this evidence can only be taken as suggestive; however, it seems unlikely that the findings would be much different even if sampling procedures had been more reliable.

These findings contrast nicely with the common observation that systematic arrests for driving while intoxicated act as a deterrent. Many casual observers have claimed that the practice in Scandinavian countries of arresting and severely sanctioning persons who drive while under the influence of alcohol has had the effect of greatly reducing the frequency of such events and (perhaps more importantly) of reducing the frequency with which accidents occur as a consequence of driving under the influence.[23] Since this offense would fall logically into the category of an instrumental act (the drinking may be expressive, but driving while drunk would clearly be instrumental by our definition), then such a finding is precisely what would have been expected according to the theory.

[21] Alfred R. Lindesmith, *The Addict and the Law,* Bloomington, Ind.: Indiana University Press, 1966.

[22] David J. Pittman and C. Wayne Gordon, *Revolving Door,* New York: The Free Press of Glencoe, 1958.

[23] Andenaes, "The General Preventive Effects of Punishment," p. 960.

However, persons who are likely to be deterred by the imposition of sanctions are, in general, the most likely to escape them. As Edwin Sutherland's analysis of white-collar crime has shown, violators of the Sherman Antitrust Laws are relatively free from criminal prosecution even though the imposition of punishment would be maximally effective with this type of offense.[24] Professional thieves also enjoy a surprising immunity from sanctions.[25]

The incompatibility of current legal practices with the data and theoretical perspective presented here is summed up in the way the legal system typically responds to the violation of antidrug laws. Relatively negligible amounts of the legal system's energies are devoted to the development of techniques and procedures which would increase the efficiency with which persons who are responsible for importing, wholesaling, and distributing drugs for illegal resale are prosecuted. By contrast, great ingenuity is shown in the enforcement of antidrug laws against persons who are buying drugs for their own consumption. Included in these techniques are ingenious, albeit quasi-legal, methods of searching dwellings without a warrant and then obtaining a warrant if anything is found and making a second "legal" search, of entrapping prospective buyers, and of using drug addicts as informers who are paid for informing by being given drugs for their own consumption.[26] As we have shown, the likelihood that drug addicts will be deterred by sanctions, regardless of how severe or likely they may be, is exceedingly small. The wholesalers, importers, and distributors, by contrast, are generally ignored. However, if sanctions were imposed on this latter group, they would be far more likely to be effective in controlling the illegal use of drugs. As Lindesmith has pointed out, the present policy of arresting addicts and ignoring the profiteers makes about as much sense as believing that the wholesale arrest of drunks along the Bowery would have curtailed the violation of prohibition laws.[27]

Law and Social Solidarity

Although the question of deterrence may well be the single most important question to be asked about the impact of legal sanctions, it is

[24] Edwin H. Sutherland, *White Collar Crime*, New York: The Dryden Press, Inc., 1949.

[25] A professional safecracker of the author's acquaintance estimated that he had been arrested for safecracking (burglary) three hundred times in a career spanning some forty-five years, but he had received only three prison sentences! His immunity from sanction stemmed principally from his ability to "fix" any criminal charges brought against him.

[26] For evidence of these practices, see Jerome Skolnick, *Justice without Trial*, New York: John Wiley & Sons, Inc., 1966, pp. 112–163, and Lindesmith, *The Addict and the Law*. Some of these practices are also mentioned in official publications of the Federal Bureau of Narcotics.

[27] Similar contradictions occur in the sanctioning of many, perhaps most, other types of offenses. The expressive murderer is probably more likely to be maximally sanctioned than is the instrumental murderer; the skid-row drunkard is more likely to be sanctioned than the drunken driver; the juvenile who commits vandalistic acts is more vulnerable than the one who shoplifts.

certainly not the only one. It is frequently argued that the law contributes to social solidarity through the creation of consensus about the moral foundations of society.[28] We lack the kinds of systematic data which would permit much confidence in our ability to determine the truth of this assertion but we can offer some general observations which may at least serve to stimulate further inquiry.

One need not look very far to discover examples of the law's inability to create consensus. Certainly America's experience with prohibition is a classic illustration of the failure of legal prescriptions to bring about a change in the attitude of the public. The persistence of gambling and prostitution likewise attest to such a failure. These cases in fact suggest that, where a democratically based legal order attempts to impose a morality which contradicts the morality of significant segments of the populace, not only will the effort be unsuccessful, but also the entire legal system may be corrupted as a consequence of that effort.

On the other hand, the history of the Jim Crow laws in the South supports the contention that the law creates consensus. For with the passage of Jim Crow laws there emerged in the South a high degree of consensus on the value of maintaining a strict separation of the races. Prior to the legal efforts to impose this policy there was apparently little or no public sentiment in favor of such a policy.[29]

Although these illustrations can scarcely be said to provide adequate grounds for asserting the truth or falsity of the claim that the legal order contributes to social solidarity by increasing consensus, they suggest that such a statement is probably true only if qualified in important ways. Specifically, the imposition of legal sanctions is likely to increase community solidarity only when the emergent morality also serves other interests of persons in positions of power in the community. When the laws are in conflict with or do not positively serve these interests, as is the case for most laws governing morality, then the contribution of the law to social solidarity will be negligible, if not negative.

Law as a Contributor to Crime: The Effects of Stigma

There is yet another side to the question of the impact of legal sanctions. Paradoxically, at the same time that the imposition of legal sanctions may act to deter some from crime through threat of punishment or through rehabilitation, social science theory and research both indicate that experiencing the lance of the law may in itself increase rather than decrease the likelihood of further criminality.

Theoretically, the process works by simultaneously closing opportunities for legitimate enterprises and opening opportunities for illegitimate ones. A well-established principle in social psychology is that what a person thinks of himself is a function of what others think of him. Less well-

[28] For an interesting application of this argument see Kai T. Erikson, *Wayward Puritans,* New York: John Wiley & Sons, Inc., 1966, and also "Notes on the Sociology of Deviance," *Social Problems,* vol. 9, pp. 307–314, Spring, 1962.

[29] C. Van Woodward, *The Strange Career of Jim Crow,* Fair Lawn, N.J.: Oxford University Press, 1955.

established, but a plausible corollary of this, is the principle that a person will behave in such a way as to make his actions correspond to his self-conception. By formally responding to someone as though he is a deviant, the chances are vastly increased that others in that person's milieu will alter their view of him such that they perceive him as deviant. Thus the informal reactions of others are altered by formal procedures. Someone so defined, for example, will find it more difficult to obtain employment in a legitimate occupation.[30] There is also considerable evidence that one will select as friends others who see us as we see ourselves—both our foibles and our strengths—and who respond favorably to us.[31] Thus one who is defined as deviant is likely to come to think of himself as deviant; he is then more likely to seek as friends others who see him as deviant. Those who will see him as deviant and at the same time respond favorably to him are most likely to be persons who are themselves deviant, and thus the person is drawn toward others whose way of life encourages and even values deviant acts.

When the formal sanctions include incarceration, then we would expect an even more forceful initiation of this process.

This cycle can, of course, be broken, and many societies, though not our own, have mechanisms specifically designed to do so. This is done principally through the institution of "rites of passage" back into legitimate society.[32] Among the Cheyenne, for example, if a member of the tribe stole another man's horse, the wrongdoer would be severely punished: his property would be confiscated, his right to hold office in the society would be denied, and he might even be banished. After some time the wrongdoer would be brought back to the tribe, he would be publicly forgiven, and his position and his property would be returned. There was a ceremony, as it were, to reestablish the person's legitimate role in the society.

Such a procedure contrasts sharply with the Anglo-American practice of maintaining the transgressor in the deviant role long after he has served his time "in exile." The released prisoner is generally "on parole," which means that he must prove that he is fit to reenter society. Such proof may be difficult to muster in view of the stigma attached to his having been formally processed and labeled. In general, the community and the officials will be skeptical, and the cycle of deviance-response-deviance is thereby perpetuated.

In her study of shoplifters, Cameron makes the point that the "best" response to the snitch—the nonprofessional shoplifter—is likely to be a warning with no formal sanction. Such a procedure will be effective in warding off future transgressions without initiating the dismal cycle of being labeled deviant.

Not everyone is equally vulnerable to this process. More than anything else, one's vulnerability depends on the degree to which being

---

[30] Schwartz and Skolnick, op. cit.

[31] William J. Chambliss, "The Selection of Friends," Social Forces, vol. 43, pp. 370–380, March, 1965; Theodore Newcomb, The Acquaintance Process, New York: Holt, Rinehart and Winston, Inc., 1961.

[32] Erikson, "Notes on the Sociology of Deviance."

processed as a deviant will permanently interrupt an established set of nondeviant, legitimate relationships. Most persons convicted of white-collar crimes find the disruption is only slight; their vulnerability to the process is therefore negligible. The subsequent careers of the executives of the electrical industry who were tried, found guilty, and given fines and jail sentences in 1961 illustrate this point. Of the seven vice-presidents sentenced to jail, all but one were subsequently reemployed at positions comparable to the ones they held prior to the trial.

On the other hand, an unemployed drifter who is processed is more than likely to become involved in this deviance-reinforcing cycle.

In addition to stimulating ever-increasing involvement in criminality through the effects of labeling, the organization of law enforcement also perpetuates crime by increasing the pressure on convicted persons to obtain large sums of money, sums which they rarely have. The professional thief is a case in point. As we have seen, the professional thief can generally arrange a fix to avoid imprisonment, but of course a fix costs money that the thief is not likely to have. If he is well known to the criminal lawyer or if his reputation is "sound," he can arrange a fix on his promise to pay the costs after release. No one is naïve enough to suppose that the payment will be forthcoming without the thief's engaging in another crime. In this way, the legal system perpetuates more criminality by placing the thief in the position of having to engage in further theft to avoid imprisonment for a previous crime.

The same process is true of posting bond. A good thief can generally obtain a release from jail on bail if he has a reputation for being reliable. The bail may be excessively high in view of his past record. For short-term bail bonds, a bondsman will generally be legally permitted to charge an interest rate of from 10 to 20 percent. This means that if a known thief is arrested and bond is set at $25,000 (which is not too high in view of his record), he must pay a bondsman between $2,500 and $5,000 for the "loan" of $25,000 for a period of several weeks. This money must also be raised, and raising it necessitates further criminal acts.

Bondsmen are willing to stand behind professional thieves' bail because there is really very little risk in doing so. Although the bail bondsman is permitted to charge high interest rates because of the allegedly high risk he takes in loaning money to persons accused of committing a crime, in point of fact, he takes little risk at all. Furthermore, one frequently finds that the chief bail bondsmen in a community are relatives or associates of law-enforcement officials. Even if an accused person fails to appear before the court and thereby forfeits the bond which he put up, it is very rare that the judge will insist that the bondsman pay the forfeited sum. In point of fact the judge has the discretion of not collecting the bond, and this is usually what happens if the forfeited bond was assured by a bail-bonding company. Thus the bail system has the consequence of encouraging criminality by creating a situation in which bondsmen are willing to set bail for thieves (because of the low risk), but where the thief is thereby put in the position of having to acquire a large sum of money very shortly after he has been arrested for a crime.

There is yet another way in which the bail system encourages crime in that persons arrested, even professional thieves, do not always know whom to get bond from. Jailers, sheriffs, and police officers are in a position to recommend a bondsman, and thus is set in motion the makings of a system of payoffs and "gifts" for recommending one bondsman rather than another.

By making it illegal to sell, distribute, or possess commodities for which there is substantial demand, the law inevitably contributes to increased criminality. In Part 2 it was pointed out how such laws serve to corrupt the legal system and thereby contribute to criminality. An equally important consequence of such policies is to raise the price of the commodity and thereby to make it impossible for most persons who want the item to be able to afford it on a legitimate salary. The classic illustration of this is provided by the case of drug use in the United States: Because of the heavy penalties imposed on drug peddlers, distributors, importers, and wholesalers, persons will be willing to take the risk of selling drugs only if the rewards are high. Consequently, the price of drugs becomes drastically inflated. A drug addict in the United States, in order to support the drug habit, inevitably turns to various types of theft to obtain the money to purchase drugs.[33]

The Law as a Source of Behavioral Models

One question which deserves considerably more systematic investigation than it has received is the extent to which the activities and values, implicit and explicit, in the behavior of the law and its proper representatives stimulate the expression of these same values in the behavior of the population as a whole. Geoffrey Gorer's inquiry into the impact of the character type of the policeman on the national character of the British is one such investigation. The results of this study, although highly speculative, suggest that law enforcers may indeed have their greatest impact in terms of establishing the ideal (whether this be "good" or "bad" ideal) type of behavior for the population as a whole to emulate. Gorer's conception of what the British police project is doubtless exaggerated—others have reported that many of the same illegal tactics (such as improper search and seizure) prevail among British police as among police in the United States. On the other hand, there is little doubt but that British police present a more honest and fair image in their everyday activities than do American police, and they are certainly much freer from corruption and reliance on violence than are the American police.

One area where this general question may play an extremely important role is in the general attitude toward the legitimacy of the use of extreme violence to settle disputes. It is quite possible that the general acceptance of the legitimacy of capital punishment on the part of a society encourages an acceptance of violence in the attitude and behavior of the population. In the earlier discussion of capital punishment it was surprising the extent to which states where capital punishment had been abolished had

[33] Edwin M. Schur, *Narcotics Addiction in Britain and America*, Bloomington, Ind.: Indiana University Press, 1962.

a consistently lower murder rate than states that had retained the death penalty, even when these states were contiguous and presumably culturally similar. One would not, of course, expect dramatic differences since the fact remains that capital punishment is very much a possibility in most states, and the impact on the population of a particular state would not be likely to be marked. The general trend toward less and less violence (as indicated by the gradual reduction in the murder rate over the years) may well be causally related to the reduction in the states' reliance on capital punishment, which implies that violence is an appropriate means for settling personal (if not political) disputes.

David Matza has argued that delinquent gangs reflect in their own subculture the values which dominate the legal order.[34] Delinquents typically "neutralize" their transgressions by putting their behavior in precisely the same categories as the law enforcers use to justify their own behavior. Thus, it is justifiable for a group of delinquents to mete out justice to a homosexual or a drunkard in the same way that it is justifiable for the police to rely on "street-corner justice" to handle such cases. Similarly, the delinquent gang typically feel that they respond to wrongdoings of others: they do not, in their own eyes, initiate the wrongdoing. Thus, when open violence occurs between two groups, it is inevitably because, in the eyes of each gang, the other group has committed a wrong and a violent response is quite justified. The "wrong" and the "response" and the logic justifying the response are clear reflections of the same type of official legal response which these youths have seen and been subjected to in the behavior of the police. If the police are justified in meting out street-corner justice, if the police have the right to tell a group of nonoffending (at the moment) youths to move on from a street corner, if the police can push around youths who are "suspect," then these types of acts become the right and proper way to respond. Not surprisingly, the youths so treated respond in like fashion to others over whom they have some control.

These ideas lack the empirical data necessary to verify whether they can be used to explain the behavior of individuals in society. But they shed some light on the more general relationship between the legal order and the behavior of individuals in the society.

Conclusion

The law touches every man. But it touches some more than others, and the impact of the encounter is not always consistent with ends sought. The organization of criminal justice in the United States is such that those persons most likely to be deterred by the imposition and the threat of punishment are the ones least likely to be sanctioned. The offenders most likely to be sanctioned, in turn, are the ones least likely to be effectively deterred thereby. That this is true is not particularly surprising in view of the findings from the study of the administration of criminal law, which suggest that the outcome of the interaction between the legal system

[34] David Matza, *Delinquency and Drift*, New York: John Wiley & Sons, Inc., 1964.

and its social setting leads to the imposition of sanctions against those persons who are easily processed and who can cause a minimum of difficulty for the agencies of law enforcement. Expressive offenders who have a low commitment to criminality are the most likely to be relatively defenseless, and therefore they can be sanctioned with the greatest freedom by the law enforcers. By contrast, those persons who by virtue of their position and influence could cause trouble are also the ones most likely to be effectively deterred by sanctions; however, they are the least likely to be punished.

The fact that the law is an instrument which simultaneously inhibits and encourages deviant behavior poses still other problems to be solved. Research on the legal system has shown a number of ways in which the law acts to stimulate criminal activities. In some instances the organization of criminal sanctions is such that persons sanctioned are placed in the position of having to commit further crimes in order to avoid serving prison sentences. This is especially true of the thief who must pay expensive legal fees or who must pay for a fix. It is also true of persons addicted to drugs who must pay high prices for drugs since they are only available through illegal and therefore expensive sources. The addict is thus forced to resort to theft and other illegal acts to support the drug habit.

The extent to which labeling a person criminal increases the likelihood of further criminality is another element in the criminal-legal process which must be given careful consideration. In some cases (for example, for the snitch) threatening punishment which will serve as an effective deterrent and at the same time withholding the imposition of punishment in order to avoid the criminal-labeling cycle is a process which requires considerable ingenuity.

21. The Deterrent Influence of the Death Penalty *

Karl F. Schuessler

This article analyzes certain statistical material as it bears on the question of how much the death penalty deters people from committing murder. This material, consisting principally of United States homicide and execution data for the period 1925–64, has been organized around six topics expressed for the most part as ques-

SOURCE: "The Deterrent Influence of the Death Penalty," *Annals of the American Academy of Political and Social Science*, vol. 284, pp. 54–63, November, 1952. By permission of the author and publisher.

EDITOR'S NOTE: Some of the data have been brought up to date by adding the years 1949–1964. Some minor alterations in interpretation have been made to make the text compatible with the more recent data.

* This paper was aided immensely by Professor Thorsten Sellin who made available to the author his extensive Memorandum on Capital Punishment prepared in 1950 for the British Royal Commission on Capital Punishment. The author is also indebted to Professor Clifford Kirkpatrick who read this paper critically but who is, of course, in no way responsible for its contents, and also to Mrs. Vada Gary who assisted with the statistical work.

tions: (1) the adequacy of United States statistics for purposes of measuring the deterrent influence of the death penalty; (2) the deterrence viewpoint as an explanation of murder and punishment trends in this country during the last twenty-five years; (3) whether fewer murders occur in places where murder is punishable by death than in places where it is not; (4) whether differences in the use of the death penalty correspond to differences in the relative occurrence of murder; (5) the consistency between the deterrence viewpoint and differentials in the murder rate by sex, race, and other population classifications; and (6) a general appraisal of the deterrent value of the death penalty.

This analysis in a sense represents a continuation of similar work done intermittently in this country during the last thirty-five years.[1] These previous studies have uniformly concluded that the death penalty is inconsequential as a deterrent and that the relative frequency of murder in a given population is a function of the cultural conditions under which the group lives. Deficiencies in United States data that handicapped earlier investigations of this kind have been remedied somewhat during the last twenty years, but many difficulties still face the analyst who wishes to generalize about murder and the death penalty. Before going to the data and their interpretation, the belief in the death penalty as a deterrent is briefly set forth.

THE DETERRENCE VIEWPOINT

In brief, people are believed to refrain from crime because they fear punishment. Since people fear death more than anything else the death penalty is the most effective deterrent, so runs the argument. It is further alleged that the effectiveness of the death penalty as a deterrent depends both on its certain application and on knowledge of this fact in the population; hence, the argument continues, regular use of the death penalty increases its deterrent value. It was largely on grounds of this sort that the death penalty was recently (1950) restored in New Zealand after a ten-year period of abolition, demonstrating that the deterrence line of reasoning still has considerable practical force.[*]

Involved in the deterrence argument is the assumption that men deliberately choose among rival courses of action in the light of foreseeable consequences, the criterion of choice being personal gratification. This psychological hedonism, needless to say, is not in accord with modern psychology and sociology, which see human behavior as largely unplanned and habitual, rather than calculated and voluntary. The belief in the deterrent value of the death penalty is thus seen not as a scientific proposition, but rather as a social conviction widely used to justify and reinforce existing ways of treatment that perhaps rest mainly on feelings of vengeance. Consequently, this study does not constitute a test of a carefully drawn sociological hypothesis that intends to explain differences in the prevalence of murder among human societies, but rather assembles factual evidence to test the validity of a popular belief. We now return to the topics posed in the introduction to this article.

[1] See, for example, Raymond T. Bye, *Capital Punishment in the United States,* Philadelphia: Committee on Philanthropic Labor of Philadelphia Yearly Meeting of Friends, 1919; Edwin H. Sutherland, "Murder and the Death Penalty," *Journal of the American Institute of Criminal Law and Criminology,* vol. 15, 1925, pp. 522–29; Clifford Kirkpatrick, *Capital Punishment,* Philadelphia: Committee on Philanthropic Labor of Philadelphia Yearly Meeting of Friends, 1925; George B. Vold, "Can the Death Penalty Prevent Crime?" *Prison Journal,* October 1932, pp. 3–8.

[*] EDITOR'S NOTE: In 1962 New Zealand had capital punishment only for "crimes against the state."

UNITED STATES HOMICIDE AND EXECUTION DATA

The homicide statistics collected by the United States Census Bureau [2] are ordinarily used as an index of murder, figures on murder being generally inaccessible as well as fragmentary. The use of homicide statistics for purposes of estimating the deterrent influence of the death penalty has been criticized on the grounds that (a) they include justifiable and excusable homicides and (b) they do not distinguish among differing degrees of murder. The reasoning behind this criticism is that the proportion of nonfelonious homicide and the relative amount of different kinds of murder may vary in time and space in such a way as to make unreliable regional comparisons and time trends.

Over against these reasonable objections is the fact that the homicide rate closely corresponds, both geographically and temporally, to the murder figures given in *Uniform Crime Reports,*[3] which exclude nonfelonious homicide, though they include non-negligent manslaughter. Also, the homicide rate is closely correlated, on both a geographic and a temporal basis, with murder conviction rates given in *Judicial Criminal Statistics,* and with murder commitment rates based on information in *Prisoners in State and Federal Prisons and Reformatories.*[4]

This consistency among four independent indexes of murder is probably due to the fact that the relative occurrence of different kinds of murder is similar among states and fairly constant during the last forty years. If this interpretation is correct, then the homicide rate is a reliable index of murder in general and first degree murder in particular, during approximately the last forty years.

National statistics on executions have been readily available in this country only since 1930, when they were reported in *Mortality Statistics* and also in *Prisoners in State and Federal Prisons and Reformatories.* From the standpoint of measuring the temporal relation between execution and murder, these figures are of limited value because they cover such a short period of time. The fact that executions-by-offense were not published for the period 1931–36 adds to this difficulty, although for certain states it may be safely assumed that all executions during that period were for murder.

Some material on murder convictions and death sentences is available in *Federal Judicial Statistics.* But for purposes of relating conviction and punishment trends to concurrent trends in murder, this source is limited as follows: (a) this series covers only a thirteen-year period, 1933–45; (b) the largest number of states reporting in any single year was thirty; (c) only eighteen states (including the District of Columbia) reported each year during the entire period; and (d) except for the first few years, the number of persons convicted of murder is not given, but rather the number of murder indictments resulting in conviction.

In spite of the forenamed shortcomings in murder statistics for the period 1925–64, they are probably more adequate than data hitherto employed as a check on the

[2] *Mortality Statistics,* Bureau of the Census, United States Department of Commerce, Washington, D.C. Also, *Special Reports,* National Office of Vital Statistics, Public Health Service, Federal Security Agency, Washington, D.C.

[3] *Uniform Crime Reports,* Federal Bureau of Investigation, United States Department of Justice, Washington, D.C.

[4] Both publications issued by the Bureau of the Census. The results of this correlational analysis are omitted because of lack of space, except to say that the correlation coefficients were uniformly high ($r \geq .8$).

alleged deterrent influence of the death penalty. In consequence, conclusions based on this study are less vulnerable to the objection that murder data are so unreliable as to make worthless generalizations about the death penalty as a deterrent.

UNITED STATES HOMICIDE AND
CAPITAL PUNISHMENT TRENDS

The United States homicide rate moved steadily upward from 1900 until the middle of the thirties, dropped sharply during the next ten-year period, and then at the close of World War II started an upward swing. Although homicide statistics are not available for 1950 and 1951, national police statistics indicate that the upward trend was checked in 1951; in any case, the rate is still far below the high levels of the late 1920's and early thirties.

State trends in the period 1925–49 generally correspond to the national trend, although there are several exceptions, important from the standpoint of an explanation of murder. (1) Vermont exhibited an almost constant rate during this period. (2) By 1949, Virginia, North Carolina, and South Carolina had returned to or exceeded the high level of the depression years. (3) Michigan, Nevada, and Florida started their downward trend before 1930. (4) At least one state—Connecticut—continued to climb until 1940. The homicide rate continued to exhibit large regional differences, the highest rates persisting in the South, the lowest in New England.

Also, the homicide rate continued to display large differentials by sex, race, ecological area, and season, the effect of each classification being conditioned to a certain extent by its relation to the others. These differentials suggest at once that murder is a complex sociological event rather than a simple response controlled altogether by the deterrent influence of the death penalty.

The speculation has been advanced that nowadays a smaller proportion of persons sentenced to death for murder are executed than formerly, the tendency to administer clemency being in line with a general trend to moderate punishment. This is borne out by an analysis of available judicial and penal statistics. Of those sentenced to death for murder in the courts of 25 states during the period 1933–39, 80 per cent were executed; during the period 1940–45, 81 per cent were executed—practically no change. But from 1960–64, only 34 per cent were executed.[5]

By way of summary, capital punishment policy and practice in this country was fairly stable in the period 1925–49 and the number of executions declined from 1960–64; the movement of the homicide rate and differentials in the homicide rate by various population classifications cannot be attributed to changes in the use of the death penalty. This suggests once again that differences in the homicide rate correspond to differences in social structure and culture setting, and that murder and the death penalty are unrelated except in the circular sense that more murder involves more death penalties.

COMPARISON OF DEATH PENALTY AND ABOLITION STATES

A comparison of states that provide the death penalty for murder with those that do not shows the homicide rate to be two to three times as large in the former states as in the latter (Table 21-1). Such a comparison is usually declared invalid because

[5] From 1960–64, 537 persons were formally sentenced to death and 181 were executed.

TABLE 21-1

Homicide Rates per 100,000 Population in Death Penalty States and Abolition States * for Five Years

Year	Abolition States	Death Penalty States
1928	4.2	8.8
1933	3.7	10.5
1938	2.2	7.6
1943	2.1	5.5
1949	2.2	6.0

* These two groupings include all states in the national registration area in any given year. All states were in the registration area after 1932.

the two groupings are not uniform with respect to population composition, social structure, and culture pattern. This criticism, though methodologically sound, affirms indirectly that the relative occurrence of murder is the result of a combination of social circumstances of which punishment is only one, possibly an immaterial one.

To meet the foregoing objection, the usual practice is to compare the homicide rate in states that have abolished the death penalty with their neighbors where the death penalty is legal. This comparison is illustrated in Table 21-2, and it will be

TABLE 21-2

Annual Average Homicide Rates in Fifteen States Selected According to Contiguity

State	1931–35	1936–40	1941–46	1959–64
Rhode Island *	1.8	1.5	1.0	1.0
Connecticut	2.4	2.0	1.9	1.4
Michigan *	5.0	3.6	3.4	3.8
Indiana	6.2	4.3	3.2	3.6
Wisconsin *	2.4	1.7	1.5	1.3
Illinois	9.6	5.7	4.4	4.9
Minnesota *	3.1	1.7	1.6	1.1
Iowa †	2.6	1.7	1.3	1.1
Kansas ‡	6.2	3.6	3.0	2.5
Colorado	7.5	5.5	3.7	4.8
Missouri	11.1	6.6	5.3	9.2
Nebraska	3.7	1.7	1.8	2.2
Oklahoma	11.0	7.2	5.6	5.9
Arizona	12.6	10.3	6.5	5.8
New Mexico	12.5	8.4	5.3	6.2

* Abolition state.
† Abolition state 1965.
‡ Abolition between 1931 and 1935.

seen that Rhode Island, an abolition state since 1852, is very similar to Connecticut, where the death penalty has been retained. Maine also, though not shown in the table, has been abolition since 1887, and is quite similar to the New England states which have the death penalty. The homicide rate in Michigan, where the death penalty was abolished in 1847 (except for treason, and it was abolished for treason in 1963), closely resembles Indiana and Illinois homicide rates, while Wisconsin, an abolition state for practically a hundred years, has a rate significantly below Michigan, indicating that the homicide rate is indifferent to the presence or absence of capital punishment. Homicide rates in Minnesota, where the death penalty was abandoned in 1911, and in Iowa * are very nearly alike with respect to both level and trend during the last forty years. Similarly, homicide rates in Arizona and New Mexico, both death penalty states, have been practically identical both in level and movement during the period 1930–64, although Arizona executed 38 and New Mexico but 8 in this period.

Kansas and South Dakota are of special interest because they make possible a before-and-after comparison, though extremely limited in scope. Kansas abolished the death penalty in 1907 and re-established it in 1935. The annual average homicide rate in Kansas for the period 1931–35, as shown in Table 21-2, was considerably higher than the average rate for the following five-year period, giving plausibility to the deterrence argument. However, an identical trend characterized the states bordering on Kansas (Table 21-2), and these states had the death penalty throughout this period. The experience of Kansas, then, when viewed in context, merely emphasizes that homicide trends are the resultant of social conditions rather than the resultant of changes in death penalty policy.

This notion is borne out by a comparison of homicide trends in South Dakota, an abolition state between 1915 and 1939, and North Dakota, where the death penalty has not been in force since 1915. The annual average homicide rate in South Dakota dropped from 1.8 for the period 1930–39 to 1.5 for the following ten-year period, while in North Dakota the rate dropped from 1.8 to 1.1. If changes in the homicide rate were due solely to differences in capital punishment policy, then North Dakota's greater proportional drop in homicides must have been due to the fact that the death penalty was not restored.

EUROPEAN DATA

Since the middle of the last century there has been a sustained though uneven movement among European countries to abolish capital punishment by legal annulment or by allowing it to fall into disuse. Certain European statistics therefore bear on the question of whether the removal of the death penalty has a perceptible effect on the incidence of murder. Several examples [6] are cited primarily to illustrate the fact that the independence between the murder rate and the death penalty is not a peculiarity of American culture.

Sweden formally abolished the death penalty in 1921; but the last execution occurred in 1910, this being the only one since 1900. During the preceding period, 1869–1900, there were 12 executions, roughly averaging 4 per decade. There is

---

* EDITOR'S NOTE: Iowa abolished the death penalty in 1965.

[6] Taken from Thorsten Sellin's *Memorandum on Capital Punishment*, London, 1951.

nothing in the Swedish homicide series (Table 21-3) to suggest that its movement has in any way been conditioned by the abandonment of the death penalty during the twentieth century.

TABLE 21-3

Annual Average Homicide Rate per 100,000 Population of Sweden from 1754 to 1942

Period	Homicide Rate
1754–1763	.83
1775–1792	.66
1793–1806	.61
1809–1830	1.09*
1831–1845	1.47
1846–1860	1.24
1861–1877	1.12
1878–1898	.90
1899–1904	.96
1905–1913	.86
1914–1916	.72
1920–1932	.52
1933–1938	.46
1939–1942	.47

* Exclusive of 1814 and 1818.

The death penalty in the Netherlands was not used after 1860 and was formally abolished in 1870. Although there was an upward trend (Table 21-4) in the murder and attempted murder conviction rate in the twenty-year period immediately follow-

TABLE 21-4

Annual Average Murder and Attempted Murder Conviction Rates per Million Inhabitants in the Netherlands, 1850–1927

Period	Homicide Rate
1850–1859	.96
1860–1869	1.46
1870–1880	.83
1881–1890	1.17
1891–1900	1.41
1901–1910	1.25
1911–1920	1.32
1921–1927	.60

ing abolition, during this period the rate never attained the level of 1860–70 when the death penalty was still legally in force. The rate reached its lowest level in the 1920's when the death penalty was, of course, not in effect. Moreover, the decade immediately following abolition, 1870–79, was the lowest but one in the approximately eight-decade period covered by this series.

CERTAINTY AS A DETERRENT INFLUENCE

The point has often been made that it is not so much the legal existence of the death penalty that deters potential murderers, but rather the certainty of its being used. In fact, a common criticism of the death penalty is that juries do not convict readily if the punishment is death, thereby reducing the certainty of punishment, and, in consequence, its deterrent value. The problem as to whether differences in the use of the death penalty are in some way related to variations in the homicide rate may be approached by correlating execution and homicide data distributed geographically or temporally.

That the risk of execution is not uniform among the states that have a death penalty for murder is demonstrated by the lack of consistency between homicide and execution rates. The correlation coefficient of a homicide rate based on the period 1937–49 and an execution rate for the same period was .48 for 41 death penalty states.[7] The question therefore arises as to whether the relative occurrence of murder decreases regularly as the risk of execution increases, since, under deterrence theory, the value of the death penalty as a deterrent is thought to depend on its certain application.

To test this idea, though somewhat crudely, the risk of execution, operationally defined as the number of executions-for-murder per 1,000 homicides for the period 1937–49, was statistically compared with the homicide rate in 41 death penalty states. The correlation between these two indices was −.26, indicating a slight tendency for the homicide rate to diminish as the probability of execution increases. Next, as a check on consistency in this trend, the ratio of the average execution rate to the average homicide rate was computed for four groupings of states according to size of the homicide rate, as shown in column 3 of Table 21-5. This analysis shows that the homicide rate does not consistently fall as the risk of execution increases.

TABLE 21-5

Average Homicide and Execution Rates in 41 States Grouped according to Size of Homicide Rate

Quartile by Homicide Rate	Average Homicide Rate (HR)	Average Execution Rate (ER)	ER/HR
Highest	15.4	.32	.21
Upper Middle	7.8	.14	.18
Lower Middle	4.2	.08	.19
Lowest	2.0	.05	.25

[7] Includes states that had a death penalty for murder during the period 1937–49, except South Dakota where the death penalty was restored in 1939 and Idaho where no executions occurred during this period. The product-moment correlation method was used throughout this analysis, not because it necessarily gave the best fit in all cases, but rather because its limitations and signification are well known.

To illustrate: the average homicide rate for the ten states having the highest homicide rates is almost twice as large as the average homicide rate for the states in the next quartile, but the risk of execution is slightly greater in the former group of states than in the latter group. This evidence, included primarily because of its suggestiveness, must be classed as negative from the standpoint of deterrence theory, since (a) the homicide rate does not drop consistently as the certainty of the death penalty increases, and (b) the geographic correlation between the risk of execution and the homicide rate is not impressive, failing to reach the 5 per cent significance level and statistically accounting for only 7 per cent (r^2) of the variability in the homicide rate.

To investigate further how differences in the use of the death penalty affect the homicide rate, the relationship between homicide and execution data as time series was measured within certain death penalty states. States which displayed little variability in executions for murder from year to year were not included in this analysis; also, states not having execution-for-murder figures complete for the period 1930–49 were omitted. This left a total of eleven states. On the assumption, implicit in deterrence theory, that a large number of executions relative to the frequency of murder should be followed by a reduction in the murder rate, a one-year time lag was established, with the execution risk, defined as the number of executions-for-murder to 1,000 homicides per year, as the forerunner.

The most general finding is that the homicide rate and the execution risk as time series move independent of one another. None of the correlation coefficients reached .35, and the number of negative correlation coefficients, 4, was less than the number of positive coefficients, 7, but not significantly so. This evidence, like that just preceding, fails to substantiate the belief that the deterrent influence of the death penalty is enhanced by its frequent use, as changes in the homicide rate do not correspond in a systematic way to variations in the probability of its being used.

DIFFERENTIAL HOMICIDE RATES AND THE DEATH PENALTY

A final problem is whether the deterrence viewpoint is consistent with certain population classifications. First, the death penalty is hardly ever used with women in the United States, but women, in contrast with men, seldom commit murder. Very likely the conditions of life surrounding women in most human societies operate to develop and sustain lawful attitudes and habits. Lawfulness in the female population, specifically the fact that women generally refrain from committing murder, is probably due to these positive sociocultural influences rather than to fear of the death penalty.

Second, the number of Negro murderers is relatively larger than the number of white murderers; yet it is doubtful whether the death penalty is used less often with Negro murderers than with white murderers. Suggestive in this connection is the fact that white executions for murder, 166, were 1.1 per cent of all white homicides, 15,494, in the period 1946–49, while Negro executions for murder, 265, constituted 1.5 per cent of all Negro homicides, 18,327, during the same period. The environmental factors influencing Negroes are analogous but opposite to those influencing women. The circumstances of life surrounding large numbers of Negroes in the

United States generate violence, assault, and murder,[8] and this kind of behavior, to a certain extent socially expected and socially sanctioned among Negroes, is indifferent to the use of the death penalty.

Finally, the homicide rate exhibits differentials by age, social class, ethnic background, community size, and season, but in no instance can these differences be ascribed to corresponding differences in the application of the death penalty.

DISCUSSION AND CONCLUSION

The results of the foregoing analysis are consistent with the results of previous investigations of this kind. The findings of this study, then, sustain the conclusion that the death penalty has little if anything to do with the relative occurrence of murder. Studies of this sort have been criticized on the ground that they do not *prove* that the death penalty is completely without deterrent value. Although logically sound in a very strict sense, this objection is unrealistic, since there is no way at present of contrasting personal and social situations so as to assure that all differences in murder behavior are due solely to differences in the use of the death penalty. As usual, inferences have to be based on evidence collected under conditions that most nearly approximate the methodological ideal. Moreover, the inference drawn from statistical data that the death penalty is inconsequential as a deterrent is borne out by case studies and expert opinion, material not surveyed in this paper but now briefly noted.

The alleged deterrent influence of the death penalty is contradicted by the following recurrent case study data, expressed as four rough generalizations: (1) In the events preceding murder, the murderer is usually preoccupied to the point that reflection over future consequences is virtually impossible. (2) The fear of death is relative to the situation; consequently, the death penalty may appear on reflection to be a necessary though unfortunate sequel to murder. (3) Certain cultural circumstances (underworld, marital, and others) often make murder imperative, thereby nullifying the supposed deterrent effect of the death penalty. (4) The relation between murderer and victim is usually primary, hence, one that is likely to be suffused with emotionality. This emotionality, probably heightened during a crisis, doubtless interferes with the objective assessment of future consequences. The indifference of the murderer to the death penalty is well illustrated by the following conversation between Lawes and a prisoner.

> Before Morris Wasser's execution, when I told him that the governor had refused him a last-minute respite, he said bitterly: "All right, Warden. It doesn't make much difference what I say now about this here system of burning a guy, but I want to set you straight on something."
>
> "What's that?" I asked.
>
> "Well, this electrocution business is the bunk. It don't do no good, I tell you, and I know, because I never thought of the chair when I plugged that old guy. And I'd probably do it again if he had me on the wrong end of a rod."
>
> "You mean," I said, "that you don't feel you've done wrong in taking another man's life?"

[8] Gunnar Myrdal, *The American Dilemma* (New York, 1944), pp. 558–60.

"No, Warden, it ain't that," he said impatiently. "I mean that you just don't think of the hot seat when you plug a guy. Somethin' inside you just makes you kill, 'cause you know if you don't shut him up it's curtains for you."

"I see. Then you never even thought of what would happen to you at the time."

"Hell, no! And lots of other guys in here, Harry and Brick and Luke, all says the same thing. I tell you the hot seat will never stop a guy from pullin' a trigger." That was Wasser's theory, and I've heard it echoed many times since.[9]

To summarize: statistical findings and case studies converge to disprove the claim that the death penalty has any special deterrent value. The belief in the death penalty as a deterrent is repudiated by statistical studies, since they consistently demonstrate that differences in homicide rates are in no way correlated with differences in the use of the death penalty. Case studies consistently reveal that the murderer seldom considers the possible consequences of his action, and, if he does, he evidently is not deterred by the death penalty. The fact that men continue to argue in favor of the death penalty on deterrence grounds may only demonstrate man's ability to confuse tradition with proof, and his related ability to justify his established way of behaving.

22. The Impact of Punishment on Compliance with Parking Regulations

William J. Chambliss

When social science was still speculating on the number of teeth in the horse's mouth before it had gone into the stable to count them, Jeremy Bentham was advocating a total revision of the criminal law based on a conception of man as "hedonist."[1] Among Bentham's many fascinating and intriguing notions was the theory that man would be deterred from crime if punishment for offenses were applied swiftly, certainly, and severely. While this proposition has been inextricably associated with Bentham and others of the "classical" school of criminology, it currently serves as a straw man for contemporary criticisms of the notion that punishment is an effective deterrent to *anything*, including crime.

The assumption that man is a complexity of hidden drives, motives, desires, and needs which push him to behave (in some cases) criminally is obviously incompatible with a "rational" conception of man which views him as selecting certain

[9] Lewis E. Lawes, *Meet the Murderer!* (New York, 1940), pp. 178–79.

SOURCE: "The Deterrent Influence of Punishment," *Crime and Delinquency*, pp. 70–75, January, 1966. By permission of the publisher.

[1] For an excellent summary of Bentham's position, see Gilbert Geis, "Pioneers in Criminology: Jeremy Bentham." *Journal of Criminal Law and Criminology*, July–August 1955, pp. 159–71.

courses of action in line with his assessment of the "pleasure" or "pain" likely to result from these actions. Furthermore, the theory of punishment as a deterrent has been rejected because the question of deterrence has frequently turned into a debate over the *morality* of *capital* punishment. Social scientists have generally opposed capital punishment on moral grounds and have, as an extension of this, put themselves in the position of arguing against punishment of any kind. Finally, the social scientists' opposition to the notion that punishment might act as a deterrent has been supported by a great deal of research which demonstrates that *capital* punishment does not act as an effective deterrent to *murder*.[2] This finding emerges consistently, regardless of the particular techniques used to assess the impact of capital punishment on the incidence of murder. In states where capital punishment has been abolished the murder rates have not changed. In addition, when we compare a state where capital punishment is a possibility with another "culturally similar" contiguous state where it is not, we arrive at the same conclusion: there is no difference between the percentages of murder in the two areas. Even an execution that is particularly well publicized has no subsequent effect on the propensity of others to murder.[3]

As important as these studies are in indicating that the death penalty is ineffective as a deterrent to murder, their very broad interpretation has rendered a disservice to the more general issue of punishment as a deterrent to all kinds of criminal behavior. Such an expansive conclusion is obviously not justified since murder is, in many ways, a unique kind of offense often involving very strong emotions.

In view of the foregoing it seems essential that studies be conducted on the deterrent influence of punishment on crimes other than murder.

An opportunity for conducting such an investigation presented itself in 1956 when changes were made in the policies and practices pertaining to the violation of parking regulations on a midwestern university campus. A dramatic increase in the certainty and severity of punishment for the violation of parking regulations occurred at this time and a study was made to assess the impact of these changes on the behavior of the group affected.

BACKGROUND OF THE STUDY

Because of the rapid increase of students and faculty in the early fifties, the university was faced with the problem of insufficient parking space. The university made several attempts to provide a system of control to assure parking space for all faculty and students, but eventually it became apparent that adequate space could not be provided for all the cars on campus. As a result, an attempt was made to restrict student parking to a few parking lots on the periphery of the campus; parking on curbs, in alleyways, and (as had sometimes occurred) on the grass was prohibited for everyone.

In 1951 the faculty council instituted a system of fines for violation of these rules. Faculty members were required to pay one dollar for each parking ticket received; students were required to pay one dollar for the first offense, three dollars for the second, and five dollars for the third. If a student received more than three citations

[2] See, for example, Karl Schuessler, "The Deterrent Influence of the Death Penalty," *Annals of the American Academy of Political and Social Science*, November 1952, pp. 54–82.

[3] Leonard D. Savitz, "A Study in Capital Punishment," *Journal of Criminal Law and Criminology*, November–December 1958, pp. 338–41.

in one academic year his "right to drive" in the county was revoked. Failure to pay fines or continuing to drive after receiving four or more tickets resulted in disciplinary action by the dean.

These procedures remained in effect until January 1956. Although the seriousness of the parking problem was somewhat reduced, the measures taken were far from sufficient. The university administration was plagued with complaints from faculty, students, and the campus police. It was argued that since no provision was made in the regulations for forcing faculty to pay fines, many of the faculty continued to park wherever they wished, frequently blocking traffic or taking up two parking spaces.

In 1956, responding to considerable bitterness and dissatisfaction with the system, the faculty council established a set of rules which attempted, once more, to alleviate the problem. These new rules provided that faculty members would be fined the same as students—one dollar for the first ticket, three dollars for the second, and five dollars for the third. Further, if a faculty member failed to pay his fine his right to park on campus would be automatically revoked, and if he parked on campus his car would be towed away at his own expense.

In addition to these rule changes, the staff employed by the safety division was greatly expanded, a new director (formerly a state police captain) was appointed, and the necessity of enforcing the regulations was pointed out to all the campus police (who had concluded that it was useless to give tickets to the faculty because they would "merely tear them up").

These changes increased the likelihood of a violator's receiving a parking citation (because of the increased number of personnel assigned to patrol parking areas and the increased efficiency of the safety division) and increased the severity of penalties (by increasing the amount of the fine to be paid for the second, third, and subsequent violations and by providing for a tow-away for failure to pay fines).

It would then follow that if punishment is an effective deterrent, the number of violations of the regulations should have decreased after January 1956, when the new policies were instituted.

THE SAMPLE

To see whether the number of violations did, in fact, decrease, we studied the faculty's pattern of violation before and after the changes in policy. Although there was consensus among the administrators of the university that the new procedures had "solved the problem," their conclusion was impressionistic and did not rest on an empirical analysis.

A sample of forty-three faculty members was taken at random from all faculty members who had been on campus for at least 2½ years before January 1956 and for an equivalent period after that date. They were interviewed and were asked simply to "discuss the parking situation at the university." The parking problem and the resultant turmoil were, apparently, of so much concern to the faculty that most of them talked at length about the events of the preceding five to six years with very little further prompting from the interviewer. The most important information sought, of course, was whether or not the interviewee had violated the regulations in either or both of the two periods and, if so, how often.

RESEARCH FINDINGS

Table 22-1 shows the breakdown, by reported frequency, of violations for the two periods. Respondents were considered frequent violators if they reported breaking the regulations five times or more. Thus, to be classified as a "frequent" violator *before* the change in regulations, the respondent had to report violating the regulations at least five times from 1953 to 1955. Similarly, to be a frequent violator *after* the change, he would have to have violated the regulations at least five times from 1955 to 1957. "Occasional" violators were those who broke the rules three or four times during the periods specified: "seldom" violators were those who violated once or twice; and "nonviolators" were those who reported no violations.

It is significant that fifteen of the forty-three respondents reported that they never violated the regulations during either period. Thus, the rules were obeyed by 35 per cent of the population not only when severe restrictions were instituted, but also when relatively light penalties were applied.

Of the remaining twenty-eight respondents, thirteen reported frequent violation of the regulations prior to the change. Of these, six became nonviolators after the change, four became seldom violators, one became an occasional violator, and two remained frequent violators.

These data indicate clearly that the change in regulations (and the corresponding increase in the certainty and severity of punishment) greatly reduced the number of transgressions and the number of transgressors and served as an effective deterrent. The differences are statistically significant, as shown in Table 22-1.

TABLE 22-1

Respondents by Reported Frequency of Violation before and after Change in Regulations

June 1, 1953, to December 31, 1955, and January 1, 1956, to June 1, 1958

Before Change	After Change				
Frequency of Violations	None	Seldom	Occasional	Frequent	Total
None (15)	15	0	0	0	15
Seldom (12)	0	12	0	0	12
Occasional (3)	1	0	2	0	3
Frequent (13)	6	4	1	2	13
TOTAL (43)	22	16	3	2	43

χ^2 (change in number of persons violating *zero times* in two periods) $= 5.1$, $P < .05$.

χ^2 (change in number of persons violating *one or two times* in two periods) $= 2.25$, not significant.

χ^2 (change in number of persons violating *three or four times* in two periods) $= n$ too small to be meaningful.

χ^2 (change in number of persons violating *five or more times* in two periods) $= 9.1$, $P < .05$.

χ^2 (change in total number violating in two periods) $= 5.1$, $P < .05$.

NOTE: For an explanation of the χ^2 formula used to compute these significance tests see Helen M. Walker and Joseph Lev, *Statistical Inference* (New York: Henry Holt, 1953), pp. 102–03.

Even the two persons who remained frequent violators after the change in regulations did so in a qualified manner. One of them reported violating the regulations
every day by parking in an alley beside his office. Although he said he knew that
this was against the rules, he had never received a citation for parking in this alley.
In this case, then, the certainty of punishment had not increased as it had for the
others. The other frequent violator said that although he still violated as often as
he had before, he was now limiting his transgressions to "emergency" stops of only
a few minutes rather than leaving his car parked illegally for sustained periods of
time. Thus he attempted to reduce the likelihood of apprehension, albeit violating
the rules with some regularity.

In summary, except for those who violated the regulations once or twice (seldom
violators), the differences in the number of violations prior to the change in regulations and the number of violations after the change are significant at the .05 level and
in the direction of a reduced number of violations.

Similar results obtain from an analysis of the frequency of receiving tickets in the
two periods (Table 22-2). Seventeen persons indicated receiving no tickets in either
period. As can be seen, there was a rather startling reduction in the number of persons receiving tickets after the change despite the fact that the likelihood of receiving a ticket for violating the regulations was greater after the change than it had been
before. It is also significant that no one in the sample received "five or more" tickets
after the change in the regulations, whereas nine persons were in the "five or more"
tickets category before the change. These findings, then, tell essentially the same
story as the above analysis of the reported frequency of violations before and after
the change in the regulations: the changes had the effect of substantially reducing
the number of violations.

TABLE 22-2

**Respondents by Reported Frequency of Receiving Tickets before and after
Changes in Regulations**

June 1, 1953, to December 31, 1955, and January 1, 1956, to June 1, 1958

Before Change	After Change			
Frequency of Receiving Tickets	None	Seldom	Occasional	Frequent	Total
None (19)	17	2	0	0	19
Seldom (12)	5	7	0	0	12
Occasional (3)	1	1	1	0	3
Frequent (9)	5	4	0	0	9
TOTAL (43)	28	14	1	0	43

Another indication of the deterrent influence of the change in the regulations is
the degree to which respondents reported greater caution in avoiding violations. Of
the forty-three persons interviewed, twenty-five (58 per cent) reported being more
cautious about violating the regulations after the changes. Among those not reporting more caution, five were nonviolators and six were seldom violators before the
change. Like the other findings, this indicates that the most outstanding changes took
place among the most frequent violators.

DISCUSSION

The findings give evidence that an increase in the certainty and the severity of punishment deters violation of parking regulations, except for one group. All twelve persons who reported that they were seldom violators before the change in the regulations reported that they were *still* seldom violators after the change in the regulations. In short, the change in the certainty and severity of punishment did in fact deter the more frequent violators, but it had no effect upon those who violated the rules only once or twice in a 2½-year period. The change had no effect because the seldom violators paid their fines during *both* periods where other categories of offenders did not. During the period before the change, sixteen persons violated the regulations occasionally or frequently (Table 22-1); twelve of them had received tickets (Table 22-2); but only *three* of them, according to their own admissions, had paid a fine. Clearly, then, the new regulations represented a rather drastic change for the frequent and occasional violators but did not represent much of a change for the seldom violators.

During the study period there were, of course, changes in the parking facilities. Space previously used for parking was put to other uses, and new parking space was made available. Although the total number of parking spaces for faculty did not change appreciably during the time studied, it is possible that the facilities after 1956 were, in general, better suited to faculty demands and that this, rather than the increased punishment imposed, accounts for the reduction in the number of violations. We assessed this possibility by asking all of the forty-three respondents whether they found it less difficult to find parking space during the second period covered by the study. Only six reported less difficulty after the change; nineteen reported that it was more difficult to find a parking space *after* January 1956 than it had been before. Thus, thirty-seven (86 per cent) of the respondents in our sample reported that they had at least as much difficulty in finding a parking space after the change as they had had before. The reduction in the number of violations, then, cannot be attributed to more accessible or "better" facilities.

CONCLUSION

We cannot, of course, infer from the findings of this study of parking regulations that "punishment does deter" any more than we should infer from the studies of murder that "punishment does not deter." Because we are dealing with specialized groups of offenders in both instances, generalizations to other groups are extremely hazardous. Rather than attempt to answer the question of deterrence in such an all-encompassing manner, we should pursue investigations, of the kind reported here, on other types of offenders and examine *those circumstances under which particular types of punishment do in fact act as a deterrent and those circumstances under which particular types of punishment have little or no effect*. It is naïve to suppose that punishment exists in a vacuum and is unrelated to the specific kinds of acts and the meaning which the punishment has for the actor. By keeping such differences in mind we can go beyond the polemics which have, unfortunately, characterized scientific as well as lay thinking on the subject of punishment as a deterrent.

23. Drug Addiction in America and England

Edwin M. Schur

There are in the United States about 60,000 opiate addicts, the Federal Bureau of Narcotics estimates, and some medical experts believe that 1,000,000 is closer to the actual number of those addicted to morphine, heroin, and related drugs. Neither figure, however startling, indicates in itself the far-reaching ramifications of the addiction problem. For a complicated web of corruption, degradation, vicious police practice, and secondary crime has developed around the use of narcotics in America. At its center stands the punitive anti-addict policy embodied in our narcotics laws.

The country's first major legislative effort to control narcotics, the Harrison Act, was to set the direction for all future legislation in this field. The law, passed by Congress in 1914 and still in effect, was essentially a tax measure designed to regulate the handling of narcotics by distributors and dispensers. While saying nothing about addicts as such, it was very broadly interpreted to mean that a doctor's "good faith" prescription of narcotics to an addict was itself improper; and since this law's enactment, few medical practitioners have cared to take the risk of trying to help a narcotics patient with his problems. In recent years, considerably more stringent anti-narcotics legislation has been enacted—much of it, paradoxically, tending to perpetuate the very condition meant to be curbed. The Boggs Act provided minimum mandatory sentences for all narcotics offenses—it followed the 1951 Kefauver Committee's investigations publicizing the narcotics problem. Four years later, a Senate subcommittee investigation, under the chairmanship of then Senator Price Daniel, led to the federal Narcotics Control Act of 1956, which both raises previous minimum sentences for violations and permits the death penalty to be imposed on adults found guilty of selling heroin to persons under eighteen. This law—like most of the country's drug statutes—fails to provide the proper distinction between the addict and the peddler who is a non-addict: the *mere fact* of possession, purchase, sale, or transfer of narcotics is made punishable. So, too, a vast array of state laws prohibits the unauthorized possession and transfer of narcotics; finally, in several states, addiction is in itself a crime.

The legal position of the American addict was neatly summed up by Dr. Herbert Berger in testimony before the Daniel committee: "It is illegal to prescribe narcotics for an addict, it is illegal to fill a prescription for an addict, it is illegal for an addict to possess narcotics, or in some states, even a syringe or other material which he might use for the taking of narcotics." Addicts, he continued, have been almost completely isolated from the medical profession, "the one group of individuals who might have brought to them some relief from their present deplorable state."

It is this very isolation which has pushed the addict straight into the black market. The addict's inability to get to the doctor obviously furnishes the economic incentive that supports the thriving underworld traffic in drugs. "It is precisely our law enforcement efforts," one authority has remarked, "and nothing else, that keeps the

SOURCE: "Drug Addiction in America and England," *Commentary,* vol. 30, pp. 241–248, September, 1960. By permission of the author and publisher.

price of drugs, nearly worthless in themselves, so high as to attract an endless procession of criminal entrepreneurs to keep the traffic flowing." This crucial supply-and-demand factor was granted even by Commisisoner of Narcotics Harry J. Anslinger—though seemingly he never tires of applauding the laws he administers; he wrote (along with W. F. Tompkins) that "the diversion of supplies from the regular medical channels causes a sharp rise in prices in the domestic illegal market, and the consequent large profits form a constant temptation and incentive to smugglers who are still able to obtain the drug abroad at comparatively modest prices." According to one estimate—a conservative one—a supply of heroin purchased abroad for $1,500 would be likely to wholesale in New York for around $6,000; split up for retailing throughout the country, it might eventually bring $200,000.

The high price of illegal drugs almost invariably forces the addict into crime. Although some law enforcement authorities take a different view of addict crime, social scientists generally agree that its main cause lies in the addict's need for money to buy drugs in the illicit market. Addicts have comparatively high arrest rates for nonviolent property crimes (and for prostitution), and comparatively low rates for violent offenses against the person (rape, assault, homicide). In a recent report on juvenile drug use in New York, Professors Isidor Chein and Eva Rosenfeld stated:

> The average addicted youngster spends about forty dollars a week on drugs, often as much as seventy dollars. He is too young and unskilled to be able to support his habit by his earnings. The connection between drug use and delinquency for "profit" has been established beyond any doubt. Apart from the users' own free admission of having committed crimes like burglary, there is independent evidence that in those areas of the city where drug rates went up, the proportion of juvenile delinquencies likely to result in cash incomes also went up, while the proportion of delinquencies which are primarily behavior disturbances (rape, assault, auto theft, disorderly conduct) went down. Available knowledge about the behavior of drug users in juvenile gangs also indicates that they show preferences for income-producing delinquencies, as against participation in gang warfare, vandalism, and general hell-raising.

But our narcotics laws do worse than just foster this black market situation: if only indirectly, they promote the spread of addiction. The drug peddler who profits by supplying narcotics, obviously stands to gain if he can enlarge his market. This means creating new addicts. Likewise addicts themselves turn to the selling of drugs in the effort to finance their own habit. It is not hard to understand why the illicit narcotics traffic has assumed the proportions of big business. A Daniel committee report, issued in 1956, stated that this traffic "now costs over $500 million per year, to say nothing of the human lives shortened or destroyed."

The underworld traffic in drugs is, plainly, too enormous for existing law enforcement agencies to handle. The Federal Bureau of Narcotics, with headquarters in Washington and district offices in key areas throughout the country, has a staff of only some four hundred employees; there is, in addition, a considerably wider interlocking anti-narcotics police network, comprising the Bureau and at least segments of the regular police organizations in most states. (Attempts to seize contraband drugs at the point of entry into the country have largely failed, and the failure has been viewed in two ways. Critics of current policy insist that if people want drugs badly enough to pay high prices for them, a way always will be found to make the drugs available. Enforcement officers, on the other hand, stress the prohibitive man-power requirements of effective smuggling control. All would perhaps agree with Commissioner Anslinger's oft quoted statement that the combined forces of the army, the navy, the Narcotics Bureau, and the Federal Bureau of Investigation could not stop the smuggling of narcotics.)

Narcotics agents have been forced to rely heavily on addict informers. But—as a police expert has pointed out—"whenever addicts are used as informers, the peddlers either cut off their supply, thus forcing them out of the community, or arrange to have them murdered." Although anti-narcotics drives have employed police decoys, and searches and seizures which raised serious questions of constitutionality, even these extreme methods have failed to achieve any impressive results. Recent reports of the Federal Bureau of Investigation cite some 7,000 or more annual arrests for violations of state narcotics laws alone, yet there is little reason to believe that these represent more than a fraction of all the violations that occurred.[1]

Whatever impact the enforcement effort does have is felt most strongly not by the big-time narcotics profiteer, but by the addict himself. Four grades of sellers in the American drug traffic were listed by a New York Academy of Medicine report in 1955: the importer, who is rarely an addict; the professional wholesaler, also rarely an addict; the peddler, who may be an addict; and the pusher, an addict who sells to get funds for his own drug supply. Despite those occasional—and well-publicized —exposés of "dope rings" and "drug syndicates," enforcement efforts in this country have had little effect at the "executive level" of the drug traffic. Any limited success has been mainly at the expense of the addicts, the pushers, perhaps the peddlers. Professor Alfred Lindesmith recently described the "long, shabby, pitiful parade of indigent drug users and petty offenders, mostly Negroes," seen in the Chicago Nar-cotics Court and other municipal courts throughout the country. As he points out, "The notion that punishing these victims will deter the lords of the dope traffic is as naïve as supposing that the bootlegging enterprises of the late Al Capone could have been destroyed by arresting drunks on West Madison Street or Times Square."

This perfervid anti-addict activity has been coupled with a modest effort to develop a medical treatment program for addicts. The U.S. Public Health Service hospitals for addicts at Lexington, Kentucky, and Fort Worth, Texas, accept both voluntary patients and those committed to the hospitals on conviction of violating federal nar-cotics laws. A comprehensive treatment routine includes gradual withdrawal from drugs, vocational and recreational activities, and some kind of psychotherapy. This program, too, has had only a limited success. It is recognized by most experts that relapse in addiction cases is the rule rather than the exception. Dr. Herbert Berger, already cited, has stated that the relapse rate probably approaches 90 per cent ("and most addicts seem to think it exceeds that figure"). As he points out, "We in medicine do not accept with equanimity any treatment that fails to achieve cure in even 5 per cent of the cases of any specified disease. Yet the United States govern-ment is committed to a plan of action which fails more than 90 per cent of the time."

[1] Like many social problems in America, addiction is concentrated in the big cities—and particularly in the most crowded and underprivileged areas of those cities. Thus, Negroes have a disproportionately high rate of narcotics arrests (in terms of their proportion to the general population), and police officials claim that they make up a large segment of the total addict population. Although the extent of juvenile addiction has sometimes been exaggerated, a considerable number of juveniles and young adults do use drugs.

Nor can expansion of treatment facilities be expected to solve the addiction problem. All such efforts suffer from the general tenor of American narcotics policy—a policy based upon compulsion. The addict cannot be "cured" against his will—a fact too often overlooked; and once treated, there is no way of insuring that he will remain abstinent. Commissioner Anslinger is, of course, a staunch advocate of the compulsory confinement (for treatment) of addicts; and perhaps he unwittingly reflects the attitude implicit in such an approach when he writes: "The great majority of addicts are parasitic. This parasitic drug addict is a tremendous burden on the community. He represents a continuing problem to the police through his depredations against society." In this statement of the Commissioner's, suggesting that the addict is more a public enemy than a troubled person, we see embodied the official approach to addiction in the United States. Condemned by the "public," hounded by the police, exploited by the black marketeer, and ravaged by the physiological and psychological pressures of his own condition, the addict has no choice, finally, but to act as though he really were a "public enemy."

In sharp contrast is the situation of addicts in Great Britain. At one time it was possible to obtain opiates in Britain (as it was in the United States) without prescription at the neighborhood chemist's, and unrecognized addiction was widespread. Yet today estimates of the number of addicts in the United Kingdom run from between 300 to 1200. British addicts commit little serious crime, and there are no signs that the juvenile population is succumbing to addiction. Neither is there a large-scale black market in narcotics; the government reports with confidence that, "The addict who is also a 'pusher' is seldom encountered in the United Kingdom." Most British addicts are nativeborn whites, over thirty years of age, and about one-quarter of them are in the medical and allied professions.

Underlying this altogether different, and far happier, narcotics situation in Great Britain is, I believe, the sane approach that the British have to the general question of addiction. To the British, addicts are persons in need of medical attention, and doctors may (if certain broad conditions are satisfied) legally supply the wanted narcotics—under the National Health Service at nominal cost. The Dangerous Drugs Act (Britain's major narcotics law, first passed in 1920) places stringent controls on the import, manufacture, sale, and possession of narcotic drugs. Careful records are required of all drug transactions, subject to periodic inspection, and the Home Office warns doctors that "the continued supply of dangerous drugs to a patient solely for the gratification of addiction" is not considered legitimate. However, the ruling principle (as established by a Ministry of Health committee in 1926) is that narcotics may properly be administered to addicts after prolonged attempt at cure if "the drug cannot be safely discontinued entirely, on account of the severity of the withdrawal symptoms produced" or if the patient, "while capable of leading a useful and relatively normal life when a certain minimum dose is regularly administered, becomes incapable of this when the drug is entirely discontinued." There is no formal registration of addicts, but doctors are requested to inform the Home Office of any addicts coming under their care. While addicts may undergo treatment at some public hospitals and private nursing homes, there is no compulsory treatment in Great Britain, nor do any state institutions specialize in the treatment of addicts.

This entire approach has worked remarkably well. Not only has the estimated number of addicts remained extremely low, it has actually decreased—from 700 in 1935 to 359 in 1957. All the evidence indicates that there are very few addicts other than those receiving their supplies through legal channels. No sizable underworld drug traffic exists. The addict furnishes no economic incentive for contraband peddling, and needn't become a thief or prostitute to pay for drugs. Apparently, the few addicts who are convicted of crimes usually have committed minor violations in order to get a little more of the drug than the doctor provided. Generally speaking, addiction and underworld life are not closely connected—one reason, perhaps, why few young people in Britain (even among the delinquents) have taken up the use of opiate drugs.

Certainly the British practice is not perfect—an addict occasionally forges a prescription for extra drugs or manages to get drugs from two doctors at once, and some doctors illegally divert drugs to their own use; but these abuses are not widespread. It would seem that by refusing to treat the addict as a criminal, Britain has kept him from becoming one. In short, the British addict is not a social menace.

What is more, not only does the British approach to addiction work—where the American does not—but the former appears to make much greater sense in light of our up-to-date medical and sociological knowledge. Misinformation about the nature of opiate addiction is widespread in the United States.[2] Many Americans continue to accept what Professor Alfred Lindesmith has labeled the " 'dope fiend' mythology." Addicts are pictured as violent and ruthless degenerates—a picture quite at odds with the known effects of opiates, which are, in fact, depressants. Opiate drugs relieve pain, decrease anxiety, relax the muscles, and induce drowsiness and euphoria; and anyone who has observed long-time addicts taking their shots knows that ordinarily the addict displays relief rather than excitement when he injects the drug. Thus, opiates, since they slow down the system rather than stimulate it, ordinarily do not propel the addict into violent crime. The claim that they promote sex orgies is equally fallacious—opiates in fact inhibit the sexual functions, often to the point of producing impotence in the male. The general deleterious effects of the drug upon the addict himself have also been greatly exaggerated. On the whole, the addict, unless deprived of his drug, probably suffers less organic harm than does the chronic alcoholic.

Yet there is little doubt that characteristic behavioral problems do arise from the regular taking of narcotics. Almost always, the addict experiences difficulties in sexual adjustment. Several American studies reveal, for example, a high rate of marital instability among known addicts. Although comparable information is not available regarding British addicts, the data that have been collected suggest that addiction interferes with normal sexual functioning even where the addict is free from persecution. American research also indicates that addiction makes satisfactory occupational adjustment very difficult. As Charles Winick has pointed out, "So akin to sleep is the effect of an opiate that the addict refers to it as being 'on the nod,' 'stoned,' 'out of this world,' 'half awake and half asleep.' His ability to earn a living is also likely to be impaired because he has to spend so much time procuring his drugs that he may literally have no time to work." Almost every study of addicts

---

[2] While marijuana is often linked indiscriminately with the opiates, opiate addiction and the habitual use of marijuana have entirely different effects. The opiate addict experiences a severe withdrawal illness if deprived of his drug; he physiologically requires it to avoid that painful syndrome. The marijuana user, on the other hand, ordinarily suffers no extreme reaction to deprivation, and has no such physiological attachment. For this reason, the use of marijuana does not pose really urgent social problems of the sort raised by opiate addiction, even though an intelligent policy regarding opiate addiction probably would reduce the use of marijuana.

has found, however, that there are some persons who can and do work effectively while taking opiates. Many doctor-addicts appear able to carry on their work satisfactorily, as have any number of creative artists who were addicted. Furthermore, the addict's ability to function in a job situation is not determined solely by the effects of the drug on him—in Britain the addict is not compelled to spend all his time seeking out drugs, nor is he under the great financial pressure of his American counterpart. But by and large, it seems indisputable that many, perhaps even most, opiate addicts find it difficult to hold down a fulltime job with any consistent regularity.

Other aspects of addict behavior are far less predictable, being determined almost entirely by social rather than physiological factors. Thus, the assertions that addicts are basically "criminal types" is unsound. If addicts are basically criminal or if the drugs themselves cause criminal behavior, why do we find in Britain a low rate of addict crime? All available evidence indicates that it is not addiction itself, but the punitive approach to addiction, which produces anti-social behavior in addicts.

An increasing emphasis, in recent years, on the question of causation has served to advance our total understanding of addiction and of the addict. Much of the professional literature on the causes of addiction asserts that drug-taking is a form of (or a result of) mental illness. Psychoanalysts, for instance, stress such factors as oral fixation and unconscious homosexuality, and many psychiatrists attribute addiction to unsatisfactory family relations, feelings of inadequacy, and similar personality matters. In essence, the psychological approach holds that particular individuals are predisposed to addiction; that addiction is primarily a symptom of some underlying psychic disturbance. But this kind of explanation is not entirely satisfactory. As Lindesmith has pointed out, the belief in a predisposition to addiction ignores the fact that probably all "normal" persons who have imagined themselves immune and who have taken opiates steadily for any length of time, have become addicted. Furthermore, even the psychologists have recognized that some addicts are not otherwise abnormal; this category of "normal addicts" would seem to contradict the idea of psychological predisposition. Then too, psychologists have studied the personalities of addicts only after they became addicted and there is no way of distinguishing between resultant and causative traits. Starting with the assumption that a person must be abnormal to become an addict, it is all too easy to find the addict's personality problems. Lindesmith believes that disapproval of addiction invariably colors the diagnosis:

> Addicts are said to become addicted because they have feelings of frustration, lack of self-confidence, and need the drug to bolster themselves up. Lack of self-confidence is taken as a criterion of psychopathy or of weakness. But another person becomes addicted, it is said, because of "curiosity" and a "willingness to try anything once" and this too is called abnormal. Thus, self-confidence and the lack of self-confidence are both signs of abnormality. The addict is evidently judged in advance. He is damned if he is self-confident and he is damned if he is not.

The belief that addiction reflects some psychological disturbance also ignores socio-cultural variations in the distribution of addiction. How does one explain the fact that in some societies the regular use of narcotics is socially acceptable? Or that in Britain and America there is a disproportionately large number of addicts in the medical profession? Clearly psychological predisposition is not a complete explanation.

Sociologists and social psychologists have related addiction to slum dwelling, family background, minority-group status, and subcultural influence. But these approaches, too, fail as universal theories. Lindesmith, in his book *Opiate Addiction*, has perhaps developed the only really comprehensive theory acceptable to sociologists. He was intrigued by the fact that some of the persons receiving prolonged administration of narcotics (e.g., for relief of pain) do not become addicts—even though experiencing the drug's physiological effects, they develop no independent craving for the drug which persists when tolerance and withdrawal distress are no longer experienced. On the basis of intensive interviews with sixty addicts (together with a careful reading of addiction literature), Lindesmith concluded that ultimately addiction must be attributed to the learning process: "The knowledge or ignorance of the meaning of withdrawal distress and the use of opiates thereafter determines whether or not the individual will become addicted." The addicts Lindesmith interviewed had all understood the withdrawal symptoms and then used drugs to avoid them; furthermore, he could find no case in which this process did not result in addiction. This approach does not, it is true, provide a basis for selecting out from the general population those individuals destined to become addicts, but this was not Lindesmith's aim. What his theory does, is describe the general process by which people (whoever they may be) become drug addicts. The doctor's peculiar susceptibility to addiction, in the light of this explanation, becomes understandable. Knowing that narcotics relieve pain and anxiety, and having easy access to them (and often believing he can take opiates without becoming addicted), the doctor, not surprisingly, may succumb. Once addicted, he realizes he must continue taking the drug. Lindesmith's approach may not be a particularly dramatic one, but it does explain, at least in part, *all* cases of addiction.

Clearly, none of these findings supports the American treatment of the addict: as a public enemy. Whether the addict is in fact sick or not, criminal he is not. Why then is it that Americans continue to treat addicts as they do? The persistence of our blatantly ineffective drug laws suggest that they are crucially bound up with other social values and institutions.

It has already been noted here that the narcotics traffic has developed into a form of big business, and as Robert Merton states, "in strictly economic terms, there is no relevant difference between the provision of licit and illicit goods and services." Specifically, then, the drug peddler serves positive economic functions by providing goods for which there is a very real demand. (Such illicit entrepreneurship seems particularly well adapted to the American ethos. Rum-running during Prohibition was, of course, the classic case; another good example is the continuing provision of illegal abortion facilities.) Max Lerner has argued that the narcotics pusher "represents the principle of creating a market, inherent in the market economy." This particular market is vitally dependent upon current drug policies; if addicts were supplied legally with low-cost drugs, the market would collapse.

In some respects, law enforcement authorities may also have a sort of vested interest in maintaining the status quo. Rufus King has argued that the Narcotics Division of the Treasury Department (the early enforcement arm of the narcotics laws, known since 1930 as the Federal Narcotics Bureau), "succeeded in creating a very large criminal class for itself to police (i.e., the whole doctor-patient-addict-peddler community), instead of the very small one that Congress had intended (the smuggler and the peddler)." How else can one explain the continuing support of policies which run counter to common sense and the vast bulk of available evidence—policies which cannot help but perpetuate the drug traffic? Why else would Commissioner Anslinger keep on asserting, as he did in a recent article, that the essence of the addiction problem is "hoodlumism," and that, "In a sense it may be true that every hoodlum is a psychiatric problem but in a practical sense one must treat the bank robber, the gambler, and the thief as criminals"?

The American treatment of addicts may also be attributed to the addict's serving as a convenient scapegoat—one more enemy in the perpetual battle against crime and immorality of which Americans seem so fond. In his perceptive essay, "Crime as an American Way of Life," Daniel Bell stressed that, "In no other country have there been such spectacular attempts to curb human appetites and brand them as illicit, and nowhere else such glaring failures. From the start America was at one and the same time a frontier community where 'everything goes,' and the fair country of the Blue Laws. . . . In America the enforcement of public morals has been a continuing feature of our history." Even well-informed persons who have discarded the stereotyped image of the addict as a violent criminal may continue to condemn him, instead, for his passivity, since opiates, because of their slowing-down effects, produce the "un-American" reaction of avoiding encounters with the environment. In the United States, where a gospel of work (of the sort Max Weber described in *The Protestant Ethic and the Spirit of Capitalism*) may be said to prevail, even part-time idleness is not easily tolerated. Indeed, opiate addiction produces the kind of behavior which, in many respects, is directly opposite to that most highly prized in our society. Erich Fromm has referred to the "marketing orientation": "Success depends largely on how well a person sells himself on the market, how well he gets his personality across, how nice a 'package' he is; whether he is 'cheerful,' 'sound,' 'aggressive,' 'reliable,' 'ambitious.' . . ." The addict is hardly likely to conform to this model.

An additional support for the official position regarding addicts has been the medical profession's failure to insist on its responsibility for their treatment. Only recently have there been indications of a change in this attitude. In 1955, a committee of the New York Academy of Medicine, holding that "the most effective way to eradicate drug addiction is to take the profit out of the illicit drug traffic," proposed a national network of federally controlled clinics at which addicts could receive low-cost drugs. In 1958, a joint committee of the American Medical Association and the American Bar Association called for the establishment of an experimental clinic to see what would happen if a group of addicts received drugs free under medical supervision. This proposal followed a report by the American Medical Association's Council on Mental Health urging that "narcotic addiction should be viewed, much more than it has been in the past, as an illness and that there should be a progressive movement in the direction of treating addiction medically rather than punitively." The Council approved the idea of eventually "endorsing regulations somewhat similar to those currently in force in England." The Narcotics Bureau and other law enforcement agencies have vehemently opposed all such proposals, arguing that there really is nothing new or special about the British approach. It is pointed out (with supporting British quotations) that Britain permits no "indiscriminate" prescribing of narcotics; that prescribing for "the mere gratification of addiction" is not allowed;

and that narcotic drugs are subject to "strict control." These statements are true enough, but when used, as here, to suggest that the British practice is no different from our own, they are totally misleading. As already mentioned, in Britain it is the doctor who decides when a person should receive narcotics. Doctors are not imprisoned for treating addicts (as some have been in the United States). The few prosecutions for over-prescribing have in fact been unsuccessful—the court upholding the doctor's professional judgment in such matters.

Critics sometimes indiscriminately link the British approach and all reform proposals with a "clinic system" which, they point out, was once unsuccessfully attempted in the United States. It is not certain, however, that these clinics—which operated between 1912 and 1925 in over forty American cities and dispensed low-cost drugs to addicts—were a complete failure. Some accounts would indicate that certain clinics were quite successful, and that the government (with the support of organized medicine) shut them all down largely on the evidence of the least efficient one, that in New York. The 1957 American Medical Association report on addiction states that, "Reasons for closing the clinics are obscure." The AMA's stand in the 1920's undoubtedly was based in part on medical considerations (some doctors still believe that to supply the addict with drugs is to abandon the attempt to "cure"), but at the same time it constituted an easy way out; the treatment of drug addiction is a bothersome and often unrewarding process. If the recent change in medical opinion is followed by pressure for actual changes in policy, there may be substantial hope for a new approach to addiction in the United States.

Just as there are many factors which have inhibited addiction reform, so there is no simple explanation for the great hold narcotic drugs seem to have upon Americans. The apolitical hipster may think to develop a new type of radicalism by deliberately courting psychopathy—drugs, violence, and mystical sexuality are his answer to the bomb, the cult of commodities, and the miseries of the mass society. The intellectual who comes to despair of the value of reason alone may seek through drugs to "transcend the self," to achieve new insights and experience new kinds of intense feeling. The minority-group or disturbed adolescent may attempt to create around the use of drugs a way of life which appears to offer him the prestige and self-esteem he is deprived of by the larger society. The general combination of tension and tedium which plagues many Americans today may lead to narcotics use, just as it may lead to reliance on alcohol, aspirin, or tranquilizers. Whatever the case, short of eradicating all the social conditions breeding addiction we must concentrate on formulating a sane policy toward the addicts.

Although legislative committees and other official bodies constantly demand "narcotics reform," they almost always take for granted the general desirability of our current policies. It is quite clear that American policies have not worked, primarily because of the vicious supply-and-demand cycle they set in motion. What is needed is an absolute reversal of our current attitudes and laws. The addict will get his drugs, no matter how hard the law enforcers try to stop him, and the only sensible course of action is to try to substitute medical supervision for police persecution. But, one may ask, would something like the British approach work in the United States? There is no way of knowing until we actually put such a policy to the test. It has been argued that supplying addicts with drugs will not reduce criminality; the addict, critics of the British system say, will not be content with the amount he gets legally. While it is true that with increasing tolerance to his drug the addict usually wants more and more of it, the British experience indicates that some addicts can, under favorable circumstances, get along reasonably well on legally prescribed limited doses. Certainly we have everything to gain and nothing to lose by instituting at least an experimental clinic through which to test the British approach.

Some would yet argue that we must condemn addiction, if for no other reason than that it is a "vice." Yet on what grounds can we call drug addiction a vice? Is it as morally reprehensible as the criminality and degradation to which we in this country have driven the addict? Similarly, is it really true (as officials sometimes contend) that the American public would never countenance a non-punitive approach to addiction? Public condemnation of the addict is as much a product of our current policy as it is a cause of that policy. The British people (though equally decent and "right thinking") appear quite capable of accepting intelligent efforts to deal with addiction. Americans may very well be able to do the same, once they are aware of the basic facts about addiction and addiction policies.

24. Two Studies of Legal Stigma

Richard D. Schwartz and Jerome H. Skolnick

Legal thinking has moved increasingly toward a sociologically meaningful view of the legal system. Sanctions, in particular, have come to be regarded in functional terms.[1] In criminal law, for instance, sanctions are said to be designed to prevent recidivism by rehabilitating, restraining, or executing the offender. They are also said to be intended to deter others from the performance of similar acts and, sometimes, to provide a channel for the expression of retaliatory motives. In such civil actions as tort or contract, monetary awards may be intended as retributive and deterrent, as in the use of punitive damages, or may be regarded as *quid pro quo* to compensate the plaintiff for his wrongful loss.

While these goals comprise an integral part of the rationale of law, little is known about the extent to which they are fulfilled in practice. Lawmen do not as a rule make such studies, because their traditions and techniques are not designed for a systematic examination of the operation of the legal system in action, especially outside the courtroom. Thus, when extra-legal consequences—e.g., the social stigma of a prison sentence—are taken into account at all, it is through the discretionary actions of police, prosecutor, judge, and jury. Systematic information on a variety of unanticipated outcomes, those which benefit the accused as well as those which hurt him, might help to inform these decision makers and perhaps lead to changes in substantive law as well. The present paper is an attempt to study the consequences of stigma associated with legal accusation.

From a sociological viewpoint, there are several types of indirect consequences of legal sanctions which can be distinguished. These include differential deterrence, effects on the sanctionee's associates, and variations in the degree of deprivation which sanction imposes on the recipient himself.

SOURCE: "Two Studies of Legal Stigma," *Social Problems*, vol. 10, pp. 133–142, Fall, 1962. By permission of the authors and publisher.

[1] Legal sanctions are defined as changes in life conditions imposed through court action.

First, the imposition of sanction, while intended as a matter of overt policy to deter the public at large, probably will vary in its effectiveness as a deterrent, depending upon the extent to which potential offenders perceive themselves as similar to the sanctionee. Such "differential deterrence" would occur if white-collar anti-trust violators were restrained by the conviction of General Electric executives, but not by invocation of the Sherman Act against union leaders.

The imposition of a sanction may even provide an unintended incentive to violate the law. A study of factors affecting compliance with federal income tax laws provides some evidence of this effect.[2] Some respondents reported that they began to cheat on their tax returns only *after* convictions for tax evasion had been obtained against others in their jurisdiction. They explained this surprising behavior by noting that the prosecutions had always been conducted against blatant violators and not against the kind of moderate offenders which they then became. These respondents were, therefore, unintentionally educated to the possibility of supposedly "safe" violations.

Second, deprivations or benefits may accrue to non-sanctioned individuals by virtue of the web of affiliations that join them to the defendant. The wife and family of a convicted man may, for instance, suffer from his arrest as much as the man himself. On the other hand, they may be relieved by his absence if the family relationship has been an unhappy one. Similarly, whole groups of persons may be affected by sanctions to an individual, as when discriminatory practices increase because of a highly publicized crime attributed to a member of a given minority group.

Finally, the social position of the defendant himself will serve to aggravate or alleviate the effects of any given sanction. Although all three indirect consequences may be interrelated, it is the third with which this paper will be primarily concerned.

FINDINGS

The subjects studied to examine the effects of legal accusation on occupational positions represented two extremes: lower-class unskilled workers charged with assault, and medical doctors accused of malpractice. The first project lent itself to a field experiment, while the second required a survey design. Because of differences in method and substance, the studies cannot be used as formal controls for each other. Taken together, however, they do suggest that the indirect effects of sanctions can be powerful, that they can produce unintended harm or unexpected benefit and that the results are related to officially unemphasized aspects of the social context in which the sanctions are administered. Accordingly, the two studies will be discussed together, as bearing on one another. Strictly speaking, however, each can, and properly should, stand alone as a separate examination of the unanticipated consequences of legal sanctions.

Study I. The Effects of a Criminal Court Record on the Employment Opportunities of Unskilled Workers

In the field experiment, four employment folders were prepared, the same in all respects except for the criminal court record of the applicant. In all of the folders

---

[2] Richard D. Schwartz, "The Effectiveness of Legal Controls: Factors in the Reporting of Minor Items of Income on Federal Income Tax Returns." Paper presented at the annual meeting of the American Sociological Association, Chicago, 1959.

he was described as a thirty-two year old single male of unspecified race, with a high school training in mechanical trades, and a record of successive short term jobs as a kitchen helper, maintenance worker, and handyman. These characteristics are roughly typical of applicants for unskilled hotel jobs in the Catskill resort area of New York State where employment opportunities were tested.[3]

The four folders differed only in the applicant's reported record of criminal court involvement. The first folder indicated that the applicant had been convicted and sentenced for assault; the second, that he had been tried for assault and acquitted; the third, also tried for assault and acquitted, but with a letter from the judge certifying the finding of not guilty and reaffirming the legal presumption of innocence. The fourth folder made no mention of any criminal record.

A sample of one hundred employers was utilized. Each employer was assigned to one of four "treatment" groups.[4] To each employer only one folder was shown; this folder was one of the four kinds mentioned above, the selection of the folder being determined by the treatment group to which the potential employer was assigned. The employer was asked whether he could "use" the man described in the folder. To preserve the reality of the situation and make it a true field experiment, employers were never given any indication that they were participating in an experiment. So far as they knew, a legitimate offer to work was being made in each showing of the folder by the "employment agent."

The experiment was designed to determine what employers would do in fact if confronted with an employment applicant with a criminal record. The questionnaire approach used in earlier studies [5] seemed ill-adapted to the problem, since respondents confronted with hypothetical situations might be particularly prone to answer in what they considered a socially acceptable manner. The second alternative—studying job opportunities of individuals who had been involved with the law—would have made it very difficult to find comparable groups of applicants and potential employers. For these reasons, the field experiment reported here was utilized.

Some deception was involved in the study. The "employment agent"—the same individual in all hundred cases—was in fact a law student who was working in the Catskills during the summer of 1959 as an insurance adjuster. In representing himself as being both an adjuster and an employment agent, he was assuming a combination of roles which is not uncommon there. The adjuster role gave him an opportunity to introduce a single application for employment casually and naturally. To the extent that the experiment worked, however, it was inevitable that some employers should be led to believe that they had immediate prospects of filling a job opening. In those instances where an offer to hire was made, the "agent" called a few hours later to say that the applicant had taken another job. The field experimenter attempted in

[3] The generality of these results remains to be determined. The effects of criminal involvement in the Catskill area are probably diminished, however, by the temporary nature of employment, the generally poor qualifications of the work force, and the excess of demand over supply of unskilled labor there. Accordingly, the employment differences among the four treatment groups found in this study are likely, if anything to be *smaller* than would be expected in industries and areas where workers are more carefully selected.

[4] Employers were not approached in pre-selected random order, due to a misunderstanding of instructions on the part of the law student who carried out the experiment during a three and one-half week period. Because of this flaw in the experimental procedure, the results should be treated with appropriate caution. Thus, chi-squared analysis may not properly be utilized. (For those used to this measure, $P < .05$ for Table 24-1.)

[5] Sol Rubin, *Crime and Juvenile Delinquency*, New York: Oceana, 1958, pp. 151–56.

such instances to locate a satisfactory replacement by contacting an employment agency in the area. Because this procedure was used and since the jobs involved were of relatively minor consequence, we believe that the deception caused little economic harm.

As mentioned, each treatment group of twenty-five employers was approached with one type of folder. Responses were dichotomized: those who expressed a willingness to consider the applicant in any way were termed positive; those who made no response or who explicitly refused to consider the candidate were termed negative. Our results consist of comparisons between positive and negative responses, thus defined, for the treatment groups.

Of the twenty-five employers shown the "no record" folder, nine gave positive responses. Subject to reservations arising from chance variations in sampling we take this as indicative of the "ceiling" of jobs available for this kind of applicant under the given field conditions. Positive responses by these employers may be compared with those in the other treatment groups to obtain an indication of job opportunities lost because of the various legal records.

Of the twenty-five employers approached with the "convict" folder, only one expressed interest in the applicant. This is a rather graphic indication of the effect which a criminal record may have on job opportunities. Care must be exercised, of course, in generalizing the conclusions to other settings. In this context, however, the criminal record made a major difference.

From a theoretical point of view, the finding leads toward the conclusion that conviction constitutes a powerful form of "status degradation" [6] which continues to operate after the time when, according to the generalized theory of justice underlying punishment in our society, the individual's "debt" has been paid. A record of conviction produces a durable if not permanent loss of status. For purposes of effective social control, this state of affairs may heighten the deterrent effect of conviction —though that remains to be established. Any such contribution to social control, however, must be balanced against the barriers imposed upon rehabilitation of the convict. If the ex-prisoner finds difficulty in securing menial kinds of legitimate work, further crime may become an increasingly attractive alternative.[7]

Another important finding of this study concerns the small number of positive responses elicited by the "accused but acquitted" applicant. Of the twenty-five employers approached with this folder, three offered jobs. Thus, the individual accused but acquitted of assault has almost as much trouble finding even an unskilled job as the one who was not only accused of the same offense, but also convicted.

From a theoretical point of view, this result indicates that permanent lowering of status is not limited to those explicitly singled out by being convicted of a crime. As

---

[6] Harold Garfinkel, "Conditions of Successful Degradation Ceremonies," *American Journal of Sociology,* 61 (March, 1956), pp. 420–24.

[7] Severe negative effects of conviction on employment opportunities have been noted by Sol Rubin, *Crime and Juvenile Delinquency,* New York: Oceana, 1958. A further source of employment difficulty is inherent in licensing statutes and security regulations which sometimes preclude convicts from being employed in their pre-conviction occupation or even in the trades which they may have acquired during imprisonment. These effects may, however, be counteracted by bonding arrangements, prison associations, and publicity programs aimed at increasing confidence in and sympathy for, ex-convicts. See also, B. F. McSally, "Finding Jobs for Released Offenders," *Federal Probation,* 24 (June, 1960), pp. 12–17; Harold D. Lasswell and Richard C. Donnelly, "The Continuing Debate over Responsibility: An Introduction to Isolating the Condemnation Sanction," *Yale Law Journal,* 68 (April, 1959), pp. 869–99; Johannes Andenaes, "General Prevention—Illusion or Reality?" *J. Criminal Law,* 43 (July–August, 1952), pp. 176–98.

an ideal outcome of American Justice, criminal procedure is supposed to distinguish between the "guilty" and those who have been acquitted. Legally controlled consequences which follow the judgment are consistent with this purpose. Thus, the "guilty" are subject to fine and imprisonment, while those who are acquitted are immune from these sanctions. But deprivations may be imposed on the acquitted, both before and after victory in court. Before trial, legal rules either permit or require arrest and detention. The suspect may be faced with the expense of an attorney and a bail bond if he is to mitigate these limitations on his privacy and freedom. In addition, some pre-trial deprivations are imposed without formal legal permission. These may include coercive questioning, use of violence, and stigmatization. And, as this study indicates, some deprivations not under the direct control of the legal process may develop or persist after an official decision of acquittal has been made.

Thus two legal principles conflict in practice. On the one hand, "a man is innocent until proven guilty." On the other, the accused is systematically treated as guilty under the administration of criminal law until a functionary or official body—police, magistrate, prosecuting attorney, or trial judge or jury—decides that he is entitled to be free. Even then, the results of treating him as guilty persist and may lead to serious consequences.

The conflict could be eased by measures aimed at reducing the deprivations imposed on the accused, before and after acquittal. Some legal attention has been focused on pre-trial deprivations. The provision of bail and counsel, the availability of habeas corpus, limitations on the admissibility of coerced confessions, and civil actions for false arrest are examples of measures aimed at protecting the rights of the accused before trial. Although these are often limited in effectiveness, especially for individuals of lower socio-economic status, they at least represent some concern with implementing the presumption of innocence at the pre-trial stage.

By contrast, the courts have done little toward alleviating the post-acquittal consequences of legal accusation. One effort along these lines has been employed in the federal courts, however. Where an individual has been accused and exonerated of a crime, he may petition the federal courts for a "Certificate of Innocence" certifying this fact.[8] Possession of such a document might be expected to alleviate post-acquittal deprivations.

Some indication of the effectiveness of such a measure is found in the responses of the final treatment group. Their folder, it will be recalled, contained information on the accusation and acquittal of the applicant, but also included a letter from a judge addressed "To whom it may concern" certifying the applicant's acquittal and reminding the reader of the presumption of innocence. Such a letter might have had a boomerang effect, by reemphasizing the legal involvement of the applicant. It was important, therefore, to determine empirically whether such a communication would improve or harm the chances of employment. Our findings indicate that it increased employment opportunities, since the letter folder elicited six positive responses. Even though this fell short of the nine responses to the "no record" folder, it doubled the number for the "accused but acquitted" and created a significantly greater number of job offers than those elicited by the convicted record. This suggests that the procedure merits consideration as a means of offsetting the occupational loss resulting from accusation. It should be noted, however, that repeated use of this device might reduce its effectiveness.

[8] 28 United States Code, Secs. 1495, 2513.

The results of the experiment are summarized in Table 24-1. The differences in outcome found there indicate that various types of legal records are systematically related to job opportunities. It seems fair to infer also that the trend of job losses corresponds with the apparent punitive intent of the authorities. Where the man is convicted, that intent is presumably greatest. It is less where he is accused but acquitted and still less where the court makes an effort to emphasize the absence of a finding of guilt. Nevertheless, where the difference in punitive intent is ideally greatest, between conviction and acquittal, the difference in occupational harm is very slight. A similar blurring of this distinction shows up in a different way in the next study.

TABLE 24-1

Effect of Four Types of Legal Folder on Job Opportunities (in Per Cent)

	No Record (N = 25)	Acquitted with Letter (N = 25)	Acquitted without Letter (N = 25)	Convicted (N = 25)	Total (N = 100)
Positive response	36	24	12	4	19
Negative response	64	76	88	96	81
TOTAL	100	100	100	100	100

Study II. The Effects on Defendants of Suits for Medical Malpractice

As indicated earlier, the second study differed from the first in a number of ways: method of research, social class of accused, relationship between the accused and his "employer," social support available to accused, type of offense and its possible relevance to occupational adequacy. Because the two studies differ in so many ways, the reader is again cautioned to avoid thinking of them as providing a rigorous comparative examination. They are presented together only to demonstrate that legal accusation can produce unanticipated deprivations, as in the case of Study I, or unanticipated benefits, as in the research now to be presented. In the discussion to follow, some of the possible reasons for the different outcomes will be suggested.

The extra-legal effects of a malpractice suit were studied by obtaining the records of Connecticut's leading carrier of malpractice insurance. According to these records, a total of 69 doctors in the State had been sued in 64 suits during the post World War II period covered by the study, September, 1945, to September, 1959.[9] Some suits were instituted against more than one doctor, and four physicians had been sued twice. Of the total of 69 physicians, 58 were questioned. Interviews were conducted with the approval of the Connecticut Medical Association by Robert Wyckoff, whose extraordinary qualifications for the work included possession of both the M.D. and LL.B. degrees. Dr. Wyckoff was able to secure detailed responses to his inquiries from all doctors contacted.

Twenty of the respondents were questioned by personal interview, 28 by telephone, and the remainder by mail. Forty-three of those reached practiced principally in cities, eleven in suburbs, and four in rural areas. Seventeen were engaged in gen-

---

[9] A spot check of one county revealed that the Company's records covered every malpractice suit tried in the courts of that county during this period.

eral practice and forty-one were specialists. The sample proved comparable to the doctors in the State as a whole in age, experience, and professional qualifications.[10] The range was from the lowest professional stratum to chiefs of staff and services in the State's most highly regarded hospitals.

Of the 57 malpractice cases reported, doctors clearly won 38; nineteen of these were dropped by the plaintiff and an equal number were won in court by the defendant doctor. Of the remaining nineteen suits, eleven were settled out of court for a nominal amount, four for approximately the amount the plaintiff claimed and four resulted in judgment for the plaintiff in court.

The malpractice survey did not reveal widespread occupational harm to the physicians involved. Of the 58 respondents, 52 reported no negative effects of the suit on their practice, and five of the remaining six, all specialists, reported that their practice *improved* after the suit. The heaviest loser in court (a radiologist), reported the largest gain. He commented, "I guess all the doctors in town felt sorry for me because new patients started coming in from doctors who had not sent me patients previously." Only one doctor reported adverse consequences to his practice. A winner in court, this man suffered physical and emotional stress symptoms which hampered his later effectiveness in surgical work. The temporary drop in his practice appears to have been produced by neurotic symptoms and is therefore only indirectly traceable to the malpractice suit. Seventeen other doctors reported varying degrees of personal dissatisfaction and anxiety during and after the suit, but none of them reported impairment of practice. No significant relationship was found between outcome of the suit and expressed dissatisfaction.

A protective institutional environment helps to explain these results. No cases were found in which a doctor's hospital privileges were reduced following the suit. Neither was any physician unable later to obtain malpractice insurance, although a handful found it necessary to pay higher rates. The State Licensing Commission, which is headed by a doctor, did not intervene in any instance. Local medical societies generally investigated charges through their ethics and grievance committees, but where they took any action, it was almost always to recommend or assist in legal defense against the suit.

DISCUSSION

Accusation has different outcomes for unskilled workers and doctors in the two studies. How may these be explained? First, they might be nothing more than artifacts of research method. In the field experiment, it was possible to see behavior directly, i.e., to determine how employers act when confronted with what appears to them to be a realistic opportunity to hire. Responses are therefore not distorted by the memory of the respondent. By contrast, the memory of the doctors might have been consciously or unconsciously shaped by the wish to create the impression that the public had not taken seriously the accusation leveled against them. The motive for such a distortion might be either to protect the respondent's self-esteem or to preserve an image of public acceptance in the eyes of the interviewer, the profession, and the public. Efforts of the interviewer to assure his subjects of anonymity—intended to offset these effects—may have succeeded or may, on the contrary, have accentuated an awareness of the danger. A related type of distortion might have

[10] No relationship was found between any of these characteristics and the legal or extra-legal consequences of the lawsuit.

stemmed from a desire by doctors to affect public attitudes toward malpractice. Two conflicting motives might have been expected to enter here. The doctor might have tended to exaggerate the harm caused by an accusation, especially if followed by acquittal, in order to turn public opinion toward legal policies which would limit malpractice liability. On the other hand, he might tend to underplay extra-legal harm caused by a legally insufficient accusation in order to discourage potential plaintiffs from instituting suits aimed at securing remunerative settlements and/or revenge for grievances. Whether these diverse motives operated to distort doctors' reports and, if so, which of them produced the greater degree of distortion is a matter for speculation. It is only suggested here that the interview method is more subject to certain types of distortion than the direct behavioral observations of the field experiment.

Even if such distortion did not occur, the results may be attributable to differences in research design. In the field experiment, a direct comparison is made between the occupational position of an accused and an identical individual not accused at a single point in time. In the medical study, effects were inferred through retrospective judgment, although checks on actual income would have no doubt confirmed these judgments. Granted that income had increased, many other explanations are available to account for it. An improvement in practice after a malpractice suit may have resulted from factors extraneous to the suit. The passage of time in the community and increased experience may have led to a larger practice and may even have masked negative effects of the suit. There may have been a general increase in practice for the kinds of doctors involved in these suits, even greater for doctors not sued than for doctors in the sample. Whether interviews with a control sample could have yielded sufficiently precise data to rule out these possibilities is problematic. Unfortunately, the resources available for the study did not enable such data to be obtained.

A third difference in the two designs may affect the results. In the field experiment, full information concerning the legal record is provided to all of the relevant decision makers, i.e., the employers. In the medical study, by contrast, the results depend on decisions of actual patients to consult a given doctor. It may be assumed that such decisions are often based on imperfect information, some patients knowing little or nothing about the malpractice suit. To ascertain how much information employers usually have concerning the legal record of the employee and then supply that amount would have been a desirable refinement, but a difficult one. The alternative approach would involve turning the medical study into an experiment in which full information concerning malpractice (e.g., liable, accused but acquitted, no record of accusation) was supplied to potential patients. This would have permitted a comparison of the effects of legal accusation in two instances where information concerning the accusation is constant. To carry out such an experiment in a field situation would require an unlikely degree of cooperation, for instance by a medical clinic which might ask patients to choose their doctor on the basis of information given them. It is difficult to conceive of an experiment along these lines which would be both realistic enough to be valid and harmless enough to be ethical.

If we assume, however, that these methodological problems do not invalidate the basic finding, how may it be explained? Why would unskilled workers accused but acquitted of assault have great difficulty getting jobs, while doctors accused of malpractice—whether acquitted or not—are left unharmed or more sought after than before?

First, the charge of criminal assault carries with it the legal allegation and the popular connotation of intent to harm. Malpractice, on the other hand, implies negligence or failure to exercise reasonable care. Even though actual physical harm may be greater in malpractice, the element of intent suggests that the man accused of assault would be more likely to repeat his attempt and to find the mark. However, it is dubious that this fine distinction could be drawn by the lay public.

Perhaps more important, all doctors and particularly specialists may be immune from the effects of a malpractice suit because their services are in short supply.[11] By contrast, the unskilled worker is one of many and therefore likely to be passed over in favor of someone with a "cleaner" record.

Moreover, high occupational status, such as is demonstrably enjoyed by doctors,[12] probably tends to insulate the doctor from imputations of incompetence. In general, professionals are assumed to possess uniformly high ability, to be oriented toward community service, and to enforce adequate standards within their own organization.[13] Doctors in particular receive deference, just because they are doctors, not only from the population as a whole but even from fellow professionals.[14]

Finally, individual doctors appear to be protected from the effects of accusation by the sympathetic and powerful support they receive from fellow members of the occupation, a factor absent in the case of unskilled, unorganized laborers.[15] The medical society provides advice on handling malpractice actions, for instance, and referrals by other doctors sometimes increase as a consequence of the sympathy felt for the malpractice suit victim. Such assistance is further evidence that the professional operates as "a community within a community," [16] shielding its members from controls exercised by formal authorities in the larger society.

In order to isolate these factors, additional studies are needed. It would be interesting to know, for instance, whether high occupational status would protect a doctor acquitted of a charge of assault. Information on this question is sparse. Actual instances of assaults by doctors are probably very rare. When and if they do occur, it seems unlikely that they would lead to publicity and prosecution, since police and prosecutor discretion might usually be employed to quash charges before they are publicized. In the rare instances in which they come to public attention, such accusations appear to produce a marked effect because of the assumption that the pressing of charges, despite the status of the defendant, indicates probable guilt. Nevertheless, instances may be found in which even the accusation of first degree murder followed

---

[11] See Eliot Freidson, "Client Control and Medical Practice," *American Journal of Sociology*, 65 (January, 1960), pp. 374–82. Freidson's point is that general practitioners are more subject to client control than specialists are. Our findings emphasize the importance of professional as compared to client control, and professional protection against a particular form of client control, extending through both branches of the medical profession. However, what holds for malpractice situations may not be true of routine medical practice.

[12] National Opinion Research Center, "Jobs and Occupations: A Popular Evaluation," *Opinion News*, 9 (Sept., 1947), pp. 3–13. More recent studies in several countries tend to confirm the high status of the physician. See Alex Inkeles, "Industrial Man: The Relation of Status to Experience, Perception and Value," *American Journal of Sociology*, 66 (July, 1960), pp. 1–31.

[13] Talcott Parsons, *The Social System*, Glencoe: The Free Press, 1951, pp. 454–73; and Everett C. Hughes, *Men and Their Work*, Glencoe: The Free Press, 1958.

[14] Alvin Zander, Arthur R. Cohen, and Ezra Stotland, *Role Relations in the Mental Health Professions*, Ann Arbor: Institute for Social Research, 1957.

[15] Unions sometimes act to protect the seniority rights of members who, discharged from their jobs upon arrest, seek re-employment following their acquittal.

[16] See William J. Goode, "Community within a Community: The Professions," *American Sociological Review*, 22 (April, 1957), pp. 194–200.

by acquittal appears to have left the doctor professionally unscathed.[17] Similarly, as a test of the group protection hypothesis, one might investigate the effect of an acquittal for assault on working men who are union members. The analogy would be particularly instructive where the union plays an important part in employment decisions, for instance in industries which make use of a union hiring hall.

In the absence of studies which isolate the effect of such factors, our findings cannot readily be generalized. It is tempting to suggest after an initial look at the results that social class differences provide the explanation. But subsequent analysis and research might well reveal significant intra-class variations, depending on the distribution of other operative factors. A lower class person with a scarce specialty and a protective occupational group who is acquitted of a lightly regarded offense might benefit from the accusation. Nevertheless, class in general seems to correlate with the relevant factors to such an extent that in reality the law regularly works to the disadvantage of the already more disadvantaged classes.

CONCLUSION

Legal accusation imposes a variety of consequences, depending on the nature of the accusation and the characteristics of the accused. Deprivations occur, even though not officially intended, in the case of unskilled workers who have been acquitted of assault charges. On the other hand, malpractice actions—even when resulting in a judgment against the doctor—are not usually followed by negative consequences and sometimes have a favorable effect on the professional position of the defendant. These differences in outcome suggest two conclusions: one, the need for more explicit clarification of legal goals; two, the importance of examining the attitudes and social structure of the community outside the courtroom if the legal process is to hit intended targets, while avoiding innocent bystanders. Greater precision in communicating goals and in appraising consequences of present practices should help to make the legal process an increasingly equitable and effective instrument of social control.

25. Modification of National Character: The Role of the Police in England

Geoffrey Gorer

To my understanding, the concept of national character is essentially an aspect of social anthropology, and only becomes meaningful within the context of the social structure and component institutions which compose the culture of the society under

[17] For instance, the acquittal of Dr. John Bodkin Adams after a sensational murder trial, in which he was accused of deliberately killing several elderly women patients to inherit their estates, was followed by his quiet return to medical practice. *New York Times,* Nov. 24, 1961, p. 28, col. 7. Whether the British regard acquittals as more exonerative than Americans is uncertain.

SOURCE: "Modification of National Character: The Role of the Police in England," *Journal of Social Issues,* vol. 11, pp. 24–32, 1955. By permission of the publisher.

investigation. The techniques of observation and interviewing that are habitual in all aspects of social anthropology are the necessary techniques for studying national character also. All anthropological statements tend to be generalizations or normative statements abstracted from a series of observed or recounted acts or expressions of opinion or belief. The study of national character describes the observed or deduced motives and values dominant within a given society at a given time in a way little different from that in which a study of primitive law describes the legal norms and sanctions operative in a given society at a given time. Studies of primitive law will often deduce generalizations that would probably not have occurred to any member of the society being studied, and will employ (often with a redefinition for the special circumstances) terms derived from the specialized study of jurisprudence as developed in the anthropologist's own society.

In quite an analogous way,[1] studies of national character have deduced unconscious motives as explanations for a variety of observed or recounted acts that would probably not have occurred to any member of the society being studied. But the observations or recorded information are primary; the deduced unconscious motives, like the deduced legal generalizations, have the status of *hypotheses* which are offered as being the principles underlying the disparate statements or behavior recorded. The usefulness of such hypotheses depends on their being applicable to a further series of observations within the same society; in other words the hypotheses concerning national character, like any other scientific hypotheses, are tested by the predictions that can be made when they are employed consistently.

Just as most generalizations about primitive law are phrased in terms drawn from contemporary jurisprudence, so are most generalizations about national character phrased in terms drawn from contemporary psychology and perhaps especially psychoanalysis. This has probably been a source of confusion; for though, to a certain extent, psychoanalysts and social anthropologists studying national character are dealing with the same endopsychic events, their observational viewpoints are different.

As an example of these different observational viewpoints, let us consider the attitudes towards authority. Both psychoanalysts and anthropologists have noted that in many instances there is similarity or congruity in the attitudes felt or expressed towards the representatives of authority in varied institutions—parent, king or president, officer, priest, teacher, representative of the law, and so on. The psychoanalyst, engaged with the historical development of a single individual, knows or infers that the individual being studied had relations with his parents prior to relations with any other holder of authority, and therefore, *for that individual*, his attitude to kings, priests or teachers, and the like will tend to generalize from his attitude to his parents; and, within this individual context, it is legitimate to speak of kings, priests, and so on, as "father-surrogates."

The social anthropologist, on the other hand, takes as his basic observation the fact that infants are born into a society in which the patterns of authority, of subordination and deference, are already established, and that these patterns include proper and expected, or improper and censured, behavior and attitudes for parents

---

[1] It should perhaps be emphasized that the analogical elements lie in the deductions the anthropologist makes from his observations and interviews, rather than in any very close parallel between legal principles and unconscious motives. That there is a connection, however, is demonstrated in my study of English character (4), where it is shown that unsophisticated English parents are likely to judge their children's conduct on the same basis as that which underlies the McNaghten rules for crimes committed by the legally insane.

of young children. Despite the variations of personality and temperament, the parents' roles are to a very considerable extent determined before a child is born by the existing patterns of authority within the culture, so that, from an anthropological point of view, a father can be considered a "king-surrogate" or "policeman-surrogate," and so on.

In psychoanalytic theory, and within the aims of individual psychotherapy, the parents' behavior is "given" or arbitrary, and the patient's adaptation to, or interpretation of, this parental behavior is the object of investigation. In the study of national character, the ideal and actual roles of parents are important objects of investigation; but they are considered to be no more "given" or arbitrary than any other aspect of the society under investigation. From this observational viewpoint, a change in the authority structure within a society can theoretically modify the expected role of the parent within the family and so, in course of time, the national character of the members of a given society.

In this paper, I wish to explore the hypothesis that the national character of a society may be modified or transformed over a given period through the selection of the personnel for institutions that are in constant contact with the mass of the population and in a somewhat superordinate position, in a position of some authority. If the personnel of the institution are selected chiefly for their approximation to a certain type of character, rather than for specific intellectual or physical skills; if persons of this type of character have not hitherto been consistently given positions of authority; and if the authority of the institution is generally felt to be benevolent, protective, or succoring: then the character exemplified by the personnel of this institution will to a certain degree become part of the ego ideal of the mass of the population. The mass of the population will then tend to mold their own behavior in conformity with this ideal, and will reward and punish their children in conformity to this adopted pattern. As generations pass, the attempt to approximate this ideal will become less and less conscious, and increasingly part of the unconscious mechanisms that determine the content of the superego; with the ultimate consequence that a type of character that may have been relatively very uncommon when the institution was first manned will subsequently become relatively common, even perhaps typical of the society as a whole, or of those portions of it with which the members of the institution are in most continuous contact.

The English police forces are the institution that I propose to examine in detail; but the evidence that is available to me suggests that strictly analogous functions were performed by the public school teachers in the United States (3, 8), particularly during the period of the great immigrations of the half century ending in 1914, when masses of immigrants' children were transformed into "hundred per cent Americans" and given new models of the parental roles. It also appears that a similar attempt is being made in the U.S.S.R. (1, 9) (and presumably in China), where the members of the Communist Party are consciously presented as models for the mass of the population.

The modern English police force had its inception in the Metropolitan Police Act of Sir Robert Peel in 1829; it was a generation before police forces became mandatory all over the country, through the County and Borough Police Act of 1856 (5). In one important respect the Metropolitan police is anomalous; it is directly responsible to the Home Secretary, to the centralized government; all the other police forces in the country are controlled by local authorities. In the counties the chief officer of police has the legal power to promote and recruit other members of the force; in the borough forces of England and Wales the power of appointment lies (at least legally; in practice it is usually the chief constable who exercises the authority) in the hands of the watch committee (10). In its relationship to the community it serves and protects, the Metropolitan police is on a different footing from the numerous other forces in Britain (in 1857 there were 239 separate forces, a number gradually reduced by amalgamation to 129 in 1949); but its practices and standards have always served as a model to the other forces.

The chief novelties in Peel's conception of the police appear to be: (a) the institution of a force for the prevention of crimes and the maintenance of public order, rather than for the apprehension of criminals after the crime has been committed; (b) the high visibility of the police in a distinctive uniform, what Inspector J. L. Thomas has called the "scarecrow function" of the police (11); (c) the fact that the police were on continuous duty during the whole 24 hours (their immediate predecessors, the Bow Street runners, were not in uniform and only patrolled during the evenings, invariably finishing duty by midnight) (11); (d) the fact that the police were unarmed, except for the truncheon, which was no more formidable than the "life-preserver" which many gentlemen of the early nineteenth century carried on their walks abroad; (e) the fact that every complaint against the conduct of the police was publicly investigated, with considerable publicity in the earlier years (6); (f) the fact that the police were never segregated in barracks nor treated as a paramilitary formation, as occurred in a number of European countries; and (g) the fact that, apart from certain qualifications of height and age, the police were recruited entirely on the basis of their character, and not on their previous employment, or through patronage, or for the possession of any special skills beyond an unfixed minimum of education. Neither examinations nor tests (other than medical) have ever preceded recruitment into the English police force, though new entrants are naturally given training after they have been accepted.

The great bulk of the English police has almost continuously been drawn from the ranks of skilled and semiskilled labor, from the working, upper working, and lower middle classes. In 1832, three years after its inception, Peel's Metropolitan force was composed of former members of the following callings: 135 butchers, 109 bakers, 198 shoemakers, 51 tailors, 402 soldiers, 1,151 laborers, 205 servants, 141 carpenters, 75 bricklayers, 20 turners, 55 blacksmiths, 151 clerks, 141 shopkeepers, 141 "superior mechanics," 46 plumbers and painters, 101 sailors, 51 weavers and 8 stonemasons (12). The heterogeneity of this list is probably typical of the composition of most of the English police forces over the last 120 years, with two exceptions: the proportion of former military and naval personnel is rather high, except for recruitment in the years immediately following a major war (12); and in this first metropolitan force there is no special mention of the agricultural laborers (unless the "laborers" without specification were country workers) who for a great part of the nineteenth century made up a very high proportion of the police recruits (12). Agricultural laborers were considered to excel in physique and stamina; and, in the words of a former Commissioner of the Metropolitan Police to the American writer, R. B. Fosdick: "They are slow but steady; you can mold them to any shape you please" (2). With the increasing industrialization and urbanization of England, the proportion of agricultural laborers has steadily dropped; and today most police recruits were formerly industrial workers, office workers, commercial travellers or shop assistants (12). It also seems probable that the type of character sought for in a police recruit was formerly much more common in the rural population than in the violent and lawless urban mobs; but with the modification of character that has been hypothesized in the mass of the English population, people of suitable character can be found in all strata of the English population, except possibly in the lower working class.

The following are the only conditions laid down by the Home Secretary for the selection of police recruits. He, or she, must be (a) within certain age limits; (b) not less than a stated height; (c) of a good character and with a satisfactory record in past employments; (d) physically and mentally fitted to perform the duties of a constable; and (d) sufficiently well educated (5). Apart from the criteria of age and height, this means in fact that the selection of recruits depends almost entirely on the result of interviews with the Chief Constable of the force concerned; his experience and skill in assessing character by unformalized techniques of observation and interrogation replace the selection boards, psychological tests, and other techniques of examination that are used for screening the entrants to most life-time careers of responsibility and authority.

In connection with the character of the members of the police force, the criterion of height may merit a little consideration. The minimum fixed by the Home Secretary is 5 feet, 8 inches for men, which already excludes more than half the male population, since the average height of the British male is 5 feet, 7½ inches (7). In point of fact, only three of the country's police forces, though of these two are the largest (Metropolitan, Birmingham, and Buckinghamshire) in 1949 were content with the Home Secretary's permitted minimum; about 30 forces will take men of 5 feet, 9 inches, and another 20 of 5 feet, 9½ inches; the remainder—somewhat more than 70 forces—insist on a minimum of 5 feet, 10 inches (10). This means that most of the police recruits come from a small and (statistically speaking) physically unrepresentative section of the population, perhaps some 10 per cent of the whole; and, although the connection between physique and character is still comparatively undetermined,[2] the folk observation that big men are likely to be easy-going, eventempered, just, and slow to anger may well have some foundation in fact. Although the minimum height was probably imposed with the intention of securing physically strong and impressive men, it may well have had the secondary effect of securing that recruits were selected from people of constitutionally equable temperament.

From its foundation, the emphasis of the British police force has been on the preservation of peace, on the prevention of crime and violence, rather than on the apprehension of criminals and rioters. The swearing-in oath, taken by each constable on entering the force, reads:

> I, A.B., do swear that I will well and truly serve our Sovereign Lady the Queen in the office of Constable. . . . without Favour or Affection, Malice or Ill-will; and that I will to the best of my Power cause the Peace to be kept and preserved, and prevent all offences against

---

[2] Attempts to correlate physique and character or temperament have been made by a number of researchers, notably Kretschmer: *Physique and character* (English translation 1925) and W. H. Sheldon: *The varieties of human physique* (1940), *The varieties of temperament* (1942), and *Varieties of delinquent youth* (1949); but to date there has not been either general acceptance of their hypotheses, nor convincing application of them by other researchers.

the Persons and Properties of Her Majesty's Subjects; and that while I continue to hold the said Office I will to the best of my skill and knowledge discharge all the Duties thereof faithfully according to Law (5).

Similarly, the regulations drawn up in 1832 by Mr. Mayne, one of the first two Commissioners of the Metropolitan police, emphasize:

> The absence of crime will be considered the best proof of the complete efficiency of the police. . . . In divisions where this security and good order have been effected, the officers and men belonging to it may feel assured that such good conduct will be noticed by rewards and promotions. . . .
>
> The Constable must remember that there is no qualification more indispensable to a police officer than a perfect command of temper, never suffering himself to be moved in the slightest degree by any language or threats that may be used: if he do his duty in a quiet and determined manner, such conduct will probably induce well-disposed bystanders to assist him should he require it (6).

This emphasis on the prevention of aggression, on the preserving of the peace by a uniformed group of powerful men demonstrating self-restraint, would appear to have been a real novelty in English public life; it was not originally accepted without a great deal of opposition and abuse both from the press and from many representatives of the governing classes (6). Before the establishment of the Metropolitan police, wearers of uniform tended to be either symbolically or potentially oppressors and exploiters rather than protectors of the mass of the population: members of the armed forces, proverbially licentious and lawless, or the liveried servants of the rich and mighty. The policeman in uniform was still a member of his class in the hours off duty, had social as well as official contacts with his neighbors, and very much the same standard of living as most of the working class.

I have been able to find very little discussion of the motives that impel a young man or woman of "superior physique and character" to take up a profession or occupation that even today is not particularly rewarding financially. I do not think any systematic research has been done on the subject, but Inspector (now Chief Inspector) J. L. Thomas of the City of Bradford Police has some illuminating observations to make (12). He writes:

> In other callings with a high age of entry such as the Church and the teaching profession, the tyro must previously devote a number of years to studying and training for his future work, and the Police Service is probably unique in taking on men aged twenty years and upwards, who have no preliminary training whatsoever for the work they are to perform. It follows therefore that it has to attract men already engaged in an occupation, and the question which presents itself is: What were the motives that induced young men to quit a diversity of jobs to become policemen?

Among the answers he suggests are: pay steady and not subject to the caprice of trade or industry, though not high; a reasonable pension at a comparatively early age; unemployment following a "dead end" job; lack of specialized training after a period in the armed forces; and similar circumstances. He continues:

> Minor causes, such as the power a policeman is supposed to wield may have influenced some men. . . . While it is acknowledged that some men now serving did cherish over a long period an ardent desire to become policemen, it is suggested that they are in the minority, and that most policemen more or less drifted into their present job, through force of circumstances, such as those already described, rather than having been impelled by a strong sense of vocation. . . . "How then," it may be asked, "has the English police service succeeded in gaining such a large measure of public approbation?" This can only be attributed to the rigid observance of a number of fundamental rules. . . . the principal ones are: selecting the best men available; preserving the civilian character of the Force by recruiting from the population at large and from a wide diversity of occupations; maintaining a high standard of discipline, integrity and *esprit de corps;* and observing the principle of promotion by merit. Consequently, the nature of the occupation previously followed by a policeman has little direct bearing on his new career. . . . The motive which prompted a man to enlist is not such a vital factor as may have been thought at first. As a matter of fact, it is often the men with the strongest inclination to become policemen who are the most unsuitable for the position.

These perspicacious remarks omit, I think, consideration of one motive which, though it may not play a large role in the decision to enlist, may quite probably be influential in keeping the new recruits in the calling they have chosen: that is the respect with which the members of the police force are regarded by their fellow-citizens. The evidence for the attitudes of the English towards their police in the nineteenth and early twentieth century is only anecdotal and inferential: music-hall songs, jokes, descriptions of members of the police in novels by Charles Dickens or Wilkie Collins and the like.[3] But today this affectionate respect is extremely widespread. In January, 1951, a scattered sample of over 11,000 English men and women filled in for me a long and detailed questionnaire. One of the questions was "What do you think of the police?" No answers were indicated, and four lines were left for volunteered comments.[4]

This large sample were overwhelmingly appreciative of the police, to the extent of 73 per cent; a mere 5 per cent were really hostile, though 13 per cent had some criticisms to make. The answers were categorized in a considerable number of ways; for this question the most significant is by social class, self-ascribed.

Although, as could have been foreseeen, appreciation of the police diminishes as one descends the social scale, it is only in the lower working class that appreciation falls below two thirds of the total.

I should like to suggest that, increasingly during the past century, the English

---

[3] E.g. Inspector Bucket in Charles Dickens' *Bleak house,* or Sergeant Cuff in Wilkie Collins' *The moonstone.*

[4] For full details of the sample from which the following figures are drawn, see my study (4). It was a mail survey, and had the very high return of 75 per cent of filled-out questionnaires. This study also gives the justification of the summary description of the ideal male character for the English outlined in the subsequent paragraphs.

TABLE 25-1

English Attitudes toward the Police, by Social Class

Question: *What do you think of the police?*

Social Class	Per Cent Favorable	Per Cent Neutral	Per Cent Critical	Per Cent Hostile	Per Cent No Answer or Irrelevant
Upper middle	79	0	13	2	6
Middle	74	2	13	5	6
Lower middle	74	1	17	3	5
Upper working	72	1	17	3	3
Working	74	1	21	3	3
Lower working	65	2	12	7	14
Total Sample	73	2	13	5	7

policeman has been for his fellow-citizens not only an object of respect but also a model of the ideal male character, self-controlled, possessing more strength than he has ever to call into use except in the gravest emergency, fair and impartial, serving the abstractions of Peace and Justice rather than any personal allegiance or sectional advantage. This model, distributed throughout the population (in 1949 there were 59,000 police officers, averaging one police officer for every 720 inhabitants (5)) has, I suggest, had an appreciable influence on the character of most of the population during recent decades, so that the bulk of the population has, so to speak, incorporated the police man or woman as an ideal and become progressively more "self-policing"; and with this incorporation there has been an increasing amount of identification, so that today, in the words of one typical respondent:

> I believe the police stand for all we English are, maybe at first appearance slow perhaps, but reliable stout and kindly. I have the greatest admiration for our police force and I am proud they are renowned abroad.

If this hypothesis be correct, then what started as an expedient to control the very great criminality and violence of large sections of the English urban population (6, 11) has resulted in a profound modification of the character of this urban population. In a somewhat similar fashion, the need to provide a common language and literacy for the children of immigrants to the United States placed the American public school teacher in a position of prestige that was not shared by her colleagues in any European society and turned her into a model of ideal American conduct. If the metaphor be allowed, the American has an incorporated schoolteacher as part of his or her superego, the English man or woman an incorporated policeman.

There is not yet sufficient evidence to show whether the Communist Party member in the U.S.S.R. is producing analogous results in the mass of the Soviet population. The Communist Party is a much more recent institution than the two others hitherto discussed, but its personnel are distributed throughout the population in much the same proportions and similar relationship as the policeman or the schoolteacher. The major contrasts are that the policy is quite self-conscious on the part of the regime, and that Communist Party members are publicly connected with the whole apparatus of state power, in a way that neither the police nor the teachers, both under the control of local authorities, are. This public connection with state power may interfere with the processes of identification by the powerless; and, it would seem, it is by means of the more-or-less complete and more-or-less conscious identification with the members of an admired and succoring institution that the characters of the mass of a population and the ways in which they interpret their roles as parents are gradually modified or transformed.

REFERENCES

1. BAUER, R. A. *The new man in Soviet psychology*. Cambridge, Mass., 1952.
2. FOSDICK, R. B. *European police systems*. New York, date unknown.
3. GORER, G. *The Americans*. London, 1948.
4. GORER, G. *Exploring English character*. *London* (Cresset Press, 1955).
5. HART, J. M. *The British police*. London, 1951.
6. LEE, W. L. M. *A history of police in England*. London, 1901.
7. MARTIN, J. *The physique of young adult males*. Memor. Med. Res. Coun. 20, London, 1949.
8. MEAD, MARGARET. *And keep your powder dry*. New York, 1942.
9. MEAD, MARGARET. *Soviet attitudes toward authority*. New York, 1951.
10. *Oaksey report on police conditions of service, Part II*. London, 1949.
11. THOMAS, J. L., The scarecrow function of the police. *Police Journal*, 1945, *18*.
12. THOMAS, J. L. Recruits for the police service. *Police Journal*, 1946, *19*.

EPILOGUE

"Between the idea
 And the reality
 Between the motion
 And the act
 Falls the Shadow"
            —T. S. Eliot

When the legal process is examined, it is invariably found to deviate rather drastically in practice from the idealized blueprint. More often than not, the cause of the hiatus between the idea and the reality of the law is seen as residing in the individuals who occupy the particular roles involved. Thus, when a police force or an entire legal system is found to be engaged in a symbiotic relationship with professional criminals, the cause of this unfortunate circumstance is seen as residing in the inherent corruptibility of the individuals involved. The theoretical discussions and the research studies in this book stand in total opposition to such a simplistic and individualistic interpretation. The legal process must be understood as taking the form that it does because of characteristics of the social system which are independent of, and which render relatively inconsequential, the motives, character, or personality of the particular people who occupy positions in the system.

Obviously, the two interpretations above have quite different implications for social change. When problems in the administration of criminal law are attributed to deficiencies in the role-incumbents, then the implications for change focus on changing the people. According to this argument, better police will be had by recruiting more highly educated and (therefore?) less corruptible individuals. Another implication is that what is needed to make the legal process more just is to increase the salaries of law-enforcement personnel and to develop more highly professionalized roles.

Although each of these suggestions may have beneficial consequences, it is unlikely that either would substantially alter the present state of affairs. So long as the agencies and individuals who administer the criminal law must enter into extralegal relationships with criminal and non-criminal segments of the population in order to function efficiently as organizations, and to the extent that these relationships interfere with the operation of the law as it is supposed to function, then the hiatus between the legal process and the expressed goals of the criminal law must persist. An alteration of these circumstances can only be brought about by changing those features of the legal system which lie at the root of the problem.

So long as law-enforcement agencies are subject to the will and desires of middle- and upper-class members of the community but are free to behave as they wish without fear or reprisal toward lower-class members of the community, then the legal system will continue to function in the highly discriminatory way that it now does. This situation will not be altered one iota by changing the educational requirements or socialization process of persons occupying positions in the system. The situation will be altered when and only when the political and economic power of the lower classes approaches that of the middle and upper classes. To suppose that this will transpire without some very fundamental and deep changes in the structure of American society is exceedingly naïve. One senses that such changes may be in the making with the black-power and hippie movements, which demonstrate the ability of these minority groups to sustain an increased membership in the face of politically and economically powerful opposition. But even if these changes are in fact in the making, it remains to be seen whether they will amount to anything more than the replacement of one group of people in positions of power by another. Certainly the history of most nations in the modern world does not allow one to be overly optimistic about the possibility of establishing a system of justice that is equally fair to all persons irrespective of their political and economic power.

In terms of specific problems, however, altering the present state of affairs may require less thoroughgoing changes in the social structure. The symbiotic relationship between various types of criminals and the legal system might be dissolved by eliminating those features of the legal system which make such a relationship rewarding. The most fundamental alteration in the legal system required to effect this change would be to eliminate as crimes those types of behavior which are prohibited but where consensus is lacking and where large members of the community demand their right to engage in these acts irrespective of the opinions of others. Specifically, this would require voiding laws which prohibit homosexuality, drug use, gambling, and prostitution.

The problems raised by such a turnabout in legal policy would be considerable. If, for example, gambling were simply legalized, there is little doubt but that organized criminals would continue to operate and manipulate these enterprises.[1] A successful initiation of legalized gambling in America would necessitate concomitant legislation establishing a government-supervised agency to organize and run the gambling enterprises. Undoubtedly such a system would have its faults, but these faults would pale by contrast with the devastating consequences inherent in allowing gambling to support organized crime to the extent that it does in the United States.

The law would also be substantially more effective if more attention were paid to its empirically demonstrable consequences. Laws could be written which would take into account such things as the instrumental or expressive character of criminal acts. Laws could be written so as to take into account the degree of commitment the person has to crime as a way of life. Although the task is not a simple one, the law has proved its capacity for distinguishing far greater subtleties than these. Indeed, in many instances similar distinctions are already being made. Laws imposing different penal sanctions for the habitual offender some close to selecting out persons who are "committed to crime as a way of life." Unfortunately, such laws are also applied, more often than not, against persons who are habitually *expressive* offenders. Such laws are used more often to incarcerate sexual offenders (who are likely to be expressive types of offenders) permanently than to incarcerate professional thieves permanently.

Similarly, laws differentiate between persons who have intent and those who do not. The notion of intent is not sufficient to differentiate expressive and instrumental acts, but the possibility of defining such a difference through setting up corresponding legal categories is certainly not far fetched. The law could well prescribe different punishment for offenders who commit a criminal act as a means of achieving some other goal than for persons who commit an act because it is an end in itself. Courts and penal institutions currently make similar distinctions: for example, arsonists are likely to receive quite different treatment if they burned a building for the pure pleasure of it than if they burned the building because it was insured for more than it was worth.

These current practices in the law suggest that the precedent and even the mechanisms exist for making such distinctions within the legal order. The problem, then, is not that the law is unable to take such things into account; the problem, rather, is to institute the required changes.

The solutions to these and other legal problems pinpointed in this book will not be found easily. One can say without fear of contradiction that between the idea and the reality of American law there is a shadow. The challenge to lawyers and social scientists is to continue to look for ways which will contribute in some measure toward erasing that shadow.

---

[1] As they have, for example, in Nevada.

Selected Bibliography

GENERAL REFERENCES

ABRAHAM, HENRY J.: *The Judicial Process,* Fair Lawn, N.J.: Oxford University Press, 1962.

ALLEN, FRANCIS A.: *The Borderline of Criminal Justice: Essays on Law and Criminology,* Chicago: The University of Chicago Press, 1964.

———: "Criminal Justice, Legal Values and the Rehabilitation Ideal," *Journal of Criminal Law, Criminology and Police Science,* vol. 50, pp. 226–232, September–October, 1959.

———: "Offenses against Property," *Annals of the American Academy of Political and Social Science,* vol. 339, pp. 57–76, January, 1962.

ARNES, RICHARD, and HAROLD D. LASSWELL: *In Defense of Public Order: The Emerging Field of Sanction Law,* New York: Columbia University Press, 1961.

AUBERT, VILHELM: *The Hidden Society,* Totowa, N.J.: The Bedminster Press, 1965.

———: "White Collar Crime and Social Structure," *American Journal of Sociology,* vol. 58, pp. 263–271, 1952.

AUERBACH, CARL, LLOYD K. GARRISON, WILLARD HURST, and SAMUEL MERMIN: *The Legal Process,* San Francisco: Chandler Publishing Co., 1961.

BARTH, ALAN: *Law Enforcement versus the Law,* New York: Collier Books, 1963.

BECKER, HOWARD S.: "Marihuana Use and Social Control," *Social Problems,* vol. 3, pp. 35–44, Spring, 1955.

BOSLOW, HAROLD M., DAVID ROSENTHAL, and L. H. GLEIDMAN: "The Maryland Defective Delinquency Law," *British Journal of Delinquency,* vol. 10, pp. 5–13, July, 1959.

BRAMSTED, ERNEST J.: *Dictatorship and Political Police,* London: Routledge & Kegan Paul, Ltd., 1945.

CAPPON, DANIEL: "Punishment and the Person," *Ethics,* vol. 67, pp. 184–195, April, 1957.

CARDOZO, BENJAMIN: *Nature of Judicial Process,* New Haven, Conn.: Yale University Press, 1922.

CARLSTON, KENNETH S.: *Law and Structures of Social Action,* New York: Columbia University Press, 1956.

CHAMBLISS, WILLIAM J., and JOHN T. LIELL: "The Legal Process in the Community Setting," *Crime and Delinquency,* pp. 310–317, October, 1966.

CHANDRA, SUSHIL: "Penal Reform Movement and Correctional Work in Uttar Pradesh," *India Sociology,* vol. 4, pp. 9–18, March, 1962.

CHORLEY, LORD: "Law and Society behind the Iron Curtain," *British Journal of Sociology,* vol. 11, pp. 277–284, September, 1960.

COHEN, ALBERT K.: "Differential Implementation of the Criminal Law," unpublished master's thesis, Indiana University, Bloomington, Ind., 1948.

COHEN, JULIUS, REGINALD A. H. ROBSON, and ALAN BATES: *Parental Authority: The Community and the Law,* New Brunswick, N.J.: Rutgers University Press, 1958.

DASH, SAMUEL, RICHARD F. SCHWARTZ, and ROBERTA E. KNOWLTON: *The Eavesdroppers,* New Brunswick, N.J.: Rutgers University Press, 1959.

DAVIS, F. JAMES, HENRY H. FOSTER, JR., C. RAY JEFFREY, and E. EUGENE DAVIS: *Society and the Law: New Meanings for an Old Profession,* New York: The Free Press of Glencoe, 1962.

DAY, FRANK: *Criminal Law and Society,* Springfield, Ill.: Charles C Thomas, Publisher, 1964.

DEUTSCHER, IRWIN: "The White Petty Offender in the Small City," *Social Problems,* vol. 1, pp. 70–73, August, 1953.

EHRLICH, EUGEN: *Fundamental Principles of the Sociology of Law,* Cambridge, Mass.: Harvard University Press, 1936.

EVAN, WILLIAM M.: "Due Process of Law in Military and Industrial Organizations," *Administrative Science Quarterly,* vol. 7, pp. 187–207, September, 1962.

———: "Organization Man and Due Process of Law," *American Sociological Review,* vol. 26, no. 4, pp. 540–547, August, 1961.

FALK, RICHARD: "The Relations of Law to Culture, Power, and Justice," *Ethics,* vol. 72, pp. 12–27, October, 1961.

FALK, RICHARD A.: *Legal Order in a Violent World*, Princeton, N.J.: Princeton University Press, 1968.

FEIFER, GEORGE: *Justice in Moscow*, New York: Dell Publishing Co., Inc., 1965.

FELDBRUGGE, F. J.: "Soviet Criminal Law—The Last Six Years," *Journal of Criminal Law, Criminology and Police Science*, vol. 54, pp. 267–272, September, 1963.

FOOTE, CALEB: "The Bail System and Equal Justice," *Federal Probation*, vol. 19, pp. 43–48, September, 1955.

———: "Vagrancy-type Law and Its Administration," *University of Pennsylvania Law Review*, vol. 104, pp. 603–650, 1956.

FOSTER, HARRY H., JR.: "The 'Comstock Load'—Obscenity and the Law," *Journal of Criminal Law, Criminology and Police Science*, vol. 48, pp. 245–258, September–October, 1957.

FRIEDMAN, LAWRENCE M.: "On Legalistic Reasoning—A Footnote to Weber," *Wisconsin Law Review*, vol. 1966, pp. 148–171, Winter, 1966.

GURVITCH, GEORGII DAVIDOVICH: *Sociology of Law*, London: Routledge & Kegan Paul, Ltd., 1947.

HALL, JEROME: *Theft, Law and Society* (revised), Indianapolis: The Bobbs-Merrill Company, Inc., 1952.

HALL, J. GRAHAM: "The Prostitute and the Law," *British Journal of Delinquency*, vol. 9, pp. 174–181, January, 1959.

HALL, WILLIAMS J. E.: "The Wolfenden Report—An Appraisal," *Political Quarterly*, vol. 29, pp. 132–143, April–June, 1958.

HARPER, F. V.: "Law in Action and Social Theory," *International Journal of Ethics*, vol. 40, 1929.

HART, H. L. A.: *Law, Liberty and Morality*, Stanford, Calif.: Stanford University Press, 1963.

JAMES, T. E.: "Law and the Sexual Offender," in Ismond Rosen (ed.), *The Pathology and Treatment of Sexual Deviation*, Fair Lawn, N.J.: Oxford University Press, 1964, pp. 461–492.

JEFFREY, CLARENCE R.: "Crime, Law and Social Structure," *Journal of Criminal Law, Criminology and Police Science*, vol. 47, pp. 423–435, November–December, 1956.

JOHNSON, EARL, JR.: "Organized Crime: Challenge to the American Legal System, Part III," *Journal of Criminal Law, Criminology and Police Science*, vol. 54, pp. 127–145, June, 1963.

KAMISAR, YALE, FRED INBAU, and THURMAN ARNOLD: *Criminal Justice in Our Time*, Charlottesville, Va.: The University Press of Virginia, 1965.

KEESKEMETI, PAUL: "Punishment as Conflict Resolution," *Archives of Criminal Psychodynamics*, vol. 4, Fall, 1961.

KEPHART, WILLIAM M.: *Racial Factors and Urban Law Enforcement*, Philadelphia: University of Pennsylvania Press, 1957.

KREMI, FRANKLIN M.: "Police, Prosecutors, and Judges," *Annals of the American Academy of Political and Social Science*, vol. 320, pp. 42–52, November, 1958.

Law and Society, supplement to Summer, 1965, issue of *Social Problems*.

LINDESMITH, ALFRED R.: *The Addict and the Law*, Bloomington, Ind.: Indiana University Press, 1965.

McMILLAN, GEORGE: *Racial Violence and Law Enforcement*, Atlanta, Ga.: Southern Regional Council, 1960.

McMULLEN, M.: "A Theory of Corruption," *Sociological Review*, vol. 9, pp. 181–201, July, 1961.

MARSHALL, GEOFFREY: *Police and Government*, London: Methuen & Co., Ltd., 1965.

MEAD, GEORGE HERBERT: "The Psychology of Punitive Justice," *American Journal of Sociology*, pp. 577–602, vol. 23, 1917–18.

MERRIAM, CHARLES E.: *Chicago: A More Intimate View of American Politics,* New York: The Macmillan Company, 1929, pp. 24–69.

MERRILL, LOUIS T.: "The Puritan Policemen," *American Sociological Review,* vol. 10, pp. 766–776, December, 1945.

MICHAEL, JEROME, and MORTIMER ADLER: *Crime, Law and Social Science,* New York: Harcourt, Brace and Company, Inc., 1933.

NAGEL, STUART: "Off-the-bench Judicial Attitudes," in Glendon Schubert (ed.), *Judicial Decision Making,* New York: The Free Press of Glencoe, 1963, pp. 29–54.

POUND, ROSCOE: *Criminal Justice in America,* Cambridge, Mass.: Harvard University Press, 1945.

————: *Social Control through Law,* New Haven, Conn.: Yale University Press, 1942.

REITH, CHARLES: *A New Study of Police History,* Edinburgh and London: Oliver & Boyd, Ltd., 1956.

ROSE, ARNOLD M.: "Does the Punishment Fit the Crime? A Study of Social Valuation," *American Journal of Sociology,* vol. 61, pp. 247–259, November, 1955.

ROSS, ALF: *On Law and Justice,* Berkeley, Calif.: University of California Press, 1959.

SAWER, GEOFFREY: *Studies on the Sociology of Law,* Canberra: Australian National University, 1961.

SCHUR, EDWIN M.: *Drug Addiction in America and England,* Bloomington, Ind.: Indiana University Press, 1962.

SIEVERTS, RUDOLF: "The Administration of the Juvenile Penal Law in the Federal Republic of Germany," *British Journal of Delinquency,* vol. 7, pp. 206–227, January, 1957.

SOWLE, CLAUDE R. (ed.): *Police Power and Individual Freedom,* Chicago: Aldine Publishing Co., 1962.

STINCHCOMBE, ARTHUR L.: "Institutions of Privacy in the Determination of Police Administrative Practices," *American Journal of Sociology,* vol. 69, pp. 150–160, September, 1963.

STONE, JULIUS: *The Province and Function of Law: Law as Logic, Justice and Social Control: A Study in Jurisprudence,* Cambridge, Mass.: Harvard University Press, 1961.

SZASZ, THOMAS: *Law, Liberty and Psychiatry,* New York: The Macmillan Company, 1963.

THOMPSON, CRAIG: *The Police State,* New York: E. P. Dutton & Co., Inc., 1950.

TIMASHEFF, N. S.: *An Introduction to the Sociology of Law,* Cambridge, Mass.: Committee on Research in the Social Sciences, Harvard University, 1939.

VAN VECHTEN, COURTLANDT C.: "Differential Criminal Case Mortality in Selected Jurisdictions," *American Sociological Review,* vol. 7, pp. 833–839, December, 1942.

WOOD, ARTHUR L.: "Informal Relations in the Practice of Criminal Law," *American Journal of Sociology,* vol. 62, pp. 48–55, July, 1956.

I. THE EMERGENCE OF LEGAL NORMS

CHAMBLISS, WILLIAM J.: "A Sociological Analysis of the Law of Vagrancy," *Social Problems,* vol. 12, pp. 67–77, Summer, 1964.

JEFFREY, CLARENCE R.: "The Development of Crime in Early English Society," *Journal of Criminal Law, Criminology and Police Science,* vol. 47, pp. 647–666, March–April 1957.

LINDESMITH, ALFRED R.: *The Addict and the Law,* Bloomington, Ind.: Indiana University Press, 1965.

————: "Federal Law and Drug Addiction," *Social Problems,* vol. 7, pp. 526–538, Summer, 1959.

LYMAN, J. L.: "The Metropolitan Police Act of 1829: An Analysis of Certain Events Influencing the Passage and Character of the Metropolitan Police Act in England," *Journal of Criminal Law, Criminology and Police Science*, vol. 55, pp. 141–154, March, 1964.

RANULF, SVEND: *Moral Indignation and Middle Class Psychology*, New York: Schocken Books, 1964.

SUTHERLAND, EDWIN H.: "The Diffusion of Sexual Psychopath Laws," *American Journal of Sociology*, vol. 56, pp. 142–148, September, 1950.

WALKER, NIGEL: *Crime, and Insanity in England: One: The Historical Perspective*. Edinburgh: Edinburgh University Press, 1968.

II. THE ADMINISTRATION OF CRIMINAL LAW

A. Arrest

BANTON, MICHAEL: "Police Discretion," *New Society*, vol. 2, pp. 6–7, Aug. 29, 1963.

———: *The Policeman in the Community*, New York: Basic Books, Inc., Publishers, 1965.

BARRETT, EDWARD: "Police Practices and the Law—From Arrest to Release or Charge," *California Law Review*, vol. 50, pp. 11–55, March, 1962.

BEELEY, A. L.: "Parenthood, the Police Power and Criminal Justice Administration," *Western Political Quarterly*, vol. 12, pp. 799–807, September, 1959.

BLUM, RICHARD H.: "The Problems of Being a Police Officer," *Police*, pp. 10–13, November–December, 1960.

BLUMBERG, ABRAHAM S.: "The Practice of Law as Confidence Game," *Law and Society Review*, vol. 1, pp. 15–39, June, 1967.

BORDUA, DAVID J. (ed.): *The Police: Six Sociological Essays*, New York: John Wiley & Sons, Inc., 1967.

———, and ALBERT J. REISS, JR.: "Command, Control and Charisma: Reflections on Police Bureaucracy," *American Journal of Sociology*, vol. 72, pp. 68–76, July, 1966.

CHAPMAN, SAMUEL G.: *The Police Heritage in England and America*, East Lansing, Mich.: The Michigan State University Press, 1962.

CLARK, JOHN P.: "Isolation of the Police: A Comparison of the British and American Situations," *Journal of Criminal Law, Criminology and Police Science*, vol. 56, pp. 307–319, 1965.

COATMAN, JOHN: *Police*, Fair Lawn, N.J.: Oxford University Press, 1958.

CRAMER, JAMES: *The World's Police*, London: Cassell & Co., Ltd., 1964.

CUMMING, ELAINE, IAN M. CUMMING, and LAURA EDELL: "Policeman as Philosopher, Guide and Friend," *Social Problems*, vol. 12, pp. 276–286, Winter, 1965.

DEUTSCH, ALBERT: *The Trouble with Cops*, New York: Crown Publishers, Inc., 1955.

FARALICQ, RENÉ: *The French Police from Within*, London: Cassell & Co., Ltd., 1933.

FOOTE, CALEB: "Vagrancy-type Law and Its Administration," *University of Pennsylvania Law Review*, vol. 104, pp. 603–650, 1956.

FOSDICK, RAYMOND: *European Police Systems*, New York: Century Company, 1915.

GOLDSTEIN, HERMAN: "Police Discretion: The Ideal versus the Real," *Public Administration Review*, vol. 23, pp. 140–148, September, 1963.

GOLDSTEIN, JOSEPH: "Police Discretion Not to Invoke the Legal Process: Low-visibility Decisions in the Administration of Justice," *Yale Law Journal*, vol. 69, pp. 543–594, 1960.

HART, J. M.: *The British Police*, London: George Allen & Unwin, Ltd., 1951.

HERSEY, JOHN: *The Algiers Motel Incident*, New York: Alfred A. Knopf, Inc., 1968.

INGERSOLL, JOHN E.: "The Police Scandal Syndrome," *Crime and Delinquency*, vol. 10, pp. 269–275, July, 1964.

JEFFREY, SIR CHARLES: *The Colonial Police,* London: M. Parrish, 1952.

LAFAVE, WAYNE R.: *Arrest: The Decision to Take a Suspect into Custody,* Boston: Little, Brown and Company, 1965.

————: "The Police and Non-enforcement of the Law," *Wisconsin Law Review,* part I, pp. 104–137, January, 1962; part II, pp. 179–239, March, 1962.

MACNAMARA, DONALD E. J.: "American Police Administration at Mid-century," *Public Administration Review,* vol. 10, pp. 181–189, Summer, 1950.

MILLER, FRANK W., and FRANK J. REMINGTON: "Procedures before Trial," *Annals of the American Academy of Political and Social Science,* vol. 339, pp. 111–141, January, 1962.

NELSON, TRUMAN: *The Torture of Mothers,* Boston: Beacon Press, 1968.

NIEDERHOFFER, ARTHUR: "A Study of Police Cynicism," unpublished doctoral dissertation, New York University, New York, 1964.

PILIAVIN, IRVING, and SCOTT BRIAR: "Police Encounters with Juveniles," *American Journal of Sociology,* vol. 70, pp. 206–214, September, 1964.

PITTMAN, DAVID J., and C. WAYNE GORDON: *Revolving Door: A Study of the Chronic Police Case Inebriate,* New York: The Free Press of Glencoe, 1958.

SKOLNICK, JEROME H.: *Justice without Trial: Law Enforcement in Democratic Society,* New York: John Wiley & Sons, Inc., 1966.

SMITH, BRUCE: *Police Systems in the United States,* 2d rev. ed., New York: Harper & Row, Publishers, Incorporated, 1960.

SOLMES, ALWYN: *The English Policeman, 1871–1935,* London: George Allen & Unwin, Ltd., 1935.

TREBACH, ARNOLD S.: *The Rationing of Justice,* New Brunswick, N.J.: Rutgers University Press, 1964.

VIRTUE, MAX BOORD: "The Two Faces of Janus: Delay in Metropolitan Trial Courts," *Annuals of the American Academy of Political and Social Science,* vol. 328, pp. 125–133, March, 1960.

WESTLEY, WILLIAM A.: "The Police: A Sociological Study of Law, Custom and Morality," unpublished doctoral dissertation, Department of Sociology, University of Chicago, Chicago, 1951.

————: "Secrecy and the Police," *Social Forces,* vol. 34, pp. 254–257, March, 1956.

————: "Violence and the Police," *American Journal of Sociology,* vol. 59, pp. 34–41, July, 1953.

WILSON, JAMES Q.: "Generational and Ethnic Differences among Career Police Officers," *American Journal of Sociology,* vol. 69, pp. 522–528, March, 1964.

————: "The Police and Their Problems: A Theory," *Public Policy,* vol. 12, pp. 189–216, 1963.

WILSON, O. W.: "Police Arrest Privileges in a Free Society: A Plea for Modernization," *Journal of Criminal Law, Criminology and Police Science,* vol. 51, pp. 395–401, November–December, 1960.

B. Prosecution

GOLDMAN, NATHAN: *The Differential Selection of Juveniles for Court Appearance,* National Council on Crime and Delinquency, 1963.

NEWMAN, DONALD J.: *Conviction: The Determination of Guilt or Innocence without Trial,* Boston: Little, Brown and Company, 1966.

————: "Pleading Guilty for Considerations: A Study of Bargain Justice," *Journal of Criminal Law, Criminology and Police Science,* vol. 46, pp. 180–190, March–April, 1956.

SUDNOW, DAVID: "Normal Crimes," *Social Problems,* vol. 12, pp. 255–276, 1965.

C. Trial and Sentencing

BLUMBERG, ABRAHAM: "The Criminal Court: An Organizational Analysis," unpublished doctoral dissertation, New School for Social Research, New York, 1964.

CALDWELL, ROBERT G.: "The Juvenile Court: Its Development and Some Major Problems," *Journal of Criminal Law, Criminology, and Police Science,* vol. 51, pp. 493–511, January–February, 1961.

CAVENAGH, W. E.: "Justice and Welfare in Juvenile Courts," *British Journal of Delinquency,* vol. 7, pp. 196–205, January, 1957.

DIONA, LEWIS: "The Rights of Juvenile Delinquents: An Appraisal of Juvenile Court Procedures," *Journal of Criminal Law, Criminology and Police Science,* vol. 47, pp. 561–569, January–February, 1957.

DUNHAM, H. WARREN, and MARY E. KNAUER: "The Juvenile Court in Its Relationship to Adult Criminality," *Social Forces,* vol. 32, pp. 290–296, March, 1954.

GAUDET, F. J., G. S. HARRIS, and G. W. ST. JOHN: "Individual Differences in the Sentencing Tendencies of Judges," *Journal of Criminal Law, Criminology and Police Science,* vol. 23, pp. 811–818, January, 1933.

GREEN, EDWARD: *Judicial Attitudes in Sentencing,* New York: St. Martin's Press, Inc., 1961.

————: *Sentencing Practices,* London: Macmillan & Co., Ltd., 1963.

————: "Sentencing Practices of Criminal Court Judges in Philadelphia," *American Journal of Corrections,* vol. 22, pp. 32–35, July–August, 1960.

JAMES, HOWARD: *Crisis in the Courts,* New York: David McKay Company, Inc., 1968.

JAMES, RITA M.: "Jurors' Assessment of Criminal Responsibility," *Social Problems,* vol. 71, pp. 58–69, Summer, 1959.

MORRIS, RUDOLPH E.: "Witness Performance under Stress: A Sociological Approach," *Journal of Social Issues,* vol. 13, pp. 17–22, 1957.

NEWMAN, CHARLES J.: "Trial by Jury: An Outmoded Relic?," *Journal of Criminal Law, Criminology and Police Science,* vol. 46, pp. 512–518, November–December, 1955.

ROBINSON, W. S.: "Bias, Probability and Trial by Jury," *American Sociological Review,* vol. 15, pp. 73–78, February, 1950.

"Sentencing," *Law and Contemporary Problems,* vol. 23, pp. 399–582, Summer, 1958.

SIMON, RITA JAMES: *The Jury and the Plea of Insanity,* Boston: Little, Brown and Company, 1966.

SORENSEN, ROBERT C.: "The Effectiveness of the Oath to Obtain a Witness' True Personal Opinion," *Journal of Criminal Law, Criminology and Police Science,* vol. 47, pp. 284–293, September–October, 1956.

STRODTBECK, FRED L., RITA M. JAMES, and CHARLES HAWKINS: "Social Status in Jury Deliberations," *American Sociological Review,* vol. 22, pp. 713–719, December, 1957.

ZEISEL, HANS: "The Jury and the Court Delay," *Annals of the American Academy of Political and Social Science,* vol. 320, pp. 46–52, March, 1960.

————, HARRY KALVEN, JR., and BERNARD BUCKHOLZ: *Delay in the Court,* Boston: Little, Brown and Company, 1959.

III. THE IMPACT OF LEGAL SANCTIONS

ANDENAES, JOHANNES: "Determinism and Criminal Law," *Journal of Criminal Law, Criminology and Police Science,* vol. 47, pp. 406–413, November–December, 1956.

————: "The General Preventive Effects of Punishment," *The University of Pennsylvania Law Review,* vol. 114, pp. 949–983, May, 1966.

CHAMBLISS, WILLIAM J.: "The Deterrent Influence of Punishment," *Crime and Delinquency,* pp. 70–75, January, 1966.

CHAMBLISS, WILLIAM J.: "Types of Deviance and the Effectiveness of Legal Sanctions," *Wisconsin Law Review,* Summer, 1967.

GORER, GEOFFREY: "Modification of National Character," *Journal of Social Issues,* vol. 11, pp. 24–32, 1955.

HULIN, CHARLES L., and BRENDAN A. MAHER: "Changes in Attitudes toward Law Concomitant with Imprisonment," *Journal of Criminal Law, Criminology and Police Science,* vol. 50, pp. 245–248, September–October, 1959.

SAVITZ, LEONARD D.: "A Study in Capital Punishment," *Journal of Criminal Law, Criminology and Police Science,* vol. 49, pp. 338–341, November–December, 1958.

SCHUESSLER, KARL F.: "The Deterrent Influence of the Death Penalty," *The Annals,* vol. 284, pp. 54–63, November, 1952.

SCHWARTZ, RICHARD D., and JEROME H. SKOLNICK: "Two Studies of Legal Stigma," *Social Problems,* vol. 10, pp. 133–142, Fall, 1962.

SELLIN, THORSTEN: *The Death Penalty,* Philadelphia: American Law Institute, 1959, pp. 19–24, 34–38, 52–59.

SRAMOTA, WENZEL: "Reactions of Criminals and Political Prisoners to Impending Death Sentences," *Journal of Offender Therapy,* vol. 6, pp. 40–43, September, 1962.

INDEXES

NAME AND CASE INDEX

SUBJECT INDEX

DATE DUE

MR 2 '70		
OC 2 '70		
NO 11 '70		
AP 15 '71		
MY 16 '72		
NO 14 '72		
FE 9 '73		
MY 29 '74		
FEB 11 '77		
DEC 2 1980		
FEB 2 1981		
APR 26 '85		
DEC 3 '85		
FEB 16 '88		
MAR 27 '89		PRINTED IN U.S.A.